FIFTH EDITION

BECOMING AN
EFFECTIVE POLICY ADVOCATE
FROM POLICY PRACTICE TO SOCIAL JUSTICE

BRUCE S. JANSSON
University of Southern California

WADSWORTH
CENGAGE Learning™

Australia • Brazil • Japan • Korea • Mexico • Singapore • Spain • United Kingdom • United States

WADSWORTH
CENGAGE Learning

**Becoming an Effective Policy Advocate:
From Policy Practice to Social Justice**
Bruce S. Jansson

Social Work Editor: Dan Alpert

Development Editor: Tangelique Williams

Assistant Editor: Ann Lee Richards

Editorial Assistant: Stephanie Rue

Technology Project Manager: Julie Aguilar

Marketing Manager: Meghan McCullough

Marketing Assistant: Teresa Marino

Marketing Communications Manager:
Shemika Britt

Project Manager, Editorial Production: Tanya
Nigh

Creative Director: Rob Hugel

Art Director: Vernon Boes

Print Buyer: Nora Massuda

Permissions Editor: Joohee Lee

Production Service: GEX Publishing Services

Text Designer: Lisa Henry

Copy Editor: GEX Publishing Services

Cover Designer: Terri Wright Design

Cover Images:
Top left: © Bob Daemmrich/PhotoEdit
Center: © Rachel Epstein/PhotoEdit
Right: © Jeff Greenberg/Index Stock Imagery
Bottom: © AP/Wide World Photos

Compositor: GEX Publishing Services

For product information and technology assistance, contact us at
Cengage Learning Customer & Sales Support, 1-800-354-9706

For permission to use material from this text or product, submit all requests online at **cengage.com/permissions**
Further permissions questions can be emailed to
permissionrequest@cengage.com

Library of Congress Control Number: 2006937190

ISBN-13: 978-0-495-00623-7

ISBN-10: 0-495-00623-8

Wadsworth
10 Davis Drive
Belmont, CA 94002-3098
USA

Cengage Learning is a leading provider of customized learning solutions with office locations around the globe, including Singapore, the United Kingdom, Australia, Mexico, Brazil, and Japan. Locate your local office at: **international.cengage.com/region**

Cengage Learning products are represented in Canada by Nelson Education, Ltd.

For your course and learning solutions, visit **academic.cengage.com**

Purchase any of our products at your local college store or at our preferred online store **www.ichapters.com**

Printed in the United States of America
2 3 4 5 6 7 11 10 09 08

CONTENTS

SPECIAL FEATURES

Policy Advocacy Challenges

PREFACE

When I first developed the concept, "policy practice," in the early 1980s, I hoped that others, too, would reconceptualize social welfare policy as a multifaceted intervention that would help social workers actually change policies to advance such ethical principles as social justice.

While the term "policy practice," and the related term "policy advocacy" have become part of social work's lexicon, I'm not convinced that many social work students truly incorporate them into social work practice after they graduate. This may partly be due to realities they confront in jobs that do not require or even encourage policy advocacy—or by professional culture that restricts social workers to clinical practice.

Policy curriculum may itself be partly at fault. Many schools of social work restrict policy practice to a residual part of policy curriculum—such as by devoting only several sessions to it. How can policy practice, any more than clinical practice, be mastered if it occupies such a small part of social work curriculum?

Some faculty may fail to make policy practice a vital part of policy curriculum because of the insufficiency of courses targeted to policy in some Schools and Departments. In such settings, faculty understandably do not wish to omit important content about the substance of existing policies. To them, I can only ask whether teaching students how to engage in policy interventions to advance social justice ought to receive primacy over knowledge of the policies of the current American welfare state particularly when only a single session is devoted to such areas as health, mental health, and child welfare policies?

For those faculty who fear that a course or text on policy practice will omit sufficient emphasis on policy analysis, I have substantially increased content on policy analysis in this edition. I provide a six-step policy-analysis framework at the start of Chapter Seven—and use it to help students understand how to analyze problems, develop innovative proposals, and engage in policy debates and make policy presentations in Chapters Seven, Eight, and Nine.

Faculty not only need to devote substantial space in their curriculum to policy practice, but need to teach it in ways that will engage even those social work students who have been socialized to a narrowly clinical perspective. I hypothesize that many students will incorporate policy advocacy into their professional role *only* if their curriculum exposes them to models of policy practice through case examples, critical thinking, experiential involvement, and video aids.

I have markedly revised this 5th edition to include these teaching strategies. To make the subject engaging and challenging, I use two "live examples" throughout this edition: New Orleans before, during, and after Hurricane Katrina and Los Angeles County as it seeks policy remedies to end the homelessness of the roughly 90,000 persons who reside on its streets each night. I've deliberately chosen these two dramatic examples to elevate students' interest in policy practice, to illustrate policy advocacy, and to demonstrate that, absent it, the needs of vulnerable populations will not be met in coming decades.

With the assistance of Michele Baggett, a former resident of New Orleans and documentary film maker who is now a master-degree student at the School of Social Work of the University of Southern California, I've inserted 16 videotapes from four policy advocates in New Orleans as well as 15 videotapes from policy advocates in Los Angeles. (Nine of the LA videotaped segments were contributed by Bob Erlenbusch, the Chair of the Board of the National Coalition Against Homelessness based in Washington, DC as well as the Executive Director of the Los Angeles Coalition to End Hunger and Homelessness.) The videotapes average 3 minutes in length and can easily be accessed by students at the Web site academic.cengage.com/social_work/jansson. I've coupled these videotapes with documentaries from the Public Broadcasting Service (PBS) that provide graphic footage of the lethal destruction of Hurricane Katrina, the failure of governmental authorities at all levels to provide timely assistance to vulnerable populations, and the failure of public authorities to rebuild the city expeditiously. Both New Orleans and Los Angeles provide, then, laboratory examples of policy advocacy and why it is essential if we wish to advance social justice.

To these, I have authored another 21 Policy Advocacy Challenges about policy issues and advocacy in New Orleans. Most chapters conclude with a case example from New Orleans that discusses a specific challenge that policy advocates confronted, such as placing issues on agendas, writing proposals, getting proposals enacted, and troubleshooting operating programs.

I've included, as well, some Policy Advocacy Challenges and video-tapes by Professor Ralph Fertig and some of his master-degree students who engaged in policy advocacy in Los Angeles as part of a policy course in advocacy at USC. I've also included videotapes from bachelor-degree and master-degree students who won prizes for their policy-practice projects at the 2006 annual conference in Washington, DC of the organization, Influencing State Policy. It is my hope that these exemplars of policy advocacy by social work students will demonstrate that actual involvement in policy advocacy helps to demystify it.

I've included, as well, an additional 57 video tapes and policy advocacy challenges in the text that cover such topics as running for office, lobbying, and working with the media. Some of them feature the work of policy advocates in other parts of the nation.

With the assistance of Michele Baggett, I've provided yet another aid to faculty, the Thomson NOW online product available through Thomson–Brooks/Cole. This powerful resource includes pre-tests and post-tests for every chapter of the book. After taking the pre-test, students are provided with a custom study plan which directs them to review specific pages of the text available in electronic form. The NOW product also provides easy access to the aforementioned original video clips in addition to ABC news footage related to the Katrina disaster. Contact your local Thomson representative for ordering information. This text also comes

with a teaching manual. To receive a copy, faculty should contact their Thomson representative.

I've included a new chapter (Chapter Five) on policy issues and policy advocacy related to globalization that I co-authored with doctoral student Dennis Kao. We now live in a world where a host of social problems are linked to the rapid movement of capital, labor, and pollution across national boundaries—whether in the United States or in developing nations. I give many examples of social problems caused by globalization, such as the large increase in migration across national boundaries, social and economic problems in developing nations, and economic problems in the United States as illustrated by the purchasing and wage policies of mega-corporations like Wal-Mart.

I've also introduced students in this edition to the emerging use of the Internet and software in policy advocacy by inserting several Policy Advocacy Challenges from organizations, political movements, and policy advocates that use them to develop and sustain coalitions that seek policy changes.

I hope that this text helps students incorporate policy practice into their professional role. If so, future generations of social workers will remain true to the vision of the profession held by some of its founders who envisioned it as a vehicle for achieving policy reforms in a nation that was often insensitive to the needs of its vulnerable citizens.

This edition:

- invites students to join a tradition of social reform in Chapter One.
- discusses four ethical rationales for participating in policy advocacy in Chapter Two.
- provides a dynamic model of policy practice and policy advocacy in Chapter Three—and this model is used throughout the text.
- discusses the ecology of social policy in the United States in Chapter Four.
- analyzes how globalization creates a variety of social problems in the United States and abroad in Chapter Five—and how policy advocates can work to ameliorate them by changing existing policies
- discusses how to get issues on policy agendas in Chapter Six.

- provides a six-step model of policy analysis in Chapter Seven and then uses it to discuss the six steps in the balance of Chapter Seven, as well as Chapters Eight and Nine. These materials not only help students learn how to do policy analysis, but to develop proposals, engage in debates, and make effective presentations.
- analyzes power and political strategy in Chapters Ten, Eleven, and Twelve showing how

- policy advocates can develop campaigns to change policies in community, agency, and legislative settings.
- discusses why ballot-based advocacy is vital to effective policy advocacy and how social workers can participate in electoral politics in Chapter Thirteen.
- analyzes policy troubleshooting in policy implementation as well as the need to assess implemented policies in Chapter Fourteen.

ACKNOWLEDGMENTS

Forty-four persons have contributed written materials or videotapes to this edition. Many of these contributors can be found on page xvi at the outset of the book. I particularly want to acknowledge the four persons in New Orleans and Baton Rouge who contributed videotaped interviews: Russell Henderson, Rebecca Kendig, Ron McClain and Norma Rutledge. I also want to thank Professor Ralph Fertig not only for initiating a policy-advocacy project on homelessness that incorporated six sections of students, but for his materials on the law and social work. Rachel Katz expertly updated many of the Internet sites in this book. Bob Erlenbusch contributed superb video tapes on advocacy that draw on his unparalleled advocacy for homeless persons in Los Angeles and Washington, DC. Dennis Kao co-authored Chapter Five on globalization.

I want to thank in particular Michele Baggett, a native of New Orleans and a student at the USC School of Social Work, who traveled to New Orleans to collect videotaped interviews that appear throughout this text—and who gathered other videotaped interviews in Los Angeles relevant to the MSW homelessness project. Not only did she gather the videotapes, but she produced the NOW software package that faculty who use this text can elect to use.

I want to thank Professor Bob Schneider for hosting the annual conference of Influencing State

Policy, where I collected some videotapes and was delighted to listen to presentations by many faculty who give policy practice a prominent position in their curriculum.

Thanks to Dan Alpert, Editor at Wadsworth Publishing Company, for his assistance in incorporating innovative features into this edition, as well as Tanya Nigh, the production manager at Wadsworth for this book.

Reviewers of the manuscript that led to this edition include the following:

Paul Maiden, University of Central Florida
Martha C. Bial, Fordham University
David Stoesz, Virginia Commonwealth University
Katharine V. Byers, Indiana University–Bloomington
Stephen Marson, University of North Carolina–Pembroke
Louise Simmons, University of Connecticut
Betty Blythe, Boston College
Eloise Rathbone-McCuan, University of Missouri–Kansas City
Suzie T. Cashwell, Western Kentucky University

Thanks to my wife, Betty Ann, for her support during this revision process.

—*Bruce Jansson, Pasadena, California*

AN INVITATION TO STUDENTS USING THIS TEXT

This text contains unique features that can help you to learn how to become an effective policy advocate and leader. It contains more than 32 video clips that feature the work of 10 policy advocates, averaging three minutes in duration. They feature policy advocates in New Orleans who have sought to help vulnerable populations in the wake of Hurricane Katrina, advocates in Los Angeles who have addressed that county's massive homeless issue, social workers who have won elective office, and social-work experts on using the media.

It is easy to access these videos. Visit the Web site at academic.cengage.com/social_work/jansson.

These videos are supplemented by many Policy Advocacy Challenges (PACs) in this book that feature written presentations by social work leaders who have obtained key policy reforms that have benefited vulnerable populations as well as the general population. Many of them discuss problems and challenges confronted by policy advocates.

Consider this text, then, to have a policy faculty of 25 persons including myself. They are:

1. Gail Abarbanel, MSW and LCSW, is the founder and Executive Director of the Rape Treatment Center in the Santa Monica-UCLA Medical Center.
2. Mimi Abramovitz, DSW and Professor in the School of Social Work and Director of the Social Welfare Program of the Graduate Center of the City University of New York. She has written extensively on social policy issues in such areas as welfare and policy discrimination against women.
3. Laura Chick, MSW, Controller of the City of Los Angeles. She is the first woman to win an election for a city-wide office in Los Angeles and is frequently featured on news programs of the mass media in Southern California.
4. Stephanie Davis, M.A., is the Research Librarian at the University of California at Irvine.

5. Ron Dear, DSW, who was a lobbyist for the University of Washington for many years in Olympia where he was a faculty member at the School of Social Work of the University of Washington.
6. Sarah-Jane Dodd, MSW, Ph.D. is Associate Professor at the School of Social Work at Hunter College and has written extensively on ethics.
7. Bob Erlenbusch, Ph.D., Chair of the Board of the National Coalition Against Homelessness in Washington, DC and Executive Director of the Los Angeles Coalition to End Homelessness and Hunger.
8. Ralph Fertig, JD and M.A., Clinical Associate Professor at the School of Social Work of the University of Southern California. He was a freedom rider in the civil rights movement, Executive Dirctor of the Metropolitan Washing Planning and Housing Assocation, and Executive Director of the War on Poverty in Los Angeles City, as well as an administrative judge. He orchestrated the homelessness project by social work students at USC.
9. Emanuel Gale, Ph.D., is Professor Emeritus of Social Work and Gerontology at the School of Social Work at the California State University at Sacramento.
10. Melony G. Griffith, MSW, Appropriations Committee, Maryland House of Delgates. She is the representative to the State of Maryland's House of Delegates from the 25th legislative district.
11. Russell Henderson, MSW and LCSW. He is the Organizer of the Rebuilding Louisiana Coalition, has been a lobbyist with the Louisiana legislature for 21 years, and teaches social policy and community organization at Dillard University in New Orleans.
12. Rachel Katz, MPP, is a program analyst in the Finance Department of the City of Long Beach, California.

13. Dennis Kao, MSW, served as an advocate for many years with the Asian Pacific American Legal Center focusing on immigrant rights.
14. Rebecca Kendig, MSW and LCSW, is the Executive Director of Case Services Management of the Youth Empowerment Project in New Orleans.
15. Patsy Lane, MSW, Director of the Department of Human Services of the City of Pasadena.
16. Ron McClain, MSW, LCSW and JD, is the President and CEO of Family Service of Greater New Orleans.
17. Victor Manola, MSW, Ph.D. is an Assistant Professor in the Department of Social Work at California State University at Los Angeles. Having run for political office twice, he plans yet another campaign in the near future.
18. Norma Rutledge, M.Ed., and B.C.P.S., is the Executive Director of the Baton Rouge Crisis Intervention Center.
19. Ramon Salcido, DSW, is an Associate Professor at the School of Social Work at the University of Southern California. He has consulted extensively with political candidates and heads the macro concentration at USC's School of Social Work.
20. Bob Schneider, Ph.D., and Professor at the School of Social Work of Virginia Commonwealth Unversity. He founded INFLUENCING STATE POLICY and has written extensively on advocacy.
21. Anneka Scranton, MSW, DPA, formerly a Clinical Professor at the School of Social Work of the University of Southern California and currently a community activist, who has served on the boards of many social agencies and led many policy advocacy projects.
22. Samuel Taylor, DSW and Associate Professor Emeritus from the School of Social Work at the University of Southern California, who has consulted extensively with community leaders and organizations.
23. Carol Turner, A.M., has been a School Board Member for the City of Portland, Oregon and a member of the staff of the Mayor of Portland.

I have included, as well, some videotapes and policy advocacy challenges from the policy advocacy projects of bachelor and master-degree social work students at the University of Kansas, Boston College, and the University of Southern California including Michele Baggett, Jessie Buerlein, Kaela Byers, Alicia Case, Bob Hernandez, Anne Milder, Carol Ryan, Lis Soujourner, Jessica Van Tuyl, Chris Veeh, and Ali Wagner.

I am the Driscoll/Clevenger Professor of Social Policy and Administration at the School of Social Work at the University of Southern California. I invented the term "policy practice" so that social workers would develop a policy intervention to be used to reform social policies to advance such ethical principles as social justice. I truly hope that this interactive text with a faculty of 24 persons, along with contributions from 11 social work students, will broaden your social work practice to include policy changing work that will make our society a more humane place for vulnerable populations.

PART 1

BECOMING MOTIVATED TO BECOME A POLICY ADVOCATE AND A LEADER

POLICY PRACTICE AND POLICY ADVOCACY AS THE FOURTH DIMENSION OF SOCIAL WORK PRACTICE

Many social problems beg creative solutions in the United States and in the world that require the determined work of social reformers. Social workers should engage in policy advocacy to become leaders to create a more humane society.

Chapter One argues that policy practice and policy advocacy are as important to social workers as their other three interventive disciplines: direct service, community, and administrative practice. Social workers must be conversant with social policies, and must be able to seek changes in these policies to advance such values as social justice and fairness, and to advance the well-being of citizens and specific groups. They also need to work to change the composition of government to increase the likelihood that decision makers will seek policies that truly help citizens. We argue that policy advocates often encounter barriers, such as opposition from persons and groups with different values, entrenched interests, and mistaken beliefs about the causes and nature of specific

social problems and issues. Since policy changing work is often associated with controversy and conflict, policy advocates must obtain perspectives and skills that enable them to be effective change agents. By becoming policy advocates, we join social-reform traditions not only in American society but in the social work profession—whether we work for policy reforms in communities, social agencies, local governments, state governments, the federal government, or through the courts. We discuss how electoral politics is pivotal to policy advocacy. We discuss key attributes that policy advocates need, such as a vision, persistence, and the ability to tolerate uncertainty.

Chapter Two discusses moral, political, and ethical imperatives for policy practice and policy advocacy. Using the moral principles of beneficence, justice, and fairness, we argue that ethical professionals should supplement their one-on-one counseling by changing policies in agencies, communities, and legislatures.

1

Joining a Tradition of Social Reform

A POLICY PREDICAMENT	When Hurricane Katrina hit New Orleans on August 29, 2005, it devastated vast portions of this city and brought enormous trauma to its citizens, who were forced to evacuate the city with an unknown future. We discuss in Policy Advocacy Challenge 1.9 at the end of this chapter why policy advocacy is so critical to the well-being of vulnerable populations like the low-income persons displaced from such areas as the Ninth Ward in the wake of Hurricane Katrina.

We discuss in this chapter a tradition of social work advocacy that long has existed both within American society and within the social work profession and how policy advocates do the following:

- Seek changes in policies to improve the well-being of members of vulnerable populations or out-groups
- Seek policy reforms that are in the general interest
- Work from an ecological or systems perspective
- Change many kinds of policies including informal ones
- Prioritize policy changes that assist oppressed populations
- Encounter and surmount barriers to reform
- Join a tradition of social reform in American society and in the social work profession
- Develop attributes that support policy advocacy
- Try to change the composition of government by participating in electoral politics

Diversity and Policy Advocacy

When discussing diversity, most people focus on the unique cultures and perspectives of specific groups, such as women, African Americans, Asian Americans, Native Americans, gay men and lesbians, persons with physical and mental disabilities, older Americans, and children. Indeed, clinicians need extensive knowledge of different cultures and perspectives when working with members of various groups, lest they be insensitive to their needs and preferences.

But social workers risk ignoring many of the social and economic needs of these groups if they limit themselves to knowledge of their cultures and perspectives. Members of each group have experienced various kinds of discrimination and prejudice in American history, both in distant times and in recent history—discrimination and prejudice that remain active in contemporary society, even though civil rights and other protections have been enacted. Moreover, each of these groups experiences structural discrimination—a series of obstacles that, singly and together, interfere with the advancement of their members into the social and economic mainstream of American society.

American society has a variety of *vulnerable populations* or *out-groups*, who have experienced discrimination and prejudice over an extended period—and whose members' well-being (as measured by economic and other criteria) often reflects the structural barriers they have encountered. These vulnerable populations include *racial groups* such as African Americans, Latinos, and Native Americans. They have been subjected not only to overt racism in personal interactions with employers, teachers, physicians, the police, and people in other professions, but to policy discrimination as reflected in schools, training programs, housing, community amenities, and correctional and law enforcement programs that give poorer services or fewer resources to them than they give to Caucasian populations. They include *sociological groups*, such as women, older persons, and people with disabilities, whose members are often expected to assume relatively dependent roles in society, whether in places of employment or in the broader society. They are often denied access to certain kinds of jobs, to promotions, and to roles within decision-making bodies because of widespread beliefs that they are incapable of moving beyond residual or lower-level roles within society. Disabled persons are often encouraged by the medical system to be dependent. They include *dependent groups,* such as children, who often must rely upon society for basic amenities, such as financial assistance, health care, dental care, and adequate housing, but who are often given inadequate governmental support because they lack political clout. They include *nonconformist groups,* who are subjected to discrimination because they are widely viewed as violating important social norms, such as sexual norms (gay men and lesbians), social norms (criminal offenders and juvenile delinquents), or social expectations (persons with mental illnesses). They include *model groups,* such as Jewish Americans, Asian Americans, and some white ethnic Americans, who are denied resources and services because many Americans believe they have no social problems. They include *economic groups* including persons in low- and moderate-income groups who often lack sufficient resources, well-paying employment, or stable employment. Lack of resources, in turn, precludes them from some life options, such as safe neighborhoods, adequate housing, and economic security, that are available to more affluent persons.

Discrimination against members of vulnerable populations, whether expressed in personal encounters with others or through policy discrimination, often shows up in statistical measures of the economic and social well-being of members of specific out-groups. Members of racial groups tend to have, for example, fewer resources, lower life expectancies, and poorer educational achievement than Caucasian populations. Women are more likely to be poor than men, particularly when they are single heads of households. Persons with physical and mental disabilities are far more likely to be poor than other members of society. Gay youth are more likely than nongay youth to commit suicide. Children are more likely than adults to live in poverty.

A critic might ask: "But don't these differences in economic, health, and other measures of well-being stem from the intrinsic problems of members of these vulnerable populations (such as medical problems in the case of the disabled) or from the culture or work ethic of members of impoverished groups?" It is true; members of these groups do sometimes contribute to their own problems. For example, a disabled person may simply choose not to seek employment because he has accepted norms of dependency widely ascribed to disabled persons or because he possesses a mental problem such as depression. Similarly, low-income persons of color sometimes exacerbate the problems of other persons in their communities by resorting to violent behavior or abusing drugs.

Yet efforts to generalize actions of specific persons to entire populations are doomed to failure. When entire groups have economic, education, health, and other indicators of well-being that are sharply divergent from the dominant population, we rightly can surmise that external forces and policies impact them adversely and contribute to these outcomes. When a disproportionate percentage of single female heads of households are immersed in poverty, we can rightly ask what factors, singly and in tandem, affect or influence the economic outcomes of this population so that, as a group, its members suffer disproportionate poverty when compared to double-headed families or single females with no children.

When examining structural discrimination, we identify policies, familial factors, cultural factors, life experiences, community factors, and economic factors that *systematically* shape the lives of specific groups so they fall behind other groups that are not subject to structural discrimination. We can understand why such groups as low-income African Americans or single heads of households lag behind white males with college degrees in income only by examining a constellation of factors that systematically impinge on them. In the case of low-income, inner-city African Americans, such factors include the following:

- Overt discrimination on the basis of race
- Subtle discrimination that relegates African Americans to poorly paid positions and to education tracks that steer them away from college preparation
- Segregated communities that are distant from places of employment
- Lack of family and community role models who have secured higher levels of education
- Overcrowded schools
- Low expectations from school personnel, including excessive tracking
- Childhood poverty exacerbated by governmental policies such as the absence of family allowances
- Family stress stemming from poverty
- Lack of recreational programs
- Exposure to violence, such as from gangs
- High rates of mortality among adolescent males
- Lack of user-friendly health systems that provide preventive services
- Lack of well-paying, accessible, and stable employment
- Lack of access to the old-boy networks that give some people an inside track to jobs and educational opportunities

If we compare suburban white children whose parents have college educations with African American inner-city residents, the harsh workings of structural discrimination immediately become evident. These suburban children rarely confront these barriers—and if they do encounter specific ones, they rarely encounter a constellation of barriers. It is not surprising that suburban white residents are often unsympathetic to inner-city African Americans. Assuming from their own experiences that a level playing field does exist, many of them believe the inner-city residents lack personal characteristics, such as the work ethic, that would bring them out of poverty.

Consider single women who have high school diplomas or less. Regardless of their ethnicity, these women are likely to secure only relatively low-paying work because they cannot compete for the higher-paying jobs usually filled by persons with higher levels of education. As single parents, moreover, they must frequently support their children without financial assistance from another parent, even though governmental authorities have placed more emphasis in recent years on collecting funds from absent parents. Because the United States does not fund day care for many women for sustained periods, their meager paychecks are often depleted by day-care costs. Because employers are not required by law to provide fringe benefits, many low-wage-earning women do not have health insurance, so they must obtain health care for themselves or their children in crowded, difficult-to-access public clinics. Some of these women cannot afford cars, so they must use a time-consuming public transportation system that sometimes does not even have routes convenient to their workplaces. It is small wonder, then, that millions of poorly educated single mothers and their children remain mired in poverty for extended periods, no matter how hard they work to achieve a better economic standard. As with inner-city African Americans, poverty brings additional stresses to individuals and families who must struggle to make ends meet, who cannot afford amenities that others take for granted, and who often must live in blighted communities where rents are relatively low. (See Policy Advocacy Challenge 1.1.)

We should not merely take a short-term perspective when we examine the effects of external forces and policies. Most African Americans, for example, were deprived of land, civil liberties, and education in the 19th century—often relegated to rural areas of the South where they lived in appalling poverty. Unlike white immigrants from Italy, Ireland, and eastern Europe, they were not allowed to participate in the emerging industrial order of northern cities in the 19th century. African Americans only began moving to the North in large numbers well into the 20th century. They were consigned to play catch up under equally appalling conditions in northern cities, such as segregated communities, exclusion from trade unions, hiring and promotion prejudice in the workplace that consigned them to unskilled and uncertain jobs, poor health care, and poor schools—not to mention police brutality. It is hardly surprising that gangs and substance abuse festered in low-income African American areas, which further impeded upward mobility. Policy developments of preceding eras, then, impeded the ability of contemporary African Americans to achieve parity with Caucasian Americans, whose upward economic assent was built upon generations of their children obtaining education, the accumulation of assets (such as savings and houses), and heightened expectations.

Policy advocates are sometimes not content merely with equalizing policies of vulnerable populations and the dominant population. Because of the effects of long-term oppression on members of these populations, we should sometimes favor *compensatory* strategies, such as extra tutoring or smaller classes in schools, outreach health services to encourage persons who do not usually use the health care system services to do so, or providing community-based services in areas where persons are particularly impoverished. Similarly, affirmative action is sometimes needed to move members of vulnerable populations more rapidly into employment and education—particularly when we conclude that their members would not otherwise achieve parity with the dominant population in the foreseeable future.

When identifying a variety of factors that lead certain vulnerable populations to lag behind the population with respect to specific indicators of well-being, we must beware of several dangers. These include excessively stigmatizing groups, viewing them as excessively dependent, or relying on panaceas. Many individuals do make it up and out despite structural discrimination, such as African Americans who enter professions, single heads of households who successfully juggle raising children and careers, and paraplegics who use technology to care for themselves and enter the workforce. Nor should we view members of vulnerable populations as passive victims of fate. American history is replete with advocates' determined efforts from these groups to mobilize resources, self-help projects, networks, alliances, and policy advocacy to better their condition. Our challenge is to empower them to develop creative solutions for overcoming barriers they encounter—and to provide them with social policies that allow them to obtain resources, housing, and services from different levels of government and from the private sector. We should not succumb to the belief that specific policies will have a magical effect. To help single mothers improve their economic condition, for example, we need multiple, interacting policies that help them improve their lot, such as greater funding for child care, increases in the minimum wage, expansion of the earned-income tax credit (which gives low-income workers a tax rebate), increases in housing subsidies, more training and remedial education, expansion of food stamp subsidies, and expansion of health insurance for children and families.

POLICY ADVOCACY CHALLENGE 1.1

Mapping Structural Discrimination

RON MCCLAIN, JD, MSW, LCSW

Go to
academic.cengage.com/ social_work/jansson
to watch this video clip

Take any vulnerable population that lags behind the general population on specific social or economic indicators. Identify a constellation of factors that lead to structural discrimination against this group by contrasting it with another group in the population that is not as subject to structural discrimination.

Identify specific kinds of policy reforms that have been enacted to ameliorate such structural discrimination. What additional reforms would help the subgroup's members improve their economic and social status?

Why are social workers' clinical skills not sufficient to redress structural discrimination?

Discuss why many low-income African Americans did *not* flee New Orleans when warned a hurricane was imminent. View Policy Advocacy Challenge Video 1.1 where Ron McClain, JD, LCSW, President and CEO of Family Service of Greater New Orleans, and adjunct faculty member of the School of Social Work of Southern University at New Orleans, discusses the plight of this vulnerable population in Hurricane Katrina's immediate aftermath. To what extent did racism and classism exist in New Orleans prior to Hurricane Katrina? What realities did many African Americans confront in New Orleans that made flight difficult or impossible? Would the federal government have taken the problems encountered by African-American residents in New Orleans after Hurricane Katrina more seriously had they mostly been affluent Caucasian persons?

In policy practice and policy advocacy, then, social workers must consider diversity at more than just the cultural level. This allows social workers to address environmental factors that stack the deck against a subgroup's members and that powerfully shape their collective destinies. Social workers can use policy advocacy to remedy or address problems like the following:

- Inner-city poverty concentrations of African Americans, Latinos, Asian Americans, and Native Americans
- The feminization of poverty, with roughly one fourth of American children living in impoverished households
- Extraordinary differences in educational attainment between white people and many people of color
- Large disparities between men and women in earnings and high-level positions in employment
- Extraordinary poverty among persons with physical and mental disabilities
- Discrimination against gay men and lesbians
- A dearth of services for people who abuse substances
- Problems of frail older people who need various kinds of tangible assistance but who are impoverished
- Inadequate safety-net programs to allow low-income persons to overcome excessive economic problems
- Violence against women
- Affordable housing for low-income Americans

POLICY ADVOCACY CHALLENGE 1.2

Enhancing the Rights of Children Who Are Sexually Assaulted in School

GAIL ABARBANEL, M.S.W., L.C.S.W., EXECUTIVE DIRECTOR, RAPE TREATMENT CENTER, SANTA MONICA—UCLA MEDICAL CENTER

As a social worker, I view social policy reforms as a way to give meaning to the experiences of my clients, as well as a means to serve them better. The following case example illustrates these two functions: Jennifer, a 12-year-old girl attending a Los Angeles middle school, was raped by another student—during the school day—on the school campus. After she reported the crime, she was revictimized by her eighth-grade classmates, who ridiculed and harassed her. Jennifer also was ostracized by some of her friends, who informed her that their parents had told them that they could no longer associate with her.

When the school district scheduled a disciplinary hearing, Jennifer received very little notice and no information about the procedures. When Jennifer and her parents arrived at the hearing, they were told that this 12-year-old child would have to go into the hearing room alone. No one was allowed to accompany her—no parent, no counsel, no support person—while she was subjected to cross-examination by the accused student's representative. The accused student, however, was allowed to have his parents and a legal representative present to support him during the entire proceeding.

Jennifer had been profoundly traumatized by the rape. She was too fragile psychologically, as most other 12-year-old children would be, to testify under the conditions set by the school district. However, she was informed by school officials that, without her testimony, there would be no disciplinary action. The hearing was postponed.

(continued)

**POLICY
ADVOCACY
CHALLENGE 1.2**

(continued)

As a result of the Rape Treatment Center's efforts on the victim's behalf, when the hearing was finally held, Jennifer was allowed to be accompanied by an ACLU attorney.

However, the attorney was required to remain silent. The school district officials seated Jennifer very close to, and directly opposite, the father of the boy who had raped her. The accused student's representative who questioned Jennifer insulted and taunted her. She also asked Jennifer to demonstrate some of the degrading things that had been done to her during the assault, an abusive practice called "reenactment" that would not be permitted in most legal proceedings involving either child or adult victims.

The hearing process was devastating for Jennifer. She was powerless, just as she had been during the rape. Again, she was revictimized—this time by the school district's disciplinary system.

As the founder and director of the Rape Treatment Center (RTC) at Santa Monica–UCLA Medical Center and a longtime advocate for victims of sexual assault, I intervened to protect this child, *and* I sought a remedy that would provide legal protection for other child victims and would prevent this kind of discriminatory treatment in the future. I turned to Assemblywoman Sheila Kuehl (D-Santa Monica), our representative in the state legislature. Together, we drafted legislation to establish rights for children who are sexually assaulted in their schools.

Under the new law, which became effective January 1, 1997, child victims are given many of the same rights afforded accused students in school disciplinary hearings, such as the right to have a support person accompany them during their testimony and to request a closed hearing. In addition, the victim's irrelevant sexual history is protected from disclosure. Sexual assault victims have had these rights in the criminal and civil justice systems for many years. However, in most states, the education codes recognize the rights only of accused students while overlooking the needs of victims. The new law corrects this inequity.

Passage of this legislation is only a first step. Students must be informed about the new rights and protections available to them if they are victimized. Schools must change their policies and procedures to implement the reforms required by the new law. The RTC has an established, school-based, sexual abuse prevention program that reaches thousands of students each year, as well as administrative personnel in schools throughout the community we serve. This program has enabled us to educate school personnel and students about the new law. Ten years later, in 2007, it educates new student cohorts and teachers.

Advancing the Public Interest at Home and Abroad

While policy advocates often focus on problems and issues affecting vulnerable populations, they also tackle problems of citizens in general, which we call the public interest. They want child-care services, for example, that improve the developmental and cognitive well-being of *any* children who use them. They want schools that provide first-rate counseling services to children so that any children who develop mental-health or substance-abuse problems can obtain quality services. They want preventive services that diminish the incidence of major social problems that afflict citizens whether or not they are members of a vulnerable population. For example, policy advocates might seek laws that disallow smoking in public places and require health-risk notifications on cigarette packages, seek antipollution measures, fight for better public transportation systems, or seek a living-wage policy for all workers.

As we discuss in Chapter Five, policy advocates do not limit their activity to the United States. With the reduction of trade barriers, for example, many American corporations have relocated their operations abroad to escape high wages, antipollution regulations, and corporate taxes they confront in the United States. To the extent that they impose inhumane practices on other nations in a quest to expand their profits, policy advocates battle for international standards that govern wages and pollution, and seek to protect wages of American workers who often are given an ultimatum to accept lower wages to forestall their company from replacing their jobs with lower-wage workers abroad. Issues of immigration across national borders are germane, as well, to policy advocates who grapple with such issues as when immigrants should receive citizenship, and how immigrants' rights should be protected in the United States. Since policy advocates are interested in the well-being of persons no matter their location, some of them pursue issues of global social justice, such as how wealthy nations like the United States can assist third-world nations with poverty and such illnesses as AIDS.

Using an Ecological Perspective

An ecological or systems perspective is highly useful in policy advocacy. As our discussion of vulnerable populations suggests, citizens' lives are impacted by multiple factors, including economic, cultural, social, community, and physiological, as well as discrimination or prejudice. Existing policies are part of their ecology: they limit resources, services, and opportunities that they receive, but also provide them. When developing policy proposals, advocates often examine the problems and populations that will be impacted by these proposals from an ecological perspective. They ask, for example, what forces and factors in the lives of welfare recipients influence whether they can secure and retain employment; then they seek policies that address these ecological factors. (We discuss an ecological perspective at greater length in Chapter Seven.)

What Policy Practitioners and Advocates Seek to Change

Policy advocates aim to change social policies. This book uses a simple, problem-solving definition of *social policy* as "a collective strategy that *prevents* and *addresses* social problems." Our definition is similar to that of the late Richard Titmuss, an English social policy theorist.[1]

Defining social policy as goal-driven problem solving has several advantages. First, it makes clear that policies are established to prevent and address social problems that include the following:

- Victimization of persons by landlords, corporations, businesses, realtors, restaurant owners, and others—such as by providing them with unsafe rentals, providing unsafe products, not providing consumers with sanitary food, and not paying employees sufficient resources to allow them to survive. These kinds of problems are often addressed by *regulations* such as the federal minimum wage, housing codes, regulations of the federal Food and Drug Administration, and local living-wage regulations.
- Inability of citizens to meet their survival needs, thus imperiling their nutritional, housing, health, and other basic needs. These kinds of policies lead to *needs-meeting policies* that provide basic health and economic benefits to citizens, such as food stamps, Medicaid and Medicare health benefits, Supplemental Security Income (SSI), and rent-supplement programs.

- Inability of citizens to obtain skills and knowledge to find employment or to find employment that can meet their basic needs. These kinds of *opportunity-enhancing policies* include public education, job-training programs, and vocational education.
- Inability of citizens to cope with mental health, marital, substance abuse, and familial problems. These *social-service policies* include a wide range of mental health, child welfare, and substance abuse programs.
- Inability of citizens to navigate complex service-delivery systems. *Referral and linkage policies* establish case management, ombudsman, and outreach programs.
- Discriminatory treatment of members of specific o ut-groups by employers, schools, public facilities, transportation companies, landlords, and others. *Civil rights policies* prohibit specific infringements of the civil rights of out-groups' members, including the Civil Rights Acts of 1964 and 1965, local antihate laws prohibiting attacks on members of out-groups and defiling places of worship, and the Americans with Disabilities Act.
- Excessive inequality between low- and high-income persons. *Equality-enhancing policies* have targeted resources to low-income populations, such as the federal Earned Income Tax Credit (EITC); progressive features of federal, state, and local tax codes that tax affluent citizens more heavily than low-income citizens; and a host of programs that target services or resources to low-income populations, such as Medicaid, SSI, and food stamps.
- Inability of low-income Americans to accumulate assets such as savings accounts and real estate. *Asset accumulation policies,* such as federal legislation stimulating individual investment accounts, give citizens tax incentives and resources to initiate savings accounts and to purchase houses.
- Citizens lack public amenities necessary for recreation and commerce. Federal, state, and local governments enact *infrastructure development policies* that promote construction of roads, parks, bridges, and public transportation.
- Certain portions of cities lack sufficient jobs to support their citizens. Various levels of government offer *economic development policies* such as tax incentives and loans to businesses that locate themselves in low-income areas.
- Low rates of participation in the political process by low-income persons that increases the disinclination of government to adequately fund programs to help them. Policies geared toward *facilitating political participation and increasing the political power of oppressed populations* include state and federal policies that prohibit excessive campaign contributions by special interests and that reapportion political districts so that they do not discriminate against persons of color.
- Insufficient resources are devoted to specific problems or issues by governments or even specific agencies or organizations requiring *budget-changing policies.*
- *Protective policies* that help persons who are subject to abusive or violent behaviors and actions of others, such as protective-services programs for children and policies that protect women from battering.

We include *prevention* in our definition of social policy because policy advocates want not only to address existing social problems, but to prevent them when possible. Much like public health advocates have succeeded in obtaining many anti-smoking, gun-control, and auto-safety measures that have saved many lives and averted injuries, social work advocates have put in place early detection programs for such mental health problems as depression, programs to prevent youth from leaving school prematurely, programs that help isolated persons join day-treatment programs, and daycare and job-training programs to help persons improve their economic condition.

We should note, as well, that many policies are geared toward improving defects in the operations of agencies that implement specific social policies. Imagine, for example, that a legislator succeeds in enacting legislation that provides prenatal services meant to decrease premature births and birth defects. Imagine, as well, that the person who sponsored the legislation finds, several years later, that it has had little impact on the rates of premature births or birth defects in an inner-city Latino area. Assume the legislator also discovers that neither bilingual nor outreach staff have been hired, that clinic hours are limited to daytime hours, and that programs are located at inconvenient sites for Latinas, such as at a distant public hospital. The following are problems in the human services system that are often the targets of policy reform in specific agencies, in specific service networks, or in legislation establishing new programs.

- *Fragmentation.* Barriers make it difficult for clients or consumers to obtain services from multiple programs.
- *Discontinuity.* Clients cannot obtain consistent, accessible services over a period of time.
- *Lack of access.* Barriers make services hard to use at specific sites.
- *Discrimination.* Service providers are hostile or indifferent to specific kinds of clients.
- *Creaming.* Providers deliberately seek clients with less serious problems.
- *Wastage.* Different providers serve the same population for the same problem, or services are not provided efficiently.
- *Lack of outreach.* Providers make little effort to seek persons who do not currently use services.
- *Incompetent staff.* Staff are asked to perform tasks for which they have little training.
- *Lack of cultural sensitivity.* Providers make little effort to match their services to the cultural perspectives of the clients they serve such as by having bilingual staff or staff versed in specific cultures.
- *Inadequate funding.* Services are funded at such low levels that important activities are compromised or deleted.

Our definition of social policy as collective strategy to prevent and address social problems makes clear that policies are developed in many places, as the example of commitment procedures for people with mental illness illustrates. Policies may come down from the highest levels, including state mental health officials, county mental health departments, various courts, and even federal authorities. Although these *high-level policies* influence their work, staff in county mental health units may implement them in strikingly different ways. The staff at one county hospital may commit many more persons than the staff at another hospital, because each defines *imminent threat* differently.

Social welfare policies are often divided into mental health, health, child and family, income maintenance, school, industrial, corrections, housing, and other sectors. This division of policies into sectors partly reflects specializations among professionals, providers, and funders, as well as specific legislative committees that write legislation in these areas. While the division of policies into these sectors usefully allows us to identify policies that are directed to specific kinds of needs and issues, it can also contribute to excessive fragmentation between the sectors. Many consumers of health services, for example, need mental health services, but they must often go to different agencies to get them—and may find their mental health needs, such as depression, not recognized or treated by health professionals. Rather than coordinating their services, specialized agencies sometimes erect turf barriers.

It is useful to portray social policy as a kind of ladder extending from federal authorities to persons in the population who use services or programs. Policy advocates can intervene at any point in this policy ladder—or at several points. They sometimes seek to change the policies of individual agencies, such as specific not-for-profit, for-profit, or public agencies. They may seek to change the policies of higher-level agencies in counties, municipalities, or townships. They may seek redress in state or federal venues. Or they may seek court rulings that place restrictions on how local mental health agencies commit mental patients involuntarily to mental institutions.

Our definition of social policy eliminates the problem of establishing rigid boundaries between social policy and other kinds of policies. Most commentators agree that public welfare, child welfare, medical, and job-training policies are social policies, but they are less certain about income tax, environmental, economic, transportation, and other policies. Our definition suggests that specific policies become social policies whenever they influence social problems. For example, income tax proposals that increase or decrease the resources of poor persons become social policies when they affect poverty and unemployment. By the same token, tax policies that regulate how corporations depreciate their equipment are not social policies unless they can be shown to be relevant to such problems as poverty and unemployment.

Thus far, we have emphasized the content or substance of policies by focusing on the kind of social problems that specific policies address. Now we turn our attention to the different forms of policies and where they are located. *Statutes* containing policies often become established when local, state, and federal governments approve legislation. *Policy objectives* (or mission statements) are a kind of policy because they shape the actions and choices of officials, executives, and staff. When a state mental health agency decides to drastically reduce the populations of mental institutions, its officials and staff are committed to this objective and to programs consonant with it. Imagine how services might change if, instead, top officials wanted to increase long-term institutional services for a range of mental conditions. (See Policy Advocacy Challenge 1.3.)

By the same token, *rules and regulations* are a kind of policy because many social policies constrain the activities of officials, staff, and consumers. For example, rules and regulations place many restrictions on mental health personnel when they wish to commit someone involuntarily to a mental hospital. They must base their commitment on evidence that the person will harm themselves or others if not committed—and they must go through specific procedures, including holding hearings and providing legal counsel to the person being committed. The operations of every publicly funded program are shaped by administrative regulations issued by government agencies, including who is eligible, what kinds of staff are hired, how records are kept, and the content of services. (Some of these operating policies are also defined in statutes.)

Budgets are a kind of policy since they determine what resources are devoted to specific, enacted policies—resources that determine whether a policy will be effective and who will receive it. Budgets also determine priorities, such as what programs are and are not emphasized. In the wake of Hurricane Katrina, for example, advocates fought hard in Washington, DC to obtain budget commitments sufficient to rebuild New Orleans and to make it safer from future natural disasters.

POLICY ADVOCACY CHALLENGE 1.3

The Impact of Hurricane Katrina on the Mission of a Social Agency in New Orleans

RON McCLAIN, JD, MSW, LCSW

Go to **academic.cengage.com/ social_work/jansson** to watch this video clip

Hurricane Katrina changed not only New Orleans' landscape, but the missions of many social agencies that now had to engage in different activities or prioritize different kinds of services as they sought to help persons and families devastated by the storm. Speculate how the missions of specific child welfare, mental health, school, or other social agencies might have shifted as a result of Katrina. See Policy Advocacy Challenge Video 1.3 as Ron McClain, JD, LSCW, President and CEO of Family Service of Greater New Orleans, and adjunct faculty member at the School of Social Work of Southern University in New Orleans discusses how Katrina impacted the mission of his agency. What new or different services did his agency provide?

Court rulings are another important kind of policy. Courts have made many rulings, for example, that require social workers to protect the confidentiality of information given to them by clients, patients, or consumers. They sometimes rescind cut-backs in services and benefits.

Formal or *written policies* can certainly be considered social policy, whether they are issued by legislation, or are court rulings, administrative guidelines, or budget documents. It is less immediately clear whether *informal* or *nonwritten policies* qualify. The issue requires some examination. When written policy contains relatively vague and ill-defined terms, officials must often develop informal policies to fill in the gaps. For example, some laws restrict involuntary commitment to persons who pose an imminent danger to themselves or others. Staff who require a strict standard may resist committing someone who has not actually attempted suicide, whereas other staff may believe that merely threatening suicide falls within this restriction. Though such standards have not been recorded in official policy, they are policies because they have the same effect as written policy. They are collectively defined rules that profoundly shape the actions of direct-service staff and their administrators.

Informal policies are absolutely critical to social policy because they cover a wide range of issues. For example, in a child welfare department, informal policies shape how staff conceptualize child welfare. Do they see their job exclusively as helping children who have been seriously abused or neglected, or do they also want to construct preventive programs to educate at-risk parents about parenting? Do they believe it is their job to link their services with schools, medical services, and job-training programs for parents, or do they see their work as isolated from other programs? Do they want to work with troubled families over an extended period, or do they see their responsibility primarily to remove children from such families?

Our definition of social policy, then, emphasizes both *formal* and *informal* policies. If the former includes rules, procedures, court rulings, and budgets that bind specific persons to specific courses of action, then subjective views of persons and groups constitute the latter. We cannot understand the workings of social agencies, legislators, or heads of governments without understanding both dimensions of social policy.

Without suggesting that any of them is more or less important than the others, we might distinguish four categories: (1) official, written policies; (2) informal, unwritten policies; (3) personal orientations toward policy, such as an aversion to specific rules or strong support of a specific policy; and (4) personal policy actions, such as obeying or disobeying a policy in a specific work setting. Bisno calls the fourth type "policy-in-action," whereas I have named it *actualized policy*.[2] All of these policy-related categories are important in social policy.

What Are Policy Practice and Policy Advocacy?

We define *policy practice* as efforts to change policies in legislative, agency, and community settings, whether by establishing new policies, improving existing ones, or defeating the policy initiatives of other people. By this definition, people of all ideological persuasions, including liberals, radicals, and conservatives, engage in policy practice. People who are skilled in policy practice increase the odds that their policy preferences will be advanced.

By *policy advocacy*, we mean policy practice that aims to help relatively powerless groups—such as women, children, poor people, African Americans, Asian Americans, Latinos, Native Americans, gay men and lesbians, and people with disabilities—improve their resources and opportunities. Thus, policy practice refers to efforts generally to change policies, and policy advocacy refers to efforts to help powerless groups improve their lot.

Because social workers usually work with people who are relatively powerless, their policy practice usually is policy advocacy. Therefore, we often refer to social workers' policy practice as policy advocacy in this book. Yet social workers as policy advocates need to ground their work in a range of tasks, skills, and competencies that also apply to policy practice. Sometimes we can even apply the tactics of skilled policy practitioners with whom we disagree to *our* policy advocacy.

This distinction between policy practice and policy advocacy is important for several reasons. First, it allows us to discover the differences between the policy practice of social workers and, for example, that of the U.S. Chamber of Commerce, the National Association of Manufacturers, and the National Rifle Association. They are policy practitioners, but they often do not advocate for relatively powerless populations.

Second, this distinction allows us to develop a general framework for any policy changing work (policy practice) that advocates can adapt to their own purposes. Were we to discuss only policy advocacy, we would be leaving out the general underlying principles of policy changing work. Policy advocacy is hard work that requires its practitioners to use an underlying policy changing framework, as well as specific tasks, skills, and competencies.

Finally, this distinction allows us to evaluate the results of policy changing work in terms of its ultimate purpose. We might admire the National Rifle Association's ability to gain and use power to block gun control, but this tactical skill (the means) should not imply that the ends are praiseworthy.

Policies rarely emerge suddenly—but always during a developmental process. Policy advocates need both to understand this process and to be able to work skillfully within it. We discuss throughout this text the tasks and skills you will need to become an effective policy advocate. When presenting problems to agency, community, and legislative decision makers, advocates engage in *agenda-setting tasks.* When they use social science research that probes their causes and when they analyze policy options to find a policy that they prefer, practitioners perform *problem-analyzing tasks.* They also analyze social problems, such as homelessness, not only analyzing its causes but trying to find solutions based on the best available knowledge, including research.

Practitioners *develop proposals* when they create solutions to specific problems, whether legislation, to improve agency services. Proposals may be relatively simple, such as those that change an agency's intake policies; or complex, such as those that establish major social programs. They make presentations and engage in debates to convince others to support their proposals.

Practitioners engage in *policy-enacting tasks* when they develop strategies to have a policy approved. When complex political processes are involved, strategy may consume major amounts of time and resources and demand frequent revisions. On other occasions, strategy may consist of one presentation at a critical meeting or personal discussions with highly placed decision makers.

Policy implementation involves identifying why a policy has not been adequately implemented and developing corrective strategies. *Policy-assessing tasks* require evaluating a policy and deciding what changes to make if the evaluation is negative.

Policy practitioners (and therefore policy advocates) use four basic skills as they engage in each of the stages of the policy-development process. They use *analytic skills* to obtain data, identify policy alternatives, compare their relative merits, and develop recommendations. *Political skills* help practitioners assess the policies' feasibility, identify power resources, and develop and implement political strategy. *Interactional skills* help practitioners make contacts, develop networks, build personal relationships, identify old-boy networks, and facilitate coalitions and committees.

Points made during the policy-making process require *value-clarification* or *ethical-reasoning skills.* Policy makers have to decide what objectives they favor when analyzing problems and developing policy proposals. Do they want drastic reforms or merely modest changes in existing policies? Values arise as well when policy makers define their motivations and loyalties. Do they identify with and seek to help certain powerless groups, the agency that employs them, or their particular work unit? Do they seek personal advancement through policy changes? Do they seek fundamental or incremental change? Policy practitioners must also determine what risks they will take in questioning existing policies, such as the loss of their jobs, in extreme cases. In addition, policy practitioners must wrestle with ethical issues related to procedural matters. Under what circumstances are deceptive, dishonest, or manipulative behaviors ethical? When is it ethical to undermine the credibility of another person or faction? When seeking support for a policy, is it ever ethical to make exaggerated claims about it? Ethical issues also arise about the substantive content of policies. For example, ethical principles are involved in involuntarily committing homeless persons with mental problems: Should laws protect homeless people's well-being or maximize their autonomy and self-determination?

Challenges Encountered by Policy Advocates

Policy advocacy is important—and challenging—work. By changing laws, rules, regulations, budgets, and objectives, policy advocates can positively impact the lives not just of specific individuals or families (as in direct-practice social work), but of large numbers of individuals and families. For example, prior to the enactment of the food stamp program, millions of low-income families lacked the resources to provide proper nutrition to their members. Another example is a social worker who persuades an agency to hire a bilingual worker, thus allowing services to be provided to scores of families that otherwise might not have received them.

If policy advocacy is often rewarding, it is also challenging for several reasons. Indeed, policy advocates often encounter opposition or controversy when they try to change specific policies. Controversy or opposition are likely for several reasons, including a crowded field, divergent interests, divergent values and ideology, and different beliefs about whether a specific policy is, or will be, effective in addressing a specific social problem.

A Crowded Field   Unlike direct-service work, for example, policy advocates rarely have the field to themselves. This is because social policies—and policies generally—commit or bind large groups of persons and organizations to specific courses of action by establishing ground rules that guide or direct their activity. Therefore, many groups, persons, and interests take an interest in specific policies—especially when someone wants to initiate a new one or change an existing one.

Influencing Tangible Interests of Persons, Groups, and Corporations
When examining interests, policy advocates often ask, "Who benefits from the status quo, and who believes their practical interests would better be met by some or major reforms?" Since specific persons, interest groups, and corporations often benefit from specific policies, they often oppose changes in them—or only want changes that advance their own needs. As persons who have sought to reform American medical care have frequently discovered, for example, pharmaceutical companies, insurance companies, health plans, and the American Medical Association have often blocked needed reforms. Indeed, consumers are often the least represented in policy deliberations that can be dominated by persons and groups with resources to hire lobbyists and to give funds to politicians and political parties.

Divergent Values and Ideologies   People often support or oppose policies because they believe they impinge on their fundamental values. As developments in the United States during the 1980s, 1990s, and first portion of this century suggest, conservatives and liberals often battle over policies. Indeed, *ideology* is a shorthand way of summarizing persons' values, as can be seen in Table 1.1.

Conservatives prioritize such values as freedom (or liberty), localism in social policy, and individualism. Because conservatives also tend to believe that the private markets are relatively effective and humane in distributing societal resources, they are less inclined than liberals to favor regulations of corporations. Such persons as Ronald Reagan, Newt Gingrich, and George W. Bush share a world view that emphasizes policies that flow from these basic values. They favor relatively low taxes, believing that citizens' resources belong to themselves. They favor diminution of federal power, preferring to transfer to state and local governments many federal policy roles. They want to increase the role of private charity in American society while reducing public expenditures. They often oppose regulations that constrain corporations, such as anti-pollution laws, increases in the minimum wage, work-safety regulations, and proposals to allow consumers to sue health maintenance organizations. Of course, not all conservatives are alike in their views. So-called moderate Republicans often want relatively more public spending, more government regulations, and less military spending than more conservative Republicans. Those drawn from fundamentalist churches often take

TABLE 1.1 Comparison of different ideologies

	Conservatives	Libertarians	Liberals	Radicals
Views of federal government	Negative, except in military and international policy and as source of subsidies for business	Negative	Relatively positive	Positive, unless it is under control of monied interests
Views of state and local government	Relatively positive	Negative	Divided, but federal government is often preferred	Less positive than views of federal government
Views of causes of social problems	Emphasis on personal and cultural factors	Unclear	More emphasis than conservatives on environmental factors	Environmental factors generated by monied interests
Views of capitalism	Positive	Positive	Positive, but regulations are favored	Negative, unless workers are empowered
Views of human nature	Relatively optimistic about affluent people, less optimistic about poor people	Favor policies that maximize the liberty of all people	Relatively optimistic about poor people but less optimistic about rich people	Pessimistic about monied interests, but optimistic about other people
Views of safety net	Want relatively meager safety net	Unclear	Want relatively generous safety net	Favor generous safety net
Attitudes toward abortion and other moral issues	Divided, but a significant faction favors government controls	Dislike government regulation of social matters	Usually oppose restrictions on abortion but favor restrictions on drugs	Often oppose restriction of social matters
Core value	Liberty, though some government incentives and regulations are favored	Liberty	Liberty, but social justice is also important	Social justice
Views of nongovernmental and governmental programs	Favor nongovernmental initiatives	Favor nongovernmental initiatives	Favor a mixture of both	Favor governmental programs, but often recommend worker or citizen inclusion in government decisions
Views of subgroups that lag behind others in economic status or that experience discrimination	Tend to deny their existence or minimize discrimination	Unclear	Favor some redistribution and strong civil rights	Emphasize oppression of out-groups and seek major corrective action

positions on so-called social issues (such as abortion and regulations regarding pornographic literature) that differ from other Republicans.

One need only contrast the positions of Reagan, Gingrich, and Bush with those of Bill Clinton, Jesse Jackson, and Ted Kennedy to see that significant ideological differences exist between conservatives and liberals. (See Table 1.1.) Liberals place somewhat greater emphasis than conservatives on social justice, favoring somewhat more redistribution of resources to low-income persons. They have traditionally been in the forefront of efforts to secure social reforms that require greater expenditure of government resources or expansion of government regulations, even when these efforts require higher taxes. They are somewhat more critical of private markets in distributing resources or advancing other goals—making them more likely than conservatives to favor a minimum or living wage, work-safety regulations, antipollution measures, and proposals that would allow consumers to sue health maintenance organizations. Liberals have traditionally been somewhat less suspicious of the government than conservatives, often turning to the federal government to implement and fund an array of social programs. Even in state and local jurisdictions, liberals are more likely than conservatives to propose and support government programs. While many conservatives have favored civil rights legislation, liberals have often been even more supportive of efforts to assist persons of color, women, the disabled, and gay men and lesbians with regulations that curtail discrimination in employment and elsewhere.

Libertarians emphasize liberty or freedom. They oppose, for example, the so-called War on Drugs on grounds that citizens should be able to make their own lifestyle choices. They do not favor heavy taxation of personal income, believing citizens should be able to keep most of their resources. They oppose restrictions on abortion, censorship of pornographic literature, and most other policies that restrict individuals' liberty to make basic choices for themselves.

It is difficult to define radicalism with precision in an American society that lacks a strong socialist tradition. (See Table 1.1.) Yet we can find many persons in American history, such as the social work leader Bertha Reynolds, who have been more insistent on equalizing wealth and power in the United States than liberals. They believe that capitalism, even when somewhat regulated by government, distributes wealth in an unfair manner. Radicals favor far higher taxation of private wealth than conservatives or liberals. They want government to redistribute resources aggressively to diminish economic inequality. They sometimes favor proposals to allow workers to acquire partial or complete ownership of corporations.

Different Opinions about What Works Best   Policy advocates sometimes encounter opposition from persons and groups who contend that their proposals will not work or are too expensive. They might be told "you can't solve problems by throwing money at them," or "that solution is too expensive," or "your solution will corrupt the work incentive of welfare recipients." Sometimes, they are told "we have tried that before and it didn't work."

In truth, it often is difficult to know precisely what policy solutions will ameliorate or solve social problems—especially complex ones like poverty, low school achievement, and some kinds of mental illness. It is difficult, as well, to know how to prevent some social problems, for instance high rates of cancer, heart disease, and mental illness or delinquency, substance abuse, and truancy. We know that diet and lifestyle changes would cut the rates of many health problems, but we do not know how to entice many people to make these changes.

POLICY ADVOCACY CHALLENGE 1.4

Ideological Cleavages About Rebuilding New Orleans Post-Katrina

REBECCA KENDIG, MSW, LCSW

Go to **academic.cengage.com/ social_work/jansson** to watch this video clip

To what extent would you anticipate that conservatives, liberals, radicals, and libertarians would disagree about how to rebuild New Orleans post-Katrina? Consider the relative emphasis they might place on market forces, government programs, regulations, the extent they wished to help persons of color, and environmental reforms. See Policy Advocacy Challenge Video 1.4 where Rebecca Kendig, MSW, LCSW and Executive Director of Case Services Management for the Youth Empowerment Project, discusses different views of African-American youth who have interacted with the juvenile justice system in New Orleans. How might ideology influence these views as well as policy recommendations that specific persons might make to improve the condition of such youth?

The efforts of policy advocates to demonstrate that certain proposals will be effective and not too costly are made more difficult by disagreements about the proper goals or objectives of the policies. For example, advocates of welfare reform often want to know whether specific policies will allow female heads of households to increase their net income as they enter and remain in the workforce—and whether the well-being of their children will also be enhanced. So they are willing to spend considerable amounts of money on job training, child care, health care, social services, housing subsidies, and transportation to achieve these goals. By contrast, some conservatives consider the rapid movement of women and children off welfare rolls to be a priority so the government saves considerable resources. With these objectives in mind, such conservatives do not give precedence to increasing the net income of women over time or even the well-being of children. They may assume that rapid movement into the labor force will improve women's and children's well-being just because the women are now working, no matter at what pay or in what job, or whether the children have adequate child care. In this example, then, policy advocates and conservatives talk at cross-purposes because they possess very different objectives. Advocates are likely to see conservatives' solutions as ineffective and conservatives are likely to see advocates' solutions as ineffective, partly because they emphasize different objectives.

Even when policy advocates share the same objectives with others, honest differences of opinion may exist about what policies will and will not be effective. Making different assumptions about human behavior, people sometimes disagree about the likely effect of a particular policy. In the case of welfare reform, for example, conservatives often believe that female single heads of households will not diligently seek and retain employment without a strong work requirement and economic incentives that make work more attractive than welfare. By contrast, some policy advocates may believe that such women will more likely respond to policies that they believe will enhance their future earnings and contribute to the well-being of their children, such as job training and day care.

Using Data   Policy advocates can sometimes find and use research data to buttress their case that a specific policy will or will not work. Such data can be an invaluable tool for securing support for a policy recommendation, such as extensive research findings that followed the enactment of federal welfare reform legislation in 1996. To the extent considerable numbers of women have remained in or near poverty in the wake of welfare reform, policy advocates can cite research to support their case that new approaches are needed, that the minimum wage needs to be raised, that child-care subsidies need to be increased, or that living-wage legislation is needed in local jurisdictions. Policy advocates can use research data, as well, to make the case that certain social problems are serious, whether in terms of their incidence, their effects on people, or the costs they impose on society. They can draw upon program and policy evaluations to propose policies supported by research data. Indeed, the Internet provides invaluable research data on myriad social problems and policies. (See Policy Advocacy Challenge 1.5.)

Joining a Tradition of Policy Advocacy

Policy Advocates Stand on the Shoulders of Many Preceding Reformers

An overview of recent American history shows that policy advocates have improved considerably the well-being of millions of Americans. Assume, for example, that Medicaid had not been created in the mid-1960s. Without Medicaid, the health care needs of low-income populations, already seriously underserved by public clinics, would have reached catastrophic proportions, because local and state governments lack the resources to address them. Older citizens who have exhausted their Medicare benefits would be unable to rely on the Medicaid program, and hundreds of thousands of them would be forced into nursing homes even worse than those they would have encountered in the 1970s. Many persons with AIDS, often financially devastated by the expense of medical procedures, would receive no services unless physicians and hospitals donated them.

POLICY ADVOCACY CHALLENGE 1.5

Using the Web as a Policy Advocate

STEPHANIE DAVIS, RESEARCH LIBRARIAN, UNIVERSITY OF CALIFORNIA, IRVINE

As an MSW student, you have a wide range of resources you can use to learn more about policy issues and to stay informed about the issues relevant to your studies and/ or clients.

Libraries

Libraries are the best source of information because their mission is to serve the people in their community by providing access to information. Your local public library or your university or college library is not only a place to find books on your topics, but it's the place to find librarians, who can help you form your research strategies and navigate the library system. Most libraries subscribe to electronic databases and catalogs that allow you to find citations and full text to articles, news, legislative information, political information, statistics, funding sources, and more. Before you start your research, visit your college or university library and talk to a librarian to get an overview of the databases your library subscribes to, and how to access those tools.

Government Depositories

Some university and college libraries are Government Depositories. This is a federal program that provides thousands of government documents for research and community purposes. If you're looking for any kind of federal government information, a government documents library is the place to start. Check with a librarian at your institution to see if there is a library in your area that collects government documents.

The federal government is also publishing many documents on the Web. In the following chapters you'll learn more about how to find that information.

The Internet

The Web is, in general, a great tool for finding information. Searching the Web is easy, and the quality of search engines has improved greatly since the Internet became part of the public consciousness. A few recommendations for general information search engines are:

- Google: Simple, easy to search, easy to navigate, and provides relevant results. **http://www.google.com**
- TeRespondo: Spanish metacrawler that searches on the more popular search engines. It also has a database of questions and answers that aid the user when searching, similar to Ask Jeeves. (**http://www.askjeeves.com**) **http://www.terespondo.com**
- FirstGov: The federal government's search engine, connecting you to government agencies, reports, statistics, and much more. **http://www.firstgov.gov**
  Local, state, and federal governments have also been jumping on the Internet bandwagon.

Many states and the federal government have mandates to make as much information accessible to citizens on the Web. The best place to start looking for information is usually your city or state Web site (for example, City of Chicago, Cook County, Illinois State Web site).

∽ EXERCISE ∽

Visit your library to investigate the information resources available to you at your university or college.

- Are there any Government Depositories at the libraries in your area?
- What kinds of databases are accessible at your library?
- Find your city or state Web site and write down the URL for future reference and exercises in this book.
- Use the preceding Web sites to find several policy reports relevant to the rebuilding of New Orleans after Katrina.

Indeed, we can proceed through each of the major enactments of the 1960s and the succeeding decades and render a similar prognosis. Assume, for example, that Medicaid, SSI, and the food stamp program did not exist. Would that not have led to a homeless population many times the size of that existing in the 1980s and 1990s? Would economic inequality in the United States, already far greater than in European nations and Canada, not have become even worse? Considerable progress has also been made in addressing poverty among older persons; challenges to the civil rights of vulnerable populations; unemployment and lack of services for persons with disabilities; malnutrition; the health needs of certain groups in the population, such as persons with kidney failure; the preschool needs of low-income children; and psychological conditions such as depression. Many persons of color markedly improved their economic and social situation in the decades following the 1960s, and many African Americans and Latinos entered the middle and upper-middle classes, partly as a result of affirmative action and civil rights laws that prohibited job-related discrimination.

We should not ignore the short-term humanitarian function of social programs. Even when they do not solve social problems, they provide resources and support to people who are experiencing such problems as unemployment, catastrophic health conditions, and mental trauma. Whether we are guided by specific religious teachings or by ethics, we realize that persons who experience hardship or trauma need assistance to diminish their suffering. This simple maxim guided the giving of alms to impoverished people in the Middle Ages, the providing of economic resources to impoverished people during recessions and the Great Depression in the United States, and the development of shelters for homeless people in contemporary society.

In many cases, problems that had seldom been recognized in prior eras were publicized and addressed by new policies because of the determined work of policy advocates. Rape, child abuse, Alzheimer's disease, spousal abuse, reading and learning disorders, discrimination against gay men and lesbians, and the needs of people with disabilities have existed throughout American history, but they have come to be widely recognized as important problems only recently. Victims of rape, for example, were subjected to punitive treatment, such as imputations of blame by judges and doctors, until many jurisdictions enacted laws that protected their rights. People with developmental disabilities often were placed in institutions in the 1950s instead of being mainstreamed in schools, communities, and employment. Children with reading difficulties routinely were dropped from school rolls in the 1950s, whereas now they often receive special services. Policy reforms emanated from a heightened public awareness of these problems and contributed to the public's knowledge of them, as individuals saw social programs' benefits to themselves, their relatives, and their friends. Moreover, social programs often have raised public expectations about the rights and needs of specific groups in the population. Americans in 1950 commonly assumed, for example, that people with paraplegia would be bedridden and institutionalized. By the 1990s, many Americans were aware of these individuals' rights and capabilities, including access to mechanized wheelchairs, independent living arrangements, occupational therapy, and employment. We can reasonably argue that the nation would have suffered harm in the absence of reforms enacted in the Progressive Era, the New Deal, and the Great Society; expansions of civil rights and entitlements in the 1970s; the Child Care and Development Block Grant of 1990; and the expansion of the EITC in the 1990s.

Reformers also have prevented the enactment of many reforms that would have harmed many Americans. Some conservatives have wanted, for example, to bar gay men and lesbians from teaching in public schools, to retain antisodomy laws of states that would allow gay men to be imprisoned for engaging in consensual sex with other men, to bar immigration of gay men and to deny them citizenship, to exclude gay men and lesbians from civil rights legislation prohibiting discrimination by employers, and to ban gay men and lesbians from the military. Only by assertive action through legislative and legal channels were advocates able to overturn these policies or their enactment.

While specific policies have failed or have had mixed results, the combined effects of social reforms have transformed the lives of tens of millions of Americans in positive ways. Most contemporary Americans cannot remember and can barely comprehend the institution of slavery, imprisonment for indebtedness, capital punishment for relatively minor crimes, poorhouses, 14-hour workdays, unsafe working conditions, child labor, routine denial of civil rights, lynching of African Americans, flagrant violations of the legal rights of radicals, the incarceration of people who publicly discussed birth control, the routine firing of gay men and lesbians, widespread malnutrition, and the denial of education to persons with disabilities.

Yet much remains to be done with respect to homelessness, huge inequalities, specific kinds of discrimination, eradication of such diseases as AIDS, poor education, and underfunded services. Effective policy advocacy is needed to address these and many other problems—and to prevent serious problems from arising in the first place among specific populations.

Joining the Reform Tradition Within Social Work

Most professions are relatively conservative and are concerned mostly with licensure, training, and the enhancement of the remuneration of their members. Like public health, which also has had a strong activist tradition, social work has had a social reform tradition extending back to the formation of the social work profession. Such founders of social work as Jane Addams militantly supported an array of social reforms in the Progressive Era at the beginning of the 20th century, including housing codes to protect tenants, governmental inspection of food to avert illness, factory regulations to protect workers, and pensions for single mothers with children to avert dire poverty.[3]

In succeeding eras, many social workers joined this reform tradition by working for policy reforms in local, state, and federal jurisdictions. Their work was bolstered by numerous theorists who developed a systems or environmental perspective on human behavior, arguing that social inequality, blighted neighborhoods, inadequate resources, unemployment, environmental pollution, discrimination, and economic uncertainty cause human suffering and contribute to clinical conditions such as depression and poor health.[4]

But narrower perspectives about social work coexisted with the reformist vision of Addams. Even at the profession's outset, such persons believed the profession should focus on casework, with scant involvement in social reform.[5] Myriad other theorists in succeeding decades adhered to this narrower view of the profession as they developed numerous clinical strategies that gave scant importance to environmental factors, discrimination, or poverty.[6]

Narrower perspectives are deficient on at least three grounds, however, as is discussed at more length in Chapter Two. By failing to address the societal factors that contribute to inequality, they neglect such values as social justice and fairness. With attention riveted exclusively on the problems of individuals, they do nothing to reform the human services delivery system so that it will provide services that are congruent with recent medical and social science findings. By abandoning the political arena, they allow other groups, with values and perspectives in opposition to the needs of clients, consumers, and citizens, to dominate public policy.

This book describes interventions, which I call *policy practice* and *policy advocacy*, that enable social workers to join the social reform tradition of the profession. They may seek changes in policies in social agencies or communities or in public arenas at local, state, and federal levels. They may integrate social reform work with other professional duties, such as clinical work, or they may specialize in it as planners, policy analysts, or organizers.

Policy Devolution, Technology, Globalization, and Policy Advocacy

As the nation moves further into the 21st century, policy advocacy should become an even more vital component of social work practice. In a sweeping departure from the growth of policy powers of the federal government in the Great Society of the 1960s, many federal policies were devolved to state and local governments in the 1980s and 1990s. In the case of so-called block grants, the federal government provides funds to the states for social policy purposes and allows them to decide how to use these resources with minimal federal guidelines.[7] (For example, in Chapters Seven and Eight we discuss how the federal government supplanted the AFDC program in 1996 with a block grant.)

This devolution of authority has meant that many policies influencing the lives of clients, consumers, and citizens are shaped by state legislatures, county boards of supervisors, and municipal governments. The social work profession used to be able to focus much of its reforming energies on the federal government; now it must establish a reforming presence in hundreds of locations around the nation.

In short, devolution has accentuated the need for policy-reforming work by dispersing key decisions to smaller units of government and disseminating many policies that used to be decided at the national level. If social workers do not actively lobby for policies that will help their clientele in numerous jurisdictions, other groups will dictate these policies, often with scant interest in the well-being of stigmatized or impoverished populations. Indeed, through policy practice and policy advocacy, the profession works to shape devolution so that it will help rather than harm clients, consumers, and citizens.

Policy advocacy also is needed to help equalize conditions and opportunities for tens of millions of Americans whose economic and social well-being have deteriorated in the wake of the technological revolution that has transformed the American economy as well as the impact of globalization. As recently as the 1960s, huge numbers of Americans earned good wages in union jobs in automobile, steel, and other manufacturing industries. As these basic industries relocated to other nations and were replaced by low-paying service industries, such as fast-food establishments, the wages of many Americans plummeted. An economic chasm has widened between persons with limited education and work experience and persons with college degrees and advanced skills.[8]

The social work profession has an ethical obligation to work to diminish this inequality. It needs to support social and economic opportunities that enable less affluent persons to better their lot through such programs as job training, remedial education, substance abuse counseling, preschool education, and family services. The profession also should work for redistributive programs that will provide resources and services to less affluent persons by such vehicles as an expanded EITC, housing subsidies, preventive medical care, and health insurance.

As we discuss in more detail in Chapter Five, policy advocacy must span international boundaries due to the accelerating movement of capital and labor between nations and due to global warming. Large numbers of immigrants now exist, for example, in virtually every state—immigrants who are subject to considerable prejudice, poor working conditions, and low pay. The movement of jobs across national boundaries often adversely impacts domestic workers—and undermines their ability to get wage concessions from employers. Global warming could endanger vast numbers of persons in coastal areas in the United States and elsewhere.

But social workers can work for these kinds of reforms only if they develop intervention skills that allow them to be effective policy advocates. This book's aim is to foster social reform work by discussing the specific tasks, skills, and competencies that social workers must master to become effective policy advocates.

Becoming an Effective Policy Advocate

Just as in direct-service, administrative, or community-organizing practice, we become *effective* policy advocates only as we learn key concepts and develop pivotal skills. Moreover, we need certain perspectives to deal with the uncertainties of changing policies. Let's discuss some concepts, skills, and perspectives as a prelude to examining them in greater detail in succeeding chapters.

Developing a Vision

Policy advocates need a vision of a preferred state of affairs, whether in specific agencies, communities, regions, states, or the nation. If we cannot envision an ideal state of affairs, we are unlikely to find fault with existing policies. This vision derives from our values, beliefs, and ideology, as well as from a desire to help vulnerable or oppressed people who receive inferior or negligible assistance. We do not attempt to define the vision in narrowly ideological terms because policy advocacy benefits from a variety of perspectives. The vision is nonetheless promoted and fueled by discontent with how existing policies and institutions measure up to an ideal.

Indeed, not only is a vision a driving force, but it can enhance a practitioner's political interests and build his or her credibility. A person has succeeded in communicating that vision when others describe him or her as someone who "has principles and really cares" or "is committed to changing things." By contrast, we tend to mistrust people who we feel are "only in it for themselves" or who "bend with the wind." Of course, inflexibility and dogmatism detract from policy practice, so people have to compromise between pragmatism and the beliefs or values that constitute their vision.

Social workers can create a vision by learning how policies have evolved in specific agencies and communities. They also should understand the policy implications of broad theoretical frameworks, such as an environmental approach. The vision may derive from identifying with the needs and aspirations of powerless or oppressed populations.

Assuming that we have some empathy for the downtrodden, historical perspectives sensitize us to the discrimination, racism, inequality, and suffering that have prompted various policy reforms. We have inherited the missions of the reformers before us, including some of the profession's founders, such as Jane Addams, who devoted remarkable energy to policy practice in a society that lacked the policies that we now take for granted. In a compelling argument, Jerome Wakefield contends that "distributional justice" provides a central mission for the social work profession, distinguishing it from other professions and from traditional psychotherapy.[9]

Seeking Opportunities for Policy Advocacy

Social workers of all stripes can assertively seek opportunities for policy advocacy, whether as part of their employment or outside their work. To be effective advocates, social workers must ask: "What systemic or environmental factors cause or exacerbate specific kinds of problems that my clients experience?" (See Policy Advocacy

Challenge 1.6.) We can try to change policies in the community or in our agencies, for instance, on task forces or committees. Within our agencies, as part of our employment, we can modify policies that we view as deficient, or develop new programs. In each case, we take a broader perspective that allows us to see more factors that adversely affect our clients and need to be remedied.

<table>
<tr>
<td>

POLICY ADVOCACY CHALLENGE 1.6

A Clinical Social Worker Engages in Case Advocacy in New Orleans

Rᴇʙᴇᴄᴄᴀ Kᴇɴᴅɪɢ, MSW, LCSW

Go to **academic.cengage.com/ social_work/jansson** to watch this video clip

</td>
<td>

All social workers are familiar with case advocacy where they "go to bat" for specific clients, patients, or consumers to help them get better or needed services or assistance "one by one." See Policy Advocacy Challenge Video 1.6 where Rebecca Kendig, MSW, LCSW, and Executive Director of the Case Services Management for the Youth Empowerment Project, discusses how she engaged in case advocacy for a specific person in New Orleans after Hurricane Katrina. Why was such case advocacy particularly needed in Katrina's wake? How does case-based advocacy differ from policy advocacy? Identify three specific needs shared by large numbers of persons after Hurricane Katrina that could only be addressed through policy advocacy.

</td>
</tr>
</table>

Social workers can engage in policy advocacy outside their working hours by helping advocacy groups, working with their professional association, or participating in political campaigns. They can work to educate the public about important issues in their communities by participating in forums, writing letters to the editor or op-ed pieces, or working with the mass media to disseminate information.

Policy advocacy sometimes aims at ambitious changes such as the enactment of legislation. Other kinds of policy advocacy are more modest, such as changing a specific policy in an agency or even initiating an idea in a staff meeting.

Taking Sensible Risks

Policy advocates have to be sensible risk takers. Each of us has a finite amount of time and energy. It is unwise to squander them on trivial or hopeless causes, even though ethical considerations sometimes prompt us to participate in difficult battles. However, we also need to be willing to take risks. As we discuss in Chapter Ten, some of us refrain from seeking policy changes because we underrate our own power (or that of our allies) or exaggerate the power of our opponents. (See Policy Advocacy Challenge 1.7.) Indeed, failures of omission are as important as errors of commission. In some cases, it is better to commit errors in trying to correct flawed policies than to avoid participating at all.

Balancing Flexibility with Planning

Policy advocates must develop plans to guide their work, but they must also be able to improvise during unexpected events. Planning helps organize their work into a purposeful, coherent pattern and clarifies which tasks to accomplish. Improvising allows them to seize unexpected opportunities, to counter their opponents' arguments, and to adopt new strategies that they did not anticipate in an earlier game plan. A policy practitioner makes plans by asking: "In light of the time and risk that I wish to take, what actions and arguments will help me obtain my objectives?" The advocate considers various strategies, either simple or more complex. The resultant plan then represents a decision that certain actions and arguments, rather than others, will yield an acceptable outcome. In light of the uncertainties of many situations, however, these hypotheses must often be guarded and subject to modification when circumstances dictate. Policy practice plans are made to be altered, because they reflect our best initial guesses.

Policy advocates need to be flexible enough to alter their style or approach situationally; like administrators, community workers, and direct-service practitioners, they need to improvise strategies as events unfold.

Being Appropriately Assertive

Policy advocates must become appropriately assertive if they wish to change policies in agencies, communities, and legislatures. They have to initiate discussions with key decision makers—or locate intermediaries who can assume this role. They must learn not to be intimidated by powerful persons such as authority figures, legislators, and government officials. Yet they need to carry themselves in ways that do not unnecessarily antagonize possible allies or persons who might prove helpful in making specific policy changes. Just as direct-service practitioners develop their clinical skills, so also must policy advocates learn to be appropriately assertive in specific situations. Such noteworthy persons as Eleanor Roosevelt—who was shy and withdrawn as a younger woman—gradually developed skills that made her a highly successful policy advocate.

POLICY ADVOCACY CHALLENGE 1.7

A Social Worker Assertively Lobbies Politicians

RUSSELL HENDERSON, MSW, LCSW

Go to **academic.cengage.com/ social_work/jansson** to watch this video clip

Listen to Policy Advocacy Challenge Video 1.7 by Russell Henderson, MSW, LCSW, the Organizer of the Rebuilding Louisiana Coalition, and a teacher of social policy and community organization at Dillard University in New Orleans. As someone who has lobbied legislators in the Louisiana State Legislature for 21 years and participated as a consultant or organizer in many political campaigns, he has immersed himself in policy advocacy as can readily be observed in this video. What knowledge do social workers possess that many legislators might value? Can social workers' listening and interactional skills, not to mention their diagnostic skills, help them when making contacts with public officials?

Developing Multiple Skills

Advocates who believe they can reduce policy practice to a simple set of recommended rules or a single style are likely to be disappointed when they discover that those rules or that style are not useful in some situations. Policy advocates need an array of analytic, political, interactional, and value clarification skills to use, singly or together, in specific situations and during extended policy deliberations. Because external realities require a combination of skills, a one-dimensional policy advocate is likely to be frustrated.

Policy advocates, just like direct-service, community, and administrative practitioners, need several skills. Some skills are analytic; we need good ideas about the reforms we want in order to be effective advocates. Other skills are process and people oriented, as our discussion of political and interactional skills throughout this book suggests. Still others involve ethical reasoning, particularly when we confront moral dilemmas.

To develop these skills into competencies, we need to work at them in the same way that we hone direct-service, administrative, or community work skills.

Being Persistent

Policy advocates often need persistence, as the inspirational lives of such social reformers as Jane Addams and Martin Luther King, Jr., suggest. These people had an ability to persevere even in the face of repeated defeats and formidable obstacles. Unlike some of their colleagues who left reform causes after early battles, Addams and King maintained their devotion to social reform. Indeed, Jane Addams, who founded the pioneer social settlement Hull House in 1889, persevered not only during the Progressive Era, but also during the 1920s to support innumerable social reforms. If Martin Luther King, Jr., had not been assassinated, no doubt he would have been active in social reforms for decades more, because he had demonstrated that he was not inclined to rest on his laurels after any of his victories in the civil rights movement of the 1960s.

Of course, few of us have the persistence or the energy of these heroic figures. However, every community has particularly dedicated social workers who participate in many policy frays in their agencies and communities, and in broader arenas, even while they perform heavy direct-service, administrative, or community work functions. We do not know why some people persevere while others cannot, but we can learn from people who have this ability, and we can seek to emulate them. Perhaps their persistence stems, in part, from a combination of their vision or moral purpose and an ability not to be deterred by personal attacks or policy defeats. A vision provides a rationale for policy practice, independent of the vagaries of particular moments or the defeats and recriminations that any policy advocate experiences.

Policy advocates need perspective to avoid pessimism and self-recrimination in the wake of defeats or partial successes. No single person or group is likely to prevail on the complex playing field of policy deliberations. Advocates must realize that defeats are more likely when people champion the needs of stigmatized and relatively powerless groups, which lack the clout of more powerful interests.

Tolerating Uncertainty

Policy advocates must be able to tolerate uncertainty, because policy practice often lacks structure and boundaries. While relatively few people participate in specific direct-service transactions, an open field often exists in policy practice, which continually draws new people into issues. Policy advocates often do not know what to expect when they initiate a proposal. Will it be associated with conflict, consensus, or apathy? And often, they cannot predict how much time and energy an issue will require.

Becoming a Policy Advocate

Policy practice can serve many purposes. In some cases, we want to advance our own interests or those of the profession, perhaps by seeking new licensing laws or better reimbursement from insurance companies. Using policy practice to advance personal or professional interests is not unethical if they have ethical merit. If professional social workers give persons counseling that elevates their well-being, then policy advocacy that seeks licensing and reimbursement for professional social workers is ethically sound.

At the same time, social workers should include policy advocacy in their policy practice, which means helping relatively powerless and oppressed populations. Ethical principles, such as social justice, fairness, and beneficence, which we discuss in Chapter Two, dictate that practitioners should engage in this work even if it brings no tangible return to them or to the profession.

When evaluating the outcome of policy advocacy, we should take into account the degree of difficulty encountered. People who undertake difficult tasks or encounter formidable opposition will lose relatively frequently, no matter how skilled they are. Conversely, people who work only on simple issues will probably emerge victorious on numerous occasions. If we were to evaluate policy practitioners solely on the basis of their policy victories, we would risk giving high marks to excessively cautious people.

Indeed, defeats do not necessarily suggest that policy practitioners have been unsuccessful. When people take the initiative to propose policies, they sensitize or educate other people who may not have been aware of specific issues. While this result brings no immediate successes, the defeated policy practitioner can reintroduce another proposal at a more propitious moment and hope that people who are now aware of the issue will change their position.

Combining Pragmatism with Principles

Policy advocates often must compromise for political reasons. With respect to controversial issues in organizational, community, and legislative settings, people rarely realize all of their goals. Yet there is a danger of making premature or excessive compromises that unnecessarily dilute a policy practitioner's goals. There is no simple way to resolve the tension between a pragmatic desire to achieve policy gains and a desire to retain provisions that a policy practitioner values. Indeed, policy advocates often encounter ethical dilemmas that they can resolve only by considering the merits of alternative courses of action and making difficult choices among them.

The Rewards of Policy Advocacy

Social workers who surmount barriers to policy practice, who bridge the various chasms discussed earlier in this chapter, and who develop policy changing skills and competencies are often richly rewarded for their tenacity. Sometimes they attain notable successes when new programs are established, when funding is enhanced for a program, or when deficient policies are ended or modified. In such cases, social workers help entire populations and communities.

However, policy advocates who take on difficult challenges realize that they may not prevail in specific battles. Entrenched or conservative interests sometimes have the resources and power to circumvent or defeat policy advocates. Or when new policies have been enacted, they may receive inadequate resources or may be sabotaged by opponents during implementation. In such cases, advocates are still amply rewarded by the realization that they gave policy reform their best effort—and that they have joined legions of prior reformers who fearlessly tackled difficult issues. Some of these failures led to tangible victories farther down the road, educating citizens to the need for policy reforms and inspiring other reformers at some future point to resume the reforming effort.

Consider policy advocacy to be an adventure that expands the boundaries of professional practice in new and challenging areas. It can begin even during one's student career in a school of social work. (See Policy Advocacy Challenge 1.8 that discusses policy advocacy by award-winning social workers.)

POLICY ADVOCACY CHALLENGE 1.8

How Five Social-Work Students Engaged in Policy Advocacy

BRUCE JANSSON, PH.D.

Professor Robert Schneider from the School of Social Work at Virginia Commonwealth University organized a national committee of social work educators in 1996 and 1997 that came to be known as INFLUENCING STATE POLICY (ISP). He has remained the driving force behind ISP in succeeding years and has received a national award for his innovative work. ISP encourages and facilitates the teaching of policy practice in Schools and Departments of Social Work around the nation. It issues a newsletter, maintains a Web site (**http://www.statepolicy.org**), organizes annual conferences, and develops videotapes on such policy-advocacy tasks as lobbying. It encourages and keeps track of the number of visits to state legislatures by social work students, documenting that 8,078 visits took place in the academic year 2005–2006.

ISP also gives annual awards to specific policy-advocacy projects jointly undertaken by social work faculty and their students. Two of the seven winning projects in 2006, video taped at the national ISP conference in Washington, DC in June were:

1. MSW student Jessie Buerlein of Boston College and her field instructor, Ms. Stacey Auger. Jessie advocated for the restoration of adult dental benefits to 700,000 persons in Massachusetts that had been rescinded by recent legislation. Partly because of the distribution of educational materials to legislators that documented adverse effects that this policy would have on children and adults, the State legislature restored the benefits in a health reform bill in April 2006. Listen to Policy Advocacy Challenge Video 1.8A where she discusses her project.
2. BSW students Kaela Byers, Lisa Crook, Lis Sojourner, and Chris Veeh of the University of Kansas successfully advocated for SB 47 that sought to reduce racial, geographical, and other biases that fostered overrepresentation of minority youth in the Kansas juvenile justice system. Listen to Policy Advocacy Challenge Video 1.8B where the students discuss their project

Go to
**academic.cengage.com/
social_work/jansson**
to watch this video clip

Changing the Composition of Decision Makers

No matter how skilled policy advocates are, they cannot obtain needed reforms in social policy unless they attract support from decision makers—whether legislators, mayors, members of county boards of supervisors, governors, presidents, or top appointees in government agencies. Even in agency settings, the composition of boards of directors, as well as persons in key administrative positions, powerfully shape what kinds of reforms are possible.

Policy advocates cannot, of course, easily change the composition of decision makers —but they are ethically derelict if they do not try. One vehicle is electoral politics, which is the nation's institutionalized method of selecting decision makers. It is true that electoral politics is often a corrupted process. Special interests often gain disproportionate power by contributing heavily to those candidates who represent their interests. Moreover, many poor people and members of some out-groups tend to vote less frequently than persons in the middle, upper-middle, and upper classes—an unfortunate tendency that tilts policy making away from those who would make the United States a more just society.

Yet policy advocates have had striking successes both in American history and in recent years. The Democratic Party, which has been somewhat more reformist than the Republican Party during and since the New Deal, has often controlled one or both chambers of Congress, as well as the presidency. Progressive governors and mayors have often been elected in state and local jurisdictions, and are frequently members of state assemblies and Senates, city councils, and boards of supervisors. Had this *not* been true, the many policy reforms of the 20th century would not have been enacted.

We will discuss in Chapter Thirteen many ways that policy advocates can participate in the electoral process, such as volunteering during campaigns, serving as official campaign aides, registering voters, initiating or working on propositions that are placed on the ballot, and donating (or raising) funds to and for specific candidates or parties. We will also discuss how policy advocates can actually build public-service careers by running for elective office themselves and by taking civil-service or appointive positions in government agencies. In the 2000 elections, for example, 14 social workers ran for elective office in federal elections—four social workers were members of the House of Representatives and two social workers were U.S. Senators. Many more held office at local and state levels, including many who were members of special government commissions, planning boards, and school boards.

Policy advocates can also seek administrative positions in social agencies, since these positions give them an inside track in shaping agency policies and implementing them.

Getting Started

Some readers of this text may think, "It is fine for others to participate in policy advocacy, but it isn't something I can do." For persons who envision careers limited to counseling or administration, for example, the world of policy advocacy can sound daunting. It is more complex. Its outcomes are sometimes uncertain. It requires time commitments. It requires knowledge of new subjects like policy analysis and politics.

Do remember two things, however: policy advocates seldom act alone—they usually work in tandem with existing advocacy groups or with persons who have experience in policy advocacy. Many of you will select an issue or policy that interests you while you are reading this book. You will soon discover that some persons and groups already have done policy advocacy work with respect to it. In some cases, lobbyists for the National Association of Social Workers or other professional organizations closely linked to social workers will be quite familiar with your issue or policy. So you may be volunteering for them or working in concert with them—or, at the very least, learning about specific issues from them. In succeeding chapters, we will discuss how you can forge linkages with persons and groups familiar with your issue.

Remember, as well, that many social work students have not only read about policy advocacy, but have actually made a strong beginning, even during their professional training in critically analyzing existing policies and seeking changes in them, whether in their field placements or in policy advocacy projects.

Becoming Leaders

Policy advocacy provides a route toward leadership in the profession and in society. By seeking to change social policies that impact vulnerable populations, policy advocates aspire to change existing rules, policies, and budgets. As they assume these broader functions, they become leaders who are recognized by their peers and others as trying to make a difference in the lives of citizens.

POLICY ADVOCACY CHALLENGE 1.9

Policy Advocacy in Hurricane Katrina's Wake in New Orleans

Bruce Jansson, Ph.D.

Natural and man-made disasters, such as hurricanes, earthquakes, terrorism, and wars provide social policy laboratories that create immediate and large-scale human suffering. Many persons are killed or injured during disasters. Many persons become ill or die in their wake from exposure, lack of water, or inability to obtain medical care for injuries or illness caused by the disaster—or because they cannot get health care or drugs either for injuries sustained during the disaster or for preexisting conditions.

They also create mid- and long-term human suffering by devastating local economies, family and social networks, housing, and local communities. Many evacuees are subjected to the trauma of long-term relocation, with its psychological trauma as well as uncertain assistance from health, mental health, housing, and other programs in their new locations. Many evacuees experience economic, health, housing, and other problems when they return to their communities in the wake of disasters.

While natural and man-made disasters impact persons from all social classes and ethnicities, many members of vulnerable populations, such as poor persons, persons of color, children, and elderly persons, often experience disproportionate hardships *during and after* natural or man-made disasters such as the following:

- They may find it harder to escape due to lack of cars.
- Their possessions are more likely to be totally or largely destroyed since they often lack back-up resources.
- They suffer greater harm from destruction or damage to local employers.
- They are more likely to have preexisting health problems that are aggravated by disasters.
- They have fewer economic options for finding new employment.

The well-being of vulnerable populations is even more dependent than affluent persons on the expansion of social programs during and after disasters. They are more likely to require:

- Evacuation assistance.
- Housing subsidies.
- Temporary shelters.
- Temporary or longer-term access to health programs.
- Temporary or longer-term income subsidies.
- Relocation assistance away from and back to their places of residence.
- Short- and longer-term unemployment insurance.
- Community rebuilding
- Publicly funded social services.
- Job training and job placement.

Go to **academic.cengage.com/ social_work/jansson** to watch this video clip

- Restored and improved public education systems.
- Restored and improved public services.
- Restored and improved police and fire services.

Citizens who survive natural or man-made disasters not only need subsidies, housing, medical, and social-service assistance to allow them to meet their basic needs during and after them, but social-development assistance to allow them to regain their economic footing. They need loans to allow them to rebuild their homes and businesses, and resources to obtain education to change careers (if necessary). They need community development assistance, not only to repair infrastructure like roads, sewage systems, water systems, and bridges, but schools and businesses. They need help from social service systems that provide mental health, child welfare, job training, and health services to help them surmount the trauma of disasters and its effect on their well-being.

Citizens who evacuate a locality in the wake of a natural disaster need assurances to make them want to return. They need community amenities, city services, social services, and decent schools. In the case of evacuees traumatized by Hurricane Katrina, they need guarantees that the Army Corps of Engineers has repaired levees so that they can withstand another major hurricane almost certain to strike New Orleans in the near future.

The response of public officials to specific disasters is *highly variable*. If public officials actively mobilize public and private resources in the wake of some disasters, they are relatively passive in the wake of others. While minimal disaster relief is provided in the wake of virtually all large disasters, such as food and shelter from such programs as the American Red Cross and the U.S. Federal Emergency Management Agency (FEMA), more ambitious assistance to citizens and communities is not provided after some disasters. Nor do low-income persons, as well as members of vulnerable groups, receive special assistance that they often need.

Precisely because the response of public officials *is* highly variable, policy practice and policy advocacy are urgently needed in the wake of specific disasters. We can learn a lot about what kinds of social policies are—and are not—proposed, enacted, and implemented by examining what persons and groups assume major roles in shaping policies. If powerful interests with scant concern about vulnerable populations dominate policy activity in the wake of disasters, such as speculators, special interests, or affluent citizens whose property was not affected by them, we can expect that needed reforms will not be enacted and necessary resources will be diverted to their interests. If policy advocates emerge with the skills to gain policy reforms, we can expect that vulnerable populations will be assisted by a range of ameliorating policies that attend both to their short-term survival needs and their long-term economic, housing, and social needs.

Hurricane Katrina provides a case example of the dynamics of policy practice and policy advocacy before, during, and after an immense national disaster.

Residents of New Orleans at first believed they had dodged a bullet when they learned that Hurricane Katrina had shifted from a category-5 status (with winds exceeding 170 mph) to a category-4 status (with winds around 130 mph or less)—when they learned that the storm's center had veered just to the east of their city when it made landfall at 6:10 a.m. on August 29, 2005. They soon discovered in the early hours of August 30 that the water-surge from Katrina had begun to flood portions of New Orleans when three levees breached that had been constructed long before Katrina to keep water from Lake

(continued)

Pontchartrain from flooding sections of New Orleans that lay as much as 9 feet below sea level. While Homeland Security Secretary Michael Chertoff became aware that the New Orleans breached levee—which now included other levees—could not be plugged by noon on August 30, many public officials remained incredulous, including Senator David Vitter (R-LA) who said: "I don't want to alarm everybody that . . . New Orleans is filling up like a bowl. That's just not happening." By 10 p.m. on August 30, about 80 percent of New Orleans was under water as sandbagging of the broken levees failed.

The damage from the Hurricane, coupled with the flooding, caused more devastation than any other hurricane in recorded American history. Tens of thousands of houses were flooded. Entire communities were destroyed. Thousands of businesses no longer existed. Hurricanes had been a fact of life in the Gulf Coast for centuries, but Hurricane Katrina was on an order of magnitude unprecedented during the past century. For discussion of this hurricane in its historical context, see Policy Advocacy Challenge Video 1.9 that features comments by Norma Rutledge, M.Ed, B.C.P.S, and Executive Director of the Baton Rouge Crisis Intervention Center. How did this Hurricane impact the region's residents in unprecedented ways that would eventually escalate suicide and mental-illness rates to dangerous levels?

The human devastation was monumental. Responding to voluntary and mandatory evacuation orders issued by Mayor Ray Nagin and Governor Kathleen Blanco in the days preceding landfall as the hurricane moved toward New Orleans, most of the city's population left the City going to an array of cities and towns that included Baton Rouge. Most of them would face months, even years, of uncertainty about whether to return to New Orleans or to abandon it with their housing and communities often destroyed, as well as their places of work. Many of them would experience health and mental health problems caused by their trauma.

While most of New Orleans' population had fled, about 15,000 persons remained stranded in New Orleans—often the most vulnerable persons in New Orleans. Partly because Louisiana, along with nearby states of Mississippi and Alabama, had chosen to fund their safety-net programs at the lowest levels in the nation and had relatively poor education systems, extreme inequality existed in a city where affluent tourists and residents comingled with extremely poor persons who were disproportionately African American. The city also had a large frail elderly population living in their own homes, as well as in nursing homes, convalescent hospitals, and hospitals. Large numbers of poverty-stricken or elderly persons couldn't obey the evacuation orders because they lacked the cars, resources, and contacts to leave the city, stay in hotels or motels, or find sanctuary with friends or relatives. Some were stranded in their homes. Thousands were evacuated to the Superdome, a large indoor sports arena. Yet others found refuge on bridges—or departed New Orleans by foot on interstate highways.

The nation witnessed the breakdown of the nation's disaster-relief system in the days following landfall on television. They saw poor people begging for water and medicines. They viewed deplorable conditions in the Superdome—with relief supplies not arriving until August 31. They saw innumerable people waving to helicopters from their roofs. They saw corpses floating in the flood waters. They discovered that Michael Brown, the Director of FEMA, was out of touch with developments in the city even to the point of not knowing that large numbers of persons were stranded in the Superdome. They saw scattered looting that led the New Orleans' police force to commit its 1,500 members to law enforcement, thus abandoning search and rescue missions, to the detriment of many stranded persons.

Vast numbers of Americans—and even some foreign governments—contributed resources to address the survival needs of Katrina's survivors. Yet it became clear that the problems of evacuees as well as those persons who returned to New Orleans could only be addressed over a period of months and years by specific *policies, programs, and resource allocations* by city, state, and federal legislatures; private businesses; and non-governmental organizations (NGOs).

Absent the emergence of skilled and powerful policy advocates, opportunities to help vulnerable populations regain their footing could be squandered. Special interests might seek a large share of rebuilding resources. Conservatives might insist that private markets would suffice, making government programs irrelevant. New Orleans might be rebuilt in ways that favored affluent persons. Misdirected policy initiatives might be enacted. Insufficient resources might be allocated to the rebuilding of New Orleans and surrounding areas by local, state, and federal governments. Public officials might fail to orchestrate a planning process in New Orleans to determine which areas could or could not be safely rebuilt, leading to uncertainty and delays in reconstructing the city. The federal government might fail to rebuild levees to withstand a Category-5 hurricane, making persons and businesses unwilling to return to New Orleans. With memories of Katrina's devastation fading, the nation might fail to commit itself to evacuees as well as those persons who returned to New Orleans.

We will refer to Hurricane Katrina at many points in succeeding chapters. We provide videos inserted into specific Policy Advocacy Challenges in succeeding chapters where four policy advocates in New Orleans and Baton Rouge discuss policy advocacy strategies that they used to help vulnerable populations in New Orleans.

POLICY ADVOCACY CHALLENGE 1.10

A Video Depiction of Events Preceding and After Hurricane Katrina

PUBLIC BROADCAST SERVICE'S FRONTLINE SHOW

An excellent depiction of events that preceded and followed Hurricane Katrina was developed by the PBS *FRONTLINE* television show called The Storm. View this 1-hour video at **http://www.pbs.org/wgbh/pages/frontline/storm/**. Discuss these questions:

- How does the video illustrate how policy makers often ignore key data and research?
- How does the video illustrate the role that policy advocates could have assumed prior to the hurricane to allow New Orleans to be better prepared for it? Why were their voices often not heard?
- How does the video demonstrate that the needs of vulnerable populations are often ignored in policy making?
- How does the video illustrate the adage that the implementing of policies is often as important as enacting them?
- How does the video show that natural disasters provide a laboratory for understanding policy practice and policy advocacy?

Readers of this text may wish to help the citizens of New Orleans and the Gulf Coast whose communities were damaged not only by Hurricane Katrina, but Hurricane Rita. Some options are discussed in Policy Advocacy Challenge 1.11.

POLICY ADVOCACY CHALLENGE 1.11

How Social Workers Can Help Persons in New Orleans Impacted by Katrina

BRUCE JANSSON, PH.D.

Go to
**academic.cengage.com/
social_work/jansson**
to watch this video clip

Social workers who read this text can assist the residents of the Gulf Coast in several ways. See Policy Advocacy Challenge Video 1.11 where Rebecca Kendig, MSW and LCSW and Executive Director of Case Services Management for the Youth Empowerment Project, urges social workers to place pressure on federal legislators from their districts or states to commit sufficient resources to the rebuilding of the Gulf Coast and to an array of human service programs that help its citizens.

Social workers can directly donate to charities that assist persons in the Gulf Coast region, but they should be certain that these charities effectively use their funds. For ratings of charities that help victims of Hurricanes Katrina and Rita by the American Institute of Philanthropy, go to **http://www.charitywatch.org**. A full list of charities can be found on Google by using the search words, "charity" and "New Orleans" as well as other rating services of charities.

Social workers who wish to work through a specific religious organization should consult responsible leaders in specific denominations—and should consult ratings of the American Institute of Philanthropy of specific charities associated with specific religious denominations as well as other rating services.

Persons who wish to donate time to specific charities in the Gulf Coast, such as Habitat for Humanity, should consult them directly.

Persons who wish to volunteer to rehabilitate houses or to work in myriad other positions should contact the Hands On Network at **http://www.handsonnetwork.org** or research other charitable organizations that use volunteers.

What You Can Now Do

CHAPTER SUMMARY

You are now equipped with an orienting perspective that will start you on the road to being a policy advocate. You can do the following:

- Articulate an ethical rationale for becoming a policy advocate from a social justice perspective.
- Identify an array of policies, formal and informal, that shape human services and the well-being of specific vulnerable populations, as well as the public interest.
- Distinguish between policy practice and policy advocacy.
- Identify specific barriers to policy advocacy.
- Discuss different ideologies.
- Identify social-reform traditions in the nation and in the profession.
- Identify some attributes of effective policy advocates.
- State why policy advocates often try to change the composition of government.
- Understand how Hurricane Katrina provided a context for policy advocacy and demonstrated why it is needed to help vulnerable populations.

The next chapter will equip you to understand how globalization has also created a context that underscores the need for policy advocates to broaden their horizons to issues and problems created by remarkable changes in the world's economy and international system.

NOTES

1. Richard Titmuss, *Commitment to Welfare* (New York: Pantheon Press, 1968), p. 156.
2. Conversation with Wilbur Finch, who attributed this phrase to Herb Bisno.
3. Stanley Wenocur and Michael Reisch, *From Charity to Enterprise: The Development of American Social Work in a Market Economy* (Urbana: University of Illinois Press, 1989), pp. 47–60.
4. For example, see Carol Meyer, *Social Work Practice: A Response to the Urban Crisis* (New York: Free Press, 1970), and Carel Germain and Alex Gitterman, *The Life Model of Social Work Practice* (New York: Columbia University Press, 1980).
5. Mary Richmond, *Social Diagnosis* (New York: Russell Sage Foundation, 1917).
6. Harry Specht, "Social Work and the Popular Psychotherapies," *Social Service Review* 64 (September 1990): 345–347.
7. Bruce Jansson and Susan Smith, "Articulating a 'New Nationalism' in Social Policy," *Social Work* 41 (September 1996): 441–451.
8. For discussion of inequality in American society, see Claude Fischer et al., *Inequality by Design: Cracking the Bell Curve Myth* (Princeton, NJ: Princeton University Press, 1997).
9. Jerome Wakefield, "Psychotherapy, Distributive Justice, and Social Work, Parts 1 and 2," *Social Service Review* 62 (June & September 1988): 187–210, 353–384.

SUGGESTED READINGS

Definitions of Policy and Social Welfare Policy

Brian Hogwood and Lewis Gunn, *Policy Analysis for the Real World* (London: Oxford University Press, 1994), pp. 12–31.

Martin Rein, *Social Policy: Issues of Choice and Change* (New York: Random House, 1970), pp. 5–8.

Richard Titmuss, *Commitment to Welfare* (New York: Pantheon, 1968), p. 156.

Materials That Link Policy to Direct-Service Practice

Chauncy Alexander, "Professional Social Workers and Political Responsibility," in Maryann Mahaffey and John Hanks, eds., *Practical Politics: Social Work and Political Response* (Washington, DC: National Association of Social Workers, 1982), pp. 22–25.

Robert Goodin, *Reasons for Welfare: The Political Theory of the Welfare State* (Princeton, NJ: Princeton University Press, 1988), pp. 123–228.

Seymour Halleck, *Politics of Therapy* (New York: Science House, 1971), pp. 11–38.

Yeheskel Hasenfeld, "Power in Social Work Practice," *Social Service Review* 61 (September 1987).

Alvin Schorr, "Practice as Policy," *Social Service Review* 59 (June 1985): 178–196.

Michael Sosin and Sharon Caulum, "Advocacy: A Conceptualization for Social Work Practice," *Social Work* 28 (January–February 1983): 12–17.

Harold Weissman and Andrea Savage, *Agency-Based Social Work: Neglected Aspects of Clinical Practice* (Philadelphia: Temple University Press, 1983).

Overviews of Policy Deliberations

James Anderson, *Public Policy-Making* (New York: Praeger, 1975).

Bruce Jansson, *Theory and Practice of Social Welfare Policy: Analysis, Processes, and Current Issues* (Belmont, CA: Wadsworth, 1984), pp. 49–55.

Policy Practice and Policy Advocacy

Mimi Abramovitz, "Should All Social Work Students Be Educated for Social Change?" *Journal of Social Work Education* 29 (Winter 1993): 6–11, 17–18.

Josephina Figueira-McDonough, "Policy Practice: The Neglected Side of Social Work Intervention," *Social Work* 38: 179–188.

Norman Wyers, "Policy Practice in Social Work: Models and Issues," *Journal of Social Work Education* 27 (Fall 1991): 241–250.

Policy Practice and Policy Advocacy in Specific Settings

Ron Dear and Rino Patti, "Legislative Advocacy," *Encyclopedia of Social Work*, 18th ed., vol. 2 (Washington, DC: National Association of Social Workers, 1987).

Karen Haynes and James Mikelson, *Affecting Change: Social Workers in the Political Arena* (New York: Longman, 1999).

Maryann Mahaffey and John Hanks, eds., *Practical Politics: Social Work and Political Response* (Silver Spring, MD: National Association of Social Workers, 1982).

Herman Resnick and Rino Patti, *Change from Within: Humanizing Social Welfare Organizations* (Philadelphia: Temple University Press, 1980).

Ramon Salcido and Essie Seck, "Political Participation among Social Work Chapters," *Social Work* 37 (November 1992): 563–564.

C H A P T E R

2

Articulating Four Rationales
for Participating in Policy Advocacy

A POLICY PREDICAMENT

Once Hurricane Katrina had wreaked its destruction on New Orleans and its surrounding communities, many persons and organizations donated vast quantities of funds and materials to its victims. We discuss in Policy Advocacy Challenge 2.9 at the end of this chapter, four ethical rationales for supplementing these meritorious charitable activities with policy advocacy for vulnerable populations in the months and years following Hurricane Katrina.

We discuss in this chapter, four reasons social workers should engage in policy reforming work:

1. To promote the values that lie at the heart of social work and that are included in the profession's code of ethics, such as social justice, fairness, self-determination, and confidentiality

2. To promote the well-being of clients, consumers, and citizens by shaping the human services system to conform to the latest findings of social science and medical research

3. To create effective opposition to groups and citizens that run counter to the code of ethics and to the well-being of clients, consumers, and citizens, and to put pressure on decision makers to approve and retain policies that advance citizens' well-being

4. To change the composition of government so that legislators and decision makers are more likely to advance such values as fairness and social justice, and promote the well-being of citizens

The Ethical Rationale for Policy Advocacy

We develop the ethical rationale for policy advocacy in two stages. First, we discuss why, in their direct-service interactions with clients, social workers should include policy-sensitive and policy-related activities. (These terms are defined later in this chapter.) Second, we discuss why social workers should also engage directly in policy advocacy.

Beneficence and Professional Practice

Professionals of all kinds are bound by codes of ethics to place their clients' needs first. We describe this moral imperative to enhance clients' well-being as beneficence because it is a term widely used in moral philosophy.[1] Professionals, including social workers, act unethically when they knowingly harm clients, such as by providing them with unnecessary or inferior services. Professionals also are morally obligated to select interventions, diagnostic tests, and treatments that will most enhance their clients' well-being.

However, clients' well-being extends beyond the scope of the professionals they consult. A woman who cannot afford an adequate diet, for example, is unlikely to achieve physical well-being no matter how skillfully a physician treats her. The doctor who takes no interest in referring this patient to the food stamps program, to a social worker, or to someone else who can link her with this program is not acting beneficently toward the patient. Similarly, a lawyer is morally derelict if he or she helps a client obtain a divorce but has no interest in the client's economic fate after the divorce is final. (So many women have become mired in poverty when they must raise children single-handed that terms such as feminization of poverty have evolved.) Like the physician in the previous example, this lawyer should expand her or his professional work beyond mere technical responsibility.

Indeed, we can say that both the physician and the lawyer have two moral obligations: to make their professional recommendations with sensitivity to their clients' economic, social, and policy realities; and to engage in brokerage, liaison, and advocacy work for specific clients to improve these economic and policy realities.[2] The first moral obligation illustrates *policy-sensitive practice,* where professionals giving technical advice are aware that the client or patient may also confront negative policy-related consequences. Examples of professionals who are not policy sensitive abound: physicians who prescribe diets or medications that clients cannot afford, lawyers who obtain divorces for clients with no thought to the economic difficulties the clients are likely to face after the divorce is final, and teachers or school administrators who remain unaware of environmental factors, such as poor diet, that influence children's ability to learn. These professionals are morally obligated to shape even their technical advice to help their clients cope with external realities. Physicians must take the time to discuss patients' situational realities rather than merely saying, "Take this tablet three times daily for three weeks." Lawyers must speak with clients about the needs they will have during and after specific legal actions. Teachers must include parents in their teaching strategies. We call this policy-sensitive practice because it requires professionals to take into account their clients' economic and social realities, many of which derive from societal policies.

Professionals should also use brokerage, liaison, and advocacy services for specific clients. We call these *policy-related services* because they involve skills, such as mediation and conflict management, which resemble the skills used in policy practice.

Brokerage is the negotiation of services for specific clients with other institutions and persons. A teacher, for example, may broker an agreement with a welfare office to obtain resources for a child with dyslexia.

Professionals need liaison skills to connect clients to related services. When a battered woman comes to a lawyer for divorce services, the lawyer may need to help her obtain access to a shelter. A physician should help low-income pregnant women obtain free food from the Women, Infants, and Children (WIC) program.

These professionals ought also to go to bat for their clients by engaging in case-based advocacy when they are unfairly denied services.[3]

We know, of course, that physicians, attorneys, and teachers often provide neither policy-sensitive nor policy-related services. Perhaps because they are unaware of the realities that affect their clients, they have been trained to provide only a technical, narrow range of services, or maybe they lack the resources to expand their work. These individuals may not want to take the time to discuss these external factors and, as a result, they may fail to address their clients' needs. Because we judge people's morality by both their omissions and their commissions, we can contend that professionals who do not engage in policy-sensitive and policy-related activities are morally deficient, even though they plead lack of time or knowledge.

Policy-Sensitive and Policy-Related Practice

We have deliberately begun this discussion with examples from professions other than social work to emphasize three things. First, all professionals are morally obligated to use beneficence to advance their clients' well-being. Second, they cannot do so without policy-sensitive and policy-related practice. Third, we can make moral judgments about all professionals' work on the basis of acts of both commission, such as lying to a client, and omission, such as not using policy-sensitive and policy-related practice. We are not holding social work to a standard and moral code different from those that apply to other professions.

We argue, however, that social workers are even more morally deficient than other professionals if they do not engage in policy-sensitive and policy-related practice, because they occupy a unique position in the human services system. Although surgeons should be concerned about their patients' welfare after they leave the hospital, their role in human services is relatively focused and specialized. They are primarily concerned with surgical procedures, are trained to perform them, and are reimbursed by insurance carriers exclusively to perform surgery. Notwithstanding our moral objections to a narrow scope, we often do not expect surgeons to go beyond their specific duties.

But beneficence takes on a broader meaning for social workers than for other professionals because of the profession's unusual nature. Many social work clients are trying to negotiate relationships not just with individuals, but with institutions. Social workers in child welfare agencies, hospitals, mental health clinics, homeless shelters, AIDS treatment programs, schools, or family courts do not merely address specialized needs, such as the need for medical treatment. They often deal with clients who have emotional trauma that cannot be resolved without negotiating interpersonal and institutional relations. Consider a patient who has been disabled by a car accident and who, after a year of intensive rehabilitation, is about to be released from the hospital. This patient will need assistance in renewing his family life, rekindling marital relations, obtaining disability benefits, seeking vocational assistance, and surmounting prejudice against people with disabilities as he re-enters the job market. The ethical social worker has to engage in brokering, liaison, and case advocacy to help this client, rather than limiting self to narrow clinical services.[4]

Beneficence requires social workers to help clients resolve emotional trauma, such as the uneasiness of someone with a disability about his loss of physical abilities. He might feel inferior because he has internalized cultural images of persons with disabilities that emphasize their helplessness or inadequacies. Policies, services, and programs greatly influence clients' well-being. A person with a disability, for example, is likely to feel threatened by inadequate disability benefits, denial of those benefits by punitive bureaucrats, lack of governmental enforcement of the rights of people with disabilities, and inadequate homemaker aides during recovery.

Our discussion suggests that beneficence cannot easily be conceived of in narrow terms. No matter how skilled professionals are, they cannot help improve their clients' well-being without addressing the clients' dysfunctional relations with their environment. Nor can social workers improve clients' well-being if the clients are continually exposed to oppressive relationships in their families, communities, or jobs. Clients must grapple with any cultural images that demean them by examining how oppressive ideology affects their personal activities and self-esteem. In all of these cases, helpers have to supplement traditional direct-service interventions, which focus on intrapsychic matters, with other remedies. They might teach survival skills or assertiveness; help persons deal with discrimination; or use brokering, liaison, or advocacy interventions.

Ethical social workers also realize that they have limited time in which to help clients. Therefore, they need to teach clients skills to help them confront barriers, find resources, and manage their own cases. The social worker seeks to equip clients with the ability to take charge of their personal destinies in the future. The term *empowerment* is commonly used to describe these survival skills.[5]

While physicians can use their knowledge of physiology to declare an infection to be a pathology, social workers need to wrestle with the proper definition of pathology when they work with specific clients. Assume, for example, that a member of an oppressed minority appears paranoid—seeming to be excessively suspicious of other persons. Is this true paranoia or a reflection of actual encounters with oppressive persons and institutions? Assume that a client does not seem to know how to make and execute plans. Could this apparent pathology stem from living in an oppressive environment where planning is relatively futile because positive outcomes are unlikely? Does spanking one's children reflect pathology or the common child rearing practices of a specific group? In each of these cases, social workers have to consider environmental and cultural realities even before making diagnoses, unlike the physician, who can diagnose an infected appendix without recourse to these realities. The social worker needs to educate oppressed people, such as battered women, about cultural forces such as sexism, which they may have internalized. For example, many women return to oppressive spouses, not just for economic reasons, but because they believe they somehow caused abusive treatment.[6]

When social workers perform policy-sensitive activities, they should recognize the following:

- Some problems or pathologies reflect situational and environmental pressures rather than deep-seated characteristics.
- Some apparent problems or pathologies are functional adaptations to oppressive realities.

- Survival skills are often as important to people (particularly persons who have been excluded from mainstream institutions) as intrapsychic interventions.
- Some persons need help to overcome feelings of inferiority that stem from exposure to oppressive ideology and institutions.
- Some people need help to become more assertive.
- Empowerment, or learning skills that will counter oppressive realities, is often as important as purely intrapsychic interventions.

When social workers perform policy-related activities, they should realize the following:

- Often, they will need to negotiate service arrangements between clients and family members or institutions such as schools, welfare departments, child welfare departments, and clinics (brokerage).
- Often, they will need to connect persons to other persons, networks, or institutions (liaison).
- Often, they must be personal advocates for clients or must empower clients to become their own advocates (case advocacy).

Moving Toward Policy Advocacy

We have argued, thus far, that all professionals need to broaden their work to include policy-sensitive and policy-related practice in their interactions with clients. We also have argued that the unique role of social workers in child welfare, hospital, clinic, school, industrial, and other settings means that they in particular need to be attentive to environmental realities. We have made three related assertions: (1) benefits to clients are intimately linked to their relationships with institutions, oppressive relationships, and oppressive ideologies; (2) social workers have to address or be aware of these relationships if they want to improve the well-being of many of their clients; and (3) social workers' failure to acknowledge key elements of clients' personal predicaments can be criticized on moral grounds as not being beneficent to their clients.

We now move beyond direct-service practice to focus on changing policies in agency, legislative, and government settings. Possible activities include developing and working in coalitions, using power, developing tactics, lobbying, engaging in political campaigns, using persuading techniques, conducting policy-related research, drafting proposals, and reforming operating programs. (Recall that policy-sensitive and policy-related practices allow us to enrich and broaden our work with specific clients but do not emphasize interventions that will change policies in agencies or legislatures.) We make the moral case that *policy advocacy* seeking to advance ethical principles falls in the domain of all social workers, no matter what their role in the human services system.

To determine whether a moral imperative exists, let us again examine other professions, such as medicine, law, and teaching, before returning to social work. Assume that physicians know that people's health depends on regular access to primary health care and that millions of Americans currently lack this access because they have no health insurance. Given the importance of access to health care, we can clearly raise moral questions about physicians as a group and as individuals who do not invest extraordinary effort in changing the existing medical system. They also can be indicted if their profession does not lead the effort to educate others about AIDS and to distribute condoms. Similarly, attorneys can be criticized morally if they fail to support expansion of the government programs that provide legal aid to poor people. As Kozol's work suggests, many inner-city teachers must contend with staggering teaching loads in facilities that are far inferior to those in suburban districts,[7] and teachers can be lambasted on moral grounds if they fail to fight overcrowding in inner-city schools.

We know that physicians, attorneys, and teachers often overlook these policy defects. Moreover, the American Medical Association often has seemed more concerned about maintaining the fees and autonomy of physicians than about supporting reforms in the American medical system.[8] But social work is in moral jeopardy equal to that of other professions if its members do not try to change policies. More than most other occupations, social work serves stigmatized populations. Because of their relative lack of power and because of societal discrimination, these groups most need assistance from government laws, regulations, and programs. However, their powerlessness makes them vulnerable to the whims of the broader electorate, government budget crunches, cuts in regulatory agencies' staff, and the backlash in the general public's attitude toward social programs. Were social workers not to serve as policy advocates for these populations, they would risk the moral charge of not caring about them. No matter how skillful, policy sensitive, and policy related, direct-service assistance cannot compensate for inadequacies in the broader society.

More often than many other professionals, moreover, social workers serve as salaried employees in organizations. Their ability to advance their clients' well-being depends largely on organizational matters, such as employee morale, organizational policies, staff members' ability to collaborate with one another and with other organizations, and adequate resources. While agency executives possess disproportionate influence, lower-level staff can participate in the deliberations and politics of organizations to enhance their ability to deliver quality services that advance the well-being of their clients. Staff who are wholly uninterested in organizational matters risk the moral accusation (as would social workers who never try to change societal policies) that they do not care about the well-being of their clients.

Far from constituting a distraction from ongoing social work practice, policy advocacy is integral to it. An ethical social worker needs skills, concepts, and sensitivities drawn from policy advocacy to be a complete (and ethical) social worker. All social workers seeking to advance their clients' well-being should practice policy advocacy sometime in their careers at all levels: agency, community, and legislative. (See Policy Advocacy Challenge 2.1.)

POLICY ADVOCACY CHALLENGE 2.1

Policy Advocacy Fitness Plan

BOB ERLENBUSCH, PH.D.

Bob Erlenbusch, Ph.D., Chair of the Board of the National Coalition Against Homelessness in Washington, DC and Executive Director of the Los Angeles Coalition to End Hunger and Homelessness, authored this plan, which he implemented when he was the Director of a shelter for homeless persons. All staff, including security staff, cooks, and social service staff, engaged in policy advocacy as a part of their work.

Advocacy Fitness Plan: Aerobics for Advocates

Becoming politically fit is a lot like become physically fit . . . just as your muscles need regular exercise and increased activity over time, so do your political muscles. Stop using them and you'll quickly become politically flabby, use them and your advocacy fitness will soar.

So what follows is a quick and easy, *10 Step Advocacy Fitness Plan,* a kind of Aerobics for Advocates—low, medium, and high impact:

LEVEL 1. LOW IMPACT   This level is like the exercises where your feet don't leave the floor and your movements are quite gentle. Even if you do not get further than Level 1, by the end of the year you will be better informed, and will have gotten a few more people thinking about the issue.

Low Impact: Every MONTH do at least one of the following:

1. ***Get on the mailing list:*** Get on a mailing list of an advocacy organization that focuses on an issue that your organization cares about. . . .
2. ***Join a coalition:*** Join a coalition that embraces the issue your organization care about. . . .
3. ***Invite a speaker:*** Invite a speaker to educate your organization about an advocacy issue . . . (from) the coalition that you have just joined. This will give your agency board of directors, staff, volunteers, and clients an opportunity to be educated about issues directly affecting them.
4. ***Know your nonprofit advocacy rights:*** Educate yourself, agency staff, and board of directors about your agency nonprofit advocacy rights. For example . . . you can educate all you want (on an advocacy issue) . . . but are limited to how much of your budget can be applied to lobbying. You can register clients to vote on site. You cannot . . . take positions on candidates running for public office (but) you . . . can take positions on local state initiatives and/or referendums.

LEVEL 2. MEDIUM IMPACT   This level is comparable to exercises where body movements are more energetic, the pace is faster . . . but the impact is far more dramatic.

Medium Impact: Every WEEK do at least one of the following:

1. ***Write a policy-maker (local, state, or federal) on an issue you care about:*** Practice what you already know; exercise your political muscles. Once you've done it a few times, it will get easier. As with most things in life, the first time is the hardest. The more you do it, the better advocacy aerobic shape you will be in.
2. ***Call a policy-maker (local, state, or federal):*** Ditto. Especially at the federal level, it is good to know that all U.S. senators and representatives have local telephone numbers, and some have toll-free numbers. Always ask to speak to the person who handles the issue that you are calling about.
3. ***Visit a policy-maker (local, state, or federal):*** Ditto again. It's not enough to read about making a visit; sooner or later you need to use what you have learned. Try it; you may like it. Always remember that you are the expert and that policymakers are relying on input on issues from community-based organizations like yours.

LEVEL 3: HIGH IMPACT   This level is like the exercise routine where you jump up and down, fling your arms, and legs, and quickly work up a sweat. At this point you will be a true citizen activist, with advocacy muscles that are taut and working at their peak. Go for it!

1. ***Involve your clients in writing, calling, visiting policymakers:*** In an exercise program, no one knows how your body feels, where it hurts, where it is tired, better

(continued)

than you. So too in advocacy aerobics. No one knows the issue better than those affected by the issue, whether it is experiencing homelessness, or being on welfare. Unfortunately, this voice is often left out in policy debates, but it is the most moving when policymakers hear it. Your role as an employee in a nonprofit can be to facilitate this voice.

2. ***Bring your clients to testify at hearings:*** Nothing is more moving than to hear the impact of policymakers in real human terms. As agency staff, we can describe an issue, but our clients bring that issue to life—they put a face on it for policymakers. Remember, usually policymakers will be moved by this kind of testimony and want to "fix" it for that client. Your job is to make sure that the systemic issue that person symbolizes is addressed.

BONUS POINTS

1. ***Five percent of all your staff job descriptions are devoted to advocacy:*** Direct service is difficult work. But it is often made more difficult because your staff are working on the symptoms of larger systemic problems (lack of housing, lack of health care) with no way to affect the issues. By taking advocacy into their job description they now have a way to address the larger issues, either through joining a coalition, calling, writing, visiting policymakers, testifying, or attending or organizing a rally. Your nonprofit can move beyond case advocacy to systemic advocacy with your vision to do so.

   Discuss this Advocacy Fitness Plan with respect to the following points:

1. Is it feasible to implement this Plan in most not-for-profit agencies?
2. Should policy advocacy be conceptualized not only as an activity that occurs "off the job" but as integral to professional work?
3. Can employees of public agencies engage in policy advocacy?

Social workers can initiate social reform projects or work through chapters of the National Association of Social Workers (NASW) or other professional organizations, or they can help existing advocacy and community groups. Indeed, empowerment, or helping individuals assert their needs, extends to helping oppressed groups assert their rights collectively, whether through community-based organizations or broader advocacy groups.[9] Social workers can volunteer their services to these advocacy groups, serve as consultants to them, help them find resources, and conduct research for them. Policy advocacy can realize fully the environmental approach to social work practice.

If we change an agency's intake policy, develop a new program in an agency, or modify an existing law, we change the terms of service for many people, even if we initially engaged in our policy changing work to help a single person or family. Clients' lives are powerfully shaped by societal and environmental factors that only policy practice can change, whether in agency, community, state, or national arenas. Without policy advocacy, the social work profession becomes, in effect, an apologist for existing institutions rather than a force for social reform.

Ethical social workers need to operate on several fronts during their careers. They must provide policy-sensitive direct-service practice, policy-related direct-service practice, and policy advocacy. They cannot engage in these disparate activities at all points in their careers; indeed, they are likely to engage only in episodes of policy practice. But these episodes ought to be a prized part of social work practice. Even relatively modest projects require social workers to possess skills and concepts not covered in direct-service literature and courses. We believe that policy practice curriculum should fill the gap by devoting considerable time to them.

Policy Advocacy and Powerless Groups

So far, we have justified policy advocacy in terms of individual clients' well-being. For example, we discussed helping persons with disabilities to obtain benefits, services, access to job training and jobs, transportation, homemaker aides, and other forms of assistance that derive from high-level policies. In this perspective, we engage in policy advocacy to enhance the well-being of individuals with disabilities by getting them more benefits, services, and rights.

But we can also justify policy advocacy from the vantage point of social justice, because we find inequalities in society morally objectionable, whether they exist among social classes or between mainstream society and a specific population, such as persons with disabilities. But should we be concerned about inequality in society? Let's discuss varieties of inequality, some reasons inequalities violate ethical standards, and the ways in which policy practitioners use policy practice to decrease inequality.

Varieties of Inequality   If we were to analyze the current status of groups of American citizens on an array of dimensions, such as housing, income, neighborhood amenities, and health, we would find vast disparities among them. Social class provides a shorthand method of summarizing many of these disparities, because persons in the upper classes tend to possess more income (and therefore better housing, better neighborhood amenities, and better health) than those in the lower classes. We can also analyze disparities in current status between specific populations and the mainstream population. If we define white adult males as the mainstream population, for example, we can compare their average income with that of a specific other population, such as women, Latinos, African Americans, or children.[10]

We could also analyze the disparities among citizens not by current income and related indicators, but by access to opportunities, such as education, health services, assets (such as houses), networks (for example, acquaintances with clout), and rights (for instance, freedom from discrimination in jobs or promotions). Opportunity is, to some extent, the flip side of current status, since having opportunities allows us to obtain or improve our current status, such as in income. The feminists' complaint that women are often excluded from old-boy networks, for example, recognizes that promotions and jobs (current status) often depend on contacts that give persons an inside track; excluded from these networks, women often lose jobs and promotions to males. Indeed, current status and access to opportunities are reciprocal; people whose income increases, for example, can afford expensive housing, which tends to be near better schools and jobs, which gives them access to opportunities, which, in turn, allows their income to increase again.

When Inequalities Violate Ethical Standards   Inequalities of status and opportunity are inevitable in any society. Short of a fiat by someone with complete control over the economy who wants full equality, certain persons, classes, and populations will have greater current status and access to opportunities than others. Such inequalities exist even in noncapitalist societies, as illustrated by differences in wealth and status within Native American tribes or between nobles and serfs in feudal society. But inequalities emerge in a particularly striking fashion in capitalistic societies, where those who control corporations or work in highly paid occupations such as law and medicine secure vastly greater income, assets, and access to opportunities than other people. Moreover, patterns of inheritance perpetuate these differences and these discrepancies. The descendants of wealthy persons not only inherit wealth but also obtain access to opportunities by virtue of contacts, schooling, and other advantages.[11]

POLICY ADVOCACY CHALLENGE 2.2

Empowering Clients or Citizens to Seek Social Justice

REBECCA KENDIG, MSW, LCSW

Go to **academic.cengage.com/ social_work/jansson** to watch this video clip

View the Policy Advocacy Challenge Video 2.2 where Rebecca Kendig, MSW, LCSW, and Executive Director of Case Services Management for the Youth Empowerment Project in New Orleans discusses how she links African-American youth to an advocacy organization that seeks to decrease police brutality and unfair treatment of young African-American adults. What information did the youth provide to the advocacy group to facilitate their work?

We confront formidable intellectual challenges when we ask, "What degrees and kinds of inequalities are morally objectionable?" We have to be clear, for example, whether we are questioning inequalities in status or access to opportunities. We need to discuss issues of threshold: At what threshold, or degree, is inequality morally objectionable? We also have to decide why inequality is objectionable, if at all. To the extent that we dislike inequalities, we must decide what kinds of policies should be used to reduce them.

We do not have the ethical field to ourselves. Many philosophers have wrestled with issues of equality. It is beyond the scope of this book to summarize and analyze their different conclusions and arguments, but to introduce the topic, we will briefly analyze some tenets of a leading contemporary philosopher, John Rawls. In his seminal work, *A Theory of Justice*, Rawls argues that we can best construct our moral vision of a good society by trying to imagine its internal arrangements from behind a "veil of ignorance," which obscures our own current status (such as income) or personal access to opportunities.[12] Rawls says that if we are aware of our current status and are, for example, relatively well off, we are likely to want a society that will perpetuate our economic well-being, even if others do not share in it. Therefore, we should retreat behind this veil, where our personal income and opportunities are not known to us. When conceptualizing the ideal society from this vantage point, we are likely to conclude that society should allow only those inequalities that will preserve or further the common good of society. We will reach this conclusion because we would not want to take a chance on being stuck in the lower reaches of a relatively inegalitarian society. We realize most people are in those lower reaches, whereas in egalitarian societies, people have similar statuses and opportunities. The rational person would, Rawls concludes, opt for an egalitarian society but would accept some inequalities. Occupations that require particular skills and training, such as brain surgery, would carry relatively high salaries to attract the most skilled and dedicated persons.

We can express Rawls's argument in simpler form by asking, "If you had the choice at the start of your existence—not yet favoring any specific society, and not knowing what social position you would hold—would you choose to live in the United States (with its relatively inegalitarian arrangements) or in a more egalitarian society such as Sweden, where discrepancies between the affluent and the less affluent classes are less marked, particularly when relatively equal access to health care and education are factored into the equation?" Rawls asserts that you would be likely to select Sweden because, on balance, you would not want to risk ending up in the American lower classes, many of whom live in blighted inner-city neighborhoods and lack health insurance.

Rawls's argument can be restated as the Golden Rule: Do unto others as you would have them do unto you. If you are not willing to experience the inequalities of the inner city, for example, you should not support policies that perpetuate such inequalities. This argument suggests that failure to engage in any social reform, whether as a private citizen or as part of one's professional role, is tantamount to violation of the Golden Rule. If we do not want to live in inner-city areas without adequate health care and other amenities, we have a moral duty to try to improve the lot of inner-city residents and other persons who experience inequality.

We can also support efforts to reduce inequalities with economic arguments. Extreme inequalities produce undesirable economic effects on the nation.[13] At a time when Americans are competing with foreign nations, for example, they can ill afford vast reservoirs of relatively uneducated, unhealthy, and nonproductive citizens in the inner cities. But Americans have decreased the productivity of many inner-city residents by failing to invest sufficiently in people, jobs, and infrastructure.

Similarly, vast disparities in status and opportunities produce undesirable social consequences. Persons in the lower reaches of relatively inegalitarian societies often despair of their chances to improve their lot. Such alienation often induces them to improve their lot through crime and drug dealing, which harms their neighborhoods and the broader society. If they despair of being able to work through the political system, they also may participate in violent collective uprisings at enormous cost to themselves, their neighborhoods, and the nation, as the domestic disturbances of the 1960s and the 1992 Los Angeles uprising suggest.[14]

We can also advocate reducing inequality in the name of the common good. (See Policy Advocacy Challenge 2.3) In recent decades, it has been fashionable to argue that self-interested and individualistic behavior constitutes the highest or best activity. Society benefits, conservatives have often said, when persons work hard, take risks, and build businesses to improve their incomes. Carried to an extreme, however, self-serving behavior can yield unfortunate consequences. If society fails to fund quality schools and infrastructure, for example, it jeopardizes, economic growth, and alienates persons who believe they cannot improve their lot.[15] Conservatives' contention that "confiscatory taxes" will jeopardize economic growth is belied by satisfactory rates of economic growth in many European nations, whose level of taxation is often far higher than the United States.[16]

POLICY ADVOCACY CHALLENGE 2.3

Imagining a Better Society

ANNEKA SCRANTON, M.S.W., DPA. COMMUNITY ACTIVIST AND FORMERLY CLINICAL ADJUNCT PROFESSOR, SCHOOL OF SOCIAL WORK, UNIVERSITY OF SOUTHERN CALIFORNIA

All of us need to develop a vision of a better society as we aim to be policy advocates. (Policy advocacy is, after all, geared to improving society in some respect.) We can do this by a "dream exercise," where, singly or in groups, we try to imagine a better American society in ten or more years.

- What is your dream of a more just society?
- What is the most important change that would take place?
- How might policy advocates begin working on this agenda?

Alternatively, we can develop a vision by discussing the impact that specific policies have had upon members of our families, ourselves, or a specific client. (Select one of these persons as your point of reference.)

- How have existing policies proven inadequate to redress some specific problems or issues of your family member, yourself, or a client?
- What is the most important change that needs to take place?
- How might policy advocates begin working on this agenda?

One thing is certain: the United States currently has extraordinary rates of economic inequality. Millions of Americans live from paycheck to paycheck, possess no savings, have scant retirement accounts (save for Social Security), and do not have such assets as houses. A recent study of economic inequality in Los Angeles County, one of the most populous metropolitan areas of the United States, discovered that one in four workers was poor, including such diverse workers as janitors, maids, teachers, health practitioners, sewing machine operators, actors, parks and recreation workers, and parking lot attendants.[17] (The study defined poverty for the working poor as an annual income of $33,098 for a family of four based on the actual cost of living—or a higher threshold than federal poverty standards of $16,700 since the federal standard does not accurately measure survival needs of citizens in L.A. County.) They discovered that inequality between the top 20 percent and the middle 20 percent of earners in Los Angeles grew significantly in the 1990s—and nationally the net worth of the top 1 percent grew by 17 percent when adjusted for inflation while the bottom 40 percent lost an amazing 80 percent of their net worth. In the late 1990s, the top 1 percent of U.S. households owned 40 percent of the nation's wealth. Other findings included the following:

- The vast majority of the working poor—77 percent—work full time.
- Of persons in two-adult households with children where at least one adult reported income in the prior year, 45 percent were poor.
- Nearly 7 of 10 people in Los Angeles with no high school education were working poor.
- While Latinos make up 40 percent of the workforce, they account for 73 percent of the working poor.
- Thirty-three percent of persons in manufacturing and 51 percent of workers in the personal service sector were poor.
- Of the working poor, 59 percent lack health insurance, and half of these have children.

Policy Advocacy for Vulnerable Populations

Rawls's approach to moral reasoning has considerable merit because his arguments force us to ponder ideal, or preferred, social and economic arrangements. But some readers may find Rawls's arguments relatively abstract. Why not proceed to social justice more directly by discussing specific groups who are clearly unequal to the dominant population? Why not seek to improve their lot on the grounds that it is unfair for such groups to be unequal? Our goal should be to move toward a situation where economic resources and opportunities are randomly distributed in society rather than existing disproportionately in specific out-groups. For example, all children should have access to preschool programs rather than tolerating (as now) a situation where many low-income children lack such access due to inadequate funding of the Head Start program.

Considerable evidence suggests that neither prized things nor inequalities are randomly distributed in the population. As we argued in Chapter One, American society has a variety of vulnerable populations with a disproportionate share of social malaise, including *racial groups* (for example, African Americans, Latinos, and Native Americans); *sociological groups* (such as women, older people, and people with disabilities), which employers often expect to occupy relatively low positions or to leave the workforce entirely; *dependent groups* (for instance, children), which need other people's assistance but are often denied supportive programs because they lack political clout; *nonconformist groups*, which have different sexual orientations (such as gay men and lesbians), have violated social norms (for example, criminal offenders and juvenile delinquents), or have stigmatizing social problems (for example, persons diagnosed with mental illness); *model groups* (such as Asian Americans, white ethnic Americans, and Jewish Americans), which find it difficult to obtain support because society believes that they have no social problems, and *economic groups* (such as members of the lowest two economic quintiles) who often lack resources to meet important needs.

Professionals, and social workers in particular, should work to ameliorate such inequalities, both by getting these out-groups more and better services in specific agencies and by seeking changes in local, state, and federal policies. (See Policy Advocacy Challenge 2.4.)

POLICY ADVOCACY CHALLENGE 2.4

Thinking Critically When Using the Web

Stephanie Davis, Research Librarian, University of California, Irvine

Many Web sites have been developed by groups that favor particular causes or populations. Many of these Web sites provide invaluable information—but others provide less reliable information. If you have experience doing research, you know that society is facing information overload. In the course of your research, you will access many different types of information using the resources above: Web sites, books, journal articles, magazine articles, think tank reports, agency reports, case studies, government documents, electronic journals, electronic books, and more.

So how do you know if information is credible or not? What is "good" information?

Throughout the research process, you will need to develop criteria for yourself to help you identify and best use the information you find. For starters, be aware that the purpose of every piece of information you find will be trying to convince you of something—they may be trying to sell you a product, persuade you to believe a certain idea or issue, influence you to vote a certain way, etc. Be a critical consumer whenever you are doing research, whether you're looking at Web sites or journal articles.

(continued)

**POLICY
ADVOCACY
CHALLENGE 2.4**

(continued)

∽ EXERCISE ∽

On the Internet, go to the Checklist for an Advocacy Web page at **http://www.widener .edu/Tools_Resources/Libraries/Wolfgram_Memorial_Library/Evaluate_Web_ Pages/Checklist_for_an_Advocacy_Web_Page/5717/**. Assess the following two sites based on the checklist criteria and the questions on the Advocacy Web page.

- National Rifle Association
  http://www.mynra.com/
- The Brady Campaign to Prevent Gun Violence
  http://www.bradycampaign.org/

It is important to note that part of the evaluation is whether you agree with the ideas presented on each site. However, when doing research, especially if your ultimate goal is to persuade a group to agree with you, you need to be aware of what your opposition is saying so you can respond intelligently.

Many Web sites present information about out-groups and the advocacy groups that represent them. Here are several examples.

- The Center for Law and Social Policy. CLASP is a national nonprofit organization with expertise in both law and policy affecting the poor. Through education, policy research, and advocacy, CLASP seeks to improve the economic conditions of low-income families with children and to secure access for the poor to our civil justice system.
  http://www.clasp.org
- The National Mental Health Association. The NMHA is "dedicated to improving the mental health of all individuals and achieving victory over mental illnesses." It is principally an advocacy organization comprising a large network of supporters. Resources, publications, activities, and a calendar of events are offered here.
  http://www.nmha.org
- The National Organization for Women. The principal political organization for women in the United States, NOW is a progressive advocacy group seeking equality for all women. This site offers multiple and varied coverage of the policy agenda, including links to resources and an on-line newsletter.
  http://www.now.org
- Institute for Women's Policy Research. The institute's Web site contains information about legislation or issues affecting women in general, as well as low income women.
  http://www.iwpr.org
- Center on Budget and Policy Priorities. The center is a leading advocate for legislative and budget reforms to help low- and moderate-income persons.
  http://www.cbpp.org
- Children's Defense Fund. The leading advocacy group for children.
  http://www.childrensdefense.org
- American Public Health Association. A major player in health reform.
  http://www.apha.org

BOX 2.1 | Reference Works Listing Advocacy and Professional Groups

Encyclopedia of Associations, National Organizations of the U.S., 3 vols. (Detroit: Gale Research, 2004).

Regional, State, and Local Organizations, Encyclopedia of Associations, 5 vols. (Detroit: Gale Research, 2006).

Washington Information Directory: Guide to Government Agencies, Associations, Congressional Committees, Congressional Staff, and Congressional Caucuses (Washington, DC: Congressional Quarterly, 2006).

We can use the principles of beneficence and social justice to support such efforts, but we also can draw on the doctrine of fairness when we try to decrease disproportionate inequality. Consider the case of expanding the Head Start program to serve all low-income African-American children. We support the program because it enhances fairness by giving low-income African-American children the educational, health, and child development services many white, middle-class families have long taken for granted. White, middle-class families send their children to nursery schools, have easy access to medical care, and purchase computers and other educational aides for their children. While expanding Head Start hardly reduces societal inequality on a grand scale, as implied by Rawls's framework, it reduces some of the inequalities of low-income African-American children.

It is relatively simple for social workers to work to help members of vulnerable populations through policy practice. Advocacy groups have developed in local, state, and national jurisdictions to assist various out-groups; you can find these groups by word of mouth or by consulting directories in your local region. (See Box 2.1.) Social workers can participate in policy action by linking themselves to an advocacy group, whether as a volunteer, a member, a staff person, or a board member. Other avenues exist, such as local and state chapters of the NASW. Social workers can also initiate their own projects, singly or together.

POLICY ADVOCACY CHALLENGE 2.5

Linking to an Advocacy Group

BOB ERLENBUSCH, PH.D.

Go to **academic.cengage.com/ social_work/jansson** to watch this video clip

Listen to the Policy Advocacy Challenge Video 2.5 where Bob Erlenbusch, Ph.D., the Chairman of the Board of the National Coalition Against Homelessness in Washington, DC and Executive Director of the Los Angeles Coalition to End Hunger and Homelessness, discusses how social workers can link themselves to advocacy groups.

Discuss the following:

1. Why individual policy advocates, operating by themselves, can rarely influence major policies single-handedly
2. How you can find out about specific advocacy groups, whether through tapping key informants or using the Web
3. How you can learn more about a specific advocacy group
4. How you can work with a specific advocacy group

The doctrine of social justice, sometimes leads to painful predicaments, as with affirmative action. To decrease a specific vulnerable population's inequalities, we sometimes must take away opportunities from a privileged group, such as white males. Say we have a limited number of positions in an organization and want to increase the number of women in those positions. We believe that women are underrepresented because of past discrimination. We can increase the number of female employees, at least in the short term, only by reducing the proportion of male employees. Does favoring female applicants (which our doctrine of social justice supports) deny social justice to male applicants? The answer depends partly on our time frame and our ultimate objectives. The doctrine of social justice dictates a random distribution of problems, such as unemployment or lower-paying jobs. Thus, positive discrimination for female applicants is justifiable because it makes men and women more equal (hence, it is fairer) with respect to jobs and higher positions, even if only within a particular organization. Were we to consider hiring women only when female applicants were better qualified than males, it would take decades to achieve parity. Affirmative discrimination for women was developed to move the clock ahead. From this perspective, it is hard to find an ethical alternative to affirmative action because any other policy would fail to redress historic patterns of inequality—at least until resources and opportunities are more randomly distributed in our population.[18]

Other Ethical Principles in Policy Advocacy

We have emphasized the ethical principles of beneficence, social justice, and fairness as rationales for policy advocacy. We have argued that these principles require ethical social workers to engage in policy practice. But what about other ethical principles, such as honesty, self-determination (or autonomy), confidentiality, and preservation of life; namely, the other ethical principles discussed widely in religious and philosophical literature?[19] When ethicists discuss various principles, they commonly refer to the following:

- *Autonomy.* The right to make critical decisions about one's own destiny
- *Freedom.* The right to hold and express personal opinions and to take personal actions
- *Preservation of life.* The right to continued existence
- *Honesty.* The right to correct and accurate information
- *Confidentiality.* The right to privacy
- *Equality.* The right of individuals to receive the same services, resources, or opportunities as other people
- *Due process.* The right to procedural safeguards when accused of crimes or when benefits or rights are withdrawn
- *Societal or collective rights.* The right of society to maintain and improve itself by safeguarding the public health and safety

Many philosophers have declared that right-living persons should adhere to these principles, as well as to the principles of beneficence and social justice we have already discussed. These principles often arise, of course, in professionals' interpersonal work, whether they are physicians, attorneys, teachers, or social workers. Professionals are urged by their codes of ethics to share information with their clients and not to deceive them (honesty); to let their clients make the important decisions that arise during their interaction with professionals (self-determination); to preserve clients' privacy by not divulging information about them to other people (confidentiality); and to act to advance clients' well-being (beneficence).[20] These ethical principles apply, as well, to policy advocacy, which often seeks to advance them.

Other Types of Ethical Reasoning

→ first principle ethicists

We have just discussed moral reasoning that relies on various ethical principles such as honesty—an approach philosophers call *deontology.* Another approach to ethical reasoning, known as *utilitarianism,* uses a different method of reasoning to formulate ethical recommendations. Utilitarians criticize reliance on ethical principles on the grounds that people often differ on the definitions or weighting of principles—or because the principles sometimes conflict. When terminal patients want assistance in dying, for example, the principles of autonomy (or self-determination) and not killing conflict, so ethical resolution is difficult.

Preferring to use empirical data to make ethical choices, utilitarians analyze the likely outcomes or consequences of specific choices, and choose the option that has the best outcomes.[21] When comparing two treatment options for people with depression, for example, they would select the option that was most effective as demonstrated by empirical data. Their approach is similar to persons in direct practice who support evidence-based practice that aims to provide interventions that have been shown to be effective by empirical outcomes research—with utilitarians supporting policies shown to be effective. For example, policies opposing smoking in public places might be supported by utilitarians who cited evidence showing that second-hand smoke often causes adverse health outcomes like lung cancer

Utilitarians examine not only the outcomes associated with specific options, but their relative cost. They might oppose a medical treatment that costs $2 million per patient even if it helped some patients recover, on grounds that the ratio of cost ($2 million per patient) to benefit (the numbers of patients cured) was too high. They might prefer a policy or treatment option with a relatively low cost-to-benefit ratio, such as prenatal care that is relatively inexpensive to provide but that averts serious health problems.

Utilitarians, in turn, are criticized by first-principle ethicists. Good data about the effects of specific proposed policies are often lacking or conflict. In the case of obesity, for example, experts differ in their appraisal of its effects on health outcomes—even if they could agree on a definition of it. We sometimes support policies that do not have low cost-to-benefit ratios, such as providing expensive medical interventions to persons with relatively poor prospects of survival on grounds they would otherwise die or be severely harmed as in the case of drug cocktails for persons with AIDS that can often cost $60,000 per year. In some cases, preoccupation with advancing the nation's well-being can lead us to flawed positions. In the infamous Tuskegee experiment, for example, African-American men with syphilis were not treated deliberately so that researchers, able to study the unchecked course of the disease, could increase their knowledge of the disease. While the researchers supported their work on grounds it might reveal useful information about syphilis, they were correctly criticized by many persons for violating norms of honesty and for putting the men's lives and well-being at risk.

Both utilitarians and first-principle ethicists are, in turn, criticized by *relativists* (sometimes called *intuitivists*), who contend that most people make ethical choices not through an extended process of reasoning, but through norms they derive from their culture.[22] When people in our colonial period placed wrongdoers on public display, they accepted a widely held norm that this punishment was morally acceptable. Some relativists also contend that ethical choices are often shaped by self-interest. When

Congress debates health policy, for example, such groups as the American Medical Association, the American Hospital Association, and the American Association of Retired Persons often support policy options that will benefit the members of their associations. It seems at first glance that choices based on self-interest must be morally flawed. In fact, however, moral people often couple their personal interests with ethical choices. Take the case of social workers who support expanded funding for mental health programs. While they take this position partly to advance the well-being of persons with mental conditions, they also realize that enhanced funding would provide employment for more social workers. Likewise, advocates for specific populations, such as women, African Americans, or Latinos, try to advance the collective interests of these groups. If we contend that all self-interested choices are immoral, we wrongly call into question an array of meritorious policies.[23]

Yet relativists also draw criticism from other ethicists. Without any first-order principles or any consideration of consequences, ethical choices would have no basis. We could even use relativism to justify the rampant discrimination against African Americans in the South in the 1950s on the grounds that it was consonant with the culture of the region—a conclusion that would clearly be ethically erroneous.

We also cannot ignore practical matters when making ethical choices. Some choices may be ethically meritorious, but impossible to get approved by legislatures or other decision makers. In the case of health care reform in the United States, for example, a universal single-payer approach, such as is used in Canada, has considerable ethical merit on grounds of fairness and beneficence—and on utilitarian grounds to the extent it improved patients' well-being—but American politicians are unlikely to enact such a plan in the near future based on their opposition to it in the past.

Toward an Eclectic Approach to Ethical Reasoning

In light of the criticisms of each of the preceding approaches to ethical reasoning, a good case can be made that we should ask a variety of questions that reflect all of the philosophical stances considered here. We should consider first the principles that have a wide following in Western societies, whether derived from a reasoning process, as in the case of Rawls, or from religious sources. We should examine the likely consequences of specific choices, as suggested by utilitarians. We should realize that cultural norms as well as self-interest shape ethical choices, as argued by relativists. And we should not ignore practical considerations, such as the political feasibility of specific options.

POLICY ADVOCACY CHALLENGE 2.6

Ethical Reasoning by Firing-Line Social Workers

BRUCE JANSSON, PH.D.

Take the example of Tenet Healthcare, a huge national healthcare corporation that was known until recently as National Medical Enterprises.[1] Assume that you worked as a social worker in one of their psychiatric hospitals, where patients were effectively imprisoned rather than being released once their treatment was finished. Wanting to exhaust patients' health insurance to enhance their revenues, some Tenet psychiatrists even sanctioned strapping down patients for months at a time, while making other patients remain silent for 12-hour stretches. Only when a task force of 600 federal

---

[1] This case is discussed by Barry Meier in "For-Profit Care's Human Cost," *New York Times* (August 8, 1997), pp. C1, C4.

agents investigated 20 facilities was the magnitude of this patient victimization made clear. (Eventually 700 claims were filed, and the corporation agreed to pay $100 million to settle them.) Had you seen these practices, which clearly reflected informal and formal policies of the corporation, and alerted federal authorities, you would have engaged in policy advocacy, since you would have sought not merely to redress the conditions for specific patients, but to change the formal and informal policies of the corporation itself.

What ethical principles did Tenet psychiatrists violate? Discuss why many Tenet staff did not report ethical violations to external authorities. How does this case illustrate how self-interest can sometimes lead people to make unethical choices?

As Box 2.2 shows, ethical reasoning forces us to consider many kinds of information when making ethical choices.[24] It requires us to integrate or synthesize this information in a process of ethical reasoning. In this process, we look for points of convergence and divergence. If deontological and utilitarian perspectives converge to suggest that a specific course of action or a specific policy choice is more meritorious than others, we can be fairly certain of our resulting decision. If these different perspectives lead us in diverging paths—that is, suggest different actions or choices—we have to devote more time and thought to seeking some resolution.

BOX 2.2	An Eclectic Approach to Ethical Reasoning

Some Considerations Drawn from Deontologists
- Identify ethical principles that are relevant to an ethical dilemma and decide, on balance, which choices or actions best satisfy them.
- When ethical principles conflict—that is, point to different choices—seek a compromise solution that satisfies each to some degree.

Some Considerations Drawn from Utilitarians
- Conduct research to identify the likely consequences of specific options or actions, or when data are lacking, use knowledge about human behavior to infer the likely effects of specific policies.
- Select the option or choice that will maximize the positive consequences for society or for one (or more) of its subunits.

Some Considerations Drawn from Relativists
- Analyze cultural factors that shape the ethical choices of people in specific historical periods, while considering other factors, such as institutional and fiscal realities.
- Analyze how the interests of people—including ourselves—shape policy choices.

Practical Considerations
- Consider the practical implications of specific policies, such as their political feasibility and their cost, as well as administrative aspects.

We may face an ethical dilemma when we have two or more options, each with some ethical merit.[25] We must then engage in a protracted process of ethical reasoning to decide which option, on balance, is preferable when principles, outcomes, self-interest, and practical considerations are entered into the balance. Reasonable people often come to different conclusions in such cases.

Returning to Ideology

When discussing values as they shape policy choices, we can usefully return to our discussion of conservative, libertarian, liberal, and radical ideologies in the first chapter. Each ideology rests on values or its own first principles. If conservatives and libertarians emphasize the value of liberty or freedom, liberals and radicals place somewhat (or considerably) more emphasis on social justice. When we link ideologies with a discussion of ethics in this chapter, we can see that affiliation with an ideology is, at least in part, an ethical choice because one has to decide which value to emphasize. This choice, in turn, is not a trivial one because it has important consequences for the well-being of citizens.

It should be clear when discussing ideology that none of us can be wholly "objective" when discussing many policy issues. Policy solutions to complex social problems often require us to draw upon our values and our ideologies. Even centrists or moderates have values that induce them to select middle points or compromise positions as compared to radicals and conservatives.

Yet Social workers' policy choices not only can be, but should be, shaped by values as defined in the NASW Code of Ethics. They must prevent and eliminate discrimination against any person or group, They must act to ensure that all persons have access to the resources, services and opportunities they require. They must act to expand choice and opportunity for all persons with special regard for disadvantaged or oppressed persons or groups. They must advocate changes in policy and legislation to improve social conditions and to promote social justice. In other words, policy advocacy is defined by the Code of Ethics as integral to the professional role and in ways that will assist vulnerable populations.

Let's begin with some consequences of conservatism and libertarianism. If society structures itself around the first principle of liberty, it maximizes the wealth and status of individual citizens as well as corporations. It taxes them relatively lightly. It issues relatively few regulations that circumscribe actions of corporations. It develops a relatively weak set of governments at local, state, and federal levels by limiting them to such housekeeping functions as funding the military, police and fire departments, sanitation, and infrastructure (such as roads). (Some conservatives concede that government should fund some things that private markets would not otherwise develop, such as parks, environmental clean-up programs and welfare programs that would provide a basic economic floor under the poorest members of society.) Both conservatives and libertarians contend that these relatively minimal government functions would suffice because private markets, if left alone, would take care of the economic affairs of the nation in an acceptable manner. Indeed, they contend that extensive regulations of private markets harm those markets. A relatively high minimum wage would, they argue, harm the natural efficiency of private markets, where labor is reimbursed at appropriate levels as determined by the automatic adjustment of supply to demand. (If some workers receive low wages, this is caused by their relative value in the natural workings of markets—and excessive subsidies merely make those markets inefficient from a conservative's perspective.) Acceptance of a conservative or libertarian ideology is, then, a vote for maximizing the interests of individuals and corporations as they would exist in a relatively unregulated society with minimal government intrusion.

POLICY ADVOCACY CHALLENGE 2.7

Using Different Ideologies to Frame Issues— and Taking a Position

BRUCE JANSSON, PH.D.

Take any important social issue facing the United States, such as growing economic inequality, homelessness, or substance abuse. Frame conservative, libertarian, liberal, and radical approaches to it, using the differences among these ideologies found in Table 1.1.

Defend *one* of these approaches, using ethical arguments germane to social justice, and discuss in ethical terms why another approach is less preferable from a social justice point of view.

Ponder these questions.

1. Can any of us be wholly "objective" when we confront social issues that are linked to values such as social justice or fairness? Are we "unscientific" if we allow values to shape our policy positions?
2. Can we use both values and empirical research to develop and defend specific policy positions? How might we do this, for example, when advocating that a specific state make the pharmaceutical "cocktail" available to Medicaid enrollees just as more affluent persons' cocktails are often funded by the private medical insurance they receive through their employers?
3. Can you think of an important social issue where definitive empirical evidence may be lacking, so that we must develop and defend our policy position primarily with respect to values?
4. How would you respond to someone who said, "why study policy advocacy, much less engage in it, if we cannot be wholly 'objective'?"
5. If we DID withdraw from policy advocacy on grounds it is not wholly "objective," would persons with an ideology different from ours ALSO withdraw? If they did not, what kinds of policies would be enacted by local, state, and federal governments?

The key ethical problem confronted by conservatism is that its tenets often lead to policies that disproportionately assist relatively affluent persons while giving less or no help to less affluent persons. At any given point in time, society is divided into social and economic strata with different levels of resources, opportunities, and services. We have already discussed, for example, how white suburban Americans are relatively more affluent than inner-city African Americans—and how single female heads of households and their children are far more likely than Americans in families with two heads of household to be poor. Left to itself, moreover, labor markets do not reimburse many unskilled and semiskilled workers at living wages, particularly when labor shortages do not exist domestically or when some corporations can threaten workers that they will relocate abroad if they are forced to raise wages. While government cannot magically undo inequality or low wages, it does have some policy tools at its disposal. These include the following:

- Redistributing some resources to less affluent persons through the tax code, such as by lowering tax rates of the working poor or by expanding the size of the Earned Income Tax Credit

- Enhancing opportunities for low-income persons through job-training programs and enhanced education programs
- Giving low-income persons in-kind goods like food stamps, medical benefits, subsidized child care, and subsidized transportation
- Raising the minimum wage or requiring a living wage
- Helping low-income persons build up assets, such as helping them start savings accounts and buy houses

When carried to its full logic, then, conservatism often denies the use of these tools by government. Each of these tools runs counter to such conservative beliefs as minimizing the role of government, lowering taxes on all citizens, not interfering with private markets, and not tampering with the existing distribution of economic resources. Of course, few conservatives or libertarians fully comply with the tenets of their ideology since they often support specific social programs. Many conservatives, for example, strongly support such programs as Medicare and Medicaid, even if they often opposed them when they were first enacted. Their opposition to programs that seem to conflict with their ideology stems not only from realization that many citizens need the benefits of these programs, but also because the conservative politicians realize they will alienate those constituents who benefit from, or support, such programs as Medicare.

While liberals and radicals are more likely to accept a significant role for government, they risk other ethical problems. They sometimes support social policies that have been ineffective as illustrated by their support of some public housing programs. When low-income persons were segregated into huge public housing complexes, such as the infamous Robert Taylor Homes in Chicago, social mayhem occurred. The tenants were bedeviled by delinquency, substance abuse, and violence—and received scant social services, much less police protection. While liberals meant well when they supported public housing, they did not think through or anticipate social and economic consequences of segregating such large numbers of low-income persons in high-rise buildings. Only recently have most of these complexes been destroyed or converted into tenant-owned facilities that operate from an empowerment approach. Some liberals and radicals can make greater use of empirical research to select policies on the basis of hard evidence. (Of course, many conservatives also fail to consult empirical research when it leads to conclusions that conflict with their ideology.)

We should not forget that both conservatives and liberals often do not act on their ethical maxims. They can be bought off by corporate contributions. They sometimes succumb to public opinion even when it runs counter to deeply held beliefs. As one example, many liberals, fearful of alienating voters, supported President George W. Bush's $1.3 trillion tax cut in 2001, as well as other tax cuts that he proposed, even though the tax cuts depleted the Treasury excessively, causing the nation to be burdened with large debt payments for decades to come and lacking resources for important domestic and international programs.

Radicals encounter a major dilemma in the United States, as was illustrated by Ralph Nader's run for the presidency as the Green Party's candidate in 2000. The Green Party subscribed to such ethical principles as social justice more completely than the Democrats or the Republicans, wanting major new expenditures on domestic needs and favoring many measures to address poverty and disease in third-world nations. The Green Party alone wanted to cut military spending to free up additional resources for the domestic agenda. But the Green Party confronted an ethical dilemma: if its presidential candidate drew more votes from the Democratic candidate (Al Gore) than from the Republican candidate (George Bush), it might give the election to Bush—a self-announced conservative. Nader's decision to run for office, then, pitted his own ethical philosophy against the risk that his candidacy might inadvertently cause many policy decisions after the election that would run strongly counter to his stated values. This risk came to fruition when Bush was narrowly elected president when he probably would have lost to Gore had Nader withdrawn or asked voters in key states to vote for Gore.

The Analytic Rationale for Policy Advocacy

We have already discussed how utilitarians emphasize the role of research in shaping policy choices. We can now amplify this argument by presenting an analytic rationale for policy advocacy. In this view, advocates should support those policies that are supported by social-science and medical research, as well as research by economists. (See Policy Advocacy Challenge 2.8.)

Take the case of schizophrenia—and the remarkable transformation that has occurred during the past 40 years in its treatment and in other mental health policies. It was widely believed in the 1950s that schizophrenia was caused by the controlling or coercive behaviors of the mothers of people with schizophrenia—and that the well-being of people with schizophrenia required them to be institutionalized for long periods, sometimes even for life, because they could not deal with the stresses of society. These two beliefs—held by legions of competent social workers, psychologists, and psychiatrists—led to treatments and policies that are hardly comprehensible to contemporary clinicians. Clinicians not only verbally chastised the mothers of people with schizophrenia for their controlling behavior but often advocated severing all ties between children and their mothers. Tens of thousands of people with schizophrenia were kept in the "chronic wards" of state mental institutions for decades, carefully segregated from the patients on "acute wards."[26]

A plethora of research after the 1960s suggested that these policies were misdirected and harmful to people with schizophrenia. Considerable research suggested that schizophrenia is a complex phenomenon that is not caused primarily (or, in some cases, at all) by mothers' behavior. If the mothers' behavior was its primary cause, why did many people with schizophrenia have siblings with no evidence of the malady? Considerable research implicated biological causes, suggesting that schizophrenia is a disease with genetic and physiological causes. Other research called into question the assumption that people with schizophrenia require institutionalization.[27]

While research strongly suggested that the long-term incarceration of people with schizophrenia was unnecessary, harmful, and wasteful, it did not demonstrate the kinds of care and supports they should receive in the community. Did they need intensive care or merely occasional contacts with clinicians? What kinds of therapy and what kinds of medication would be most useful? Because empirical data were lacking, people with schizophrenia were exposed to various arrangements. In light of the reluctance of politicians to fund outpatient services, many people with schizophrenia also lacked access to any supportive services. Some of them became homeless, living on the streets, in shelters, or in low-cost housing—often in unsafe neighborhoods where they were exposed to crime and violence. Some moved in with relatives or spouses in community settings.[28] In coming years, research findings should reveal the kinds of services and living arrangements that are helpful to schizophrenic persons—but even these will come to naught if policies and funding do not allow or implement them.

POLICY ADVOCACY CHALLENGE 2.8

Using Evidence-Based Policies in Policy Advocacy

BRUCE JANSSON, PH.D.

The quest for evidence-based policies, as well as practice, is nowhere more pronounced than in medicine. It has, in fact, become a "bandwagon" as many persons have sought to ground practice and policy in scientific evidence.[1]

Take the example of asthma, which has become an epidemic among low-income African-American and Latino children in urban communities. Considerable research has identified best practices for treating this disease—and for identifying some community factors that contribute to its incidence.

At the **practice level**, advocates want physicians to use new techniques for treating asthmatic children based on scientific research. At the **policy level**, advocates want major efforts to clean up the air in low-income areas, to get schools to do early case finding and to hire nurses, and to develop outreach programs to teach parents how best to care for asthmatic children. They want early detection services for these children to lower rates of hospitalization.

Yet even in the case of asthma, only about 68 percent of physicians follow evidence-based practice guidelines—and this rate is even higher than an adherence rate of only 54.5 percent for practice guidelines for other diseases. Many low-income urban populations continue to live, moreover, in relatively polluted areas, leading to higher rates of asthma among them—and many of them do not receive adequate assistance from schools or from outreach projects.

The United States continues not to enact many other policies in health care, moreover, that evidence suggests would save lives and money. By not providing health insurance to more than 45 million Americans, for example, the United States discourages many persons from seeking services early in the development of illnesses—leading to unnecessary deaths. By not providing health insurance to many persons, moreover, the nation encourages persons to go to emergency rooms for their care since emergency rooms are required by law to give service to all persons who enter them regardless of their insurance status. It is far more expensive, however, to treat persons in emergency rooms than through visits to primary-care physicians—forcing taxpayers to foot large and unnecessary costs and raising private-insurance premiums for insured Americans as hospitals raise their fees to fund emergency-room services for uninsured persons.

Resistance to evidence-based medicine stems from many sources at both practice and policy levels. At the **practice level**, opponents fear it will make providers treat all patients the same rather than using best clinical judgments. Practitioners are often victim to inertia and tradition. At the **policy level**, opponents oppose evidence-based policies because of their cost, because they challenge corporate interests, or because they oppose them on ideological grounds. Many conservatives opposed a proposed

---

[1] For discussion of evidence-based medicine, see Stefan Timmermans and Aaron Mauck, "The Promises and Pitfalls of Evidence-Based Medicine," *Health Affairs*, Vol. 24 (2005): 18–28 and A. Geligins, et. al., "Evidence, Pitfalls, and Technological Change, *Health Affairs*, Vol. 24 (2005): 29–40.

policy that the federal government distribute sterilized needles to drug addicts, for example, even though extensive research demonstrated that this policy would greatly reduce the transmission of AIDS and other diseases particularly among low-income African-American and Latino populations.

Yet many evidence-based guidelines for practice and policy **have** been enacted. Many states require riders of motorcycles and drivers of automobiles to use helmets or seat belts—policies that have saved thousands of lives and countless injuries. Policies requiring food labeling have allowed consumers to improve their diets. Policies that prohibit smoking in public places have reduced rates of lung cancer from secondary smoke. All of these policies were obtained by the determined efforts of policy advocates who often had to battle corporations, as well as opponents of government regulations.

See if you can identify an evidence-based policy that the United States—or specific states or localities—has not enacted? Why was it not enacted? Now identify an evidence-based policy that has been enacted. Why was it enacted? How do you account for the difference?

Our discussion of research on schizophrenia demonstrates the analytic rationale for policy advocates. If they wish to advance their clients' or patients' interests, social workers must change those policies and treatments that research demonstrates are harmful or ineffective. When less expensive approaches are found to be as effective as or more effective than more expensive approaches, they should favor them to save consumers' and taxpayers' resources.

Choosing Sides: Controversy and Research

It is incorrect to assume, however, that policy advocates, armed with the latest research, can easily modify all policies. Politicians, bureaucrats, and administrators often choose to ignore research findings that conflict with their ideology, their self-interest, or their customary practices.[29] Moreover, different researchers often reach divergent conclusions, which sometimes leads to conflict. In such cases, policy advocates must decide which researcher's data and conclusions are most meritorious—and must become advocates for those policies that rest on them rather than on nonmeritorious research.

The available research on social inequality provides an excellent example of conflicting research. Take the conflicting findings of two sets of researchers: Richard Herrnstein and Charles Murray's research was reported in *The Bell Curve: Intelligence and Class Structure in American Life;* and the findings of Claude Fischer, Michael Hout, et al., were reported in *Inequality by Design: Cracking the Bell Curve Myth.*[30] Both sets of researchers agree that American society is unequal and that African Americans are found disproportionately in the poorest classes, but they reach different conclusions about the reasons African Americans are disproportionately poorer than whites.

Publishing *The Bell Curve* in 1994, Herrnstein and Murray began their analysis by contending that scores on intelligence tests form a bell-shaped curve with a few people at the lower and upper ends, and most people falling in the middle. Drawing on data from a large national survey of 10,000 Americans who were followed from 1980 onward, they asserted that intelligence scores (as measured by the Armed Forces Qualifying Test or AFQT) are strongly associated with life outcomes. Examining white non-Latinos, they contended that people with low IQ scores are more likely than those with high scores to be poor, high school dropouts, unemployed, unmarried, unwed mothers, or welfare recipients; neglectful mothers; and criminals. When comparing the effects of social class and intelligence, they concluded that intelligence scores were better predictors of life outcomes. Herrnstein and Murray then turned to their controversial assertions about connections between race, intelligence, and life outcomes. African Americans, they asserted, score, on average, 15 points lower than whites on intelligence tests—and they attributed African Americans' higher rates of poverty, school dropout, unemployment, single parent-headed families, use of welfare, and criminality to these lower intelligence scores.

The Bell Curve caused an immediate sensation, not just because it alleged that race and intelligence are associated, but because the authors contended that government can have little influence on social problems. If social problems are caused by personal factors like intelligence—and if intelligence is both unchanging and caused by genetic factors—then society cannot assume a major role in reducing poverty, curtailing school dropouts, or decreasing the use of welfare. Nor should society use affirmative action, since it contributes to the problem by stereotyping African Americans and reducing their self-esteem, as well as placing people in jobs for which they lack the needed skills and intelligence. These authors ended their book with the pessimistic conclusion that vast inequalities are inevitable, since they are caused primarily by differences in intelligence that cannot be influenced substantially by social remedies.

Claude Fischer and many of his sociology colleagues at the University of California at Berkeley (hereafter called the *Berkeley sociologists*) reexamined Herrnstein and Murray's data. The Berkeley sociologists had been perturbed by rising inequality in the United States, such as the marked increases in per capita income for the top 20 percent of the population compared with both the middle 60 percent and the bottom 20 percent from 1959 to 1989. They doubted that inequality is inevitable, pointing to smaller rates of inequality in other industrialized nations. And they doubted that inequality is caused primarily by personal characteristics such as intelligence, believing that persons' "social milieux" (family, neighborhood, school, and community) powerfully shape their economic destinies. These sociologists, then, suspected that inequality, rather than stemming from innate characteristics, is primarily a "social construction" that stems from specific policy choices of American society, compared with those of societies with lower levels of inequality. Why otherwise, they argue, would societies with the same or similar "genetic stocks," such as the United States, Canada, England, and Sweden, vary so much in their levels of inequality? And why would levels of inequality shift over time within a single country if individual characteristics like intelligence remain relatively constant?

The Berkeley sociologists used two major strategies: They analyzed the statistical procedures used by Herrnstein and Murray, and they asked fundamental questions about Herrnstein and Murray's assumptions, such as those concerning intelligence tests and the relative effects of individual talent and social environment on life outcomes. The Berkeley sociologists began by noting that even Herrnstein and Murray had conceded that only 5 to 10 percent of the differences in life outcomes among their survey members had been caused by their intelligence scores, meaning that 90 to 95 percent of these differences had been caused by other factors. Put differently, even if all adults had identical intelligence scores, the inequality of household incomes would decrease by only ten percent. Intelligence scores assume only a modest role in shaping life outcomes—hardly the huge role suggested by Herrnstein and Murray.

The effects of intelligence scores on life outcomes become even more modest, the Berkeley sociologists contended, if intelligence is scrutinized more carefully. Scores on the AFQT test, they contended, are powerfully shaped by people's social environment, such as what they have been taught in high school, as well as by their response to the test itself (how seriously they take it and how hard they try). Moreover, people's success in employment is determined by many factors that have no relation to intelligence scores, such as creativity, persistence, and social skills. Indeed, when the Berkeley sociologists reanalyzed the data from the survey used by Herrnstein and Murray, they found that AFQT scores in 1980 did not accurately predict how the subjects had fared 10 years later in employment markets.

The Berkeley sociologists also concluded that African Americans' lower scores on the AFQT did not suggest genetic causation. "Subordinate ethnic minorities" have often done more poorly in schools and on tests than dominant groups, "whether . . . Eastern European Jews in 1910 in New York, the Irish in England, Koreans in Japan, or Afrikaaners in South Africa."[31] This historical perspective strongly suggests, they contended, that "it is not low intelligence that leads to inferior status; it is that inferior status leads to low intelligence test scores."[32]

If intelligence scores do not have a great effect on inequality—or on other life outcomes, such as criminality and welfare use—what factors do? The Berkeley sociologists discovered that a host of factors totally ignored by Herrnstein and Murray had significantly affected the life outcomes of the survey members, such as being female, unmarried, and a parent. Other factors associated with poverty included the attributes of persons' communities (such as the region of the country and the extent to which their communities were impoverished and had high dropout rates from high school), the number of years of schooling, and the academic track in high school. When these factors were included in the statistical analysis and when the technical errors made by Herrnstein and Murray were corrected, the Berkeley sociologists discovered that the AFQT scores had been eclipsed in explaining life outcomes by the combined effects of other community, economic, and social factors, including the survey members' likelihood of having out-of-wedlock births, of being incarcerated, of being on welfare, and of being divorced. They concluded that if all adults had the same family origins and environments (but still had different AFQT scores), inequality of household incomes would decrease by a whopping 37 percent. In short, the combined effects of familial and environmental factors, not AFQT scores, powerfully shape life outcomes. Moreover, AFQT test scores are themselves profoundly shaped by community and familial factors, a fact suggesting they are not intrinsic in one's nature but are artifacts of the social environment.

But the Berkeley sociologists were not content merely to criticize the statistical analysis of *The Bell Curve*. Moving beyond the survey findings of Herrnstein and Murray, they examined an array of social policies that influence income distribution. Some economic factors, such as the replacement of unionized and well-paying positions by service jobs in fast-food restaurants and other settings, had caused an economic deterioration in the wages of persons with high school or less education at the same time that the income of college graduates had increased.

These background economic factors, moreover, were supplemented by an array of American social policies that had also increased economic inequality during the previous 25 years. The Berkeley sociologists identified a system of inequality in the United States through "rules and rewards of the game" that had favored affluent persons, including the

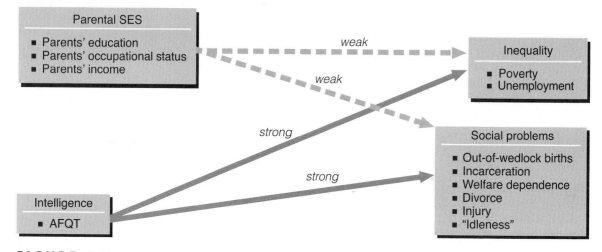

FIGURE 2.1
Herrnstein and
Murray's model

following: corporate decisions to pay well-educated and higher-level workers far more than less-educated and lower-level workers; reductions in the income tax rates for affluent Americans while the tax rates for less affluent Americans were raised or stayed the same; lack of public funding for child care (whose cost seriously depleted the incomes of less affluent Americans); affluent Americans' mortgage-interest tax deductions; linking health insurance to employment rather than providing national health insurance available to all Americans; and heavy subsidies to higher-education institutions that were used primarily by affluent Americans' children. Although Americans had made extraordinary progress in reducing poverty among elderly citizens by expanding Social Security and Medicare, they had constructed policies that had kept 20 percent of American children in poverty, compared with 9 percent of Canadian and Australian children, 7 percent of British children, and even smaller percentages of French, West German, and Swedish children. Americans had also exacerbated inequality by educational policies in secondary schools, such as having shorter school years than many other nations and tracking children from less affluent families away from college preparatory classes.

The Berkeley researchers' reexamination of the data used in *The Bell Curve,* as well as their use of findings from other social science research, suggests a causal framework radically different from that used by Herrnstein and Murray. In Herrnstein and Murray's model (see Figure 2.1), intelligence is strongly associated both with economic inequality (poverty and unemployment) and with such social problems as out-of-wedlock births, incarceration, divorce, injury, and idleness.[33] In the Berkeley sociologists' model (see Figure 2.2), "cognitive skills" (they used this term rather than intelligence) are caused by an array of environmental factors, such as the parental home environment and the adolescent community environment.[34] Although cognitive skills are associated with inequality, they share this distinction with many other factors, so their effects on inequality are diminished. Indeed, their association with inequality stems partly from their association with other variables that are also associated with inequality, such as the parental home environment and the adolescent community environment. But cognitive skills are not associated with social problems, as alleged by Herrnstein and Murray, and race bears no significant relationship to cognitive skills, inequality, or social problems.

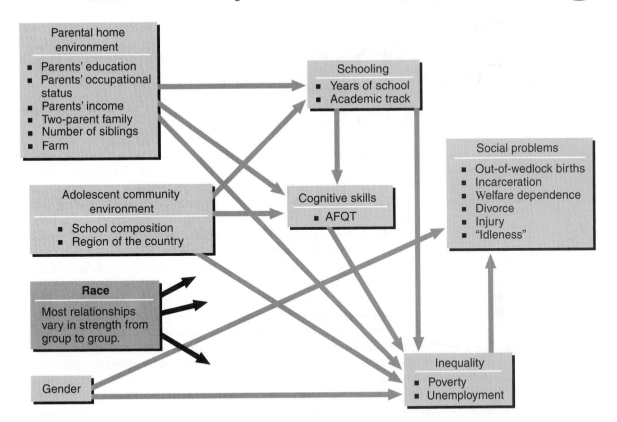

FIGURE 2.2
The Berkeley sociologists' model

Our discussion of these two research studies suggests that policy advocates must proceed carefully when basing their actions on empirical findings. Research can be misleading, simplistic, or erroneous for a variety of reasons and, as this example suggests, must be used with caution. Researchers may make technical errors in their collection and analysis of data, they may overestimate the effects of certain variables because they have excluded other factors they ought to have considered, or they may misinterpret their data. Researchers' ideology may shape not only their research, but their policy conclusions.

When research findings conflict or when they believe research is faulty, policy advocates should engage in policy debates about them. They should take sides, stating why they believe certain research as well as research findings are preferable to other research and research findings.

The Political Rationale for Policy Advocacy

Policy choices that advance fairness and social justice in American society frequently do not receive a fair hearing because the political system is rigged against poor, oppressed, and powerless groups. Powerful interest groups, whether liquor interests, the National Rifle Association (NRA), pharmaceutical companies, or the U.S. Chamber of Commerce, often wish to sustain the status quo or even to roll back social reforms. Politicians who are pledged to restrict the role of government in American affairs, even when social programs and regulations are needed to redistribute wealth and to protect oppressed groups, often control pivotal offices or possess a majority in legislative chambers. Special interests and wealthy individuals usually provide the bulk of campaign funds for the legislators of both political parties—and often receive policy concessions in return for their contributions.

Public opinion is not necessarily receptive to needed reforms. Buying the myth that any individual can succeed merely through hard work, Americans often minimize the barriers—such as low-wage jobs, lack of subsidized child care, lack of health insurance, inadequate public transportation, and unfair systems of taxation—that impede upward mobility and that cast millions of Americans into poverty. Ostensibly a liberal, Bill Clinton often moved to the center or to the right in response to public opinion polls suggesting that Americans do not want major reforms or substantial increases in programs that invest in human capital. This moderate or conservative bias in public opinion is accentuated by the disinclination to vote of millions of poor people—a group so large that it could aptly be called the party of nonvoters. Whether this stems from procedural barriers to registration and voting or from cynicism about American politics, nonvoters make policy changes in American society more difficult.[35]

If Americans who favor social justice or fairness fail to participate in the political process, they risk increasing the extent to which the political process is skewed against social reforms. One thing is certain: persons opposed to social justice, such as some conservatives, love the political vacuum created when other people do not participate in the political process. Such defections merely allow them to realize their policy preferences more easily. Indeed, nonparticipation is a vote for the values of those who do participate, including more affluent members of society who vote at far higher rates than low-income persons or persons with relatively progressive viewpoints such as many youth.

The composition of government determines what kinds of social policies are (and are not) enacted in local, state, and federal jurisdictions. The political party that obtains a majority of the members of a legislative chamber gets an extraordinary advantage in shaping the legislation that is enacted by that chamber. It gets not only the majority of votes in that chamber, but it controls the chairs of all of its legislative committees, which allows it to determine what bills are given serious attention by the committees and when they are scheduled for votes. The political party that wins head-of-government positions like mayoralties, governorships, and presidencies also gets a huge advantage over other parties. These heads of government appoint the heads and top staff of key government agencies, allowing them to shape how specific programs are implemented. In addition, they can use the media more easily than other politicians to publicize policies that they favor and to attack opponents' policies.

Presidents and governors appoint many of the nation's judges, which allows them to have major influence over controversial court decisions on such topics as abortion and affirmative action. Majority parties in legislatures control how boundaries of political districts are established (so-called apportionment), allowing them to gain seats for themselves by drawing lines in ways that give them an advantage in certain districts.

The ethical stakes are high, as well, when propositions are placed on the ballot in local and state jurisdictions. Originally intended to allow voters to bypass corrupt politicians by placing legislative proposals directly on the ballot, the proposition process has often been used by special interests and conservatives to get their policies enacted. (See Policy Advocacy Challenge 2.9.)

Some social workers believe that political activity is antithetical to professionalism, viewing the development and use of power as unethical. This view is shortsighted, however, as Jane Addams realized in the early part of this century. If persons who are committed to social justice and fairness do not use power, they simply concede to persons who are not committed to these values.

Nor is it necessarily unethical to engage in self-interested activity. When social workers seek licensing laws, which now exist in all states, they want (among other things) access to reimbursements from insurance companies and Medicare. When they try to make certain positions in public agencies classified (that is, reserved for people with social work degrees), they seek to exclude other persons from these positions because they believe that social work education enhances the help available to vulnerable populations. To gauge the ethical merits of self-interested activity, we have to ask why people are seeking resources or power and how they plan to use their gains.

As Salcido and Seck argue, however, those who act only out of self-interest are morally derelict.[36] Legendary activists, such as Martin Luther King, Jr., risked their lives and ultimately lost them to advance social justice and fairness. Despite probable bad publicity, professionals should take positions on unpopular issues, such as the economic and social needs of AFDC women, the plight of prisoners on death row, and needle exchange programs to prevent AIDS among drug addicts. Disturbingly, Salcido and Seck found evidence that some chapters of NASW engaged only in licensing issues and ignored broader issues.

Social workers need to engage in policy practice precisely because they often bring distinctive viewpoints into the policy-making process. An example is found in the comments (made during a personal conversation with the author) of Maurice Bischeff, who ran simulation games in the professional schools of the University of Southern California. He compared the tactics of business school students and social work students in a simulation game known as End of the Line, in which the participants assume the role of elderly people with limited resources, such as money and food, symbolized by paper clips; players "die" when they lose their stock of paper clips. Students in the business school usually created a win-lose situation that led to a few winners and many losers. Social workers, by contrast, often invited destitute players to join supportive groups that shared their dwindling supplies of paper clips. The social workers defined the game in win-win terms that emphasized cooperative rather than competitive strategies.

POLICY ADVOCACY CHALLENGE 2.9

Confronting Powerful Interests

RUSSELL HENDERSON, MSW, LCSW

Go to **academic.cengage.com/ social_work/jansson** to watch this video clip

Listen to Policy Advocacy Challenge Video 2.9, where Russell Henderson, MSW, LCSW, Organizer of the Rebuilding Louisiana Coalition, faculty member at Dillard University, and lobbyist with the Louisiana legislature, discusses how various special interests, as well as affluent citizens on "high ground," made his work more difficult when seeking resources and programs to rebuild New Orleans in the wake of Hurricane Katrina. What special interests does he discuss?

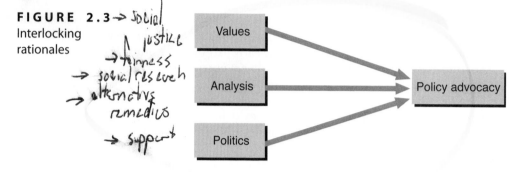

FIGURE 2.3 →
Interlocking
rationales

[handwritten annotations: social justice / fairness / social research / alternative remedies / support]

While Bischeff's observations do not provide definitive evidence, they suggest that social workers are somewhat more likely to identify with the underdogs, the downtrodden, and the oppressed. Of course, social workers with clinical interests need to move beyond empathy to policy advocacy if they want to diminish inequalities and injustices in American society.

Interlocking Rationales for Policy Advocacy

Ethical, analytic, and political rationales work together to buttress the case for policy practice and policy advocacy. (See Figure 2.3.)

Values like social justice and fairness, as well as identification with oppressed groups, prompt us to become policy advocates in the first place. Social research helps us discover effective ways of advancing these values and helping these groups, and allows us to choose from alternative remedies. No matter how meritorious our policy recommendations are on ethical or analytic grounds, we cannot have them implemented if we do not mobilize political support for them.

POLICY ADVOCACY CHALLENGE 2.10

Developing the Ethical Rationale for Policy Advocacy in the Wake of Hurricane Katrina

Bruce Jansson, Ph.D.

Go to
academic.cengage.com/
social_work/jansson
to watch this video clip

When Hurricane Katrina slammed into New Orleans on August 29, 2005, it caused vast damage to the city's infrastructure, housing, and businesses from the combined effects of winds, rain, and flooding from broken levees. It also caused untold human suffering not only to citizens generally, but to the city's and region's low-income, African American, disabled, and elderly communities. In a long-standing pattern, low-income persons disproportionately lived in areas of the city, that were below sea level. The Ninth Ward was virtually obliterated with many of its dwellings under nine feet of water after Katrina's landfall.

Seeking refuge in their homes, hospitals, and boarding houses, the Superdome, and such elevated places as bridges and interstate highways, the city's poor, elderly, and disabled experienced Katrina's wrath first-hand. Considerable numbers of them died. Yet others experienced unimaginable suffering as public officials from city, state, and federal agencies failed to provide them with water, food, and medicines in Katrina's wake. Eventually, most persons were evacuated to distant shelters and hospitals in such places as Baton Rouge and Houston, but even in these locations they faced an uncertain future in meeting their basic income, housing, and medical needs.

Persons who experienced Katrina's destruction clearly needed charitable assistance in her wake to meet their survival needs such as food, clothing, water, and medical care. But they also needed *policy advocacy* that would help them no matter where they had been evacuated. They needed:

- Emergency "Section 8" housing vouchers to allow them to get federal subsidies to rent houses.
- Changes in the existing Disaster Unemployment Program (DUA) to raise its benefits to a minimum living standard.
- Disaster assistance payments to poor families to bring their income to a level to meet their basic needs.
- Temporary revisions in the Medicaid Program to allow Katrina survivors to get access to Medicaid quickly even when they did not qualify for the regular Medicaid Program.
- Revisions in the Food Stamp Program to allow Katrina survivors to become eligible for food stamps for an extended period.
- Increases in the funding for the WIC Program as well as for the Low-Income Home Energy Assistance Program (LIHEAP) in light of increased expenditures for these programs, in light of the needs of Katrina survivors, as well as likely increases in home heating bills.
- Changes in existing regulations so that all legal immigrants who are Katrina victims can get access to a range of programs like Medicaid and Temporary Assistance for Needy Families (TANF).

Absent pressure from policy advocates, however, Katrina's low-income and legal-immigrant survivors were unlikely to obtain such policy assistance, much less robust programs to rebuild their neighborhoods or to give them economic and other assistance needed to help them re-enter the economic and social mainstream.

Those evacuees who returned to New Orleans, no matter their social class or ethnicity, would need help from a set of policies and huge resources that would rebuild their community. When President George W. Bush made a speech to the nation on September 15, 2005 when he promised "massive reconstruction" and vast resources, it appeared that he would exercise presidential leadership. Yet concerted opposition to robust programs of help for Katrina's survivors arose by the middle portion of September 2005—and intensified in following months—within his own party. The President had backpedaled from this pledge by mid-November, declaring that local officials should take the lead. While FEMA replaced Michael Brown with another director, the Army Corps of Engineers had patched the levees on a temporary basis, and FEMA had placed 10,000 trailers in the city, no authority or plan had yet emerged about when or how communities might be repaired. It remained unclear whether the Ninth Ward, a community inhabited by low-income African Americans, would be rebuilt. Speculators roamed the city seeking to buy large amounts of property in hopes of reaping profits. Huge amounts of the resources committed to Katrina had been diverted to other parishes, towns, and cities in Louisiana and Mississippi—even ones where only minor storm damage had occurred. Yet other resources were devoted to repairs of military establishments.

If debates in the Congress and press commentary had mostly assumed in the weeks following Katrina that large-scale governmental assistance would be needed to rebuild New Orleans and help evacuees, a strong conservative movement had developed by mid-October that was based upon different premises. Its spokespersons wanted the

(continued)

private sector to take the lead, wanted local units of government to assume the prime responsibility, and even sought to cut budgets of social programs required to help many evacuees such as Food Stamps and Medicaid. Influenced by the conservative wing of the Republican Party, President Bush assumed a lower profile and retreated from his promise in mid-September to orchestrate "the largest reconstruction effort in American history."

Residents of New Orleans would need far more than food, medical care, and resources, then, in coming months. They would need:

- Rebuilding of levees so that the area would withstand another severe hurricane as early as the next hurricane season beginning in August 2006—or one year after Hurricane Katrina. To the extent that specific areas would not be safe for rebuilding even with repaired levees, government officials had to identify them so that rebuilding could proceed rapidly in other areas.
- Federal assistance with private home insurance that many citizens possessed—so that they could get funds for rebuilding their houses since many of their policies limited insurance only to damage caused by wind, not water. To the extent private insurance companies did not reimburse water-caused damage, the federal government needed to grant its own subsidies to homeowners.
- A planning process that defined where persons could rebuild and what kinds of structures, roads, and other infrastructure would go where. Absent a plan, persons would not know whether and where to proceed with rebuilding the city. Improvements to New Orleans had to be made in a planned sequence if former residents were to return to the city, since they would want not just housing but grocery stores, banks, roads, mass transportation at the point that they returned to New Orleans.
- Strong federal direction to insure that homeowners and business owners received resources rapidly for reconstructing their properties.
- Strict federal monitoring to assure that corruption did not take place, such as persons getting assistance when they did not need it or contractors not providing work for which they were reimbursed.
- Holding elections even though many residents had left New Orleans, so that elected officials would be responsive to the needs of both evacuees and residents.
- Special assistance to low-income evacuees, including affordable housing, lest they be unable to return to New Orleans—and to avoid repopulating of the city by relatively affluent Caucasian persons rather than a racially-mixed population.

In addition to these imperatives, citizens of New Orleans would also need the rapid reconstruction of the social, medical, and educational services, not to mention police and fire protection. In the hurricane's wake, many professionals, including social workers, left New Orleans. Not only was it necessary for many of them to return, but local, state, and federal officials would need to provide resources to allow them to maintain services at an adequate level.

In order to develop four rationales for engaging in policy advocacy following Katrina, imagine what might have happened had *no* policy advocates emerged. In these rationales, focus on the members of a specific vulnerable population.

- ***Ethical rationale:*** Identify specific ethical principles that suggest that policy advocates were strongly needed in Hurricane Katrina's wake.

- *Research rationale:* Identify specific kinds of data that policy advocates might collect or obtain to make a case for improvements in the housing, mental health services, or health services of evacuees, as well as persons remaining in New Orleans.
- *Political rationale:* Identify some groups that would "fill the political vacuum" if no policy advocates emerged. Select one of them and conjecture what kinds of specific policies and resource allocations they might favor as compared to policy advocates. How might their proposed policies harm a specific vulnerable population?
- *Electoral rationale:* Assume that *all* elected officials in Washington, DC, the Louisiana State legislature, and the New Orleans City Council possessed conservative perspectives. Absent any opposition, what policies would they likely have sought? Does your discussion suggest the need to balance conservative legislators with legislators with different perspectives while acknowledging that moderate and liberal legislators can also develop ill-advised policies? To the extent that you believe that a mixture of legislators are needed—or that greater numbers of relatively progressive ones are needed to assist vulnerable populations—what role should policy advocates assume during specific elections?

Listen to Policy Advocacy Challenge Video 2.10 where Russell Henderson, MSW, LCSW, Organizer of the Rebuilding Louisiana Coalition, social-policy teacher at Dillard University, and legislative lobbyist, makes an ethical case for policy advocacy in Katrina's wake. What ethical arguments does he use? Were policy advocates NOT to emerge in New Orleans in Hurricane Katrina's wake, what adverse outcomes might we expect?

What You Can Now Do

CHAPTER SUMMARY

You are now equipped with skills in ethical reasoning that are needed for policy advocacy. You can do the following:

- Discuss differences between policy-sensitive and policy-related practice—and how they differ from policy practice and policy advocacy.
- Discuss Rawls's theory of social justice as it provides a rationale for working to help out-groups.
- Develop an ethical position that draws together various kinds of ethical arguments.
- Present an analytic rationale for policy advocacy.
- Present a political rationale for policy advocacy.
- Discuss why policy advocates often seek to change the composition of governments—and dangers that exist if they abandon the political arena and interests to others.
- Understand how to use the Web intelligently to obtain information from specific advocacy groups.

In the next chapter, we develop a framework for policy practice that sets the stage for discussing the skills, tasks, and competencies needed by policy advocates.

NOTES

1. Robert Veatch, *A Theory of Medical Ethics* (New York: Basic Books, 1981).

2. For example, physicians are often implored to break down the barriers that patients encounter when seeking medical care; see Elizabeth Rosenthal, "Despite an Infusion of Public Funds, Women Find Barriers to Prenatal Care," *New York Times* (January 6, 1993), p. 6.

3. Ibid.

4. See Julie Kosterlitz, "Enablement, the Disability Movement after 1990 Victory," *National Journal* (August 31, 1991): 2092–2096.

5. Barbara Solomon, *Black Empowerment* (New York: Columbia University Press, 1976).

6. See Nancy Humphreys, "Integrating Policy and Practice," *Smith College Studies in Social Work* 63 (March 1993): 182–184.

7. Jonathan Kozol, *Savage Inequities* (New York: Crown, 1991).

8. The indifference of many physicians to the obstacles that poor people encounter when seeking medical services is discussed by Paul Starr, *The Social Transformation of American Medicine* (New York: Basic Books, 1982).

9. For a discussion of how policy practitioners can help advocacy and community groups, see Kim Bobo, Jackie Kendall, and Steve Max, *Organizing for Social Change: A Manual for Activists in the 1990s* (Washington, DC: Seven Locks Press, 1991).

10. Lester Thurow, *The Zero-Sum Society* (New York: Basic Books, 1980), pp. 155–190.

11. John Rawls, *A Theory of Justice* (Cambridge: Harvard University Press, 1971), pp. 83–90, 96–100.

12. Ibid.

13. Robert Reich, *Work of Nations: Preparing Ourselves for Twenty-First Century Capitalism* (New York: Knopf, 1991), pp. 171–261.

14. Ibid.

15. Robert Bellah et al., *Habits of the Heart* (Berkeley and Los Angeles: University of California Press, 1985), pp. 275–296.

16. Thurow, *The Zero-Sum Society*, pp. 155–190.

17. Paul Moore, et al., *The Other Lost Angeles: The Working Poor in the City in the 21st Century* (Los Angeles: Los Angeles Alliance for a New Economy, 2000).

18. A defense of affirmative action is provided by John Baker, *Arguing for Equality* (London: Verso, 1987), pp. 44–51.

19. Veatch, *Medical Ethics.*

20. Various authors discuss first-order ethical principles that are applicable to social work. See Frank Loewenberg and Ralph Dolgoff, *Ethical Decisions for Social Work Practice* (Itasca, IL: Peacock, 1988); Frederic Reamer, *Ethical Dilemmas in Social Service*, 2nd ed. (New York: Columbia University Press, 1990); Frederic Reamer, *The Philosophical Foundations of Social Work* (New York: Columbia University Press, 1993); and Margaret Rhodes, *Ethical Dilemmas in Social Work Practice* (Boston: Routledge & Kegan Paul, 1986).

21. The classic statement of utilitarianism is found in Jeremy Bentham, *An Introduction to the Principles of Morals and Legislation* (London: Athlone Press, 1970). For a critique of this approach, see Mackie, *Ethics*, pp. 126–134.

22. Ibid.

23. Ibid.

24. Bruce S. Jansson, *The Reluctant Welfare State*, 3rd ed. (Pacific Grove, CA: Brooks/Cole, 1997), pp. 22–23.

25. For a discussion of ethical dilemmas, see Tom Beauchamp and James Childress, *Principles of Biomedical Ethics*, 4th ed. (New York: Oxford University Press, 1994).

26. Bernard Bloom, *Community Mental Health* (Pacific Grove, CA: Brooks/Cole, 1977).

27. Erving Goffman, *Asylums: Essays on the Social Situation of Mental Patients and Other Inmates* (New York: Anchor Books, 1961).

28. Madeleine Stoner, *The Civil Rights of Homeless People* (New York: Aldine de Gruyter, 1995), pp. 79–97.

29. Thomas Mann and Norman Ornstein, *How Congress Shapes Health Policy* (Washington, DC: Brookings Institution, 1995).

30. Claude Fischer et al., *Inequality by Design: Cracking the Bell Curve Myth* (Princeton, NJ: Princeton University Press, 1997) and Richard Herrnstein and Charles Murray, *The Bell Curve: Intelligence and Class Structure in American Life* (New York: Free Press, 1994).

31. Fischer et al., Inequality by Design, p. 177.

32. Ibid., p. 172.

33. Ibid., p. 73.

34. Ibid., p. 74.

35. Frances Fox Piven and Richard Cloward, *Why Americans Don't Vote* (New York: Pantheon Books, 1988).

36. See Ramon Salcido and Essie Seck, "Political Participation Among Social Work Chapters," *Social Work* 37 (November 1992): 563–564, for a critique of NASW chapters that focus their political activities only on issues of licensure and reimbursement.

SUGGESTED READINGS

Understanding Moral Reasoning: Utilitarian Approaches

Jeremy Bentham, *An Introduction to the Principles of Morals and Legislation* (London: Athlone Press, 1970).

Understanding Moral Reasoning: Deontological Approaches

Tom Beauchamp and James Childress, *Principles of Biomedical Ethics*, 4th ed. (New York: Oxford University Press, 1994).

Understanding Moral Reasoning: Intuitionist Approaches

Ann Fleck-Henderson, "Moral Reasoning in Social Work Practice," *Social Service Review* (June 1991): 185–202.

J. L. Mackie, *Ethics: Inventing Right and Wrong* (London: Penguin Books, 1977).

Exploring Ethical Issues That Confront Social Workers

Frank Loewenberg and Ralph Dolgoff, *Ethical Decisions for Social Work Practice*, 3rd ed. (Itasca, IL: Peacock, 1988).

Frederic Reamer, *Ethical Dilemmas in Social Service,* 2nd ed. (New York: Columbia University Press, 1990).

Margaret Rhodes, *Ethical Dilemmas in Social Work Practice* (Boston: Routledge & Kegan Paul, 1986).

Exploring Ethical Issues About the Nature of the "Good Society"

John Baker, *Arguing for Equality* (London: Verso, 1987).

Robert Goodin, *Reasons for Welfare: The Political Theory of the Welfare State* (Princeton, NJ: Princeton University Press, 1988), pp. 227–359.

John Rawls, *A Theory of Justice* (Cambridge: Harvard University Press, 1971).

Frederic Reamer, *The Philosophical Foundations of Social Work* (New York: Columbia University Press, 1993).

2

SURMOUNTING CYNICISM BY DEVELOPING POLICY-ADVOCACY SKILLS

It is easy to succumb to cynicism when we view important social problems that have festered for decades or when we understand that legislators, presidents, and other leaders are often captive to special interests or have ideologies that make them disinterested in social justice. We can surmount cynicism, however, by gaining skills, knowledge, and perspectives that allow any of us to participate effectively in policy changing work.

Chapter Three provides a framework for policy practice and policy advocacy within a political and economic context. It identifies six policy practice tasks, four policy practice skills, and various policy competencies. It provides case examples and videotaped interviews with policy advocates to demonstrate how policy can be an intervention discipline. It discusses four styles of policy practice widely used by policy advocates. It discusses how the development and use of power is important to policy advocacy, but how analytic, interaction, and value-clarification skills also are important. You should emerge from reading this chapter with a better understanding of how social workers can make policy advocacy not just a theory-building and policy-descriptive discipline, but a practice discipline that they can use in their professional careers no matter where they work.

Obtaining Skills and Competencies for Policy Advocacy

TWO POLICY PREDICAMENTS	It is worth asking how policy advocacy prior to Hurricane Katrina might have better prepared New Orleans for this catastrophe. In this chapter, we provide case examples of policy advocacy in New Orleans before and after Hurricane Katrina hit the city. We also discuss how students enrolled in a master degree program in social work (MSWs) in Los Angeles engaged in policy advocacy with respect to the city's huge homeless population.

This chapter provides a general framework for policy practice in any setting, whether legislative, organizational, or community. We discuss in this chapter how to:

- Understand a policy practice framework that places policy deliberations in their contextual setting
- Identify six policy practice tasks: agenda building, problem analyzing, proposal constructing, policy enacting, policy implementing, and policy assessing
- Identify four policy practice skills used to accomplish the policy tasks: value clarifying, political, interactional, and analytic
- Understand specific policy competencies needed to operationalize each of the policy skills
- Identify and understand four styles of policy practice that are used by policy practitioners, as well as hybrid styles
- Understand the importance of power in policy practice

A Policy Practice Framework

To be useful to policy advocates, a policy practice framework must be multifaceted and must do the following:

- Place policy advocacy in its contextual setting, because it never occurs in a vacuum
- Identify the values, ideology, interests, and goals of stakeholders in specific policy situations—including those of the policy advocate and his or her allies
- Discuss patterns of participation, because an array of participants usually shape choices and outcomes
- Identify the key tasks that policy advocates undertake in their work
- Identify the fundamental skills that policy advocates should possess
- Identify the key competencies that policy advocates should possess

Such a framework is presented in Figure 3.1, which we will now discuss and illustrate with a case example.

The Policy Context

The framework in Figure 3.1 describes the context and tasks of policy practice and advocacy as they take place in specific agency, community, and legislative settings. It encourages us to ask important questions about how policy making works, both in general and in specific situations. We can ask, for example, whether political and economic forces determine the outcome of policy deliberations. In some cases, powerful interests have such clout that they can single-handedly shape the course of deliberations. Interest groups with large constituencies and many economic resources have developed extraordinary power through mass mailing, marketing, campaign underwriting, and vote-counting technology. This has been true of corporate groups like the American Association of Automobile Dealers or groups with mass membership like the American Association of Retired Persons.[1] Concerning other issues, however, powerful external interests do not exist or are locked in opposition with one another, giving policy advocates more latitude. Even when powerful interests exist, policy advocates have won noteworthy victories, such as getting national legislation that required automobile companies to install seat belts or getting states to control smoking in public places.

Contextual factors help us understand the response of public and nongovernmental officials to Hurricane Katrina's destruction after its landfall on August 29, 2005. Many factors contributed to a *positive response* in its immediate aftermath. The nation was shocked by the extent of its devastation as it viewed hours of graphic coverage on television—coverage that included floating corpses, persons shouting for assistance from rooftops, and stranded persons at the Superdome who lacked basic amenities. Stung by the negative coverage of the Federal Emergency Management Agency's (FEMA's) immediate failure to respond to needs of citizens during and after the storm, as well as his ill-advised and premature televised praise for the work of FEMA Director Michael Brown, President George W. Bush promised a massive reconstruction of the region with unprecedented federal resources by mid-September. (His low position in political polls, as well as partisan attacks by Democrats, also spurred him into action.)

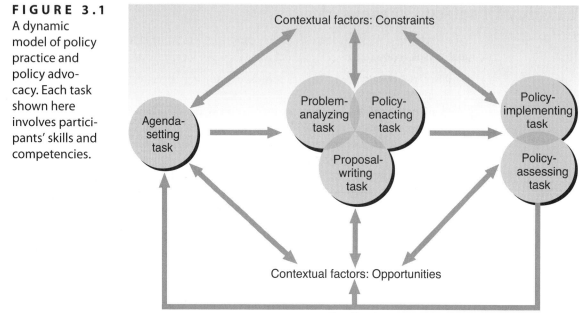

Concerned about the city and also wanting to obtain partisan advantage, Democrats lashed out at the administration for its tardy response, the bumbling response of FEMA, and Bush's early inattention—stimulating Bush and fellow Republicans to propose a massive reconstruction.

Yet other contextual factors led to a marked pullback by the president and his party by late September in a pattern that continued through the rest of fall 2005 and into 2006. Conservatives became leery of huge expenditures and a substantial federal role in redressing Katrina's destruction. Press coverage in the week following Katrina had often emphasized looting in the storm's wake, which decreased sympathy for its victims among some segments of the population. Perhaps not fully realizing that many low-income and elderly persons lacked transportation to leave the area, some persons blamed them for some of the problems they encountered when the city flooded. When they heard the President pledge massive reconstruction at unprecedented cost—and heard reports that he was considering placing it under the control of a federal agency—many members of the Republican Party influenced him to take a more cautious approach when they rebelled against him. Bush retreated from his proposal to spend as much as $250 billion on the reconstruction of New Orleans when this promise renewed attacks on the huge deficits that he had incurred as president—and when many politicians demanded that he offset these expenditures with tax increases, cuts in military spending, or cuts in popular programs. If Democrats had prioritized reconstruction in early fall 2005, they put more emphasis on criticizing Bush's policies in Iraq in succeeding months.

This curious mixture of positive and negative contextual factors allows us to understand why a *vacillating* response to Katrina evolved during the 12 months after Katrina's landfall. When positive factors prevailed, Congress and the president responded more affirmatively than when negative factors gained strength. Bush's resolve to develop a strong federal response to Katrina diminished as negative factors gained strength. Only time would tell whether, when, and how New Orleans' crisis would eventually be resolved.

Perspectives of Stakeholders and Policy Advocates

Policies are ultimately initiated, changed, or rejected by people—not by abstract forces. We can distinguish between stakeholders and policy initiators. *Stakeholders* are persons with a vested interest in a specific policy or issue being contested. These include the following:

- Leaders and members of interest groups
- Advocacy groups that have been active in seeking policy reforms in a progressive way
- Administrators and staff of existing programs
- Legislators (and their aides) who are members, or chairs, of committees that have been active with respect to the issue or policy under consideration
- Heads of government interested in a specific policy or issue, whether regarding its political importance to them or as they are charged with overseeing it
- Government agencies and funders who fund programs related to the policy, or who monitor or regulate them
- Consumers or beneficiaries of a specific policy or issue
- Regulatory bodies or courts associated with a policy or issue, such as state departments that inspect nursing homes and child-care centers
- Professional groups associated with a program or issue, such as the National Association of Social Workers regarding licensing issues related to social work
- Associations of agencies that focus on specific issues, such as the directors of child-care centers in a particular state
- Corporate interest groups such as the U.S. Chamber of Commerce or associations representing pharmaceutical companies (in the case of health legislation)
- Heads of political parties to the extent they believe a policy or issue has political ramifications for themselves

We call these persons and groups stakeholders because they have a stake in a policy or issue, whether political or economic, or because they are directly affected by it. Policy advocates need to discover at the outset who these people and groups are, because they probably will become involved when advocates try to initiate, modify, or terminate a specific policy.

Not only do policy advocates need to identify these groups, they need to understand the likely positions and perspectives they possess. (See Policy Advocacy Challenge 3.1.) Of course, stakeholders do not always act consistently. Policy advocates should be careful not to assume that past actions and perspectives always predict future ones. Sometimes conservatives support major social legislation despite their opposition to "big government," such as representatives from farm states who have strong supporters of the federal Food Stamp Program.

**POLICY
ADVOCACY
CHALLENGE 3.1**

Conducting
Research
to Support
Policy Advocacy

STEPHANIE
DAVIS, RESEARCH
LIBRARIAN,
UNIVERSITY
OF SOUTHERN
CALIFORNIA, IRVINE

On some levels, doing research to support policy practice is the same as doing research for a term paper. You still need to write clearly, state your arguments in a lucid and succinct manner, back up your position with other work in the same area or with statistics and other data, and you will need to cite any information that is not your idea.

However, in policy practice research, most likely you are casting a wider net in terms of the kind of information you want to find to support your case. In most cases, term paper research is based mostly in finding academic research articles and books. In policy practice research, your end goal is to persuade a certain group that you are right. You'll want to bring in other information such as legislation, new Congressional bills, and case studies or reports from agencies or organizations.

The following are a few research skills that will come in handy when starting your policy research:

- Know the extent of the resources in your community and make use of the expertise, such as other agencies, libraries, government departments, and educators.
- Search strategically: if you don't find the information you want at first, try searching with different keywords, in a different database, or on a different Web site.
- Inform yourself about your community, your city, and your state. This is as simple as reading a newspaper and watching the news.
- Remember that information that proves your point is just as important as information that disproves your point. You need to be aware of both.
- Familiarize yourself with the historical aspects of the problem you are trying to address in your work so you can learn how others have approached the problem in the past, and how people have been impacted by the problem.
- Evaluate the information that you find, check your facts, and cite your sources.

The sheer number and variety of stakeholders varies from issue to issue. In the case of relatively technical issues that affect relatively few people, relatively few stakeholders exist. Some minor technical change in laws that license social workers, for example, have import primarily to social workers. In contrast, any effort to reform national health care policies in major ways is relevant to scores of stakeholder groups and hundreds of politicians, not to mention the general public.

We want to know not only which stakeholders are likely to be involved, but the importance they attach to a policy initiative. Will the initiative be perceived in ideological terms; for example, will stakeholders believe that it is connected to deep-seated beliefs about society and how it should operate? In the case of national health insurance, for example, conservatives and liberals bring to the table different perspectives that have repeatedly led to marked conflict whenever this issue is raised in the Congress. Will key stakeholders see the policy initiative as affecting their basic economic and political interests, such as taking resources from them, giving them major additional resources, or impinging on their political base of support? We can ask, as well, if the policy initiative is likely to be perceived as costing a lot of money, which also raises the economic stakes to a range of persons since money is usually in short supply in legislatures and agencies. If any or all of these three factors are involved (ideology, key interests, or money), we can predict high interest by a number of stakeholders. Such interest could, in turn, suggest possible conflict or, at the very least, considerable maneuvering by stakeholders as they seek resolutions that will be consonant with their ideology, interests, and available resources.

Of course, the opposite also is true: initiatives seen as not impinging on ideology, interests, or budgets will likely attract less interest and controversy.

Policy initiators are persons or groups that initiate a change in existing policy. They may propose a new policy, or the modification or termination of an existing policy. Sometimes they are stakeholders themselves, such as a legislator or head of government who proposes new legislation. Sometimes they are advocacy groups. In rarer cases, policies are initiated by individual citizens, for example, persons who want to change existing policies because they have had bad experiences with these programs or policies. Policy initiators bring their own perspectives, values, and ideologies to the table, as well as their own interests, which we need to understand to know why they have initiated a policy proposal and whether they will invest major resources in it. Is this an issue in which they have a longstanding interest? To what extent are they connected to other stakeholders in a positive way? Do they possess the expertise and resources to be effective advocates—and do they intend to invest major resources in this initiative, such as staff time and money? How are they viewed by other stakeholders—and will these perceptions affect their likely success in obtaining collaborators and allies? Are they likely to make a credible case for the initiative, such as by drawing on available data and research?

Patterns of Participation

Policy initiators usually do not have the field to themselves because other people participate in policy deliberations. Some are *bystanders* who take no part in policy deliberations, and others are *policy responders* who seek to modify or change the policy proposals of the initiators. *Opposers* decide to block or modify proposals. These groups rarely remain fixed; people change groups as policy deliberations proceed. Initiators often want to expand their ranks by attracting people from other groups, just as opposers want to convert people to their position.

Issues spark different levels of conflict during policy deliberations. Some issues create a great deal of disagreement, and others are resolved with minimal conflict. Participants' actions and rhetoric reflect the level of conflict. In high conflict, people use emotion-laden language, make vigorous efforts to outmaneuver other participants, use extraordinary tactics (such as filibusters), publicize the issue through the mass media, and try to enlist others to support their position. Conflict may result in the polarization of factions and groups, such as political parties, conservatives and liberals in legislatures, different factions in communities, or management and line staff in organizations. An absence of such conflict and alignments usually suggests consensual deliberations.

Policy deliberations often last a long time. A piece of legislation, for example, goes through subcommittees, committees, and floor debates before it is forwarded to elected officials, such as the president or the governor, for approval or veto. Policy initiatives sometimes take years to enact as their supporters work to educate others about the merits of their initiatives. Yet other issues are processed rapidly, as when heads of government place initiatives high on their agendas and successfully rally support for them. Proposals in agencies often proceed through sequences of deliberation in meetings and committees and with officials. Policy changes can be made quickly or slowly in agencies, as well. Some initiatives languish for years until a new executive decides to push them. Other issues, however, are resolved rapidly, such as decisions made in agency staff meetings to modify internal policies.

The Six Tasks of Policy Practitioners

Policy practitioners and policy advocates undertake six tasks as we discussed in Chapter One. In the *agenda-setting task*, practitioners gauge whether the context is favorable for a policy initiative, and they evolve early strategy to place it on policy makers' agendas. In the *problem-analyzing task*, practitioners analyze the causes, nature, and prevalence of specific problems. In the *proposal-writing task*, practitioners develop solutions to specific problems. Proposals may be relatively ambitious, such as a piece of legislation, or relatively modest, such as incremental changes in existing policies. In the *policy-enacting task*, practitioners try to have policies approved or enacted.

At some point, proposals are either enacted in their original or an amended form, or rejected. When analyzing these outcomes, we often ask: Who won and who lost? Those whose proposals are enacted with few changes are clear victors. Sometimes, however, apparent victors have actually lost because their proposals are so diluted as to be meaningless, as Peter Bachrach and Morton Baratz noted in discussing "decisionless decisions."[2] An example of a decisionless decision is enacting a new program when no resources are available. Clear losers are those whose proposals are rejected.

Policy practitioners continue to work even after policy enactment when they undertake the *policy-implementing task*, in which they try to carry out enacted policies. Once a policy has been enacted, policy deliberations focus on its implementation and assessment. (See Figure 3.1.) Considerable conflict may erupt during a policy's implementation as people and interest groups try to influence the priorities and directions of social programs. Unions, professionals, civil servants, legislators, and consumers, as well as heads of government, shape implementation.

Policy practitioners evaluate programs when they undertake the *policy-assessing task* by obtaining data about the implemented policy's performance. Policy practitioners frequently assess programs after policy enactment to see if they fulfill certain objectives. For example, researchers have assessed the Food Stamp program to see if it has decreased malnutrition in specific segments of the population, evaluated the Head Start program to decide whether it enhances children's cognitive development, and analyzed the Adoption Assistance and Child Welfare Act to determine whether it has shortened children's stays in foster care. Ultimately, we ask which segments of the population have benefited or have been harmed by a policy's enactment. If a new social program distributes resources exclusively to affluent persons, for example, we might declare that poor persons have lost.

When we discuss these policy tasks as separate entities, we suggest that they are easily distinguishable. In fact, persons often engage in several of these tasks at the same time. For example, legislators simultaneously engage in proposal-writing and policy-enacting tasks when they modify a proposal to enhance its prospects of enactment. They couple the problem-analyzing task with the proposal-writing task when they create a proposal that addresses the basic causes of a social problem or the needs of a specific group.

Moreover, policy practitioners rarely accomplish the various tasks sequentially and predictably. Legislators may draft a proposal before devoting much time to analyzing the presenting problem. They may revise the proposal in response to a social scientist's comments at a legislative committee hearing. In this case, they begin with the proposal-writing task, revert to the problem-analyzing task, and return to proposal writing. Similarly, a legislator may attempt to rally support for a vague and ill-defined proposal (the policy-enacting task), only to return to the problem-analyzing and proposal-writing tasks at a later time. Of course, this seemingly chaotic approach to policy making departs from the sequential process that some policy analysts describe, but events in the real world rarely correspond to any orderly approach. (To underscore the fluid nature of policy making, we use overlapping circles in Figure 3.1 to characterize the relationships among the various roles.)

Our policy framework also poses interesting questions about the relationships among the phases of policy deliberations. The initial definition of an issue in deliberations (during the agenda-building and problem-analyzing tasks) often shapes people's perceptions and choices during the ensuing deliberations. In the year after Hurricane Katrina made landfall, for example, public officials had to determine the broad goals that would shape the reconstruction of New Orleans. Did they wish to retain its tradition as a multiethnic city that contained a mixture of affluent, middle-class, working-class, and low-income persons? Or did they want it to become primarily a tourist destination, as well as a financial center, which would primarily contain relatively affluent Caucasian persons? If the former choice was selected, then reconstruction proposals would necessarily require considerable governmental expenditures, not just to make the city safe from Category-5 hurricanes, but to provide vast amounts of subsidized housing, large resources to expand and rebuild social and educational services, and resources to restore community amenities. If New Orleans was primarily to be a tourist destination, then rebuilding proposals might primarily involve federal taxes and loans to private enterprises—and widespread use of eminent domain to clear low-income areas for recreational areas or for hotels and other amenities. It was unclear in early 2006 which goal would inform New Orleans' reconstruction, but many policy advocates feared that the latter goal might prevail if they failed to muster the power to replace it with a vision of a more inclusive and diverse city.

Policy advocacy was needed on many fronts in the wake of Hurricane Katrina, but was made more complex because the city was largely depopulated except for its more affluent portions in fall 2005. Moreover, the city of New Orleans, as well as Louisiana, did not have the resources to engage in major reconstruction because their taxes had been depleted by the destruction of houses (which severely cut revenues from property taxes), businesses (which severely cut sales-tax revenues), and tourism (which cut taxes paid by hotels, motels, and conferences). Even the federal government faced huge deficits in the wake of tax cuts by the administration of George W. Bush and the Iraq War.

In this volatile and complex environment, policy advocates in local, state, and federal locations had to place on the agenda proposals to get housing, job-training, medical, and income-maintenance proposals on *policy agendas*. They needed to *analyze* how to rebuild New Orleans in ways that would preserve its diverse nature and that would not excessively favor affluent interests and persons. They needed to write *policy proposals* not just for helping evacuees, but for rebuilding New Orleans in a humane way. They needed to be certain that the programs were *implemented* fairly and efficiently. They needed to *assess* those programs that were established to be certain they achieved their goals.

Similarly, activities in other phases of policy making also influence the outcome. Writing proposals and implementing policy are closely related. When policy makers establish lofty goals but their proposals allocate relatively few resources, for example, they decrease the likelihood that their proposals will be implemented.[3]

Four Skills That Policy Practitioners Need

When undertaking their various tasks, policy practitioners need at least four basic skills. They need *analytic skills* to evaluate social problems and develop policy proposals, to analyze the severity of specific problems, to identify the barriers to policy implementation, and to develop strategies for assessing programs. They need *political skills* to gain and use power and to develop and implement political strategy. They need *interactional skills* to participate in task groups, such as committees and coalitions, and to persuade other people to support specific policies. (See Policy Advocacy Challenge 3.2.) And they need *value-clarifying skills* to identify and rank relevant principles when engaging in policy practice. Just as many theorists have discussed the skills necessary for direct-service work, administration, and community organization, policy theorists need to discuss the skills needed in policy practice and policy advocacy.

POLICY ADVOCACY CHALLENGE 3.2

Forming a Coalition in New Orleans

RON McCLAIN, JD, MSW, LCSW

In order to pool resources and provide a more adequate response to vulnerable populations in New Orleans after Hurricane Katrina, Family Service of Greater New Orleans joined with community partners to form the Community Based Service Network (CBSN). Although large numbers of the city's poor population had either evacuated on their own or were evacuated from the city after Hurricane Katrina, many poor residents never left the city and others returned within months. The mental health and social services infrastructure had been devastated, but the needs for these services were greater than they were before the storm. . . . our coalition was formed with the goal of working together to enhance the overall well-being and circumstances of living of some of the most vulnerable populations in post-Katrina New Orleans.

In addition to Family Service of Greater New Orleans, the network included other relatively strong organizations . . . (including) Volunteers of America, Catholic Charities New Orleans, Kingsley House, Children's Bureau, Nonprofit Knowledge Works, Baptist Community Ministries and the Institute of Mental Hygiene. The group initially spent time developing a vision statement, a mission statement and core values. The vision statement is: *The Community Based Service Network envisions a partnership of health and human service agencies committed to building a safer, stronger, healthier, and economically viable Greater New Orleans community.* The mission statement is: *The Mission of CBSN is to create an effective, efficient, integrated service delivery system for children and families in need.* Our coalition also decided that it was important to identify values to which we would commit ourselves and our activities. The core values of the network are: 1) *Client Centered,* 2) *Family Focused,* 3) *Culturally Competent,* 4) *Community Based,* 5) *Use of Evidence Based Practices,* 6) *Accountability to Participants and Stakeholders,* 7) *Commitment to Quality Assurance, Outcome Measurement, and Fiscal Accountability.*

The vulnerable poor and displaced populations in post-Katrina New Orleans had significant needs including housing, the need to retrieve vital records, food and supplies, appliances, transportation, job search assistance, childcare, and mental health services. The Network's focus was to create an infrastructure where our agencies could collaborate to deliver service outcomes for families with multiple needs . . . The initial

Go to
**academic.cengage.com/
social_work/jansson**
to watch this video clip

project for the network is a contract with the Louisiana Family Recovery Corp. to assist families with emergency needs . . . Although resources are limited, the network has been extremely successful in this first service delivery project . . . with a waiting list of 1900 families.

We are also advocating for a better system response to the needs of these poor vulnerable families. The lack of quality affordable housing represents one of the most significant threats to the viability of these families . . . Our network will continue to advocate for more affordable housing and other supportive services for poor families in post-Katrina New Orleans. We have begun working to build relationships with state and legislative leaders as well as local governmental agencies in an effort to raise awareness about the needs of our city's most vulnerable families.

Policy advocates encountered a fluid power structure in the wake of Hurricane Katrina. They needed to pool their resources in order to be able to secure enlightened policies for the city's vulnerable populations, whose political strength was greatly weakened by the sheer number of them that had left the city.

See Policy Advocacy Challenge Video 3.2 where Ron McClain discusses the building of this coalition—and then discuss:

1. the multiple functions of the Coalition
2. why it facilitates policy advocacy with legislative and governmental leaders
3. whether similar coalitions should exist in many cities and localities

Policy practice seems more complicated because it involves four skills, not one, but imagine if we argued that direct-service or administrative practice required only one skill! Although many policy theorists emphasize one or another of these skills, effective policy practitioners need all of them in many situations.

Policy Competencies

Policy practitioners must use the four policy skills when taking concrete actions in organizational, community, or legislative settings. We call these skills *policy competencies*, each of which is discussed on the pages indicated in Table 3.1. We can develop these competencies only by practicing them in agency, community, and legislative settings, much as we develop skills in direct service, community organization, and administration.

Styles of Policy Practice

Just as different styles exist in direct-service practice (for example, cognitive versus psychodynamic approaches) and community-organization practice (for example, social-action versus community-development approaches), different approaches exist in policy practice.[4] Let's contrast electoral, legislative advocacy, troubleshooting, and analytic models of policy advocacy (see Table 3.2). The *electoral style* is used when policy advocates want to get someone elected to office or when they want to initiate or contest a ballot initiative (also called a proposition). The goal is to change the composition of

TABLE 3.1
Policy
competencies

	Organizational settings	Community settings	Legislative settings
Political competencies			
Using the mass media (pp. 199, 426–428)	Press releases and press conferences	Press releases and press conferences	Press releases and press conferences
Taking a personal position (pp. 356–358, 382–383)	Advocating a position in a staff meeting	Advocating a position with a community resident or official	Voting
Advocating a position with a decision maker (pp. 366, 372–376, 382–383, 391–392, 405–409, 421–426)	Talking with an executive director about a policy	Talking to a school principal about a policy	Lobbying legislators or civil servants
Seeking positions of power (pp. 123, 376–381, 382–384, 448–478)	Seeking a high position in an agency	Running for the school board	Running for elective office
Empowering others (pp. 7–8, 26, 48, 175–176, 420–421, 461, 470–471)	Enhancing staff (or consumers') participation in agency policy making	Increasing citizens' participation in policy making of community institutions	Registering voters
Orchestrating pressure on decision makers (pp. 347–351, 455–456, 361–365, 372–376, 390–409, 411–445)	Mobilizing protest within an agency	Mobilizing protest within a community	Mobilizing protest against legislators by phone trees, petitions, mass mailings, delegations, or protests
Finding resources to fund advocacy projects (pp. 321–328)	Securing agency resources for coalitions and lobbying	Raising funds for advocacy groups	Raising funds for campaigns
Developing and using personal power resources (pp. 344–386)	To mobilize support for a policy	To mobilize support for a policy	To mobilize support for a policy
Donating time/ resources to an advocacy group (pp. 51–53)	To an intra-agency coalition	To a community advocacy group	To an advocacy group focusing on legislative policy, a political campaign, or a political action committee like PACE
Advocating for the needs of a client (pp. 7–8, 26, 40–43)	With agency officials	With community officials	With public officials
Participating in a demonstration (p. 419)	Protesting an agency policy	Protesting a community policy	Protesting a public policy

	Organizational settings	Community settings	Legislative settings
Initiating litigation to change policies (pp. 130–133)	Of agencies	Of communities	Of public agencies and legislatures
Participating in a political campaign (pp. 447–485)	———	———	Working with a candidate for office
Voter registration (pp. 453–461, 470–471)	———	———	Working with a political party or advocacy group
Analytic competencies			
Developing a proposal (pp. 258–295)	Writing a grant proposal	Proposing an interagency consortium	Drafting legislation
Calculating trade-offs (pp. 279–292, 415–418)	Examining program options	Examining program options	Examining legislative options
Doing force field analysis (pp. 393–399)	Before proposing an innovation in an agency	Before proposing a community innovation	Before proposing a legislative initiative
Using social science research (pp. 61–67, 216–257)	Designing an intervention strategy	Designing an intervention strategy	Designing public policy
Conducting a marketing study (pp. 231–248, 453–457)	Designing an agency program	Designing a community program	Designing a public program
Using the Internet (pp. 20–21, 51–52, 82, 111, 163–165, 168–169, 177–178, 186–187, 221–222, 324, 345–346, 361–364, 392, 396, 413–414, 420–421, 448, 491)	Getting information germane to any policy task	Getting information germane to any policy task	Getting information germane to any policy task
Working with budgets (pp. 265–271, 323–328, 429–432)	Analyzing agency budgets	Analyzing the budget of a community institution	Analyzing a governmental budget
Finding funding sources for specific projects (pp. 321–324)	Researching foundations, private donors, or public donors	Researching foundations, private donors, or public donors	Researching foundations, private donors, or public donors
Diagnosing audiences (pp. 309–321)	When making an agency presentation	When making a community presentation	When testifying
Designing a presentation (pp. 296–325)	Before agency staff or officials	Before community representatives	Before public officials

(continued)

TABLE 3.1
(continued)

	Organizational settings	Community settings	Legislative settings
Diagnosing barriers to implementation (pp. 496–508, 512–532)	When implementing agency programs	When implementing community programs	When implementing federally funded programs
Designing strategy to improve implementation (pp. 509–511, 512–532)	In agency settings	In community settings	In public agencies
Developing political strategy (pp. 390–445)	In agency settings	In community settings	In public agencies
Analyzing the context of policies and issues (pp. 79–84, 110–155, 189–200, 216–218, 258–260, 297–300, 308–311, 393–399, 414–415, 447–456, 491–496)	In agency settings	In communities	In legislatures
Designing policy assessments (pp. 61–67, 84–85, 532–533)	In agency settings	In communities	In legislatures
Selecting a policy practice style (pp. 87–93, 343–351, 403–404, 419–420, 432, 434)	In agency settings	In communities	In legislatures

Interactional competencies

	Organizational settings	Community settings	Legislative settings
Coalition building (pp. 86–87, 382, 402, 406–408, 412–413, 429, 439–440)	Organizing a coalition in an agency	Organizing a coalition in the community to develop new programs	Organizing an advocacy group to pressure legislators
Making a presentation (pp. 296–341)	Presenting to the board	Speaking at a community forum	Testifying before a legislative committee
Building personal power (pp. 344–389)	Building networks and credibility	Building networks and credibility	Building networks and credibility
Task group formation and maintenance (pp. pp. 435–439)	Forming, staffing, and joining task groups	Forming, staffing, and joining task groups	Forming, staffing, and joining task groups
Managing conflict (pp. 300–321, 356–361, 403, 419, 432, 434, 459–460)	Mediating disputes	Mediating disputes	Mediating disputes

Value-clarifying competency

	Organizational settings	Community settings	Legislative settings
Engaging in ethical reasoning (pp. 39–75)	In agency settings	In community settings	In public settings

government by getting progressive candidates into office, and to defeat less progressive candidates, or to get a ballot initiative enacted or defeated, depending on whether they do or do not advance such ideas as social justice. Policy advocates work with campaign organizations, with political action committees (such as NASW's PACE), or with political parties. They can expect high conflict because elections and ballot initiatives are usually hotly contested. They need skills in talking with voters, framing issues, and working with campaign staff. Some policy advocates run for office themselves, as we discuss in more detail in Chapter Thirteen.

Some policy advocates use a *legislative advocacy style* by which they hope to secure the enactment of meritorious legislation or defeat ill-conceived measures. They work with advocacy groups, community-based organizations, professional associations, and lobbyists as they try to convince legislators to adopt their measure or to defeat a measure that they dislike. Depending on the specific measure, the level of conflict can vary. (So-called hot button issues that polarize legislators by party or ideology are likely to be associated with high conflict, unlike more technical issues.) Policy advocates need skills in policy analysis, developing strategy, and working with coalitions, as well as knowledge of the legislative process and lobbying.

With an *analytic style* policy advocates use data to develop policy proposals or evaluate how existing policies are working. They often work in or with think tanks, academic units, funders, or government agencies. They need skills in conducting research, using data, and making recommendations.

Policy advocates sometimes use a *troubleshooting* style to increase the effectiveness of operating programs or to evaluate them with an eye to improving them. They need to work with planning groups that consist of members of the implementing team, sometimes mixing insiders with outside consultants, government officials, funders, or consumers. In still other cases, they work with outside groups of consumers or others who bring pressure on the staff of a program to change it. In most cases, troubleshooting involves relatively low conflict because policy advocates engage in problem solving with staff and administrators to improve the workings of a particular program. Troubleshooters need skills in diagnosing why specific programs have flawed operations or outcomes, in obtaining data to assess them, and in working collaboratively with staff and administrators.

Not everyone is skilled in each of the styles, and tensions often exist among persons who like different styles. Some policy advocates like political maneuvering and excel in it, whether the electoral or legislative-advocacy style. They sometimes are critical of the analytic style, believing that proposals, no matter how meritorious on technical grounds, will come to naught absent political advocacy. Persons who like to use the analytic style are sometimes critical of persons who they perceive to be excessively political since they often want policy choices to be made primarily through the use of data and research. (We discussed evidence-based policies in the preceding chapter.) Some troubleshooters, excelling at using collaborative planning approaches to overcome such organizational problems as turf rivalries and fragmentation, are less comfortable with high-conflict strategies sometimes used by political activists.

The astute reader can see that the different policy-advocacy styles correspond to the six tasks we have already discussed. Persons who use the analytic style often are most comfortable with the problem-defining, proposal-writing, and assessing tasks since these tasks often require the use of data and research. Those who use the legislative advocacy style often are most comfortable with the policy-enacting task, and persons

TABLE 3.2
Four styles of policy practice and policy advocacy

	Ballot-Based Advocacy	Legislative Advocacy	Analytic Advocacy	Troubleshooting Advocacy
GOAL	To change the composition of governments or to get a ballot initiative enacted or defeated	To secure the enactment of—or the defeat of—specific legislative proposals	To make policy choices that are based on hard data and structured analysis	To increase the effectiveness of operating programs
PIVOTAL ORGANI-ZATIONS TO WHICH ADVOCATES ARE LINKED	Campaign organizations, political action committees, political parties	Advocacy groups, interest groups, community-agencies, based organizations, professional associations	Think tanks, academic centers, government agencies, funders	Planning or oversight groups composed of insiders, outsiders, consumers, and/or others
LEVELS OF CONFLICT	High conflict between contending campaigns in win-lose contests	Variable conflict, but usually moderate to high conflict	Conflict between stakeholders about technical issues and interpretive issues	Usually low to moderate conflict, unless outsiders protest specific implementing policies and actions
KEY SKILLS OF ADVOCATES	Developing strategy, interacting with likely voters, raising funds, media relations, using polls and focus groups	Policy analysis, lobbying, knowledge of the legislative process, building and sustaining coalitions	Research and analytic skills, obtaining and processing data, making technical presentations	Diagnosing operating programs, understanding organizational dynamics, collaborative, problem solving managing conflict

who use the troubleshooting task are most comfortable with the policy-implementing task. The electoral style, however, does not correspond to any of the six tasks. It is unique because it focuses on campaigns, whether to elect candidates or to get ballot initiatives enacted. It neither aims to guide policy initiatives through the decision-making process nor troubleshoot existing programs, but to change the composition of government so that decision makers are more receptive to accepting humane policies and reforms in the implementation of social programs. Ballot initiatives, such as propositions, aim to change policy by getting voters to select policies—thus *circumventing* the regular legislative process.

In the real world, of course, the different styles often are combined in *hybrid styles* where policy advocates combine or move between the four different styles. You cannot engage in legislative advocacy, for example, without doing at least some policy analysis, because your policy initiatives will not be credible if you use no data. You cannot be effective doing policy analysis if you are not looking ahead to political realities that your proposal will encounter when it comes before legislators. If you draft a policy that makes sense in terms of data but that has no chance of adoption by legislators, you risk spinning your wheels. Both policy analysts and legislative advocates need to anticipate issues and problems during policy implementation lest they frame and enact policies that are poorly implemented because they failed to anticipate them. All policy advocates, no matter their stylistic preferences, need to engage in ballot-based advocacy to enhance the chances that their proposals will receive a sympathetic hearing from elected public officials in local, state, and federal legislatures and offices.

Quite apart from policy styles, effective advocates need a combination of each of the four skills to be effective. Someone who relies only on good values, but does not develop and use power resources, and never uses analytic information ought to ponder whether this narrow approach to policy practice is effective in specific agency, community, or legislative settings. Similarly, people who use only political or analytic skills risk not being effective in many situations. Policy practitioners who rely on a single skill are sometimes stereotyped: *opportunists* rely on political skills, *do-gooders* rely on values, and *policy wonks* rely on analytic data.

Applications of Policy Tasks and Skills

When undertaking the six tasks, policy advocates must often use a combination of the four skills to be successful, as our succeeding discussion suggests.

Building Agendas

When they want to change existing policies, policy practitioners have to analyze the context to gauge whether it will support or oppose a specific policy initiative. If the situation is favorable, they may decide to proceed at once. If it is not favorable, they may devote time and effort to making the context more favorable, or they may decide to delay their policy changing work until a more propitious moment. Policy practitioners encounter analytic, political, interactional, and value-based challenges when they try to make the context more favorable.[5] Their analytic challenge is to provide technical information to convince others that the problem deserves serious attention. They can argue that a problem, such as alcoholism, has sufficiently serious effects on society to warrant attention. Policy practitioners often use trend data to suggest that a problem is becoming more serious with time, a tactic that suggests that inaction will increase the severity of the problem. They work to convince decision makers that they possess a policy or strategy that can more effectively address a social problem than existing policies.

Policy practitioners often use their analytic skills to create the impression that a crisis exists. When current data point to a problem's severity and trend data track the problem over time, decision makers are likely to believe that it demands immediate attention.[6] Policy practitioners use political skills to associate issues with political threats and opportunities in the minds of decision makers. Democrats got Congress to prioritize action on extending Medicare coverage to prescription drugs in early 2001, for example, by threatening to use the issue to carry favor with millions of senior citizens, whose votes would be critical in forthcoming elections.

Policy practitioners have many ways of conveying the political importance of specific issues to decision makers. They can discuss important groups or funders who would like specific policy reforms in agency or legislative settings. They can imply to members of one party that members of another party may beat them to the punch if they fail to take interest in a specific issue.

Effective policy practitioners skillfully select propitious moments to inject issues into political deliberations. John Kingdon suggests that "windows of opportunity" exist when background factors are particularly favorable.[7] Perhaps a particularly scandalous condition has just been publicized, such as the neglect of someone with Alzheimer's disease. Maybe a recently elected city mayor, whose mother has Alzheimer's disease, supports funding a new initiative. Or perhaps a new research report documents the dearth of services to families of people with Alzheimer's. Alas, windows of opportunity often close quickly as the political situation changes. Democrats' desire to extend Medicare to cover prescription drugs was frustrated by the tragic destruction of New York City's Twin Towers by terrorists on September 11, 2001, which diverted Congress's attention to military issues and "homeland defense."

Policy practitioners use interactional skills to place issues on the agendas of decision makers. Perhaps a committee chairperson agrees to address a specific issue at a forthcoming meeting, or an agency executive consents to form a task force to examine a problem. Perhaps the aide to an influential legislator agrees to discuss an issue with a powerful member of a legislative committee so that a bill will receive preferential treatment in the committee's deliberations.

To secure a privileged position for issues, then, policy practitioners need to use persuasive and coalition-building competencies. In personal discussions, they need to convince others that an issue is relevant to their beliefs, that important political threats or opportunities exist, or that credible people take an interest in the issue.

Policy practitioners confront value issues when they seek a preferred position for a specific problem in policy deliberations. To increase the prominence of an issue, practitioners sometimes inflate figures, exaggerate a problem's negative impact on the broader society, or magnify political threats or opportunities. These tactics pose ethical questions that practitioners must consider. In other cases, they may display undue caution by avoiding relatively unpopular but important issues, thus ignoring the needs of oppressed populations.

Analyzing Problems

Policy advocates must invest considerable effort in understanding the social problems that they seek to address through policy initiatives. They must understand how many persons are impacted by a specific problem. They need to understand what kinds of persons possess the problem by race, ethnicity, social class, place of residence, and other characteristics. They need to understand what causes persons to develop specific social problems such as homelessness.

When engaging in policy analysis, policy advocates often analyze research reports, census data, articles in professional journals, and articles in the mass media.

Even analysis intersects with politics, however, because a specific policy proposal must be framed to attract the attention of decision makers.[8] Words, titles, and explanations must be both comprehensible and palatable, as when advocates of Aid to Families with Dependent Children (AFDC) reform in 1988 emphasized "family support" rather than "welfare reform"—or when President George W. Bush called his education initiative in his first term "No Child Left Behind."

Rather than working alone, policy advocates usually work with advocacy groups and coalitions to develop an understanding of specific social problems and to scrutinize existing policies to begin to understand how they might be changed.

Writing Proposals

Policy advocates need to develop policy proposals that will be perceived to be meritorious by decision makers. They often make extensive use of analytic skills when they develop them. They often develop criteria, such as cost and effectiveness, that they use to rate or rank an array of policy alternatives or options that they wish to consider. A policy advocate who wants to help homeless persons in a specific locality might, for example, ask what kinds of housing arrangements might best meet their needs and how much they might cost, such as shelters, single-occupancy hotels, and subsidized private housing. Only when the advocate is convinced that one of the housing options is better than the others on the basis of cost and effectiveness would she or he approach decision makers.

Many policies are shaped and modified in the course of policy deliberations within advocacy groups or during discussions by legislators or public officials. As Ron Dear and Rino Patti note, the enactment of legislation often hinges on its advocates' willingness to accept amendments that may alter policies, such as a program's title, its administrative details, the services it offers, its eligibility standards, the type of agency that can deliver the services, or standards for the staff providing the services.[9] Policy practitioners use political and value-clarification skills to decide when to accept or oppose amendments.

Because policy practitioners can sometimes diminish conflict by leaving some controversial aspects of a proposal vague, they sometimes deliberately do not define specific provisions in a proposal. These details will have to be eventually resolved when the proposal is implemented, such as when government agencies issue administrative regulations.

Practitioners need interactional skills at many points in developing proposals. Committees may have a central position in fashioning proposals, whether in legislative or agency settings. Coalitions often play a prominent role in proposal writing; for example, they may mobilize opposition to hostile amendments or oppose efforts to make a proposal excessively vague, at least with the matters they deem particularly important. Personal discussions with a proposal's friends and foes will bolster friendly amendments and soften or avert hostile ones.

Enacting Policy

Practitioners often use analytic skills when developing a political strategy to enact policy in specific settings. They analyze the context, identify the power resources available to them, evolve a coherent political strategy, and use their political skills to implement the strategy.

Interactional skills help practitioners during the political process. They often seek access to people with inside information about the strategies their opponents are likely to use. They use their persuasive skills to convert people to their side and to keep opponents on the defensive. They use group skills, such as the ability to work with leaders or staff of legislative committees and to develop and sustain coalitions,

Policy practitioners confront some ethical issues during the political process. They must decide what tactics are ethically meritorious and which ones are not. It is difficult to establish inflexible ethical rules because realities, such as the opponents' tactics, often influence ethical choices. While blatant lying is seldom justified, they may decide to withhold sensitive information from opponents in certain circumstances.

Implementing Policy

Policy practitioners use analytic skills to decide what kinds of organizational arrangements will help implement specific policies; for example, hiring bilingual staff and establishing decentralized offices to help Spanish-speaking people obtain preventive health services.

At this stage, policy practitioners often must use political skills as well. Perhaps specific groups or individuals who wish to defend their turf decide to undermine a program's implementation or to preserve outmoded procedures; perhaps legislators who promised to support a program decide to allot it insufficient resources after it is enacted. They need to develop strategy in these cases to offset these kinds of barriers to the effective implementation of a specific policy.

Policy advocates often use interactional skills to improve the implementation of a specific policy. They may mediate disputes between persons engaged in its implementation, forge interagency agreements when several agencies need to collaborate, or provide training sessions for staff so they know how to implement a policy.

Policy advocates must use value-clarifications skills during implementation. They may need to decide, for example, what kinds of persons should receive priority in getting services when resources are insufficient to serve everyone who seeks them.

Assessing Policy

Policy practitioners often participate in assessing operating programs to ascertain whether they meet specific objectives or criteria. When using analytic skills, practitioners must decide what kinds of data are needed, how to collect them, and how to interpret their findings.

When assessing programs, policy practitioners often encounter political conflict. Some people may disagree about what criteria or measures should be used to evaluate a specific policy or how to interpret evaluation data that is collected about a specific program.

Values intrude at many points during program assessments. For example, values shape the criteria selected to decide whether a program has been successful. Is a homeless project to be assessed by its getting homeless persons into the job market, resolving specific mental or substance-abuse problems, providing them with permanent housing, or getting them off the streets?

Policy advocates who assess specific policies have to interact with other persons at numerous points as they develop an assessment methodology, gather data, and interpret findings. Stakeholders are more likely to use the findings of an evaluation project if they are involved in its design and implementation throughout the assessment process.

Analyzing Policy Practice

Using the framework shown in Figure 3.1, we can describe policy practice during specific episodes, such as when policy advocates engage in one of the six policy tasks. Or we can examine how policy practitioners perform a sequence of tasks. Indeed, we can envision a continuum extending from very brief episodes of policy practice, such as making a specific presentation, to a sequence that involves writing a policy proposal, seeking its enactment, and shaping its implementation

At the simplest level, we examine the use of a specific skill when a practitioner engages in a single policy task. We can evaluate, for example, how an advocate used her analytic skills (a single skill) in developing a policy proposal (a single task) by asking, for example, whether she became familiar with important social science research, consulted someone with technical expertise, and researched possible funding sources. We then can evaluate her political skills by asking whether she examined the proposal's political feasibility and consulted with people who could secure support for it.

At a more general level, we can inquire about a policy advocate's effectiveness in accomplishing a specific policy task that requires various skills. We can ask whether she used a combination of analytic, political, and interactional skills when developing a specific policy proposal. We might decide, for example, that she skillfully used both analytic and political skills when developing a proposal in a setting where both skills were needed, such as in a politically charged setting.

At an even more general level, we can examine the work of a practitioner who engages in several related tasks. We can ask how the practitioner not only constructed a specific proposal (one task) but also sought its enactment and implementation (two additional tasks). We might conclude, for example, that the practitioner exhibited technical expertise in writing the proposal but lacked the political skills to obtain its approval from decision makers. Or we might decide that a policy advocate successfully carried a proposal through the agenda-building, policy-analysis, and policy-enactment phases of the policy-making process.

POLICY ADVOCACY CHALLENGE 3.3

How Policy Advocacy Might Have Better Prepared New Orleans for Hurricane Katrina

BRUCE JANSSON, PH.D.

We use events prior to, during, and after Hurricane Katrina in New Orleans to illustrate policy advocacy at many points in this text. After briefly discussing the history of hurricanes in the Gulf Coast region, we will analyze how a hypothetical aide to a Congressman from New Orleans—whom we call Agnes Vermillion, might have used policy advocacy to better prepare her region for this impending disaster.

The Context

A series of hurricanes had repeatedly struck the United States throughout its history, but they were particularly numerous in the 1960s and 1970s when Hurricanes Carla, Betsy, Camilla, and Agnes occurred. Nor had New Orleans been immune from them: Hurricane Betsy flooded one-half of New Orleans, for example, in 1965. Upset that relief work in these hurricanes' wake had been inadequate partly because it was spread between 100 federal agencies, state governors pressured President Jimmy Carter to establish the Federal Emergency Management Agency (FEMA) in 1979 to coordinate federal disaster relief. But FEMA was relatively ineffectual under Presidents Ronald Reagan and George Bush, Sr., since both presidents filled its top positions with political cronies with scant expertise in natural disasters. Its inadequacies were masked, however, by the absence of major natural disasters in the 1980s.

(continued)

If FEMA's inadequacies were masked in the 1980s because the nation had few major natural disasters, it was subjected to widespread criticism when it failed to provide timely assistance to Floridians in the wake of Hurricane Andrew in 1992. A geographically small but exceedingly savage storm, Andrew, mercifully side-stepped Miami but destroyed vast portions of such cities as Florida City and Homestead—destroying or damaging 125,000 homes. When little assistance was forthcoming, irate citizens flooded the White House with phone calls—and FEMA's bumbling response may even have contributed to the electoral defeat of George Bush, Sr. in 1992, when Republicans lost Florida to Bill Clinton.

Determined not to face a similar situation, President Clinton selected the first FEMA director (James Lee Witt) with substantial experience dealing with natural disasters. He not only energized FEMA, but launched Project Impact to help an initial group of seven cities and eventually 250 cities prepare for natural disasters. (Tragically, New Orleans chose not to participate in Project Impact when it might have developed programs that could have softened the impact of major hurricanes for its residents.) FEMA performed admirably in the wakes of the Northridge Earthquake in Los Angeles and flooding of the lower Mississippi with Hurricane Floyd during the Clinton administration.

But the context swung in a more negative direction with the election of George W. Bush in 2000. Like his father, he also appointed political cronies to FEMA's top positions such as his campaign director, Joe Albaugh—who quickly enacted deep cuts in its budget including ending Project Impact. FEMA was further marginalized in the wake of the destruction of the World Trade Center on September 11, 2001, when it was placed in a subordinate position in the Home Security Agency (HSA) and when the HSA emphasized counter-terrorism over natural disasters. When Albaugh left for the private sector, he was replaced by Michael Brown, another director with no disaster experience. Even more marginalized by the HSA and with an incompetent director, FEMA's staff became so demoralized that many of its best staff left the agency.

Policy Tasks

Let's now return to the role of a hypothetical aide to a member of Congress from a hurricane-prone state—whom we call Agnes Vermillion—who astutely realized that her constituents would be placed in harm's way if a major hurricane struck her district in southern Louisiana. Worried as she observed the decline of FEMA during the first term of George W. Bush's presidency, she participated in a planning exercise (which they called "PAM") that FEMA organized in 2004 to simulate what would happen if a Category-5 hurricane (with winds as high as 170 mph) struck southern Louisiana. With technical modeling approaches developed by scientists at Louisiana State University (LSU), participants from parish, city, state, and federal agencies, as well as elected officials, received the grim news: a powerful hurricane would flood large portions of New Orleans and surrounding areas, destroy vast amounts of housing, destroy thousands of businesses, and require massive evacuations of citizens before the hurricane struck. Not only should residents take measures to strengthen their homes and office buildings, the experts urged, but the Army Corps of Engineers should proceed at once to fortify some levees, and officials from all levels of government, under FEMA's direction, should pre-position water and food at key points in the community, develop evacuation plans, and develop mobile "interoperable" communication systems so that each public agency from every level of government could easily communicate with one another if existing phone and communication systems were disrupted by a hurricane. An elaborate plan was constructed in which *each* agency promised to take specific steps.

But Vermillion soon realized that funding HSA officials cut funding for PAM's implementation. Her challenge was *to place this issue on the agenda* of President Bush and Congress, as well as state and city public officials, to ensure that PAM's recommendations were implemented. To undertake this goal, she approached a senior Democratic senator from Louisiana with considerable interest in natural disasters, as well as two Republican senators respectively from Mississippi and Texas. Working through these high-level intermediaries, Vermillion hoped to place PAM's funding on the HSA and president's agenda.

Vermillion *analyzed* what resources and leadership would be required to implement plans emanating from PAM. She decided that a lead staff person from FEMA—with the full backing of the HSA and the president, would have to be given the mandate to implement PAM's recommendations. Only with such high-level leadership, she decided, might differences between state, local, and federal officials be breeched so that each of them would contribute to the implementation plan. She identified the specific resources that would be needed to develop interoperable and mobile communication systems; to pre-position medicines, food, and water; and to evacuate persons including those who had no cars or who lacked funds to pay for lodging once they left New Orleans. She decided that community-organization staff needed to be hired to link churches, synagogues, and temples into the evacuation plan to help inform persons—particularly persons not likely to read or listen to the mass media—about the need to evacuate the city if a catastrophic storm struck.

Working with the senators, she developed a legislative *proposal* for implementing PAM's recommendations with a specific budget allocation as well as a mandate to FEMA that it implement PAM's recommendations within one year. The proposal required FEMA to report back to Congress that it had implemented PAM's proposals.

Again working with the senators to secure the *enactment* of this proposal, she worked to broaden support for it by broadening the proposal to include resources for 15 cities including New Orleans, in southern Louisiana and Mississippi, and as well as Texas from Galveston to the Louisiana border. (It is common in policy practice to modify a proposal to secure more support for it.) She increased resources for the proposal—and now included the mandate that each of the 15 cities develop mobile interoperable communication systems, pre-position supplies, and develop evacuation plans. She now included a Web site that would link churches, synagogues, and temples into the evolving plan as facilitators for evacuation plans. With these modifications in place, she and the three senators were able to approach three additional senators from the affected states, as well as 10 members of the House of Representatives whose districts included the 15 cities. All of them agreed to co-sponsor the legislation, along with the three senators—and these legislators persuaded the Director of the HSA to support the legislation.

By dint of hard work, the legislation was enacted. Vermillion kept track of the legislation's implementation. She made certain that FEMA *did* appoint a public official to oversee its implementation. She made certain that FEMA met specific implementation milestones. When the 15 cities and FEMA could not agree on which specific mobile interoperable communication device to purchase, she got the three senators to demand an emergency meeting that led to the eventual selection of a specific vendor.

(continued)

Vermillion *assessed* how well the legislation was working to prepare the cities for catastrophic hurricanes at periodic points during the year when it was being implemented. As specific milestones or objectives were *not* met, she would seek remedial actions. As it became obvious that they had underestimated the difficulty of implementing specific facets of the legislation, she worked with the FEMA director of the project to find additional resources or to develop new strategies.

Actual events were markedly different from this scenario. Because no one like Vermillion emerged to catalyze implementation of PAM's recommendations, they were not implemented. (Democratic Senator Mary Landrieu did make many efforts to prepare federal, state, and city authorities for a large hurricane, but found her efforts rebuffed by the Bush Administration, as well as many members of Congress who discounted the danger or were more committed to other projects. Indeed, FEMA and HSA *cut* the very resources needed to implement PAM's recommendations and did not put an official in charge of implementing them.) The tragic consequences became clear when Hurricane Katrina hit New Orleans on August 29, 2005, and lives were needlessly lost.

Yet policy advocates like Vermillion often *do* emerge in situations like this and do make a difference. To be effective advocates, they need familiarity with policy-practice tasks—and they need to undertake these tasks skillfully. For example, Robert Greenstein and his staff from the Center on Budget and Policy Priorities engaged in *agenda-building,* not only generating ideas about how to improve a variety of federal programs to make them relevant to Katrina victims, but placing them on the agenda of public officials by sending the policy documents and talking with them in person. He even hoped that the nation would have a long-overdue debate about persistent poverty in the United States, since Katrina had exposed the depth and amount of poverty among African Americans and other Katrina victims in New Orleans. When he became alarmed by a dramatic turn in discussion of Katrina as congressional conservatives placed pressure on President Bush *not* to dramatically expand social spending and *not* to emphasize a federal role, he used the mass media to create a more favorable environment for progressive proposals.

Greenstein and his staff engaged in *problem analysis* by estimating the cost of expanding various programs such as the food stamp program and Medicaid so that they would meet needs of Katrina survivors. He and his staff examined existing regulations to see how they might be relaxed not only for persons who lacked documents to get through current eligibility standards, but for persons who would not meet existing standards but who had temporary need for assistance in light of the loss of their homes, property, and businesses. They estimated the costs of these specific expansions of existing programs. They engaged in the *proposal-writing task* by writing specific legislative proposals that they disseminated on their Web site, to the media, to legislators, and to policy staff in the White House.

Greenstein and his staff engaged in the *policy-enacting task* by lobbying key congressional staff and legislators to get these proposals enacted, as well as by using the mass media. They looked forward to the *implementation task* when they insisted that the Department of Housing and Urban Development (HUD), rather than FEMA, should implement housing programs for Katrina's victims since they had more housing expertise and already implemented the major housing-subsidy programs of the federal government such as Section-8 housing vouchers. They engaged in the *policy assessment task* by using knowledge about the effectiveness of programs developed in the wake of prior natural disasters to help them fashion their proposals for Katrina's survivors.

Using Policy Skills to Accomplish Policy Tasks

Vermillion would have had to use analytic, political, interactional, and value-clarifying skills to accomplish six policy-practice tasks. Let's take the example of her need to place the implementation of PAM's recommendations on the agendas of the president, the heads of HSA and FEMA, and the three senators. She needed *analytic* skills to persuade them that it was important to implement these recommendations, such as by enumerating the likely destruction of a Category-5 hurricane as described by hurricane scientists at the PAM Conference. As important, she had to convince them that it was feasible to implement PAM's recommendations in the specific time frame of one year. To do this, she went to other cities that *had* implemented similar recommendations and discovered what resources and person-power that they had used. She had to help the 3 senators draft an initial legislative proposal that was sufficiently impressive that the 10 members of Congress would agree to co-sponsor it.

She would have needed *political skills* to enlist the three senators and the 10 members of Congress in the project—and to help them develop strategy to shepherd the legislative proposal through the Congress. She would have needed to work through intermediaries on occasion, such as getting a Republican senator or member of Congress to elicit the support of the president for the project.

She would have needed *interactional skills* to develop links with key public officials, participate in meetings with them, make credible public presentations, and work with task groups charged with implementing PAM's recommendations. If senators, members of Congress, staff in the White House, aides of legislators, and FEMA and HSA officials did not like and trust her, she would have found it difficult to work with them effectively.

She would have needed *value-clarifying skills* to make difficult choices at specific points. When she decided to expand the project to include 14 cities in addition to New Orleans to get the political support of more legislators for it, she might have wondered if this expansion would have had negative consequences for preparedness planning in New Orleans since it now had to share scarce resources with many other cities. Policy advocates often encounter trade-offs like this one—and must ultimately make difficult value-based choices. Her decision to devote significant amounts of time to implementing PAM's recommendations would have been based on her values because it required her to give less time to competing projects. In light of the likely suffering of citizens of New Orleans if a catastrophic storm hit—and in particular its most vulnerable citizens—she might have prioritized PAM's recommendations because she had a strong commitment to social justice.

As with its implementation task, Vermillion would have needed analytic, political, interactional, and value-clarifying skills to complete each of the other five policy-practice tasks.

We suggested in Chapter One a PBS one-hour video tape that provides an excellent analysis of the events that led up to the bungled response to Hurricane Katrina. If you have not already seen it, go to **http://www.pbs.org/wgbh/pages/frontline/storm/**. Please ask these questions:

1. What persons engaged in policy advocacy as portrayed by the PBS video tape?
2. What barriers did they confront?

(continued)

3. Could someone like Agnes Vermillion have made an appreciable difference in this case—or was the context so unfavorable to preventive actions that policy practice would have been relatively futile in this case?

4. Had PAM occurred when Bill Clinton was president, might policy advocates had more success in preparing the region for Hurricane Katrina?

Ballot-Based Advocacy

We have given an example of policy practice involving six tasks and four skills. But policy practice also includes the electoral style. We will not discuss specific political campaigns since this topic will be covered in Chapter Twelve. Suffice it to say that the six tasks and four skills also apply to developing and managing a political campaign. A candidate must decide when it is propitious to run for office in the context of background factors, her own track record, likely opponents, and likely assistance she will receive from funders and party officials *(agenda-building)*. She needs to decipher why her likely opponent is defeatable in the context of prior patterns of voting in the district and in public opinion polls *(policy analysis)*. She needs to make a case to contributors, volunteers, and party officials that her candidacy makes sense so that she stands a decent chance of winning *(proposal construction)*. She needs to actually wage the campaign by making correct strategy choices, mustering volunteers, raising funds, and using the mass media to her advantage *(policy enacting and policy implementing)*. Win or lose, she needs to *assess* her strategy and campaign organization so she can decide whether to run again, if she loses, or to develop strategy for the next campaign, if she wins.

Candidates need each of the four policy skills. They need political skills to devise strategy. They need value-clarifying skills to decide what tactics are ethical to use during the campaign, such as whether and how they would respond to (or initiate) hardball strategies like attacking opponents' records and integrity. They need analytic skills to initiate and debate campaign issues and to devise solutions to them. They need interactional skills to develop and maintain a campaign organization.

With the formation and expansion of PACE, the electoral style is becoming increasingly important to social workers. Tens of thousands of members of NASW now contribute to PACE in connection with their annual dues. PACE carefully screens candidates across the nation, both in local and national races, to decide which of them will receive financial assistance from NASW.

Hurricane Katrina illustrates how the work of policy advocates is made more difficult if elected officials do not prioritize policies that help vulnerable populations. Persons who believe that existing politicians, whether at city, state, or federal levels of government, are insensitive to the vulnerable citizens of New Orleans should engage in ballot-based advocacy. They can work in campaigns of specific candidates. They can urge PACE to support specific candidates. They can run for office themselves or encourage friends or colleagues to run for office.

The Variety of Policies

Social workers confront policy issues at virtually every turn. The services they provide are dictated by policies from different sources: legislatures, government agencies, courts, funders such as United Way, contracts and grants that governmental authorities use to purchase services from agencies, professional associations such as the NASW, licensing and accrediting bodies, boards of directors of agencies, and administrative staff. We argued in Chapter One, as well, that some policies emanate from the informal culture of the staff who implement policies.

We do not suggest that these policies are restrictive, because they often provide implementing staff with considerable discretion. However, in many ways, they do shape the lives and work of citizens, clients, and implementing staff alike.

These policies vary in their effects and importance. Trivial policies have little importance, such as some of the detailed policies in agencies and programs. Others, however, have considerable impact on citizens and professionals; reformers should give these policies attention when they believe them to be dysfunctional.

Policies also vary in their malleability. Some are relatively simple to change because of their source, nature, and context. Practitioners find it much easier to modify a relatively simple, nonconflictual administrative agency policy than to change a controversial legislative policy that requires hundreds of legislators to concur.

Practitioners need not focus on a single kind of policy in their work; they can try to change simple or complex, agency or legislative, or controversial or noncontroversial policies. Our focus in this book, indeed, is on generic concepts that apply to any policy practice, no matter what the issue or the setting.

It would be possible, of course, to study policy practice in a more specialized way by focusing on specific settings like agencies or legislatures. We could also focus on a specific style of policy making like the analytic style. Alternatively, we could gear our discussion of policy to a specific sector, such as child welfare policy, rather than using a range of policy examples.

However, a broader treatment of policy practice has many advantages. Concentration on a single kind of policy, for example agency-based or legislative, would imply that that kind of policy should take precedence over other kinds. Concentration on policies that are relatively easy to change, such as some agency-based ones, would imply that social workers should not try to change more complex and controversial ones, such as legislative policies. Concentration on a single style of policy making, like the analytic style, would imply that this style is effective in all or most situations.

A generic approach to policy practice underscores the need for flexibility. Because policy practice occurs in many kinds of settings, takes many forms, and varies with the issue and the context, we believe it is better to understand concepts, skills, tasks, and frameworks that apply to a range of policy practice situations than it is to limit ourselves to a single style or situation.

The need for versatility in policy practice stems from the diversity of policy practices that social workers can undertake. Policy practice can occur inside agencies when advocates interact with other agency staff. Or it can take place primarily outside of agencies such as policy advocates who work with community groups, social movements, and lobbyists. Policy practice can occur in formally sanctioned or official projects, as when executives establish task forces to examine policy issues, or it can be informal, as when a direct-service worker decides to pursue an issue without the approval of higher officials. Policy practice can be planned or improvised, as when someone attends a meeting and decides on the spot to make a statement. Policy practitioners can assume affirming, blocking, or bystander roles. Practice can involve an extended sequence of actions or only one or two episodes. Policy practitioners may use only one skill suited to a specific situation, or they may use several skills at once. Policy practitioners may be leaders or initiators or followers regarding a specific issue.

A generic approach to policy practice, then, sensitizes us to the wide variety of policy practice situations and actions. It does not limit policy practice to specific styles, settings, or issues. It invites us to become participants in many ways and at different points in our professional work.

This generic approach offers no quick fixes or panaceas, however. Some issues are difficult to address, and some policies are relatively intractable. Policy making does not occur on a level playing field; some people bring more power resources to the game, some can invest more time, and some have more skill than others. Policy advocates sometimes take some risks when they engage in practice, such as when employees try to change policies strongly favored by their employers. These cautionary notes should not, however, obscure the challenges and rewards associated with policy practice. Trying to change policies allows professionals to expand their boundaries and obtain the satisfaction that accompanies successful projects.

Overcoming Discomfort with Power

Although political skills are only one of four kinds of policy skills we have discussed in preceding chapters, they are essential to performing policy tasks. For example, people must use power resources, such as expertise and coalitions, to persuade highly placed officials to prioritize an agenda. Using power is crucial in the policy-enacting task, to help enact or block proposals. It is also integral to implementing and assessing policy as we have discussed. In addition to using power skillfully and assertively, effective policy practitioners must devote considerable time to developing power resources. They need to enhance their credibility by gaining access to networks of people who have information and power in specific settings.

Some social workers may believe that it is unethical to develop and use power—or even to use it in specific situations. On further reflection, however, they should realize that all of us develop and use power in our daily lives, such as when we try to convince someone to do something, no matter how trivial.

All social workers use power, moreover, in their professional work. Yeheskel Hasenfeld suggests the following:

1. Clinical social workers often use power.
2. They interpret their clients' problems in ways that conform to the mission of their agencies. They establish certain expectations about clients' roles during the helping process.
3. They use sanctions and penalties for clients whose responses to services fall outside specific norms or expectations.
4. They enforce (or choose not to enforce) agency procedures governing eligibility, referrals, and termination.
5. They proffer comments and suggestions that steer clients toward certain actions or decisions.
6. They take sides in family or other conflicts, sometimes in subtle ways.[10]

Indeed, if social workers did not use power in clinical transactions, clients would probably be disappointed. Clients expect their helpers, who presumably have considerable expertise, to guide them, offer informed suggestions, and establish realistic expectations. As agency employees, moreover, most social workers are instructed to enforce specific policies, procedures, and protocols.

We need to demystify power and declare it a professional resource vital to both clinical work and policy practice. Like other professional skills, power needs to be observed, modeled, and practiced. (We discuss power in Chapters 10, 11, and 12.)

We should realize, too, that powerless people sometimes enter a vicious circle: they are aware that they are powerless and avoid participating in policy practice, which makes them even more powerless. Social workers sometimes work in programs that receive little support from the broader society or from the bureaucracies that they often must fight if they are to save programs. Moreover, most social workers are women. Rosabeth Kanter suggests that women are frequently excluded from the inner circles of power, which may erode the confidence they need to participate in policy practice.[11] This male-dominated society has also accorded background and supportive roles to women. When women and persons of color use power in ways that white males might, they are sometimes perceived as aggressive and become the targets of animosity.

Social workers need, then, to see power as integral not only to their professional helping roles, but to their policy advocacy. Moreover, social workers need to develop leadership skills so they can initiate and assume important policy-making roles.[12] We define *policy leadership* as "taking the initiative to develop new policies and to change existing ones to improve the human condition." People who initiate policy deliberations expose themselves to some risk, but they may also receive recognition and the psychological rewards of assuming a constructive, problem-solving role. We need to perceive leadership not as a burden but, like power, as an integral part of the professional role. When social workers fail to exert policy leadership, they allow other people with less commitment to clients' well-being and to oppressed minorities' needs to shape the human services delivery system.

Social Policy's Role in Ecological Frameworks

The importance of policy practice has always been merely implied in ecological, or environmental, frameworks, which continue to receive prominence in the social work literature that discusses direct service and human behavior. Perhaps because the writers of this literature tend to come from the direct-service segments of the profession, they usually fail to devote sufficient attention to policy practice.[13] The logic of environmental frameworks is clear; social workers who wish to help their clients have a professional duty to try to reform those factors that cause or exacerbate their clients' problems.

As we discussed in the preceding two chapters, changing existing policies provides one strategy for helping citizens and clients. Members of vulnerable populations are subject to a variety of forces and policies (or the absence of policies) that make it difficult for them to improve their condition as compared to others. If social workers do not attempt to change these policies, they ignore key elements of the ecosystems of their clients.

Policy advocacy is, in short, a *professional* intervention because, like direct-service work, it is geared to improving the well-being of citizens and clients. Drawing on NASW's Code of Ethics, we also argued in the preceding chapter that it is *unethical* not to engage in policy advocacy during one's career—and not to support efforts by the profession to lobby policy makers and to attempt to get progressive candidates elected to office.

Policy Practice as a Unifying Theme

As Phillip Popple suggests, it is a romantic idea to aspire to a profession that is wholly unified, when its members work in such different settings and undertake such different tasks. Indeed, he calls social work a "federated profession" that consists of various groups with different specializations and perspectives.[14] At the same time, however, if the profession lacks cohesion, it will fail to develop united positions and political clout on important issues like licensing and funding. Moreover, social workers will lack the strong professional organizations that can influence decision makers.

Perhaps policy practice and policy advocacy can serve as one unifying theme, because it is something that all social workers do, no matter what their specialization. It will allow social workers, singly and in groups, to shape the world to be more congruent with their values and to change those policies that profoundly affect the well-being of oppressed populations. Furthermore, it will infuse social workers with the broader vision of the profession's founders, as when Jane Addams tried to persuade decision makers to enact humane policies.

What You Can Now Do

CHAPTER SUMMARY

Social policy has traditionally emphasized historical, philosophical, and descriptive content, but policy advocacy and policy practice are gaining prominence in professional literature. *Policy practice* refers to the skills and strategies of those who seek to modify policies, whereas *policy advocacy* describes efforts to change policies to gain greater resources and opportunities for powerless and oppressed out-groups. (See Policy Advocacy Challenge 3.4.)

POLICY ADVOCACY CHALLENGE 3.4

How MSW Students Engage in Policy Advocacy with Respect to Homelessness

RALPH FERTIG, JD, MA

Go to
academic.cengage.com/
social_work/jansson
to watch this video clip

Clinical Associate Professor Ralph Fertig, a former social worker, lawyer, retired federal administrative judge, and freedom rider in the civil rights movement, decided to engage the MSW students at the School of Social Work at the University of Southern California in a project to address the huge problem of homelessness in Los Angeles County. Los Angeles County is so large that the 2005 Homeless Count needed more than 1,000 volunteers to cover a geographic area of 4,000 square miles over a period of 3 days and nights in more than 500 Census tracts. Their data led to a countywide estimate of 88,000 homeless persons on any given night. Yet local, state, and federal public officials had often neglected this population despite the efforts by some policy advocates to get policies in place that would substantially reduce the size of homeless persons in the County through more affordable and accessible housing as well as many other policies.

Listen to Policy Advocacy Challenge Video 3.4A in which Professor Fertig discusses how different sections of the policy advocacy class, required of all MSW students, participated in this policy advocacy project. After listening to this video:

1. Identify specific policy tasks that MSW students undertook.
2. Identify specific policy skills that MSW students used.
3. Does this project demonstrate that social workers can make a difference?
4. Did social work policy advocates in New Orleans also make a difference in the wake of Hurricane Katrina in helping vulnerable populations?

Also listen to Policy Advocacy Challenge Video 3.4B in which MSW student, Jessica Van Tuyl, discusses how this policy advocacy project broadened her professional horizons to supplement clinical work with policy advocacy. After listening to this video:

1. Discuss her views about what she learned from the project.
2. Discuss whether clinical work and policy advocacy can be combined in social work practice.

You are now equipped to do the following:

- Diagram a policy-practice, policy-advocacy framework with a context, and six tasks.
- Discuss four policy-practice skills.
- Identify stakeholders in specific policy-advocacy situations.
- Identify four styles of policy advocacy.
- Take a case study of policy advocacy and identify policy tasks, skills, and competencies used by participants.
- Discuss why power is essential to policy advocacy.
- Discuss why policy advocacy is an interventive discipline just as direct-service practice, administrative practice, and community organization are practice disciplines.
- Discuss why policy advocacy can be a unifying theme for the social work profession.

Policy advocates not only need a task- and skill-based framework, such as the one developed in this chapter, they also need knowledge about the way policies are developed in legislative, agency, community, and electoral situations—which we provide in the next chapter as a prelude to discussing the six policy-advocacy tasks in succeeding chapters.

NOTES

1. See Hedrick Smith, *The Power Game: How Washington Works* (New York: Ballantine Books, 1988), pp. 215–269.
2. Peter Bachrach and Morton Baratz, *Power and Poverty* (New York: Oxford University Press, 1970), pp. 17–38.
3. Robert Montjoy and Laurence O'Toole, "Toward a Theory of Policy Implementation: An Organizational Perspective," *Public Administration Review* 39 (September–October 1979): 465–477.
4. Jack Rothman, "The Interweaving of Community Intervention Approaches," *Journal of Community Practice* 3 (3/4): 69–99.
5. For a discussion of building agendas, see Robert Eyestone, *From Social Issues to Public Policy* (New York: Wiley, 1978), and John Kingdon, *Agendas, Alternatives, and Public Policies* (Boston: Little, Brown, 1984).
6. Kingdon, *Agendas, Alternatives, and Public Policies,* pp. 95–105.
7. Ibid., pp. 182–184.
8. Smith, *The Power Game,* pp. 331–387.
9. Ron Dear and Rino Patti, "Legislative Advocacy," in *Encyclopedia of Social Work,* 18th ed., vol. 2 (Silver Spring, MD: National Association of Social Workers, 1987), p. 371.
10. Yeheskel Hasenfeld, "Power in Social Work Practice," *Social Service Review* 61 (September 1987): 475–476.
11. Rosabeth Kanter, *Men and Women of the Corporation* (New York: Basic Books, 1977).

12. Eleanor Brilliant, "Social Work Leadership: A Missing Ingredient," *Social Work* (September–October 1986): 327–328.
13. For an exception, see Carel Germain's contribution to Samuel Taylor and Robert Roberts, *Theory and Practice of Community Work* (New York: Columbia University Press, 1985), pp. 30–58.
14. Phillip Popple, "The Social Work Profession: A Reconceptualization," *Social Service Review* 59 (December 1985): 560–577.

SUGGESTED READINGS

Value-Clarifying Skills

Robert Moroney, "Policy Analysis Within a Value Theoretical Framework," in Ron Haskins and James Gallagher, eds., *Models for Analysis of Social Policy* (Norwood, NJ: Ablex, 1981), pp. 78–102.

Martin Rein, "Value-Critical Policy Analysis," in Daniel Callahan and Bruce Jennings, eds., *Ethics, the Social Sciences, and Policy Analysis* (New York: Plenum Press, 1983), pp. 83–111.

Analytic Skills

Brian Hogwood and Lewis Gunn, *Policy Analysis for the Real World* (London: Oxford University Press, 1984).

Carl Patton and David Sawicki, *Basic Methods of Policy Analysis and Planning* (Englewood Cliffs, NJ: Prentice Hall, 1993).

Political Skills

Eugene Bardach, *The Skill Factor in Politics* (Berkeley and Los Angeles: University of California Press, 1972).

Charles Linblom and Edward Woodhouse, *The Policy-Making Process*, 3rd ed. (Englewood Cliffs, NJ: Prentice Hall, 1993).

Hedrick Smith, *The Power Game: How Washington Works* (New York: Ballantine Books, 1988).

Building Agendas

Joel Best, ed., *Images of Issues: Typifying Contemporary Social Problems* (New York: Aldine de Gruyter, 1989).

John Kingdon, *Agendas, Alternatives, and Public Policies* (Boston: Little, Brown, 1997).

Marc Ross and Roger Cobb, *The Cultural Strategy of Agenda Denial* (Lawrence: University of Kansas, 1997).

Smith, *The Power Game*, pp. 331–444.

Analyzing Problems

Hogwood and Gunn, *Policy Analysis for the Real World*, pp. 67–87, 108–127.

Patton and Sawicki, *Basic Methods of Policy Analysis and Planning*.

Enacting Policy

Donald deKieffer, *The Citizen's Guide to Lobbying Congress* (Chicago: Chicago Review Press, 1997).

Eric Redman, *The Dance of Legislation* (New York: Simon & Schuster, 1973).

Smith, *The Power Game*.

Implementing Policy

Yeheskel Hasenfeld, "Implementation of Social Policy Revisited," *Administration and Society* 22 (February 1991): 451–479.

Robert Montjoy and Laurence O'Toole, "Toward a Theory of Policy Implementation: An Organizational Perspective," *Public Administration Review* 39 (September–October 1979): 465–477.

Assessing Policy

Richard Nathan, *Social Science in Government: Uses and Misuses* (New York: Basic Books, 1988).

Patton and Sawicki, *Basic Methods of Policy Analysis and Planning*, pp. 300–328.

3

THE ECOLOGY OF POLICY IN THE UNITED STATES AND IN A GLOBAL WORLD

Chapter Four analyzes the ecology of policy in the United States. It discusses key institutions, legislatures, and funding bodies that provide the ecology of policies in local, state, and national settings. It illustrates the ecology of policy with New Orleans in the wake of Katrina. Consider this chapter a policy roadmap to be negotiated when engaging in policy advocacy.

Chapter Five discusses the global context of policy. Policy advocates have to understand how many domestic problems are caused or exacerbated by international factors, such as relocation of corporations abroad, migration of people across national boundaries, and environmental factors created by the combined effects of industry and citizens. Since globalization looms large in the contemporary world, policy advocates have to broaden their horizons to understand many social problems and find ways to ameliorate them. Consider this chapter to be a policy roadmap to globalization.

CHAPTER

4

Understanding the Ecology of Policy in Governmental, Electoral, Community, and Agency Settings

POLICY PREDICAMENT

When Hurricane Katrina hit New Orleans on August 29, 2005, policy advocates faced a dilemma. On one hand, a multitude of potential sources existed for helping Katrina survivors and for rebuilding New Orleans. On the other hand, it was difficult to determine how to proceed precisely *because* so many agencies and programs existed in public, not-for-profit, and for-profit sectors. Each of them possesses different application processes and priorities. We discuss the ecology of policy in New Orleans after Hurricane Katrina in Policy Advocacy Challenge 4.7 at the end of this chapter.

This chapter provides a road map to legislatures, communities, agencies, and electoral politics in the United States. The map does not tell us what route to take or how fast to drive, but it orients us to the landscape so that we can better find our direction once we have started the trip.

To be effective, policy advocates must understand how decisions are made in each of these four arenas, how broader forces influence decision making, what rules or procedures are commonly used, who the key players are, and what are the mindsets of key officials.

We discuss the following in this chapter:

- The cast of players in governmental settings
- The mindsets of public officials
- The legislative process
- Social agencies in their political and economic context
- The players in organizational settings

• Community-based organizations that influence policies
• Electoral politics

The Players in Legislative and Governmental Settings

Anyone who conducts policy advocacy in the governmental sector must know who the key players are and what motivates them. (See Policy Advocacy Challenge 4.1.)

Let's discuss elected officials (politicians), bureaucrats (unelected officials), lobbyists, and the interest groups with which they are affiliated. (See Figure 4.1.)

POLICY ADVOCACY CHALLENGE 4.1

Finding Information About Political Institutions on the Web

Stephanie Davis, Research Librarian, University of California, Irvine

Political institutions have an enormous impact on social policy. The importance of maintaining an awareness of the happenings of the political scene cannot be stated strongly enough. The sites below will help you to become knowledgeable about the structure of the government, how it works, and who the major players are.

• How Our Laws Are Made: A detailed description of the federal legislative process. **http://thomas.loc.gov/home/lawsmade.toc.html**
• THOMAS (Library of Congress): Search engine for federal bills and laws, links to biographical information, and links to additional congressional Internet services. **http://www.thomas.loc.gov**
• United States Senate: Links to senators' Web sites, legislative agendas, votes, and more. **http://www.senate.gov**
• United States House of Representatives: Links to representatives' Web sites, legislative agendas, votes, and more. **http://www.house.gov**
• The White House. **http://www.whitehouse.gov**

∽ EXERCISE ∽

Using the search engines discussed in Chapter One, and the evaluation techniques discussed in Chapter Two, visit these Web sites and answer the following questions:

• Who are your state senator and your U.S. senator?
• What are their top legislative agenda items?
• Is there any information about their campaign finances on their Web sites?
• Who is their constituency?

Vulnerable Populations and Stakeholders   One of the best uses of the Web is to promote social justice. Organizations that represent out-groups and stakeholders often use the Web to focus on the issues and challenges faced by a specific population. One excellent example is the National Organization for Women. Another good example that focuses on an issue rather than a population is the National Mental Health Association. Locate a Web site for a vulnerable population that interests you.

Using the previously mentioned resources (do not forget the checklist), find additional Web sites for out-groups or other stakeholders that measure up to your criteria standards.

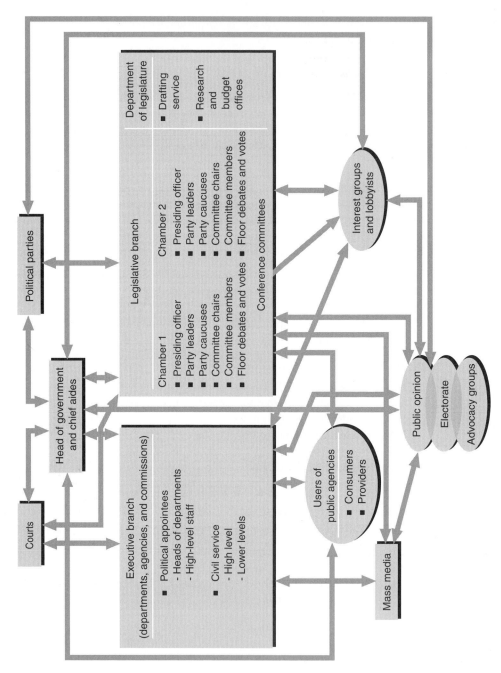

FIGURE 4.1
A schematic view
of government
and key players

Elected Officials

We can distinguish three kinds of elected public officials: heads of government, such
as mayors, governors, and the U.S. president; legislators, such as city councilpersons,
members of county boards of supervisors, state legislators, and federal legislators; and
officials elected to specialized public entities such as school boards.

Heads of Government   The head of government (or chief executive) is the elected official charged with developing an administration. Thus, we name an administration after its leader, as in *the Bush Administration.*

Although some local governments have nonpartisan elections, heads of government are often the titular heads of their political party in their specific jurisdictions.[1] Once he was inaugurated, for example, George W. Bush effectively became the national head of the Republican Party, just as many mayors and governors head their political parties in their jurisdictions.

Heads of government usually have some guiding principles that shape their approach to the central issues they confront. As the differences between Ronald Reagan and Franklin Roosevelt show, a head of government can often be characterized as relatively liberal or conservative. Of course, ideology does not always predict how a politician will vote on specific issues.

Heads of government and other elected officials want to establish positive, popular records for their administrations that appeal to members of their own party as well as to other groups that they hope will enlarge their political base.

Their central position in government and their constitutional powers make heads of government pivotal in the unfolding of policy while they are in office. First, the U.S. president is in charge of the executive branch of government, which comprises the myriad agencies that implement federal governmental policies. These agencies are usually called *departments,* such as the Department of Health and Human Services (DHHS). State and local governments have similar organizations, with a head and executive branch. Heads of government appoint the high-level officials in the executive branch's departments or agencies.

Second, heads of government usually initiate a budget, even though the legislators make many of the final budgetary choices. This initiating role represents an important power because it allows chief executives to influence priorities within the executive branch.[2]

Third, chief executives usually develop a legislative agenda to which they often refer in general terms in speeches, such as the president's State of the Union speech. They have vast resources to help them fashion this legislative agenda. For instance, they have personal aides in their own office, their political appointees in the executive branch, and political allies who occupy powerful positions on legislative committees or in the party in the legislature.[3] Because heads of government have a central position in government and a high profile, their legislative proposals, which members of their own party or political allies introduce into the legislature, often have an advantage over individual legislators' proposals. Even with such power, the legislative proposals of many heads of government are defeated, particularly when the opposing party holds a majority in the legislature.

Fourth, chief executives often use their central position in government as a bully pulpit.

Capitalizing on the extensive coverage the mass media usually accords them, heads of government often try to gain support for legislative measures, rally opposition against legislators who may block their policies, and educate the public about specific issues.[4]

Finally, heads of government can veto legislation that the legislature has approved, an important power since legislatures often cannot muster the votes (such as the two-thirds of each chamber required in the federal government) to override a veto. Some governors have line-item vetoes over the budgets that legislatures have approved; line-item vetoes allow heads of government to unilaterally change budget figures.

Legislators   Under the division of powers in federal, state, and local constitutions, legislatures have responsibilities and powers that often rival those of heads of government.

Foremost, legislatures can develop, approve, and reject legislation. They use this power both to respond to legislation proposed by heads of government and to introduce their own legislation.

Legislators possess extraordinary powers over budgets. When they write legislation covering particular programs, for example, they often include the amount of the funds to be used for those programs in a specific year. Heads of government cannot exceed these sums when they make up their annual budget. In a separate process, legislators decide the total of the appropriations for a specific year and how to divide it among various programs. They usually begin with the budget proposed by the head of government but often make major changes in it.[5]

While not charged with actually implementing enacted legislation or writing the administrative regulations that will shape this implementation, legislatures engage in administrative oversight. Many of their standing committees hold hearings during which they ask high-level executive branch officials to discuss the operations of specific programs. Legislators also learn from their constituents about the operations of programs. When legislators believe they have found problems in programs, they have several remedies. First, they can amend the legislation that established the program. Second, they can convince executive branch officials to correct problems in programs by modifying their administration. For example, if legislators find that an existing program does not serve people with disabilities, even though they were intended to be part of the program when it was originally enacted, they might convince the program director to devote considerable resources to informing people with physical disabilities about the program. Third, legislators often use public hearings to expose issues, educate the public, hear feedback on proposed legislation, and put political pressure on heads of government and their appointees to correct problems. Indeed, as Hedrick Smith notes when discussing Congress, many legislators like to use the mass media to publicize specific issues, often in defiance of or without consulting senior legislators or party officials, whose power has diminished in the decades since Watergate.[6]

Legislatures seem formidably complex; in fact, they are all structured rather similarly.

A diagram of the Wisconsin state legislature shows the essential structure of most legislatures. (See Figure 4.2.) Legislatures are usually divided into two houses, such as the House of Representatives and the Senate at the federal level, or the Senate and the Assembly at the state level, as in Wisconsin. Usually, both houses must assent to legislation or a budget before it can become operative. Many legislatures, like the U.S. Congress, convene annually, but some state legislatures convene only every two years. Moreover, the length of legislatures' sessions varies widely; Congress meets almost nonstop each year, but other legislatures convene only for several months.

The members of each house or chamber of a legislature, whether local, state, or federal, are elected by districts, whose precise shape changes over time. Districts are reapportioned as the population shifts and as the courts decide that existing district

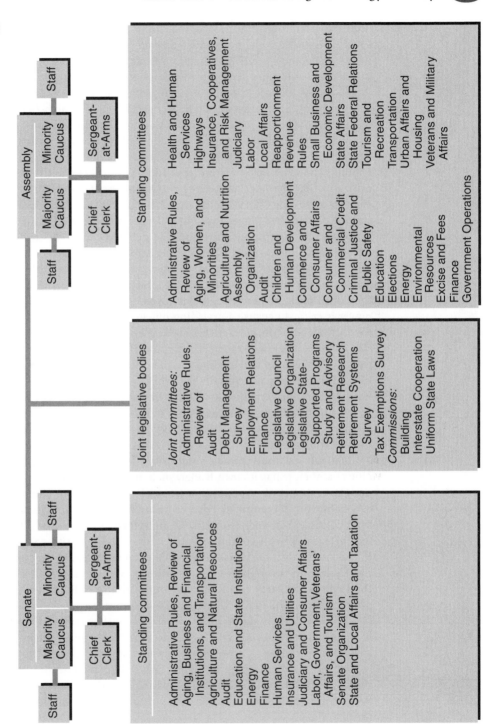

FIGURE 4.2
The structure of the Wisconsin state legislature

lines are unfair to specific groups, such as Latinos or African Americans. To understand specific legislators, then, we must analyze the characteristics of their constituents, whose preferences influence their positions on myriad issues. We might ask: Is the district relatively affluent or poor? Does it have a mix of ethnic and racial groups, or is it dominated by a single group? Is it urban, suburban, or rural? Is it dominated by a single party or evenly divided between two parties?[7] We can also ask whether specific legislators occupy relatively safe seats or whether they will face closely contested elections.

To understand how specific chambers of legislatures operate, we must first ask: Which party controls a majority of the legislature's members? The majority party appoints the chairs of all committees and has a majority of the members on each committee of that chamber. Moreover, the members of the majority party in each house elect the presiding officer of that chamber, such as the president of the U.S. Senate and the Speaker of the House. These high-level leaders have considerable power in determining when specific measures will be debated on the floor, in mobilizing support for or against measures, and in making important parliamentary decisions at critical junctures in floor debate. Presiding officers often have the authority to establish committees, assign members to committees, and appoint chairs of committees. In addition, they often have the power to decide where to route specific bills for deliberation. This power is critical because a presiding officer can often kill a bill by insisting that it go through specific committees that are known to be hostile to it.[8]

Each chamber has a second tier of powerful leaders: the floor leaders, which are also elected by caucuses and include the majority leader and the majority whip. Working in tandem with the presiding officer, these party leaders shepherd legislation through floor deliberations and decide which measures their party will support or oppose.[9]

A third tier of leaders, the chairs of the important committees of a chamber, are members of the majority party and have considerable power over the fate of legislation in their committees.[10]

Though at a disadvantage, a minority party often has considerable power in a specific chamber. It has its own leader, such as the U.S. House minority leader, who can mobilize support of or opposition to pieces of legislation. The minority party is allocated seats on all committees of a chamber in proportion to its share of the chamber's total membership, and its members sometimes obtain a majority vote on a committee by teaming with committee members of the majority party. Thus, in the era of Presidents Reagan and Bush, Republicans could defeat congressional legislation that the Democrats strongly favored by joining with southern Democrats, even though the Democratic Party had a majority in the House of Representatives throughout the period and controlled the Senate from November 1986 onward.

Because of their size and the myriad issues they consider, legislatures are divided into specialized committees. In the federal House of Representatives, for example, the Ways and Means Committee processes Social Security, Medicare, and tax legislation; and the Committee on Labor and Public Welfare processes social programs such as Head Start. (See Figure 4.2, which lists the committees in each chamber of Wisconsin's legislature, and Box 4.1, which lists the committees in each chamber of the U.S. Congress.)

As we have discussed, the presiding officers of each chamber often have considerable discretion in referring measures to committees. Many pieces of legislation go to multiple committees when they pose issues that cut across committee divisions. In other cases, certain kinds of legislation are automatically referred to a specific committee. Social

BOX 4.1 | Standing Committees of the U.S. Congress

Senate	**House**
Agriculture, Nutrition, and Forestry	Agriculture
Appropriations	Appropriations
Armed Services	Armed Services
Banking, Housing, and Urban Affairs	Banking, Housing, and Urban Affairs
Budget	Budget
Commerce, Science, and Transportation	District of Columbia
Energy and Natural Resources	Education and Labor
Environment and Public Works	Energy and Commerce
Finance	Foreign Affairs
Foreign Relations	Government Operations
Government Affairs	House Administration
Judiciary	Intelligence
Labor and Human Resources	Interior and Insular Affairs
Rules and Administration	Judiciary
Small Business	Merchant Marine and Fisheries
Veteran Affairs	Narcotics Abuse and Control
	Post Office and Civil Service
	Public Works and Transportation
	Rules
	Science and Technology
	Small Business
	Standards of Official Conduct
	Veteran Affairs
	Ways and Means

Security and Medicare legislation, for example, are always considered by the House Ways and Means Committee and the Senate Finance Committee in the U.S. Congress.

Each legislative committee has its own internal structure. Its chairperson may be elected by the committee's members or appointed by the chamber's presiding officer. Committee chairs are usually powerful figures. Like presiding officers of the overall chamber, they can kill legislation by not placing it on the committee's agenda, by referring it to a hostile subcommittee, or by merely raising strong objections to it when the committee discusses it.[11] Each legislative committee has subcommittees that specialize in certain issues, within the whole committee's purview. Subcommittee chairs also have considerable power over issues that fall within their domain.

Legislation that presiding officers refer to a committee falls into two categories. Some of it is consigned, more or less at once, to the legislative junk heap because the committee, much less the full chamber, does not consider it seriously. The subcommittees and committees take other legislation seriously and mark it up in committee deliberations; that is, they amend it in various ways.

Legislative proposal introduced in House

House version now considered in the Senate

Process initiated to resolve differences in House and Senate versions

Bill assigned to a specific established committee

Committee assigns bill to a subcommittee

Committee approves a final version of bill

Rules of debate decided

Committee version of bill forwarded to the full House

Bill considered, amended, and passsed in the House

Bill forwarded to the Senate

Bill assigned to a specific established committee

Committee assigns bill to a subcommittee

Committee approves a final version of bill

Rules of debate determined

Committee version of bill forwarded to the full Senate

Bill considered, amended, and passed in Senate

Bill forwarded to the conference committee

House-Senate conference committee established

House-Senate version of bill established

Bill sent back to House and Senate to ratify conference committee version

Bill forwarded to the president

Bill becomes law if signed by the president

FIGURE 4.3

The route that a typical bill follows in the U.S. Congress

Most legislation, then, evolves in the course of deliberations that take weeks, months, or even years, and it can be amended on the floor of the chamber when the whole chamber decides whether to amend, accept, or defeat a bill.

Figure 4.3 shows the usual trajectory of legislative proposals, though many variations are possible. A bill usually starts in one chamber, progresses from committees to a floor debate and then a vote. It is then referred to the other chamber, where it follows a similar course. After the second chamber enacts its own version, representatives from each chamber seek a common version, which usually requires both chambers to make concessions. If the conference committee creates a joint version, each chamber must then ratify it before it goes to the president (or governor), who then signs it into law or vetoes it. Congress can override a veto if each chamber musters a two-thirds vote. Otherwise, the legislation dies.

Some legislative deliberations are relatively straightforward; relatively few amendments are offered and legislators move quickly to a decision. Other legislative deliberations, particularly those concerning controversial issues, are marked by various parliamentary maneuvers, such as the opponents' efforts to derail the legislation. In unusual cases, opponents in the Senate will even filibuster a bill by talking nonstop to prevent a concluding vote. Filibusters are not allowed in the House.[12]

Officials Elected to Special Bodies Officials elected to some special political bodies, such as school boards, wield considerable power within their areas. Other political bodies, such as county boards of supervisors and city councils, have markedly different structures from those of the state and federal legislatures. They consist of a single chamber, and the election of their members is often nonpartisan; that is, the candidates have no party affiliations on the ballot. Many differences exist among cities; for example, some have mayors elected by the public, and others elect their mayors on a rotating basis from the city council. It is beyond the scope of this discussion to elaborate on the differences in city governments, but policy practitioners need to be versed in them to participate in local politics.[13]

Unelected Officials or Bureaucrats

Legislators are far outnumbered by unelected public officials who work in government agencies in city, county, state, and federal jurisdictions. These public officials are either political appointees or civil servants.

Political Appointees Political appointees are high-level persons appointed to top jobs by heads of government, such as mayors, governors, or the president. They serve at the pleasure of the heads of government. They do not have long-term job security, because their mentor may dismiss them if they fall into disfavor, if they are considered to be a political liability, or when a new head of government comes into office. This new leader usually dismisses the prior staff and appoints his or her own nominees. Political appointees become spokespersons and representatives of their mentor, as when they discuss their administration's policy positions at press conferences. They are likely to have the same ideology as their mentor.[14]

Civil Servants Unlike political appointees, civil servants obtain their jobs through competitive exams. They are hired at a specific level or grade in the civil service hierarchy and then are promoted to higher grades based on annual job reviews by superiors. Those in higher grades have more power than those in lower grades, though there are many exceptions. Unlike political appointees, civil servants usually have job security, though they can be terminated as a result of funding cutbacks.[15]

Civil servants are the engines of government bureaucracies; they administer programs, draft regulations, collect data, and disburse funds to programs. Most civil servants outlast particular administrations. Indeed, civil servants are the permanent government, with real powers that equal or even exceed those of some political appointees.

Even though they receive their positions by competitive exam rather than by political appointment, some civil servants have close ties with legislators. They may have worked in the legislature as aides, and they may have developed relationships with other aides or with the staff of legislative committees.[16]

Lobbyists and Interest Groups

Lobbyists are professional advocates who represent interest groups or causes. Hired by corporations, trade associations, professional organizations, or groups representing specific populations or issues, they voice their perspectives to legislators and to officials in the executive branch of governments.[17]

We can distinguish between powerful lobbyists, who represent interest groups with considerable money and clout, and shoestring lobbyists, who represent groups with relatively little money and clout. Lobbyists' power depends on several factors. Truly powerful lobbyists not only have funds to make campaign contributions to the legislators they wish to woo, but also to entertain them by hosting special events, taking them out to meals, paying them to address special meetings or conferences, and even funding special trips for them. Powerful lobbyists often have considerable technical resources; their affluent interest groups can hire researchers and consultants to provide legislators with proposals and technical reports. Powerful interest groups in various states and in Washington, DC, such as the American Medical Association, do not hire single lobbyists; they often hire teams of lobbyists large enough to speak to most of the people in a specific legislature during a given period. They increase their clout further by forming coalitions with other lobbyists and interest groups with similar concerns. The American Medical Association, for example, may team with other medical interest groups and even with some corporations to support or oppose specific pieces of legislation.[18]

By contrast, shoestring lobbyists serve smaller and poorer groups. Often acting alone, they lack the resources to make even minimal contact with many legislators, to make large donations to campaign coffers, or to entertain legislators. Their relative poverty should not imply, of course, that they are powerless; they can shape public policy on certain issues by carefully using their resources, establishing coalitions with like-minded interest groups and lobbyists, and mobilizing their constituencies to pressure public officials—for example, by writing letters to them—on important occasions.

Lobbyists' character also shapes their effectiveness. While the general public widely views lobbyists as slippery and devious, they need reputations as straight shooters to be successful with legislators. Lobbyists who are caught telling lies, such as claiming someone supports a measure when she or he does not or giving deliberately misleading information, soon lose their credibility. Lobbyists must be persistent and must not let specific defeats deter them. They must like to engage in endless networking with legislators, civil servants, and interested citizens to form relationships that will help them achieve their goals.

Lobbyists' power hinges, of course, on the groups they represent. When we examine external pressures on legislators, then, we need to consider the power of specific interest groups. They obtain their power partly by hiring skilled lobbyists, but they also offer carrots (rewards and incentives) and sticks (implied or actual threats). The incentives include campaign contributions from political action committees (PACs) to specific politicians, volunteers to help with campaigns, and technical assistance on issues. The threats include withdrawal of these carrots, the endorsement of opponents in primaries and general elections, and the provision of funds and volunteers to opponents.[19]

Some interest groups that begin with relatively scant resources augment their power by building a reputation for the quality of the technical information they give legislators. The Children's Defense Fund and the Center for Budget and Policy Priorities in Washington have, for example, attained key positions concerning an array of issues, even though they lack the resources of the American Medical Association. By securing foundation funds, with which they have built a core of sophisticated researchers and have evolved a national constituency, these groups have developed credibility for their research and their principled positions.

Think tanks, which are institutions that conduct policy research and disseminate evaluations of specific policies, have also emerged to represent a range of perspectives. They issue periodic reports that carry considerable clout in Washington, as well as in the state capitals.[20]

Connections Among Interest Groups, Legislators, and Bureaucrats

Important relationships exist among lobbyists, legislators, and bureaucrats. Many lobbyists, for example, are former legislators, civil servants, or political appointees. Many civil servants are former aides to legislators, with whom they maintain important relationships, such as passing them "inside information."[21]

While commentators sometimes exaggerate their power, iron triangles link civil servants, legislators, and lobbyists (or interest groups) when the legislature considers specific issues. For instance, if legislation about child abuse goes through a state legislature, several people who know each other and have worked together in the past may become active. Such a collaboration may include lobbyists associated with children's advocacy groups; an association of the directors of public child welfare agencies around the state; professional associations, such as the state chapter of the National Association of Social Workers; a key civil servant in the state's welfare department; and an aide to a legislator with a long-standing interest in child abuse. Sharing similar points of view and past patterns of collaboration, these people may cooperate and bargain to develop a mutually acceptable policy and then may pool their resources to seek its enactment.

We do not want to imply that such relationships exist on all issues or that their power precludes important roles for other participants. But those who try to change policy in legislative settings need to be aware that these relationships exist and that they can be tapped into for technical advice or for the support of a specific measure.

Public Opinion

Politicians, bureaucrats, and lobbyists work in an environment of uncertainty. They realize that voters can end a politician's career and can bring down an administration.[22] Bureaucrats are also vulnerable to public opinion because scandals or unpopular decisions can ruin political appointees' and even civil servants' careers.[23] Legislators often try to implement programs in ways that will please their constituents, as illustrated by politicians who oppose placing mental health facilities and prisons in their districts.

However, measuring public opinion is an uncertain art. Politicians often read polls, but they realize that even accurate polls cannot predict future changes in public opinion. Politicians often gauge public opinion through mail from constituents and from talking to constituents in their legislative offices and in their home districts.[24]

Advocacy Groups

Advocacy groups place pressure on decision makers in city councils, boards of supervisors, and state and federal legislators. They may be community groups, coalitions, think tanks, public interest groups, groups of consumers, or professional groups like the National Association of Social Workers. Some advocacy groups exist for long periods of time, while others are relatively short-lived, such as ones developed to address a specific issue at a specific time. Advocacy groups vary in their size and staff: if some a relatively small, others have substantial resources from foundations and other sources. Policy advocates often work with advocacy groups when they seek to change policies as we discuss in succeeding chapters.

The Electoral Process

To say the very least, the electoral process is highly competitive, because very few elections are uncontested at any level of government. The electoral process is the institutionalized guts of any democracy; it provides a nonviolent way of solving the problem of succession to office. It is competitive because it is a win-lose conflict where only one candidate can win.

The precise formats of elections are described in legal statutes and regulations that prescribe how candidates get on ballots, how votes are counted, how runoffs are held, how campaigns can be financed, and how long the terms of office are.

These precise rules vary widely not only between jurisdictions, but regarding specific kinds of offices. Rules that govern school board elections, for example, are very different from rules that govern federal elections.

Let's discuss the electoral process from a developmental perspective, from the early maneuvering by possible candidates through the actual elections.

Early Maneuvering

Long before most elections are held, potential candidates decide whether they want to make a run for a specific office. Potential candidates are sometimes approached by other persons, such as leaders of local, state, or national parties who want strong candidates who will have a chance at winning an office. Incumbents (persons already holding office) ponder whether they wish to run for office again—or whether they want to retire from public service, move into a government bureaucratic job, or seek yet another, often higher, office.

When deciding whether to run or rerun for a particular office, people consider various factors. Nonincumbents consider whether specific incumbents are vulnerable, whether because of their track record in office, weakness in public opinion polls, access to funds, or the extent that they are backed by other opinion setters or party officials. They consider, as well, which other nonincumbents might run for a specific office; because their chances diminish to the extent other formidable candidates enter the race. They take into account the degree of name recognition they already possess or might develop in the course of a campaign, because name recognition is crucial in many elections. They also think about whether they can develop grassroots support during a campaign, such as by eliciting support from community groups, local leaders, and volunteers. (Such successful candidates as social work Democratic Senators Debbie Stabenow and Barbara Mikulski gained early success in electoral politics by cultivating relationships with local community groups.)

Nonincumbents' motivation to run for office is often increased when their positions differ markedly from those of the incumbents. By winning, they not only gain office but substitute their positions for those maintained by specific incumbents.

Candidates with a commitment to social justice often see their public service in ethical terms—not just as a way to advance their personal self-interest.

Nonincumbents face a hard reality: the overwhelming majority of incumbents win elections when they decide to rerun for office. This is so for several reasons. Incumbents tend to have relatively high name recognition because of media coverage of their prior elections and their actions while in office. They can often raise money relatively easily from special interests they have helped through their policy decisions while in office. They know the electoral ropes because they have already been through one or more prior campaigns, and they often have support from local, state, or federal party officials who do not want to lose the incumbents seats to the opposing party.

We should not overstate the difficulties faced by nonincumbents, however.

Incumbents sometimes are vulnerable. A nonincumbent can run for an empty seat when an incumbent retires or runs for another office. Nonincumbents realize, moreover, that some races are less demanding than others in terms of the resources, name recognition, and time that they require. Nonpartisan elections, such as for school board, local planning councils, and positions on township or city councils, usually do not require the level of resources and name recognition required in partisan elections. Many nonincumbents begin their careers by not running for office at all: they get appointed to commissions in local jurisdictions or start their careers by obtaining jobs in government agencies or as aides to office holders. With a public-service base established, they can then scan the horizon for possible electoral races.

Seeking elective office is not for everybody. It takes time and effort, and it exposes persons to attacks from opposing candidates. Yet the rewards are numerous for persons who are elected to public office; they can make vitally important public-policy decisions because they are insiders whose votes count. Social workers possess characteristics that make many of them ideal candidates for public office. (See Policy Advocacy Challenge 4.2.)

POLICY ADVOCACY CHALLENGE 4.2

How Social Workers Run for Office

MELONY G. GRIFFITH, MSW

Go to
academic.cengage.com/
social_work/jansson
to watch this video clip

Melony Ghee Griffith was elected to the Maryland General Assembly in 1998 after spending years in community activism and political service, including serving as voter registration director for the Maryland Democratic Party. Like most social workers who run for political office, she had a substantial social work career even before thinking about running for office. After getting her MSW from Howard University, she was a hospital social worker and even a psychotherapist and program coordinator for the National Basketball Players Association Health Education Project at the Johns Hopkins University in Baltimore.

When she discovered that her neighborhood was not well represented by the incumbent politician in the Maryland General Assembly, she decided to run for office—winning an election to represent her district.

Listen to Policy Advocacy Challenge Video 4.2 where she discusses her decision to run for office, as well as the attributes of social workers that make them effective candidates, as well as public officials. After you have listened to this video, ask:

1. what attributes do social workers possess that makes them effective candidates?
2. what attributes do social workers possess that makes them effective public officials?
3. could you imagine running for office at some point?

Running Campaigns

Once nonincumbents decide to run for specific offices, they must wage successful campaigns to secure those offices. Their first challenge is to get on the final ballot by prevailing in primaries or in nonpartisan races with more than two candidates. Primaries are partisan elections in which representatives of specific parties must defeat members of their own parties to get on the final ballot where they are pitted against the representatives of opposing parties. Al Gore and George W. Bush emerged on the final ballot in 2000, for example, by defeating such opponents as Bill Bradley and John McCain in primary contests. In nonpartisan contests with multiple entrants, the two candidates with the highest vote totals often appear on the final ballot if neither of them received more than 50 percent of the vote.

The key objective in any campaign is to get more votes than ones opponent. To accomplish this, candidates must find ways to persuade the voters who are already sympathetic to their positions to vote, and must get some undecided or swing votes as well.

This requires them to engage in such tasks as the following:

- Develop positions on key issues that both speak to their natural constituency and appeal to some swing voters
- Make personal contact with many voters through campaign appearances and precinct walking
- Recruit and use volunteers to make personal contact with voters by phone and by precinct walking
- Reach voters through the mass media, such as through press conferences and debates with opponents
- Reach voters through advertisements in the mass media and mailings
- Increase the pool of sympathetic voters through voter registration, particularly in areas where public opinion is supportive

These activities, in turn, require candidates to raise campaign funds. These funds can come from friends, from political parties, from political action committees, and from personal resources. The amount of political resources required for a specific campaign varies widely depending on the competition for a particular office. In general, partisan races, hotly contested races, and races involving positions that imbue holders with great political power (such as races for state and federal offices) are more expensive than other races.

Once candidates face off, their ability to win partly depends on their skill in devising campaign strategy. They have to decide which issues to surface, what parts of the constituency to emphasize, how to respond to opponents' attacks, and how to get sufficient resources and volunteers to implement their campaigns. (We discuss campaigns in more detail in Chapter Twelve.)

Implementing Public-Service Careers   Once candidates win their first election, they begin a public-service career. Some of them will be content to serve one or more terms in that office, but others will begin a decades-long public service career that takes them into multiple positions and offices. For example, Senator Debbie Stabenow, a social worker, became a U.S. senator only after an extended career in which she held various lower-level offices. Some persons alternate between elected offices and offices in appointive positions in the government.

The Mindsets of Elected Officials

Those who engage in policy practice in governmental settings need to understand the mindsets of heads of government, legislators, political appointees, and civil servants. Success in changing policy hinges on obtaining the help and support of these people. Policy practitioners can understand officials' mindsets only by examining the environment that shapes their choices.

The Environment of Public Servants: Elected Officials

Imagine that you have just spent two years planning, fund-raising, and campaigning to obtain your job. You have narrowly defeated a determined opponent who has already pledged to prevail in the next election, which is several years away. In response to this threat, you are likely to have reelection on your mind throughout your tenure. You will look at most issues with an eye to their effect on your reelection, and you will spend hours wondering about the general public's preferences. To deduce their views, you will study the following:

- Public opinion polls
- Recent outcomes of other elections in comparable districts
- The mail you receive
- The views of subgroups within your constituency, particularly those that you believe will support you in the next election
- The preferences of state or national organizations—for example, professional associations or groups such as the American Association of Retired Persons—that might contribute funds to your next campaign

Moreover, you will nervously eye the statements and positions of potential opponents in the next election. In some cases, you will support an issue to steal the thunder of your likely opponents, and in other cases you will openly support issues that they oppose to publicize your differences from them. In districts divided between liberals and conservatives, relatively liberal candidates often support liberal issues to solidify their support among liberals. They realize that without committed support from this constituency, they may lose to conservative opponents.[25]

This nonstop campaigning will make you sensitive to the political ramifications of certain choices. Some issues, such as increasing funds for city parks, will cause you little or no concern. However, issues seen as more controversial by important segments of your constituency will make you hesitate before committing yourself.

If elected officials often have their ears to the ground, they are also extraordinarily busy. Assume that you are a member of several major committees and subcommittees, each of which handles many issues on which you need to brief yourself before and during policy deliberations. As you hurriedly read technical reports and briefing papers, you simultaneously try to raise funds for your reelection bid. You make weekly trips back to your district to meet with its citizens and convene regularly with lobbyists from various interest groups. Constituents also come to your offices every day to speak with you. While a caseworker (this title is used even though these persons are not usually social workers) helps you process many constituent requests, you also devote some of your energies to specific requests, such as that of an older woman who wants help in coping with her husband's Alzheimer's disease.[26]

You also are concerned about your relationships with your legislative and party colleagues.

Although at times you are a relatively independent legislator who wants to make a name for yourself, you also are part of larger systems that, much like an organization controls an employee, place some limits on your actions, such as pressuring you in certain situations to go along with policies and procedures you dislike. Because you want to increase your status within these systems, you must play by their rules. As a member of legislative committees and subcommittees, you know that the chairperson holds great power and can often determine which issues will receive a serious airing in the committee and which amendments will be enacted. You belong to a political party, as well, which meets regularly, agrees collectively to support or oppose certain measures, and parcels out rewards and penalties, such as committee assignments and campaign funds. If you are a complete renegade, you will suffer reprisals from high officials on your legislative committees and in your party.

Shortcuts: Aides, Lobbyists, and Priorities

With such a full agenda, you need to develop shortcuts. You have to rely heavily on aides to manage the bulk of your interactions with constituents, lobbyists, and others.[27] You are not afraid to delegate much of your work to these trusted aides, because without them, you cannot function. You create a division of labor by hiring specialists in legislative matters, in handling constituent demands (such as the woman who wants help with her husband's Alzheimer's disease), in fund-raising, and in public relations. In other cases, you rely heavily on lobbyists to do technical work for you, to do reconnaissance work with other legislators, to help you draft legislative proposals, and to help you write amendments to existing legislation.[28]

Early in your term, you decide that you have to develop priorities by taking some pieces of legislation seriously, and only giving glancing attention to others. Suppose a constituent wants you to sponsor a piece of legislation (by sponsoring it, you place your name at its head with those of other sponsoring legislators), but you decide the legislation is not a priority for you. Although you agree to sponsor it as a symbolic gesture to keep your constituent's goodwill, you know you will not invest energy in promoting it. You decide, instead, to expend your political capital (your power resources) liberally on issues that may bring you large political dividends when you come up for reelection, or that appeal to you for other reasons.

The Calculus of Choice

Any policy practitioner soon discovers that several factors shape legislators' choices. Indeed, precisely because so many factors intrude, policy practitioners should refrain from discounting legislators whose voting records make them appear unpromising. We can divide the determinants of choice into eight categories. We have already discussed the *electoral considerations* that lead politicians to support or oppose measures, based on the preferences of voters, interest groups, and campaign donors.

However, electoral calculations are not always easy to make, because politicians often have poor information on which to base predictions of how the public will respond to an issue in a future election. Politicians often try to gauge what positions *existing and potential opponents* will take on issues. Then, these politicians can upstage their rivals, take important issues from them, or take the opposite position.

Personal values and life experiences also shape politicians' positions; for example, many politicians who have had cancer show strong support for medical research.

Politicians sometimes support measures because they want to *obtain credit* for initiating a measure by going public before rival politicians take action. For this reason, politicians in the House of Representatives often vie with senators to develop legislative initiatives, and Democrats often try to develop a measure before Republicans take the initiative.

Some politicians support measures in areas where they hope to become known as *personal experts.* In the late 1980s, Senator Christopher Dodd (a Democrat) and Senator Orrin Hatch (a Republican) sought reputations as experts on day-care legislation by vigorously and publicly supporting the Act for Better Child Care.

Although they often focus on the needs of specific interest groups, politicians sometimes attend to the *public interest,* particularly when they believe voters will hold them accountable for decisions that hurt the public interest.[29] Indeed, politicians sometimes support budget cuts and corporate tax hikes, even in defiance of powerful special interests.

Politicians often base their choices on *political feasibility.* They do not want to invest effort in measures that have little or no chance of passage. In some cases, of course, politicians support measures that they believe will not be enacted. They do this to publicize their position to important parts of their constituencies.

Policy advocates must also remember that many issues have surfaced before in legislative settings. Like the rest of us, legislators often are creatures of habit; *habit* or *tradition* shapes their position on some issues. Of course, people often change their minds as they receive new information or as political realities shift.

Politicians have to decide not only how to vote, but whether to invest considerable energy in specific issues. When they want to avoid offending someone but are not really committed to a measure, they may give it only symbolic support. In other cases, when they personally favor an issue but fear negative consequences, they try to keep a low profile in their support. Sometimes, they openly campaign for an issue. At other times, they act as bystanders and may even absent themselves from the final voting to avoid offending either the supporters or the opponents of the legislation. In still other cases, they may openly oppose it.

Public advocates for an issue are aware, of course, that their measures are most likely to succeed if they have the support of especially powerful political leaders, such as committee chairs, the presiding officer of a chamber, and party leaders. These high-level leaders have extraordinary power, not merely in expediting measures through the legislative process, but also in attracting support for them from other, less powerful legislators. Policy practitioners' chances also increase as they obtain sponsors from both parties and from both relatively liberal and relatively conservative politicians. Of course, such breadth of sponsorship is not always possible.

Our discussion of the mind-sets of elected officials suggests that policy advocates need to exercise caution in making premature judgments about legislators' choices. Many factors can impel them to support or oppose a measure and to invest energy in it. For example, advocates of food stamp legislation were tempted to write off some conservatives who usually opposed social reforms. However, they soon found that many conservatives were becoming ardent supporters, whether because they were beholden to agricultural interests (who believed the food stamp program would enhance

128   **PART 3**   **The Ecology of Policy in the United States and in a Global World**

markets for farm products) or because they were genuinely troubled by the specter of malnutrition. Moreover, some Republicans did not want Democrats to get sole credit for enacting and expanding the food stamp program, which they believed would be politically popular. Liberal advocates for enacting and expanding the food stamp program, who would have faced an uphill political battle, found these conservative allies indispensable on numerous occasions.[30]

The Mindsets of Nonelected Officials

Policy practitioners frequently seek assistance from nonelected officials, whether political appointees or civil servants.

Political Appointees

When dealing with political appointees, one must always remember that they were appointed by high-level political allies, such as heads of government. Appointees will not usually support, at least openly, legislation that these mentors would not approve. Therefore, one can expect political appointees to seek permission from higher authorities before they commit themselves publicly to a measure.

In the real world, however, high-level political appointees, such as the U.S. Secretary of Health and Human Services, often make choices in a relatively ambiguous context. They may like a measure (or an amended version of it) but may fail to get a definite opinion about it from higher authorities who want the measure to evolve in the legislative process before they decide whether to support or oppose it. In this situation, a high-level appointee might have some aides work on the issue and might even give technical assistance to advocates of the measure. In other cases, political appointees receive word from their mentors, such as a governor or the president, that certain features of a measure are unacceptable to them and will elicit a veto, but other features are acceptable. In these cases, the head of government attempts to influence a measure by threatening to veto it if the final version contains certain provisions. In yet other cases, high-level appointees engage in a dangerous game of defiance; they quietly give background support to a proposal's advocates, even when they know that the head of government opposes the measure.[31]

Heads of government decide to support or oppose specific measures in much the same way legislators do. However, they are probably more attuned to a measure's budgetary implications than many legislators, because governors, mayors, and the president initiate budgets.

The political appointees in government agencies are likely to be interested in the facets of a measure that they will be called on to implement. They will attend to details such as what resources the measure will need, what relationships will exist between different levels of government, and what rules (such as eligibility procedures) will be left vague or will be defined. Like heads of government, political appointees will be interested in a measure's budgetary implications, because part of its funds may come from the department or agency.

Civil Servants

As nonelected officials who do not depend on politicians for their job tenure, civil servants often have a different perspective from that of politicians or political appointees. They commonly view themselves as professionals with specific expertise, and are not under the same compulsion to act political. Nor can they commit their bureaucracies to a specific measure, because that prerogative is reserved for political appointees who head agencies.[32]

At the same time, however, civil servants work in a political environment. They have to be sensitive to the desires of the high-level political appointees who administer their departments, because they work under them, and their job promotions and job assignments are influenced by these executives. As lower-level staff in the elaborate chain of command of government, they often receive directives from high officials and may receive reprimands if they do not heed them.

Policy advocates who approach lower-level civil servants about proposed legislation should not expect them to endorse it, because departmental or agency approval can come only from the director. However, lower-level civil servants can provide indispensable technical information, such as reports, studies, and data germane to writing a proposal.[33]

The degree of cooperation that a policy advocate receives from civil servants varies widely. Some civil servants are extraordinarily helpful to those who ask for technical assistance, but others are relatively cloistered and appear to be irritated by external requests. Their cooperativeness is often related to their personal disposition, their values (whether they like the proposed project), and their perceptions of the advocate (whether they trust him or her). Advocates must often be persistent when seeking help from civil servants, but they must also be aware that civil servants are responsible for numerous tasks.[34]

Like political appointees, civil servants sometimes give low-profile assistance to causes that they like, even without high-level departmental or agency approval. Advocacy groups sometimes find reliable contacts in government agencies who give them inside information that enhances their work.

Strategy in Legislative Settings

We have provided an overview of legislative and other governmental settings. With knowledge of the procedures used in these settings and the mindsets of the legislators and officials who inhabit them, policy advocates have to devise strategy for having legislation enacted. They need to know how to obtain assistance in developing strategy, how to find sponsors for their legislation, how to testify before committees, and how to use phone calls and letters to pressure politicians. Moreover, practitioners often try to create favorable conditions for their policies in legislatures. A practitioner might, for example, participate in a politician's campaign, attend political club meetings or parties, and contribute resources and time to a political action committee (such as PACE, the political action committee of the National Association of Social Workers). Chapters Twelve and Thirteen are devoted to methods of developing and implementing political strategy.

Advocating for Resources

Policy advocates often seek legislation that establishes new programs or regulations. Such legislation is enacted by *authorizing committees* that write and enact legislation. Yet advocates also often want enhanced resources for a specific committee, which requires then to work through and with *appropriations committees* that decide what resources to allocate to specific programs and departments. It is important both to get meritorious policies, but they become ineffective if they are not given sufficient funding by legislatures for them to make them effective. Policy advocates need to put pressure on appropriations committees in both legislative chambers, then, to secure adequate funding for specific programs.

Policy advocates need to realize, as well, that resources for social policies hinge upon the kind and level of tax revenues that governments collect. Minus sufficient taxes, governments lack resources to fund meritorious policies—particularly if available resources are wasted or siphoned toward programs and policies that lack merit. In the case of the federal government, for example, Joseph Stiglitz, a Nobel-Prize economist, contended that the Iraq War would ultimately cost the United States $2 trillion—resources that might otherwise have been used for social programs at home and abroad.

The Law and Social Policy

The courts assume a major role in social policy, issuing many rulings that directly impact social policies. Indeed, as can see in Policy Advocacy Challenge 4.3, policy advocates often use legal strategy to obtain specific objectives, including with respect to such social problems as homelessness.

POLICY ADVOCACY CHALLENGE 4.3

The Use of the Law in Policy Advocacy

RALPH FERTIG, A.M. AND J.D.[1]

Once the meeting of a need is defined as a right, then those in need may secure the protection of the law. Social welfare advocates may help define such rights through litigation or legislation, and may ensure the application of those rights through administrative tribunals.

Litigation

Some 12 to 16,000 homeless people regularly cluster in an area of downtown Los Angeles known as Skid Row. A number of social agencies provide social services and some housing. Still, there is not enough temporary shelter (in missions and those provided by social agencies), transitional (single room occupancy hotels and programs designed to help selected homeless people get through a crisis), or long term assisted housing to meet the needs of all.

The result is that thousands of the homeless sleep on the streets of Skid Row. A lucky few huddle in cardboard boxes, under a highway bridge, or in dumpsters. Their 24 hour presence impacts the streets of the area. They constitute a sub-society, a magnet for other homeless people, many of those released from prison or hospitals, and for social work agencies that serve them.

But the real estate that they occupy is alongside a burgeoning commercial and high rent residential area. Developers want to clear the seamy sights of homeless people from the neighborhood and claim their sites for luxury high rises. Elected officials are often influenced by wealthy contributors to their campaigns, and are tempted by the

Go to
academic.cengage.com/ social_work/jansson
to watch this video clip

---

[1] Clinical Associate Professor at the University of Southern California School of Social Work, a former social worker, lawyer, and a retired federal administrative judge.

prospect of private developments that would generate more taxes to provide increased services for everyone.

So complaints about the homeless blocking the sidewalks, creating a sanitary problem on the public way, or intimidating shoppers and office workers in nearby buildings, together with concerns about their drawing dope dealers and prostitutes to Skid Row, led the city council to pass an ordinance (L.A, Cal. Mun. Code § 41.18(d) 2005), used by the police to clear the homeless away, tear down their cardboard shelters, and arrest those who slept on the streets.

Social workers led the protest and linked the homeless to ACLU lawyers. Two who were convicted and sentenced for violating the ordinance, along with four others who were threatened with arrest, prosecution, incarceration and conviction for violating it, sought an injunction against the ordinance and the arrests. Under a federal civil rights statute (42 USC 1983), alleging that enforcement of the municipal code violated their constitutional rights, they filed suit in the U. S. District Court for the Central District of California. (*Edware Jones v. city of Los Angeles*).

Though they lost at the trial court level, they appealed. On April 14, 2006, the Ninth Circuit reversed and remanded the case (444 F.3d 1118), ruling that because there was substantial and undisputed evidence that the number of homeless persons in the city far exceeded the number of available shelter beds at all times, the city encroached on the rights of the homeless by criminalizing the unavoidable act of sitting, lying, or sleeping at night on public sidewalks while being involuntarily homeless. The court found that the Eighth Amendment (which bars cruel and unusual punishment) prohibits the state from punishing an involuntary act or condition if it is the unavoidable consequence of one's status or being, here a consequence of being human and homeless without shelter in the city.

Legislation

So long as there are not enough shelters for the homeless, their right to sleep on the streets was secured in *Jones v. city of Los Angeles* (above). But they still need housing of all sorts, assisted with social services. That calls for private charities, public funds, and the backing of local governments. Since the homeless are scattered throughout the state, and to minimize their further concentration in Skid Row pockets of vulnerability, all communities should provide their fair share of housing. But the spirit of NIMBY ("Not In My BackYard") dominates much of local politics.

Students in USC's Social Welfare Policy classes met with State Senator Gil Cedillo, whose district includes Skid Row. He then introduced SB 1322, which would require every city or county in California to identify sites, in the housing element of their general plan, where emergency homeless shelters and residential service providers would be allowed to locate without the ability of the local governing body to change the plan once it is adopted. With these anti-NIMBY provisions, the bill establishes "Housing by Right." The sites identified in the plan would be available for emergency shelters and assisted transitional and long term housing within the planning period, sufficient to shelter families and individuals in need of such service. Localities are free to finance the housing, regulate developers to set aside a proportion of new housing for low income rentals, perhaps in exchange for density bonuses or other incentives, or fashion their

(continued)

own solutions. But they are mandated to do something to plan for and enable the housing of their homeless.

Some students went to Sacramento to lobby State Senators, others visited them in their local offices. The bill passed the Senate and at this writing is before the State Assembly, where the Speaker and key sponsors have assured us of its passage. Then it will go to the Governor. If he vetoes SB 1322, USC classes will follow through in 2007 to spur re-re-introduction of the bill and to help it pass with a sufficient margin to override another veto. *Whenever* it is signed into law, USC students will fan out to social agencies in the cities of Los Angeles and Orange Counties in organizing efforts to assure its implementation at the local level. Where they run into resistance, they will turn to lawyers to seek injunctions, ordering local communities to comply with the provisions of the new law.

Administrative Law   Once rights are established and programs are authorized (as seen in the examples above), programs have to be established to implement them. Generally, the enabling legislation delegates responsibility for administering such programs to a new or ongoing public agency, authorizing it to use rules and procedures for carrying out its work. A first draft of such regulations is submitted for a period of public review and comments are invited. Social workers frequently offer input to the proposed rules and procedures which are considered by the agency and may be integrated into the final regulations. Once they are adopted, their implementation typically provides for an administrative tribunal to allow appeal, review, and possible modification of any actions taken with regard to any individual or group. Such tribunals are run by neutral Administrative Judges who can order the agency to change its practice, pay compensation, and make the client whole.

Social workers may advise their clients that they can appeal changes in their benefits from most federal and state programs such as Social Security, disability or unemployment compensation. And you can either link them to a lawyer (who in most cases will be paid a statutory fee, one set by law that will not cost your client anything). They can seek administrative review of discrimination on their jobs due to race, gender, religion, national origin, age (if 40 or older), or disability, drawing upon lawyers provided (without cost to the client) by the Equal Employment Opportunity Commission or the State Fair Employment and Housing Commission. They can appeal denial of proper compensation for overtime, and the denial or constriction of countless benefits established in law.

As an Administrative Judge with the EEOC, I was able to order the hiring of a qualified man, represented by a social worker, who had applied in vain to be a mail carrier. The Postal Service had repeatedly passed him over because he wore a large turban and insisted on his right, as a Sikh, to wear it on the job, while delivering mail. I found the Post Office had violated the law against religious discrimination. He was given the job and back pay to the time when he was first denied a position, and because the government appealed my ruling to the federal court, he got more. My order was upheld, the Post Office had to pay him full salary for the years his case was tied up in appeal, and the Post Office was enjoined to never deny any work benefits to anyone because he wore a turban.

Such rulings take place in administrative tribunals, but getting to them can intimidate or confuse clients. Often, the details of a client's claim are lost in the bureaucratic procedures of the agencies and overloaded intake workers through which one must begin the process. But Social workers can go with their clients to the administrative agencies to assure that their entreaties are properly understood, filed, and properly moved on to the administrative tribunal.

Social workers may also work with lawyers in preparation for and at the hearing held by the administrative judge and be witnesses their behalf. All administrative tribunals recognize the right of social workers to fully represent their clients as advocates in place of lawyers, as in the case above.

Furthermore, it is in the interaction between the intended beneficiaries of social programs, those who manage and distribute those benefits, and lawyers that social workers can discern needs and help transmute them into rights by changing the system, its policies, procedures, and regulations. Sometimes that means going to court for injunctive relief (as in *Jones v. city of Los Angeles*); sometimes that means seeking new laws (as in *SB 1322*, above); and sometimes it means serving as an advocate for your clients, one at a time, before an administrative tribunal.

After reading Policy Advocacy Challenge 4.3, listen to Policy Advocacy Challenge Video 4.3 as Professor Fertig discusses how policy advocates can use the law to facilitate their work. Please address these questions:

1. how can the law be an ally to policy advocates?
2. why must social work policy advocates sometimes work in tandem with, or consult, attorneys?

The Political Economy of Social Agencies

Just as policy advocates need to understand the structure and operations of legislatures, they must also be familiar with organizational processes to understand how social agencies work. It is useful to analyze social agencies' political economy as a prelude to examining their policies.

To survive, social agencies require ongoing, regular resources to meet their payrolls and other overhead costs. A few lucky social agencies are massively endowed by private donors, but the officials of most social agencies must frequently interact with institutions, accrediting bodies, and clients to maintain a steady flow of resources. When social agencies stop receiving support from external sources or find these sources severely constricted, they go out of existence, downsize, merge with other agencies, or renegotiate their relations with the external world by changing their mission, their fund-raising strategies, or their marketing strategies.[35]

Social agencies, which have always been shaped by their political and economic context, were subjected to a particularly harsh set of realities in the 1980s and 1990s. Traditional sources of public funds were constricted during the budget cuts and tax revolts of those decades, when many citizens sought to reduce property taxes or objected to the budget levels of local, state, and federal governments. Agencies that receive funds from campaigns such as United Way and the United Jewish Communities, which raise funds for a coalition of agencies joined in a federation, often found their allocations diminished. The resources of federated campaigns have been depleted by competition from other fund-raising groups, national economic difficulties that have decreased corporations' contributions, and scandals (in the case of the national United Way, whose chief executive was accused of a misuse of funds).

The restricted flow of money from governmental agencies and federated campaigns has meant that larger numbers of social agencies have competed for the scarce resources of foundations, corporations, and private donors. Many social agencies have also found it difficult to maintain a large enough proportion of paying clients. (The clients of many agencies have become poorer and are beset by serious mental, economic, and other problems in an era of increasing inequality in the United States.)[36]

The revenues of social agencies come from a variety of sources. To survive, agencies need resources from fees, foundations, donors, and government. They also need clients.[37] Some clients come directly to agencies through word of mouth, advertising, and outreach programs. Others are referrals, as when one agency suggests that a client use another agency's services, or when courts or probation departments require people to obtain specific agency services. Interorganization exchanges often shape the flow of clients to an agency, as when the staffs of two organizations agree to enter a reciprocal relationship. Two organizations may negotiate an agreement whereby each agency focuses only on certain kinds of clients, while referring other clients to the second organization. Agencies may also develop joint programs funded by collaboration in writing a grant proposal or seeking a contract.

Demographic, cultural, social, and technological factors also affect agencies profoundly, as when the population shifts, public opinion changes, and new perceptions of social problems, such as family violence, evolve. These changes influence the extent to which people use agency services, the social problems they have, and the agencies they believe are relevant to their problems. While we usually think that agencies, once established, are permanent, many agencies cease to exist when their environment changes. For example, many agencies used to provide residences for pregnant teenagers, where they stayed before giving their newborns up for adoption. With legalized, safe abortions usually available and with many young women choosing to keep their babies, many of these agencies have disappeared or markedly changed their mission.

Various pieces of legislation impose procedural requirements on social agencies, such as the Americans with Disabilities Act of 1990, which requires agencies to accommodate people with chronic physical and mental disabilities. Various state laws require agencies to report certain social problems, such as child abuse; to inform patients or clients of the risks of certain procedures; to adhere to severe procedural limits when taking children from their natural parents; and to work within restrictions when committing people involuntarily to mental institutions. Federal legislation places restrictions on the use of restraints in nursing homes. Court rulings, such as those forbidding discrimination against members of specific ethnic or racial groups, also influence the procedures of many social agencies.

As we discussed earlier in this chapter, legislation that establishes and funds social programs often dictates the kinds of policies that agencies must follow in implementing them. Some program details that were left vague in the original legislation are defined later when the high-level government agency charged with implementing the program adds administrative regulations.

Some nongovernmental bodies issue regulations that agencies must follow to be accredited, and inspect the agencies regularly to ensure that these regulations are being followed. Because unaccredited agencies may have difficulty hiring staff or recruiting clients, such regulations powerfully shape agencies' choices.

Community pressures on social agencies include community groups, organized groups of clients, or individual clients who may request or demand policy changes.

Citizens can place pressure on agencies, particularly governmental agencies, by complaining to government officials about specific services or policies they dislike. Pressure sometimes also emanates from the mass media, as in horror stories about services that clients have or have not received.

Competition within the broader community places pressure on organizations and undermines the security that agencies find in relatively stable streams of clients and resources. In the face of competition, agencies sometimes have to alter their programs or face retrenchment or termination. For example, by the 1970s, many YMCAs and YWCAs were depending increasingly on fee-based recreation and exercise programs for middle-class people but found their resources imperiled by the rise of profit-oriented exercise centers.[38] Many Ys were forced to retrench when they were unable to develop alternative programs.

To secure resources in the harsh era of the 1980s and 1990s, organizations had to negotiate and manage relations with their political and economic environments by building relationships with existing and potential funders; by developing services that appealed to sufficient numbers of clients to provide revenues; by satisfying external funders that their services met specific evaluative criteria; by developing public relations campaigns to attract funders and clients to the agency; and by modifying their services as competitors encroached on their traditional sources of clients. Funders and clientele shape organizations' policies, as do agencies' adjustments to their turbulent environment. Although rarely reaching the levels described in Policy Advocacy Challenge 4.4, conflict can occur in agencies as people develop different positions in the context of their values and the agency.

POLICY ADVOCACY CHALLENGE 4.4

Agency in Policy Turmoil

SAMUEL H. TAYLOR, DSW

Exactly one year ago, Dr. George Breeze came to San Marcos, a metropolitan suburb of Los Angeles with a population of 60,000 people, to direct the recently established San Marcos Community Mental Health Center. Dr. Breeze had previously worked in Philadelphia, where he had acquired a reputation as the innovative, inspiring, and flexible director of Manford University's Outreach Mental Health Services Department.

When Dr. Breeze initially interviewed for his position, several board members expressed some reservations about how he would fit in, since he did not wear a tie and seemed almost overconfident. Dr. Sedgwick, the retiring director, calmed the board by saying that, as a young psychoanalyst, he too had been fairly unconventional. The board had to keep in mind that this was no longer the San Marcos Clinic, it was a new mental health center, and it needed new ideas and the dedication of the youth. "He will work out," Dr. Sedgwick reassured them.

Shortly after George Breeze arrived at the San Marcos Community Mental Health Center, he made it clear to the staff that waiting lists, long-term therapy, and supervision were outdated. In the following months, he:

1. urged short-term, crisis-oriented management of cases
2. requested and received permission to establish an advisory board of citizens from the catchment area and another board composed of consumers
3. abolished the supervision system and established a flexible peer-consultation system
4. asked staff members to work evenings in order to see families

(continued)

5. got into an argument with the Chief of Police about how officers were handling youngsters and emotionally ill persons
6. hired paraprofessionals from a human services program of a community college to serve as community aides
7. told the staff that he wanted to know personally about the service and disposition of each case that involved a racial or ethnic minority client because he suspected that the staff members were allowing biases to influence case management

Within 6 months, the staff in the agency had become deeply divided. Three major groups had formed and developed leadership. First, some of the original clinic staff members (who had helped Dr. Sedgwick prepare the mental health center application) resented Dr. Breeze's nontraditional ways and felt that they had no chance to introduce their ideas. They rallied behind Dr. Jones, met privately, and decided that they must take their case to other agencies, in San Marcos and to local civic leaders and then must present their complaints to the agency board with the support of these other groups and leaders.

The staff hired by Dr. Breeze (young activist professionals and community aides) learned of the strategy and immediately alerted Asian, black, and Chicano groups in San Marcos and rallied behind Dr. Smith, who contacted both the National Institute of Mental Health (the prime federal funder of the center) and the Citizen and Consumer Advisory Boards. They were ready to ask for termination of federal and state funds if Dr. Breeze was fired.

Finally, a number of agency supervisors formed a group behind Dr. Virtue that advocated "responsible change." They were not opposed to all the changes instituted by Dr. Breeze but particularly opposed to those that deprived "professionals" of their rightful positions of authority and prestige within the agency. They wanted restoration of the supervisory system and curtailment of hiring of new careerists.

The issue reached crisis proportions when a patient being cared for by a community aide committed suicide in a most sensational manner. A reporter from the newspaper interviewed a member of the original staff and was told that "this would never have happened if Dr. Sedgwick had been there; Dr. Breeze's ideas just don't work." The board decided to hold a meeting to settle the issue, and they agreed to allow representatives of all sides to present their evidence. They felt that Dr. Breeze had introduced some good programs but also felt that he was unconventional. At this meeting, they hoped to reach a final decision as to whether Dr. Breeze should be fired, retained (but only after placing limits on the reforms he had issued), or given a vote of complete confidence.

"Traditionalists," then, rallied behind Dr. Jones and wanted to restore the traditional mission of the agency—long-term therapy with white and middle-class clients. "Insurgents" supported Dr. Breeze and his various reforms with no qualifications. "Advocates of responsible change" wanted some innovations but not at the expense of the traditional prerogatives of professionals. The board wished to bring unity to the agency as soon as possible to avoid further adverse publicity as well as possible loss of funds.

Source: This case was developed by Professor Samuel H. Taylor: Names and locations have been altered.

We do not mean to suggest that political and economic factors wholly determine organizations' actions. Not-for-profit agencies have latitude in deciding, for example, which public contracts or grants to seek. Governmental policies that descend on public and nonpublic agencies are often vague or ill-defined on many points, so the staff in these agencies has considerable discretion in shaping many details of their services. While noncompliance with governmental policies poses legal and ethical questions, agencies sometimes disobey specific policies or bend the rules.

The description of the harsh atmosphere for social agencies in the 1980s and 1990s, such as funding restrictions, should not suggest that they cannot maintain humane, caring services. Even when such restrictions stretch staff resources to the limit, many agencies deliver effective services. Skilled leadership allows many agencies to keep up staff morale even in difficult circumstances.

As they manage and plan relations with their environment, agencies also must attend to their internal operations: They have to build and maintain a staff, design programs, mediate internal disputes and conflicts, develop decision-making processes, produce budgets, attend to logistical tasks, and maintain their facilities. Indeed, social agencies may be unable to obtain a steady flow of resources if they lack a reputation for delivering quality services. In the case of not-for-profit agencies, for example, foundations often ask community leaders about a specific agency's reputation in the community. This reputation depends on people's perceptions of the services and staff of the agencies they interact with or hear about.[39]

The executive of an agency, then, must juggle many tasks if the agency is to flourish, devoting attention to the agency's relations with its environment while trying to develop internal processes that enable the agency to maintain quality services. Of course, executives often delegate tasks, as when they use fund developers and planners for external relations and program directors for internal matters.

The Political Economy of Programs and Social Work Units

We have discussed social agencies' political economy, but many social workers operate in large organizations dominated by other professions, like hospitals, public welfare departments, corporations, and schools. Others work in specialized units within a broader social service organization, such as adoption units within child welfare departments, programs for homeless persons within mental health clinics, and programs to help single mothers within family counseling agencies.[40]

Our discussion of social agencies' political economy applies in double measure to these units or programs within larger organizations. They depend on their host organizations for resources and for permission to perform specific roles or functions. In turn, the political and economic factors that impinge on the host organization influence the subsidiary programs' ability to command resources and mandates from that host organization.

To illustrate, consider the case of a social work unit in a hospital. Such a unit must hire sufficient staff to help patients in many parts of the hospital, including the emergency room and the oncology and outpatient departments. It also needs permission from various units of the hospital, as well as the top management of the hospital, to assign personnel to these areas. To obtain these resources and permissions, the social work unit must be exceedingly adroit in managing its relationship with the hospital's officials and staff; indeed, the hospital is a key part of the social work unit's political economy. (A more detailed discussion of the political strategies the social work unit can use to obtain resources appears in Chapter Eleven.) In turn, the hospital's willingness to allocate resources to the social work unit hinges on factors in its political and economic environment, such as hospital accreditation standards and the extent to which Medicare and private insurance will or will not fund social work services.[41]

Some program units within larger agencies derive funds from both the host organization and special external funders. A project for homeless persons in a mental health clinic, for example, might receive funds from a governmental agency or a foundation and funds or supplies from the host organization. The directors and staff of such a program would need to be attentive to both sets of funders to ensure the program's survival. If the external funding ended or decreased, the program's staff would have to try to convince the clinic itself to increase its funding of the program.

Mapping Agencies' Policies

Our discussion of social agencies' political and economic context leads us to consider the nature, varieties, and content of agencies' social policies. To better understand the nature of agency policies, try to imagine a social agency without policies. In such an agency, the staff members would do their own thing without the guidance of agency rules, regulations, protocols, or priorities. There would be no written mission statement and no manual to define procedures. It would be impossible for the staff members to describe the agency's activities to outsiders, such as clients and funders. And how would clients using an agency with no policies know which services they could obtain and for how long? How would they know their rights, or what protections or safeguards were in place?[42]

Policies govern the relationships among agency staff members as well, so staff members in an agency lacking policies would find themselves in a chaotic and unpredictable environment. There would be no personnel policies to establish staff's duties and rights, rules for termination, or protection from arbitrary treatment. Nor would such an agency have clear priorities established by the agency budget, which is itself a kind of policy.

Although policies cannot shape every detail of an agency's internal organization or internal dynamics, they typically provide an agency with a central direction, priorities, guidance for its operating programs, and some protections for staff and clients.

Figure 4.4 maps the variety of agency policies. It is a complex diagram because of the wide range of policies, which cannot be easily summarized.

POLICY ADVOCACY CHALLENGE 4.5

Map of Agency Policies

Ron McClain, J.D., MSW, LCSW

Go to **academic.cengage.com/ social_work/jansson** to watch this video clip

Using Figure 4.4 as an orienting framework, select a specific program in a social agency. Trace the following:

• Its history
• What combination of policies exist within it or define it
• What money streams are relevant to it
• How it is (or is not) supported or shaped by informal policies in the agency
• Whether it has implications for relations between the agency and other agencies
• How it might be changed or reformed in the context of agency politics so that it provides better services

Listen to Policy Advocacy Challenge Video 4.5 where Ron McClain, J.D., MSW, LCSW discusses how Hurricane Katrina's destructive effects on New Orleans power-fully shaped and transformed the map of his agency. Please answer these questions:

1. What changes took place in his agency's mission and why?
2. How did the programs of the agency change?
3. Speculate whether he was able to tap into new funding sources that helped his agency implement its transformed mission?

The missions and programs of many social agencies are not static. Not only do funding sources change through time, but so also do flows of clients. In Hurricane Katrina's wake these shifts in funding and clientele occurred rapidly, whereas they may change more gradually at other times. Effective executive directors and agency boards of directors work hard to position agencies in their environments so that they can not only fiscally thrive, but meet important community needs.

Some policies are originally external to agencies but are then internalized, like the policies agencies accept when they take funding from governmental programs.

These internalized policies establish specific rules, such as intake procedures, staffing requirements, content of services, reporting mechanisms, and a general state-ment about the program's purposes. An agency that has a number of externally funded programs (not-for-profit agencies now receive the majority of their funds from the government and from foundations) will have multiple sets, or clusters, of these exter-nally established policies. Some details of funded programs are left relatively vague, so the agency's staff must fill the gaps with their own policies. (Of course, agency staff may ignore or even violate some of the funder's policies, though they run the risk that their omissions or violations will be detected during audits and monitoring.)

Court rulings shape agency policies as well, such as the *Tarasoff* decision, which requires social workers to inform intended victims when a client tells the worker that he or she intends to inflict bodily injury on them. Social workers who neglect to inform the threatened targets may be sued.[43]

The stipulations of nongovernmental agencies that purchase services that reim-burse agencies (or their clientele) for specific kinds of services, such as health insurance companies, also affect agency policies.

Other agency policies are centrally established, even though external economic and social forces may influence their content. For example, most not-for-profit agencies have a mission statement that defines their priorities and direction.[44] One agency defines its mission as "a career and job resource center created to serve a broad spectrum of women by helping them recognize and attain their employment and earnings potential in the work world through providing job and career resources in a supportive environment."

As you can see, mission statements are relatively vague; nonetheless, they establish the agency's general philosophy. In this example, the mission statement affirms certain activities, such as providing job and career resources, but not others, such as counsel-ing services or mental health services. In addition to a mission statement, staff often has certain objectives, goals, or priorities in common. A staff member who says, "What makes us unique is that we like preventive services," or "We like to use outreach," sug-gests an overall approach to services that, she thinks, distinguishes her agency from other agencies.

FIGURE 4.4
Map of agency
policies

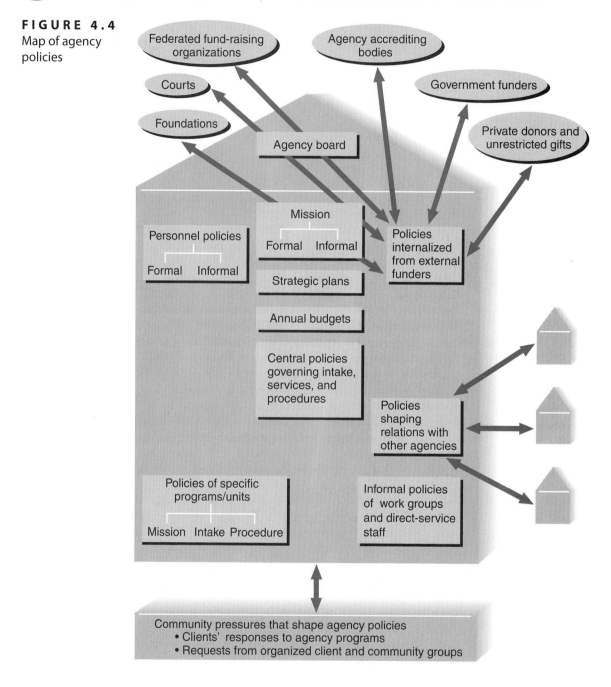

Agencies' annual budgets also serve as policy statements, at least in part. They shape agencies' priorities by distributing resources to various programs, perhaps cutting funds for one program while increasing them for another. To fully understand an agency's policies, then, one must examine both its present and its previous budgets to determine its priorities and how they have changed.[45]

For services that it funds by itself, the agency must establish its own internal policies, such as intake procedures and the content of services. For example, a not-for-profit mental health clinic, might receive 50 percent of its annual operating funds from external funders (which shape the policies for those programs) and make up 50 percent of its budget from its own funds. The clinic would decide internally how to govern the intake, services, and other details of those programs funded with its own money.

Many nonprofit agencies receive funds from federated fund-raisers, who then impose some of their own policies. They monitor the agency regularly and may make recommendations about the agency's internal priorities.[46]

In complex organizations, such as hospitals or government bureaucracies, many policies exist at the level of the unit, the bureau (or department), or the program. These smaller units often have their own mission statements. The following is the mission statement of one social work unit in a hospital:

> It is the mission of the Social Service Department to enhance the delivery of comprehensive health services by providing social services to the patients and their families of the University of Minnesota Hospitals and to assist in the resolution of social and emotional problems related to illness, medical services, and rehabilitation.[47]

These units usually have their own budgets, which the staff of the host organization review and approve, and their own policies. A social work department in a hospital may decide, for example, to fund social work services in one unit, such as the emergency room, but not in another, such as the neurology unit.

In addition to the budgets; mission statements; and official policies of agencies, units, or departments, many other policies are fashioned through informal systems and networks. While not documented, informal policies shape staff's actions and choices at many points in their work and deliberations. Informal policies may vary from official written policy, but they may also fill gaps when official policy is ambiguous.[48]

To illustrate the importance of informal policy even in the higher reaches of an agency, we will return to the discussion of an organization's mission. A written mission statement conveys a unity that is usually absent from organizations, because different staff members often have diverse and subjective notions concerning their organization's mission. While the official mission may, for example, stress services to families with single heads of households, some staff may want the agency to place more stress on serving intact families. Staff members may also disagree about the extent to which the agency should seek or accept governmental funds or about how intake policies should be structured. Sometimes, divergent notions of the agency's mission erupt into conflict, as when the organization selects a new director or when it deliberates over the agency's budget.[49] In other cases, however, staff may sublimate their differences and may even be unaware of some of them.

And on a very basic level, each agency employee will have a set of personal policies, or approaches, to his or her work. When confronting virtually identical client problems, for example, one staff member may provide services based on traditional psychotherapy, while another may emphasize survival skills, advocacy, and empowerment.

Personal policy preferences, as well as binding informal policies that many staff share, are neither good nor bad; they must be judged by their specific outcomes for the clients and the agency. If we decide that a worker's personal policy preferences or the informal policies of a group of staff result in prejudices against certain kinds of clients, such as gays, we will want to modify them. But sometimes these preferences and policies lead to positive outcomes, such as advocacy and outreach, constructive efforts to help clients, and extraordinary efforts to assist clients above and beyond the call of duty.[50] In addition, they sometimes help place legitimate limits on official policies, as when elderly patients are under pressure by hospital and Medicare administrators to leave the hospital as soon as possible after medical treatment. Disoriented by surgery and medications, such older persons often resist early discharge and find ready allies in social workers who help delay their discharge for one or more days. While operating in apparent violation of higher-level policy, these social workers can often justify their actions as being necessary for the well-being of their clients.

The Players in Organizational Settings

Anyone who seeks to change organizational policies encounters hierarchies and divisions of labor. These are the formal and structural characteristics of organizations that Max Weber emphasized in his classic writings.[51] A hierarchy is the chain of command that gives high-level executives such powers as creating high-level policies, hiring staff, and making budgets. The division of labor, or specialization, divides staff into units that focus on specific tasks, such as protective services, adoptions, and foster care in a child welfare office. While many organizational theorists have sought ways to soften hierarchy and specialization within organizations, they remain enduring, important features.

Some may associate these structural characteristics with control, rigidity, and fragmentation, but they also serve positive purposes. As productive collectives, organizations need powerful officials who focus on functions such as developing overarching policies, a mission, budgets, and planning. The complexities of the tasks in the modern welfare state often require specialization, both in the work of specific units or departments within the larger organization and in the work of the individuals within the units or departments.

Figure 4.5 provides useful clues to hierarchy and division of labor in a sample organization. The organizational units include those that provide specific kinds of services to clients and those that perform work for the larger organization, such as research and accounting. The figure also shows the distribution of power within the organization: The people toward the top of the hierarchy have certain formal powers.

Were we to attend only to the organizational chart, however, we would have an incomplete and distorted conception of the organization. Policy practitioners often want to know how power is distributed in organizations with respect to certain issues. While the organizational chart offers clues, it may overstate or understate the power of specific individuals.[52] The director of a relatively small unit, for example, may have considerable power with respect to certain issues and less power with respect to others.

To obtain a more complete understanding of organizational power, and other organizational dynamics and processes, we need to understand the interactions among the staff of an organization. We can conceptualize organizations as transparent overlays, placed on top of one another, that depict (a) the formal organizational chart, which displays the official hierarchy and division of labor; (b) the resources allocated to specific units, programs, or functions within the organization; (c) employees and internal programs that generate revenue, clientele, and prestige for an organization; and (d) informal relationships and patterns of consultation between members of the organization.[53] Of course, such overlays do not exist in the real world, but they

FIGURE 4.5
Sample organizational chart

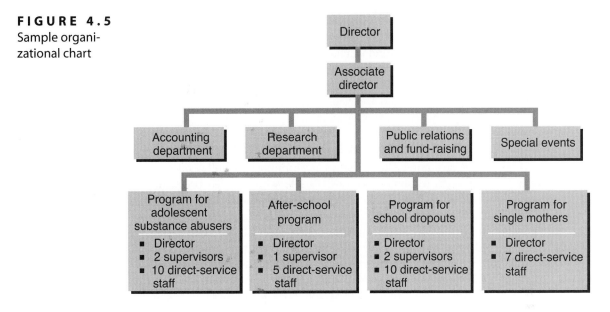

provide a useful means of conceptualizing power and relationships within organizations. Together, these overlays provide useful, important information that allows us to build a fuller understanding of the dynamics of a specific agency.

Overlay 1: The Organizational Chart

Organizational charts tell us a great deal about the players in a specific organization. As we have discussed, people at high levels in the hierarchy, whether in specific units of the organization or in the broader organization, usually have powers and prerogatives that enable them to shape decisions. They help make budgets; participate in hiring, firing, promoting, and supervising lower-level staff; obtain access to information about the personnel, programs, and budgets of the agency; and have access to information about the resources and institutions in the agency's external environment.

We can sometimes infer a person's perspective from her or his position in an organization.

Top executives are often concerned about the budget implications of specific choices, whereas lower-level professional staff often emphasize budget implications for clients and staff workloads. As intermediaries between management and direct-service staff, supervisors often share the perspectives of both higher-level and lower-level personnel. Those who direct or work in a specific program often view policy choices and agency budgets only from the perspective of that program.

The board of directors of nongovernmental agencies makes many important policy decisions. The board establishes an agency's high-level policies, such as its mission; hires its executive director; oversees the development of personnel policies; examines the agency's budget; and serves as the general overseer. Some public, or governmental, agencies also have advisory boards that offer suggestions to the top staff of the agency.[54] (The top executives of public agencies are ultimately responsible to those elected officials who appoint them, as discussed in the first portion of this chapter.)

An organizational chart, however, may be misleading. Some people in the higher ranks of organizations defer to persons who are horizontal to them or even below them in the formal chart. Organizational charts do not tell us which units or programs in an organization have considerable resources, and which ones the top executives favor. In addition, organizational charts imply that high-level persons make most general policy choices, but they do not tell us who has power with respect to specific issues. Many political scientists have observed that the distribution of power often varies with the issue; persons who are exceedingly powerful concerning certain issues may have little or no power regarding other issues.[55]

Overlay 2: Budget Priorities

We have noted that a budget is an important policy document because it establishes an organization's priorities. People who oversee program units with considerable resources, for example, often have more power than those who oversee units with relatively few resources. Examining budget trends in organizations can prove useful; if one unit has been losing staff positions while another has been gaining them, we can deduce that the power of each unit has changed. However, when considered individually, budgets may give us misleading impressions. Some persons who direct units with relatively small budgetary resources may have extraordinary power that derives, for example, from their close personal ties with other persons in the organization.

Overlay 3: Boundary Spanners and Mission Enhancers

Some persons are boundary spanners who have links with institutions, officials, and agencies that can bring substantial resources to an agency. They may have links to funders, such as staff in a foundation; a knowledge of funding sources or grant-writing skills; connections to elected officials (or their aides) who have power over the funds that go to the agency; a seat on an important committee in the host organization or in the community; or connections with key sources of referrals to an agency. Such people, who enhance agencies' resources and clientele, often derive power from these roles.[56]

Mission enhancers promote goals that highly placed persons in organizations favor. If the top officials in a hospital want to increase the number of older clients, they are likely to view with favor those units or officials within their hospital who they believe can advance this goal. Conversely, we can assume that units or staff whose activities are peripheral to the organization's central objectives are likely to have less power.

Overlay 4: Informal Relationships among Organizational Members

Some of the connections between persons in organizations are predicted by the organizational chart, but proximity in the organization's hierarchy does not tell us about patterns of friendship and trust, enmity, or social distance. Nor does it tell us about human contacts that span different units of an organization or that cut across levels of the hierarchy. Policy practitioners need to know about these relationships to understand processes and choices in organizations.

The formal organizational chart cannot tell us which persons will band together to enhance their power within an organization. Groupings take many forms. Some are ongoing informal clusters of persons who share knowledge and who support one another. Other groupings are constructed during specific controversies or crises, such as to oppose the termination of a program. Some groupings are relatively large; others consist of only a few staff members.

The Political Economy of Communities

Many kinds of communities exist. They may be so heterogeneous that they cannot easily be described, or they may be dominated by a specific group. Most neighborhoods within communities can be described by social class or economic variables, as well as by ethnic, racial, and age characteristics.[57]

As sociologists have long noted, communities have vertical and horizontal dimensions. When we discuss their vertical dimensions, we analyze the economic, political, and social institutions that descend on communities from the outside, such as supermarket chains, corporations, state or federal policies, the mass media, and social movements with local chapters or supporters. When we discuss their horizontal dimensions, we examine local civic associations (groups that advance a neighborhood's well-being), advocacy groups (local groups that promote specific causes), social agencies, public agencies, neighborhood groups, and churches. Moreover, social movements—that is, broad movements that foster social change, such as the civil rights movement of the 1960s and the Rainbow Coalition in the 1980s—sometimes develop local offshoots or chapters.[58]

When addressing specific issues in communities, such as where to place social service institutions or how to mobilize opposition to certain policies, policy advocates need to discover which community residents, leaders, politicians, and institutions have traditionally focused on this issue. Rather than power elite that controls all issues, most communities have a series of elites that specialize in specific issues.

In seeking specific reforms in communities, policy advocates often affiliate with, consult, or enlist the support of community-based groups. These groups may include civic associations; advocacy groups; local chapters of national groups, such as NOW or the National Association for the Advancement of Colored People (NAACP); or local offshoots of social movements. Policy practitioners sometimes form coalitions representing social agencies and community groups when they want to oppose a specific measure, such as a cut in welfare benefits, or when they want to establish new programs, such as programs to help abused children.[59]

The mass media, including local papers, television stations, and radio stations, often assume a pivotal role in local communities. Of course, the mass media may be relatively conservative in local areas, so astute policy practitioners cultivate relationships with sympathetic reporters.

Many kinds of policy issues develop in communities. Some pertain to where buildings are, or are not, placed, such as whether a half-way house for persons with specific problems is placed in a certain neighborhood. Some pertain to the policies of institutions, such as local schools. Advocates might question, for example, whether a particular school provides sufficient tutoring to certain kinds of students, sufficient outreach to truants, or sufficient public health services. Some pertain to a local government's budget: should it allocate greater resources to specific programs or needs? Still other issues involve patterns of citizen participation in decision making, such as whether certain boards are representative of the jurisdiction's population. Advocates sometimes seek establishment of task forces to analyze problems such as inadequate child care, lack of after-school recreation programs, or gangs.

The community politics of many issues can be highly conflicting. For example, when a county welfare office wanted to establish a branch office in a certain community, remarkable conflict ensued that pitted policy advocates against persons and businesses who feared the office would lower property values and bring undesirable people into the area. Only after protracted conflict and some court rulings was the branch office finally established.

Different Layers of Government and Policy

We have discussed policy within specific levels of government, such as federal, state, city, and community levels. Different policies and resources exist at each of these levels in the American federal system. Policies that are germane to homelessness exist, for example, at each level. The federal government funds programs for homeless persons run by local jurisdictions or nongovernmental groups, such as shelters. Some federal programs exacerbate homelessness, such as inadequate funding of construction of affordable housing, failure to enact a sufficient minimum wage, and insufficient funding for substance abuse and mental health programs. States, too, fund service programs, housing and social-service programs. Local units of government sometimes cooperate with advocates who seek to end homelessness, but often enact policies that harm homeless persons, such as by local ordinances that allow the police to place them in jails. States have assumed larger policy roles in recent decades with the devolution of federal policy to them, such as through block grants and federal mandates that require states to address specific problems.

When addressing issues like homelessness, policy advocates have to understand specific policies and funds that exist at each level of government so that they not only can tap resources, but know what policies they wish to change.

Nor should we forget the private sector. In the case of homelessness, for example some foundations fund programs to help or empower homeless persons. Not-for-profit groups that build affordable housing are often key resources in specific communities. Advocacy groups and some churches work to eradicate homelessness in specific communities. Some private developers, particularly if required to do so by local or state ordinances, include affordable housing in their projects—or can be pressured to do so.

The multiplicity of policies that bear on specific social problems like homelessness often presents challenges to advocates, who need to get officials from different levels of government, and from the public and private sectors, to collaborate. (See Policy Advocacy Challenge 4.6.)

POLICY ADVOCACY CHALLENGE 4.6

Challenges in Getting Officials to Collaborate

BOB ERLENBUSCH, PH.D.

Go to academic.cengage.com/ social_work/jansson to watch this video clip

When different units of government have different policies for addressing problems like homelessness, policy advocates have to try to get them to work together. Listen to Policy Advocacy Challenge Video 4.6 as Bob Erlenbusch, Ph.D., Chair of the Board of the National Coalition Against Homelessness in Washington, DC and the Executive Director of the Los Angeles Coalition to End Hunger and Homelessness, discusses his challenges in trying to link programs and policies of Los Angeles County with those of the city of Los Angeles when trying to end homelessness in Southern California.

Maneuvering in a Multi-Layered Policy Ecology

Americans have created a complex policy ecology that involves policies from different levels of government, including federal, state, and local levels, as well as public and private sectors. This complex policy ecology was nowhere more obvious than in post-Katrina New Orleans. We discuss this context in Policy Advocacy Challenge 4.7.

POLICY ADVOCACY CHALLENGE 4.7

The Ecology of Policy in Post-Katrina New Orleans

BRUCE JANSSON, PH.D.

Policy advocates in New Orleans had to decide *who* to contact or *who* to pressure in this maze of different levels of government, elected officials, government agencies, civil service staff, nongovernmental agencies, religious institutions, and the private sector—not to mention government associations and advocacy groups.

It was certain from the outset that the federal government would have to assume a pivotal role in the rebuilding of New Orleans, as well as meeting the survival needs of its residents. The city of New Orleans and well as the State of Louisiana were bereft of resources in the Katrina's wake because it destroyed many of their tax revenues. Their traditional sources of revenues, such as property, income, and tourism taxes, were devastated by the Hurricane's destruction of homes, the forced evacuation of many citizens, and the destruction of hotels and casinos. Minus massive federal spending, New Orleans would not be able to rebound from Katrina and many of her citizens would have encountered even greater hardships than they already had to endure.

Massive federal resources would be needed, too, to help citizens deal with economic and housing losses. Homeowners who lacked flood insurance, for example, would suffer huge losses unless they received resources from the federal government. Renters would be unable to find or afford rental units in New Orleans due to the destruction of many of them. Those homeowners or renters who evacuated to other cities, such as Houston and Baton Rouge, would often be unable to afford rents due to loss of employment and assets unless they received major federal subsidies. Not only would citizens and evacuees need rent subsidies, but they would need trailers in which to live, since many of them would be unable to find privately-owned units. Only the Federal Emergency Management Agency (FEMA) would have the resources to provide trailers on a massive basis in New Orleans and surrounding areas.

Citizens could not easily return to New Orleans if they could not find employment—but many businesses had been destroyed by Katrina. Such federal agencies as the Small Business Administration (SBA) would have to give grants and low-interest loans to small businesses. The federal government would need to waive or reduce corporate taxes of damaged or destroyed businesses for specific periods of time to help them find resources to rebuild—and give tax breaks to victims of Katrina. The federal Department of Commerce would need to provide economic-development funds for businesses and infrastructure, such as roads, bridges, and ports.

Nor could many citizens meet their survival needs without massive federal assistance. Persons lacking medical insurance but whose income and assets precluded them from receiving Medicaid would need to have normal eligibility levels raised so that they could receive it. Eligibility for Food Stamps would also need to be raised. Because residents of New Orleans would not easily be employed due to the destruction or

(continued)

evacuation of many businesses, they would need to have their unemployment benefits extended beyond the time limit usually placed on unemployment benefits by the federal government—as would many evacuees who would could not find employment in those locations where they moved.

Federal resources would be needed not only by communities struck by Hurricane Katrina, but by communities that hosted evacuees. Such cities as Houston would, for example, face higher TANF, Medicaid, school, police, and social-service costs as thousands of evacuees moved to them. Minus substantial federal assistance, they would (in effect) be punished for being good Samaritans.

Massive federal resources would be needed because Hurricane Katrina was the worst natural disaster in American history. Even nine weeks after it hit, 123,000 customers had no electricity, 190,000 persons had no dial tone on their telephones, all schools were closed with many of them destroyed, only two hospitals were functioning, about one-half of physicians and three-fourths of psychiatrists had evacuated the city, and roughly 1500 persons had died. Mountains of debris littered many neighborhoods that often were piled with it even a year after Katrina. Ninety percent of the city's 8,000 public housing units were deemed uninhabitable after Katrina.

The federal government had always assumed a major role in helping states and local units of government that were devastated by natural disasters, whether hurricanes, tornados, floods, fires, or earthquakes. FEMA was the lead federal agency for providing immediate survival resources to citizens, cleaning up debris, and providing temporary housing. The federal Environmental Protection Agency was charged with addressing environmental problems in the wake of disasters, such as the chemicals entered flood waters in the wake of Katrina when industrial sites were partly or completely destroyed. The federal Army Corps of Engineers had long been the principle agency for building levees and other devices for averting floods—even if its flawed work in New Orleans on levees were later found to have caused much of the devastation of New Orleans. Only it had the resources and expertise to reconstruct the levees—and many businesses and citizens would return to New Orleans only if they were convinced that it had repaired levees to a level that would withstand future major hurricanes. FEMA and the Army Corps of Engineers would be responsible, moreover, for undertaking technical studies to determine where citizens and businesses could safely rebuild in light of flood planes—information that would also shape what homes and businesses could receive insurance coverage in coming years since insurance companies would be reluctant to cover homes and businesses at high danger of destruction when another hurricane hit New Orleans.

If the federal government would have to take the lead in funding the rebuilding of New Orleans and survival needs of its citizens and evacuees, the state of Louisiana and the city of New Orleans would also need to assume major roles. Beginning in the early 1980s, the federal government continued to fund many programs, but gave states enhanced powers to implement them in housing, community development, social service, public health, welfare, health and economic development areas. This devolution meant that the federal government still gave states considerable resources, but it required them to determine what specific programs were funded in various cities and towns within them—and even to establish many guidelines for their implementation and monitoring. Devolution meant that the State of Louisiana would determine how many of the federal resources that would rebuild New Orleans and help its citizens were used. Governor Kathleen Blanco decided within five weeks of Katrina to establish the Louisiana Recovery Authority that would receive and distribute much of the federal funds directed to New Orleans and its citizens. The State would also continue to over-see the implementation of Medicaid and TANF while receiving considerable federal resources for them.

The city of New Orleans would also have pivotal roles in rebuilding New Orleans. Because it was in charge of its police, fire, transportation, and sanitation services, it could decide what communities received them and in what amount—decisions that would shape what areas were settled and which ones remained largely vacant since citizens would often choose not to return to communities that lacked these amenities. It would similarly shape settlement decisions by citizens and businesses by deciding what streets, bridges, and other infrastructure would be repaired and when. Lacking the resources to fund many of these services and repairs, the city would depend heavily on the federal government for subsidies until its tax revenues resumed as persons and businesses came back to the city and as tourists returned.

Like other cities, moreover, the city was vested with the power to develop city plans, such as by zoning certain areas for residential, industrial, and recreational uses. It also had the power of eminent domain that allowed it to purchase property even from owners who did not want to sell it—such as to obtain land for public uses such as for schools. Unless states specifically enacted laws that restricted them, cities even have the power to purchase land from unwilling owners to re-sell them to private developers who wish to build malls, hotels, or housing developments as several recent court deci-sions had determined in Ohio and other states. These planning and economic powers, as well as control of city services, meant that Mayor Ray Nagin and the city council would powerfully shape New Orleans' redevelopment.

To develop a plan for the city, Mayor Nagin formed the Bring New Orleans Back Commission in Katrina's wake. He soon discovered, however, that local units of gov-ernment within New Orleans and on its periphery—called parishes in Louisiana—had views of their own about the rebuilding of their areas. With their own elected officials, a number of them began their own planning projects in the year after Katrina hit.

It was unclear in Katrina's aftermath, then, just how key decisions about New Orleans' rebuilding would be made because the federal government, state, city, and parishes each had significant powers and roles. George W. Bush and Congressional conservatives, while realizing they had to fund much of the rebuilding of New Orleans, mostly wanted to leave key decisions to local authorities. Some Democrats wanted to create a strong federal agency, like the Tennessee Valley Authority (TVA) with a strong "czar" at its head, to redevelop New Orleans and the Gulf Coast. Governor Blanco and Mayor Nagin wanted respectively to assume a leading role in the planning process, as did public officials and citizens in some of the parishes. It was unclear in Katrina's immediate aftermath just who would take the lead in planning how the city would be rebuilt, such as which neighborhoods would be razed, which would be developed, what mix of housing would be constructed, and what parts of the city would be devoted to industry or recreation.

A host of private-sector players would also assume important roles in Katrina's aftermath. The New Orleans Chamber of Commerce, as well as Greater New Orleans, Inc., would represent the interests of businesses to public officials. Private developers and speculators would shape the rebuilding of the city by purchasing property and seeking approval for housing, hotels, businesses, and other structures. Various trade

(continued)

unions would protect jobs and workers' interests in an area certain to have a labor shortage in light of the evacuation of many workers. Social service providers would establish the Community Based Service Network to seek funds and develop collaborative programs. Many faith-based charities would come to New Orleans to address food, shelter, and other survival needs of citizens and to supplement the services of the American Red Cross. An army of volunteers would come to the city from other cities and states to help rebuild the city and address its citizens' survival needs.

The courts would assume a major role in Katrina's aftermath. They would have to determine the legal responsibilities of insurance companies to the extent that they did not reimburse homeowners and businesses in a timely way for damages covered by their policies or if they contended their policies precluded damages from floods. Civil rights suits might be filed if African Americans or other ethnic groups believed that they received discriminatory treatment from public officials, such as if their neighborhoods were not rebuilt when others were. Environmentalists might sue the EPA if it failed to address environmental hazards in a timely way. Suits might be filed against the city if it made plans for the redevelopment of neighborhoods without adequate citizen participation.

Everyone also realized that the rebuilding of New Orleans and the meeting of its citizens' needs would take place in a political context. President George W. Bush and several of his top aides, such as FEMA Director Michael Brown and Home-Security Director Michael Chertoff had been widely criticized for their initial tepid response to Hurricane Katrina—and Bush's popularity had plummeted in Katrina's wake. If they were perceived not to care about New Orleans or not to meet its needs effectively, they might suffer political repercussions—particularly because leading Democrats would be likely to make the rebuilding of New Orleans a campaign issue in federal, state, and local elections in succeeding years. Governor Blanco and Mayor Nagin had also been criticized in Katrina's wake for not orchestrating an orderly evacuation of the city and not responding more rapidly to citizens' needs. Were citizens to perceive them as inept, they might be replaced by opponents in primary or general elections in New Orleans and Louisiana.

Governor Blanco's effectiveness as an advocate for New Orleans would partly hinge on her ability to work with the Louisiana delegation, which consisted of representatives and Senators to the Congress from the State including Senator Mary Landrieu. This delegation would be critical to getting resources and policies from the federal government. She cleverly persuaded recently retired Senator John Breaux, the former Democratic Senator from Louisiana with close ties to Congressional leaders from both parties as well as the White House, to work as a liaison to the Administration and Congress for the Louisiana Recovery Authority. His links to both parties would be particularly important because the Republican Party controlled both houses of Congress as well as the presidency.

Much would depend, too, on the outcome of struggles within the Administration and the Republican Party. Some conservative Republicans did not want to commit huge resources to New Orleans—and wanted them mostly to take the form of tax credit and incentives rather than large spending programs. Some Democrats wanted, by contrast, to create a new federal agency modeled after the Tennessee Valley Authority (TVA) with a federal czar who would oversee and even control the rebuilding process.

Bush soon took a middle position: he would commit more than $100 billion to rebuilding New Orleans and the Gulf Coast, but he would leave most key policy and planning decisions to the State and to the city in keeping with conservative values.

The politics of the rebuilding of New Orleans would inevitably be complicated by racial issues. While citizens from all social classes and races suffered devastating losses from Katrina, African Americans suffered particular losses. A disproportionate number of them lived on "low ground" due to the historic placement of their neighborhoods in low-lying areas that were at greater risk during hurricanes that had repeatedly struck New Orleans during the past 150 years. The Ninth Ward, a community that was almost completely occupied by African Americans, had the misfortune to be located by the Industrial Canal even if it was not one of the lowest areas in New Orleans. When its levees were breeched, a huge torrent of water rushed through the community with such force that it destroyed virtually all of its residences and businesses.

Almost at once, the status of the Ninth Ward became a symbolic issue. If many officials wanted *not* to rebuild it, including Mayor Nagin in early fall 2005, many African Americans insisted that it *should* be rebuilt. Even soon after Katrina, moreover, it became clear that many relatively affluent persons as well as some owners of businesses viewed the Hurricane as a way to "cleanse" the city of low-income African-American persons that they perceived to have high rates of crime and welfare. In turn, many African Americans were equally determined that they not receive discriminatory treatment by public officials.

Another racial issue was certain to arise. To the extent that certain low-lying areas that had been places of residence for African Americans were not rebuilt, their former residents could return to New Orleans only if they could find housing in integrated or mostly-white areas higher areas that had sustained less damage or that would be rebuilt—or in relatively white suburban areas. This policy would require the construction of affordable housing and public housing in largely Caucasian neighborhoods. In a city and region that had been among the most segregated in the United States, it remained to be seen if public officials would support integration in the rebuilding of New Orleans.

Policy advocates would need to be creative in post-Katrina New Orleans in seeking allies, sources of resources and favorable policy decisions in parishes, the city, the state, and the federal government. Some of them would have to resort to litigation. They would need to form coalitions. They would need to lobby public officials. They would need to supplement social services with policy advocacy.

New Orleans post-Katrina also illustrates how direct services would both be highly necessary to help citizens recover from their trauma, and insufficient if it became the complete preoccupation of social workers. If policy advocates did not help them secure favorable policies and work to empower them, vulnerable populations might find themselves excluded from New Orleans—or living in a city increasingly dominated by relatively affluent persons with scant interest in keeping them in the city or providing a humane environment for them.

Key elections would assume a major role in shaping outcomes by determining which public officials would make key decisions. Mayor Nagin would face reelection

(continued)

in summer 2006 and Governor Blanco in November 2007. Congressional elections would take place in November 2006—and again, along with presidential elections, in November 2008. The politics of Katrina a would be further complicated, moreover, by that fact that most of the citizens of New Orleans had evacuated the city—with less than half returning a year later. Would African-American evacuees vote in forthcoming elections, even if they could be located and provided absentee ballots—and, if increasingly not, would the changed composition of the city's electorate favor local policies and politicians that favored the interests of relatively affluent citizens?

Policy advocates had a full agenda in New Orleans. They would have to get resource commitments from the Congress by pressuring not only legislative but appropriations committees. They would have to persuade Congress to enact many modifications of current programs for the victims of Katrina, such as extending the weeks persons could receive unemployment insurance and raising eligibility levels for Food Stamps, TANF, and Medicaid to assist non-welfare persons who had lost their homes and jobs. They would need federal commitments to homeowners who had lost homes that were not fully or sufficiently covered by private insurance policies. They would need huge resource commitments so that FEMA could clear and dispose of hundreds of tons of debris from New Orleans and surrounding areas, provide trailers for displaced persons, and meet other survival needs of citizens.

Post-Katrina New Orleans illustrates, as well, how considerable information about specific areas can be gleaned from the Internet. At the federal level, many agencies possessed programs and resources that could be potentially useful to New Orleans and Katrina survivors, including the Department of Defense, FEMA, the National Institute of Mental Health, the National Institute of Health, the Centers for Disease Control and Prevention, the Department of Housing and Urban Development, the Department of Labor, the Department of Commerce with its Small Business Administration and other programs, the Department of Education, and the Department of Transportation. Many of these agencies possessed scores of programs relevant to New Orleans and Katrina's survivors. (Use Google to find their Web sites and to locate relevant programs.)

A large list of agencies existed, as well, at the level of state government—and in the city of New Orleans itself. Go to the State's Web site at **http://www.louisiana.gov**. Or go to the Web site of New Orleans at **http://www.cityofno.com** to find relevant sources in the city. For private charitable agencies in New Orleans post-Katrina, go the Web site of the American Institute of Philanthropy at **http://www.charitywatch**. org. Lists of nongovernmental agencies in New Orleans can be accessed by going to **http://www.neworleanscvb.com/listings/index.cfm/catID/13/**—including ones with specific mental health, child-based, health, and job training programs.

The private sector also should not be ignored. Banks give loans and mortgages crucial to businesses and homeowners. Groceries, large retailers, pharmacies, and other businesses need to be in place for communities to rebuild. The New Orleans Chamber of Commerce, with its list of area businesses that belong to it, can be found at **http://www.neworleanschamber.org**.

What You Can Now Do	# CHAPTER SUMMARY

You are now equipped to do the following:

- Understand how governments are structured
- Understand relations between legislators, lobbyists, interest groups, public opinion, and members of the executive branch
- Find names of key committees in state and federal jurisdictions
- Understand the mindsets of elected officials such as legislators and heads of government
- Know the mindsets of nonelected officials such as civil servants and political appointees
- Understand the political economy of social agencies
- Understand the political economy of programs and social work units within agencies
- Be able to map agencies' policies
- Be able to draw an organizational chart
- Use four overlays to develop a dynamic understanding of a specific social agency
- Understand the political economy of communities

NOTES

1. See James McGregor Burns, *The Power to Lead* (New York: Simon & Schuster, 1984).
2. For discussion of the budget roles of the president, see Aaron Wildavsky, *The New Politics of the Budgetary Process* (Glenview, IL: Scott, Foresman, 1988), pp. 166–186.
3. Abraham Holtzman, *Legislative Liaison: Executive Leadership in the Congress* (Chicago: Rand McNally, 1970).
4. Hedrick Smith, *The Power Game: How Washington Works* (New York: Ballantine Books, 1988), pp. 388–428.
5. Wildavsky, *The New Politics*, pp. 165–212.
6. Smith, *The Power Game*, pp. 41–57.
7. Smith, *The Power Game*, pp. 145–150. For a classic discussion of the different orientations of conservative and liberal constituencies to social legislation, see Lewis Froman, "Interparty Constituency Differences and Congressional Voting Behavior," *American Political Science Review* 57 (March 1963): 57–61.

8. Marilyn Bagwell, *A Political Handbook for Health Professionals* (Boston: Little, Brown, 1985), pp. 63–64.
9. Ibid., pp. 64–66. See also Richard Cheney and Lynne Cheney, *Kings of the Hill* (New York: Continuum, 1983).
10. Bagwell, *Political Handbook*, pp. 67–68.
11. Judith Meredith, *Lobbying on a Shoestring* (Dover, MA: Auburn House, 1989), pp. 65–78.
12. Lewis Froman, *The Congressional Process: Strategies, Rules, and Procedures* (Boston: Little, Brown, 1967).
13. Glenn Abney and Thomas Lauth, *The Politics of State and City Administration* (Albany: State University of New York Press, 1986), pp. 130–212.
14. Laurence Lynn, *Managing Public Policy* (Boston: Little, Brown, 1987).
15. Smith, *The Power Game*, pp. 270–326.
16. For a discussion of links between legislatures and civil servants, see J. Weatherford McIver,

Tribes on the Hill (New York: Rawson Wade, 1981), pp. 87–111.

17. Interactions between lobbyists and legislators are discussed throughout Jeffrey Birnbaum and Alan Murray, *Showdown at Gucci Gulch* (New York: Vintage Books, 1987).

18. See Policy Advocacy Challenge 11.1 in this book for a detailed discussion of the tactics used by lobbyists.

19. The role of funds from special interests and affluent Americans in campaigns and politics is discussed by Thomas Edsall, *The New Politics of Inequality* (New York: Norton, 1984).

20. See, for example, James Smith, *Brookings at Seventy-Five* (Washington, DC: Brookings Institution, 1991).

21. McIver, *Tribes on the Hill*, pp. 87–111.

22. See R. Douglas Arnold, *The Logic of Congressional Action* (New Haven, CT: Yale University Press, 1990), pp. 1–87.

23. Lynn, *Managing Public Policy*, pp. 68–73.

25. Arnold, *The Logic of Congressional Action*, pp. 60–87.

25. Ibid.

26. Smith, *The Power Game*, pp. 119–159.

27. Ibid., pp. 119–159; and Willard Richan, *Lobbying for Social Change* (New York: Haworth Press, 1991), pp. 53–54.

28. Smith, *The Power Game*, pp. 270–284.

29. Arnold, *The Logic of Congressional Action*, pp. 141–144.

30. For a discussion of the need not to write off conservatives when developing coalitions, see Nancy Amidei, "How to Be an Advocate in Bad Times," *Public Welfare* 40 (Summer 1982): 41.

31. As an example of the ambiguous signals that high-level political appointees often receive from heads of government, see the roles of Elliot Richardson and Edward Zigler in my case study titled "An Extended Policy-Practice Case: Child Development and Daycare," in *Social Welfare Policy: From Theory to Practice* (Belmont, CA: Wadsworth, 1990), pp. 350–377.

32. Richan, *Lobbying for Social Change*, pp. 60–62.

33. See Ron Dear and Rino Patti, "Legislative Advocacy: Seven Effective Tactics," in Maryann Mahaffey and John Hanks, eds., *Practical Politics: Social Work and Political Responsibility*

(Silver Spring, MD: National Association of Social Workers, 1982), pp. 107–108.

34. An example of a civil servant's resistance to a policy advocate is provided by William Bell and Budd Bell, "Monitoring the Bureaucracy: An Extension of Legislative Lobbying," in Mahaffey and Hanks, *Practical Politics*, pp. 128–130.

35. Yeheskel Hasenfeld, *Human Service Organizations* (Englewood Cliffs, NJ: Prentice Hall, 1983), pp. 43–49.

36. Economic pressures on human service organizations in the 1980s and 1990s are discussed by Stepen Webster and Mary Wylie, "Strategic Planning in a Competitive Environment," *Administration in Mental Health* 15 (Fall 1988): 25–44.

37. Hasenfeld, *Human Service Organizations*, pp. 50–83.

38. Mayer Zald, *Organizational Change: The Political Economy of the YMCA* (Chicago: University of Chicago Press, 1970).

39. Jean Potuchek, "The Context of Social Service Funding: The Funding Relationship," *Social Service Review* 60 (September 1986): 421–436.

40. Bruce Jansson and June Simmons, "The Survival of Social Work Departments," *Social Work* 31 (September 1986): 339–344.

41. Bruce Jansson and June Simmons, "The Ecology of Social Work Departments," *Social Work in Health Care* 11 (Winter 1985): 1–16, and Bruce Jansson and June Simmons, "Building Department or Unit Power within Human Service Organizations," *Administration in Social Work* 8 (Fall 1984): 41–56.

42. Robert Goodin, *Reasons for Welfare* (Princeton, NJ: Princeton University Press, 1988), pp. 190–193.

43. See *Tarasoff v. Regents of the University of California*, 1976. 17 Cal. 4d 425.

44. Hasenfeld, *Human Service Organizations*, pp. 84–109.

45. For a discussion of the politics of money in organizations, see Burton Gummer, *The Politics of Social Administration: Managing Organizational Politics in Social Agencies* (Englewood Cliffs, NJ: Prentice Hall, 1990), pp. 46–67.

46. For a critical view of federated fund raising, see Stanley Wenocur, "A Pluralistic Planning Model for United Way Organizations," *Social Service Review* 50 (December 1976): 586–600. See also Eleanor Brilliant, *The United Way: Dilemmas of Organized Charity* (New York: Columbia University Press, 1990).

47. Murray Gruber, ed., *Management Systems in the Human Services* (Philadelphia: Temple University Press, 1981), pp. 87–96.

48. A case study of the divergence between high-level official policy and the actual operative policies in agencies is provided by Franklin Chu and Sharland Trotter, *The Madness Establishment* (New York: Grossman, 1974).

49. Gummer, *The Politics of Social Administration*, pp. 10–11, 19–20, 162–163.

50. Goodin, *Reasons for Welfare*, pp. 190–193.

51. Hans Gerth and C. Wright Mills, eds., *From Max Weber: Essays in Sociology* (New York: Oxford University Press, 1946).

52. Gummer, *The Politics of Social Administration*, pp. 11–13.

53. Existing organizational theory, which presents a variety of factors that shape outcomes and behavior, is suggestive of the concept of overlays. Different authors emphasize different structural, political, and economic factors, as well as the informal culture of organizations. While placing organizational behavior in a political-economic framework, for example, Hasenfeld discusses these various factors in *Human Service Organizations.*

54. See, for example, Sheldon Gelman, "The Board of Directors and Agency Accountability," *Social Casework* 64 (February 1983): 83–91.

55. Robert Dahl, *Pluralist Democracy in the United States* (Chicago: Rand McNally, 1967).

56. Hasenfeld, *Human Service Organizations*, p. 8.

57. For a discussion of neighborhoods, see James Cunningham, "Are Neighborhoods Real? A Review Essay," *Urban Resources* 1 (Winter 1984): 19–22.

58. Roland Warren, *New Perspectives on the American Community* (Homewood, IL: Dorsey Press, 1977), pp. 260–365.

59. Milan Dluhy, *Building Coalitions in the Human Services* (Newbury Park, CA: Sage, 1990).

SUGGESTED READINGS

Legislatures

R. Douglas Arnold, *The Logic of Congressional Action* (New Haven, CT: Yale University Press, 1990).

J. Weatherford McIver, *Tribes on the Hill* (New York: Rawson, Wade, 1981).

Hedrick Smith, *The Power Game: How Washington Works* (New York: Ballantine Books, 1988), pp. 119–160, 270–326.

Government Bureaucracies

Laurence Lynn, *Managing Public Policy* (Boston: Little, Brown, 1987).

Interest Groups and Lobbyists

Marilyn Bagwell, *A Political Handbook for Health Professionals* (Boston: Little, Brown, 1985).

Hedrick Smith, *The Power Game: How Washington Works* (New York: Ballantine Books, 1988), pp. 215–269.

Policies of Social Agencies

Burton Gummer, *The Politics of Social Administration: Managing Organizational Politics in Social Agencies* (Englewood Cliffs, NJ: Prentice Hall, 1990).

The Political Economy of Services

Michael Fabricant and Steve Burghardt, *The Welfare State Crisis and the Transformation of Social Service Work* (Armonk, NY: Sharpe, 1992).

Yeheskel Hasenfeld, *Human Service Organizations* (Englewood Cliffs, NJ: Prentice Hall, 1983).

Expanding Policy Advocacy
Across National Borders

**(This chapter is co-authored with Dennis Kao, MSW
and doctoral student at the USC School of Social Work)**

POLICY PREDICAMENT	If the last chapter focused on policy institutions and processes within the United States, this chapter broadens the horizon to include global realities and institutions—not only as they contribute to social problems abroad but within the United States. In Policy Advocacy Challenge 5.7 at the end of this chapter, we will discuss some ways that globalization shaped events in New Orleans, including greatly expanding its homeless and migrant populations

Social Problems in an Interdependent World

Globalization is a broad and complex phenomenon that impacts almost every aspect of the United States and most nations, including their economies, educational systems, health and human service systems, relations among ethnic groups, patterns of immigration and emigration, mass media, and cultures. Even though many definitions of globalization exist, most of them emphasize the massive movement in recent decades of capital, jobs, labor, and culture across national boundaries. (Such movements have long existed, but their magnitude has vastly increased to the point that virtually all nations are deeply enmeshed in these global movements.)

Banks and financiers in industrialized nations make loans, for example, to governments and entrepreneurs in developing nations. American firms outsource jobs to developing nations, such as having personnel in India respond to inquiries from American consumers about credit applications. American and other industrial nations place automobile plants and garment factories in developing nations such as Mexico and Thailand. Often lured by the prospect of jobs, millions of migrants have crossed international borders from developing nations to industrial nations in the last decade—just as entrepreneurs in industrial nations often relocate in developing nations to gain access to their markets. Even diseases and pollution cross national boundaries—and the world risks the effects of global warming that will impact all nations in coming years.

The Internet represents the most dramatic example of globalization. Persons in remote parts of developing nations who have Internet access can reach thousands of Web sites that give them music, news, and entertainment from many other nations. Improvements in transportation across national boundaries has also speeded globalization as persons routinely fly between distant nations.

Globalization has brought many benefits to nations and citizens. It has created jobs in many developing nations. It has fostered the sharing of technology and information across national boundaries—even allowing citizens in developing nations to obtain a considerable portion of their education from distance education on the Internet from industrial nations. It has created markets for industries in industrialized nations. It has stimulated technological innovation.

But globalization has a darker side in industrialized nations like the United States. It has led to the loss of jobs of many American workers—and sometimes led to reductions in their pay and benefits. It has undermined some American trade unions. It has widened the gap between relatively well-educated and skilled workers and many relatively uneducated and unskilled workers in some regions of the United States. It has sometimes degraded environmental standards and working conditions. It has increased the vulnerability of some Americans to illnesses that spread across international boundaries. It has led to huge migration flows to the United States, whose members are often victimized by American employers in agri-business, tourist, construction, restaurant, and other businesses.

It has also had a darker side in many developing nations. It has sometimes destabilized their economies, exposed workers to harsh working conditions and low pay, and encouraged child labor. It has sometimes contributed to growing inequality. It has undermined indigenous traditions with American culture, whose music and films have dramatically impacted other nations. It has increased pollution in some nations. It has fostered such rapid movements of persons from rural to urban areas in some nations that huge numbers of rural migrants face poverty and disease in urban areas in nations that lack resources and human service systems to help them. It has fostered, as well, massive movements of persons across borders—with some of them occupying a marginal and illegal status that had accentuated their poverty and other problems in the destination nations.

Policy advocates must therefore expand their horizons to include issues and problems that cross international boundaries in coming decades if they wish to help vulnerable populations that are impacted by globalization—both at home and abroad. They need to develop social policies that will prevent or offset some of globalization's negative consequences while embracing some of its positive impacts.

Why Globalization Sometimes Harms Vulnerable Populations in the United States

Globalization is viewed by many Americans as a positive phenomenon, but support seems to have waned somewhat in the past 5 years according to a 2004 poll conducted by the Program on International Policy Attitudes (PIPA).[1] In its study, PIPA found that

40 percent of Americans viewed the process of globalization in 2004 as "more positive," down from 53 percent in 1999. The report also saw increases in the percentages of Americans who viewed the process of globalization as "equally negative and positive" (from 30 percent in 1999 to 39 percent in 2000) and "more negative" (15 percent to 19 percent). Furthermore, twice as many Americans felt that the goal of the United States should be to either "try to slow it down" or "try to stop or reverse it" (38 percent) as opposed to "try to actively promote it" (19 percent).

These growing reservations in the United States stem in considerable measure from the fact that many Americans attribute their erosion or stagnation of living standards to globalization even if economists disagree about globalization's contribution to them. The gap between the richest fifth and the poorest fifth of Americans has widened as compared to the late 1960s as the United States has replaced a significant portion of its unionized and relatively well-paying industrial jobs with lower-paying service jobs. The living standard of many American workers has remained stagnant, moreover, during the past 5 years. In 2004, 37 million people, or 12.7 percent of the total population, were living under the federal poverty level, including 13 million children and 3.5 million seniors.[2]

It is appropriate to ask to what extent these income and job losses and economic stagnation have been caused by globalization or other factors—and to note that globalization has sometimes facilitated economic growth in the United States. It is nonetheless clear that many American industrial jobs have migrated to developing nations as corporations seek higher profits by replacing American workers with low-wage workers. Some corporations also increase their profits by not investing sufficiently in work safety and anti-pollution equipment in developing nations, aided by scant environmental or work safety regulations in them. They enhance their profits, moreover, by paying little or no taxes in many developing nations, inhibiting their ability to fund social programs.

The exodus of jobs from the United States began in the 1960s when automobile companies began to place their plants in such nations as Mexico, dealing a mortal blow in succeeding decades to the economies of such cities as Flint and Detroit, Michigan. Other industries followed suit, including textile, steel, furniture, and many manufacturing jobs. More recently, service jobs have been outsourced to companies in other nations, such as certain clerical, customer service, and engineering jobs.

Many American workers and trade unions became even more worried when American presidents and many congressmen embraced free-trade agreements, such as the North American Free Trade Agreement (NAFTA) during the presidency of Bill Clinton—and subsequently many additional trade agreements. While protective tariffs had often shielded American workers from foreign companies that exported goods to the United States that were cheaper than American goods, many of these tariffs had been markedly reduced or even terminated in the 1990s and during the administration of George W. Bush.

Some positive benefits have accrued from economic globalization. American consumers reduced their cost of living by purchasing inexpensive imported goods. The United States found new markets for its products in developing nations. Globalization spurred greater attention by many nations to their shared pollution risks—even though the United States failed to sign the ground-breaking Kyoto Treaty in 1997 or subsequently that required assenting nations to reduce carbon dioxide gas emissions that were widely believed to cause global warming.

If optimists contended that "all boats rise" during globalization, other experts predicted a "race to the bottom" among nations. In this scenario, nations cut corporate taxes, protections for labor, and protections for the environment to lure corporations to their shores. As they cut corporate and other taxes, nations are forced to cut their welfare states. Some experts fear that this competitive dynamic has increased economic inequality in many nations, not to mention the well-being of their vulnerable populations (See Policy Advocacy Challenge 5.1).

**POLICY
ADVOCACY
CHALLENGE 5.1**

Issues Raised by
Wal-Mart in a
Global Context

A fierce debate about the merits of Wal-Mart, the corporate giant of American retailing, exemplifies the emerging controversy within the United States about globalization and corporate responsibility. Founded in 1962 in Rogers, Arkansas, Wal-Mart had developed a worldwide chain of discount stores, grocery stores, and hypermarkets by 2006 that produced revenues of more than $315 billion dollars and was the largest private employer in the United States and Mexico. One of its founders, Sam Walton, viewed its corporate mission as providing products at discount prices to consumers— viewing it as a friend of low-income persons who could save resources by purchasing its products.

Its critics contended, however, that Wal-Mart achieved its low prices by purchasing many of its products from contractors and producers in developing nations who underbid other producers by paying excessively low wages and giving poor working conditions to their employees. They argued, as well, the Wal-Mart followed similar policies with its own employees, not only paying low wages, but denying many of them health and other benefits. These purchasing and employee policies, they argued, often forced more ethical competing companies—out of business since they could not successfully compete against Wal-Mart.

Wal-Mart was not the only American corporation to be criticized for aggressively obtaining its products from contractors and manufacturers in developing nations that underpaid workers and subjected them to poor working conditions. As one example, Nike, the seller of athletic shoes, had widely been criticized for underselling competitors by using similar tactics. If Nike diminished this criticism by monitoring the labor policies of contractors and manufacturers abroad, however, Wal-Mart was not able to quell controversy surrounding it as competing groups argued for and against Wal-Mart. Wal-Mart supported its policies by forming a group called Working Families for Wal-Mart in late 2005 with the former civil rights activist, Andrew Young, as its chairperson. Trade unions, in turn, formed several organizations that sought to change Wal-Mart's labor policies at home and abroad, including Wake Up Wal-Mart (the United Food and Commercial Workers) and Wal-Mart Watch (the Services Employees International Union).

The groups formed by trade unions mostly criticized Wal-Mart's labor policies, as well as the aggressive strategies it used to obtain approval from local areas to construct its stores. They criticized, for example, its low wages and its refusal to provide many employees with health insurance—policies that often contributed to local poverty and that required American taxpayers to foot the bill for such programs as Medicaid that were widely used by Wal-Mart employees. But they also criticized Wal-Mart's

(continued)

exploitation of labor in other nations. In Bangladesh where the average annual income of citizens is only $400, nearly 2 million workers produce clothing exports worth $5 billion with most of it purchased by such American companies as Kmart, GAP, and Wal-Mart.[1]

These companies *did* require contractors and manufacturers not to use child labor in Bangladesh after opposition from human rights groups in the 1990s, but many abuses remained in 2006. When NBC News set up a fictional American company wanting to purchase clothing from manufacturers in Bangladesh, they discovered that their promises to heed working and pay regulations for their workers were often violated. Workers frequently were denied breaks, required to sit on stools with no backs, and provided with no air conditioning so that temperatures often exceeded 90 degrees. Employees often were given excessive production quotas with the stipulation that they had to work overtime with no pay if they failed to meet them. Many workers were required to work more than 70 hours per week—or 10 hours greater than permitted by local laws. Some workers were required to work 18 hours straight to meet production deadlines. When American companies sent inspectors to check on working conditions, workers often gave them false information for fear they would be fired.

Nor were workers reimbursed at levels they often promised American companies. In one factory, for example, workers were paid 12 cents per hour to start, rising to 19 cents when they became "senior operators." These low wages, in turn, place workers in extreme poverty with more than 30 families sometimes sharing one cooking area, with little protein in their diets,

While many contractors and manufacturers in Bangladesh are greedy, some might raise wages if they received even slightly higher purchase prices from companies like Wal-Mart. Intent on keeping its prices low and increasing its profits, however, Wal-Mart often refuses not only to accept products even a cent more costly—but often insists that manufacturers in Bangladesh *lower* their prices each year.

Such hard-fisted purchasing policies by corporations like Wal-Mart not only allow them to undersell other American corporations, but to pocket huge profits. When a worker from Bangladesh was flown to the United States, she was astonished to find that a single pair of pants sold for the equivalent of a single week's pay for her—or $12.84.

Wal-Mart's spokespersons, in turn, argue that its hard-fisted purchasing policies led to lower prices for its hard-pressed American consumers, many of whom cannot make ends meet. They contend, as well, that "the wages and benefits we provide have helped improve the lives of many thousands of workers of the world." They also deny that they require lower prices each year from manufacturers in developing nations. Not only did Wal-Mart deny allegations against it, but it sought to convince the WTO in late 2005 at its meeting in Hong Kong to pass a regulation forbidding any nation from restricting the placement of foreign-owned businesses in specific neighborhoods—and attempted to stop other nations from following the example of many American communities that refused to allow Wal-Mart stores to be constructed in their neighborhoods.

The Wal-Mart controversy continues to simmer in the United States. The Chair of the group it formed to defend its policies, Andrew Young, resigned from his position in August 2006 after apologizing for a statement he made that argued that Wal-Mart had emancipated low-income African American persons from Jewish, Arab, and Korean

──────────

[1] See the NBC Dateline hidden camera investigation of labor practices in Bangladesh, "The Human Costs Behind Bargain Shopping" at http://msnbc.msn.com/id/8243331/

shop grocery-store owners who had "ripped off" urban communities for years by "selling us stale bread and bad meat and wilted vegetables. . . . you see those are the people who have been overcharging us (before) they sold out and moved to Florida."

Controversies surrounding Wal-Mart illustrate corporations from industrialized nations are enmeshed in globalization. Consider these questions:

1. Can "responsible corporations" that truly insist upon human labor practices abroad compete with corporations that do not? If not, what kinds of international regulations, such as ones stated in treaties, are needed—and what kinds of monitoring procedures?
2. To the extent that the United States has high levels of poverty, is it ethically correct for Wal-Mart to lower prices for these persons through purchasing policies abroad that create hardships for workers in developing nations?

Why an Economic Gap Developed Between Developing and Developed Nations

To understand why developing nations have often been harmed by globalization, we need to understand why a substantial economic gap developed between them and developed nations. Virtually the entire world was impoverished as recently as 1820 when the average income of European nations was only about 90 percent of the current income of African nations and when Europeans' average life expectancy was merely 40 years of age. The world population barely grew from 1000 AD to 1800 AD from its base of roughly 1 billion persons.

Then everything changed. World population zoomed upward by six times from 1800 to the present. World per capita average income climbed nine times in the same period (or 15 times in Europe and 25 times in the United States). Total world economic output increased by 49 times.

This revolution in the world's economy and population created a new phenomenon: a gap between relatively affluent and less affluent nations. If average income had been roughly the same in different nations in 1800, the gap between American average income had become 20 times greater than African average income by 2000—and Europe and Japan developed similar disparities against most other nations in Africa, Asia, Central America, and South America. These disparities between developed and developing nations did not grow overnight, but over the long haul as more affluent nations grew annually two to three times more rapidly than African nations, yielding an enormous discrepancy over a period of 200 years.

Many scholars argue convincingly that the economic gap between developed and developing nations was *not* caused by intrinsic differences between their citizens, such as in their intelligence or other personal characteristics. Instead, some nations moved forward economically as compared to others because they gained access to technology that allowed them to produce and harness power primarily from fossil fuels such as coal and (later) petroleum. They used this power to create the industrial revolution that allowed them to mass produce a wide array of products in factories. They used it to allow them to produce crops of vast size. They harnessed power, moreover, to develop mass transit, to make machines that allowed them to farm large tracts of land with relatively little labor, to manufacture ships driven by engines, to build infrastructure, and to distribute electricity to large segments of their populations. They also used power to mine minerals such as iron ore and copper which they used to make steel and many other products that were essential to the construction of machines and the transmission of energy. They developed market economies as they created systems of banking and currency that allowed businesses to get loans and to invest their resources.

These technological advances, in turn, led to a geometric increase in per capita wealth in industrializing nations. Emancipated from reliance on manual labor to farm and to make goods, persons could mass-produce goods and could farm large tracts of land with relatively little labor. With the growing profits that they received, entrepreneurs could hire large work forces and reimburse them at steadily increasing rates, even if recessions often led to periodic economic turndowns.

Europeans got access to technology by a series of fortuitous circumstances. Even before the industrial order began, Europeans benefited from inventions made by persons in the Middle East who learned how to domesticate many kinds of animals such as cattle, horses, goats, pigs, and sheep. These animals, in turn, not only gave them relatively large quantities of food and fiber, but allowed them to cultivate crops relatively efficiently with horses, mules, and oxen. (Close proximity to these animals also immunized them to those many diseases that spread from animals to people—diseases that would soon kill as much as 90 percent of the populations of indigenous persons in South and North America in the aftermath of European immigration to these areas because they lacked this immunity partly because they had not domesticated many animals.) They learned from Middle-Easterners how to smelt iron ore to make iron and how to make gunpowder, swords, and guns, which helped them to conquer large areas in Africa, South and Central America, and North America where they got access to gold and timber and other commodities that fueled their economic growth.

Great Britain had other kinds of good fortune that helped it to begin to industrialize even in the latter part of the 18th century. With its traditions of political liberty, it was relatively open to new ideas such as breakthroughs in science, mathematics and technology that led to many inventions. Since it protected property rights, entrepreneurs had an incentive to increase their holdings. Because it was an island and had a powerful navy, it could protect its emerging industries from invasion. It had copious quantities of coal and iron ore that it could transport with its many rivers and canals—and then with its railroad system. It could feed its urbanized citizens with a robust agricultural sector due to its climate and soils, as well as emerging agricultural technology.

With similar advantages, other European nations, as well as the British colonies and the United States, replicated Britain's movement toward industrialization with remarkable speed as steam engines, railroads, telegraphs, ocean steamers, electrification, and the internal combustion engine following in rapid succession. Europeans, British colonies, and the United States had colonized or controlled large sections of the globe by 1900.

It seemed that Europe, the United States, and former British colonies, as well as Japan, would squander their economic advantage over the rest of the world when they engaged in two world wars in the early and middle portion of the 20th century and experienced marked economic downturns that included the Great Depression of the 1930s. As we discuss subsequently, however, they evolved various international organizations and treaties, as well as internal banking systems and economic policies, that allowed them to mitigate the economic chaos caused by these difficult events.

As Europe, the United States, and other nations made this transition from reliance on human labor to machines, large parts of the rest of the world failed to gain access to technology, so their economies remained powered primarily by human labor rather than machines and fossil fuels. Their per capita incomes barely rose. They were victimized by Europeans who invaded them, plundered them, took their timber and minerals, and killed vast numbers of them with diseases to which they had little immunity. They mostly provided raw commodities to industrialized nations rather than trading with them as equals.

A series of interrelated factors enmeshed these nations in poverty. Many of them did not possess minerals or their lands were arid or landlocked. People who lived in tropical areas were often devastated by tropical diseases. Lacking resources that industrializing nations developed as their economies grew, the governments of developing nations could not invest in infrastructure and educational systems. They often had governments that were relatively corrupt—and they lacked judicial systems and ways of protecting property rights for those persons and corporations that might invest in their domestic economies or develop innovations. They often denied women basic rights; diminishing their contributions to the economy. They had such small local markets that few incentives existed to develop innovations. With high fertility rates, women could not contribute to economic growth because they were mired in family roles—and these large families often lacked the resources to invest in their children's education.

Large parts of the world were relatively poor as compared to Europe, former British colonies, the United States, and Japan during the 20th century. (Japan had industrialized before and after World War II.) Even the Union of Soviet Socialist Republics (USSR), before its dissolution in 1991 into separate republics, was relatively poor—even if it had developed an industrial order in the middle and latter part of the 20th century.

Considerable differences nonetheless existed among developing nations by 2000. Some of them, such as India and China, had made considerable economic progress. Others, such as Bangladesh, had promoted growing numbers of small businesses. Yet others, such as Malawi, remained mired in deep and persistent poverty. Jeffrey Sachs, a leading development economist, estimates that about one-sixth of the world's population resembles Malawi whereas one-half of the world's population is relatively poor but making progress toward less infant mortality, more education, and better sanitation.[3] According to the World Bank, about 2 billion persons lived in poverty in 2002.[4] (For information about how to learn more about developing nations, see Policy Advocacy 5.2.)

POLICY ADVOCACY CHALLENGE 5.2

Using the Web to Find International Data

RACHEL KATZ, MPP

Researching international social policy issues can be difficult because the quality and quantity of information available varies widely across sources. Some Web sites contain comparative country data that allow you to examine differences and similarities between countries. These tend to be Web sites of international organizations, which collect data from individual countries and compile it in a central location. Other Web sites, specifically national Web sites, provide only data limited to specific countries. Because national Web sites vary in content and quality, it may be difficult to find the information you need and you should assess the reliability of the data. An additional challenge when accessing national Web sites may be language. Because a country's Web site is likely available only in the national language, you must be familiar with the language in order to navigate the site.

(continued)

Here are some sources of international data:

Organisation for Economic Co-operation and Development   This is an international organization with 30 member nations. It is a good source of information on economic and social issues in these countries, with much data on social and welfare indicators and policies as well as analyses of social conditions. You can access comparative data or data by country.
http://www.oecd.org

United Nations   The UN currently has 191 member nations, and its Web site is a good source for comparative data on social indicators. The UN Web site also contains a database listing that may provide links to organizations involved in advocacy efforts, including humanitarian relief agencies and international NGOs.
http://www.un.org

CIA   The Central Intelligence Agency publishes The World Factbook every year, which provides a basic set of data on every country, including statistics related to population, government, and health systems.
http://www.cia.gov/cia/publications/factbook/

U.S. Census Bureau   Within the Population Division, the Census Bureau operates an International Programs Center, which provides demographic and socioeconomic statistics on 227 countries or "independent states" and "areas" of the world. The IDB offers both historical data dating back as far as 1950 and projections available out to 2050.
http://www.census.gov/ipc/www/

Government Web Sites   You may search for data through national Web sites. Here are two Web sites that provide links to the Web sites of individual countries:

- **http://www.psr.keele.ac.uk/official.htm**
- **http://www.library.northwestern.edu/govpub/resource/internat/foreign.html**

Some national Web sites offer links to statistical databases. For example, Mexico has a National Institute of Statistics Geography and Informatics, which can be accessed at **http://www.inegi.gob.mx/inegi/default.asp** (available in Spanish only). Taiwan has a Government Information Office, with information available in English at **http://www.gio.gov.tw/**.

University Library Resources   Many university libraries subscribe to database services that can provide additional international data sources. Visit the reference or database listing section of your university library's Web site or talk to a reference librarian for assistance. Here is a listing of some of the databases with information on international topics that your university library may subscribe to:

- Columbia International Affairs Online. CIAO offers basic comparative data on all countries, including birth rates, mortality rates, GDP, etc.

- Economist Intelligence Unit. EIU offers data on approximately 200 countries including information on social issues in their Country Reports and Country Profiles.
- Statistical Universe. This database is accessed through LexisNexis, and allows you to search for comparative data on a wide range of topics.

∽ EXERCISE ∾

Visit the U.S. Census Bureau International Programs Center Web site and collect data for all available years on the infant mortality rates of Latin America and the Caribbean, eastern Europe, and western Europe. Look at how the rates have changed over time and how they are projected to change over the next several decades in these three regions. Which region has the highest infant mortality rate today? Which has the lowest? Which region is projected to have the highest infant mortality rate in the year 2050? Which is projected to have the lowest? Based on this data, think about what types of efforts a policy advocate interested in public health might undertake in one or more of these regions to decrease the incidence of infant mortality.

The challenge facing the world is to cut extreme poverty in the world—and then to end it. When endorsing the UN Millennium Development Goal in 2000, 191 nations pledged to cut world poverty by one-half by 2015 and to end extreme poverty by 2025. To accomplish this goal, however, such nations as the United States will have to pledge far greater resources to other nations than they currently contribute.

Why Globalization Sometimes Harms Vulnerable Persons in Developing Nations

When globalization accelerated in the 1980s, it was accompanied by a policy consensus known as the Washington Consensus among top officials in the United States, as well as some European nations, about ways to foster it. They wanted to promote it in ways that would advance an *economic model of "free market capitalism"*—a theory widely credited to the British economist David Ricardo who postulated that free trade should be developed so that specific nations specialize in producing only those goods and services where they have a competitive advantage, producing these goods not only for internal consumption, but for export. In turn, they should import products from other countries that are produced more efficiently elsewhere. In his best-selling book on globalization, *The Lexus and the Olive Tree*, New York columnist and Pulitzer Prize recipient Thomas Friedman (2000) wrote, "Those countries that are most willing to let capitalism quickly destroy inefficient companies, so that money can be freed up and directed to more innovative ones, will thrive in the era of globalization." (p. 11)[5]

If advocates of the Washington Consensus favored eventual elimination of tariffs, they also believed that nations should gradually reduce special subsidies or corporate tax concessions that might give their products an unfair advantage in a free-trade world. They favored, as well, fiscal discipline in government spending so that nations had relatively little budget deficits and debt, reduction of marginal tax rates, free movement of capital from developed into developing nations, privatization of public enterprises, and developing private property rights.

Many of the advocates of the Washington Consensus wanted to use international organizations and treaties to pressure developing nations to adopt these economic principles—including Russia and China as well as many nations in Latin and South America, Africa, and Asia. They had at their disposal the International Monetary Fund (IMF) that was created in the wake of World War II to rebuild Europe by providing loans and grants to specific nations that come from contributions of different nations. It is dominated by the major developed nations—and particularly by the United States which is the only nation that has a veto over its decisions. The IMF was supplemented by the World Bank, which lent money to nations for projects like roads and dams. The General Agreement on Tariffs and Trade (GATT) was also established after World War II to promote tariff-reduction agreements between nations. Wanting even greater reduction in tariffs, policy makers established the World Trade Organization (WTO) in 1995 to serve as a forum for trade negotiations between nations, as well as to enforce their decisions through specific penalties and fines. (Individual nations can file grievances against other nations that unfairly seek advantages for their corporations in international trade through protective tariffs or governmental subsidies.)

In his *Globalization and its Discontents*, Joseph Stiglitz (2002), a Nobel-prize winning economist, documents how the IMF, World Bank, and WTO were often dominated not only by the United States, but by the Washington Consensus particularly from the 1980s onward.[6] (Both the IMF and the World Bank have their headquarters in Washington, DC) Prigoff (2000) discusses how British economist John Maynard Keynes had lost the fight to actually locate the World Bank in London because he felt that "the fund might be more independent of the U.S. government than it would be in Washington, DC." (p. 116).[7]

Imposition of the views of the Washington Consensus on developing nations often exacerbated their economic problems partly because these nations faced a catch-22 dilemma. In order to stimulate economic growth, they had to invest considerable resources in their infrastructure (such as roads, public buildings, and dams) as well as their citizens (such as schools, human services, and health services). Yet they often possessed relatively meager tax revenues to cover these expenditures precisely because their national economies were relatively small. When they sought loans and grants from the IMF and World Bank to help them fund these expenditures, they often discovered that these institutions would give them resources *only* if they cut their spending markedly to reduce their budget deficits—a policy that forced them to cut spending on programs for vulnerable populations and their infrastructure. These spending cuts not only increased inequality in their nations, but curtailed programs needed to stimulate their economic growth.

Stiglitz (2002) contends, moreover, that the IMF and World Bank wrongly pressured some developing nations to privatize publicly held firms, such as banks, energy-producing companies, and utilities. This policy sometimes led, he argues, to acquisition of these concerns by criminal elements at cut-rate prices—a development likely to occur in nations that did not yet possess law enforcement and monitoring procedures of more advanced economies. Better, he contends, to move more gradually toward private property than to impose this policy all at once.[8]

The IMF, World Bank, and WTO sometimes stimulated greater inequality in developing nations, as well, when they demanded deep reductions in some of their tariffs. In the case of agricultural products, for example, large American agricultural concerns, which operate efficiently due to their very size and their use of expensive equipment, have an economic advantage over the small agricultural producers of developing nations, such as peasants in the Chiapas region of Mexico. When pressured to cut tariffs on agricultural products, peasants were often forced into bankruptcy—hastening their migration to cities or across borders where they often faced extreme poverty such as in shanty towns that ringed many Mexican cities. To add insult to injury, the United States sometimes gave its agricultural producers large subsidies at the very time that it asked developing nations to end their agricultural tariffs, giving the American producers an even greater advantage over peasants.

Other forms of victimization of developing nations took place. As corporations shift their production to these countries, they are also focusing their sales efforts in these emerging markets. Unfortunately, they sometimes sell "lower-quality products or products that are outright toxic and thus banned in the industrialized countries" (Khor, 1996, p. 49), such as: pharmaceutical drugs or contraceptives that have been banned in Europe, the United States, or Japan; cigarettes with high tar or nicotine content; and diluted or contaminated baby formulas.[9]

Corporations also victimized many of their workers in developing nations. They often used child labor; exposed workers to unsafe working conditions; paid excessively low wages; made workers work for excessive hours per week; did not give workers benefits; and laid workers off with no advance notice. They often failed to install anti-pollution equipment on their factories.

Another Vulnerable Population: Migrants Within and Between Nations

Globalization has been associated with unprecedented movements of people in the last five decades—both within specific nations and between nations. As nations like China have rapidly industrialized, roughly 120 million rural migrants have migrated to urban areas in just the past decade—persons who have often experienced great hardships because they are denied public education, health care (aside from brief emergency care), and other amenities. Such migrations to urban areas have taken place in all developing nations with similar adverse consequences for many migrants. Yet these migrants choose to move to urban areas precisely because their economic situation is intolerable in rural areas, where population increases often mean that insufficient arable land or jobs exist to support them. (Even the low wages of many factories in developing nations far exceed the incomes persons can receive in rural areas.)

Migrants to urban areas in many developing nations have uncertain legal status. In China, for example, migrants who move to urban areas without required permits lack residency status, so many of them are not even allowed to use public schools or to get benefits from many government programs. Huge shanty towns have developed on the periphery of Mexico City, Beijing, and Caracas where migrants living in unhealthy settings and in dire poverty.

Massive migrations have also occurred between nations (see Policy Advocacy Challenge 5.3). Approximately 175 million people live outside their nations of birth in 2000. Approximately 16 million of them were recognized refugees and almost 1 million were asylum seekers who were involuntarily displaced from their homes by actual or feared persecution by the governments of their nations of origin.[10]

POLICY ADVOCACY CHALLENGE 5.3

Web Sites Pertaining to Migrants or Immigrants in the United States and Abroad

Dennis Kao, MSW, Doctoral Student, School of Social Work, University of Southern California

UNITED STATES

Asian American Justice Center   Founded in 1991, AAJC (formerly the National Asian Pacific American Legal Consortium) works to "advance the human and civil rights of Asian Americans through advocacy, public policy, public education, and litigation." In addition to immigrant rights and immigration issues, AAJC also works on affirmative action, hate crimes prevention/race relations, census, language access, and voting rights. **http://www.advancingequality.org**

Center for Immigration Studies   CIS—founded in 1985—is an independent, nonpartisan, nonprofit research organization devoted to research and policy analysis dealing with the economic, social, demographic, fiscal, and other implications of immigration for the United States. Its mission is "to expand the base of public knowledge and understanding of the need for an immigration policy that gives first concern to the broad national interest." **http://www.cis.org/**

Federation for American Immigration Reform   FAIR is a national nonprofit membership organization of more than 198,000 members, which "seeks to improve border security, to stop illegal immigration, and to promote immigration levels consistent with the national interest." **http://www.fairus.org**

Migration Policy Institute   Founded in 2001, MPI is an independent, nonpartisan, nonprofit research organization, which conducts research on the movement of people worldwide and provides analysis, development, and evaluation regarding local, national, and international migration and refugee policies. In 2002, MPI launched the Migration Information Source, which provides up-to-date data on international migration. **http://www.migrationpolicy.org** and **http://www.migrationinformation.org**

National Council of La Raza   As the "largest national Hispanic civil rights advocacy organization in the United States," NCLR is a nonprofit organization which strives to improve opportunities to the nation's Hispanic American population. Through a network of nearly 300 community-based organizations in 41 states, Puerto Rico, and the District of Columbia, NCLR works on five key issue areas: assets/investments, civil rights/immigration, education, employment/economic status, and health. **http://www.nclr.org**

National Immigration Forum   The Forum's mission is to "embrace and uphold America's tradition as a nation of immigrants" and advocates for public policies that "welcome immigrants and refugees and are fair and supportive to newcomers in the United States." **http://www.immigrationforum.org**

National Immigration Law Center   Founded in 1979, NILC is "a leading expert on immigration, public benefits, and employment laws affecting immigrants and refugees." Committed to protecting and promoting the rights of immigrants and their families, NILC's work includes policy analysis and advocacy, impact litigation, coalition building, technical assistance, publications, and training. **http://www.nilc.org**

National Network for Immigrant & Refugee Rights   Committed to the rights of immigrants and refugees in the United States, NNIRR is a national organization which "serves as a forum to share information, to educate communities and the general public, and to develop and coordinate plans of action on important immigrant and refugee issues." **http://www.nnirr.org/**

International

The International Migration Policy Programme   IMP is an inter-agency program of the United Nations Population Fund, UN Institute of Training and Research, the International Organization for Migration, and the International Labour Office, which works to promote government capacity building and cooperation around migration and refugee policies. Hundreds of government officials representing 115 countries have benefited from IMP activities since its establishment in 1998. **http://www.impprog.ch**

International Organization for Migration   Established in 1951, IOM is the world's primary intergovernmental organization focused on the issue of migration and is dedicated to "promoting humane and orderly migration for the benefit of all." With 116 member states as of March 2006, IOM focuses on four areas: migration and development, facilitating migration, regulating migration, and addressing forced migration. **http://www.iom.int**

Migrants Rights International   MRI—founded during the 1994 United Nations International Conference on Population and Development in Cairo—is a membership organization of migration and human rights experts and practitioners. **http://www .migrantwatch.org**

Population Reference Bureau   PRB works to "inform people around the world about population, health, and the environment, and empower them to use that information to advance the well-being of current and future generations." PRB's work is focused around four themes: reproductive health and fertility, children and families, population and the environment, and population futures (which include migration). **http://www.prb.org**

Office of the United Nations High Commissioner for Refugees   Established on December 14, 1950, the Office of UNHCR was created and mandated by the UN General Assembly to "lead and coordinate international action to protect refugees and resolve refugee problems worldwide" and "safeguard the rights and well-being of refugees." Since its inception, the agency has helped approximately 50 million refugees looking to restart their lives. **http://www.unhcr.ch**

United Nations Population Fund   The UN Population Fund (UNFPA) is an international development agency which "promotes the right of every woman, man, and child to enjoy a life of health and equal opportunity." UNFPA works with governments to develop policies that lead to reduced poverty and improved sustainable development and also assists countries with their population data collection and analyses. **http://www.unfpa.org**

Most immigrants cross borders for economic reasons, seeking higher wages in more affluent nations. Indeed, immigrants constitute about 6 percent of the populations in rich nations as opposed to just 1 percent in poor countries. These migrants often remain linked to their families in the countries of origin sending remittances back to their families, which then constitute an important source of capital for many developing countries or for the rural areas from which they migrated.[11] For example, India received the largest volume of remittances ($21.7 billion in 2004), followed by China ($21.3 billion) and Mexico ($18.1 billion).[12] The United States has attracted the greatest number of immigrants relative to other countries with 31.1 million foreign-born (11.1 percent of its total population in 2000)—with the majority of the immigrants in the United States from Mexico, Central America, and Asia.[13]

Migrants to other nations are a heterogeneous group with respect to their legal status. Many of them are "undocumented," i.e., crossed borders without the approval of host nations. Undocumented persons often exist in a state of limbo. They are frequently exploited by employers who pay them low wages and deny them benefits. While they often work and even pay taxes, they find it difficult to get access to social programs and education—whether because host nations deny them these benefits or they fear deportation if they claim benefits. Others have temporary status in host nations, such as immigrants to the United States who possess "green cards." Still others occupy an uncertain status, such as applying for a green card but not yet receiving it. Yet others get official citizenship.

Controversy swirls around immigrants in many nations. They are often subject to harassment by persons who believe they place downward pressure on wages of naturalized citizens—or who contend that they create a burden on nations' social, health, and education systems.[14] This harassment surfaced in riots in 2006 in France by Muslim immigrants who contended that they were subject to extreme persecution by French citizens. Yet other persons contend that immigrants benefit host nations because they often take jobs that most citizens would not fill (such as low-paid unskilled work in agriculture, hotels, and restaurants) while *not* making extensive use of social, health, and educational programs. With the aging of populations in Europe, Asia, and the United States, moreover, immigrants will increasingly be needed to ease labor shortages caused by the exodus of retirees from the labor force.

Globalization's Impact on the Environment

Recent global issues, such as the depletion of the atmospheric ozone layer, climate change due the greenhouse effect, and the depletion of the Earth's natural resources (e.g., forests and land), have gained increasing attention. Scientists differ in their estimates of the rate of global warming, but they mostly agree that the huge releases of carbon dioxide from fossil fuels has already led to increases in temperatures on earth and accelerated the melting of glaciers and ice caps in many places. Many scientists offer dire predictions of consequences that nations will suffer if carbon dioxide emissions are not slowed and capped, such as was advocated by the Kyoto Treaty of 1997 that the United States refused to sign. If just the icecap over Greenland were to melt, for example, the seas could rise more than twenty feet, inundating such areas as New Orleans, coastal areas of Florida, and some of Manhattan with water at some point during the coming century.

Were the oceans to rise markedly, citizens in coastal regions around the world would have to evacuate to higher ground, causing massive migrations, huge industrial losses, and the destruction of hundreds of ports that undergird the world's economy. The warming of the atmosphere would cause large sections of the globe to have insufficient rain to support agriculture, possibly contributing to famine in many nations. Global warming will have unknown consequences for the world's oceans and fisheries, but some evidence already exists that it will disrupt them by endangering some of the organisms that form the diets of various species of fish.

Globalization when coupled with rapid industrialization in many nations will pose other problems for the world's economy. While abundant fossil fuel reserves still exist, they will probably become increasingly expensive during the 21st century—not to mention many other minerals like copper, iron ore, and bauxite. Unless other means of producing power are discovered that can produce comparable levels as fossil fuels, such as solar and wind-generated energy, a melt-down of the world's economy could take place since it is currently based upon use of fossil fuels. Escalating prices for fossil fuels could, as well, incite conflict between nations for control of deposits of oil, gas, and coal—and could widen the gap between affluent nations and poor nations as industries within affluent nations outbid industries in developing nations for fossil fuels.

Nations will have to grapple with the difficult issue of sustainability. To what degree can escalating industrialization and consumption of goods be sustained with the world's existing stock of fossil fuels and minerals—particularly when global warming and the world's population is considered? (See Policy Advocacy Challenge 5.4.)

POLICY ADVOCACY CHALLENGE 5.4

Global Warming's Threat to New Orleans

BRUCE JANSSON, PH.D.

The flooding of New Orleans after Katrina was shaped by an array of erroneous decisions that were made by the Army Corps of Engineers, as well as by international oil companies.

The Army Corps had built levees around New Orleans incorrectly, often not giving them a deep enough base to withstand rising waters from a Category-5 hurricane. Nor had it sufficiently maintained the levees over a period of many decades so that cracks developed in many of them.

Both the Army Corps and oil companies had made yet another set of errors by constructing canals and water diversion projects that prevented soil from washing down the Mississippi River into the extended delta, wetlands and islands South of New Orleans that buffered the city from upsurging water from hurricanes. This build-up of soil and land had protected New Orleans for centuries from hurricanes, but it had increasingly become depleted in the decades preceding Hurricane Katrina. Many scientists contended that, useful as levees were, they would prove insufficient to protect New Orleans if environmental policies were not put in place to rebuild these wetlands, the delta, and offshore islands.

Many experts doubted, however, that *either* the levees *or* rebuilding of wetlands would be ultimately effective if nations of the world failed to contain and place a ceiling on carbon dioxide emissions that derived from the burning of fossil fuels that would arrest global warming. If the seas rose more than 25 feet *just* from the melting of the

(continued)

ice cap over Greenland at some point in the 21st century—and many more feet when the Artic and Antarctic ice caps are considered—New Orleans and the entire Gulf region would be inundated with water forcing mass and permanent evacuations. This would occur not all at once, as happened with Hurricane Katrina, but over many decades.

The United States was the worst culprit in the sheer quantity of its emissions, but industrial countries, with about 25 percent of the world's population, currently consume almost 70 percent of the world's commercial energy whether from, oil, natural gas, coal, nuclear energy, and hydroelectricity.[1]

As India and China rapidly industrialize, not to mention other nations like Brazil and Mexico, carbon dioxide emissions will accelerate as the world's stock of forests, which slow global warming, rapidly decline with deforestation in Asia, South America, and elsewhere.

The international trading system, as well as international regulations regarding pollution caused by fossil fuels, remain ill-prepared in 2007 to address these difficult issues. For example, nearly 80 percent of the world's international trade is carried by ocean ships that use an enormous amount of fossil fuel and are highly polluting.[2] The push for free trade has often led to the "ratcheting-down" of environmental regulations, which are viewed as costly obstructions to deregulation, even leading the WTO in one of its earliest actions to rule against the United States' Clean Air Act on grounds that its guidelines for controlling pollution were excessively strict.[3]

Global warming is merely one manifestation of globalization because carbon dioxide emissions cross international boundaries and nations share the world's atmosphere. Only international treaties and policies that mandate and fund the use of alternative fuels, the installation of anti-pollution devices in factories, fuel-efficient cars, and other initiatives can control it and prevent the devastation of coastal regions around the world from rising seas where the bulk of the world's population lives. The future of New Orleans is linked to these global realities.

---

[1] Jose Goldemberg, "Energy and Sustainable Development." In *Worlds apart: Globalization and the environment,* edited by James Gustave Speth (Washington, DC: Islander Press, 2003): pp. 53–65.
[2] Jerry Mander, "Intrinsic negative effects of economic globalization on the environment" In *Worlds apart: Globalization and the environment,* edited by James Gustave Speth (Washington, DC: Islander Press, 2003): pp. 109–129.
[3] Ibid.

Threats to Public Health

Similar to environmental problems, public health problems—such as communicable diseases—are not bound by national borders, as evidenced by recent scares about SARS and Bird Flu epidemics. With increased movement of both goods and people, preventing the spread of potentially deadly diseases has become increasingly challenging for national governments. The United States Department of Agriculture estimates that the number of travelers to the United States was 66 million in 1996, an almost three-fold increase from 1984 and there were 400 million border crossings in 1996. The Harvard Working Group on New and Resurgent Diseases (HWG) argue that "increased travel and trade have greatly increased the opportunities for pathogens and vectors (e.g., insects) to spread to new areas. This problem is not a new one—but the rapidity with which goods and people now move around the globe has augmented the likelihood of 'microbial traffic.'" (p. 164–165).[15]

Despite advances in healthcare and public health knowledge and technology, infectious diseases remain a leading cause of death globally, accounting for a quarter to a third of the world's deaths in 1998.[16] The international community has seen not only the arrival of new diseases, but also a resurgence of old diseases. In a recent television series and Web-based educational program, entitled *Rx for Survival: A Global Health Challenge*, the Public Broadcasting Corporation (PBC) found that "some 38 new diseases—including avian flu, West Nile virus, severe acute respiratory syndrome (SARS), and mad cow disease—have appeared since 1973. Further, 20 diseases that had been suppressed—including malaria and tuberculosis—are again on the rise."[17] These reemerging diseases are also spreading to new geographic areas. With globalization leaving many countries and communities behind, these populations face extreme poverty, malnutrition, and lack of access to safe drinking water, thus making them more vulnerable and susceptible to the spread of a disease.[18]

Creating a Mono-Culture?

Harvard University Professor Marcelo Suarez-Orozco (2001) writes that "globalization decisively undermines the once imagined neat fit between language, culture, and the nation" (p. 346).[19] Not surprisingly, this "global monoculture" generally reflects the values and lifestyles of the United States, as Friedman (2000) argues that "culturally speaking, globalization has tended to involve the spread (for better and for worse) of Americanization—from Big Macs to iMacs to Mickey Mouse" (p. 9).[20] Similarly, Barnet and Cavanagh (1996) write that "the entire planet is being wired into music, movies, news, television programs, and other cultural products that originate primarily in the film and recording studios of the United States... American culture products are sweeping the globe" (p. 72).[21]

The Great Caveat: Globalization's Positive Effects

As countries have entered the global economy, they have often experienced overall higher standards of living. Marber (2004/2005) writes that "no matter how one measures wealth—whether by economic, bio-social, or financial indicators—there have been gains in virtually every meaningful aspect of life in the last two generations ... most people are living longer, healthier, fuller lives" (p. 29).[22] In fact, overall improvements can be shown in a broad range of measures: life expectancies; literacy rates and public education; economic output and trade; poverty, per capita income, and income equality; access to technology (e.g., televisions and automobiles); quality of life (e.g., work hours per year); and political participation (i.e., the right to vote). In its 2002 report, *Globalization, Growth, and Poverty*, the World Bank shows that the "more globalized" developing countries, such as China and Mexico, fared better along several of these indicators, than "less globalized" countries, such as Pakistan and Kenya. For example, in the newly globalized countries, the number of individuals living in extreme poverty (less than $1 per day) declined by 120 million in the 5-year period between 1993 and 1998.[23]

It is clear, however, that this prosperity has not been shared by everyone or every country. Even the World Bank—one of the key institutions driving globalization—admits that "the fact that globalization does not on average increase inequality within countries disguises the reality that there are specific winners and losers in each society" (p. 2).[24] After touting the benefits of globalization, Marber writes that "even with its positive trends, globalization is not a perfect process. It is not a panacea for every problem for every person at every moment in time" (p. 37).[25] Even a critic of some of globalization such as Joseph Stiglitz argues that, while "those who vilify globalization too often overlook its benefits" while then proceeding to say that "the proponents of globalization have been, if anything, even more unbalanced. To them, globalization (which typically is associated with accepting triumphant capitalism, American style) is progress; developing countries must accept it, if they are to grow and to fight poverty effectively. But to many in the developing world, globalization has not brought the promised benefits" (p. 5).[26]

Policy Advocacy for Populations Harmed by Globalization

Policy advocates need to develop and secure the enactment of an array of policies that decrease the negative impact of globalization upon vulnerable populations, whether in the United States or by working with advocacy groups that seek to address social problems abroad or in the treaties and international organizations that regulate or deal with issues associated with globalization. We provide a few illustrative examples.

Policy Options in the United States

Local, state, and federal governments need to invest more resources in relatively unskilled workers so that they can rebound when they lose their jobs as corporations close plants or move abroad. These workers need job training assistance and relocation assistance. In some cases, they need financial assistance so that they can obtain educational credentials from high schools, community colleges, and colleges.

Policy advocates need to enact policies that require corporations to give advance notice of their intention to close or move their operations—and that require them to help fund assistance to workers who become unemployed. To the extent some corporations undercut American corporations by selling low-cost imports that rely on victimization of workers in developing nations, policy advocates need to place pressure on them to set and enforce minimum wage and work-safety standards in the developing nations where their products are manufactured.

Policy advocates need to develop policies to help migrants. Persons who are defined as "illegal" or "undocumented" immigrants are subject not only to prejudice, but to victimization by landlords, criminal elements, and employers who realize that they cannot easily seek protection from the police or courts for fear of deportation. The United States needs to give substantial groups of these persons—without whom the American economy cannot function at its current level—a combination of amnesty and other legal protections—as a concerted social movement of immigration reforms sought in widespread demonstrations in the United States in 2006. Since efforts to keep such persons from entering the United States are futile as long as the economic gap is so large between the places of origin and the destinations of immigrants, efforts to rely exclusively or primarily on strengthening border patrols will not succeed in keeping many persons from crossing borders.

For an example of policy advocacy for immigrants, see Policy Advocacy Challenge 5.5 where Dennis Kao discusses his advocacy for immigrants to the United States.

**POLICY
ADVOCACY
CHALLENGE 5.5**

Serving as an
Intermediary
Between
Immigrant
Communities
and Sacramento:
Lessons Learned

DENNIS KAO,
MSW & DOCTORAL
STUDENT, SCHOOL
OF SOCIAL WORK,
UNIVERSITY
OF SOUTHERN
CALIFORNIA

Like other disadvantaged groups, immigrants and their families often feel disconnected from the policymaking process. However, immigrants also encounter another layer of unique barriers. For example, while other disadvantaged groups may be perceived to be low-propensity voters, immigrants, by definition, cannot vote and consequently, often are unable to participate in public elections or legislative decisions. Many immigrants also may not yet have attained a strong grasp of the English language and therefore, often lack knowledge regarding their basic rights and have difficulty communicating their needs and concerns. Depending on the current political climate and/or their own experiences in their home countries, many immigrants may also feel a sense of fear or distrust towards the government. Given these challenges, it is often difficult for immigrant families to feel that they can have a voice. For several years, I had the opportunity to work for a nonprofit immigrant rights organization in Los Angeles County, which was also a part of a statewide coalition of organizations. Our primary role was to serve as an intermediary, i.e., to facilitate communication between the immigrant communities we served and the policymakers in Sacramento. Here are some of the lessons I learned during my time there.

Engaging Community Leaders and Organizations

We felt that a single organization couldn't possibly outreach to or engage the broader immigrant community, given its diversity and size. Much of our time, therefore, was spent working closely with community leaders and organizations (i.e., service agencies, churches, membership organizations, etc.), who can then work to engage their own members or clients. To help build their advocacy capacity, we conducted ongoing advocacy trainings (e.g., legislative/budget process, advocacy skills, lobbying rules for nonprofits, etc.). We also held monthly regional meetings that pulled in many of our partner organizations, as well as other groups. The purpose of these meetings was to discuss current policy issues that were important to the local organizations and to strategize regional campaigns.

Investing in Communities Long-Term

We often found that the community work necessary to build capacity and momentum operated on a much slower timeline than the fast and unpredictable policy-making process. It was important, therefore, to establish short-term policy goals and campaigns, but to always keep in mind the longer-term goal of capacity-building. In our case, it was also important to redefine what "policy success" meant to us. In most circles, policy success simply means achieving legislative victories. While this obviously was important to us, we also felt that we were successful if more organizations or individuals were meaningfully engaged in the process each year. The challenge then is how we measure this type of success. Examples of outcome measures included: number of advocacy trainings/workshops, number of legislative visits organized, number and types of organizations who participated in those legislative visits, attendance at regional meetings, response to our policy updates (see below), and the extent we are engaging immigrants and their families.

Facilitating Ongoing Communication

Before the start of each legislative session, we conducted surveys and consulted with key partners to assess the key state policy issues for that year. Based on this process, these issues became a part of our policy agenda for that legislative session. We established a

(continued)

rapid-alert network which at one point grew to about 400 organizations and individuals in the county. Either through fax or e-mail, we would provide timely state policy and budget updates regarding the issues on our agenda, as well as other issues impacting immigrants. These updates often included simple actions that individuals and organizations could take, e.g., writing a letter or making a call (in which case, a sample letter or script would also be included). Having a presence in Sacramento can be important and in our case, our statewide coalition had established an office in Sacramento with a full-time policy advocate who provided us with timely information and updates. Understanding that this isn't possible in most cases, there are also a number of Sacramento-based organizations that would be open to working closely with local groups.

Providing Space for Individuals to Tell Their Story

The most important lesson for me was to learn that everyone has a story to tell if given the chance and that these personal stories/testimonies can be extremely effective in conveying a strong message and influencing policy. In addition to providing opportunities for individuals to express their concerns via letters or phone calls, we coordinated group visits with state legislators in their district office. Depending on the issue, these groups could consist of community leaders, providers, advocates, and immigrants themselves. We have also compiled the stories of immigrants directly impacted by specific policies and distributed them (e.g., in a brochure, weekly fax, or a larger report) to legislators. Finally, each year in May (a crucial time in the state budget process), we and our statewide partners coordinated an "immigrant advocacy day" in the state capitol, which pulled together hundreds of advocates and immigrants. Throughout the day, participants would take part in a number of activities, such as legislative visits, rally, and training. For many, this day was the first opportunity to speak directly to a policymaker.

Policy Options to Help Vulnerable Populations Abroad

Policy advocates need to pressure international organizations, such as the IMF and World Bank, as well as the WTO, to implement policies that do not victimize vulnerable populations in developing nations, such as policies that require them to reduce their spending excessively on social programs. (Their discontent with the WTO was apparent when thousands of demonstrators disrupted the WTO's 1999 Ministerial Meeting in Seattle, WA, and for the most part, shut down the city).[27] They should support efforts to eliminate barriers to imports from developing nations that curtail the well-being of vulnerable populations. This was illustrated when some policy advocates sought a detailed agreement at the WTO meetings in mid-December 2005 to eliminate all duties and quotas on the exports of at least 32 of the world's poor countries—with considerable support for this policy coming from Europe and Japan. (Faced with pressure from such states as North Carolina over cuts in American quotas on cotton imports, the Bush Administration withheld its support for such far-reaching policies.) They can, moreover, support or work with groups that provide assistance to vulnerable populations in developing nations. They can support projects to help developing nations retain some of their protective tariffs when their removal would excessively harm vulnerable populations such as peasants. (See Policy Advocacy Challenge 5.6.) Policy advocates can lend support to advocacy groups that pressure governments to include minimum standards for wages and working conditions in trade treaties approved by the WTO and by NAFTA, the FTAA, and the GATT.

Many international organizations work as advocates for socially vulnerable groups across the globe. Some work at the community level to provide direct relief services or to empower people and groups in developing nations to fight for social justice at the community level, while others focus on political campaigns and lobbying to effect broader policy changes. Below are descriptions of several organizations involved in international advocacy efforts.

Oxfam International   Oxfam is a group of 12 humanitarian organizations around the world, which together work to fight poverty and social justice. Oxfam engages in three types of advocacy work: (1) leading organizing efforts for people living in poverty around the world, (2) conducting political lobbying, and (3) building alliances across organizations and groups. A current project of Oxfam focuses on advocating for debt relief, increased foreign aid, and better trade conditions for developing nations. This project is based in Washington, DC, and the advocacy targets of this effort are the World Bank and the International Monetary Fund.
http://www.oxfam.org

CARE   CARE is a humanitarian organization made up of 12 member organizations in different nations around the world. CARE member organizations work to fight poverty in over 70 nations. Like Oxfam, CARE advocates both through empowerment initiatives and lobbying for policy changes.
http://www.care.org

United Nations Children's Fund   UNICEF advocates for the rights of children in 157 nations around the world. UNICEF's focus areas include education, health, environmental safety, and violence and abuse. UNICEF provides direct services within these areas—for example, delivering food to hungry children or helping a county to launch an AIDS education campaign. UNICEF also conducts policy analysis and other research, which it disseminates throughout its partner organizations. UNICEF does not affiliate itself with political parties, and does not engage in political lobbying efforts.
http://www.unicef.org

USAID   USAID is an independent agency of the U.S. federal government. USAID carries out U.S. foreign aid projects in many areas, including health, humanitarian assistance, and conflict prevention. Because USAID is a federal agency, it does not engage in political lobbying, though it does publish reports on strategies to address global issues.
http://www.usaid.gov

Global Trade Watch   GTW is an international organization that advocates against what it calls "corporate globalization," arguing that free trade does more harm than good. GTW conducts both grassroots advocacy and political lobbying efforts in many areas of

(continued)

**POLICY
ADVOCACY
CHALLENGE 5.6**

(continued)

globalization, including environmental, health, and responsible government. The targets of GTW lobbying efforts include the WTO (World Trade Organization), NAFTA (North American Free Trade Agreement), and FTAA (Free Trade Area of the Americas). **http://www.citizen.org/trade**

Just as many organizations advocate protecting vulnerable populations in developing nations from the effects of globalization, other groups actively promote globalization with the argument that it spurs economic growth and improves living standards around the world. These groups tend to be business associations, which focus on the economic and trade aspects of globalization. Some examples include the Business Roundtable (**http://www.businessroundtable.org**), an association of business leaders in the United States with an international focus; and the International Chamber of Commerce (**http://www.iccwbo.org**), an association of business executives from over 130 countries.

Policy advocates also need to obtain legislation in the United States that protects migrants from victimization by employers and by citizens. The need for these protections is illustrated by New Orleans in the wake of Hurricane Katrina when its housing, businesses, and infrastructure had to be rebuilt at a time when an acute labor shortage existed due to the evacuation of many residents. This labor shortage was met by an influx of immigrants, who included large numbers of persons from Mexico and Central America. These persons often worked under deplorable working conditions and encountered other problems, such as poor housing and inadequate medical care. (See Policy Advocacy Challenge 5.7.) Such measures should be considered as extending amnesty to those persons who have resided in the United States for a specific period, as well as policies that guarantee and monitor rights of immigrants who have guest-worker status. When large numbers of persons live in the United States who are undocumented, many of them will be victimized since they lack rights given either to citizens or to persons with visas. As fugitives, they cannot easily report crimes done to them or use medical or other programs when they need them. Nor are they likely to report employers' unfair treatment of them.

**POLICY
ADVOCACY
CHALLENGE 5.7**

How Globalization
Powerfully Shaped
Social Problems
in Post-Katrina
New Orleans

BRUCE JANSSON, PH.D.

When a huge portion of New Orleans' population evacuated the city in the wake of Katrina—and when many of them chose not to return to the city even a year later—the city encountered a major labor shortage. Vast amounts of debris had to be collected and moved. Many of the city's structures had to be demolished. Those structures that could be salvaged often had to be gutted to remove mold- and mildew-infested plaster, dry wall, and wood. The electrical and plumbing systems of houses often had to be replaced. Roads and bridges had to be repaired or rebuilt. Levees had to be repaired or rebuilt.

One source of labor were African American evacuees and residents—since they had comprised about 67 percent of the population of New Orleans prior to Hurricane Katrina.[1] So also would have been African American contractors who had been

---

[1] I draw heavily on a Report titled "And Injustice for All: Workers' Lives in the Reconstruction of New Orleans" (2006) issued by the a Washington Legal Aid Group called the Advancement Project, co-authored by Judith Browne-Dianis, and Jennifer Lai of the Project, as well as Marielena Hincapie of the National Immigration Law Center and Saket Soni of the New Orleans Worker Justice Coalition. The Report can be found online at http://www.advancementproject.org/reports/workersreport.pdf.

a vital part of New Orleans' business community before Katrina. Other sources of labor included not only the Caucasian residents and evacuees, but sizeable numbers of immigrants from Vietnam and Honduras who had settled in New Orleans before Hurricane Katrina.

Once the city had been devastated by the hurricane, however, local employers and companies were often supplanted by out-of-state contractors, such as construction firms with links to powerful public officials in Louisiana and in Washington, DC. These firms often wanted to reap the benefits of substantial contracts from the federal government—benefits that would be greatly increased if they could pay low wages, offer no or few benefits to workers, and ignore work-safety regulations.

It is not surprising, then, that the contractors obtained the enactment of many policies that relaxed regulations that protected workers' rights and safety. President Bush suspended by executive order, for example, provisions of the Davis-Bacon Act that required federal construction contractors to pay no less than the prevailing wage rates for private construction workers in September 2005—allowing them to cut their pay even below the already low rates in Louisiana. Only pressure from unions and others forced him to restore these provisions in November 2005. The Occupational Safety and Health Administration (OSHA) suspended enforcement of work safety and health standard in August 2005—and they were still suspended in late 2006. The Department of Labor assigned virtually no staff to monitoring whether employers actually paid their employees.

Any hope that African American contractors would obtain many contracts were dashed when the Department of Labor suspended affirmation action requirements. While it lifted this suspension in late 2005, the tone had been set: few contracts went to these firms. Then many contracts were given to specific contractors without using a competitive bidding process—again putting minority contractors at a disadvantage as compared to contractors with links to powerful government officials. Nor did the Small Business Administration (SBA) give many loans or grants to small businesses so that they could get going after many had lost their equipment and supplies from Hurricane Katrina. Many African Americans could not get jobs, moreover, due to job discrimination by employers, whether because they were racially prejudiced or because they believed that they could pay immigrants from abroad at lower rates.

Many African American evacuees and residents of New Orleans could not reenter the labor force for practical reasons. Many did not own or had lost automobiles, so they could not get to job sites due to the dearth of local busses. Affordable day care was hard to find in New Orleans. Many could not return to New Orleans because the State of Louisiana, which took over most of the city's public schools, was so slow to repair and reopen them—and Charter Schools had long waiting lists. Nor could they often find affordable housing as many, unable to afford skyrocketing rents in New Orleans, lived in FEMA trailer camps distant from New Orleans or on its periphery. Some of them alleged, as well, that some employers systematically discriminated against them in favor of hiring migrants, thinking that migrants would be less likely to complain to government officials about working conditions and their low pay for fear of being deported.

Out-of-state contractors aggressively sought workers in Mexico and some Asian nations such as Thailand by advertising in newspapers where they promised housing and relatively high wages. Believing these advertisements, immigrants went to

(continued)

American consulates in such places as Mexico City and obtained H-2A visas for "non-immigrant workers," which gave them the right to temporarily enter the United States if they were sponsored by a specific employer. This kind of visa allowed them to stay in the United States only as long as they worked for *this* employer.

Louisiana had never been a pro-labor area, lacking even a minimum wage law unlike most other states. It became even less so in the wake of Katrina when vast sums of money were dispatched to contractors in a short span of time with an Administration not inclined to protect laborers. Between 30,000 and 100,000 persons streamed into New Orleans to get work—with roughly half of them Latinos from Mexico. Many of these persons became embroiled in a "national crisis of civil and human rights." Many of them received meager pay. They often worked in toxic environments in areas with mold, mildew, and chemicals, but with little or no protective gear. They often discovered that they were not paid for their work, or only partially paid; not reimbursed for overtime; and sometimes given checks that bounced. They often lived in motels with as many as ten persons in a room—or were homeless. Even when they possessed temporary-worker visas, they were often harassed by police and immigration officials, who often used racial profiling when they accosted them. Many of these laborers received no health insurance and no workman's compensation—and some were fired when they developed illnesses, such as eye infections from working in toxic areas. Some migrants where told that they would be reported to immigration officials if they complained to authorities about their working conditions.

Tragically, Latino and African-American workers seldom made common cause against their victimization, partly because many of them subscribed to beliefs that pitted them against one another. If many African Americans often viewed themselves as the rightful residents of New Orleans who were overrun by Latinos, Latinos often subscribed to the view that African Americans were too lazy to work. Mayor Ray Nagin contributed to this view when he said on October 10, 2005, "How do I make sure that New Orleans is not overrun by Mexican workers?" In the same vein, Senator Mary Landrieu said about the same time, "they (Mexicans) aggravate our employment crisis and depress earnings for our workers." Both public officials might better have focused on the victimization of workers of both racial and ethnic groups by federal contractors— a practice that was promoted by the laxness of the Bush Administration in enforcing federal wage, work-safety, and wage-payment policies and not moving even faster to get affordable childcare, housing, and medical care back into New Orleans.

The inability of African Americans to obtain jobs in New Orleans was frustrated, as well, by the decisions of some corporations to relocate their facilities abroad in developing nations where they could pay lower wages, use child labor, and avoid American environmental and work-safety regulations.

Globalization powerfully shaped employment in post-Katrina New Orleans, whether through the in-migration of workers from abroad or from the exodus of some American corporations to developing nations.

Policy advocates also need to work to increase the amount of foreign aid that the United States gives to developing nations, such as for infrastructure, technology, health programs, education programs, job training programs, and family planning services. To the extent that this foreign aid reduces poverty and unemployment in developing nations, it will cut rates of migration of poor persons into the United States. The United States ranks very low among developed nations in its foreign aid, giving less than 1 percent of the federal budget even after significant increases during the presidency of George W. Bush.

Policy advocates also need to work on environmental and public-health fronts. They should pressure the United States to sign treaties like the Kyoto treaty and successor treaties that commit nations to reduce carbon dioxide emissions that threaten global warming—and that aim to reduce other ills such as over-fishing of the seas and air pollution that crosses international boundaries. They need, as well, to pressure the United States to increase its fiscal commitments to public health so that the nation has an infrastructure that can protect Americans from diseases that spread across national boundaries.

As you consider this case, ponder the following questions:

1. To what extent does globalization pit low income groups against on another in the United States—or to what extent do immigrants take jobs that residents would not seek?
2. To what extent can Americans help to create economic growth in Mexico and other developing nations through the provision of foreign aid?

What You Can Now Do

CHAPTER SUMMARY

You are now equipped with knowledge about social problems caused by globalization, as well as the role that policy advocates can assume in addressing them. You can do the following:

- Define globalization
- Identify specific problems caused by globalization in the United States
- Identify links between globalization and global warming
- Analyze why a large economic gap arose between developing and developed nations
- Identify specific international institutions and treaties that have shaped trade and economic relations among nations
- Identify specific problems caused by globalization in developing nations by international, organizations
- Know where to gain more information about developing nations
- Identify some policy options that policy advocates can use to address problems caused by globalization at home and abroad
- Identify key international advocacy groups

The next chapter will enable you to articulate four central reasons why social workers should participate in policy advocacy.

NOTES

1. Steven Kull, Clay Ramsay, Stefan Subias, and Evan Lewis, *Americans on globalization, trade, and farm subsidies* (Washington, DC: Program on International Policy Attitudes, January 22, 2004).

2. United States Census Bureau, *Poverty: 2004 Highlights* (Washington, DC: U.S. Census Bureau, August 30, 2005).

3. Jeffrey Sachs, *End of Poverty. Economic Possibilities for Our Time* (New York: Penguin Press, 2005).

4. The World Bank, *Globalization, Growth, and Poverty: Building an Inclusive World Economy* (Washington, DC: World Bank and Oxford University Press, 2002).

5. Thomas L. Friedman, *The Lexus and the Olive Tree: Understanding Globalization* (New York: Anchor Books, 2000), p. 11.

6. Joseph E. Stiglitz, *Globalization and its Discontents* (New York, NY: W.W. Norton & Company, 2002).

7. Arline Prigoff, *Economics for social workers: Social outcomes of economic globalization with strategies for community action* (Stamford, CT: Brooks/Cole Thomson Learning, 2000): p. 116.

8. Stiglitz et al., *Globalization and its Discontents*.

9. Martin Khor, "Global Economy and the Third World." In *The Case Against the Global Economy and for a Turn Toward the Local*, edited by Jerry Mander & Edward Goldsmith (San Francisco, CA: Sierra Club Books, 1996): p. 47–59.

10. Michael W. Doyle, "The Challenge of Worldwide Migration," *Journal of International Affairs* 57, no. 2 (Spring 2004): 1–5.

11. The World Bank, *Globalization, Growth, and Poverty: Building an Inclusive World Economy*.

12. Sridhar Krishnaswami, "Remittances: India is World no. 1," *Rediff India Abroad*, November 17, 2005, http://us.rediff.com (accessed November 21, 2005).

13. The World Bank, *Globalization, Growth, and Poverty: Building an Inclusive World Economy*.

14. George Borjas, "The Economics of Immigration," *Journal of Economic Literature* 22 (1996): 1667–1717; Council of Economic Affairs, *Economic Report of the President* (Washington, DC: United States Government Printing Office, February 2005); and Barry Edmonston and Ronald Lee, eds., *Local Fiscal Effects of Illegal Immigration: Report of a Workshop* (Washington, DC: National Academy Press, 1996).

15. Harvard Working Group on New and Resurgent Diseases, "Globalization, Development, and the Spread of Disease." In *The Case Against the Global Economy and for a Turn Toward the Local*, edited by Jerry Mander & Edward Goldsmith (San Francisco, CA: Sierra Club Books, 1996): pp. 160–170.

16. Erica Bark-Ruggles, "The globalization of disease: When Congo sneezes, will California get a cold?" *The Brookings Review* 19, no. 4 (2001): 30–33; and Harvard Working Group on New and Resurgent Diseases, "Globalization, Development, and the Spread of Disease."

17. Public Broadcasting Corporation, *Rx for Survival: A Global Health Challenge*, October 2005, http://www.pbs.org (accessed November, 18, 2005).

18. Erica Bark-Ruggles, "The globalization of disease: When Congo sneezes, will California get a cold?"; and Yach, D. & Bettcher, D. (1998). The globalization of public health, I: Threats and opportunities. *American Journal of Public Health* 88, no. 5 (2001): 735–738.

19. Marcelo M. Suarez-Orozco, "Globalization, Immigration, and Education: The Research Agenda." *Harvard Educational Review* 71, no. 3 (2001): 345–635.

20. Friedman, *The Lexus and the Olive Tree*.

21. Richard Barnet and John Cavanagh, "Homogenization of Global Culture." In *The Case Against the Global Economy and for a Turn Toward the Local*, edited by Jerry Mander & Edward Goldsmith (San Francisco, CA: Sierra Club Books, 1996): pp. 71–77.

22. Peter Marber, "Globalization and its Contents," *World Policy Journal* 21, no. 4 (2004/2005): 29–37.

23. The World Bank, *Globalization, Growth, and Poverty: Building an Inclusive World Economy*.

24. Ibid

25. Marber, "Globalization and its Contents."

26. Stiglitz et al., *Globalization and its Discontents*

27. Jay R. Mandle, *Globalization and the poor* (Cambridge, United Kingdom: Cambridge University Press, 2003).

4

COMMITTING TO PROBLEMS AND SOLUTIONS THROUGH BUILDING AGENDAS AND POLICY ANALYSIS

Policy advocates are driven by the desire to improve society. As a prelude to their work, they need to identify specific problems or issues where they believe they can make a difference—and get them placed on the policy agendas of decision makers. They also need to find meritorious solutions by engaging in policy analysis, as well as ones that appear to have a reasonable chance of enactment and implementation. (We discuss how policy advocates get policies enacted or approved in Part 5 and how they implement them in Part 6.)

Chapters Six through Nine discuss this preparatory work, which often determines whether policy advocates will succeed in changing existing policies and implementing policy innovations.

Chapter Six discusses how advocates place issues, problems, or solutions on policy agendas of decision makers so that they will take them seriously.

Chapter Seven introduces a six-step model of policy analysis which policy advocates can use to develop policy proposals. Chapter Seven focuses upon the first step of this model where policy advocates familiarize themselves with a social problem or issue.

Chapter Eight focuses on the second, third, and fourth steps of the six-step model of policy analysis where policy advocates develop specific policy proposals by identifying various policy options and then selecting one

Chapter Nine focuses on the fifth and sixth steps of the policy analysis model where policy advocates seek to persuade other persons to accept or fund specific proposals, whether by making presentations to them, engaging in negotiations or debates, or writing grant proposals.

CHAPTER

Committing to an Issue:
Building Agendas

<table>
<tr><td>

**POLICY
PREDICAMENT**

</td><td>

The Gulf Coast of the United States has a long history of catastrophic hurricanes for centuries. As the area became densely populated during the past 50 years, these hurricanes wreaked mounting havoc with persons in the area. Yet policy makers in the region, as well as in the federal government, often failed to place preparedness high on policy agendas—so years would often go by without them making serious efforts to prepare for upcoming hurricanes. Once specific hurricanes strike, policy advocates try to place on policy agendas an array of social problems caused by them, such as the need for affordable housing; reconstruction of human services, medical, and education delivery systems; and policies to help vulnerable populations. Similarly, policy advocates in specific jurisdictions try to place the issue of homelessness on policy agendas when public officials often place it on a back burner because homeless persons are often a stigmatized population with little political clout. We use Hurricane Katrina and homelessness in Los Angeles County to illustrate how policy advocates place issues on policy agendas.

</td></tr>
</table>

Experienced policy advocates realize that their first challenge is to get a specific policy issue on decision makers' agendas in agency, community, or legislative settings. Before an issue can advance into the later phases of policy practice, where proposals are actually refined, enacted, and implemented, decision makers must decide that a specific issue is important enough to merit serious consideration. It must compete with myriad other issues for the scarce time and resources of staff, executives, boards of directors, governmental officials, legislators, mayors, boards of supervisors, community leaders, and presidents. Policy advocates often have to use a combination of political, interactional, and analytic skills to place their issues on decision makers' agendas.

We discuss the following in this chapter:

- The importance of agenda-building processes to policy practice
- The three stages of agenda building: diagnosing, softening, and activating
- How social problems and solutions reach agendas
- How political processes shape agendas
- How windows of opportunity and policy entrepreneurs shape agendas
- How direct-service staff can build agendas
- The challenges policy advocates face in shaping agendas

How do we know when an issue is on the agenda? In legislative settings, this has happened when legislation has been introduced into the legislative process and referred to a committee, and has attracted the serious attention of some legislators—preferably ones with clout. In agency settings, an issue is on the agenda when it has become part of the agency's deliberations. Perhaps the executive director has formed a task force or committee to study it. Maybe the staff or the agency's board plans to discuss the issue in a meeting. A group in the agency may have decided to rally support for a policy change. In communities, an issue is on the agenda when community leaders and decision makers have decided to take it seriously enough to convene meetings to consider solutions.

Of course, placing issues or proposals on these agendas does not necessarily have a positive outcome; many factors, such as opposition, can defeat them. Indeed, many issues never reach the agenda because opposing groups successfully use tactics to keep them off the agenda.[1] Also, placement on the agenda does not tell us precisely what kind of proposal or solution will finally emerge, because proposals are finalized in the give-and-take of deliberations. But placement on the agenda does tell us that a proposal is well positioned to receive serious attention and that it has received an initial impetus, unlike many issues that do not even achieve this status. Were we *not* to discuss agenda building, it might seem that policy reforms can be easily initiated without any preliminary work, such as discussing the proposed reform, analyzing its feasibility, convincing others that it merits attention, considering who might get the ball rolling, and deciding on the right time to introduce the issue to others.

In this chapter, we discuss some policy practice skills that help get proposals onto agendas.

Taking the First Step

Assume that you work in an agency that provides job referrals and career assistance to women. You are perturbed because the agency provides little service to a specific client group, such as single teenage mothers. While some services are available to them, none of the services, you decide, focus on employment needs. While your distant challenge is to develop a proposal to help this population and perhaps secure funding for this help, your immediate challenge is to convince others, preferably decision makers at the agency, that the problem merits their serious attention. At this very moment, you are engaged in building an agenda. In this preliminary phase, you must place the issue on the agenda so that someone—perhaps an executive, a staff committee, or a committee of the agency's board—will examine the issue in more detail or delegate it to others for further exploration.

Agenda building is a critical phase of the policy development process. Skillful policy practitioners who are building an agenda try to create favorable conditions, interest, and support for a policy reform at the outset.

Why Agenda Building Is Needed

Legislatures

It is easy to see why most proposals fall by the wayside when we consider some simple realities that confront legislators and agency executives. Legislators must limit the number of issues they consider and must rank them in some order. Thousands of pieces of legislation are introduced into each session of state legislatures and Congress conceived by the legislators themselves, lobbyists, citizens, or professional associations. (See Policy Advocacy Challenge 6.1.)

Were legislators to debate a large fraction of these proposals, they would work themselves to exhaustion and not give careful attention to any of them. When many people with different perspectives and constituencies are involved, it takes time and effort to consider even simple pieces of legislation. In each chamber of Congress, for example, subcommittees consider the policies and forward them for further debate and votes to the full legislative committee, which forwards them to the full chamber for floor debates and votes. If each chamber enacts a different version, they may have to be sent to a conference committee composed of members of both chambers, and then to the president for his signature. Moreover, during this process, many legislators must spend endless hours with lobbyists and other citizens. It is no wonder, then, that leaders of legislatures decide not to put most measures on the legislative agenda, thus reserving their scarce time for those pieces of legislation they want to concentrate on.

POLICY ADVOCACY CHALLENGE 6.1

Finding Emerging Legislation in State and Federal Jurisdictions

STEPHANIE DAVIS, RESEARCH LIBRARIAN, UNIVERSITY OF CALIFORNIA, IRVINE

Federal Government Information

In 1995, a team of librarians and technologists from the Library of Congress created THOMAS under a federal mandate from the 104th Congress to make federal legislative information freely available to the public via the Internet. THOMAS, located online at **http://thomas.loc.gov**, is named for Thomas Jefferson, and provides access to many different types of political and government information:

- Legislation: text of bills and information about those bills introduced into the House and Senate, text of laws passed by Congress, record of how members of Congress vote on bills, motions and more (roll call votes)
- Congressional Record: an index to and full text of the official record of the speeches, remarks, issues, and other happenings in Congress
- House and Senate Committee information: membership, charges, schedules, text of hearings
- Senator/Representative directories: links to homepages with contact information, constituency information, profiles, legislative agendas; finding aids for locating a specific member by ZIP code and state

- Other Congressional Internet Services such as the Government Printing Office, General Accounting Office, Congressional Budget Office, and others
- Links to guides on the legislative process in the House and Senate, database of historical documents, and more

Your library may have access to a subscription database called *Congressional Universe,* which provides much of the same information as THOMAS. Both are excellent resources for finding federal legislative information.

State Legislative Information

Finding state information is, in general, not as streamlined as finding federal information. States generally do not have the same mandate to place their legislative information on the Internet. There is a subscription database called *State Capital Universe* that provides access to state bills, regulations, statutes, policy and issue information, and biographical information about state senators and politicians.

Often the best way to find state information is to find your state's homepage on the Internet, and look for links to government, legislature, agencies, elected officials, and state libraries or archives. These are excellent starting points.

∽ EXERCISE ∾

First, spend some time getting acquainted with THOMAS at **http://thomas.loc.gov**. Select a topic of interest to you, and search for bills or laws on that topic (i.e., health care, welfare, children).

Next, using the search engines we discussed in Chapter One, find your state's homepage, and then find your state legislature's Web site. If the Web site allows for searching introduced and passed legislation, repeat the search you did in THOMAS.

- Compare the results of your searches—how are the bills or laws similar? Do they address the same or similar problems? How is the state's approach different from the federal, and vice versa?
- Who introduced or sponsored each piece of legislation? Find their homepage and compare their legislative agendas.
- From your perspective, is the solution to the problem addressed in the legislation a good solution or a poor solution? Critique each piece of legislation as if you were a member of the state legislature faced with voting on that piece of legislation.

Legislators often avoid issues that appear to give them little or no political advantage in reelection, such as not selecting issues that will not help them obtain or retain constituents' support. A particular issue may seem too controversial or may antagonize an important faction or interest group, even if it pleases other people. Yet legislators sometimes do select issues that they realize will be difficult to enact or controversial so it is important not to assume that such issues cannot attract attention from those legislators who may be willing to invest political capital on them, such as when various presidents from both parties sought to enact national health insurance when they knew it would be controversial.

Unlike agency executives who often want to avoid contentious issues that could disrupt their agency, politicians are often attracted to issues associated with conflict if such issues can gain them support among their constituents. For example, liberal politicians may deliberately support an issue to anger conservatives and thus prove their ideological leanings to their liberal supporters. Legislators may opportunistically select issues that will give them media exposure and a resultant advantage over their opponents in an upcoming election battle. On other occasions, however, specific legislators decide not to invest their limited time and resources in issues that stand little or no chance of success.

Agencies

Agency executives must manage organizations, raise funds, hire staff, adjudicate conflicts, and plan—tasks that occupy most of their working hours. Executives also confront myriad policy issues, such as deciding what kinds of clients to serve and which social problems fall within the purview of the agency, naming overarching objectives or goals, developing policies and procedures within specific grant proposals, deciding whether to be advocates for their clients in the broader community or in a legislature, determining what kind of staff to hire, and developing policies and procedures to guide their staff. Some of these policies concern internal, procedural matters, while others concern the goals or mission of the organization in its political and funding context.

In light of these many tasks, executives must ignore or defer many issues, even ones that seem important to a staff member, a board member, or a client. Were executives to try to examine each issue in considerable detail, they would become exhausted and frustrated.

Executives also ignore or defer certain issues because they would embroil the agency in conflict. Even seemingly mundane issues such as changing an agency's intake procedures may impassion people who want the issue left alone. Often, they act only when they are convinced that an issue merits attention in spite of possible political conflict and the time and effort it may take. Perhaps they like an existing policy because it furthers their own interests, as when it facilitates a steady flow of certain kinds of clients to their units. Often more than staff, executives take a strategic view of their agencies, wanting policies that will give them a competitive advantage over other agencies. Policy advocates who can argue that a specific policy innovation will help an agency increase its resources and clientele may attract more support to it than if it is perceived as diminishing or having no effect on an agency's ability to survive. [2]

Executives may like an existing policy or one that is proposed by a policy advocate for ideological reasons. They may be committeed for instance, to serving a specific vulnerable population and be unwilling to diminish services for it. Or they may be committed to a specific approach to serving a specific population, believing it most effectively and efficiently meets their needs.

Policy advocates must develop a strategy to convince agency executives that their issues merit attention. When policy advocates succeed in placing an issue on the agendas of executives and agency boards, they do not necessarily succeed in getting them to enact new policies or to accept policy innovations, but at least they have a better chance than if these executives and boards develop little or no interest in the issue.

Communities

Agenda building also occurs in community settings as various issues vie for attention.Community activists may introduce ideas to community groups, the media, city or town councils, school boards, and other community influentials. These ideas could include blocking a freeway that will split the community, expanding a school, securing approval for a community park, or opening a counseling program for substance abusers. Activists may draw attention to a policy proposal by getting a story in the mass media, holding a community forum, or staging a protest. Or they may inject the issue into a campaign for city council or school board elections, with the ultimate objective of persuading community decision makers to prioritize it in their deliberations.

Three Challenges in Agenda Building

Agenda building can be conceptualized as a funnel. (See Figure 6.1.) We will discuss this agenda-building framework from the top down. Policy practitioners face three challenges when considering specific reforms: they (or their allies) must *diagnose* the context, *soften* the context, and *activate* change.

The top funnel illustrates the process that policy practitioners use to winnow a few issues from the multitude of issues that could be presented for active consideration. At the top of the funnel are the context and the practitioner's diagnosing role. Just beneath these are the modified context and the policy practitioner's softening role. The numbers *1* through *10* just above the funnel represent the many potential issues that exist in any setting. Policy entrepreneurs, who are discussed in more detail later, engage in the activating role when they pull a specific issue (in this case, number 8) into the funnel, where it is placed on the decision agenda when someone or some group prioritizes it for systematic deliberation. (See the decision agenda at the bottom of the top funnel in Figure 6.1.)

After an issue is placed on the decision agenda, such as on to the agenda of a meeting or committee, it then enters policy deliberations where it is waylaid, defeated, or enacted. (See the bottom funnel in Figure 6.1.) This is a second winnowing process; relatively few policies are actually enacted after they enter policy deliberations.

We can tell the stage of an issue in Figure 6.1 by asking several questions: Has the issue been floated with little or no discussion? If so, it is in the original context or the modified context. Has the issue been forwarded to a committee, a task force, or some other deliberative entity for further discussion? If so, it is on the decision agenda. Have systematic deliberations begun? If so, it is in policy deliberations. Has the issue been enacted by decision makers? If so, it is positioned for implementation at the bottom of the second funnel.

Policy advocates need to diagnose the context to identify contextual constraints and opportunities. If they decide that specific policies will be extremely difficult to change, they must do considerable work to change the context or to focus on alternative policy changes. When they decide that the contextual opportunities far outnumber constraints, they can initiate a policy changing strategy at once. In some cases, the prognosis will be guarded or unclear.

Having diagnosed the context, policy advocates must soften it; that is, they must make it more amenable to a specific policy initiative. Even when the context appears

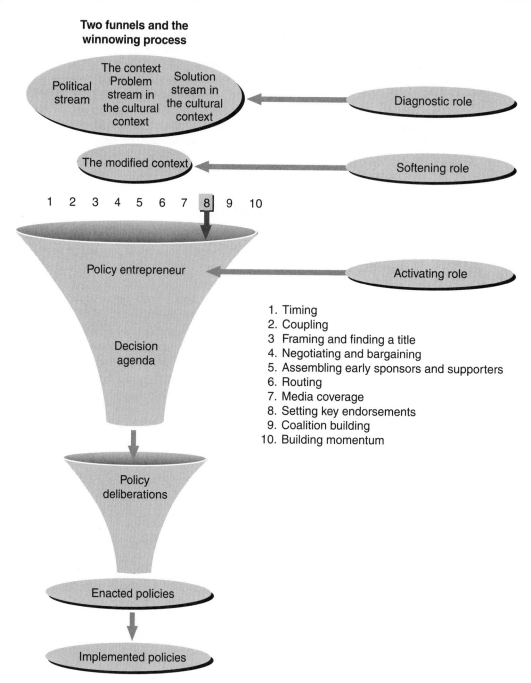

Two funnels and the winnowing process

Political stream
The context
Problem stream in the cultural context
Solution stream in the cultural context

Diagnostic role

The modified context

Softening role

1 2 3 4 5 6 7 8 9 10

Policy entrepreneur

Activating role

Decision agenda

1. Timing
2. Coupling
3 Framing and finding a title
4. Negotiating and bargaining
5. Assembling early sponsors and supporters
6. Routing
7. Media coverage
8. Setting key endorsements
9. Coalition building
10. Building momentum

Policy deliberations

Enacted policies

Implemented policies

FIGURE 6.1
The agenda funnel

bleak, they may discover that a few conversations with strategically placed persons will make the prognosis more optimistic or will indicate that their pessimistic forecast was unwarranted. Or they may work with a coalition on advocacy group to pressure decision makers to take interest in a specific issue, such as by sending a delegation to them or by getting the issue placed on the meeting of a city council or school board.

At some point, of course, policy advocates need to activate change. They need to get a decision maker or legislator to put an issue on the agenda of the other decision makers in the agency, community, or legislative setting. The chairperson might place the issue on the agenda of an agency committee or staff meeting. Perhaps a legislator drafts a piece of legislation and initiates a search for cosponsors. Or maybe a state's director of health and human services presents a detailed analysis of a particular problem in the administration of his or her program.

Agenda building is, then, often a precursor to other policy practice tasks, although in some cases policy advocates may proceed with other tasks, such as developing a policy proposal, even before decision makers have shown an interest in a specific issue. Even in this case, however, policy advocates must return to agenda building to get the issue on decision makers' agendas lest they find their issue stymied for lack of interest by them. And, if policy advocates have successfully softened the context, they may make ultimate success in placing an issue on decision makers' agendas more likely.

I rely heavily on the pathbreaking work of political scientist John Kingdon in our discussion of agenda building. Before Kingdon wrote his classic work, *Agendas, Alternatives, and Public Policies,* many people ignored the agenda-building task altogether, conveying the misleading impression that policy reforms magically appear with no prior work by policy practitioners.[3] Or they used simplistic explanations. Some *rationalists* assumed, for example, that decision makers placed issues on agendas whenever they received technical reports or data that recommended a specific change. While this assumption is sometimes true, issues are often placed on agendas without empirical studies—and technical reports often gather dust in agency, community, and legislative settings. Indeed, legislators and even agency executives sometimes retain policies that they know to be ineffective if they are supported by powerful lobbyists or bring revenues to an agency. Some *incrementalists* assumed that administrators and legislators often introduced modest changes in existing policies in response to complaints or pressures, as when federal legislators expanded the Head Start program to include children with physical and mental disabilities in response to lobbying by groups representing these children. While incremental change often takes place, Kingdon rightly argues that decision makers, in both agency and legislative settings, often support major changes in existing policy.[4] Legislators sometimes seek a major overhaul of a program or the enactment of a major social reform. Agencies sometimes launch new programs that diverge markedly from their existing programs.

Another theorist developed the *garbage can theory* of agenda building. Emphasizing organizations, he noted that many ideas bubble up regarding problems (e.g., social problems, service delivery problems, and administrative problems) and solutions (e.g., service delivery, program, or administrative innovations).[5] These problems or solutions may surface at staff or committee meetings, or at a retreat of the executives and the board. Even when agency members and executives consider an issue fleetingly, these problems and solutions often retain a place in their memories, remaining in a state of limbo—a figurative garbage can—until they are placed on the agendas of decision makers at a later point in time as they recall them. Similarly, we can say that myriad problems and solutions exist in the "garbage cans" of legislatures. These problems and solutions derive from such sources as lobbyists, reform-minded legislators, think tanks, professional associations, and citizens. The garbage can theory suggests a more fluid and dynamic process than the rationalist or incrementalist theories, but it does not discuss in sufficient detail how certain issues are activated, or placed on policy agendas.

While we draw on Kingdon's theory, we also modify it. We include more factors in the context than he does, and we add the diagnosing, softening, and activating stages because they clarify the roles of policy advocates in bringing issues to the agenda.

As can be seen in Figure 6.1, agenda building is a precursor to actual deliberations. Agenda building merely gets specific issues or policies on the table to be followed by actual deliberations where they are processed by committees and legislatures. In this deliberative process, some of the issues and policies are also sifted out. Some are defeated. Some are cast aside. Some are tabled. What we have, then, are two funnels that each winnow issues and policies. What is actually enacted or approved—a small fraction of the issues and policies that began this trip at the top of the first funnel—comes out the bottom of the second funnel.

Even though many issues, problems, or solutions do not emerge from the bottoms of the funnels—or only make it through one of them—it is important to realize that many of them do emerge from both funnels as is illustrated by the many policies are enacted or approved by legislatures, communities, and agencies.

The Diagnosing Stage

When diagnosing the context, policy advocates must analyze streams of problems and solutions, recent professional decisions and trends, and political realities.

Streams of Problems and Solutions   When policy advocates begin their work, they must carefully consider the kinds of problems and solutions that have already been considered in a setting. Indeed, we can use Kingdon's language, as he refers to problem and solution "streams" in specific settings.[6]

In many agencies, one need merely examine developments in the agency during, say, the last 5 years to see that a problem stream exists. Take the earlier example of a small agency that provides job placement and career counseling services to women. The social worker who directs these services also founded the agency. In the beginning, the agency had a relatively narrow set of services, consisting mostly of posting job openings from area firms on a bulletin board and holding career-planning seminars for women. In the 10 years since its founding, the staff, the executive director, and the members of the board have identified problems that the agency could address. They initially discussed some of these ideas in meetings or in personal conversations, but over time, many of the ideas have led to new programs, funded grant proposals, and cooperative projects with other agencies. The agency has added special job placement and career planning services for Latinas, single teenage mothers, and displaced homemakers; a job placement program for unemployed women funded by the federal Job Training Partnership Act; and job fairs for high school women in a local school district. Each of these programs stemmed from a problem that someone placed in the agency's general problem stream in conversations or meetings. Of course, many other problems have been discussed that never reached solution. For example, the agency staff decided not to pursue a suggestion to provide a support group for unemployed women with a mental health orientation, because they believed it fell outside their mission, which emphasizes concrete services like job referral, job search, and career development services.

A stream of problems exists in legislative settings, too. Policy practitioners interested in reforming the child welfare system of a specific county, for example, would be likely to interview advocates and highly placed officials to find out what kinds of problems concerning the child welfare system have already been discussed. (See Policy Advocacy Challenge 6.2 for ways to search for legislative proposals that are in the hopper.)

POLICY ADVOCACY CHALLENGE 6.2 Using the Mass Media to Discover Issues that Might be Placed on Policy Agendas BRUCE JANSSON, PH.D.	Over a period of several weeks, collect stories in a local newspaper that suggest items problems or solutions that might be candidates for policy agendas in your jurisdiction. Group them under issues, problems, and solutions. Also analyze which public officials, parties, high-level officials or advocacy groups might be candidates to champion them, and at what level of government or in the private sector. Are persons and parties with different ideologies likely to approach the issues differently? To find out what issues are percolating in New Orleans, go to its leading newspaper, the Times-Picayune, at **http://www.nola.com**. You can use its search engine with such key words as "Hurricane Katrina" to find articles printed during the past 14 days. Engage in the same exercise to identify what issues, problems, or solutions might be candidates for policy agendas in New Orleans.

Similarly, a stream of solutions exists in agency, community, and legislative settings. In our women's job placement agency, the staff, the board, and the executive director have considered decentralizing services, adopting a sliding-fee schedule, merging with a local YWCA, developing joint programs with a community college, and developing a computer lab to help job seekers find positions. In a specific county, the board of supervisors and child welfare officials may consider new management systems, new record-keeping systems, partnerships with local schools, use of evidence-based practice, and different ways of recruiting foster parents.

We can classify solutions into three broad groups. Some propose specific programs, such as interventions to help children, single mothers, or older people. Others aim to correct institutional problems, such as financing a program, changing an agency's fee structure, or enhancing the collaboration of different agencies in serving a specific client group. Still others propose methods of making decisions, such as setting up a task force, establishing a committee, or organizing an interagency planning committee.

We rarely begin policy practice with a blank slate. By examining streams of problems and solutions in specific settings, policy advocates discover where their issue fits into this larger picture. They might discover, for example, that others have already introduced the issue, but that it went nowhere because of budgetary implications. Or they might discover that their issue has never been discussed, but that related issues were the subject of initial discussion several years ago. As they piece together the recent history of streams of problems and solutions, policy advocates get a better sense of their issue's prognosis.

Recent Professional Developments and Trends   Fads and trends can powerfully shape the prognosis of a policy reform. For example, partnerships and collaborations between agencies became widely popular in the mid-1990s, partly because many professionals, public officials, and funders came to believe that their clients required more intensive and complicated services than specific agencies could give. A policy reform encouraging collaboration would have fared better in this environment than if it had been introduced a decade earlier, when less attention was given to collaboration. More recently, evidence-based practice has been widely emphasized in professional literature—making it more feasible for policy advocates to put forward policies that are grounded in existing research, such as proposals for different or new interventions in a specific agency. Fads and trends can be discerned by examining professional journals, talking with professionals, and analyzing the kinds of innovations that funders (such as foundations and government agencies) prioritize.

Problem and solution streams exist in a cultural context whether in nations or in specific settings. "Problems" in one setting are not perceived to be problems in other settings. Americans are less likely to view great discrepancies in wealth as a problem as compared with many European nations. High levels of conflict between staff may be viewed as problematic in one agency but not another. Similarly, some solutions, such as national health insurance, are widely accepted in European nations but not the United States. It is important, then, to be familiar with the culture of specific settings to better understand the kinds of innovations that are relatively feasible in them, while also realizing that decision makers sometimes make policy choices that are discrepant with these traditions.

Political Realities   Background political developments powerfully influence whether specific issues will be placed on policy agendas, as our discussion of the big picture in Chapter Four suggests. Let's start with legislative settings. When working on a policy issue or reform, policy advocates need to consider the viewpoint of important officials by finding out what position they have taken on similar issues or reforms in the past. This consideration should include the following:

- The viewpoints of heads of government or chief executives
- The viewpoints of legislators, particularly those who have official positions (like majority speaker or committee chairperson) or who have influential roles in specific caucuses such as a women's caucus
- The viewpoints of the legislators from one's own district, since they often support proposals made by their constituents
- The viewpoints of legislators who have assumed leadership on similar issues in the past, such as legislators who have taken a personal interest in child welfare issues
- The viewpoints of key members of government bureaucracy, whether political appointees or civil servants, particularly those who oversee programs and policies relevant to the present issue
- The viewpoints of lobbyists or the heads of interest groups that are active on the issue or policy
- The viewpoints of the public as reflected in polls or in recently contested elections
- The extent to which a policy reform is likely to receive sympathetic coverage in the mass media as reflected by media coverage of similar issues in the past

Read Policy Advocacy Challenge 6.3 to better understand how high-level policy officials can sometimes have significant impact on agendas, even when they do not themselves have considerable resources that they can contribute to programs addressing issues they place on agendas.

POLICY ADVOCACY CHALLENGE 6.3

The Role of a High-Level Appointee in Placing Homelessness on Policy Agendas in Many Urban Areas

BRUCE JANSSON, PH.D.

In a little known campaign, more than 20 cities adopted a "housing first" policy in 2005 and 2006 where they sought to place homeless persons into apartments with "no strings attached."[1] Rather than placing them in drug treatment programs or transitional housing, homeless persons are "coaxed" into rooms of their own, i.e., supportive housing. A key catalyst for this movement has been an unlikely person, Phillip F. Mangano. Formerly the director of the Massachusetts Housing and Shelter Alliance, Mangano was appointed by President George W. Bush to head the United States Interagency Council on Homelessness. Mangano spent five years visiting many mayors and governors "brandishing successful examples, cost-benefit studies, and his own messianic fervor along with modest amounts of federal money." Mangano informed them that they would save money by investing in projects to place homeless persons in apartments, saving expenditures on shelters, soup kitchens, emergency rooms, detoxification centers and jails. Not only should public officials adopt policies, he said, to immediately move persons into apartments, but they should give them medical, mental health, and detoxification services in these settings, as well as job-finding services. A key feature of this supportive housing is monitoring by social workers who help them and link them to other services. Even if they continue to use drugs or alcohol, they can remain in their apartments.

Even with his motivational successes, however, Mangano could not easily surmount a key problem: cuts or lack of increases in key federal programs that might help homeless persons. So many cities had to combine federal funds with local, foundation, and corporate resources to even make a dent in the problem. The results have been impressive in such cities as New York, San Francisco, Philadelphia, Dallas, and Raleigh-Durham.

Meanwhile, such groups as the National Coalition Against Homelessness, chaired by Bob Erlenbusch, worked to place increases in federal funding for housing for homeless persons on the policy agendas of Congress and the president.

---

[1] For further discussion of this national movement, see Erik Eckholm, "New Campaign Shows Progress for Homeless," *The New York Times* (June 7, 2006), A1, A19.

Policy advocates also need to consider court rulings that are germane to their issue. With respect to homeless people, for example, court rulings have required some local jurisdictions to provide shelters for homeless people.

In agency settings, policy advocates must consider a range of factors that shape the prognosis of a specific reform or issue, including the following:

- The extent to which a policy reform is consonant with the agency's mission
- The state of the agency's budget, such as whether it is running a deep deficit or is balanced
- The amount of interest that specific agency funders are likely to have in a specific issue or problem

- The viewpoints of the key agency officials, such as the director, top administrators, or members of the board of directors, and the directors of important agency programs, as surmised from their position in prior years on similar issues
- The viewpoints of the agency officials or staff who are likely to be most impacted by a reform or issue
- The viewpoints of union leaders (if staff are unionized)
- The likely effects of a specific reform on an agency's clientele
- The likely position of the agency's accrediting bodies

In community settings, policy advocates must consider the following:

- The viewpoints of key community leaders
- Local public opinion
- The perspectives of the local media

When considering the prognosis of policy changes in any setting, several factors often suggest when specific policy innovations will be relatively difficult to achieve:

- The sheer magnitude of a policy change (large changes are often more difficult to obtain than more modest changes)
- Whether an issue is already politicized (if the issue has already excited considerable political conflict, it is likely to be associated with political conflict when it is reintroduced)
- Whether persons with considerable power believe that specific policy changes will harm their economic, professional, or political self-interest (if they have this negative orientation, policy reform will be more difficult)
- Whether a specific reform will be expensive or difficult to implement (policies that present logistical or funding problems are often opposed by agency executives)

When engaging in diagnostic work, policy advocates should not prematurely abandon an issue even when they believe it has a negative prognosis. Reforms that will help powerless or oppressed populations, for example, often encounter opposition. Had Martin Luther King, Jr., abandoned civil rights in the 1950s because of its poor prognosis, the subsequent enactment of civil rights legislation in the United States would have been significantly delayed.

The Softening Stage

Policy advocates can sometimes attempt to enhance the prognosis of a policy reform even before it enters policy deliberations by working in problem and solution streams and by building political support.

Working in Problem and Solution Streams As Kingdon suggests, those who want decision makers to take their problem seriously have to convince them that it is a problem and not merely a condition.[7] Unlike a condition, a problem poses a threat or danger to someone, whether a group in the population, an agency, or politicians. When a condition is perceived as a problem, legislators, agency officials, and others are more likely to view it as important—and even to believe that someone (or they themselves) will suffer dire consequences if it is not addressed. If agency executives believe that their agency will suffer important consequences if they do not support a reform, such as loss of resources or clientele, they will be more likely to support it. If proponents of measures to end homelessness can persuade public officials in a specific jurisdiction that they will save resources by helping homeless persons find affordable housing and jobs—such as by cutting welfare costs and the use of emergency rooms—they increase the odds that they will support reforms.

But how do we convince other people that certain conditions *are* problems? We can use data to argue that a condition is serious in its absolute numbers, that some subset of the population is afflicted far more than other portions of the population, or that the problem is becoming steadily worse.[8] Absolute numbers, such as the percentage of women with inadequate or no child care, can shock decision makers into believing that a condition is a problem. Someone with data indicating that Latinas lack adequate child care in far greater numbers than white women may be able to use these data to persuade legislators to fund day care for Spanish-speaking children. Data showing that a problem is worsening may convince legislators that it will reach crisis proportions without governmental intervention.

Policy advocates can use data to demonstrate that a specific social problem has important implications that extend beyond a specific issue or population. If persons who want greater federal support for measures to protect wetlands and offshore islands in the Gulf region can convince public officials that specific environmental measures will save the nation billions of dollars by saving Gulf Coast fisheries and other businesses, they will be more likely to succeed in obtaining their support.

Advocates for corrective action often use words such as *crisis* to describe a condition. Because this word is overused, the advocate needs some evidence or rationale for its use. Take, for example, the dramatic spread of tuberculosis in the United States in the 1990s, which particularly affected AIDS patients and immigrants. When drug-resistant strains of the disease spread because many persons failed to take the prescribed medications long enough, advocates of greater funding for tuberculosis programs were able to convince federal, state, and local officials to prioritize funding for public health programs.

Policy advocates also need to demonstrate that a problem is not hopeless and can be ameliorated. For example, advocates have often found it difficult to secure support for inner cities, the underclass, and even people who are homeless, because many legislators see these problems as unsolvable, in contrast to simpler ones. Advocates can buttress their cases by citing research or finding successful pilot projects that demonstrate that specific reforms will yield positive outcomes.

In addition, policy advocates can appeal to values such as the ethical principles of beneficence, social justice, and fairness by arguing that society (or a legislature) has a duty to address an issue. They can use value-based arguments, and they can illustrate them with specific case studies of persons who suffer from problems. In the case of Hurricane Katrina, for example, the testimony of persons who suffered grievous harm made a compelling case for policy reforms that would provide them with resources, services, and opportunities.

Because politicians often consider how taking corrective action will affect their careers, advocates often try to state problems in relatively broad terms. They may stress the absence of child care for working women rather than merely for persons on welfare, the increased incidence of Alzheimer's disease among all social classes and races, or inadequate sex education in American schools. By presenting problems in general terms, advocates increase the likelihood that more politicians will see the problem as important to significant segments of their constituencies.[9]

Terminology is important when describing problems. For example, some policy advocates may refer to a social program as "investing" in human needs rather than merely "spending" resources. Legislators and citizens are more likely to respond to this terminology because it suggests that society will receive a return on its expenditure of funds. Nomenclature can also appeal to socially acceptable symbols.[10] With the Adoption and Safe Families Act of 1997, congressional child welfare advocates used the term "safe families" in its title rather than a more technical term, knowing that few persons would want to oppose legislation with this goal.[11]

POLICY ADVOCACY CHALLENGE 6.4

Framing Issues to Attract Support for Policy Reforms

Bob Erlenbusch, Ph.D.

Go to **academic.cengage.com/ social_work/jansson** to watch this video clip

Policy advocates often have to ponder how to "frame" issues so that other persons are more likely to take them seriously. They have to decide what symbols, words, values, and proposed outcomes will make other persons listen to them. Listen to Policy Advocacy Challenge Video 6.4 where Bob Erlenbusch, Chair of the Board of the National Coalition Against Homelessness and the Executive Director of the Los Angeles Coalition to End Homelessness and Hunger, discusses how he is wrestling with ways to make homelessness an issue that persons who own their own homes can understand.

When faced with harsh fiscal realities, policy advocates try to show that a specific policy, such as increasing Head Start funding, will avert subsequent costly problems, such as welfare and crime. They may propose a pilot program and hope to expand it later.

Advocates encounter a double-edged sword when they use the word *prevention* to seek support for a problem. Prevention is, on the one hand, a culturally acceptable symbol because everyone prefers preventing a problem to fixing it afterward. On the other hand, decision makers often perceive preventive programs negatively. They may wonder if a specific problem, such as teenage pregnancy or drug use, can be prevented. They may want to prioritize services for persons who are already afflicted with a specific problem rather than to fund prevention. Those advocating preventive programs, then, need to find evidence that they can successfully avert problems when proposing a specific innovation.[12] In the case of preschool programs, for example, a significant body of research has emerged in the last two decades that demonstrates that they avert cognitive and other problems, as well as decrease school drop-out rates even in high schools years later.

Our discussion suggests that policy practitioners need to anticipate likely objections or opposition to a specific policy so they can diminish or rebut them. They should develop arguments to counter claims that a particular problem is not solvable or cannot be prevented, that a remedy is too expensive or too difficult to implement, that a particular issue does not fall within an agency's mission, that a specific problem is unimportant, or that voters will punish legislators who support a specific reform. As they successfully counter these objections, they soften the context, making it easier not only to get an issue placed on the agenda, but to get a reform enacted.

The media can serve as an important educational tool in policy practice. Stories in the press, on the radio, and on television about social problems can create powerful images in the minds of citizens and elected officials, who may decide to give them serious attention. A social worker in an agency found, for example, that a reporter from a local paper became a frequent ally.[13] When the social worker wanted the city to replace junkyards with low- and moderate-income housing in a specific neighborhood, several stories in the newspaper about the blighted area prompted local politicians to take the neighborhood's problems seriously, and to help find federal and state programs to build affordable housing and recreation areas in it.

Social workers can help to shape agendas by using the mass media. This is not easy to do because the media ration their scarce time among many claimants. With their proximity to many social issues and problems, however, social workers increasingly should seek air time and print space in local and national media.

POLICY ADVOCACY CHALLENGE 6.5

Using the Mass Media to Place Issues on Agendas

Bob Erlenbusch, Ph.D.

Go to **academic.cengage.com/social_work/jansson** to watch this video clip

Policy advocates increase their chances of getting media coverage if they develop a compelling story that has human interest. They need to be able to express the basic theme of this story in several sentences because they will not have the luxury of an extended story in the media in most cases. They can seek coverage from a single reporter with whom they have contact or who they call, telling him or her about their story. Additionally, they can put out a press release which they send to many print and visual media outlets, where they also convey in a succinct but compelling way what they will discuss at it, and who will make the presentation. They need to remember, however, that intensive competition exists for media space in light of the many possible stories that the media can cover. Their chances for coverage increase if the presenter or interviewee is a well known community leader. For more discussion of strategies for relating to the media, see Policy Advocacy Challenge Video 6.5 where Bob Erlenbusch, Chair of the Board of the National Coalition Against Homelessness and Executive Director of the Los Angeles County Coalition Against Homelessness and Hunger, discusses strategies for getting media coverage.

As with social problems, only certain solutions make it to agency or legislative agendas. Those who examine solutions often test their fiscal, administrative, and political feasibility.[14] Assume that a staff person in a job-counseling agency for women is advocating not only referring women to jobs, but actually training them. Some staff may be skeptical about this idea's feasibility. They may ask whether the agency, which has emphasized job referrals and job search, can develop training programs in fields such as computer literacy. Can it find facilities to house these services, foundations or government funders to fund them, and the needed staff? Can it place the graduates in actual jobs? Since this program represents a marked departure from current programs, it is likely to encounter political opposition from some staff, as well as some board members, who will question whether the proposal falls within the agency's mission. Some staff may fear as well that the proposed service will detract from existing services. Decision makers also judge a solution's likely effectiveness and technical merits. Will a proposed program actually help clients, and will it be sufficiently inexpensive to prove feasible in light of the agency's budget? Policy advocates can counter such skepticism, of course, by citing evaluative research or by showing how a solution has been success-fully used in model programs elsewhere. They can find possible funding sources for the proposed policy innovation.

Our discussion suggests that policy advocates must try to place a solution in a favorable light if they want it to get onto decision makers' agendas. They must accomplish this task, moreover, in settings where specific solutions vie with one another for the scarce space on agendas. They should also recognize that they may encounter opposition from persons or groups that do not like their solution and that want to cast it in an unfavorable light.

Political Realities   Policy advocates can also soften the context by diminishing opposition to a specific reform. They can talk with persons in strategic positions to educate them about the need for a specific reform. They can directly address the concerns or objections these persons have, and they can correct erroneous information.

As Tip O'Neill, the late Democratic Speaker of the House, suggested, it is often effective to co-opt others by asking for their suggestions.[15] Policy practitioners can ask people to offer suggestions about getting a policy reform on the agenda. As these people offer guidance about how to proceed, they sometimes unwittingly become part of the change effort.

When softening the political context, it is important not to prematurely dismiss some people on the basis of their ideology or prior positions. To the extent they can, policy advocates often want to construct a "big tent" that contains an array of persons, even those with divergent perspectives, to build a coalition that can support a policy reform. To achieve this objective, they must be open to input from a variety of people, have good listening skills to understand various perspectives, and be willing to compromise.[16]

Of course, this approach is not always feasible in highly polarized situations, where policy advocates sometimes have to rely on the support of a specific faction. Indeed, in some situations, policy advocates have to create a ruckus to get decision makers to pay attention to an issue, such as organizing demonstrations, picketing, or sit-ins. Disruptive activities sometimes backfire by hardening decision makers against a proposal or issue, but they can also mobilize popular opinion if used skillfully.

When an agency staff member wants to make the political context more favorable to a problem or solution, he or she can point to funding trends, court rulings, or professional developments that support a specific change in agency policy.

The Activating Stage

Now we turn our attention to the activating stage, which appears inside the top funnel in Figure 6.1. A policy entrepreneur is a decision maker, a legislator, a chairperson, an executive, or another person who has the power to pull an issue onto an agenda so that it will receive serious consideration.[17]

To pull an issue into the decision funnel, policy entrepreneurs use tactics that often include timing, coupling, negotiating, assembling early sponsors and supporters, and routing.

Timing and Windows of Opportunity   Calling key times "windows of opportunity," Kingdon suggests that they represent relatively brief moments when "the time is ripe" for specific initiatives. In legislative settings, key events often sensitize legislators to a specific issue. Dramatic and publicized stories, such as a homeless person's death from exposure or a flagrant example of child abuse, may make them suddenly aware of specific needs. A task force may issue a report that alerts people to a problem, such as the one issued in 2006 that described the extent construction workers in New Orleans were victimized by their employers through low wages, unpaid wages, unreimbursed overtime, and unsafe working conditions. When the media cover such events extensively, public opinion may encourage legislators or heads of government departments to consider a legislative proposal.

Pivotal events in the political stream stir up support for a specific problem or solution. With Bill Clinton's victory in November 1992, after 12 years of Republican rule, many people hoped that issues that had lain dormant would now reach congressional agendas, such as national health care reforms, parental leave bills, expanded programs for children, job-training initiatives, changes in military policies concerning gay men and lesbians, and pro-choice issues. With renewed hope that their issues would now reach decision or choice agendas, people invested time and resources in publicizing and championing them. As this example suggests, though, the placement of issues on decision agendas does not mean they will be successfully resolved. Political opposition and budget deficits stopped many of Clinton's reforms. This example also illustrates how windows of opportunity often close rapidly. When the Republicans captured control of both houses of the Congress in 1994 and retained this control in 1996, they aborted many of Clinton's reforms as did President George W. Bush and the Republican Congress from 2001 to 2007.

Policy reformers expected deep cuts in many social programs in the wake of George W. Bush's ascension to the presidency in November 2000. While the funding of some programs were cut during the two terms of his presidency, they were not cut as deeply as might have been expected from a relatively conservative president. Indeed, federal domestic discretionary spending, as well as spending on entitlements, rose markedly during the Bush presidency even if specific programs were cut. Also, unlike many preceding Republican presidents, Bush had not vetoed any spending bills even by September 2006. This was due in part to the narrow political balance in the Congress between conservatives on the one hand and liberals and moderates on the other hand. Key Republican moderates, such as Senator Olympia Snowe from Maine, insisted that many social programs not be cut. Bush wanted to woo moderates and independents in the electorate, moreover, who were critical to Bush's goal of retaining control of the Senate and the House of Representatives in many jurisdictions, and many of them supported funding of many domestic programs.

Similarly, Republicans hoped when George W. Bush won the White House in 2000, that many issues that conservatives had suggested during the preceding eight years would come to the surface. They hoped that large tax cuts would be enacted particularly for middle-, upper-middle, and upper-class Americans. Some of them wanted large increases in military spending. Even during the presidential campaign, Bush had discussed "faith-based initiatives" to give religious institutions federal dollars to provide services to poor people, the homeless, and others. Conservatives hoped that proposals to privatize Social Security—letting citizens invest their own resources rather than turning over their payroll taxes—would soon be enacted. They favored vouchers for schools so citizens could select whatever schools they wanted with vouchers funded by the government.

Here, too, fast-moving events shifted the agenda. The tragic destruction of the Twin Towers in New York City on September 11, 2001 propelled issues of national and domestic security to the forefront while putting many domestic policy issues on the backburner. Hurricane Katrina similarly forced attention to the policy issues of the Gulf region, and diverted about $110 billion to its problems even if much of these resources had not yet been spent even in a year after Katrina hit.

Regular, predictable windows of opportunity exist in legislative settings during annual budget preparations, when advocates can seek a discussion of expanded resources for specific programs.[18] When legislation is being reauthorized—that is, renewed—advocates sometimes obtain reforms in the legislation. When tax revenues increase more rapidly than had been expected, more resources exist for spending on social programs at home and abroad.

Pivotal events in social agencies also create opportunities for changing policy. A governor, mayor, or large foundation might announce a new program for dealing with a problem related to an agency's mission, thereby creating a positive milieu for policy changes. Dramatic events may sensitize an agency's executive director or board members to a problem that the agency does not currently address; Hurricane Katrina forced the federal government to pay more attention to the levees in New Orleans after neglecting them for decades. An affluent person may bequeath unexpected funds to an agency, enabling it to start a new program. Fiscal crises sometimes force an agency to reconsider its priorities or to search frantically for resources from new funding sources. Perhaps an accrediting agency is about to make a visit, causing the agency to make some changes that will guarantee a favorable report.

New tides in an agency's politics also create opportunity, such as the arrival of a new executive director or other high-level staff.[19] While executives are not omnipotent, their critical position allows them to chart new directions for agencies. Changes in the leadership of an agency's board of directors may also create a positive milieu for policy changes. When agencies engage in systematic planning about their mission and programs—often called *strategic planning*—their staff and boards are often open to program and policy reforms. Indeed, strategic planning is a formal planning approach to finding issues, problems, and solutions that should be placed on agendas. (See Policy Advocacy Challenge 6.3.)

In similar fashion, a change of presidents and governors or a shifting of majorities from one to another party in one or both legislative branches of the federal government or state government can signal a window of opportunity for a policy that had a poor prognosis before these shifts in leadership.

Timing allows policy entrepreneurs to capitalize on windows of opportunity. Their strategy involves (a) preparing for an opportunity by analyzing an issue or problem, (b) recognizing when a window of opportunity augurs well for it, and (c) seizing the moment by seeking support for placing it on the decision agenda.[20] In government settings, the policy entrepreneur is often an enterprising legislator with persistence, creativity, respectability, and good timing, or a creative lobbyist or advocate who convinces a legislator that the time is ripe to draft and introduce legislation on a specific issue before the window of opportunity closes. In agency settings, policy entrepreneurs can come from anywhere within the organization, recognizing a window of opportunity for a specific issue and persuading others to place it on the decision agenda.

Alas, windows of opportunity often close, and often in a relatively short time. Perhaps crises emerge that divert attention of public officials to other issues. Perhaps leaders change, people think that a problem has been adequately addressed by some other measure, and new issues supplant older ones. Perhaps the momentum of a specific policy proposal is lost as persons haggle over the details of a suggested reform, as opposition emerges, as budget exigencies intervene, or as other issues surface. In the case of New Orleans, policy advocates had to try to keep many of the problems that they confronted before federal and state legislators who often wanted to move onto other issues when the newspaper headlines about Katrina's destruction had vanished. Indeed, the editors of the *Times-Picayune*, the New Orleans newspaper, chose to put their newspaper online (http://www.nola.com) so that public officials and the news media in other parts of the nation would possess nonstop coverage about the many needs of citizens of New Orleans even many months after Hurricane Katrina.

Coupling

Policy practitioners sometimes try to make imaginative connections between the solution, problem, and political streams depicted in Figure 6.1. Perhaps someone in an agency has discussed decentralizing services (a solution) while someone else has noted the relative lack of services to the Latino population (a problem). A policy entrepreneur in the agency may suggest writing a grant proposal to develop outreach stations for the Latino population, a proposal that would couple the problem with the solution.[21] Or perhaps someone links the many problems of public schools in New Orleans prior to Hurricane Katrina, including high drop-out rates and poor student achievement levels, with the solution "charter schools," where schools are placed under the control of parents and administrators rather than the public bureaucracy that had governed them. Quite apart from whether it was good policy to do so, the vast bulk of public schools in New Orleans had become charter schools within a year of Hurricane Katrina because of this coupling.

Framing and Finding Titles

Policy entrepreneurs put a twist on proposals to make them appealing to decision makers. For example, they may portray a benefit as an *earned* benefit to make it difficult for opponents to argue that it is a *welfare* benefit. This strategy is illustrated by arguments used to support the enactment of the Earned Income Tax Credit given to families with working parents in 1973, and to increase its size so that it is now the largest anti-poverty program funded by the federal government. Had the Earned Income Tax Credit been framed as a *welfare* program, it probably would not have been enacted in light of widespread political opposition to welfare. Even critics of George W. Bush's program, No Child Left Behind, would agree that the title cleverly makes it difficult for opponents to marshal opposition to it, because we would all agree that no child *should* be left behind.

Negotiating and Bargaining

Even before an issue appears on the decision agenda, policy entrepreneurs need to accommodate different points of view. Even though policy proposals are not fully developed until an issue has entered policy deliberations (see the bottom of the funnel in Figure 6.1), policy entrepreneurs often develop their tentative outlines even before this. They often try to create a *win-win* atmosphere that allows different people and factions to believe they will each have a piece of the action. By contrast, if a *win-lose* atmosphere exists even before an issue reaches policy deliberations, public officials are more likely to have a combative mood that will sometimes imperil the policy's enactment.[22]

Negotiating and bargaining take place in agency and community settings, as well, Assume, for example, that a planning commission in a specific city is deciding whether the approve the placement of a residential treatment center for substance abusers in a specific neighborhood. If the supporters of this center give residents a chance not only to discuss the proposed center, but to offer suggestions about how it might be administered so that it does not cause crime or other neighborhood problems, opposition to it is likely to decrease—and the planning commission is more likely to approve it.

Assembling Early Sponsors and Supporters

In legislative arenas, policy entrepreneurs actually enlist people to sponsor a legislative proposal by placing their names on it. The characteristics of these sponsors is very important: If they are powerful politicians who also represent an array of perspectives, the chances of the legislation passing are much better than if the legislation is sponsored by only a narrow range of politicians who lack power.[23] Even in agency settings, policy entrepreneurs often enlist an array of persons during the agenda-building process by soliciting their advice and by making them part of the planning process.

To return to our example of the residential treatment center, a policy advocate would be well advised not only to invite persons in the neighborhood to come to meetings about it, but would cultivate highly respected neighborhood leaders, whose support would be most helpful to getting residents to support it.

Routing

Policy entrepreneurs must find a home base for their issue by routing it to decision makers who want to resolve it in ways that the entrepreneurs find acceptable. When a choice exists in legislative settings, they have to decide which committee should get jurisdiction. Naturally, a policy entrepreneur does not want an issue routed to a committee whose chairperson or members do not want to act on it or have contrary views. By discussing the routing with highly placed politicians and members of a special committee (called the Rules Committee in the U.S. House of Representatives), policy entrepreneurs can sometimes influence routing decisions.[24] Policy entrepreneurs influence routing decisions in agency settings as well; they may seek jurisdiction by a specific committee, the general staff, the agency's board, an ad hoc committee, or the executive director. Of course, some issues, such as fundamental changes in agency policies, have to be considered by the agency board.

Media Coverage

Timely coverage of proposals is often critical in projecting them onto decision agendas in the case of legislation and community decisions. Policy entrepreneurs who are state or federal legislators often use the media to get stories about their activities printed or placed on television in their home districts.

POLICY
ADVOCACY
CHALLENGE 6.6

The Competition
for Policy
Agendas—and
Diversions
from Them

BRUCE JANSSON,
PH.D.

The scramble for scarce resources in the wake of Hurricane Katrina illustrates the challenge that policy advocates often encounter. All experts agreed: the hurricane's wrath was most concentrated in New Orleans, as well as in specific cities in southern Mississippi and Alabama such as Gulfport, Biloxi, and Mobile. Yet considerable FEMA assistance was given to counties and cities that experienced only tropical storm-force winds not exceeding 74 mph. Jackson, Mississippi, for example, received $21 million when only 50 to 60 homes were declared uninhabitable. Mississippi requested the Bush Administration to broaden the initial disaster area to extend as far as 220 miles inland. The Red Cross followed FEMA's example and also gave extensive aid to outlying and relatively undamaged areas, some of it to persons who fraudulently claimed damage when none or little existed. A large amount of resources directed toward New Orleans actually went to repairing military facilities—resources not taken from the already-large military budget.

Some policy advocates feared that large amounts of federal loans and grants would go to private commercial interests intent on rebuilding New Orleans as a tourist center—thus bleeding funds needed for affordable houses, schools, and other basic needs of vulnerable populations.

Policy advocates in New Orleans had to contend, then, with intense competition for space on policy agendas. Wanting to prioritize the needs of vulnerable populations whose housing had been destroyed, they found that other claimants for resources often succeeded in getting on policy agendas even when their needs were not as large as vulnerable populations and even when their resources could have come from existing military and other budgets.

They also had to contend with diversions of resources from those resources supposedly dedicated to the needs of vulnerable persons, such as from fraud and corruption. Government investigators revealed in June 2006 that over $1 billion of FEMA resources was fraudulently claimed by criminals. Still other resources were wasted because FEMA staff miscalculated the benefits that specific persons were due. All told, the overall estimate of $2 billion in fraud and waste amounted to nearly 11 percent of the $19 billion spent by FEMA on Hurricanes Katrina and Rita by June 2006. According to Senator Susan Collins (R., Maine) who chairs the U.S. Senate's Homeland Security and Governmental Affairs Committee, "The blatant fraud, the audacity of the schemes, the scale of the waste—it is simply breathtaking."[1]

Listen to Russell Henderson, MSW, LCSW, in Policy Advocacy Challenge Video 6.6 as he discusses competition for policy agendas and waste in New Orleans.

Go to
academic.cengage.com/
social_work/jansson
to watch this video clip

[2] Eric Lipton, "Breathtaking Waste and Fraud in Hurricane Aid," New York Times (June 27, 2006, pp. A1, A13.

Can Direct-Service Staff Help to Build Agendas?

Our discussion suggests that policy advocates in agency and legislative settings can diagnose and soften the context, as well as search for a policy entrepreneur.

Is agenda building restricted to legislators and high-level agency staff, such as executive directors? To be sure, these persons are best situated to assume pivotal roles in building agendas, but direct-service staff can participate in agenda building in both agency and legislative settings. They can begin by working within their agencies and agency networks, by locating unaddressed or poorly addressed community needs. They can read professional literature and find evidence-based practices that could be (but are not) implemented in specific settings, drawing this to the attention of other staff members as well as executives. They can join coalitions and advocacy groups that already exist in the community and lend them volunteer and other support. As persons who directly serve persons, they gain credibility from their direct observations of persons and communities that their agency or program seeks to serve.

Direct service staff ought, as well, to move beyond their agencies into the broader policy world. They can talk with legislative aides about specific unaddressed or poorly addressed issues that they have seen in their work. They can encourage their clients to call high-level officials within agencies and agency networks, and within legislatures or commissions at the local, state, and federal levels. They can help their clients draft letters to these officials.

To the extent that their agency is not involved in trying to shape policies that are relevant to its clientele or to the community, direct-service staff can ask whether voter registration projects can be organized by their agency or by other agencies in their area, or whether informational materials can be distributed by agencies about specific propositions or initiatives on the ballot. Agencies cannot endorse specific candidates, but they can endorse propositions or initiatives.

Persons do not have to—and should not—wait to become policy advocates until they have risen to executive positions in agencies. If they limit their work only to clinical practice at the outset of their careers, they risk limiting their horizons thereafter as well. If it is ethically meritorious to be a policy advocate, as we discussed in Chapter Two, why not begin this trajectory not only while in a school or department of social work, but in the initial phases of one's career?

To find windows of opportunity, staff can identify strategic times in the workings of agencies or legislatures when conditions will favor advancing specific initiatives. Finally, staff can search for policy entrepreneurs who can place a specific issue on their agency's or a legislature's agenda, or on the agenda of a city council, school board, commission, or county board of supervisors.

Policy Advocacy for Powerless Populations and Unpopular Issues

Thus far, our discussion about agenda building has emphasized how agenda processes work and how a pragmatic policy practitioner can use these processes to reach policy goals. When we discuss how agenda processes actually work, however, it is important to remember that they are often skewed against unpopular issues and powerless groups. For example, the Children's Defense Fund, established in 1973, sought for more than 15 years to convince Congress to place day care on its agenda, finally succeeding in 1989. Advocates of initiatives to end homelessness have made considerable success, but still have a long way to go as homeless populations in major cities—and even some suburban and rural areas—suggest. Those who want to change the American federal tax structure to truly reduce economic inequality have been relatively unsuccessful for decades, although they have succeeded in taking many persons with low income off federal tax rolls, even if they must continue to pay Social Security and Medicare taxes.

Groups that plug away for unpopular issues and populations may be laying the groundwork for subsequent policy changes. In the case of day care and the Children's Defense Fund, advocates' diligent and sustained lobbying, as well as their assistance to grassroots reform groups throughout the United States, doubtless educated many politicians about the specific problems and needs of children. When pressure from feminist groups and corporations that hired large numbers of women finally placed day care on Congress's decision agenda in the 1980s, the Children's Defense Fund spearheaded a coalition to seek specific legislation. Had they not promoted the issue in the preceding two decades, however, they might not have been successful in legislation they enacted in 1990; had they not been active over an extended period, this legislation, which was hardly adequate in its funding and scope, might have been even more limited.

We have mostly discussed policy change through conventional channels, such as by working with public officials in legislative settings or with executives in agency settings. We should note, however, that some policy advocates conclude at specific points in time and in specific places that they cannot secure policy initiatives working solely through conventional channels. Abolitionists in the 1850s, suffragettes in the early part of last century, and civil rights advocates in the 1950s and 1960s used nonviolent protest strategies to force neglected issues onto public officials' agendas, as did a national movement of persons seeking reforms in immigration legislation in 2006. They persisted despite criticism that their tactics were unethical or unwarranted, or that they were counterproductive.

Policy advocates who use protests as a part of their strategy to secure policy changes should realize that they can sometimes harden the positions of some public officials against the reforms that they seek, or that protests can sometimes lead to a backlash by persons who oppose their policies. Yet some policy advocates believe they must use nonviolent protests and demonstrations because decision makers will not otherwise pay attention to them, and the general public will remain ignorant or opposed to their positions. The organizers of nationwide protests to secure more human immigration policies in the United States came to this precise conclusion in 2006, leading to a series of massive, nationwide demonstration of hundreds of thousands of persons. Consider public demonstrations, then, to be an arrow in policy advocates' quivers, but realize, too, that they are not a panacea and must, in any case, be supplemented with efforts to work through conventional channels to get specific proposals enacted.[25]

Electoral Processes

Agenda setting often takes place within electoral politics as politicians, parties, and activists try to find issues that can be used to distinguish themselves from their opposition. They want issues that will appeal to their natural constituencies while also allowing them to appeal to swing voters. Sometimes they want issues (so-called "wedge issues") that will divide the opposing party. If they do not find new issues and their opponents do, they lose a strategic advantage in upcoming elections.

The search for new issues is particularly intense after a party loses an election. When George W. Bush won the White House in 2004, for example, Democrats wondered where they should go next in terms of issues. Liberals in their ranks wanted Democrats to focus on health care reform, policies to help working families (such as child care, college tuition subsidies, increasing the Earned Income Tax Credit), and tax increases for affluent Americans. More moderate or conservative Democrats were more leery of major social reforms or tax increases—and often opposed a time schedule for withdrawing troops from Iraq.

Republicans, in turn, wanted issues that would appeal to their natural constituencies while also retaining support of swing suburban votes. Playing the same card that he had used in the 2002 and 2004 elections, as his party neared congressional elections in 2006, President George W. Bush sought to convince voters that Republicans were tougher on terrorism than Democrats, often stating or hinting that the latter favored "cutting and running" from Iraq. In turn, many Democrats sought to focus the campaign not on terrorism, which favored Bush, but on the "failed Iraq policies" of the president. They reminded voters that many experts had shown that Saddam Hussein, the Iraqi leader deposed by the United States, had not had links with known terrorists and had no role in the attack on the World Trade Center on September 11, 2001.

Local candidates also engage in agenda building as they seek issues that will generate support for themselves as compared to their opponents.

In this nonstop process of agenda setting, ideology assumes a key role partly because the two major parties have somewhat different bases of political support. A large segment of Republicans' constituencies derives from relatively affluent segments of the population, farmers, and southerners, as well as residents of so-called "Red States" in the Midwest and Rocky Mountain area. In contrast, the more urban, northern, and working-class population, as well as the so-called coastal "Blue States" like New York and California, provide a base of support for Democrats. Republicans' natural base of support is relatively more conservative than Democrats', so the two parties gravitate toward somewhat different ideologies and, therefore, positions on issues.

Ideological differences between the two parties ought not to be overstated, however. Both parties often compete for swing votes, such as in the suburbs, where many citizens are somewhere in the middle. So both parties often battle for the center, seeking issues and policies that will appeal to centrist voters so they can gain a winning edge.

Developing Links with Advocacy Groups

Policy advocates who wish to build agendas in the broader community, but who do not know how to get started, should consider connecting with an established advocacy group. (See Box 2.1.) Effective advocacy groups try to shape public officials' agendas by pressuring them to consider solutions or problems, presenting research that underlines the importance of addressing specific social needs, and publicizing stories in the mass media that dramatize certain issues. Would-be advocates can join a local group or a local chapter of a national group, meet the director of the advocacy group, subscribe to its newsletters and other materials, volunteer to work on its outreach and education projects, help its staff conduct research, and help the group lobby public officials. Those who want to be involved can work with local and state chapters of the National Association of Social Workers (NASW), whose leaders and lobbyists pressure legislators. Both advocacy groups and the NASW not only generate ideas for policy agendas, such as specific pieces of legislation, but also put pressure on politicians to move these ideas toward choice or decision agendas. They often try to convince the chairpersons of pivotal legislative committees, for example, to hold hearings and seriously discuss proposals, rather than let them slip into oblivion.

Policy advocates can also campaign for politicians they believe will put certain issues on policy agendas. For example, PACE, the political action arm of NASW that backs politicians who support issues favored by NASW, regularly canvasses NASW members to work for the candidates it supports.

Using Multiple Skills in Agenda Building

Policy advocates use the four skills that we discussed in Chapter Three when they try to influence policy agendas. They use *political skills* to analyze and engage in the political stream; *analytic skills* to develop and use data in the problem and solution streams; *interactional skills* to help problems and solutions reach policy deliberations in agency and legislative settings, persuade people to take specific problems and solutions seriously, participate on committees and task forces, and organize coalitions and *value-clarifying skills* to decide whether to invest energy in promoting an issue in the first place and to decide how to frame it.

POLICY ADVOCACY CHALLENGE 6.7

Challenges in Placing Vulnerable Populations on Policy Agendas in New Orleans Post-Katrina

Bruce Jansson, Ph.D.

Hurricane Katrina played no favorites in its destruction of New Orleans and surrounding areas. If shanty houses of low-income African Americans in the Lower Ninth Ward were mostly destroyed by it, so also were homes of many middle-class and affluent persons of all social classes and ethnicities.

Yet policy advocates, who often focus their work on issues of vulnerable populations, encountered particular challenges in placing them on policy agendas in Washington, DC, in Baton Rouge (where Louisiana's legislature meets), and in New Orleans.

Many policy advocates sought policies that would help vulnerable populations in Katrina's wake including the Baton Rouge Crisis Intervention Center, Common Ground, the Grassroots Legal Network, the Hispanic Apostolate, Catholic Charities, the Archdiocese of New Orleans, the Family Service of Greater New Orleans, Hope House, INCITE (Women of Color Against Violence), the Latino Health Outreach Project, the Loyola Poverty Law Clinic, the Mary Queen Vietnam Catholic Church, the Mississippi Workers Center for Human Rights, the NAACP (in Lafayette, La.), the NAACP Gulf Coast Office, the New Orleans Worker Justice Coalition, the People's Hurricane Relief Fund and Oversight Coalition, the People's Institute for Survival and Beyond, the Rebuilding Louisiana Coalition, the Southern Poverty Law Center (in Montgomery, Alabama), the Safe Streets/Strong Communities, the Student Hurricane Network, and the Youth Empowerment Project—just to name a few of them. Policy advocates also included specific trade unions, local politicians, faculty at many New Orleans and Louisiana colleges and universities, and many private citizens—not to mention local, state, and federal public officials. These policy advocates sought to place issues, problems, and solutions on policy agendas in the city council, the mayor's office, specific planning groups in parishes and in the city, and also in state and federal agencies and legislatures.

Agenda-Building Challenges in Washington, DC

Within a month of Katrina, the nation's capitol became a hotbed of agenda-building activities that was dominated by members of both political parties. To an extraordinary degree, media coverage of Hurricane Katrina had brought before the nation a

(continued)

topic that it had not focused upon since the 1960s: issues presented by low-income African Americans as they crowded into the Superdome or waved at cameras while stranded on the tops of buildings, highways, or bridges.

Congress immediately enacted funds for FEMA in the wake of Katrina, but many public officials wanted to think beyond the immediate relief needs of citizens in New Orleans.

This hurricane opened the policy agenda of the Congress and presidency to issues of intractable or severe poverty. Reeling from criticism of him and his administration for inaction in Katrina's wake, President George W. Bush promised in mid-September "one the largest reconstruction efforts the nation has ever seen." Democratic leaders, in turn, wanted to offer their own proposals for rebuilding New Orleans.

President Bush's solutions to this problem came from solutions that he had long proposed. He wanted to build in New Orleans and the Gulf region an "ownership society" that focused on giving poor persons $5,000 "spending accounts" so that they could purchase job training and education, and providing them with educational vouchers so they could purchase education from for-profit schools established after the hurricane. He wanted to give businesses tax incentives to stimulate their renewal in the region. He wanted rebuilding efforts to be "locally driven" rather than dictated by the federal government.

Democrats, in turn, argued that an ownership-society approach would not work. They wanted more activist solutions like a "New Deal-style authority that would coordinate the rebuilding of the region and put thousands of people to work rebuilding their communities."[1] They wanted to integrate low-income persons in middle-income neighborhoods rather than relying on FEMA trailers in their low-income and segregated areas, or merely rebuilding the 8,000 units of public housing that had been placed almost exclusively in low income areas.

It seemed, then, that members of both parties would place many solutions onto Congress's policy agenda. In fact, both Congress and the Bush administration soon lost interest in rebuilding New Orleans in fall 2005. Many conservatives and some moderates came to view the destitute African Americans who had been so apparent in media coverage during and after the hurricane in negative terms. Should they not have evacuated like many other citizens? Were they not persons of poor character who would not have been poor had they worked hard? Would "handouts" merely make them dependent on welfare? Many Republicans were offended, moreover, by the Louisiana delegation's estimate that $250 billion in federal funds would be needed to rebuild the Gulf Coast—a staggering sum at a time that the federal government had a massive federal deficit.

Other events crowded New Orleans off the policy agenda including the war in Iraq and unrest in other parts of the Middle East—not to mention foreign-policy issues in other parts of the world. Despite diligent efforts by the Louisiana congressional delegation to keep the issue on policy agendas, it seemed that major legislation and significant resources would not be forthcoming.

Then another set of actors entered the situation—influential and frustrated Mississippi officials. Unlike public officials from Louisiana and New Orleans who mostly were Democrats, the Mississippi public officials were mostly Republicans. Their Gulf

---

[1] "Reinventing the War on Poverty," *Congressional Quarterly Weekly*, September 19, 2005, p. 2479

communities, too, had been harmed by Katrina when it turned east even before it hit New Orleans. They, too, wanted massive resources and myriad programs. They played a critical role in keeping the rebuilding of the Gulf Coast on policy agendas.

Then, too, top Republican strategists came to realize that the response to Hurricane Katrina could become a major issue in the congressional elections of November 2006—only one year off. Public opinion polls had disclosed that Bush's popularity had fallen after Katrina. Were they not to improve or to get worse, Democrats chances of controlling Congress would be greatly increased.

With pressure from Mississippians supplementing the Louisianans, and with Bush renewing his interest in the issue, the way was set for movement of a $29 billion package for rebuilding levees, schools, and highways, as well as aiding state and local governments whose tax revenues had plummeted in the storm's wake in late 2005. Local governments would get $11.5 billion of these funds through the Community Development Block grant program that gave states wide discretion in their use of the funds. Bush signed into law, as well, a $7.8 billion measure providing tax incentives to stimulate investment in hurricane areas to go along with the tax relief that had been enacted in September for individual victims and businesses.[2]

Even with these victories, however, public officials from Louisiana failed to get another key initiative: a program that would fund federal subsidies of $150,000 to each homeowner whose home had been destroyed or damaged. Minus this assistance, many homeowners would not be able to rebuild or repair their homes since many of them had insurance policies that only covered wind damage, not flood damage. This issue was on the agenda of the president and Congress by fall 2005, even if it would take many more months for legislation finally to emerge in summer 2006.

Once again, policy advocates feared in February 2006 that the Bush Administration had lost interest in rebuilding New Orleans since he hardly mentioned it in his State of Union speech. Would he once again prioritize it, and would he commit the far larger resources to New Orleans and the Gulf Coast? Once again, policy advocates would have to push issues onto the administration's agenda, perhaps once again getting help from public officials in Mississippi. Once again, the president would decide he had no choice but to help New Orleans, such as promising by late February to fund a proposal to help homeowners repay, rebuild, or relocate by giving them up to $150,000 each, minus whatever insurance payments they had received.[3]

Even as some policy advocates focused on the needs of New Orleans, others sought federal help for evacuees from New Orleans that had gone to cities like Houston, Baton Rouge, and Dallas. These cities needed federal assistance in funding the school, housing, and social-service needs of evacuees, who mostly remained unemployed even a year after Katrina. Even a year after Katrina hit, many of the leaders of these cities complained that insufficient federal resources had reached them to fund the additional costs they had footed for evacuees.

---

[2] Joseph Schatz, "End-of-Session Gift for the Gulf Coast," *Congressional Quarterly Weekly*, December 12, 2005, pp. 3401-3403.
[3] Joseph Schatz, "Navigating Crossfire on the Gulf Coast," *Congressional Quarterly Weekly*, March 6, 2006, 583-586.

(continued)

**POLICY
ADVOCACY
CHALLENGE 6.7**

(continued)

Agenda-Building Challenges in Baton Rouge and New Orleans

Policy advocates also had to get proposals and problems on the policy agendas of public officials in the city of New Orleans and the state of Louisiana. They had to work in a city and state that had not been particularly kind to African Americans prior to Hurricane Katrina. About 28 percent of New Orleans' citizens fell beneath federal poverty lines, as compared, for example, to only about 14 percent in Kansas City, which was roughly the same size. Poor persons were mostly African American (67 percent of them) and Caucasian (28 percent of them) with only small numbers of low-income Asian and Latino residents in New Orleans prior to Katrina. Like many other cities, the low-income African-American population was concentrated in specific areas, including New Orleans East, the Lower Ninth Ward, Central City, Holligrove, and Treme.

New Orleans' economy had stagnated for years. With its economy focusing on shipping and tourism, it had failed to develop industries that could provide resources to its low-income population. Indeed, New Orleans' population had declined from 600,000 to 460,000 persons from 1960 to 2005—and this population had become even more segregated by race and class as many white persons fled the area or moved to suburbs.

New Orleans had one of the worst correctional, police systems and school systems in the nation even before Hurricane Katrina. It had the second highest murder rate for a city in the nation. Its police department made 114,000 arrests in 2004—or almost one in every four adults—but it mostly released these persons with no follow-up or social services.

Nor were the public schools generally effective—with about 40 percent of the city's population illiterate. Its teachers were seriously underpaid, with salaries in Louisiana the third lowest of any state. The city's public system of health care lacked resources to cope with very high rates of infant mortality, chronic diseases like diabetes, heart disease, and AIDS. It had such poor outpatient services that citizens' use of emergency rooms was far higher than the national average.

Nor had New Orleans' political structure been responsive to the needs of vulnerable populations. With notable exceptions, members of the city council had taken few initiatives to assist vulnerable populations in prior decades. Ray Nagin, the African American mayor, was widely viewed by his own community to be nonresponsive to their needs, instead prioritizing the local business community. The state's legislature had also neglected New Orleans as its legislators prioritized the needs of rural areas and relatively small towns and cities.

Policy advocates, then, had to work hard to get the needs of vulnerable populations on the agendas of city and state officials to address their urgent needs. Most residents of major cities take city services for granted, such as the provision of water, electricity, and sanitation ones, as well as road maintenance. They also assume that police and fire services will be readily available. None of these assumptions could be made in Katrina's wake since city facilities had often been destroyed, and many personnel had fled the city never to return. The problem of delinquent services was most acute in many low-income areas as compared with more affluent areas. A key challenge to policy advocates, then, was to get city-service issues onto the policy agendas of the mayor and the city council.

Mayor Nagin had established a commission called "Bring New Orleans Back" soon after Katrina hit, but it was mostly inactive and finally ceased to exist. Rarely a politician who took decisive action, Mayor Nagin preferred to play a background role—partly because he realized that many planning decisions would be highly controversial. Someone would have to decide, for example, what areas to rebuild, and what areas not to rebuild. He had already been widely criticized when he seemed to repudiate African Americans when he implied that the Ninth Ward should not be rebuilt, and was also criticized by many Caucasians when he said that New Orleans would remain "chocolate" in its makeup.

With the Mayor on the sidelines, each parish attempted to develop its own rebuilding plan. With funding from the Rockefeller Foundation, each parish received funds to hire consultants to develop its plan—which would then be merged into a single citywide plan to be submitted to the City Planning Commission, the city council, Mayor Nagin, and (finally) the Louisiana Recovery Authority.[4]

This planning process meant that policy advocates had to get onto the agendas of local planners those issues that impacted the lives of vulnerable populations—such as affordable housing, mixed-income housing, transportation systems, childcare centers, job training centers, and sources of employment. They had to try to get planners in relatively affluent areas to accept some mixed-income housing as well as housing vouchers for low-income African Americans.

As they engaged in the planning process, policy advocates would also need to get officials in the private sector to place important issues on their agendas. They would need to convince the leaders of charter schools—public schools emancipated from city and state control—to accept a considerable number of African-American children. They would need to convince private developers to include a fair share of low-income and subsidized units in their projects.

As if these challenges were not enough, policy advocates would also need to get key issues onto the agenda of public officials in Baton Rouge, where the state's governor and legislature resided. Because a considerable portion of federal funds for the rebuilding of New Orleans came through the Louisiana Recovery Authority, policy advocates would need to make certain that its officials focused on important needs of vulnerable populations. Soon after Katrina, the state took over control of most of New Orleans' public schools, giving it extraordinary power over public education. Because the state established many of the policies that govern the Medicaid program, it had extraordinary power over medical issues confronting low-income populations.

The Importance of Agenda Building

Whether vulnerable populations would emerge with important policy victories in New Orleans, Baton Rouge, and Washington, DC would partly hinge on policy advocates' ability to get their issues onto the agendas of public officials. Placement on agendas would not guarantee their enactment, but it would be an important first step.

To be effective, policy advocates would have to engage in agenda building at federal, state, and local levels of government, as well as in the private sector. Were they *not* sufficiently assertive and skilled, other interests—such as private developers and speculators—would assert *their* policies onto policy agendas, perhaps shoving the needs of vulnerable populations to the side.

---

[4] Bruce Eggler, "Public Meetings Set on Storm Recovery Plan," *Times-Picayune*, July 26, 2006

What You Can Now Do	# CHAPTER SUMMARY

You are now equipped with skills to do the following:

- Diagnose agendas in legislative, agency, and community settings
- Enhance support for a problem or solution by softening the context
- Develop support for a problem or solution by using such tactics as timing, coupling, negotiating, finding sponsors, and routing
- Place items on the agenda as a direct-service worker
- Be able to engage in agenda building at different levels of government as well as in the private sector

We discuss methods of analyzing problems in the next chapter.

NOTES

1. Marc Ross and Roger Cobb, *The Cultural Strategies of Agenda Denial* (Kansas City: University of Kansas, 1997).
2. Robert Eyestone, *From Social Issues to Public Policy* (New York: Wiley, 1978), pp. 20–21, and Frank Baumgartner and Bryan Jones, *Agendas and Instability in American Politics* (Chicago: University of Chicago Press, 1993), pp. 250–251.
3. John Kingdon, *Agendas, Alternatives, and Public Policies* (Boston: Little, Brown, 1984).
4. Ibid., pp. 83–88.
5. Michael Cohen, James March, and Johan Olsen, "A Garbage Can Model of Organizational Choice," *Administrative Science Quarterly* 17 (March 1972): 1–25.
6. Ibid., pp. 95–121.
7. Kingdon, *Agendas, Alternatives, and Public Policies*, p. 115.
8. Ibid., pp. 95–108.
9. The work of advocates to place Alzheimer's disease on national policy agendas illustrates how advocates seek to dramatize the severity or pervasiveness of a social problem—even when precise data are lacking. See Julie Kosterlitz, "Anguish and Opportunity: Alzheimer's Disease," *National Journal* 23 (March 9, 1991): 2728–2732.
10. See Reich's use of the term *investment* rather than *spending* in Robert Reich, *The Work of Nations: Preparing Ourselves for 21st-Century Capitalism* (New York: Knopf, 1991), pp. 252–261.
11. Bruce Jansson, *The Reluctant Welfare State,* 5th ed. (Pacific Grove, CA: Brooks/Cole, 1993), p. 393.
12. The political problem of securing funds for prevention is illustrated by the AIDS epidemic; see Julie Kosterlitz, "AIDS Wars," *National Journal* 24 (July 25, 1992): 1727–1732.
13. For uses of the media to place issues on an agenda, see Hedrick Smith, *The Power Game: How Washington Works,* (New York: Ballantine Books, 1988), pp. 331–387; and Baumgartner and Jones, *Agendas and Instability in American Politics,* pp. 103–125.
14. Ibid., pp. 138–139.
15. Chris Matthews, *Hardball: How Politics Is Played* (New York: Summit Books, 1988).
16. Donald deKieffer, *The Citizen's Guide to Lobbying Congress* (Chicago: Chicago Review Press, 1997), pp. 19–20.
17. Kingdon, *Agendas, Alternatives, and Public Policies,* pp. 174–193.
18. Ibid., pp. 110–115.
19. Ibid., pp. 160–162.
20. Ibid., pp. 188–193.
21. Ibid., pp. 181–188.
22. Clinton decided not to use the single-payer Canadian system not only because health provider groups opposed it, but because the federal government would have been required to fund the entire package of benefits just as Clinton was trying to reduce the federal deficit. Ibid., pp. 1, 9.

23. Ron Dear and Rino Patti, "Legislative Advocacy: Seven Effective Tactics," *Social Work* 26 (July 1981): 289–297.

24. Ibid.

25. Kingdon, *Agendas, Alternatives, and Public Policies,* pp. 134–138.

SUGGESTED READINGS

Joel Best, ed., *Images of Issues: Typifying Contemporary Social Problems* (New York: Aldine de Gruyter, 1989).

John Kingdon, *Agendas, Alternatives, and Public Policies* (Boston: Little, Brown, 1997).

Julie Kosterlitz, "Anguish and Opportunity: Alzheimer's Disease," *National Journal* (April 28, 1990), pp. 1008–1015.

Marc Ross and Roger Cobb, *The Cultural Strategies of Agenda Denial* (Lawrence: University of Kansas, 1997).

Jeffrey Schmalz, "Whatever Happened to AIDS?" *New York Times Magazine* (November 28, 1993), pp. 55–86.

Hedrick Smith, *The Power Game: How Washington Really Works* (New York: Ballantine Books, 1988), pp. 331–387.

Rochelle Stanford, "Child Care Quagmire," *National Journal* (February 27, 1993), pp. 55–86.

CHAPTER

7

Analyzing Problems in the First Step of Policy Analysis

POLICY PREDICAMENT

When Hurricane Katrina hit New Orleans, it quickly forced nearly all of its residents to take refuge in other towns, cities, and states. A key policy issue soon emerged. Should New Orleans be rebuilt with large areas of concentrated poverty or should the city be rebuilt to emphasize mixed-income and integrated communities? This issue triggered a debate about the extent low-income African Americans are harmed by living in communities where many persons fall near or below federal poverty standards as compared to living in mixed-income and integrated areas. We discuss this debate at the end of the chapter in Policy Advocacy Challenge 7.9 as it illustrates challenges in analyzing problems.

Putting It All Together: A Six-Step Policy Analysis Framework

The part of policy practice and policy advocacy that leads to concrete proposals to address specific problems or issues is called "policy analysis." Let's examine a step-by-step framework for conducting it.[1] (See Figure 7.1.)

A Six-Step Policy Analysis Framework

1. **Familiarize oneself with a specific social problem or issue—or interrelated problems or issues.** Policy analysis begins with the selection of a specific social problem or issue that can include victimization of persons by landlords and others; inability of persons to meet their basic or survival needs; inability of persons to obtain opportunity-enhancing services; inability of persons and families to get help with specific needs or issues; infringement of the rights of members of specific outgroups by employers or others; excessive levels of inequality; inability of persons

FIGURE 7.1
Developing
and defending
policy proposals
using a six-step
policy analysis
framework

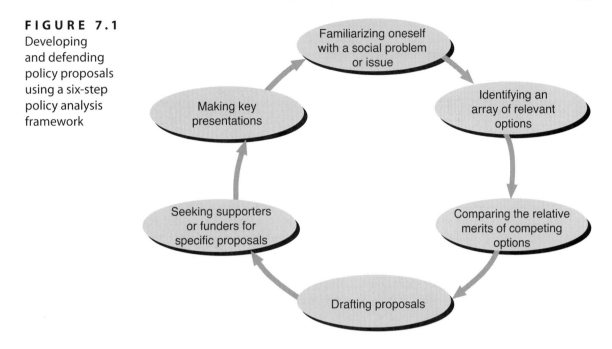

to acquire needed assets such as housing and savings; insufficient access to loans, capital, and resources by specific geographic areas; and inequities in the political process such as unfair electoral districts. It can involve ways to rebuild disaster-torn areas, such as New Orleans after Hurricane Katrina. Or the problem or issue can involve defects in the implementation of specific programs or regulations. Perhaps a specific program, such as medical services in the Latino community, fails to connect with substance abuse programs even when a substantial number of Latinos possess this problem. Perhaps public schools do not implement the main-streaming of developmentally challenged youth in their classrooms as required by federal law.

Policy advocates need to ask:

- What political, fiscal, cultural, or other factors led to a specific festering problem or issue—which often can be stated by using words like "too many people possess XYZ condition or problem" such as homelessness, poverty, or lack of access to specific services. Or "too few persons with depression receive optimal services for their condition." Or they can use a value-based perspective to state a specific problem, such as by contending that too many low income persons lack adequate housing when compared with the broader population.
- What remedies or solutions (if any) currently exist for the social problem or issue—and why are they insufficient either in strategy, relative size, or implementation? Can they be reformed or changed—and, if so, how—or are new remedies or solutions needed?

- What is the magnitude of current expenditures on the program or issue? From what sources do these funds come? Are they sufficient or insufficient?
- What adverse consequences does the current problem or issue pose for specific persons, communities, and society? What is the level or amount of these consequences? Do the adverse consequences suggest that the problem requires urgent action? (If policy advocates cannot make a strong case that the problem or issue is trivial or unimportant, they will find it difficult to generate support for solutions from decision makers.)

When developing proposals that address specific social problems, policy advocates need to use social science and other literature to better understand how they evolve or develop in specific populations. They need to understand where these populations go for assistance with these problems or issues both within organized programs and from nontraditional agencies. They need to understand how specific populations perceive specific conditions—and whether they even view them as "problems." They need to examine an array of strategies currently used to redress or solve them, such as empowerment approaches, remedial strategies, use of regulations, or some combination of these approaches.

Policy advocates sometimes develop strategies for preventing specific problems. They might propose specific policies to curtail exposure to toxic substances such as smoke or pollution. They might seek greater funding for child care as it helps children prepare for school or avoid neglect. They need to examine social-science, public-health, and other literature, as well as Internet sites, that discuss prevention strategies.

They also need to ask where policy solutions might be considered:

- In what specific policy arenas can remedies for this social problem or issue be developed and enacted, including local, state, or federal legislatures; specific local, state, or federal bureaucracies; the courts; the private sector; specific social agencies, whether public ones or nongovernmental organizations (NGOs); and nonpublic entities such as faith-based or for-profit organizations.
- Or should the issue or problem be addressed by a combination of these organizations, such as by a strategy that links public and non-public agencies?

Even at the outset, policy advocates often involve other persons in their work. Policy advocacy usually involves collaborative work by task forces, teams, coalitions, or advocacy groups that seek solutions to specific social problems or issues.

2. **Policy advocates brainstorm an array of relevant policy, programmatic, and resource options that, singly and together, might define a strategy for addressing the social problem or issue.** These can consider several, or many options depending on the complexity of the proposal that is ultimately developed during the analytic process including:

- Elements of a new social program, such as its intake procedures, the content of its services or benefits, where the program is positioned in an existing or new agency, the nature of its staff, and how it is linked to other social programs.
- Content of a proposed or modified regulation, such as ones that protect rights of members of specific out-groups.
- Proposed modifications in an existing social program—or in the way it is implemented.

- A proposed change in the amount of resources dedicated to a specific program or issue, such as a proposal to increase these resources.
- A proposed modification in a specific protocol or procedure for helping specific persons, such as a proposal to require social workers' involvement in end-of-life decision making.

To identify and compare options, they collect information from a variety of sources including interviews with persons knowledgeable about existing programs and policies. They use social-science and other research and theory to develop options that appear promising for addressing or solving a specific social problem like homelessness or substance abuse. (We provide flowcharts in this chapter that can be used to generate promising policy options.)

3. **Policy advocates analyze the relative merits of competing options** so that, on balance, they can select a specific one from two or more options. To make these comparisons of options, they must first identify specific criteria that they will use to contrast the options and to decide, on balance, which of them is meritorious.

Several kinds of criteria are commonly used in policy analysis. Value-based criteria are critical since they provide a normative basis for comparing options. A policy analyst might want to consider, for example, whether and to what extent specific options meet social-justice or fairness criteria, whether they preserve persons' confidentiality or self-determination rights. To underscore the importance of values, imagine a proponent of free-market capitalism developing a proposal for rebuilding New Orleans as compared to a policy advocate determined to help displaced low-income African Americans return to their neighborhoods. Unlike the policy advocate, the free-market advocate might not even include such values as "social justice" or fairness in her analysis—and this decision would lead her to favor policy options, such as letting private developers decide how to rebuild specific areas, even if their housing was primarily purchased by affluent persons. As this example reveals, *the selection of criteria pivotally shape the recommendations of policy analysts, so they must be chosen with care.*

Most policy analyses also include criteria that deal with the effectiveness of specific options. Decision makers usually want to know whether a specific option will actually prevent, address, or solve an issue or problem effectively—particularly given the competition for programs for scarce resources. In the case of rebuilding New Orleans, for example, federal HUD officials would want to know how to get affordable housing constructed in a timely way in key parts of the city. In the case of social problems like homelessness or substance abuse, policy analysts *have to* use available social-science research and theory to make the case that a specific option will effectively address a specific social problem.

They also would want to compare policies by their cost. If the cost of a specific option is prohibitive in light of available resources, decision makers may reject it even if it scores high on other criteria.

Decision makers sometimes combine criteria, such as asking if they are "cost-effective." In this case, they favor policy options that are *both* effective *and* relatively inexpensive.

Still other criteria have to do with practical political and implementation considerations. Assume, for example, that a specific option is cost effective, but will attract such opposition from legislators that it has no chance of passage. In this case, a policy analyst might recommend a policy option that is less cost-effective, but that has a greater chance of being enacted. Policies that cannot easily be implemented may also be rejected. Perhaps, for example, a policy option is sufficiently complex that implementing agencies will be unlikely to understand it, much less to put in place some of its provisions. Here, too, an otherwise meritorious option may be rejected by decision makers on implementation grounds.

The term "trade-offs" is used to describe how policy analysts deal with the fact that a specific policy often ranks high on one or more criteria but lower on others. Faced with this situation, a policy analyst might conclude that *on balance* she prefers a specific policy option even though it does not rank high on all criteria.

Criteria often include:

- Cost
- Effectiveness
- Political feasibility
- Ease of implementation
- Specific values such as social justice, fairness, confidentiality, and self-determination

In simple proposals, such as changing an intake procedure in an agency or changing a protocol for helping certain kinds of persons, such as battered women in hospital settings, relatively few options will need to be considered. Policy advocates who advance more complex proposals may need to examine a variety of options with respect to several or more facets of this larger proposal. (We discuss how proposals are fashioned in more detail in Chapter Eight.)

4. **Policy advocates draft a specific policy proposal that flows from their brainstorming and conceptual work during the preceding three stages of policy analysis.** The proposals can be relatively simple or complex; relatively modest or ambitious; or relatively inexpensive or costly. They can propose new policies or modifications of existing ones. They can propose new programs or improvements in existing ones. They often include proposed budgets.

   Policy advocates often get feedback during the drafting process from other policy advocates and from decision makers—and modify their proposals as needed. They might decide, for example, to downsize or to upsize proposals. They might decide to delete certain contentious provisions from them—or to add some if they think they have sufficient political support for them.

5. **Policy advocates seek supporters for their proposals**—although as we noted in Step 1, above, they will have involved other persons in their work from the outset.

6. **Policy advocates make key presentations** to public officials or decision makers to persuade them that their policy proposal is meritorious as they enter the policy-enacting phase of the policy-advocacy process as discussed in Chapters Nine, Ten, and Eleven.

Do Policy Advocates Have to Analyze Problems?

Some people may believe that policy advocates do not have to analyze problems because their work is driven by their progressive values, such as their commitment to social justice and fairness. In fact, advocates must analyze problems for several reasons. Were they not to base their recommendations (at least in part) on hardheaded analysis of specific problems, including the use of up-to-date research, they would often find their proposals dismissed as lacking a substantive base. (See Policy Advocacy Challenge 7.1.) Moreover, a candid assessment of the social reforms of prior eras suggests that they often have not worked, partly because their advocates lacked sufficient knowledge of specific problems when they proposed specific reforms. The classic example is public housing for low-income persons. Believing they were providing a long-term solution, reformers in the late 1930s and the next two decades obtained federal funding for huge public housing projects, not fully realizing they would become segregated by class and by race—and bedeviled by high rates of crime and drug use.

POLICY ADVOCACY CHALLENGE 7.1

Using the Web as a Tool in Policy Analysis

STEPHANIE DAVIS, RESEARCH LIBRARIAN, UNIVERSITY OF CALIFORNIA, IRVINE

Analysis is an essential part of policy work and advocacy. Analysis can take many forms, i.e. statistics, reports, case studies, etc. The goals of analysis (in part) establish a definition for the problem, investigate the causes, history and impacts of the problem, and determine who the problem affects. Your research will lead you to ask these questions and more. A few examples of sites that present analysis are listed below:

- Center on Budget and Policy Priorities **http://www.cbpp.org**
- Fedstats **http://www.fedstats.gov**
- John F. Kennedy School of Government at Harvard University **http://www.ksg.harvard.edu**

Using these sites and others you find for your specific issue or problem, assess how well the sites address your topic or issue.

Web sites are also useful for finding statistics. Why are statistics important? First of all, they provide a picture of our country—information about our population, pastimes, habits, how we spend our money, where we work, and the problems we face as a nation. Using statistics to back up your words or to show the impact of a specific problem on a population can be powerful.

As part of your research you may be asked to find statistics, such as the number of children in foster care, or the percentage of women without health care. There are many places to find statistics, online and in print sources such as books and journal articles.

Here are a few resources to get you started:

- *Dictionary of U.S. Government Statistical Terms.* Alfred N. Garwood and Louise Hornor. 1991.
- *Historical Statistics of the United States: Colonial Times to 1970.* 2 vols. 1975.
- *Social Work Almanac.* Leon Ginsberg. 1995.
- *Statistical Abstract of the United States.* U.S. Bureau of the Census. 1878–.
- *The World Almanac and Book of Facts.* 1923–.

There are also three indexes that provide comprehensive access to statistical information, available in print and through the subscription database *Statistical Universe:*

- *American Statistics Index* (U.S. Federal Government statistics)
- *Index to International Statistics* (International statistics from inter-governmental organizations, including the United Nations)
- *Statistical Reference Index.* (Statistics collected by states, private agencies, non-profit organizations, and research organizations)

(continued)

Online Sources:

- FirstGov, the Federal Government Search Engine
  http://www.firstgov.gov
- Fedstats, One-Stop Shopping for Federal Statistics
  http://www.fedstats.gov
- University of Michigan Documents Center Statistical Resources
  http://www.lib.umich.edu/govdocs/stats.html
- United States Census Bureau
  http://www.census.gov

Evaluating Statistics:

Locating your statistics is only the first step. You need to evaluate this information critically as you would a journal article, report or book.

Here are criteria to consider when evaluating statistics:

- Where does the information come from—the government, corporation, private agency, state or regional agency?
- Did the government pay for the study that produced the statistics? If not, who paid?
- How old is the statistical information? Is it based on the current census, or the previous census?
- What was the sampling size and sampling error?

∽ EXERCISE ∽

Go to the library and find the most recent edition of *Statistical Abstract of the United States* (it's published every year). Find statistics about your research topic or an issue that interests you. Then look at the Appendix titled "Limitations of the Data" (usually Appendix III). Do these limitations have a possible impact on the data you found? Give three reasons how the data you found could be incorrect or inconsistent.

When searching for new solutions to problems, policy advocates must realize that persons, groups, and institutions often select policies that will enhance their prestige, revenue, and power, sometimes with scant regard for citizens who need assistance. Tradition often shapes policies, even when existing policies are obviously outmoded and ineffective. Professional wisdom, which often fosters effective services, sometimes promotes dysfunctional policies, such as many surgeons' excessive reliance on radical mastectomies, hysterectomies, and heart bypass operations. Policy makers are not immune to societal prejudices and misconceptions, as well as fads and presumed panaceas. So policy advocates must subject their policy choices to careful deliberation to minimize the effects of power, tradition, fuzzy intentions, and intuition.

Using a Flowchart to Analyze Some Social Problems in Step 1

It is useful to diagram social problems so that we can develop solutions or ameliorating policies. Flowcharts are particularly useful when seeking policy solutions to social problems that social workers emphasize, such as welfare reform, homelessness, and substance abuse since they place the problems in a developmental context. Let's begin with an overarching diagram that can be used, in whole or part, to analyze many social problems. Then let's develop a diagram specifically geared to the welfare-to-work problem to show how to apply the overarching diagram to a specific problem.

Five Cells in a Flowchart Format in Step 1

Our overarching diagram has five cells placed in a context that includes familial, community, and economic factors. (See Figure 7.2.) Let's begin with the context, because human services always exist in a context.

Family members, peers, and social networks powerfully shape how people address their needs, whether they seek organized services, how they respond to organized services, and whether they develop specific problems and how they deal with them. Persons in affluent communities with outstanding schools and services, for example, have a head start compared with persons in low-income communities with poor schools, poor housing, and high rates of crime. We also should not forget cultural factors that influence how people define specific problems and whether they seek help from organized institutions and programs.

The cell at the far left of Figure 7.2 represents the prevention arena which describes persons who have not yet developed a problem like substance abuse, mental illness, poverty, or diabetes. The prevention arena shows interventions we can use to stop persons from developing specific problems. We can sometimes identify at-risk factors that allow us to target interventions that decrease the odds of a specific person developing a specific problem. In some cases, we find out by luck that specific interventions prevent certain problems, such as when medical researchers discovered that the daily intake of small amounts of aspirin lessened persons' likelihood of contracting colon cancer. In other cases, we have no idea how to prevent certain problems, and sometimes considerable controversy exists about the effectiveness of specific interventions. Preventive strategies sometimes require the active involvement of people, for example, changing their lifestyles (such as diet) in an effort to avert a specific social problem. In addition, society sometimes attempts to prevent certain social problems, by instituting changes in peoples' environment, such as decreasing pollutants, improving the safety of automobiles, or preventing cigarette sales to youth.

POLICY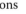
ADVOCACY
CHALLENGE 7.2

Preventing
Homelessness
Among LGBTQQ
Youth

JESSICA VAN TUYL,
MSW STUDENT

Go to
academic.cengage.com/
social_work/jansson
to watch this video clip

Prior to pursuing a masters degree in social work, I worked with lesbian, gay, bisexual, transgender, queer, and questioning youth (LGBTQQ). I became shocked by the prevalence of homelessness among these youth.

According to a report by the Lambda Legal Defense and Education Fund, LGBTQQ youth comprise 20 to 40 percent of the national youth homeless population each year.[1] LGBTQQ youth become homeless for a number of reasons both related and unrelated to their sexual orientation or gender identity. Many become homeless due to forced departure from their homes as a result of family rejection of their sexual orientation or gender identity. In addition, LGBTQQ youth become homeless due to family discord, abuse, neglect, and religious or cultural conflict. Some LGBTQQ homeless youth

---

[1] C. Sullivan and S. Sommer, *Youth in the Margins: a Report on the Unmet Needs of Lesbian, Gay, Bisexual and Transgender Youth in Foster Care.* New York: Lambda Legal Defense and Education Fund, 2001.

(continued)

do not identify as LGBTQQ upon becoming homeless, but discover their identities through exposure to the LGBTQQ community while homeless.[2]

After they become homeless, LGBTQQ youth under the age of 18 are funneled into the foster care system, often times to families who are not affirming their identities. Consequently, many LGBTQQ youth run away from their foster care placements, beginning an endless cycle in the child welfare system.[3] These youth may be placed in congregate care settings where they are often verbally and physically harassed by youth and/or staff and are unable to access the services they need.[4]

After emancipation from foster care at age 18, a disproportionate number of LGBTQQ youth end up back on the streets.[5] While the experience of homelessness often allows LGBTQQ youth to explore their identities and attain a sense of belonging through membership in the larger LGBTQQ community, they face a number of challenges while homeless including emotional distress, depression, post traumatic stress disorder, suicidal ideation, drug and alcohol abuse, coming out issues, homophobia, and invisibility. They often struggle to come to terms with the withdrawal of love and acceptance from their families. Research shows that these youth are more likely to engage in prostitution and to report higher rates of sexual victimization than their heterosexual peers. They are more likely to contract HIV while homeless than heterosexual youth.[6]

Broad based structural change is needed within the child welfare system to prevent homelessness in this population. First, LGBTQQ family reunification programs must be created. Second, child welfare agencies must offer training for foster parents and child welfare workers to improve their skills in working with this population to promote greater success in placements. Third, child welfare agencies must recruit foster parents interested in helping these youths and create additional LGBTQQ congregate care settings. Fourth, child welfare agencies must offer transitional housing services, life skills training, education, substance abuse treatment and preventive programs, and mental health services. Fifth, child welfare agencies must offer mentorship programs to LGBTQQ homeless youth to help them develop support networks.

Social workers are uniquely able to design and deliver these preventive services in the child welfare system to prevent many LGBTQQ youth from becoming homeless. See Policy Advocacy Challenge Video 7.2 where Jessica Van Tuyl discusses prevention strategies for LGBTQQ youth. Discuss:

- causes of homelessness in this population.
- remedies that Jessica Van Tuyl identifies both from reunification, within the child welfare system, and through services given to homeless youth.

---

[2] S. Pendergast, G. A. Dunne, and D. Telford, "A Story of 'Difference,' A Different Story: Young Homeless, Lesbian, Gay, and Bisexual People," *The International Journal of Sociology and Social Policy*, Vol. 21, 2001, 4–6, 64.

[3] National Center for Lesbian Rights, *LGBTQQ Youth in the Foster Care System*. Retrieved on March 1, 2006 from http://www.nclrights.org

[4] M. Freundlich and R.J. Avery, "Gay and Lesbian Youth in Foster Care: Meeting Their Placement and Service Needs," *Journal of Gay and Lesbian Social Services*, Vol. 17, 2005, p. 4.

[5] G.P. Mallon, "There's No Place Like Home: Achieving Safety, Permanency, and Well-Being for Lesbian and Gay Adolescents in Out-of-Home Care Settings," *Child Welfare*, Vol. 51, 2002, p. 2.

[6] R.C. Savin-Williams, "The Disclosure to Families of Same-Sex Attractions by Lesbian, Gay, and Bisexual Youths," *Journal of Research on Adolescence*, Vol. 8, 1998, pp. 49–68.

FIGURE 7.2
An ecological
model of social
problems

If we are successful in preventing specific problems—or if some people simply do not develop them—they stay within the preventive arena. People who do develop specific problems move into one of the three cells in the middle of the diagram.

- the top-middle cell describes persons who remain outside the orbit of all organized systems of care. To the extent they get help from others, it is from family and neighborhood members, persons at their place of employment, the clergy, and others in their support systems.
- the middle-middle cell describes organized systems of care, such as social agencies, hospitals, clinics, schools, job-training programs, and professionals.
- the middle-bottom cell describes programs that operate on an empowerment or self-help perspective such as Alcoholics Anonymous, programs for persons who are physically challenged, and community-based programs for persons with persistent mental problems.

This distinction between those who remain outside institutions and programs and those who remain in them is critical to understanding social policy. In many cases, only a small percentage of persons with specific problems actually seek organized services for them. For example, huge numbers of persons with mental illness, medical problems, poverty, reading disorders, and delinquency are not helped by organized institutions and programs—whether because they do not know about them, they believe they are not eligible, they do not want to present a stigmatized condition to others, they drop out of services, or they do not perceive themselves as having a problem.

We should not prematurely conclude that persons outside the orbit of organized programs do not cope with or even solve their problems. Many people solve problems on their own or with help from support networks in their own communities, and a certain number, such as substance abusers, mature out of their problems over the course of time.

Yet some persons clearly harm themselves by not using organized programs. People with diabetes or cancer, for example, may die from their malady if they do not get medical help—as may persons with clinical depression. Persons with severe reading disorders are unlikely to deal with their condition without assistance. It is important to ask why some people do not avail themselves of organized programs. Some people lack the resources needed to use organized programs as in the case of medically uninsured Americans. Some may not know about organized services, and others may be given services that they perceive to be intrusive, demeaning, or ineffective. Finally, organized services may be so severely underfunded that people cannot gain access to them, as is true with substance abuse counseling.

Other people do use organized services and programs to address specific problems, whether voluntarily or because they are required or coerced into using them. Voluntary entrants enter organized services because they want assistance with specific problems and believe that organized services can help them. To understand how they fare during such service transactions, we need to understand not only what is provided to them, but how other factors (such as family and support networks, economic conditions, and peer factors) shape how they perceive and benefit from services.

Involuntary entrants are forced to get certain services, often by the courts, which require persons to use them to avoid incarceration or other penalties. Implied, stated, or perceived threats can also lead some persons to seek services, such as a parent who fears she will lose custody of her children if she does not solve a substance abuse problem or accept services from a child welfare agency.

Some people turn not to organized programs, but to programs or activities that use a self-help or empowerment paradigm. Examples include community-based programs to help physically, mentally, or developmentally challenged persons, Alcoholics Anonymous, and community-based programs that help people purchase their own houses. In each of these cases, people have problems, whether physical disabilities, substance abuse, or poverty, but these programs focus on persons' strengths in dealing with them. (Many programs that help physically challenged persons do not even use words like disability, clients, or diagnosis.) They want to mobilize peoples' existing skills and motivation or help develop them. For example asset-building programs operate under the assumption that poverty can best be averted by helping persons obtain assets, like houses or savings accounts, that middle-class and upper-class people commonly use to advance their well-being. These empowerment programs not only use different language and different strategies, but they are not structured like traditional social agencies.

They are more likely to have informal organizational structures and less likely to have charts on their clients. In addition, their staff are less likely to be credentialed professionals.

Consider the case of a self-help agency that assists persons with persistent mental problems such as schizophrenia. Psychiatrists, mental institutions, and counseling by professionals comprise the central thrust of traditional mental health services. By contrast, community-based programs with an empowerment perspective aim to inculcate problem-solving skills in persons with persistent mental problems. They may provide them with low-cost housing, encourage them to seek employment while providing job training and referral services, and give them skills to develop social supports such as going to specific organized activities. They are taught to monitor their medications so they can seek technical assistance when certain symptoms emerge. The community-based program establishes an advisory council, comprised of persons with persistent mental problems, to develop additional empowerment strategies.

Typologies within the Middle Cells   It is important to remember that populations with specific problems are not homogeneous in the prevention. Indeed, considerable evidence suggests that specific interventions often do not work for many people, who may respond to different approaches. Later we discuss in more detail, using welfare reform as our example, how policy advocates need to develop typologies identifying subgroups within a larger population that possesses a specific problem.

Relationships among the Cells   People move among the three cells in the middle of Figure 7.2 in interesting and complex ways. For example, someone may begin in organized services, drop out of them, and then be helped by a community-based empowerment program. Someone else may solve a problem with the assistance of family members and move back into the prevention arena. Or people can use organized institutions and empowerment programs simultaneously, such as when a physically challenged person uses traditional health services while getting help from a community-based organization run by physically challenged people. (See Policy Advocacy Challenge 7.3)

An important issue in social policy is whether the organized system of services can successfully draw upon family and neighborhood resources (the top-middle cell in Figure 7.2) or the work of agencies using an empowerment paradigm (the bottom-middle cell). It would seem advisable for social agencies, for example, to use community leaders and caregivers, such as barbers and beauticians, to refer cases (such as depressed persons) to trained professionals working in agencies—and even to use them to give therapeutic services that supplement professional ones. It would also seem logical for organized systems of care to organize support networks for persons with mental and other problems, since considerable research suggests that persons with social supports fare better than many others in addressing their problems.

POLICY ADVOCACY CHALLENGE 7.3

Diagramming a Social Problem

BRUCE JANSSON, PH.D.

Take a social problem that interests you and diagram it following the format of Figure 7.2. Be certain to include the prevention arena, persons who are not part of the organized service-delivery system, and persons who do receive help from the organized service-delivery system. What does this exercise teach about the following?

- The relative numbers of persons who remain outside the human services system
- The role of families, communities, and self-help groups
- The potential promise of preventive strategies
- The sheer number of outcomes that are possible for clients, patients, and consumers of service
- The sheer number of policies that influence whether and how persons move through and access the organized human services system

---

However, these courses of action need to be taken with the awareness of certain risks, as a number of researchers and theorists suggest. Social supports are not always helpful to clients, such as when dysfunctional relationships exist within them that may even exacerbate someone's problems. When family and neighborhood persons relate to professionals, they may lose their natural way of relating to a client. It takes time for professionals to organize and relate to community and family supports—and it is not always clear how to do it.

Nor is it easy for organized systems of care to relate to empowerment-focused programs such as those for persons who are physically challenged. Empowerment-focused groups are often suspicious of professionals, such as physicians, who they believe label them and treat them paternalistically. They may fear overmedication and excessive use of surgery. In some cases, traditional organized systems of care incorporate units or programs with an empowerment perspective, such as a birthing clinic in a hospital that uses midwives and places less emphasis on traditional medical ways of delivering babies.

Outcomes   On the far right side of Figure 7.2, outcomes are depicted. Successful outcomes can include eradicating a problem or lessening its severity or impact. If we use an empowerment approach, successful outcomes would include mobilizing persons' personal strengths to allow them to cope with specific issues in their lives or to overcome such challenges as physical disability. Unsuccessful outcomes can include failure to solve or redress a problem or to develop personal coping strategies. We sometimes try to assess the effectiveness of specific programs by using techniques of program evaluation—whether quantitative or qualitative approaches.

Illustrating a Flow Chart with Welfare Reform

We will illustrate the use of a flow chart with the welfare-to-work issue. We do not have to use all of the cells in Figure 7.2 because we focus on organized systems of care in this case—we use only the prevention arena, the center-middle cell, and the right-hand cell. (See Figure 7.3.)

By way of background, recall that President Bill Clinton and the Congress revolutionized the American welfare system when they approved the Personal Responsibility and Work Opportunity Reconciliation Act in 1996. It replaced AFDC with state-run welfare programs to be funded by a combination of federal block-grant funds and state resources. (Grants under the new state-run program were called Temporary Assistance for Needy Families, or TANF, grants.) The legislation ceded virtually all decisions to the states. Only prohibiting them from reducing their current spending on welfare more than 20 percent, it even allowed them not to fund welfare for specific families if the state's allotted funds ran out, to replace cash payments with in-kind assistance (such as food items), and not to provide fair hearings if recipients believed their rights had been violated.[2]

Rather than establishing statewide rules, as under the AFDC program, states could let each of their counties establish their own programs drawing on state block-grant funds. The federal government did not add significant training and day-care funds to the federal block-grant funds. The legislation also cut food stamp allotments deeply, ended welfare payments under the Supplementary Security Income program (SSI) for legal immigrants, and proposed the removal of many disabled children from SSI rolls. This welfare reform legislation set in motion developments that would profoundly shape the well-being of millions of women and their children, requiring 50 percent of single-parent recipients to be participating in work or work-related activities by the year 2002.

Welfare reform is an excellent example of how policymakers analyze social problems, using such methods as quantitative research. Yet it also demonstrates that perceptions of social problems, as well as proposed solutions, are profoundly shaped by such non-rational factors as values, culture, and politics. Indeed, persons with radical, liberal, and conservative perspectives disagreed sharply about the advisability of the welfare reform legislation. Indeed, these divergent perspectives will come into play whenever Congress reauthorizes welfare legislation in coming years.

We use welfare reform throughout this chapter as a case example of policymaking in the United States. It demonstrates that policy advocates must assert their analyses of social problems, lest other analyses prevail.

Figure 7.3 presents a flowchart of single heads of households who are susceptible to joining welfare rolls, who currently use welfare, or who have left welfare rolls. It includes various *stages of development*, as seen from an analysis of the model from the left to the right, moving from a susceptible population not yet using welfare to an array of users of welfare to former users who have left the rolls. Policy advocates are also interested in understanding the *dynamics* of a problem, such as patterns of movement between the different phases as depicted in Figure 7.3 by arrows between the different stages. They might ask, for example, what percentage of susceptible persons actually seek and obtain welfare benefits; what percentage of recipients obtain jobs and for how long; how many recipients leave the welfare rolls permanently; what percentage of former recipients find themselves with a net income lower or higher than when they were on the welfare rolls; and how many recipients move repeatedly between welfare and work during a brief period.

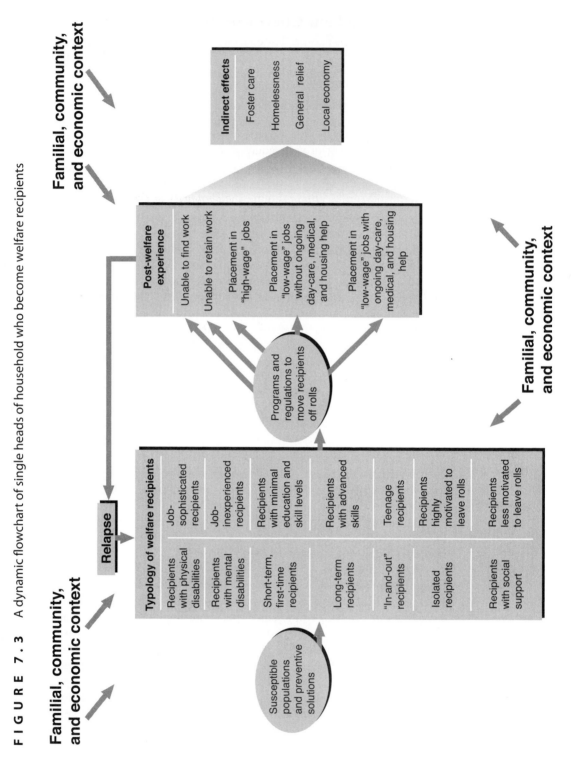

FIGURE 7.3 A dynamic flowchart of single heads of household who become welfare recipients

A typology of welfare recipients can classify them with respect to their manifestations, chronicity, and demographic characteristics (see the center portion of Figure 7.3, titled "Typology of welfare recipients"). *Manifestations* are outward behaviors, symptoms, or characteristics that differentiate people with specific problems. They are widely used to establish typologies of illness in medicine and mental health, as illustrated by the diseases and illnesses listed in any medical encyclopedia or in the *DSM-IV.*[3]

We can develop a typology of welfare recipients based on such characteristics as whether they have extensive or little job experience, whether they possess job-related skills, and the extent of their education. Or we could establish categories based on recipients' views about job seeking, such as "discouraged job seekers versus optimistic job seekers."[4]

Policy advocates often examine the *chronicity* of problems. For example, welfare recipients can be classified as chronic users, in-and-out or oscillating users, brief one-time users, and occasional users.

By using manifestations, chronicity, and demographic factors, policy analysts develop typologies of persons who have a specific problem. Typologies are useful because they make clear that populations with a specific problem are not homogeneous and consist of specific subgroups with distinguishing characteristics. Some single heads of household who receive welfare, for example, have had extensive working experience, and others have never been employed. Some of them are teenagers, and others are considerably older. Some have physical or mental disabilities; others have no disabilities. Some are highly educated; others have not completed the eighth grade.

POLICY ADVOCACY CHALLENGE 7.4

Developing a Typology of Homeless Persons

ANNE MILDER, MSW STUDENT

When my fellow students and I were required, as part of our first year policy sequence at University of Southern California School of Social Work, to advocate for the homeless in Los Angeles and Orange counties, many of us followed the individual passions which had influenced our decision to become social workers. For instance, a student previously interested in women's rights looked at homeless women, another previously interested in LGBTQQ youth looked at homeless LGBTQQ youth, and, as I was previously interested in young children, I investigated the needs of and services offered to homeless children, ages 0–5, in Los Angeles county, and the policies which govern them.

As social work students, we knew that the face of homelessness is quite different from the cliché, more than the popular image of the disheveled and smelly old man living on a park bench, taking swigs from a bottle, too lazy to work. We knew the population is multifaceted, and we soon became aware that it is important to describe our particular homeless population of interest, their numbers and needs, and the policies affecting their status, in order to think about advocating for them and, ultimately, developing preventive strategies and securing services for them.

What took us—or at least me—longer to understand is that any discussion of the subgroups under the umbrella of the term homelessness assumes that there is a uniform working definition of homelessness, a commonly agreed upon definition. How homelessness is defined is a legal and political battle in and of itself. The legal definition of homelessness determines literally who is counted, how monies are distributed, and

(continued)

who is eligible for support and services. Thus, an essential point of advocacy must be to determine the legal definition of who is homeless.

The legal definition of homelessness varies across Federal law and is currently the subject of much political debate. A USC professor indicated that there are something like 14 different Federal definitions of homelessness. But, as Barbara Duffield, Policy Director, National Association for the Education of Homeless Children and Youth, indicated to me, what is at issue is not so much the number of definitions, but the extreme limitation of the HUD definition of homelessness. According to the HUD Web site, "[g]enerally speaking, homeless individuals and families are those who are sleeping in places not meant for human habitation, such as cars, parks, sidewalks, and abandoned buildings, or those who are sleeping in an emergency shelter as a primary nighttime residence."

While the HUD definition may sound perfectly reasonable (homeless people lack homes), it excludes many homeless subgroups, and it disproportionately excludes families and children. Unlike the education subtitle of the McKinney-Vento Act, the HUD definition excludes those who are living with relatives or friends (commonly called "doubled-up"), those who are "couch surfing" (moving from one relative's or friend's home to another), and those living in motels or hotels because they lack other options. As a result, the HUD definition excludes a number of families who opt not to live on the streets, either for child-safety reasons, or to avoid the involvement of child protective services, or, as in the city of Los Angeles, because public policy prevents them from doing so (the new policy of the Los Angeles Board of Supervisors is one of "zero tolerance" for families on skid row).

When designing programs and services, of course, one can't simply assume that all homeless people need the same services, or even that all homeless people need shelter. When touring skid row, we were told that certain individuals refuse shelter because the shelter regulations are more than they can endure. One homeless individual said he just wanted to live as he is, on the street; he didn't want any more people trying to help; he thought a section of the city should be available for those wanting to live un-housed. Yet, there are many different subgroups of homeless people, and to treat them all as one homogeneous group means that the needs of many will be neglected. An elderly woman recently homeless due to the lack of affordable housing will need different services than a pregnant teen kicked out of her parents' home, or than a veteran with PTSD. If public officials limit homelessness to only one type of person, then only one type of homeless person will be served. The HUD definition is so limited that it focuses services only on one type of persons—chronically homeless persons.

Since I'm biased towards the care of young children, I, of course, am advocating that the current HUD definition be made more inclusive.

Typologies are useful for several reasons. Because they divide people with specific social problems into smaller subgroups, they force policy practitioners to develop an array of interventions rather than relying on a single approach.[5]

Indeed, many theorists in social marketing contend that policy advocates must segment populations into smaller groups, much as we have done in Figure 7.3.[6] As these theorists identify smaller groups, they can use so-called focus groups to find out what kinds of services or resources the members of these groups believe they need. A policy advocate forms a focus group of five to eight people who fit into a subgroup like those in Figure 7.3, choosing people who are likely to articulate the needs of this subgroup.

She develops five or six broad questions framed to capture their definitions of their problems and the interventions that they believe will be effective. She poses the questions, allowing 15 to 25 minutes of discussion per question, carefully eliciting the views of all group members. Taking careful notes or recording the session, she analyzes the group's responses at a later time to develop policies and programs geared to this group's needs.[7] (See Policy Advocacy Challenge 7.5.)

Typologies facilitate evaluations of programs and policies as well. A welfare-to-work program may be highly successful with a specific subgroup, such as highly educated recipients who have had prior work experience, but may have poor rates of success with less educated recipients with scant work experience. Were policy practitioners to rely on global evaluations of welfare-to-work recipients, they would fail to detect variations between subgroups, thwarting efforts to design strategies designed to address their specific needs.

POLICY ADVOCACY CHALLENGE 7.5

A Focus Group in Action

BRUCE JANSSON, PH.D.

A social worker wants to establish outpatient services for older citizens in a major hospital but wants to obtain their perspectives. She segments this population into ambulatory but relatively healthy older people and those with more acute rather than chronic conditions. Realizing that older people in her hospital's service area are Caucasian and Asian, she draws from these two groups to form two focus groups of well older people.

She develops the following broad questions:

1. What kinds of medical problems or issues do well older people have?
2. Where do you currently receive outpatient medical services?
3. What problems do you experience with the services that you currently receive?
4. If you could establish the ideal outpatient agency for well older people, what would it be like?
5. What dangers or pitfalls would you advise the staff of this outpatient agency to avoid?

The policy advocate gains important insights from the older people she has consulted. For example, she finds that they value continuity of care (i.e., having a regular doctor) more than promptness of service.

Armed with insights from her use of focus groups, she develops a proposal for outpatient services that she hopes will be accepted by the hospital's board of directors.

ᕦ EXERCISE ᕤ

Now imagine that you are conducting a focus group with evacuees from the Ninth Ward of New Orleans—and you wanting to know what they would want in terms of amenities and quality of life to induce them to return to New Orleans from another city. Develop a set of questions that you might ask.

Typologies also allow policy practitioners to establish priorities. If research suggests that certain subgroups are most likely to become long-term users of welfare, for example, state authorities can prioritize programs to assist them. Typologies help us understand not only welfare populations, but also people who have other social problems, such as mental illness, poverty, child abuse, and marital discord.

Of course, typologies are not a panacea, as we discuss at more length later. Critics may ask, for example, whether the subgroups in Figure 7.3 are mutually exclusive, since welfare recipients often fall into several of them. Persons who construct typologies often encounter a dilemma regarding the breadth of their categories. If relatively few categories are used, it is difficult to develop specialized programs that focus on the needs of specific subgroups. If too many categories are used, policy practitioners may fail to see the commonalities of persons in different subgroups, such as the common problems that welfare recipients confront as they enter job markets.[8] In the case of mental health typologies, such as the DSM-IV, many critics wonder whether some of the categories have been invented by psychiatrists or actually describe existing mental conditions.[9]

Analyzing the Causes of Social Problems in Step 1

Problems are caused by physiological, personal, familial, community, and societal factors. (See Box 7.1 for various causes of welfare dependency.) Welfare dependency is linked to such personal and familial factors as levels of education; job-related experiences; family size; whether a woman has been divorced or widowed or has had children out of wedlock; how much child support a woman receives; personal orientations toward welfare; the physical or mental disabilities of a head of household; and whether a woman has a child or children with disabilities.[10] These personal factors operate not only singly but together to cause welfare dependency. A woman's risk of dependency increases, for example, if she is the single head of a household, does not receive child support, and has a child with disabilities.

Welfare is also shaped by a host of community factors, such as rates of unemployment, wage levels, the availability of child care, the receptivity of employers to hiring welfare recipients, the availability of transportation, and the availability of job-training programs.[11] The likelihood of high rates of welfare in a community increase as multiple factors interact, such as low-wage employment, unavailability of day care, and high rates of unemployment.

Various personal, familial, and environmental factors often act together to place some people in higher risk categories than persons who are exposed to only one factor. A woman may experience short-term risk, for example, when her husband leaves, rendering her economically dependent on government programs. But her chances of securing employment that pays enough to allow her to leave the welfare rolls increase if she has prior work experience, has a college degree, lives in a neighborhood with expanding economic opportunities, and has access to affordable transportation and child care. By contrast, a woman who lacks all of these advantages and who is also left by her husband is less likely to find employment that pays enough to make her economically independent.

Policy advocates use both quantitative and qualitative research to analyze the causes of specific problems. Four approaches are common. First, they compare persons with a social problem with persons who do not have it, to infer from their differences why certain persons develop the problem. Because welfare dependency is strongly associated with single-parent families, for example, we can infer that persons in families that

BOX 7.1   Some Causes of Welfare Dependency

1. Physiological causes
   a. Physical disabilities
   b. Developmental disabilities
   c. Mental disabilities
2. Personal and familial causes
   a. Age (e.g., teenage mothers)
   b. Educational deficits
   c. Skill deficits
   d. Lack of work experience
   e. Lack of role models that facilitate job entry
   f. Lack of child support
   g. Subjection to abuse by spouse or others
3. Environmental causes
   a. Lack of jobs in local area
   b. Lack of jobs in local area that pay sufficiently to allow economic independence
   c. Lack of job placement and training programs
   d. Lack of public or subsidized transportation to job sites
   e. Discrimination by employers against welfare recipients
   f. Competition for scarce jobs from other people, such as unemployed persons, new job entrants, persons reentering the labor force, and immigrants
4. Interacting causes placing some people at higher risk of welfare dependency
   a. Persons associated with two of the preceding at-risk factors
   b. Persons associated with three of the preceding at-risk factors
   c. Persons associated with four or more of the preceding at-risk factors

are supported by a single wage are more vulnerable to poverty—and welfare—than persons in families with dual wages.[12] Second, they follow people through time to discover why they develop a problem, such as following teen women to discern why some of them become pregnant and join welfare rolls. It is more difficult to conduct this second kind of research, because it requires gathering data at many intervals from participants who must agree to participate for an extended period.[13] Third, they evaluate existing programs to find clues to a problem's causes. If recipients who received ongoing and substantial day-care subsidies after they left the rolls have lower rates of recidivism than recipients who did not receive them, policy practitioners can surmise that day-care expenses force many women onto the rolls.[14] Fourth, they get information directly from persons who are experiencing a specific problem, by observing them (as in anthropological studies) or by interviewing them.[15]

Rather than limiting ourselves to examining the immediate causes of welfare dependency, we can analyze a sequence of factors that causes dependency. If low wages cause welfare dependency for many single mothers, for example, we can ask what causes low wages. If many poverty-stricken inner-city persons do not live near job sites, what caused residential segregation by race and social class? The answers to these kinds of questions force us to consider social reforms that might address the economic and social forces that ultimately cause welfare dependency, such as raising the minimum wage or securing housing for low-income persons in suburban areas, where jobs are increasingly located.[16]

When researchers examine the causes of social problems, their perspectives influence their work, such as whether they emphasize personal, psychological, economic, biological, or environmental causes. Researchers with *public health* or *ecological perspectives* emphasize occupational, economic, familial, peer, and neighborhood factors.[17] When examining the causes of welfare, for example, these researchers implicate low-wage industries, the sheer cost of day care, the lack of transportation, and the placement of many jobs in suburban areas that are distant from inner-city residents. They also cite discrimination against welfare recipients by many employers.

Persons with *radical perspectives* implicate economic and social inequalities, the reduced economic opportunities of certain populations, and the practices of corporations as causes of specific social problems.[18] With the globalizing of the economy, for example, corporations often place their factories in low-wage nations in the developing world, thereby eliminating jobs in the United States that might have employed some welfare recipients. In addition corporations have often relocated their plants to suburban sites, making it difficult for inner-city residents to get to them. Corporations stand to benefit, moreover, from welfare reforms that force hundreds of thousands of people into the competition for jobs, allowing them to depress wages even further for relatively unskilled persons.

Analysts who use *medical* or *disease models* explore the physiological factors associated with specific problems.[19] Considerable numbers of welfare recipients are disabled or must care for children with disabilities. Medical or disease models dominate the medical and increasingly, the mental health fields, where physiological and pharmaceutical causes and solutions dominate.

Persons who emphasize *intrapsychic factors* explore personal and familial causes of social problems. Some researchers contend, for example, that teen pregnancy is often caused by a constellation of personal and familial dynamics, such as abusive parents, truancy, and poor school performance.

In a departure from traditional approaches, some persons adhere to *behavioral frameworks,* contending that certain social problems can be redressed only by providing rewards and disincentives that make welfare less attractive than employment. Persons who favor disincentives advocate reducing the levels of welfare grants or requiring teen mothers to live with their parents except when they are abused by them. Persons who favor rewards often favor allowing recipients to retain some assistance from the government even after they leave welfare so their post-welfare income will exceed their welfare income.

Some people emphasize *deterrent strategies* that penalize persons with social problems. Deterrents might include time limits for welfare or ending welfare altogether for certain groups of persons, like legal immigrants.

These different approaches often cause vigorous debates among theorists, analysts, and researchers. Persons who implicate economic and environmental factors often contend that counseling is an ineffective strategy. Radicals contend that, without remedying the inequalities in American society and the stress that poverty causes, many social problems cannot be significantly alleviated. Contending groups often selectively cite research evidence to support specific remedies and to attack the proposals of persons who use different paradigms.

These various frameworks and causal factors are not mutually exclusive, because various causes interact. Sophisticated policy practitioners and theorists believe that social problems are caused by an array of factors that combine the traditional approaches.[20] The risk of dependency increases when someone has not completed high school, has had no prior work experience, lives in a geographic area with high unemployment, has been subjected to parental abuse, and is sexually victimized by an older male. Such theorists as William Julius Wilson analyze these kinds of intersecting factors that shape complex phenomena like welfare dependency.[21] Indeed, policy advocates should take leading roles in critiquing social policies that are premised on simplistic analyses of social problems.

Developing Interventions and Programs in Step 1

Having established a typology and analyzed causation, policy advocates devise interventions to solve specific social problems. They develop curative strategies and preventive programs, measure the prevalence of specific problems, and conduct research to locate persons with specific problems.

Some policy initiatives emphasize a deterrent approach, but many policy advocates favor a public health and radical approach. Single women have children for many reasons, including coerced sex, lack of knowledge of contraception, a desire for companionship, and a desire to form a family unit. (In many cases, women believe that the father of the children will remain part of the family, only to find that he deserts, divorces, or fails to marry the mother of his children.) Research does not suggest that a diminution of welfare benefits markedly diminishes the number of single-headed families because women do not base childbirth decisions primarily on economic calculations.[22]

Once women do have children and once they are single heads of households, economic realities force them into poverty when they confront low-wage jobs and the sheer cost of day care, transportation, health care, and housing. Many of them realize from personal experience or from discussions with other women who have tried that they cannot support their families with income from low-wage jobs. So, many women stay on the rolls for extended periods or resort to on-and-off patterns as they enter and leave jobs that cannot finance their basic needs. Indeed, the decision to seek welfare in these economic circumstances is often a meritorious strategy used by women who care about their children enough to want them to have sufficient food, clothing, medical care, and housing.[23]

What is needed, then, is not deterrence but a constructive approach to make work pay enough to (at least) bring families to a poverty standard. This can be accomplished by giving all families in the lowest economic quintile in-kind help through day care, health care, and housing subsidies that continues as long as families remain below the poverty level. These in-kind subsidies need to be supplemented by direct income subsidies, such as an expanded earned-income tax credit (EITC) that gives families tax rebates as long as they remain below the poverty level.

Also needed are programs to help people employed at low wages to upgrade their earning potential. Persons with minimal skills and limited education must be prepared for jobs that are geared to their abilities and must receive sophisticated job placement services. To the extent that their skills and education can be enhanced to improve their long-term prospects, they should receive extended services, education, and job training. Some recipients need help moving to areas with less unemployment and those with disabilities might need jobs geared to their capabilities.

Even these remedies, however, ignore the reality of growing inequality in the wage structure of the United States. Dramatic increases in the minimum wage, as well as an increase in the power of American trade unions, are needed to raise wage levels for low-wage workers whose economic status has been eclipsed by the dramatic growth of wages for highly skilled and educated workers. Many advocates participate in a movement to require "living wages" in jobs that flow from government contracts.

Another set of interventions must be directed to employers in the private and public sectors. It is tempting to portray private employers as villains, but it is understandable that they would try to fill specific slots with job seekers who already have the requisite skills and job experience, which many welfare recipients do not possess. Without economic incentives for employers to hire them, many welfare recipients will not get jobs except during booming economic periods—and they are likely to be the first persons to be laid off when the nation enters a recession.[24] Moreover, federal, state, and local governments must create large numbers of public service jobs and retain them as long as the private sector does not absorb welfare recipients. These public service positions are needed particularly by recipients who are physically or mentally challenged. The government ought also to offer massive tax incentives to corporations that locate in low-wage areas, rather than the minor incentives offered under the current tax code.

Of course, booming economic growth will reduce the welfare rolls in some states even without these ameliorative policies. It will make deterrent strategies appear successful in the short term because employers, facing labor shortages, will hire many welfare recipients into low-wage jobs and will even promote some of them into moderate paying ones. In the long term, however, the deterrent approach to welfare is not likely to be effective because it does not upgrade the skills and education of recipients; consequently, they will be vulnerable to layoffs when economic growth slows. Services and policies tailored to the needs of specific subgroups are needed rather than a single set of policies. (See Policy Advocacy Challenge 7.6.)

To protect the rights of single heads of households and to safeguard their children, the welfare reforms of 1996 should have included a *bill of rights* for welfare recipients. If they participate in activities that prepare them for work, diligently seek employment, and secure employment, they should not fall beneath poverty standards or beneath the combined AFDC, food stamp, housing, and health benefits that welfare recipients received just before the enactment of welfare reforms. This bill of rights is needed to prevent the victimization of recipients by states that push recipients into poverty by insisting they take low-wage jobs, while cutting off the child-care, health, housing, and transportation.

POLICY ADVOCACY CHALLENGE 7.6

Designing Services for Homeless Children

ANNE MILDER, MSW STUDENT

When I learned, last December, that I, like every other first year MSW student at the University of Southern California School of Social Work, would be required to advocate for a specific homeless population in Los Angeles or Orange Counties, to do real policy analysis and advocacy, I complained and I complained loudly. *This was not what I had signed up for when I enrolled in the program; I just wanted to be a practitioner, working with infants and toddlers and their mothers. How could I, a student, know enough to tackle a problem as large and seemingly unsolvable as homelessness? Besides, wasn't it obvious that the homeless just needed homes? I couldn't provide houses. . . .* The task felt not only unrelated to the conceptualization of social work practice I held at the time, but, worse, it seemed like a futile exercise.

Given my on-going interest in young children, from the prenatal stage through age five, and the crucial brain development which takes place at this juncture (and its interrelationship, at least according to the postulations of affective neurobiology, with attachments to primary caregivers), I chose, as my area of focus, homeless children under the age of five.

None of my roughly 250 fellow students were looking at the 0–5 age range, and, in my studies, I was surprised to discover the many ways in which the 0–5 homeless population is commonly overlooked. For instance, at the time I began my analysis, I was told that First 5 LA—a public institution created by funds from Proposition 10 in Los Angeles County by a statewide ballot initiative designed to increase and improve services for children 0–5—had not yet designed programs specifically for homeless children. Also, I was told that LAUP—the institution created by LA First 5 to promote universal preschool—was not yet specifically thinking about preschool issues for homeless children. And I was told that ICARE—a network coordinated by the Department of Mental Health, specializing in children from birth to five years of age—had not yet concentrated on homeless children. I was told that many front line staff in local schools do not understand the McKinney-Vento definition of homelessness and do not know that children who are "doubled-up" with other relatives or friends are legally homeless. Most surprising to me was that the homeless count often did not include these children—or lumped them in a broader group of youth from birth to age 18—thus not recognizing them as a subgroup with its own needs.

I believe this is a particularly good example of just how subtle, how insidious and pervasive, is the prejudice embodied by the HUD definition of homelessness. Even though I had come to USC precisely because of my interest in young children, and even though I had studied the work of Emmi Pikler's Budapest orphanage the summer before starting school, and even though I had spent the first semester thinking about relief efforts for young children relocated to Los Angeles due to Hurricane Katrina, I had never thought of children as homeless persons even though many orphans and Katrina children evacuees become homeless.

Without knowing the depth of the problem, in terms of numbers, it was difficult to do a full analysis and advocate for services. I was, however, able to speak with the Department of Mental Health, specifically the coordinators of their 0–5 program group, and propose the possibility that my School of Social Work might survey their providers to see how many homeless children they serve and determine the needs of those children. (Perhaps some students from next year's policy class will take on this task.) I was able to propose to the Los Angeles County McKinney-Vento Coordinator that a question be asked on the intake forms at all schools about the ages of all siblings, a practice I was told by those working at the controversial Pappas School in Phoenix, Arizona, is very good for identifying younger, homeless siblings who are not yet in school. Via my professor, Ralph Fertig, I was able to advocate to the Los Angeles Homeless Services Agency (LAHSA) that homeless children 0–5 be included as a separate category in the next homeless count, and also that the count adopt a broader definition of homelessness, substituting the McKinney-Vento definition for the HUD definition.

What now seems obvious to me is that these children are part of at least two outgroups. Not only are they children—thus not voters or adults with a vote or a voice—but they are homeless, another usually voiceless population, and many of them are homeless in a way not recognized or counted by HUD.

What I learned stirred me enormously, both emotionally and intellectually. These homeless children, and all children, exist within a continuum of nested systems, from

(continued)

the family system, the community systems, to the socio-political systems. To do the work I originally envisioned when enrolling in an MSW program, to work with young children and their mothers, to work at bettering those relationships, I must also become a policy advocate.

Having identified the number and location of these children, we must then go the next step and design services that will speak to their needs and that will prevent them from becoming homeless in the first place.

Developing Preventive Programs in Step 1

Both Figures 7.2 and 7.3 show prevention arenas at their left edges. Prevention is akin to apple pie and motherhood, yet Americans devote scant resources to the prevention of most social problems, including the need for welfare. The challenge is to find preventive strategies that are sufficiently effective for funders to devote resources to them.

The Promise of Prevention   We should make a distinction at the outset among primary, secondary, and tertiary prevention. We emphasize primary prevention in Figures 7.2 and 7.3 because it prevents persons from experiencing important problems in the first place. Were we to prevent some people from ever getting cancer by cutting use of pesticides, for example, we would achieve *primary* prevention. In *secondary* prevention, persons with a specific problem are given assistance in its early stages, thus averting a full-blown or serious problem. When medical and mental-health screening problems locate persons with early-stage cancer or early-stage depression, for example, they can avert life-threatening cancer and depression through early interventions even though they failed to prevent cancer and depression altogether. *Tertiary* prevention aims to arrest a well-developed problem by using interventions that stop it from evolving further into a catastrophic condition. For example, the progression of clinical depression can often be stopped in persons treated with new medications as compared with persons who only receive counseling. (We can now update Figures 7.2 and 7.3 by noting that, although primary prevention occurs in the left-most circle, secondary and tertiary prevention occur in the middle circles of the diagram as persons are engaged with organized services or with community-based empowerment programs.)

Many preventive strategies have been shown to be effective at primary, secondary, and tertiary levels. With respect to primary prevention, for example, we know that lifestyle changes such as exercise, reduction of fat intake, reduction of alcohol consumption beneath certain thresholds, and weight control can markedly change health and mental health outcomes. We know that the requirement that automobile riders use seat belts and that bicycle and motorcycle riders use helmets have saved tens of thousands of lives. We have good evidence that Head Start improves school performance years after children have graduated from it. We know that educational credentials, such as a community college or college degree, markedly increase earnings (and therefore reduce poverty) in succeeding years. With respect to secondary and tertiary prevention, we have good evidence that early treatment stops the progression of an array of medical, mental health school, and job performance problems.

All of these examples share certain characteristics. Research had established links between specific causal factors and specific problems. Prevention interventions could be

BOX 7.2 | An Array of Interventions to Increase the Resources of Low-Wage Earners

1. Direct economic assistance
   a. Expanded EITC
2. In-kind economic assistance
   a. Child-care, health, transportation, and housing subsidies
   b. Food stamps
3. Indirect strategies to elevate wages for low-wage employees
   a. Increases in the minimum wage and enactment of a living wage
   b. Encouragement of trade unions
4. Job creation
   a. Public subsidies of private wages
   b. Public service jobs
   c. Expanded tax concessions to industries that locate in areas with high unemployment
5. Encouragement of mobility
   a. Relocation assistance to promote migration from areas of high unemployment
6. Tailoring of services to the needs of subgroups
7. A bill of rights for welfare recipients

targeted to persons with identifiable at-risk factors, such as obesity, sedentary lifestyles, poor diets, and lack of educational credentials—thus allowing society to focus its interventions on persons with these at-risk characteristics. Or, in the case of seat belts society targeted everyone who rides in cars, with clear evidence that the preventive intervention, seat belts, would increase the percentage of persons who survive car accidents. In each case, the cost of prevention was not so prohibitive that opponents could contend that society could not afford it.

Yet the promise of prevention is often unfulfilled. Certain interventions are poorly funded and implemented even when data suggests their effectiveness. Relatively few resources are devoted to helping persons make lifestyle changes; for example, even when sedentary lifestyles and obesity are strongly linked to various diseases and shortened life expectancy. We often invest too little money in programs that might prevent poverty, such as tutoring and preschool programs.

We lack good research on some preventive strategies, such as whether we can prevent many mental health problems from occurring in the first place. We do not yet know whether certain asset-building strategies actually work in the long term, such as helping low-income persons to establish savings accounts or to own their own homes, though early results are promising. Therefore, we need to examine an array of factors that impede greater emphasis on prevention.

Factors that Impede Prevention A series of barriers discourage prevention, including the problem of efficiency, difficulties in marshaling evidence of the effectiveness of preventive programs, the power of special interests, and competition with curative programs.

The Problem of Efficiency   To understand the problem of efficiency, let's assume that we know precisely which persons will develop social problems, such as which teenage women will have out-of-wedlock births in high school and enter the welfare rolls. Our knowledge would be based on research about at-risk indicators, such as the various causes of welfare dependency listed in Box 7.1. Assume that this research allows us to predict with complete accuracy *true positives* (women who will join the rolls) and *true negatives* (women who will not join the rolls). Under these circumstances, we will direct our prevention efforts exclusively to the true positives, excluding true negatives from our project because we have accurately predicted they will not join the welfare rolls. Were policy advocates able to predict accurately which women would become welfare recipients and which would not, they could develop a highly efficient prevention program that targeted its preventive services and resources only to true positives and provided no preventive services to true negatives.

In the real world, however, our ability to predict which people will and will not develop a specific problem is imperfect.[25] Some women have characteristics that are frequently associated with pregnancy in high school, such as low school achievement, abusive parents, and sexual victimization by an older male, but defy the odds and do not become pregnant. These women are *false positives* because they do not become welfare recipients, even though they have at-risk characteristics. Conversely, some women do not have these at-risk characteristics and do become pregnant. These women are *false negatives.* To the extent that a prevention program makes incorrect predictions about who will and who will not develop a problem, it wrongly directs some of its resources to false positives and wrongly fails to direct its resources to some persons who will develop a problem. As it wastes resources in this manner, the prevention program's efficiency declines. (See Figure 7.4 for examples of a relatively inefficient prevention program—Program B—and a relatively efficient prevention program—Program A.)

Prevention programs further decline in efficiency, moreover, if they cannot help persons actually avert a problem. Assume, for example, that a program asks teenagers in a high school who the school staff believe are at high risk of becoming pregnant to take a pledge to be abstinent. Also assume that the staff later discovers that this intervention is relatively ineffective in averting teen pregnancy. Even if this program had correctly predicted which teens would become pregnant, it would be inefficient because its intervention—getting teens to pledge abstinence—is relatively ineffective in averting teen pregnancy. This situation is not unusual: Prevention programs must both direct resources to true positives *and* develop effective interventions.

Problems in Getting People to Participate   Efficiency also declines when prevention programs cannot persuade people who are at risk to participate. Some teens refuse to participate because they do not want to make the effort, dislike the intervention, fear the motives of its staff, or are persuaded by peers not to participate.

We need not be excessively pessimistic: Some prevention programs are highly efficient and effective. (See Figure 7.4.) For example, the Ford Foundation funded a system of mentoring for high school students deemed to be at high risk of truancy and dropping out. High school graduates were assigned students to whom they were mentors for at least three years, aggressively monitoring the attendance and performance of these students, immediately finding them when they were truant, and getting them tutorial assistance when they received failing grades. The mentors visited the homes of their

FIGURE 7.4
An efficient and inefficient preventive intervention

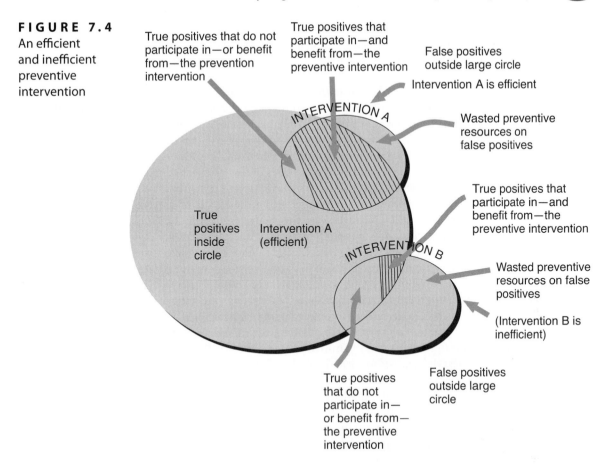

students frequently to secure the cooperation of parents and to address familial factors that impeded school attendance. In schools with dropout rates exceeding 50 percent, the mentoring program reduced dropout rates to less than 10 percent.[26]

It is useful to discuss as well the importance of passive prevention in social policy, as it is distinguished from active prevention. If active prevention helps people make corrective lifestyle changes or personal decisions to forestall a disease or problem (such as changing diets, engaging in exercise, using birth control, or stopping smoking), passive prevention changes the environments of people to diminish the likelihood that they will develop a problem. Examples of such changes are installing seat belts in cars (to prevent injuries or deaths from crashes), removing pollution from the air (to prevent lung diseases), and persuading food manufacturers to reduce the saturated fat in certain foods (to prevent heart disease). In each of these cases, people passively receive the benefits of these environmental changes without having to alter their lifestyle or to make different choices.[27] As in the case of active prevention, however, advocates must convince decision makers that the cost of these measures will be balanced by the benefits to society. For example, many advocates had to pressure legislators for years before convincing them that the cost of seat belts would be offset by the number of deaths they would prevent.

Many prevention measures fall between the active and passive poles. Banning smoking advertisements from billboards near schools, for example, is effective only if teenagers decide not to smoke.

Difficulties in Marshaling Evidence of the Effectiveness of Preventive Programs

It is often difficult to marshal the empirical evidence that specific programs actually prevent specific problems. Researchers must follow subjects over a significant period of time to demonstrate that preventive interventions actually reduce such problems as teen pregnancy or alcoholism. They also have to rule out the effects of other factors that have affected the lives of their subjects during this period. And they must demonstrate a magnitude of prevention that justifies the costs of the preventive program. The problems in demonstrating the effects of preventive programs are well illustrated by the controversy in the health field over the efficacy of dietary supplements like vitamin C; researchers remain uncertain despite myriad studies. Yet some interventions have been demonstrated to have remarkable success, such as the aforementioned mentoring program for students at risk of not finishing high school.

The Unproven Efficacy of Genetic Testing

Genetic testing has enormous promise for conditions linked to genetic factors, such as many health problems and possibly some mental health problems. If researchers can identify genetic predispositions to certain problems, they can involve persons with them in preventive programs, such as lifestyle changes for persons with a disposition for heart disease. But the efficacy of genetic testing is now limited to relatively few conditions—and it remains to be seen if persons with genetic predispositions will commit themselves to prevention programs that could allow them to avert certain problems.

The Power of Special Interests

Special interests often oppose meritorious prevention projects. Cigarette companies have successfully thwarted efforts to prevent teenagers from smoking because cigarette manufacturers consider teenagers a lucrative and growing market. Automobile manufacturers fought the installation of seat belts for years because of the cost. Right-to-life and moral majority groups have prevented many schools from providing effective sex education programs, as well as birth control services. Professionals who are socialized to medical models tend to focus on curative rather than preventive remedies.

Yet determined reformers often overcome the power of special interests. Laws requiring the use of helmets by motorcyclists and bicyclists have saved thousands of lives, even though they were strenuously opposed by motorcyclists. Even cigarette companies, despite opposition, have been required to comply with many governmental regulations.

Competition between Curative and Preventive Programs

Preventive programs must compete for funds with programs that help people who already have specific problems. In the case of welfare programs, for example, states and localities must expend vast resources to sustain dependent families, whether providing them with welfare benefits, helping them get jobs, subsidizing child care, or providing health care. Advocates who want significant resources to prevent teenage girls from joining the rolls have to convince legislators to divert scarce resources from curative to preventive programs.

We should not be deterred from developing preventive programs just because they are often inefficient, are difficult to evaluate, are opposed by special interests, or compete with curative programs. To the extent that we can prevent problems, we not only forestall human suffering but also avoid future costs. (See Policy Advocacy Challenge 7.7.)

Measuring the Magnitude of Problems in Step 1

It is relatively simple to measure the magnitude of welfare dependency among single women with children because public authorities issue data about the number of persons who receive welfare checks. Other problems, such as homelessness and substance abuse, are more difficult to measure because people who have these problems often do not seek public services. Policy advocates often have to demonstrate that specific problems are sufficiently important to merit the attention of agency staff, funders, government officials, and legislators.

POLICY ADVOCACY CHALLENGE 7.7

Developing a Prevention Program and Convincing Decision Makers to Adopt It

BRUCE JANSSON, PH.D.

Try to develop an intervention program for an inner-city school that seeks to diminish teen pregnancy. As you plan the program, discuss whether it should do the following:

- Try to increase teenagers' self-esteem
- Emphasize career and employment planning in hopes that teenagers who believe they have an economic future will be less likely to have children
- Seek to change behaviors of teenagers or attempt to change behaviors of males, to the extent that teenagers become pregnant because they are raped or pressured to have sex by older men
- Include the parents of teenagers in their project in hopes that improvements in family functioning will avert pregnancies
- Provide birth-control information and devices

Assuming that you lack resources to provide your intervention to all teenagers in the school, what at-risk factors might you use to decide whom you would try to reach?

Once you have developed a tentative strategy, discuss what strategies you might use to persuade teenagers to participate in your intervention.

Discuss some problems you might face in trying to convince the local school board to adopt your intervention for the entire school district. Discuss the problem of efficiency in this context.

Legislators, funders, and agency executives are likely to invest scarce resources in programs that they believe address widespread problems. Rates, prevalence, and incidence are commonly used to measure the relative magnitude of social problems.[28] *Rates* (expressed as percentages), for example, measure the ratio of a group of persons, such as white males between the ages of 18 and 25 who were arrested for drunk driving in a specific year, to a larger reference group, such as the total number of white males in this age bracket in the population that year. *Incidence* (also expressed as a percentage) measures the ratio of new cases—for example, the number of new arrests in 2001 of white males aged 18 to 25—to a larger reference group, such as the total number of white males in the population that year in that age bracket. *Prevalence* (again, expressed as a percentage) measures the ratio of persons who are currently experiencing a social problem to the total population. A policy practitioner might want to compare the number of persons currently being prosecuted for drunk driving to the total number of drivers on a specific day. Each measure provides a somewhat different estimate of the problem's seriousness. These kinds of data are often available from city, county, state, or federal agencies or from research literature in the social and health sciences.

Practitioners can use a variety of technical approaches when measuring the magnitude of social problems. When data are not available from government agencies or the research literature, policy practitioners measure social problems in other ways. Jonathan Bradshaw contrasts measures of felt need, expressed need, expert need, and comparative need.[29] *Felt need* measures persons' belief that they have a problem. An agency might interview a sample of working mothers with preschool children, for example, to assess their belief that they cannot afford day care. Of course, persons sometimes exaggerate their actual needs or, in the case of stigmatized conditions such as substance abuse, underreport them.

Expressed need measures persons' actual search for specific services. A policy practitioner might examine the length of the waiting lists at drug treatment centers, for example, or the number of calls that a hot line receives about substance abuse. Although a knowledge of clients' service-related behaviors is useful, these behaviors may not accurately reflect people's actual needs. Some persons do not seek services, for example, because they believe they cannot afford them, do not like social agencies, are unaware of the services, think they will receive ineffective services, fear they will be prosecuted, or fear they will be subjected to punitive services because of their stigmatized condition.

Policy advocates sometimes assess *expert needs* by asking experts, such as social scientists, social work practitioners, local agency executives, or government officials, for their estimates of the severity of specific problems. Experts can draw convincing evidence from current research, such as the extent of alcoholism among women. Of course, experts' biases and values may influence their position and credibility; someone who defines alcoholism as consuming many drinks each day will provide a lower estimate of the problem's seriousness than someone who uses a more stringent standard, such as consuming only several drinks a day.

A *comparative need* approach measures unmet needs by comparing the services offered in different communities. Assume, for example, that certain neighborhoods have many drug treatment programs, but others with similar demographic characteristics have few. We can infer a larger unmet need for drug treatment services in the neighborhoods with fewer treatment programs. One should interpret comparative need measures with caution, however, because they rely on inference rather than a direct measure of need. For example, a neighborhood with few drug treatment programs will appear to have a shortage of services when compared with neighborhoods that have too many such programs.

Using several or all of these means of assessing needs helps us gauge the importance of specific social problems. If we were trying to promote drug treatment programs in a specific neighborhood, for example, we might look into the length of the existing programs' waiting lists (expressed need), ask high school students for their perceptions of the seriousness of adolescent substance abuse (felt need), discover whether similar neighborhoods have more programs (comparative need), and get information from selected experts (expert need).

Measurements of social problems become more dramatic when they include trend data suggesting that a specific problem is becoming more serious. Such data may come from felt-need, expressed-need, comparative-need, or expert-need sources, or from rising rates, prevalence, or incidence of specific problems. A dramatic increase in a community's substance abuse problems, for example, would be documented by a rising rate of deaths from overdose and longer waiting lists for drug treatment programs (felt need).

Policy decision makers, however, do not spring into action merely because policy advocates present them with data about the prevalence of a problem or the need for specific services. Legislators often ignore overwhelming data about a problem, particularly when they are not subjected to strong pressure by voters and interest groups or when powerful interests oppose ameliorating measures. Despite large numbers of deaths and injuries from guns in inner-city areas, for example, politicians in most jurisdictions have not enacted stringent measures to control guns because of opposition by the National Rifle Association. Politicians sometimes take action not when a problem is becoming more serious, but when the public believes it is becoming more important or when party leaders believe they can improve their political fortunes by taking action. In the case of welfare reform in 1996, for example, the cost of AFDC had risen from $15.5 billion in 1970 to $22.3 billion in 1993—not a marked increase after adjusting for inflation. Yet a welfare crisis was proclaimed, leading the Congress and the president to rescind the AFDC program and to devolve welfare assistance to the states.[30]

Locating Problems Spatially

It does little good to determine that a problem is relatively widespread if we cannot locate and reach its victims or, in the case of preventive programs, its potential victims. Social science tools are one way to locate people with certain problems. The U.S. Census, done every 10 years, does not collect data about social problems such as substance abuse and mental illness but instead states demographic, economic, and housing data in aggregate terms for specific geographic regions.[31] Nonetheless its data are important to social workers because social scientists have linked demographic and economic factors with social problems. For example, poor persons are more likely than affluent persons to experience specific medical problems, to be unemployed, to have poor housing, and to be pressured by dealers to use illegal drugs. Members of certain ethnic groups are more likely than others to have some medical conditions, such as sickle cell anemia and Tay-Sachs disease. By using economic, housing, demographic, and ethnic data, policy practitioners can infer high rates of certain social problems in specific geographic areas.

Policy advocates need not confine themselves to census material. Local public health offices, various state agencies, municipal and county authorities, and some federal agencies, such as the National Institute of Mental Health, regularly collect and compile various kinds of population-based data.[32]

Census and other public data can also shape marketing, outreach, and advertising strategies. An agency could publicize its services in certain neighborhoods with a high concentration of specific groups. For example, the agency could market its services to areas with working women (day care), adolescents (substance abuse), or elderly people (home health care services). Policy advocates can even inspect neighborhoods to decide where persons with specific kinds of problems live. As a tenant organizer, for example, I discovered that I could easily locate substandard housing by observing the window frames in specific neighborhoods; from flaking paint and the absence of putty, I could often predict the overall condition of the rental unit.

POLICY ADVOCACY CHALLENGE 7.8

Using Demographic Data to Locate At-Risk Populations

BOB ERLENBUSCH, PH.D.

Go to **academic.cengage.com/ social_work/jansson** to watch this video clip

Listen to Bob Erlenbusch, Chair of the National Coalition Against Homelessness and Executive Director of the Los Angeles Coalition to End Hunger and Homelessness, in Policy Advocacy Challenge Video 7.8 as he discusses why policy advocates must often collect data from the census or from other sources to buttress their case to decision makers that a specific issue or problem should receive priority. Please ask these questions:

Why is a map showing the distribution of homeless persons in a jurisdiction an important device when talking with elected officials in that area?

Why is a map important, as well, to providers and other agencies?

Social Problems as Slippery Concepts

Flowcharts like the ones in Figures 7.2 and 7.3 are useful, but they do not reveal the subtle distinctions and philosophical issues that confront policy advocates. Social problems are human constructs, not purely objective phenomena. Indeed, by referring to social phenomena as social problems, people define them as requiring human intervention to be solved. They invent terms and classification systems, sometimes even when demonstrable problems do not exist or when it is unclear how many people have them. Part of the subject of this chapter, then—the analysis of problems—is a consideration of the basic concept of *social problem*. Let's analyze some ambiguities and philosophical issues that most social workers will confront during their careers.

When Are Social Problems Real, and When Are They Invented?

Because social problems are social conditions invested with human meaning, all of them are "invented."[33] Pestilence and famine were regarded in medieval times as inevitable and not solvable, but they are widely regarded in contemporary society as problems that demand solutions—at least in developed nations where the resources and technology exist to address them. Myriad conditions have only recently been called problems, such as dyslexia, many mental disorders, and such physiological conditions as menopause. (Successive versions of the *DSM*, which describes mental conditions for mental health professionals, have included scores of additional conditions, often with no credible evidence that they are important mental problems.)[34]

Most of us would agree, however, that we can be relatively confident in declaring some conditions to be problems. Such conditions as malnutrition, heart disease, cancer, and severe mental depression bring demonstrable suffering and death to their victims. Moreover, human service workers and health workers diagnose these conditions with high levels of reliability by using diagnostic tests that have been perfected through decades of research. But other social conditions are called problems without evidence that they are regular and identifiable phenomena in the real world. Critics of *DSM-IV* contend, for example, that research demonstrates that qualified clinicians cannot reliably make distinctions among many of the disorders listed.[35]

Social workers should view problems with healthy skepticism. As they proliferate with scant evidence that they are truly problems, human service workers are likely to treat subjects unnecessarily, to label them, and to apply remedies to conditions that do not require treatment. Indeed, the attitude toward some problems must be reversed, as is illustrated in the medical field by childbirth. For centuries, when childbirth was viewed as a normal condition rather than as a problem, women delivered their babies at home with the help of a midwife—a practice still prevalent in some European nations. Once childbirth was declared a medical problem by American obstetricians, women were taken to hospitals for delivery, drugged heavily, and subjected to extraordinarily high rates of cesarean section—policies that vastly increased the cost of childbirth without lowering the infant death rate.[36] Only recently has the pendulum reversed, as increasing numbers of women use midwives, either in hospitals or in their own homes.

Some social conditions are so complex that it is difficult to know when they are problems. Take the case of teen pregnancy, which is widely viewed as a problem. Considerable medical evidence suggests that when girls of 12 or 13 give birth, they imperil themselves and their infants, who experience high rates of birth defects. Such risks diminish sharply, however, as girls enter their mid and late teens. One researcher contends, moreover, that on a variety of indicators, including wages and amount of schooling, low-income women who have children in their mid to late teens are not worse off than women who wait to have children.[37] (The researcher contended that because they do not have to interrupt their careers with pregnancies and child rearing, women who have children early may be more able than women who wait to concentrate continuously on work and careers.) Even this cursory discussion suggests that teen pregnancy may not always be a problem. Indeed, we might well ask whether the decision of some teen mothers to have children is a legitimate lifestyle choice, particularly in light of evidence that some of them do not harm themselves or their children.

Many Social Problems Defy Simple Solutions, But Many People Favor Panaceas

Most social problems are complex phenomena that do not lend themselves to simple solutions. Yet people frequently demand panaceas, as American history amply suggests.[38] This familiar pattern reasserted itself with respect to welfare reform in the mid and late 1990s with the adoption of a deterrent strategy to deal with a complicated problem. Because of its roots in the social and economic fabric of American society, welfare dependency cannot be solved by deterrence; it is caused by such factors as low-wage jobs; residential segregation; and the high cost of day care, housing, medical care, and transportation.

Moreover, solving problems requires persistence rather than time-limited crusades. As existing welfare recipients enter the job market, additional women will require job-seeking assistance or welfare when they have children and can find only low-wage jobs. Many women who secure jobs will lose them during recessions. When welfare recipients do receive jobs, they will displace some current workers (male and female) from the labor force, particularly in areas that do not have high rates of economic growth. As even this brief discussion suggests, many social problems cannot be solved but merely ameliorated through continuing efforts.

The panaceas are sometimes promoted by class and racial prejudice. Because they have not experienced the actual circumstances of living in many inner-city and rural areas—and are not subject to the structural factors that cause and sustain social problems like high levels of crime, unemployment, disease, delinquency, welfare dependency, bad housing, homelessness, and dropping out of school—many affluent Americans seek simple solutions aimed at changing the values and viewpoints of low-income persons. Some believe that sex education programs preaching abstinence will eradicate teen pregnancy. Some favor the widespread use of volunteers to teach children to read or to offer middle-class models to impoverished children. Some support deterrent policies to diminish crime rates and welfare dependency in inner-city communities. These solutions do not take into account the realities of living in these communities.

Priorities Are Not Chosen Rationally

The literature on policy analysts sometimes conveys the misleading impression that decision makers rely on research to shape public priorities. We already have mentioned, for example, that policy analysts often try to gauge the costs to society of specific problems, such as the work absenteeism, death, and lost wages that derive from alcoholism. However, the reality that politics ultimately shapes the selection of priorities can be shown by two examples: antismoking policies and the magnitude of the resources devoted to children's programs. An extraordinary body of research has implicated smoking in hundreds of thousands of deaths annually, yet strong gains were made in regulating tobacco as a drug only in the late 1990s. Many researchers have argued that interventions directed at children, such as children's health programs, have a high benefit-to-cost ratio. Yet the United States devotes only a small fraction of its domestic budget to children—and continues not to fund medical coverage for many of them.

Solving One Problem Can Create Others

Even if some problems can be solved, others often emerge in their wake, as in the case of welfare reform. While saving money by paying reduced welfare costs, society incurs new costs as some (or many) former recipients receive lower resources from employment or from general relief. As some become homeless, they require shelter care and develop health problems that local authorities have to fund. Foster care costs rise as some mothers become unable to provide adequately for their children. Economic desperation is likely to bring increases in family violence, crime, and substance abuse. As some recipients exceed their allotted time on welfare and still are unemployed, counties and cities will have to expend more funds for general relief.[39]

The precise amount of these new costs to society will depend partly on rates of economic growth. In parts of the country with robust growth, job creation will absorb large numbers of former welfare recipients, but they will compete with other unemployed people, new job seekers (such as recent graduates from high school), and immigrants for scarce jobs in other areas. When former recipients do find jobs, some other job seekers will not find work and will be forced onto general relief. Were a recession to occur, moreover, the relief and unemployment rolls would vastly expand.

Variations in Problems

When pointing to the issues in defining, measuring, and conceptualizing social problems, many policy advocates stress the differences between groups in the population. Alcoholism appears, for example, to have different causes and to take different forms in men and women.[40] Unlike men, whose alcoholism often stems from occupational stress and peer pressure, many women develop alcoholism during times of family crisis, such as marital discord, divorce, or a child's death. Unlike alcoholic men, who tend to drink in public—in bars or with friends—many alcoholic women drink secretly. These differences in both the causes and manifestations of alcoholism suggest that men and women need different kinds of treatment, as well as different kinds of preventive services.

Moreover, cultural differences affect people's responses to services. Spanish-speaking families, for example, often defer to male heads of household before seeking assistance for specific problems. In white families, women often take the initiative in seeking services for specific problems. If they want to be successful, social service agencies that serve Latinos must try to include male heads of household in service transactions.[41] Some ethnic groups require bilingual and bicultural staff who can interpret nuances of expression and probe for the meaning of verbal and nonverbal cues that would escape staff from the dominant culture. Some persons respond favorably to one approach, such as a specific kind of counseling, whereas others respond to behavior modification or to membership in support groups, such as Alcoholics Anonymous. Deterrent measures, such as increasing the cost of alcohol or cigarettes, appear to decrease some people's use, but they may be even more effective when supplemented with counseling programs and reductions in advertising.

The vast literature that has recently evolved on "culturally sensitive practice" and "multidiversity" stresses the need to adapt programs to specific populations.[42] This sensitivity must occur on two related levels. First, we need to examine the differences in specific social problems in different populations, as our discussion of alcoholism among males and females suggests. Second, services must be adapted to the culture and norms of specific ethnic and racial groups.

We should remember as well that the problems of oppressed populations are often caused or exacerbated by the hostile environments and extreme poverty that many of their members encounter, particularly in inner-city communities. The rules of mental health, for example, whether in diagnosis or treatment, must be modified when social workers are helping persons who live in areas that look like bombed-out cities, who are exposed to violence daily, who cannot obtain secure jobs that will allow them to escape poverty, and who can obtain amenities such as health care only by waiting for days in clinics. Terms such as *paranoia, inability to make long-term plans,* and *flight,* which can be used in the diagnosis and treatment of mental conditions or problem-solving deficits in middle-class citizens, must be used cautiously in labeling persons in these high-stress environments, where trust, planning, and permanent social arrangements are less feasible.

The term *empowerment* helps us reconceptualize some of the services that social workers provide to persons in high-stress environments. (While empowerment is not limited to persons in high-stress environments, it may have particular relevance for them.) When seeking to empower persons, social workers often emphasize survival skills, such as helping persons cope with the fragmentation of services, understaffed services, and hostile bureaucrats. Rather than focusing on pathology, empowerment helps people develop personal plans to improve their lives. Indeed, some people favor terms like *consumers of service* rather than *patient* or *client* to avoid labeling people. Some social workers advocate placing less reliance on mental health diagnostic categories, such as those in *DSM-IV,* that label persons on the basis of deficits rather than strengths.[43]

Challenges for Policy Advocates

We have noted that policy advocates who help oppressed populations encounter particular challenges in policy arenas because their issues are frequently unpopular. Certain kinds of issues and populations have a relatively privileged position in American culture, as can be seen by their success in securing a disproportionate share of resources. Fund-raisers for hospitals, certain cultural undertakings, and privileged educational organizations such as private schools have an enviable job in raising funds compared to shoestring organizations that help stigmatized populations.[44]

Moreover, the broader population views the problems of stigmatized conditions, such as homelessness or AIDS, through prejudiced lenses. Rather than viewing homelessness as stemming from an absence of halfway houses, decent social services, and affordable housing, many persons stress the personal failings of those who are homeless as the major, even the sole, cause of this condition. Rather than viewing AIDS as an epidemic, similar to cholera in prior eras, some persons view many who have this disease through the lens of homophobia, seeing it as stemming from an aberrant lifestyle choice. Problems of oppressed populations are, moreover, often viewed as relatively hopeless and unsolvable, unlike those of more powerful populations.

When policy advocates suggest that inequalities in American society, such as discrepancies in the incomes and opportunities of the social classes, should be rectified, they are often dismissed as left-leaning radicals. In a society that lacks a strong radical tradition, the rhetoric of social equality is often dismissed. But advocates for powerless populations and unpopular issues often realize that without a fundamental redistribution of resources and opportunities, specific groups, such as inner-city African Americans, will remain on the periphery of American society. They will be unable even to imagine themselves significantly improving their lives.

These common perceptions of the problems of oppressed populations underline the need for their advocates to educate people, whether through the mass media or through personal discussions with highly placed officials. They must contest the definitions and conceptualizations of specific social problems, such as equating welfare with bad character rather than with limited, low-paying jobs. They have to resist people's stereotypes by arguing that certain groups do, in fact, have different needs and problems.

What You Can Now Do	**CHAPTER SUMMARY**

You are now equipped to do the following:

- Identify the six steps of the Policy Analysis Framework
- State why policy analysis is often needed in policy advocacy

- Develop flow charts to understand the development of social problems and to enhance policy analysis
- Use typologies to identify subpopulations within a broader population of persons with specific social conditions
- Identify multiple causes of social problems
- Identify different perspectives or models that shape the solutions that persons develop for specific social problems
- Develop preventive solutions to specific social problems
- Measure the magnitude of specific social problems and their spatial distribution
- Grapple with non-rational factors that shape how persons view specific social problems and the kinds of solutions that they propose
- Develop policy solutions that take into account the culture, ethnicity, race, and social class of specific populations

We discuss strategies for defending and presenting policy proposals in the next chapter.

POLICY ADVOCACY CHALLENGE 7.9

Analyzing Effects of Concentrated Poverty on African Americans in New Orleans

BRUCE JANSSON, PH.D.

Most tourists flock to the Garden District and entertainment centers of New Orleans, hardly seeing its less flattering side. Not only had its population declined by roughly one-fourth over the post 30 years, but the percentage of persons in communities with concentrated poverty—defined as neighborhoods where more than 40 percent of the population living below federal poverty levels—had considerably increased.

The communities with concentrated poverty, such as the lower Ninth Ward, were beset with myriad social problems; they had extraordinary crime and homicide rates, considerable gang violence, high school drop-out rates, and high levels of unemployment. Yet the lower Ninth Ward also had many strengths. It had many churches and small businesses. Since many families had lived in the neighborhood for generations, extensive kinship and friendship networks existed even as many families lived in or near poverty levels. Roughly 60 percent of its adult residents owned their own homes.

As social scientists viewed the lower Ninth Ward devastated by flood waters caused by Hurricane Katrina, they pondered whether the storm might open the door to an intriguing option. Might not huge federal resources be used, they wondered, to provide homes for many low-income African-American evacuees in mixed-income and integrated neighborhoods rather than rebuilding New Orleans as it had existed prior to Hurricane Katrina?

Some social scientists and public officials had long hypothesized that persons in neighborhoods with concentrated poverty would be better off if they resided in mixed-income areas.[1] Their logic seemed unassailable since they would have better housing, schools, medical facilities, grocery stores, and other amenities in mixed-income areas. They would often live closer to places of employment—and have more employment options than in areas of concentrated poverty. African-American youth would, they hypothesized, benefit from living in neighborhoods with sharply lower rates of crime,

Go to **academic.cengage.com/ social_work/jansson** to watch this video clip

[1] Julie Kosterlitz, "The Katrina Experiment," *National Journal*, November 5, 2005: 3436–3441.

(continued)

school drop-outs, and use of illicit drugs—and they would be more likely to obtain employment as they established networks with relatively affluent youth.

Jonathan Crane's research, published in 1991, appeared to confirm the deleterious impact of "ghettoes" on their residents.[2] His data indicated that such problems as dropping-out from schools and teen pregnancy rapidly escalate once they reach a certain threshold. He conjectured that teens spread these problems to their peers once they reach high thresholds, growing to "epidemic levels."

It was not surprising, then, that 176 anti-poverty experts, including William Julius Wilson, the noted African-American social scientist, urged federal, state, and local public officials to help low-income African Americans in New Orleans move to areas integrated by class and race in the wake of Hurricane Katrina rather than trying to place them back in areas of high concentrations of poverty.[3]

Relocation of low-income persons to mixed-income areas had been implemented in other cities during the several decades preceding Hurricane Katrina. To settle a class-action suit against the Chicago Public Housing Authority, for example, 7,100 African-American families had been relocated from areas of concentrated poverty to integrated or largely Caucasian areas with the use of housing vouchers with help from counselors to help them deal with this transition. The Congress had funded the movement of 4,600 low-income families to more affluent areas in five cities in so-called Moving to Opportunity demonstrations. President Bill Clinton's HOPE VI program had converted some public housing projects into mixed-income ones.

Unfortunately, however, data that was gathered at these various sites could not definitively show that the relocation of low-income persons had necessarily been responsible for encouraging outcomes, such as increased income, lower rates of drop-outs, and less drug usage. Since an experimental design had not been used, it was possible that the persons who agreed to be relocated already were more motivated than persons who chose to remain in their neighborhoods. Some data also suggested that some relocated persons did not fare better than those who remained, particularly among African-American male adolescents who sometimes developed relatively high rates of drug usage and were prone to dropping out of school.

When Katrina hit New Orleans, then, good reasons existed for hypothesizing that many low-income residents would benefit from mixed-income neighborhoods even if data was not yet definitive. Quite apart from social science theory and data, however, an excellent ethical rationale could be articulated for giving low-income African-American evacuees a range of choices so *they* could decide where they wanted to live when they returned to New Orleans. Relatively affluent persons whose homes had been destroyed or damaged by Katrina often *had* choices since they often had sufficient resources to choose whether to repair or rebuild their homes or to move to other locations. By contrast, low-income African Americans often lacked resources either to return to their old communities or to move to mixed-income areas. If they owned their homes, they often lacked resources to rebuild them even with federal subsidies. If they wanted to move to a mixed-income community, federal payments to them for their old house would be insufficient to allow them to purchase a house in a more expensive community. If they were renters, they often could not afford rents in either their old

---

[2] Jonathan Crane, "The Epidemic Theory of Ghettos and Neighborhood Effects on Dropping Out and Teenage Childbearing," *American Journal of Sociology*, Vol. 96, March 1991, 1226–1259.
[3] Kosterlitz, "The Katrina Experiment," p. 3437

community or mixed-income communities since rents had escalated throughout the New Orleans region due to a shortage of rental units in Katrina's wake.

It seemed only fair, then, to give these low-income evacuees choices that more affluent residents possessed. Indeed, evacuees who chose not to return to New Orleans but to remain in cities like Houston, deserved a similar range of choices. With use of housing vouchers and Section 8 rent subsidies, they ought to be able to choose whether to live in mixed-income areas or in low-income areas. These choices would not exist, however, if the federal government was not determined to fund mixed-income housing projects or to help low-income African Americans find rental housing—or even to purchase homes with subsidized mortgages, in mixed-income areas.

How does this case example illustrate how:

1. public officials and policy advocates had to engage in problem analysis in Katrina's wake?
2. how definitive data often does not exist when important policy decisions must be made—but public officials need often need to proceed anyway using best information about the issue at stake
3. why public policy should often seek to give vulnerable populations choices that more affluent persons take for granted

Listen to Ron McClain, JD, MSW, LCSW and CEO of the Family Service of Greater New Orleans, in Policy Advocacy Challenge Video 7.9, as he discusses some strategies for bringing some low income evacuees back to New Orleans.

• What role should residents and evacuees have in the planning process?
• To what extent do you think evacuees should have the choice of living in areas of concentrated poverty or mixed-income areas?

NOTES

1. For an eight-step model of policy analysis, see Eugene Bardach, *The Eight-Step Path of Policy Analysis: A Handbook of Practice*, Berkeley Academic Press, 1998.
2. Mary Jo Bane, "Welfare as We Might Know It," *American Prospect* 30 (January–February 1997): 47–53.
3. The *DSM-IV* is the fourth edition of the *Diagnostic and Statistical Manual of Mental Disorders*, published in 1994 by The American Psychiatric Association.
4. See the testimony of David Ellwood in the U.S. Senate, *Hearings*, Subcommittee on Social Security and Family Policy of Committee on Finance (March 2, 1987), pp. 105–111.
5. See J. K. Wing, *Reasoning about Mental Illness* (London: Oxford University Press, 1978), Chap. 2.
6. Phillip Kotler, *Principles of Marketing*, 4th ed. (Englewood Cliffs, NJ: Prentice Hall, 1989), pp. 42–46.
7. Richard Krueger, *Focus Groups: A Practical Guide for Applied Research* (Newbury Park, CA: Sage, 1990).
8. See David Mechanic, *Mental Health and Social Policy*, 3rd ed. (Englewood Cliffs, NJ: Prentice Hall, 1989), pp. 16–44.
9. Stuart Kirk and Herb Hutchins, *The Selling of DSM: The Rhetoric of Science in Psychiatry* (New York: Aldine de Gruyter, 1992).
10. Bane, "Welfare as We Might Know It."
11. Claude Fischer et al., *Inequality by Design: Cracking the Bell Curve Myth* (Princeton, NJ: Princeton University Press, 1996), pp. 102–128.

12. David Ellwood, *Poor Support: Poverty in the American Family* (New York: Basic Books, 1988).

13. Irving Piliavin et al., "The Duration of Homeless Careers: An Exploratory Study," *Social Service Review* (December 1993): 57–69.

14. Richard Berk et al., "Social Policy Experimentation," *Evaluation Review* 9 (August 1985): 387–431.

15. Claire Renzetti and Raymond Lee, eds., *Researching Sensitive Topics* (Newbury Park, CA: Sage, 1993).

16. Bane, "Welfare as We Might Know It."

17. U.S. Department of Health and Human Services, *Alcohol and Health: Report to U.S. Congress* (Washington, DC: Government Printing Office, 1987), pp. 97–119.

18. Steven Wineman, *The Politics of Human Services: A Radical Alternative to the Welfare State* (Boston: South End Press, 1984).

19. For a critique of the medical model in substance abuse, see Dorothy Nelkin, *Methadone Maintenance: A Technological Fix* (New York: Braziller, 1973).

20. William Miller and Hester Reid, "Matching Problem Drinkers with Optimal Treatments," in William Miller and Nick Heather, eds., *Treating Addictive Behaviors: Processes of Change* (New York: Plenum Press, 1986), pp. 175–204.

21. William Julius Wilson, *When Work Disappears: The World of the New Urban Poor* (New York: Knopf, 1996).

22. Melissa Healy, "Welfare 'Family Cap' Fails to Cut Birthrate in New Jersey," *Los Angeles Times* (September 12, 1997), pp. 1, 16.

23. David Zucchino, *Myth of the Welfare Queen* (New York: Scribner, 1997).

24. Louis Uchitelle, "Welfare Recipients Taking Jobs Often Held by the Working Poor," *New York Times* (April 1, 1997), pp. 1, 10.

25. Martin Bloom, *Primary Prevention: The Possible Science* (Englewood Cliffs, NJ: Prentice Hall, 1981).

26. Jonathan Smith, "Quantum Opportunities Program," *New York Times* (March 9, 1995), pp. 1, 2.

27. Bloom, *Primary Prevention.*

28. Ibid., pp. 173–174.

29. Jonathan Bradshaw, "The Concept of Social Need," *New Society* 30 (March 1972): 640–643.

30. Mary Ellen Hombs, *Welfare Reform: A Reference Handbook* (Santa Barbara, CA: ABC-CLIO, 1996), p. 54.

31. See National Institute of Mental Health, *A Working Manual of Simple Evaluation Techniques for Community Mental Health Centers* (Washington, DC: Government Printing Office, 1976), pp. 99–146.

32. Ibid.

33. Arnold Green, *Social Problems: Arena of Conflict* (New York: McGraw-Hill, 1975), pp. 67–115.

34. Kirk and Hutchins, *The Selling of DSM*, pp. 199–218.

35. Ibid.

36. Barbara Ehrenreich and Deirdre English, *For Her Own Good: 150 Years of the Experts' Advice to Women* (New York: Anchor Books, 1979).

37. See the discussion of Joseph Hotz's work in Richard Cooper, "Contrary Message on Teenage Pregnancy," *Los Angeles Times* (May 24, 1997), pp. 1, 14.

38. Bruce S. Jansson, *The Reluctant Welfare State*, 3rd ed. (Pacific Grove, CA: Brooks/Cole, 1997), pp. 352–353.

39. Wolch and Sommer, *Los Angeles in an Era*, pp. 78–80.

40. Vasanti Burtle, ed., *Women Who Drink: Experience and Psychotherapy* (Springfield, IL: Charles C Thomas, 1979).

41. Vicente Abad, "Mental Health Delivery Systems for Hispanics in the United States: Issues and Dilemmas," in Moises Gaviria and Jose Arana, eds., *Health and Behavior: Research Agenda for Hispanics* (Chicago: Simon Bolivar Hispanic American Psychiatric Research and Training Program, 1987).

42. See, for example, Wynetta Devore and Elfrieda Schlesinger, *Ethnic-Sensitive Social Work* (St. Louis: Mosby, 1981), and Donna Ferullo, *Cultural Diversity in Social Work Practice* (Boston: Social Work Library at Boston College, 1991).

43. Barbara Solomon, *Black Empowerment* (New York: Columbia University Press, 1976).

44. Jean Potuchek, "The Context of Social Service Funding: The Funding Relationship," *Social Service Review* 60 (September 1986): 421–436.

SUGGESTED READINGS

Developing Typologies

David Ellwood, *Poor Support: Poverty in the American Family* (New York: Basic Books, 1988).

Controversies in Defining and Conceptualizing Social Problems

Mary Jo Bane, "Welfare as We Might Know It," *American Prospect* 30 (January–February 1997): 47–53.

David Ellwood, "Welfare Reform as I Knew It," *American Prospect* 25 (May–June 1996): 22–29.

Claude Fischer et al., *Inequality by Design: Cracking the Bell Curve Myth* (Princeton, NJ: Princeton University Press, 1996).

Stuart Kirk and Herb Hutchins, *The Selling of DSM: The Rhetoric of Science in Psychiatry* (New York: Aldine de Gruyter, 1992).

How Culture and Values Influence Definitions of Social Problems

Joel Best, ed., *Images of Issues* (New York: Aldine de Gruyter, 1989).

Malcolm Spector and John Kitsuse, *Constructing Social Problems* (Menlo Park, CA: Cummings, 1977).

Technical Approaches to Analyzing and Measuring Social Problems

Jonathan Bradshaw, "The Concept of Social Need," in Neil Gilbert and Harry Specht, eds., *Planning for Social Welfare* (Englewood Cliffs, NJ: Prentice Hall, 1977), pp. 290–297.

Christopher Jencks, *The Homeless* (Cambridge: Harvard University Press, 1994).

Irving Piliavin, Michael Sosin, Alex Westerfelt, and Ross Matsueda, "The Duration of Homeless Careers: An Exploratory Study," *Social Service Review* (December 1993): 57–69.

Developing Policy Proposals
in the Second, Third, and Fourth Steps
of Policy Analysis

POLICY PREDICAMENT	Public officials wrestled with important alternatives as they contemplated rebuilding New Orleans in the wake of Hurricane Katrina. We discuss in Policy Advocacy Challenge 8.4 some key options that they considered and which one prevailed during the year following Katrina.

Returning to the Six-Step Policy Analysis Framework

We discuss steps 2, 3, and 4 of the six-step policy analysis framework that we presented in the last chapter. (See Figure 7.1.) Policy advocates compare and contrast policy options as a prelude to developing and drafting policy proposals.

Intersecting Arenas and Stakeholders

Before we discuss policy options, we need to make clear that proposals are fashioned through deliberations and discussions of stakeholders—key persons, groups, and institutions with an interest in a particular policy issue. They include administrators, consumers, advocacy groups, government officials, persons from the private sector (such as business leaders), and persons from so-called NGOs (nongovernmental organizations). Which stakeholders play a role in policy deliberations varies from issue to issue.

For example, deliberations about homelessness take place in many urban, and even rural, jurisdictions. If the term *intersecting arenas* describes links between the federal, state, county, and municipal arenas as well as governmental and nongovernmental

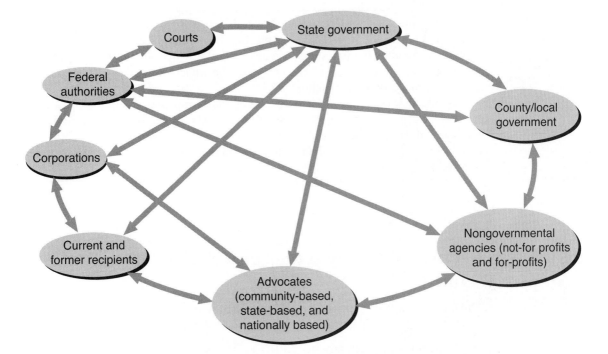

FIGURE 8.1

Intersecting
arenas
and stakeholders

sectors, *stakeholders* are the officials and advocates who operate in specific arenas. (See Figure 8.1.)

Efforts to develop policies regarding homelessness resemble a dance in which the moves of each of these stakeholders are profoundly influenced by the moves of the others. When the president or Congress make specific legislative choices at the national level, state and local officials are profoundly affected. Within specific states, governors and state officials, county officials, corporate leaders, advocacy groups, NGOs, current and former homeless persons, federal authorities, and the courts engage in a kind of dance where each assumes a key role in making choices about states' policies.

Stakeholders have various motivations and perspectives as they consider the merits of specific policies. We have discussed ideology at many points. Some stakeholders bring their ideological preferences to the table, such as when some conservatives insist that homeless persons be subjected to relatively harsh policies such as placing them in jails. Businessmen and women sometimes want streets cleared so that foot traffic that uses their businesses is not deterred. Developers of downtown housing often fear that a significant homeless population will deter persons from purchasing their units. Policy advocates, in turn, are often somewhat more likely to support spending on a variety of medical, social service, housing, childcare, job training, substance-abuse counseling, and mental health services for homeless persons. Courts have issued a number of rulings that set limits on the actions of local police and jails. Local medical providers often want special reimbursements for the costs of treating homeless persons in emergency rooms and outpatient departments.

POLICY
ADVOCACY
CHALLENGE 8.1

Stakeholders
and the Wheel
of Interaction
Bruce Jansson, Ph.D.

We can use the wheel of interaction shown in Figure 8.1 to understand the proposal preferences of specific stakeholders by placing them in the center of the wheel. In the politics surrounding homelessness in your state or local jurisdiction, for example, place community-based advocates in the center of the wheel. What demands or requests might they make of other stakeholders?

Or take the rebuilding of New Orleans as your example by assuming you are part of a planning group in the Ninth Ward. Place your planning group in the center of the wheel and identify key stakeholders with whom you would need to interact. What perspectives might they possess about whether even to rebuild this previously low-income area and how to do this?

Identifying Recurring Policy Issues and Policy Options in Steps 2, 3, and 4

When designing policy proposals, policy advocates must consider a range of issues. They can be placed in nine groups that establish the following:

1. A mission for a proposal
2. How a proposal's services will be structured
3. The resource path of a proposal
4. The content of a proposal's services
5. How a proposal's resources will be rationed
6. How agencies associated with a proposal will be linked
7. How a proposal's services will be linked to communities
8. How the implementation of a proposal will be overseen
9. How a proposal's services will be assessed

As they encounter each of these nine issues, policy advocates must choose among competing alternatives or options.

To illustrate our discussion, we will consider a hypothetical policy advocate in Washington, DC, who wants to develop a federally funded program for victims of spousal abuse.[1] She thinks abused women need the immediate protection that shelters afford and realizes that many women lack the resources to find alternative sources of safe shelter. She works for a shelter in Baltimore and is connected with a coalition of service providers, feminists, victims of spousal abuse, and professionals who want the federal government to take a more active role in addressing this problem. (The group is called the Stop Wife-Battering Coalition.) This policy advocate knows that several local programs have been initiated for this purpose, mostly by underfunded nonprofit agencies that have sought assistance from foundations, private benefactors, and public sources, such as the U.S. Department of Housing and Urban Development. Despite their founders' determined efforts, these centers have proved woefully inadequate to help the rising number of women who seek relief from spousal abuse. The coalition tentatively calls its proposed program the Federal Shelter Program.

Establishing a Mission in Steps 2, 3, and 4

While developing this program, the policy advocate must create some objectives for the Federal Shelter Program. We have noted that policies usually contain explicit or implicit objectives that provide programs with an overarching direction. Often, the preambles of legislation also provide such a rationale.

When discussing the shelters with legislators' aides, she finds no consensus on the federal government's mission in responding to spousal abuse. Some legislators are uninterested in the issue, believing that advocates grossly exaggerate its importance and magnitude; indeed, one aide contends that battering is a "figment of the imagination of do-gooder social workers, who want to create more jobs for themselves." Other legislators favor a "get-tough" strategy that would provide federal funds and policy requirements to local governmental units to find, prosecute, and imprison offenders. However, they object to direct federal assistance to shelters, which they think local jurisdictions should fund. Still other legislators want to provide federal assistance to a national network of shelters for battered women and their children.

While believing that better law enforcement is also needed, our policy advocate and other participants in the Stop Wife-Battering Coalition decide to emphasize federal assistance to shelters. The coalition also wants the shelter program to offer a service to help women cope with their predicament and link them to legal, welfare, job placement, and other services.

Their objectives, then, emphasize federal funding to establish shelters and to serve the women who seek protection there. This mission has important consequences for the policies they will develop; had they adopted a mission that emphasized prosecuting spouse abusers, their proposal would have taken an entirely different form.

Designing the Structure of Service in Steps 2, 3, and 4

Having established a general direction, this policy advocate and her allies encounter some practice questions: Who should ultimately oversee the new program? What kinds of agencies should receive funds for the program?

Fixing Ultimate Responsibility Programs and agencies are typically classified into policy sectors, such as mental health, health, child welfare, public welfare, and gerontology. Assigning a specific program to a sector is often arbitrary and sometimes contentious. For example, the federal Office of Education and the federal Office of Economic Opportunity (OEO) vied for the Head Start program at its inception. In truth, it could have been placed in either sector because it has educational components as well as the parent and community participation that OEO emphasizes.[2] Ultimately, it was placed in OEO because its key founders feared that placing it in the Office of Education would render it a mere educational program that lacked advocacy, parent-participation, and child-development dimensions.

Returning to our example, the policy advocate has to decide who should have ultimate responsibility for the program. If the Federal Shelter Program were assigned to the National Institute of Mental Health, for example, its major focus might become providing counseling services, with less emphasis on providing shelter services. If it were assigned to the Department of Housing and Urban Development, social services might be eliminated. Of course, the policy advocate could try to make it an independent agency that reports directly to the president and is possibly linked to other programs that assist victims of violence.

She not only needs to decide which governmental department should receive ultimate jurisdiction, but must also develop policies about implementation. In doing so, she must ask the following questions: Should state officials (perhaps from a state agency) or federal authorities oversee the program and who should choose which agencies are to receive federal funds? Who should collect statistics about how the shelters use their funds, to keep legislators informed? Who should attend to program problems, such as misuse of funds or failure to comply with local building codes? Who should determine the shelters' eligibility policies within a specific state? Should these policies be contained within the federal legislation, be defined by federal officials after the legislation has been enacted, or be left to the discretion of state officials?

In the 1960s, legislators made federal officials responsible for many funding and operational decisions. Indeed, in many federally funded programs in the War on Poverty, local agencies applied directly to federal authorities for funds, and federal officials inspected and audited local projects. Since then, authority increasingly has been vested in state, regional, or county officials, who ultimately report some details of local programs, such as program statistics, to federal funders. (In the Reagan administration, even this reporting was minimized because he wanted to eliminate federal roles in favor of state and local ones.)

The policy advocate must weigh the advantages of using the various levels of government.[3] If she believes that many local units will be particularly unreceptive to the needs of battered women, she can vest responsibility in the federal government.

However, it is difficult for federal officials to superintend the operational details of thousands of shelters—and the political climate bodes ill for policies that propose augmenting federal power. Alternatively, she can choose a middle course by directing the federal funds to state authorities, but requiring them to follow specific standards and report specific information to federal authorities.

Kinds of Agencies Receiving Funds   The policy advocate has to decide which kinds of agencies can receive federal funds. Should not-for-profit, public, or profit-oriented agencies, or some combination of these receive funds?[4] Not-for-profit agencies have boards of directors, but their members are not allowed to have a financial stake in the agency, nor do the boards have shareholders or other investors who receive dividends. (Agency surpluses must be reinvested in the agency, whose staff receive fixed salaries.) Not-for-profit agencies are exempt from state and federal taxes, and contributors can usually deduct donations from their income, provided the agencies have a tax-exempt status with the Internal Revenue Service and with the state authorities that oversee nonprofit agencies. Profit-oriented agencies are owned by private investors, whether owners or stockholders, who expect a financial return on their investment. (Owners may assume a major role in overseeing their agencies or may cede management to outside managers who work under their general direction.) Public agencies are usually funded exclusively by public authorities and clients' payments. In actual practice, though, complex hybrids exist. Virtually all not-for-profit agencies and some profit-oriented agencies receive contracts from public authorities; indeed, most not-for-profits receive more than 60 percent of their revenues from public contracts and grants. Some nonprofits even have profit-oriented subsidiaries.

The policy advocate has to compare these kinds of agencies when deciding whether to give them funds. Because public agencies lack a profit motive, they have no economic incentive to deceive or shortchange clients. Many critics have assailed public agencies, however, because they are often bedeviled by red tape, and by civil service and unionized employees who cannot be easily removed if they are ineffective. Although ultimately accountable to elected officials, many public agencies do not make extensive use of community resources, such as volunteers and support groups. Because public agencies often have emphasized services to poor persons, they often are shunned by working- and middle-class citizens, who also may believe them to be excessively bureaucratic.[5]

Not-for-profit agencies are perceived as more innovative than public agencies because fewer regulations constrain their programs.[6] As they tend to be smaller than public agencies and have boards composed of residents, some of them are probably more responsive to the needs of specific communities. Some critics nonetheless question whether not-for-profit agencies are actually more innovative than public agencies and note that their boards are often dominated by community elites, with scant participation by ordinary citizens.[7] Some of them engage so aggressively in marketing and fundraising that they are indistinguishable from profit-oriented agencies, which also have their defenders and detractors. Many persons advocate privatizing the human services by giving profit-oriented organizations an expanded role in delivering services. They contend that private markets enhance the efficiency of human services and the gearing of services to clients' needs. Wanting to instill market efficiency into the human services, they content that public agencies that are inefficient or unresponsive to consumers should be supplanted by for-profit or not-for-profit agencies.[8] Many critics vigorously challenge this positive portrayal of for-profit agencies. They point out that profit-oriented nursing homes and day-care centers sometimes attract clients with deceptive advertising, cut the quality of their services to increase their profits, and refrain from serving persons who cannot pay their fees.[9]

Planning the Extent of Devolution and the Resource Path in Steps 2, 3, and 4

The policy advocate realizes that fiscal resources are the lifeblood of the human services system and that shelters desperately need funds to survive. She must choose a funding source for social programs, determine how much money to give specific programs, and select a funding channel—and she must make these choices in the context of existing policy realities.

Extent of Devolution Intense controversy exists about the respective roles of federal and state governments. Indeed, a movement to devolve federal programs and policies to state and local levels has taken place during the last three decades. After establishing federal social insurance and welfare programs during the Great Depression, the United States vastly enlarged a federally directed welfare state in the following four decades; federal domestic spending rose from a paltry 2 percent of the gross national product (GNP) in 1930 (before the depression) to 17 percent by 1979.[10] This growth in the federal government was a result of widespread cynicism about the ability of state and local governments to address social problems. Even as liberals took the lead in developing this welfare state, conservatives chafed at the rise in federal power and launched three successive assaults on it. Richard Nixon, Ronald Reagan, and Newt Gingrich attempted

TABLE 8.1
Orienting framework criteria for placing social policies on the federal-to-state continuum

Criteria	Sole federal	Devolved with federal tilt	Devolved with state/local tilt	Sole state or local
Extent to which federal tax code is used	X			
Extent to which program addresses survival needs	X	X		
Likelihood that states will discriminate	X	X		
Extent to which problem requires large resources	X	X	X	
Extent to which economic competition between states inhibits socially responsive policies	X	X	X	
Extent to which problem is linked to global competitiveness	X	X	X	
Extent to which local inputs and partnerships are needed		X	X	X
Service-intensive programs		X	X	X

in the early 1970s, the 1980s, and the mid-1990s, respectively, to cut federal spending and to devolve federal programs to state and local governments using so-called block grants. (Unlike categorical programs such as Head Start, which the federal government funds, defines, and regulates, block grants distribute funds to states or localities with relatively few restrictions.) Reagan succeeded in establishing nine block grants in 1981 that redirected the funds for 77 categorical programs into block grants, and Gingrich and his allies, with some cooperation from Bill Clinton, ended AFDC as a federal program and entitlement and converted it to a block grant.

While conservatives have often framed relationships between federal and non-federal governments in either-or terms, many permutations are not only possible but desirable, as can be seen in Table 8.1. Where programs should be placed on a continuum extending from sole federal to sole state or local depends, I contend, on how the programs rank on eight criteria.[11] (Of course, many people might disagree with my recommendations, such as some conservatives who would like to turn virtually all social programs over to the state and local governments.)

National authorities should fund programs that meet survival needs, such as SSI, the food stamp program, social insurances, and the now-devolved AFDC program. Not only do these programs require huge resources, but they are unlikely to be funded sufficiently by state and local governments for several reasons. The nationwide total of state and local tax revenues is only half the total of federal tax revenues; thus, state and local governments lack the resources for large programs, particularly as they also must fund schools, highways, prisons, and the local share of such federal programs as Medicaid. Moreover, many policy experts fear a "race to the bottom" as states compete to cut their safety net programs.[12] Fearing that low-income persons will immigrate if they offer safety net programs that are more munificent than those of other states, some states offer miserly benefits. Many states restrict their tax revenues, moreover, by keeping their tax rates lower to entice corporations that like low-tax states, and these constrictions of their tax revenues diminish their resources for social programs.

Many other programs can be devolved with a federal tilt so the federal government provides some funds and considerable oversight and regulations, or they can be devolved with a state/local tilt so the government provides fewer resources, less oversight, and fewer regulations. Many social service programs that require local input and partnerships and that need to be tailored to local needs fit into these two models. But many of these programs should not be completely devolved because they will be poorly funded. Moreover, the nation has a stake in many state and local services, such as job training, that keep American citizens competitive in job markets as the economy globalizes.

Some programs should continue to be funded and administered by local and state governments, such as large components of secondary education and correctional institutions. States and localities can and should fund many social programs that fill the gaps in federal and state programs.

Sources of Funds for Social Programs

Sources of Funds for Social Programs   Policy advocates must choose from a variety of funding options.[13] The extensive general revenues of local, county, state, and federal governments fund many programs. Since the 1930s, the federal government has emerged as the major funder of social welfare programs, because it raises roughly two times the combined tax revenues of state and local governments, which include state income taxes, state (or local) property taxes, and state (or local) sales, excise, and license taxes. General revenues provide a useful source of funds for social programs because they are generally unrestricted. However, fierce competition exists over general revenues, as many groups, thousands of existing social programs, and the Department of Defense all seek them. When taxes are periodically cut, access to general revenues becomes even more difficult.

Payroll taxes fund Social Security and Medicare programs. These taxes take a certain percentage of employees' or employers' payrolls, or both. While payroll taxes are a predictable and stable source of revenues, it is virtually impossible to develop new payroll taxes because Social Security and Medicare already preempt a considerable share of people's income.

Clients' payments for services fund a significant share of the nation's social programs that are run by agencies or private practitioners. Requiring payment discourages clients from the unnecessary use of social and medical services. In the case of sliding fees, relatively affluent persons shoulder a substantial part of programs' operating costs. However, charging fees often deter poor persons from seeking needed services.

Special taxes, such as on marriage licenses, auto licenses, and alcoholic beverages, are often earmarked for specific programs, as when states use taxes on marriage licenses to fund shelters for battered women. Like payroll taxes, special taxes provide a stable source of revenues for specific programs, but political interests, such as liquor companies, often oppose them, fearing the taxes will raise the cost of their products and erode their markets.

Private philanthropy, including federated community fund-raising drives (such as United Way and appeals for Jewish and Catholic agencies), corporations, foundations, and individual donors, remains a major funding source for social programs, even though it has been eclipsed by governmental funding since the late 1950s.[14] Private philanthropy provides funds that are often less restricted than government funds because they are not usually earmarked for specific programs. As with general government revenues, however, agencies and programs compete fiercely for scarce philanthropic funds, particularly since the cuts in government funding in the 1980s and 1990s. The bulk of private philanthropic dollars is, moreover, given to educational, medical, and cultural groups rather than to agencies serving persons with stigmatized conditions or from low-income groups.

Determining Levels of Funds   Euphoric after the enactment of legislation, policy advocates often discover that the programs they have championed have received inadequate funding. The funding of public programs usually follows a two-step procedure.[15] First, legislatures authorize funds by stipulating how much money (an upper limit) a specific program can receive in a given year. Second, the legislature appropriates—that is, actually commits—a specific amount of money to the program for a specific year. As illustrated by Medicare, Medicaid, and Social Security, legislatures provide open-ended funding for some programs, in which they agree to fund whatever costs those programs incur in a specific year. However, most programs must battle for their funds in the appropriations process, often receiving far less money than was authorized for them, because of competing demands for the available funds.

We should realize that choices about the funding of social policies occur in a broader context, whether at county, state, or federal levels. Using the federal level as an example, assume that you wanted federal resources for a so-called discretionary program. (The funding of discretionary programs is determined annually in the push-and-pull of the budget process, unlike interest on the federal debt and entitlements—or mandatory spending—like Medicare, Medicaid, Food Stamps, SSI, the Earned Income Tax Credit, and Social Security, which are automatically funded to the level of claimed benefits in a given year.) When mandatory spending is subtracted from budget totals, about 36 percent of federal budget revenues remain. In turn, more than one-half of these revenues are absorbed by military spending, meaning that about 13 percent of the entire federal budget is available for domestic discretionary spending. Many claimants that are not social programs vie for these discretionary dollars, including transportation, the National Park Service, environmental clean-up, road and bridge construction, public works programs, and foreign policy. About 5 percent of the total federal budget exists for discretionary social programs of the Department of Health and Human Services, so advocates of increased funding for specific programs must realize that they play in a crowded field—and they must use considerable pressure and lobbying to convince legislators to increase funding for the program they favor. Even in agency settings, policy advocates who want greater resources for a specific program must understand the agency's budget so they can make a good case for shifting resources from existing programs to one that they favor—assuming they cannot find new resources, such as by writing a grant proposal.

Some legislative committees are authorizing committees that, essentially, decide the maximum amount of resources that can be expended on a particular program in a given year. (An example is the House Committee on Economic and Educational Opportunities that authorizes resources for the Social Services Block Grant.) Appropriations committees decide how much money will actually be given to a specific program in a given year. So advocates need to get both sufficient authorizations and sufficient appropriations for specific programs.

Funding Channels   Once funds exist for a social program and some combination of public, nonprofit, and profit-oriented agencies has been chosen to receive the money, funding channels need to be devised to distribute these resources. We can visualize

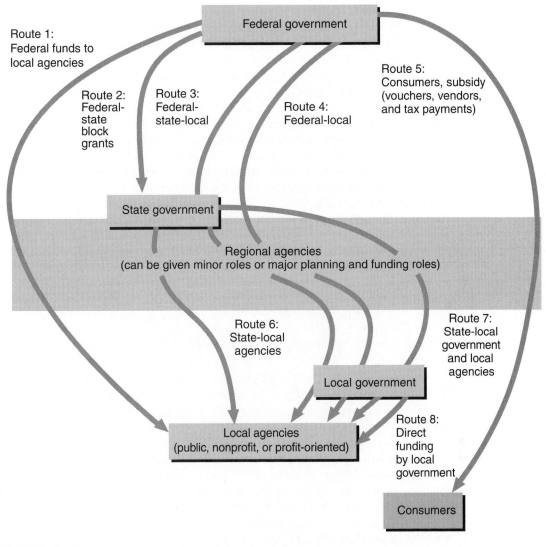

Route 1:
Federal funds to
local agencies

Federal government

Route 2:
Federal-
state
block
grants

Route 3:
Federal-
state-local

Route 4:
Federal-local

Route 5:
Consumers, subsidy
(vouchers, vendors,
and tax payments)

State government

Regional agencies
(can be given minor roles or major planning and funding roles)

Route 6:
State-local
agencies

Route 7:
State-local
government
and local
agencies

Local government

Local agencies
(public, nonprofit, or profit-oriented)

Route 8:
Direct
funding
by local
government

Consumers

FIGURE 8.2
Possible funding
channels

the funds as flowing through channels, or routes, from various levels of government to agencies or consumers. (See Figure 8.2.)

Federal funders often provide money directly to agencies, as shown in Route 1. Funding may take the form of *project grants,* in which the federal government gives funds to a shelter to provide services to battered women. If project grants usually give agencies considerable latitude, government *contracts* specify the precise services the government wishes to provide, such as "5,000 days of residential services, for battered women in Fargo, North Dakota."[16]

Alternatively, some persons argue that federal funders should provide resources directly to consumers (Route 5). For example, some persons favor the use of *vouchers,* that is, funds consumers can use to purchase specific services, such as day care. Government may place limits on the kinds of commodities that can be purchased and may require providers to meet certain licensing standards. Government funds may also take the form of *vendor payments* that reimburse providers for their services to specific clients.[17] For example, the Medicaid program directly reimburses hospitals and physicians for the medical services they provide to low-income patients.

In the federal-to-state channel (Route 2), the federal government distributes funds to the states, which then distribute the funds to specific agencies. Advocates of state government support this policy because it gives the states an enhanced role in the human services system. Indeed, advocates of block grants, which are relatively unrestricted funds that the federal government gives states or local units of government, argue that they give recipients the flexibility to use the funds as they wish and to adapt their programs to local need. Opponents of block grants contend that they provide local jurisdictions with carte blanche use of federal funds for trivial or misdirected programs, and might allow them to underserve specific groups.[18] These opponents favor the federal funding of specific programs that requires the recipient to use the money for specific purposes and to adhere to numerous federal regulations. These programs, such as the Head Start program, are often called *categorical programs.* In the Reagan administration, a number of large block-grant programs were established, including ones for maternal and child health and for social services. While the federal government placed some restrictions on how the states could use these funds, there were fewer constraints than in the 57 categorical programs that these two replaced. (As we discussed in the last chapter, welfare reform legislation in 1996 replaced the categorical AFDC program with a federal block grant.)

Alternatively, the federal government can fund local governments directly (Route 4), a tactic favored by some mayors and county supervisors who chafe at the extraordinary power of the federal government. In this case, local governments would use federal funds to fund shelters for battered women within their jurisdictions.

Similarly, the states use many channels when they distribute their funds to local programs. They may distribute the funds directly to agencies (Route 6) or they may use local governments to distribute funds to agencies (Route 7).

Each funding channel has its critics and defenders. Those who favor the use of vouchers contend, for example, that it promotes healthy competition among agencies for clientele and decreases the need for government bureaucracy. Critics, however, point to many defects in market schemes. Although armed with vouchers, many low-income consumers cannot find quality providers because relatively few of them have agencies or practices in low-income areas.[19]

Indirect Financing   We have focused on how federal and state governments finance social welfare programs directly. Social welfare services can also be financed indirectly through the tax system, as when clients are given *tax deductions* that allow them to deduct specific health, housing, or social welfare expenditures from their pretax income. In the case of interest payments on their mortgages, for example, millions of Americans receive tax deductions for their housing. *Tax credits* are direct cash rebates from the U.S. Department of the Treasury to taxpayers who meet specific eligibility standards after they have filed their taxes, such as cash received by low-income families through the EITC. Some taxpayers receive tax credits by subtracting payments for specific programs from their federal taxes; for example, many working women fund part of their day-care expenditures by subtracting a child-care credit from the taxes they would otherwise pay. *Tax exemptions* allow taxpayers not to pay taxes on part of their income. For instance, people can subtract from their taxable income an exemption for each dependent, which lowers their taxable income.

By these indirect methods of financing social welfare, then, citizens receive money not by direct government appropriations, but through tax concessions.[20] The advantage of using the tax system to finance social welfare is that it does not require appropriations and thus avoids political uncertainties. However, tax concessions often benefit wealthy persons and corporations disproportionately. (See Policy Advocacy Challenge 8.2.) For instance, the tax deductions for mortgage interest payments on expensive homes vastly exceed the deductions for modest homes, and tenants generally receive no assistance from the tax codes. Although the government gives persons with tax-subsidized benefits a free hand in choosing their services, it does not usually regulate or monitor them. For example, persons who receive day-care credits may use services that do not meet basic standards.

POLICY ADVOCACY CHALLENGE 8.2

The Upside-Down Welfare State[1]

MIMI ABRAMOVITZ, DSW, PROFESSOR, SCHOOL OF SOCIAL WORK, HUNTER COLLEGE SCHOOL OF SOCIAL WORK, DIRECTOR OF SOCIAL WELFARE PROGRAM, THE GRADUATE CENTER, CITY UNIVERSITY OF NEW YORK

It is commonly accepted that government tax and spending policies create more equality because they cushion the blows of the market economy for the poor. But a broader look at spending levels, benefit amounts, and vulnerability to budget cuts reveal, by and large, government programs favor the haves over the have-nots. Contrary to popular wisdom, as it is currently configured, social policy reinforces inequality.

Social Welfare Spending for the Middle Class.   In 2000, the federal government spent more than $1 trillion on social welfare programs or 61 percent of all federal spending including Welfare, food stamps, Supplemental Security Income (SSI), the Earned Income Tax Credit, Social Security, Medicare, among numerous other programs. Paradoxically, the majority of these dollars ended in the pockets of the well-to-do. While $235.9 billion dollars went to means-tested public assistance program for the poor, we spent a much larger $793.9 billion for programs that do not use poverty or need as a criterion for receiving aid. Programs for the have-nots absorbed 23 percent of all entitlement spending compared to 77 percent for the more affluent.[2] While the latter comprise more of the U.S. population, they profit from less restrictive and more generous programs and from the belief that they are more worthy of aid.

Tax Expenditures for the Affluent.   When tax expenditures are factored into the equality calculation, it turns out that the government spends even more on the more well-to-do. Tax expenditures—revenue losses stemming from provisions of federal tax laws that reduce income taxes that people pay[3]—represent taxes the government chooses not to collect. Few people think of the tax code as a social welfare system, yet these dollars address the same common human needs as social welfare spending including family support, retirement, health care, housing, child care, and education but are targeted to the needs of the middle and upper class.

[1] Title adapted from Huff, D. (1992, Winter). Upside-Down Welfare, *Public Welfare*, pp. 36–40. See also Abramovitz, M. (2001, October). Everyone Is Still on Welfare: The Role of Redistribution in Social Policy. *Social Work* 46 (4): 297–308.
[2] Congressional Budget Office (2001, January). *The Economic and Budget Outlook: Fiscal Years 2002–2011.* Washington, DC: U.S. Government Printing Office.
[3] U.S. Joint Committee on Taxation (2001, April 6). *Estimates of Federal Tax Expenditures for the Fiscal Years 2001–2005.* Washington, DC: U.S. Government Printing Office, pp. 2–3.

(continued)

Between 1965 and the late 1990s, the number of tax expenditures grew from 50 to 166. The cost to government in lost revenues rose from $36.6 billion in 1967 to an estimated $587 billion in 2000—$292 billion more than the $295 billion allocated to the military that year. Projections indicate that from 1996 through 2002, taxes not collected will amount to $3.7 trillion—more than enough to have paid off the $3.4 trillion national debt in 2000.[4] This tax spending on the gilded welfare state for the upper class often exceeds similar programs for the poor. The U.S. Joint Committee on Taxation[5] projected that in 1998 the federal government would spend some $72.2 billion on housing subsidies for the rich (mortgage interest tax deductions, property taxes, and capital gains on home). This contrasts sharply with the $24 billion spent by the Department of Housing and Urban Development on low-income housing and rental subsidies for the poor. On a larger scale, the $587 billion tax expenditure bill for 2000 was $352 billion more than the $235 allocated to means-tested programs for poor people; $118 billion more than the $406 billion for Social Security; and just $378 billion less than the total $966 billion spent on entitlement benefits.[6]

The benefit levels of both the social welfare and tax benefit systems also favor the affluent over the poor. Tied to the cost of living, social insurance programs serving the middle class pay significantly higher benefits than the public assistance programs for poor people that lack this built-in protection against erosion from inflation.[7] Tax benefits are even more class-biased. The 1999 tax cut amounted to nearly $32,000 more a year for the wealthiest 1 percent of the U.S. households while the bottom 60 percent suffered a $166 cut.[8] The 2001 Bush administration's $1.3 trillion, 10-year tax cut continued this uneven pattern.[9]

The differential vulnerability to budget cuts furthers the systemic inequalities resulting from government policies. The nation's leaders readily cut spending for the needy—who lack political clout and who are deemed unworthy of government aid—while protecting programs used by the better-off middle class. In the mid-1990s, low-income programs received 23 percent of all mandatory funds but suffered 93 percent of the cuts. Low-income programs received 21 percent of discretionary spending but absorbed 43 percent of the cuts.[10] Tax expenditures are particularly *in*vulnerable to the budget ax. Less visible to the wider public than direct social spending and less subject to the perils of the budget process, they win Congressional approval more easily and remain on the books longer than direct spending programs.

[4] Congressional Budget Office (2001, January). *The Economic and Budget Outlook: Fiscal Years 2002–2011.* Washington, DC: U.S. Government Printing Office.
[5] U.S. Joint Committee on Taxation (1998, December 14). *Estimates of Federal Tax Expenditures for the Fiscal Years 1999–2003.* Washington, DC: U.S. Government Printing Office, Table 1, pp. 17–18.
[6] Congressional Budget Office (2001, January). *The Economic and Budget Outlook: Fiscal Years 2002–2011.* Washington, DC: U.S. Government Printing Office.
[7] House Committee on Houseways and Means (2000). *Overview of Entitlement Programs* (2000 Green Book). Washington, DC: Government Printing Office.
[8] Lav, I. J. and Greenstein, R. (1999, August 29). *Tax Bill Contains Only Modest Benefits for Middle Class Despite Its High Cost.* Washington, DC: Center on Budget and Policy Priorities, p. 1.
[9] Shapiro, L. and Sly, J. (2001). *Bush Tax Cut and House Rate Cuts Widen Record after Tax Income Disparities.* Washington, DC: Center on Budget and Policy Priorities.
[10] Greenstein, R., Kogan, R., and Nichols, M. (1996). *Bearing Most of the Burden: How Deficit Reduction During the 104th Congress Concentrated on Programs for the Poor.* Washington, DC: Center on Budget and Policy Priorities.

Corporate Welfare.   Government aid to business and industry intensifies the upward bias of social policy. As reported by the conservative Cato Institute, every major government department is a repository for government funding of private industry.[11] The editors of *TIME Magazine* estimated that the government dispenses about $125 billion a year to companies to help them advertise their products, build new facilities, train their workers, and write off the cost of perks.[12] Corporate welfare also includes direct government grants, tax reductions, support for research and development, and discounted user fees for public resources, among others. But the vast bulk of government largesse to big business appears in special tax abatements, which in fiscal 2000 cost the government approximately $195 billion—far, far larger than direct-spending business subsidies.[13]

In sum, everyone is on welfare, but the class biases of both the highly visible social welfare system and the hidden welfare state embedded in the tax code ensure that government tax and spending policies do not benefit everyone equally. To make government a better deal for ordinary Americans in the United States—whose gap between the rich and the poor exceeds that of any other industrialized nation—social workers can help expose the gilded welfare state as undemocratic and unfair and call for a system based on real distributive justice for all.

---

[11] Hershey, R. D., Jr. (1995, March 7). A Hard Look at Corporate Welfare. *New York Times,* p. D1.
[12] Bartlett, D. L. and Steel, J. B. (1998, November 8). Corporate Welfare, *Time Magazine,* p. 38.
[13] Statement of Robert S. McIntyre, Director, Citizens for Tax Justice. Before the House Committee on the Budget Regarding Unnecessary Business Subsidies, June 30, 1999.

Some Funding Choices   The policy practitioner has to state in her legislative proposal how much funding she is requesting, to what extent the states should match federal funds, whether the states should receive funds with relatively few restrictions, and whether in some states taxes on marriage licenses should be used to fund shelters.

When examining funding channels, she has to review her attitudes toward the various levels of government. If she decides to emphasize the states' role in superintending the program, she will propose that federal authorities direct funds to states, which will then fund the shelters. If, by contrast, she wants to emphasize the role of the federal government, she will have federal authorities directly fund local agencies, or she will develop a categorical program providing funds to states, which follow specific guidelines in using the funds.

She decides to ask for an authorization level of $450 million in the first year, with authorizations to rise to $600 million within three years. Although she wants more funds than this for the program, she realizes that conservatives, as well as some moderates and liberals, will object to a larger program during a period of federal budgetary deficits. She selects Route 2 from the funding channels; that is, the federal government is to give funds to the states, which then fund local shelters. She would have preferred direct federal funding of shelters, but decides that this alternative is not politically feasible.

Defining Services in Steps 2, 3, and 4

As she develops an initial outline of the Federal Shelter Program, the policy practitioner must provide direction for the shelters' services, decide what mix of preventive and curative services to offer, and determine how to ration scarce resources.

Establishing an Orienting Framework   We can return now to our discussion of conceptual frameworks in Chapter Seven, where we contrasted public health, intrapsychic, deterrent, and other paradigms frequently used in social policy. The policy practitioner has to articulate an orienting framework on which to base her services.

The policy advocate realizes that women who have been subjected to abusive behavior often have multiple problems, such as legal, psychological, familial, medical, and economic issues. Many of them contend with divorce and police protection, suffer from anxiety and depression, have children traumatized by family violence and disruption, have serious physical injuries from the violence, and face a loss of income after separating from their spouses. These considerations prompt the policy practitioner to favor multifaceted services integrated with residential services. As she struggles to define the services, she decides she wants some combination of advocacy, crisis intervention, and referral services, integrated by a case management system.

She is certain, however, that some shelters will not provide any social services, because they will lack the funds or will be preoccupied with the residential services. Therefore, she decides to specify in the legislation the services that shelters receiving federal subsidies will need, including crisis intervention, referral services, and case management services, to attend to battered women's multiple needs. She does not want the shelters to become mere places of residence for battered women; indeed, she wants to link the shelters to their surrounding community and local feminist organizations. Moreover, she wants them to be advocates, not only for individuals, but also for battered women in general. She wants the shelters to support policies that increase the prosecution of spousal abusers and that include battered women in the existing state programs that provide financial reimbursement to the victims of violent crimes. Besides case management and other services, she decides to require advocacy for battered women, the use of volunteers, and battered women's participation on the shelters' governing or advisory boards (to be discussed later). Even with these stipulations, she realizes that many shelters will seem to offer only a residence, not a multiservice center, because it is far simpler to define facilities' formal attributes than it is to shape their informal qualities, such as sensitivity, advocacy, or responsiveness to community needs.

Staff and Licensing   The policy advocate realizes that implementing these plans requires competent staff. She also knows, however, that considerable competition may develop among social service professionals if she favors certain kinds of professionals, such as social workers, in her legislation.

Before we can understand her predicament, we need to discuss how professions, including social work, develop their power and credibility.[21] Professions develop out of both altruism and self-interest. Members of specific professions want to protect consumers from incompetent persons (altruism), but they also want to reserve certain jobs and private practices for persons who meet certain requirements (self-interest). Both altruism and self-interest encourage monopolies from which professionals exclude outsiders who have not received specific training.

Professions must establish minimal education and training requirements, both to be certain that their members have certain competencies and to distinguish their members from the general public and from other professionals. (If no minimum requirements existed, anyone could use the title of the profession and pose as a member of it. This would undermine the profession's credibility because consumers and employers would be likely to believe the title meant nothing.) To protect their members, then, professions specify minimal training and education and develop methods for monitoring them. In the case of social work, graduate schools, whose graduates receive an MSW degree, cannot be accredited by the Council on Social Work Education (CSWE) unless they follow minimal classroom and fieldwork requirements.[22] Similarly, persons who claim they have the B.S.W. degree must have completed specified undergraduate education and fieldwork requirements that CSWE specifies. Programs not accredited by CSWE can graduate students, but they would have difficulty recruiting faculty, and their graduates might have trouble finding jobs.

However, professional organizations are rarely content, again for reasons of altruism and self-interest, to rely exclusively on accreditation to enhance their status. They also want government to use its licensing powers to reserve certain titles, tasks, and positions for their members.[23] Licensing of titles means that by state law, people can use titles such as licensed clinical social worker, physician, or attorney at law only when they have met certain training requirements, including graduating from an accredited program and engaging in postgraduate training. For example, in some states, the requirements for the title licensed clinical social worker (LCSW) include working for a specified number of hours under a licensed clinical social worker's supervision.

Licensing of tasks or functions requires people to complete certain training before performing specified tasks, such as surgery or prescribing drugs. This kind of licensing represents an even more potent form of protection for a profession because—unlike the licensing of titles, which merely regulates the terms that persons use to describe themselves—it limits certain tasks to members of a profession.[24] Imagine the power that licensed clinical social workers would suddenly gain if all counseling were limited to them, just as surgery is limited to physicians!

Professions often try to keep certain positions in government agencies to themselves by having them *classified*. When government authorities require certain credentials for a civil service position, such as a master's degree in social work, they prevent members of other professions from competing for that position. It is small wonder that professional social workers have been perturbed by declassification, which removes the requirement that one must have a master's degree, or even a bachelor's degree, in social work for many positions in child welfare agencies, welfare programs, and other programs. Licensing and classification are often controversial because rival professions vie to reserve certain positions for themselves or to prevent other professions from monopolizing them.[25]

Our policy advocate must decide whether to require the shelters that receive federal funds to hire certain kinds of professionals. The legislation could stipulate, for example, that each shelter's director of social services must have an MSW degree and that only members of specific professions with a supervised practicum in clinical work can provide certain counseling and case management services. Such requirements may enhance the quality of the shelters' social services and make their services billable to insurance. But the policy practitioner realizes that such staffing requirements have some disadvantages. They will substantially increase the cost of maintaining the shelters, because the shelters will have to pay the higher salaries that professionals command. Professionals excluded from directing the shelters, such as marriage and family counselors and psychologists, may oppose the legislation.

Some people may even argue that professionalizing the shelters will detract from their use of volunteer and community support; many feminists seek to increase the contributions of nonpaid women to programs that help women. The policy advocate decides to require that the shelter directors have an MSW degree and that the direct-service staff have had a supervised practicum, but not to specify their professional affiliation.

Preventive versus Curative Services When contemplating whether to incorporate a major preventive component, the policy advocate confronts difficult dilemmas (see Chapter Six). The number of women on waiting lists for shelters makes it difficult to justify spending large sums on prevention, and it is difficult to know how to prevent abusive behavior in light of the complexity of the problem and the absence of definitive research. Abusive behaviors probably stem from some combination of exposure to abuse as a child, marital discord, substance abuse, cultural factors, sexism, situational stressors such as unemployment and poverty, ownership of a gun, a national culture that promotes violence, and possibly a genetic predisposition toward violence. While large-scale national reforms could address some of these causes, the policy practitioner cannot easily address them in her legislative proposal. If *primary prevention*, which is directed to persons not yet having a social problem, is difficult to accomplish, she nonetheless wonders whether her legislation could engage in *secondary prevention*, which aims at averting the further progression of problems that are in their early stages. As members of her coalition brainstorm the issue, they decide that properly advertised local hot lines would encourage women to seek early assistance. Thus, the policy advocate includes in her proposal a section qualifying shelters to apply for funds to set up a hot line.

Rationing Scarce Resources in Steps 2, 3, and 4

There are always many people who need assistance, so every social agency and social program must engage in some form of rationing.[26] Our policy practitioner must grapple with this issue as she plans the legislation, because the resources that Congress might authorize will not be sufficient to address the large demand for services by battered women, who have formed long waiting lists for the existing shelters. Moreover, if the Federal Shelter Program is enacted and advertised, it is likely that many women who do not currently use services will seek them.

Formal or Direct Methods of Rationing One of the most common methods of restricting access is giving free services only to those who fall beneath a minimum level, such as the official poverty line. This method is called *means testing*. Using income measures poses some problems, however.[27] Means testing requires shelter staff to check applicants' financial records, a time-consuming task. Many abused women are, moreover, in a chaotic financial situation in the wake of leaving their spouses or partners, losing access to joint banking accounts, and lacking independent sources of income. Can shelter staff accurately identify actual available income, as opposed to total family income, in these circumstances? Income-based eligibility, however, has some advantages. It allows social agencies to focus scarce resources on those who are least able to purchase services.

In addition to, or instead of, basing eligibility on income, the policy advocate can use diagnostic criteria, such as the level of danger, the frequency or severity of the abuse, or the extent of the applicants' personal trauma. Like mental health institutions, which often limit access or at least involuntary commitment to persons who are a danger to themselves or others, the policy practitioner can limit use of the shelters to women who have actually been abused rather than those who have only received verbal threats. Diagnostic criteria have the advantage of limiting the programs to the persons who appear to have the most serious problems. This is an important consideration when dealing with battered women, whose lives are sometimes in danger. However, these criteria place applicants at the mercy of intake staff, who may misread the seriousness of a woman's problem or who may allow their own preferences to shape their judgments.[28] Indeed, intake staff may be more sympathetic to certain persons, such as members of their own racial or ethnic group or women with certain kinds of problems. When analyzing her options, the policy advocate might choose to use a number of eligibility criteria. She could, for example, limit free service to persons earning less than a certain amount and require shelter staff to give priority to women in danger of serious injury.

The policy advocate cannot resolve rationing issues without considering certain values and her original mission. If she wants a national network of federally subsidized shelters that will serve most battered women, she may establish eligibility policies that are relatively nonexclusionary. She could even aim to make the shelters an entitlement, much like Medicare or Social Security, which will receive automatic funding for whatever services they provide to abused women during a given year. This option would have bleak political prospects, however, because of its high cost.

We should note that buck passing is common with respect to eligibility. In order not to make difficult and sometimes controversial choices, federal legislators, for example, may yield eligibility decisions to states or agencies, as in some block-granted programs. Such ceding of decisions on eligibility standards has some merit because standards of living and demand for services vary in different parts of the nation. Critics contend, however, that more conservative and poorer states restrict eligibility excessively when given this power.

Indirect Methods of Restricting Access

Social agencies and programs devise policies that indirectly influence clients' access. One method of rationing is to place upper limits on the intensity or duration of services. To allow more persons to receive assistance, a program administrator may decide, for example, to limit residence in a shelter to a certain number of months. When placing limits on services, policy practitioners must balance effectiveness with equity. If the intensity, duration, or number of services or benefits is markedly reduced, more consumers will receive program benefits (equity is increased), but the services may be distributed so thinly that they are ineffective or inadequate. Policy practitioners must make difficult choices when considering the relative intensity or number of program benefits.

Another common method of rationing resources in social agencies and programs is to adopt a first-come, first-served policy, in which consumers receive services in the order of their application. This approach appears at first glance to be equitable because no favoritism is possible. However, this policy has its own liabilities. People with serious problems may need preferential access, and certain kinds of clients may drop off waiting lists.

Some critics argue that social agencies should reserve resources for underserved populations, much as affirmative action has reserved employment slots for women and racial minorities. According to this argument, social agencies should also develop outreach to these populations and examine service utilization patterns in order to reach consumers who leave the service prematurely.

Some social agencies ration services by discouraging specific populations from using them. Overt discrimination is probably less serious than subtler forms.[29] Low-income populations that want tangible assistance with economic and social problems will probably not use some service approaches, such as extended talking therapies. Similarly, a lack of bilingual and ethnic minority staff will deter ethnic minorities from using services. Agency personnel may not fully realize that their forms of service or their staffing patterns powerfully influence who does or does not use the program.

Agencies ration services indirectly in many other ways, including the location of facilities, the use of specific program titles, and the selective use of outreach. Facilities located in low-income areas promote use by poor persons, just as facilities in many suburban areas favor affluent populations. The importance of titles becomes obvious when one examines the difference between "free clinic" and "women's free clinic": the latter clearly would encourage female users and discourage male users. Patterns of outreach and advertising also influence access; if an agency advertises its program to relatively affluent populations, for example, it biases access toward these persons and away from other populations.

Charging fees is another way to restrict access. As fees increase, low-income consumers are less likely to seek services and more likely to terminate as soon as possible. Some policies, such as restricting services to regular hours, impose a hidden but substantial burden on working persons and poor persons, who must, in effect, pay a fee by taking time from their employment.

Our policy advocate reluctantly decides that she has to ration the services financed by the Federal Shelter Program because of the enormity of the unmet needs. She decides to restrict access to three months of residence in the shelters unless a woman remains in imminent danger of physical abuse. She also decides to require the shelters to disseminate information about their services to a broad range of community groups, and she establishes a sliding-fee schedule that can be waived when family finances are disrupted by dislocation.

Addressing Agency Network Issues in Steps 2, 3, and 4

It was customary in the 1950s to conceptualize a social agency as an autonomous entity providing services more or less in isolation from other agencies. But in the succeeding decades, many policy theorists came to realize that agencies had to develop links with one another if they were to provide quality services. Child welfare agencies maintain hundreds of thousands of children in foster care, while serving the natural families of many of these children and the dysfunctional families whose children have not been removed.

No matter how dedicated its staff, the child welfare agency cannot provide quality services unless it links these children and families to schools, mental health agencies, job-training agencies, job search agencies, substance-abuse clinics, adult education agencies, health providers, Social Security offices, and government welfare agencies. Indeed, linkage must occur on several levels simultaneously. At a case management level, child welfare staff need to develop individualized plans for children and families that identify an array of services, make referrals, and monitor referrals to be certain that children and families actually receive them. If a child welfare agency lacks funds to purchase services, moreover, children and families will sometimes fail to receive them from referral agencies that are overwhelmed by current demands on their services. So case management has to be supplemented with purchase-of-service resources.

At a more ambitious level, however, a child welfare agency must develop partnerships and collaborations with other agencies. In some cases, it must subcontract with other agencies to help specific kinds of families and children. A child welfare agency might subcontract with a family-counseling agency, for example, to provide family support and empowerment services for dysfunctional families that show promise of improving their parenting sufficiently so that children can remain in the family. Or a child welfare agency might establish a *collaborative project* with other agencies to which each contributes staff and resources. It might, for example, establish a collaboration with a substance-abuse agency and a job-training agency, creating a new program that combines substance-abuse, job-training, job-referral, and family-counseling services. The substance-abuse, job-training, and family-counseling staff would not only meet separately with families but have frequent case conferences, both among themselves and with the families.

Links among agencies were also fostered by a *managed-care* revolution in the 1990s. It began in the health service industry in response to the double-digit annual increases in costs that confronted government funders, corporations, and insurance companies.[30] By 2002, the United States was spending about 16 percent of its gross domestic product, or GDP, on health care—far more than any other industrialized nation. Before the advent of managed care, autonomous physicians were reimbursed for each test or service, such as $1,000 for removing an appendix. Few limits were placed on their fees, and insurance companies usually reimbursed physicians and hospitals for whatever fees they charged. Such *fee-for-service* reimbursement was very costly because it encouraged physicians to do excessive surgeries and diagnostic tests, as their incomes were based on the number of services they provided.

Determined to establish limits on these costs, insurance companies formed managed-care organizations and placed physicians and hospitals under tight controls. To participate in managed care and to get reimbursed, physicians and hospitals had to agree to limit their charges and to get approval for diagnostic tests and surgeries. Variously called *preferred-provider organizations* or *health maintenance organizations*, these managed-care organizations sharply restricted the autonomy of physicians and hospitals.

It seemed at first that managed care, which began with health services, would not affect social workers, but it was soon extended to mental health services, which employ tens of thousands of social workers. Because, originally, they had provided some mental health benefits, health insurance companies placed mental health practitioners under controls similar to those on physicians: If they wanted to be reimbursed, mental health practitioners had to agree to certain fee levels and had to get approval if they wanted to provide treatment that exceeded, in many cases, 10 sessions.[31] This trend toward managed care in the mental health services was accelerated by federal legislation in 1996 that required health insurance plans to include mental health coverage. Managed care in mental health quickly spread to the public sector as well. For example, the Los Angeles County Mental Health Department, which is charged with caring for persons with chronic conditions who receive SSI, decided to subcontract its services to not-for-profit and for-profit agencies, giving them specific payment amounts per patient. This method of financing care, called *capitation*, differs markedly from fee-for-service. Whereas mental health providers had often billed insurance companies and public authorities by the hour for the clinical services they provided, capitation meant that they received a flat amount per year for each patient in their care, say,

$1,500 per patient. As with managed care generally, capitation removes any incentive to overextend services, because the more treatment provided, the less return on the time expended.

As clients soon discovered, the movement toward managed care had both positive and negative consequences. By placing providers under the control of insurance administrators and by setting limits on their fees and services, it fostered greater efficiency in health and mental health. Some managed-care health facilities, however, chose to underserve their patients and clients, increasing their revenues per capita, for example, by deciding to deny diagnostic tests, surgeries, and mental health services even to patients and clients who clearly needed them.[32]

Indeed, policy advocates in many states introduced legislation that placed restrictions on managed-care insurance companies, such as diminishing the power of their administrators to force providers to restrict their services excessively, or that gave consumers the right to appeal treatment decisions that denied them services or tests.

In some cases, policy advocates work to create regional organizations to fund local agencies and shape policy choices. For example, the Ryan White legislation provides federal funds for AIDS treatment and prevention programs.[33] This legislation created regional boards across the nation that distribute funds to agencies in their area, monitor these agencies' services, and create new programs when gaps or omissions exist. While critics view these regional organizations as yet another layer of bureaucracy, their advocates note their ability to locate unserved needs, promote joint programs, and advocate for the needs of underserved populations.

Addressing Community Factors in Steps 2, 3, and 4

We noted earlier that our policy advocate wants to embed the shelters in her program in the community. She inserts provisions in the legislation to encourage shelters to spread word of their services to local self-help groups; local professionals who have extensive contact with women (such as hair stylists); female community leaders; and agencies that link women to schools, job placement, medical services, free clinics, and other social agencies. She also requires the shelters to provide advocacy services, such as seeking greater protection by local police departments for women who have been abused.

Because shelters' staff and boards will define priorities and objectives, the policy advocate requires the boards to select 51 percent of their membership from currently or previously battered women, female leaders in the community, and local professionals who work in self-help and other agencies. These kinds of board members should be more sympathetic to her objectives than the businesspeople and professionals who usually dominate agencies' boards. To give the boards even greater powers, the policy practitioner also requires them to review programs and budgets in the hope that they will promote the full range of services in the legislation, including advocacy and outreach.

Guiding and Overseeing Policy Implementation in Steps 2, 3, and 4

As we discuss in more detail in Chapter Thirteen, implementation is a critical part of the policy process. Were policy advocates not to consider implementation in their proposals, they would ignore a vital aspect of the policy-making process. They must consider two issues: Who will establish the detailed policies that will guide the implementation of their proposal, and who will monitor their proposal's implementation?

Most proposals do not attempt to define the myriad administrative policies that will shape their implementation. While they may discuss a broad strategy for determining eligibility, for example, they may not describe detailed policies, such as how current income will be calculated if a means-tested sliding-fee approach is used. These kinds of details are frequently decided through *administrative regulations* that a high-level agency establishes. Our policy practitioner decides to give the responsibility for establishing these detailed policies to the states rather than vesting them with the federal government, partly because she fears that conservatives will oppose her Federal Shelter Program if it gives the federal government this role.

She must also decide whether the programs of specific shelters will be monitored by higher authorities to see if their services are in compliance with the policies in the legislation and the states' administrative regulations.[34] She also must decide whether shelters will be given technical assistance to help them implement these federal and state policies. She decides they will and gives state agencies the task of monitoring the shelters and providing them with technical assistance. Realizing that monitoring and technical assistance can be costly because staff must be hired and reimbursed to travel widely, she decides to earmark some of the Federal Shelter Program's resources for these two functions.

Assessing Implemented Policies in Steps 2, 3, and 4

Policy proposals often discuss how programs or services they establish will be assessed. In the case of the Federal Shelter Program, the policy advocate must decide who will perform these assessments and how they will be funded. As with monitoring and technical assistance, she decides to give this responsibility to the state agency that oversees the shelters.

An Overview of the Proposal to Fund Shelters for Battered Women

We have watched our policy advocate face a number of policy options and make some tentative choices. Here is an overview of her decisions.

She has established a mission by proposing a nationwide system of shelters for battered women. The shelters will provide these women with a range of social services. She has designed the structure of service to place the Federal Shelter Program in the U.S. Department of Health and Human Services, to use only nonprofit agencies, and to set some standards at the federal level, but requires each state to appoint a lead agency to administer the funds to the local shelters. She has planned the disbursement and circulation of resources by establishing an authorization level of $450 million, which will increase to $600 million within three years, using Route 2 from Figure 8.1. She has defined the services to be offered by using an ecological paradigm and requiring that they include referral, crisis management, case management, advocacy, legal help, and outreach; proposing a regional hot line in designated regional areas; and requiring the shelter directors to have an MSW degree and direct-service staff to have had a supervised practicum.

She has rationed scarce resources by establishing a sliding fee that can be waived when family finances are disrupted by dislocation; by limiting residence to a period of three months, which can be extended when the resident remains in imminent danger of physical abuse; and by giving admittance priority to women in imminent danger of physical abuse. She has included local coordinating boards to link the work of different shelters. The proposal addresses community factors by requiring outreach to underserved segments of the population, links with community support systems, and advocacy; and by requiring 51 percent of the board to consist of currently or previously battered women, staff in agencies or support groups for this population, or community leaders. Finally, she has arranged for overseeing policy implementation by earmarking 3 percent of funds for state agencies to monitor the shelter programs.

As we will see in the next chapter, it is relatively simple to list policy options and to make preliminary choices, as our practitioner has done. But she and other members of her coalition have not yet encountered the difficulties of the political process or persons who are not favorably disposed to the proposal. At that point, she will have to make some agonizing choices.

The Anatomy of Policy Proposals

We can conceptualize proposal writing as choosing from the competing options on various policy issues. The policy advocate maps a proposal by drawing lines between alternative options on a diagram that displays the issues and the competing options. (See Figure 8.3, which illustrates the choices made by the policy practitioner who has constructed the Federal Shelter Program. The shaded items are the options.)

Trade-Offs: Systematically Comparing Policy Options in Step 3

Policy advocates sometimes use a systematic process to compare the relative merits of competing options like the ones discussed in the previous chapter. To make systematic comparisons of policy options, policy advocates often proceed deliberately; they identify options, select and weigh criteria, rank options, and develop a decision-making matrix.[35] You should know about this analytic style of reasoning because it is often used in policy deliberations.

Identifying Options in Step 2

Policy analysts rarely feel comfortable with a single policy approach, wanting to compare and contrast alternative policies before making a final selection. Someone seeking to end malnutrition in certain segments of the population, for example, might examine the merits of distributing food directly to certain persons, changing the food stamp program, and changing existing welfare programs to give low-income persons more funds to purchase food. These three policy choices might be contrasted with expanding income tax credits to poor persons to allow them to purchase more food. By identifying these four options, the policy analyst hopes to avoid being prematurely committed to a specific policy.

Let's consider the systematic process of examining trade-offs by using as our example an MSW student intern who discovered that Spanish-speaking patients in her hospital placement had very few translation services available to them. She observed that some newly admitted patients had been hospitalized for as long as 24 hours without receiving any explanation of their medical condition or treatment. Many hospital staff were not informed about nuances of Latino culture, moreover, that powerfully shaped

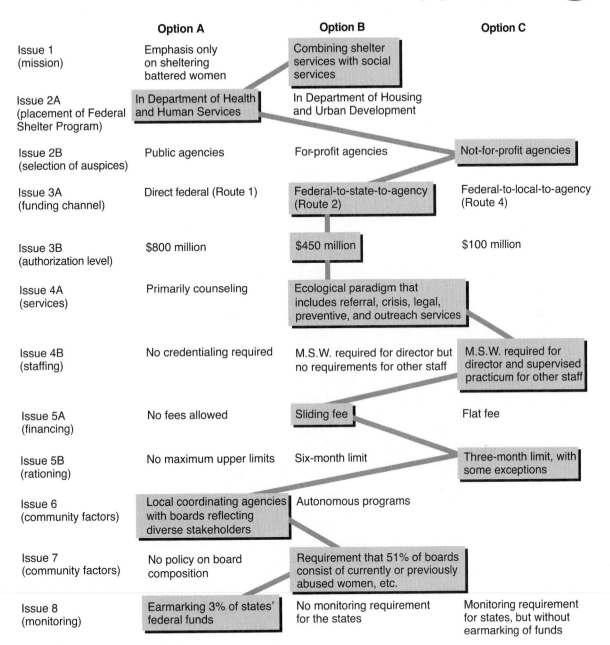

	Option A	Option B	Option C
Issue 1 (mission)	Emphasis only on sheltering battered women	Combining shelter services with social services	
Issue 2A (placement of Federal Shelter Program)	In Department of Health and Human Services	In Department of Housing and Urban Development	
Issue 2B (selection of auspices)	Public agencies	For-profit agencies	Not-for-profit agencies
Issue 3A (funding channel)	Direct federal (Route 1)	Federal-to-state-to-agency (Route 2)	Federal-to-local-to-agency (Route 4)
Issue 3B (authorization level)	$800 million	$450 million	$100 million
Issue 4A (services)	Primarily counseling	Ecological paradigm that includes referral, crisis, legal, preventive, and outreach services	
Issue 4B (staffing)	No credentialing required	M.S.W. required for director but no requirements for other staff	M.S.W. required for director and supervised practicum for other staff
Issue 5A (financing)	No fees allowed	Sliding fee	Flat fee
Issue 5B (rationing)	No maximum upper limits	Six-month limit	Three-month limit, with some exceptions
Issue 6 (community factors)	Local coordinating agencies with boards reflecting diverse stakeholders	Autonomous programs	
Issue 7 (community factors)	No policy on board composition	Requirement that 51% of boards consist of currently or previously abused women, etc.	
Issue 8 (monitoring)	Earmarking 3% of states' federal funds	No monitoring requirement for the states	Monitoring requirement for states, but without earmarking of funds

FIGURE 8.3

The anatomy of the Federal Shelter Program proposal

patients' responses to medical treatments. For example, a Latina signed an informed consent form for a hysterectomy. Her physician, knowing that her bilingual son had served as her interpreter, assumed that she favored the treatment plan, only to discover the next day that she was so irate that a hysterectomy had been performed that she was threatening to sue the hospital. Only later was the physician informed that it is culturally inappropriate for a Latino son to discuss private parts with his mother—and that the embarrassed son had told his mother that a tumor would be removed from her abdomen! In turn, the mother was furious, not only because she had not been informed about the procedure, but because hysterectomies are considered taboo procedures by some segments of the Latino community.

The intern's challenge was to develop a proposal to address this situation. To do so, she had to compare alternative strategies and gauge which one would be most effective in getting translation services to Latinos. She did not take this task lightly; she realized that the well-being of many Latinos depended on getting translation services.

The social work intern identified four options:

1. Develop a cultural awareness course for new medical residents to instill sensitivity to the culture and language of Spanish-speaking patients. In particular, the course would help the residents understand the need to engage these patients in extended discussions and caring services to offset their fear of the medical system and their inability to express their needs in English.
2. Develop a computerized list of all hospital employees and residents who speak Spanish, allowing them to be paged by medical staff when translations are needed, thus easing the burden on the seven full-time interpreters employed by the hospital.
3. Hire more interpreters.
4. Recruit 40 bilingual Latino undergraduate students to serve as volunteer interpreters two hours per week, assigning them to the nurses' station in each unit of the hospital.

Selecting and Weighing Criteria in Step 3

In order to select an optimal policy, policy advocates must first identify the criteria to use as a basis of comparison. In simple cases, a single criterion suffices; given three policy options, for example, with the single criterion being cost, the cheapest policy option would be selected. In most cases, however, advocates identify several criteria. For example, they might consider costs, administrative feasibility, and effectiveness in addressing consumers' needs.

Policy advocates can select a variety of criteria. As was discussed in Chapter Two, *value-based criteria* are reflected in terms such as equality, equity, social justice, and various freedoms, such as the right to free speech, the right to privacy, the right to receive accurate and honest information, and the right to self-determination. (Moral philosophers, religious leaders, the due process clause of the Fifth and Fourteenth Amendments to the U.S. Constitution, and the Bill of Rights discuss these value-based criteria.)

Consumer-outcome criteria define specific policies' effectiveness in ameliorating social problems. In the social services, for example, people often scrutinize how various policy options will affect clients' well-being.

Terms such as efficiency and cost reflect *economic criteria.* Having limited resources, policy advocates must assess the relative cost of competing options. *Feasibility criteria* pertain to the political and administrative practicality of specific policy options. An option may seem quite attractive but may be rejected because it cannot be implemented or is not politically feasible. For example, some people believe we should decriminalize certain drugs, such as cocaine, by selling them at cheap prices in state-regulated stores. However, many practical details confound the administration of this policy. If cocaine were legalized, what about countless other substances, including some that have not even been invented? If cocaine were legalized, the state-regulated stores might offer a wide assortment of mood-altering substances. Who would pay for growing or manufacturing the currently illegal drugs? Should poor persons be allowed to use their food stamps to purchase them? Could federal authorities easily override state laws that declare mood-altering substances illegal? Would authorities have to limit the amount of a drug someone could purchase, or could persons obtain unlimited quantities? Could drugs in such an open market be kept from adolescents or schoolchildren, or would older friends, siblings, or even some parents supply them? Some politicians would very likely assail this policy for threatening to corrode our youths' morals by making drugs too accessible.

Externalities criteria are used to assess how a policy option would affect institutions or persons who initially appear to be unrelated to the policy. If drugs, including hallucinogens, were decriminalized, policy analysts would have to ask whether driving accidents would markedly increase. This externality could not be dismissed as trivial because as many as 35,000 Americans die each year from accidents caused by driving while under the influence of alcohol, a decriminalized and accessible drug. However, some positive externalities might offset these negative ones. The reduced price of drugs and their increased availability in state-regulated stores would drive criminal elements, gangs, and foreign profiteers out of drug dealing and would make it unnecessary for addicts to steal to support their habit.

Terms such as cost-effectiveness reflect how we can combine several criteria into single measures.[36] In cost-effectiveness studies, analysts want to know which policy will most benefit consumers at the lowest cost. One policy option may yield considerable benefit to consumers, but at a prohibitive cost; another option may yield few benefits, but at a low cost; and a third option may provide considerable benefits at a relatively modest cost. A policy analyst who wants a cost-effective policy would probably select the third option because it balances cost and effectiveness.

When selecting more than one criterion, policy advocates need to weigh their relative importance. This is not a scientific undertaking; it reflects the values of the policy practitioner. When discussing alternative criteria for evaluating welfare reform (see Chapter Seven), many policy advocates would be more likely than conservatives to emphasize welfare reform's effects on the economic well-being of former recipients, whereas many conservatives would emphasize its effects in reducing the welfare rolls.

The social work intern decided to select four criteria, assigning a numerical value to each of them. To force herself to determine the relative importance of these four criteria, she decided to make the four scores add up to 1.0. She gave the most weight to cost and effectiveness in helping patients with translation needs, wanting to help patients immediately but realizing that funds were short in her hospital. (Each of these criteria was scored as 0.3.) She included the criteria of political feasibility and ease of implementation, realizing she would need high-level approval that would stem partly from the administrators' belief that the project could be easily implemented. (Each of these criteria was scored as 0.2, so the total score for the four criteria was 1.0.) Of course, someone else might have weighted the criteria differently.

Creating a Decision-Making Matrix in Step 3

To help them select policies, advocates often construct a decision-making matrix that graphically portrays the options and the criteria.[37] The social work intern placed her four options and her four criteria on a decision-making matrix that organized her options and criteria into a table. (See Table 8.2.)

Recall that she had already rated the criteria by giving scores of 0.3 to cost and effectiveness and scores of 0.2 to political feasibility and ease of implementation. (See the criteria at the top of Table 8.3, which shows how she rated the criteria and the options.)

TABLE 8.2
A decision-
making matrix

| | | Criteria | | |
Policy options	Cost	Effectiveness in helping patients with translations	Political feasibility	Ease of implementation
Cultural course for new residents				
Computerized list of Spanish-speaking employees				
Hiring more interpreters				
Recruiting 40 bilingual undergraduate volunteers				

She then rated the policy options by the criteria (Table 8.3). She decided to rank each of the options from 1 (poor) to 10 (outstanding), using information gleaned from physicians and administrators, as well as her own best guesses. She rated the cultural course as 6 with respect to cost because it would require the development of curriculum and staff to teach it. Since the computerized list would be relatively inexpensive to produce, she gave it a ranking of 8. She ranked the hiring of more interpreters as 1 because it would require more paid hospital staff. The recruiting of undergraduate volunteers was ranked 7; while they would provide free labor, staff time would be needed to recruit, train, and coordinate them. She then ranked the four policy options by the remaining three criteria. As shown in Table 8.3, she gave the lowest score on effectiveness in helping patients with translations to the cultural course (3) on the grounds that it might sensitize residents to the culture of Latinos, but it would not provide new translation services. Regarding political feasibility, she ranked the option of hiring new translators the lowest, giving it only a score of 3 because she doubted that the hospital administrators would fund this proposal. All of the options were relatively easy to implement, she decided, not giving any of them a score lower than 6.

She discovered that each option had at least one weakness: The cultural course would not make an immediate impact on the translation needs of patients; the computerized list would not prove easy to implement since bilingual staff could not interrupt their regular assignments and become translators on the spur of the moment; hiring new translators was too costly; and training and coordinating undergraduate volunteers might prove difficult to implement.

The student intern now had to calculate scores that combined her ranking of the options for each criterion and the relative importance of each criterion (the numbers in parentheses under each criterion in Table 8.3). She multiplied the option rating in each cell by each criterion score, arriving at a final score for each cell (the subscript number in italics). To score the recruiting of undergraduate volunteers by the cost criterion, for example, she multiplied 0.3 times 7, arriving at a score of 2.1 in the lower-left-hand cell.

Then, she added the scores for each option across the table to discover the total score for each option. She concluded that using undergraduate volunteers was the best solution, because it received a total score of 7.8, compared with the next closest option, the computerized list, which received a score of 7.3. (See the total scores for each option in the right-hand column of Table 8.3.) She hoped she could get a local foundation to

TABLE 8.3
Scoring policy options by using policy criteria

Policy options		Criteria			
	Cost (0.3)	Effectiveness in helping patients with translations (0.3)	Political feasibility (0.2)	Ease of implementation (0.2)	Total
Cultural course for new residents	$6_{1.8}$	$3_{.9}$	$8_{1.6}$	$6_{1.2}$	5.5
Computerized list of Spanish-speaking employees	$8_{2.4}$	$7_{2.1}$	$8_{1.6}$	$6_{1.2}$	7.3
Hiring more interpreters	$1_{.3}$	$9_{2.7}$	$3_{.6}$	$8_{1.6}$	5.2
Recruiting 40 bilingual undergraduate volunteers	$7_{2.1}$	$9_{2.7}$	$9_{1.8}$	$6_{1.2}$	7.8

provide funds for a part-time coordinator to recruit and train these volunteers. She was excited about this option for educational reasons as well: It would provide an excellent opportunity for the students to learn about the health care system.

The term *trade-off* refers to assessing the comparative advantages of policy options. The policy practitioner seeks to discover which option has the most weight, that is, the greatest net score on the criteria that the policy analyst has identified and ranked.[38] Thus, the student intern selected the fourth policy option, even though other options had received higher scores on specific criteria.

When reviewing this example of a decision-making matrix, it is important to dwell not on the details of the scoring rules, but on the style of analytic reasoning. Other approaches to scoring could easily have been used to rank the criteria and the various options and to compute the final scores. When using an analytic style of reasoning, the policy analyst breaks the selection process into a series of sequential steps that eventually lead to an overall score for specific options.

Using a policy matrix like Table 8.3 does not necessarily eliminate conflict; persons may disagree about the criteria selected, their relative importance, and specific options' scores for those criteria. When policy analysis occurs before a policy is enacted, as in this hospital case, policy practitioners must predict the outcomes, costs, and consequences of options. Such predictions often turn out to be partially inaccurate; in this case, the student intern might later discover that she had underestimated the costs of a policy option or its effectiveness in solving a social problem.

Qualitative Rankings

Had the student intern not been quantitatively inclined, she could have ranked her four policy options qualitatively. Some critics of quantitative techniques would readily support this tactic on the grounds that the existing data do not allow accurate quantitative rankings. However, persons making qualitative rankings (such as high, medium, and low) would still have to develop options and criteria and weigh the criteria to judge the relative merits of the two policy options.

TABLE 8.4
Trade-offs in
policy options

Policy options	Advantages	Disadvantages
Using intensive rather than extensive services	Provides in-depth services with greater impact	Denies services to large numbers of consumers
Developing community-based rather than agency services	Decreases stigma of service; helps integrate consumers into mainstream	Is difficult to orchestrate several community services and involve transient populations
Using generalist rather than specialized services or staff	Focuses on client as a whole person	Staff members lack specialized expertise relevant to consumers' specific needs
Providing preventive rather than curative services	Allows early detection and treatment of social problems and educates consumers to forestall development of problems	May neglect the needs of people who already have a serious problem
Using universal rather than selective eligibility	Allows staff to serve all applicants; makes imposing means tests unnecessary	Makes it difficult to target scarce resources on those with particularly serious problems
Using decentralized rather than centralized services	Makes outreach to consumers possible; improves access to services and use of community networks	Is more expensive to operate than centralized facilities
Using multiprofessional teams rather than single professions	Allows many professions to contribute to service	May promote interprofessional conflict

Table 8.4 portrays some trade-offs that social workers in agencies often encounter. Indeed, the policy advocate discussed earlier in the chapter who developed legislation to help battered women would have encountered each of the trade-offs in Table 8.4 when designing shelter programs at the local level. (See Policy Advocacy Challenge 8.3.)

POLICY ADVOCACY CHALLENGE 8.3

Micro-Level Policy: Examining Policy Trade-Offs in Agencies

BRUCE JANSSON, PH.D.

Take any social agency with which you are familiar and any of the policy options listed in Table 8.4. Discuss how the administrators and staff of the agency have wrestled with that option and what solutions they have chosen in the context of trade-offs. If possible, interview some agency staff about their choices concerning the option; otherwise, use your knowledge of the agency to speculate about the possible trade-offs they had to consider when they made their choices.

Using Different Policy Skills in Tandem in Steps 2, 3, and 4

The evolution of the Federal Shelter Program proposal demonstrates that effective policy advocates combine analytic skills in identifying, comparing, and selecting policy options with other policy practice skills. Our policy advocate *also* had to develop and maintain a coalition and make ethical choices as she (and her allies) decided whether to make compromises to get the proposal enacted.

As our example of the proposed legislation to fund shelters for battered women suggests, policy advocates must *also* be acutely aware of political realities as they construct proposals. In drafting the legislation, our policy advocate decided at several critical junctures to modify some of the provisions to accommodate political realities. She chose, for example, to propose a fiscal authorization at the rather limited sum of $450 million in the first year. She also chose to use the states to administer the funds (Route 2), rather than to give federal authorities a more expansive role. In making these concessions to conservative and moderate politicians, she had to wrestle with an ethical dilemma: Is half a loaf better than none? Recall our Chapter Two discussion of ethical dilemmas that arise when ethical principles, such as social justice, are pitted against pragmatic factors, such as political realities.

In the aftermath of Katrina, policy advocates faced a dilemma about how to plan New Orleans' rebuilding, particularly if the needs of vulnerable low-income African Americans were to be addressed. Two divergent policy options existed, but it remained to be seen which one would be chosen. (See Policy Advocacy Challenge 8.4.)

POLICY ADVOCACY CHALLENGE 8.4

Two Divergent Policy Options for Rebuilding New Orleans

BRUCE JANSSON, PH.D.

Two proposals for rebuilding New Orleans surfaced in Katrina's wake. One of them was a "free market option," which was favored by President George W. Bush. The other "guided planning" proposal, favored by some liberal politicians and think tanks, favored the development of some form of government metropolitan or regional planning entity that would use federal funds to guide the rebuilding of New Orleans to include efforts to give many African Americans the choice to come back to mixed-income neighborhoods within New Orleans or near it.[1]

The free market option had the advantages of simplicity and possibly lower costs than the guided planning option. This approach would let citizens and businesses decide whether, when, and where to return to New Orleans. The federal government's role would primarily consist of giving citizens and businesses tax incentives to rebuild or repair structures—as well as giving low-income citizens rent vouchers and by giving developers subsidies to encourage them to build rental units for low-income persons. By summer 2006, moreover, the federal government had approved a $4.2 billion block grant that allowed the state of Louisiana to give each homeowner in New Orleans up to $150,000 to repair their homes or to purchase a new home—minus whatever resources they might have obtained from insurance companies for damage caused to their home.

---

[1] For discussion of a guided planning option, see Will Fischer and Barbara Sard, "Bringing Katrina's Poorest Victims Home," Center on Budget and Policy Priorities, November 3, 2005. (It can be accessed at http://cbpp.org.)

(continued)

In the free market option, individual citizens and businesses would largely determine what New Orleans would look like after Hurricane Katrina by making relocation decisions. Homeowners, renters, and businesses would "vote with their feet" by choosing whether return to the city and where to place themselves. Persons known as "pioneers" returned in the year following Katrina, one by one, and often with little assistance from the government, to reclaim their property and then to repair or rebuild it—sometimes choosing to live in areas where no one else chose to live much like persons on the American frontier in the 19th century. Individual businesses made similar choices, but they had to consider whether sufficient numbers of persons lived near them to provide them with business.

We should not imply that supporters of the free market option believed that FEMA and other government programs should not subsidize the city of New Orleans to help it pay for the cost of municipal fire, police, and sanitation costs, as well as the cost of repairing its streets when its own tax revenues had plummeted in the wake of Katrina due to the destruction of property and businesses. They also eventually supported giving homeowners who lacked sufficient insurance up to $150,000 to rebuild their homes or to buy new ones.

Rather than large subsidies, however, advocates of the free market option mostly wanted to rely on tax incentives, housing vouchers, and tax relief to promote the relocation of persons and businesses to New Orleans, i.e., money that would grease the wheels of capitalism rather than supplant it.

Private markets were not, however, a panacea and posed real problems for the rebuilding of New Orleans. If relatively small subsidies and incentives were sufficient for relatively affluent persons whose businesses and homes had been damaged or destroyed, they were insufficient for many poor persons—particularly if they wished to relocate to a mixed income area. Assume that low income African Americans' homes had been destroyed: a $150,000 subsidy to each of them would be insufficient for them to buy new homes in mixed-income areas as opposed to communities with concentrated poverty.

Relatively small incentives to individual African-American homeowners would be insufficient to attract them to return to New Orleans, moreover, because their neighborhoods—often on lower ground—were often far more damaged than ones occupied by more affluent persons. Why would they return to rebuild or repair their homes if they do not know when: (1) key city services like electricity and water would be restored, (2) roads would be repaired, (3) city transportation services would be restored since many did not have cars, (4) sufficient numbers of their neighbors would return so that they would feel secure, (5) their churches might be rebuilt or repaired, and (6) reliable employment could be secured.

Often occupying lower ground, moreover, they would be even less likely to return to the city than more affluent persons on higher ground if they were not relatively certain that their old neighborhood would be made safe should a Category-5 hurricane, like Katrina, hit New Orleans again. Why go to all the effort of rebuilding or repairing homes if they might be destroyed or severely damaged again in the near future?

Those venturesome low-income African Americans who *did* return and who lived in FEMA trailers next to their destroyed or damaged homes or in nearby trailer camps might often decide to leave the city even after they had begun repairing their homes when these various amenities were *not* provided *and* their areas had not been rendered safe. Imagine yourself returning to New Orleans when virtually all the homes in a ten-block area surrounding your home were uninhabited and where (even) city lights were not functioning. Imagine, too, that your home was on low ground so that you did not feel comfortable that your home would not be spared if a major hurricane struck. By contrast, relatively affluent persons on higher ground and in neighborhoods less damaged by Katrina would be more likely to return to the city even if their neighborhoods had sustained considerable damage and even knowing that the Army Corps of Engineers had not repaired levees sufficient to protect against a Catetgory-5 hurricane.

Other problems existed with the free market option. With no regional agency put in place to orchestrate the rebuilding of New Orleans, no one would be held accountable for doing it in an efficient, effective, and timely way. Even a year after Katrina, for example, vast sections of New Orleans had not yet been cleaned of debris because no one had set a time schedule for doing it.

With no regional agency put in place, moreover, no authority existed for coordinating all the federal, state, and local agencies and officials involved in the rebuilding of the city. For example, who would make certain that city services, like police and firefighting services, were in place in those areas where citizens had returned?

With no regional agency, moreover, *regional* problems and solutions could not be addressed or goals established. Assume, for example, that a significant number of low-income African Americans wanted to move into mixed-income neighborhoods as compared to their former neighborhoods that possessed concentrated poverty. Without a regional agency, location of rental and for-purchase homes could not easily be located to which these persons might move.

With no regional agency, moreover, it would prove difficult to *sequence* economic, housing, service, and environmental actions in ways that would encourage expeditious rebuilding of New Orleans. If scattered persons returned to New Orleans only to find no services, insufficient employment, insufficient public transportation, few grocery stores, and unrepaired roads, they would likely not stay or would be extremely unhappy. Some entity would be needed that could facilitate the orderly sequencing of these needed amenities so that they took place all at once or soon after one another.

In contrast to the free market option, a regional body (let's call it the regional New Orleans Development Authority, or NODA) would develop a master plan for the region by drawing upon inputs from local citizens. It would develop a plan to phase the rebuilding of New Orleans into place over time. Since the city lacked the construction firms and labor to redevelop New Orleans all at once, NODA would establish priorities geared toward giving low-income African-American evacuees, as well as other evacuees, a range of housing and community choices in a number of communities.

It might begin, however, by deciding in liaison with the Army Corps of Engineers what areas of New Orleans could be protected from Category-5 hurricanes for an extended period, say 30 years. It would secure from the federal government sufficient resources to accomplish this goal *at the outset* rather than waiting for an extended period. (President Bush had rebuilt many levees by fall 2006, but they would only be sufficient to protect the city from Category-3 hurricanes.) Nor had FEMA declared certain areas of New Orleans to be unsafe for continued residency, merely suggesting that residents in some areas place their houses on stilts to avoid flood damage. Clearly, however, significant areas of New Orleans *were* unsafe—so NODA would have declared

(continued)

them off bounds until they were made safe while pressuring FEMA to strengthen levees in many parts of New Orleans to provide citizens with necessary safety.

Let's assume, then, that NODA had decided that the lower Ninth Ward could be protected against Category-5 storms and had largely rebuilt the levees by fall 2006 to accomplish this goal. Let's assume NODA polled all the evacuees it could locate, as well as residents of the lower Ninth Ward, to better understand their intentions—so that it had some idea how many evacuees would even consider returning to the lower Ninth Ward and under what conditions. Let's also assume that NODA had developed a plan by December 2006 that included some mixture of rehabilitated or rebuilt homes of prior owners and a variety of mixed-income rental, freestanding homes, condominiums, and apartments. Let's also assume that the plan for the new lower Ninth Ward contained amenities like scattered parks, athletic fields, tennis courts, bike and jogging paths. Assume, as well, that sites would be assigned to grocery stores, malls, and other commercial facilities.

To be effective, NODA would need the power and resources to purchase abandoned properties in the lower Ninth Ward once it had been determined that their owners did not want them. NODA would also need the power and resources to purchase some standing properties when it was determined that the land on which they stood needed to be used for other purposes such as parks or mixed-income housing.

Working closely with the Louisiana Recovery Authority established by Governor Kathleen Blanco soon after Katrina hit New Orleans—and that served as a conduit for federal block grant funds—NODA would decide what combination of private and public capital would be needed for specific housing and community developments. It would liaison with Mayor Nagin and the city of New Orleans to decide which city services would be implemented in the lower Ninth Ward and when. Working in liaison with the Small Business Administration (SBA), it would seek grants, loans, and tax incentives for grocery stores and other businesses to return to, or locate in, the lower Ninth Ward.

Were such a plan to exist, then, two kinds of low-income African-American evacuees could better make their plans: homeowners and renters. *Homeowners* would be more likely to use the $150,000 subsidy to rebuild or repair their homes knowing they would be returning to a neighborhood with a planned future, knowing many fellow homeowners would return, and knowing they would be secure from future hurricanes. They would also have a realistic expectation that the value of their home would appreciate as it was surrounded by a viable community. *Renters* would have a number of options. They would be given first priority for subsidized rentals in the lower Ninth Ward in mixed-income townhouses and apartment buildings. Or they could get rental units in other projects in the New Orleans region that NODA had developed. Or they could purchase a home subject to qualifying for several federal programs to help low-income persons obtain houses.

A guided planning option might avert or diminish some of the following dangers that could be associated with the free market option, such as:

- Low-income African-American homeowners from the lower Ninth Ward might abandon their destroyed or damaged homes not knowing they would become part of a vibrant community and be safe from hurricanes—and many who did return to the lower Ninth Ward could become discouraged, possibly abandoning their homes even as they were repairing or rebuilding them.

- Low-income African-American renters from the lower Ninth Ward might not be able to find rental units because developers and owners of them would fear building or repairing them in a neighborhood with an insecure future and unsafe from hurricanes. These low-income renters might not be able to afford rental units in the Ninth Ward or in other neighborhoods in New Orleans because their rents had escalated due to the sheer number of rental units that had been destroyed by Hurricane Katrina.
- The rebuilding of New Orleans might be greatly slowed without a NODA that would oversee not just the planning of specific areas, but the phasing into place of housing, parks, city services, grocery stores and services, places of employment, and repaired levees.
- Without a planned and synchronized sequence of economic, housing, public services, and environmental actions, persons and businesses might be reluctant to return to New Orleans—or could delay their decisions—not knowing when they would could expect these amenities to be put in place. Many persons and businesses could become discouraged when they *did* return and not find the other amenities in place.

Many of these dangers had already come to pass in many communities in New Orleans in the year following Katrina—and it seemed inevitable that they would continue during the coming years since the free market option had no strategy to avert them.

Bush's free market approach would be less costly than the guided planning option because the federal government would mostly let private markets fund the rebuilding of New Orleans rather than using federal resources to purchase land, make plans, and rebuild New Orleans—save for the use of tax incentives, subsidies to the city of New Orleans, and scattered housing projects with HUD funds. If persons did not reclaim their land, large tracts would simply remain undeveloped.

Yet Bush's free market approach might ultimately be *more* costly than a guided planning option. Were the free market approach to delay the rebuilding of New Orleans as compared to the guided planning option, such as by not synchronizing economic, housing, and service developments in specific areas, the city, state, and federal governments would receive lower tax revenues from businesses and housing developments. If housing and businesses relocated to unsafe areas and were again destroyed or damaged by a hurricane in coming years, the government would lose all the resources it had used to fund rebuilding in those areas after Katrina.

The free market option posed yet another danger for vulnerable populations. What if large areas were purchased by private developers or speculators who were intent on using them for relatively affluent populations, such as for hotels, high-priced condominiums, and casinos? Might land needed for housing for vulnerable populations be lost in this process?

The free market option had far better political prospects than a guided planning option in 2005 and 2006. Republicans controlled the Congress and the presidency—and most of them subscribed to a private-market approach. Mayor Nagin was himself a free market advocate who was determined to let each neighborhood make its own plans without developing a regional plan that would establish goals and implement them until well into 2007. A hands-off approach also served his political interests.

(continued)

By letting each neighborhood makes its own plan, he did not have to ask relatively affluent areas to allow affordable or subsidized housing programs where low-income African Americans would live. He did not have to share power with a regional planning authority like NODA—much less be under pressure from it to phase into place city services into specific neighborhoods at a pace that NODA wanted. Nor would he have to decide what areas in New Orleans could *not* be rebuilt due to danger from Category-5 hurricanes—a decision that would be unpopular with those African-American or other neighborhoods that were declared unsafe.

It remained to be seen, however, how the free market approach would work. By fall 2006, its report card was not favorable. Vast sections of New Orleans remained devastated and lacked even rudimentary plans for their reconstruction. Scattered pioneers had cautiously returned to their destroyed or damaged homes often living in FEMA trailers on their properties, but they often found themselves living in desolate areas with high crime rates, poor city services, and few grocery stores—and no plans for their rebuilding. The murder rate in New Orleans had returned to its pre-Katrina levels by fall 2006 even though the city only had a population half its pre-Katrina size. Not only had little *physical* planning occurred under the free market option, but scant *social* planning.

Low-income African-American evacuees faced an uncertain future. Some fared well in cities and towns outside of New Orleans, but most remained unemployed a year after they had left New Orleans. It was unclear how many would be able to return to New Orleans even if they wished to do so. In a game of musical chairs, some low-income African Americans had fled their old neighborhoods only to end up in neighborhoods with concentrated poverty in another city.

The guided planning option would not have been a panacea had it been tried, but would it have done worse that the free market option?

Take a stab at the following tasks:

1. Construct a policy matrix with guided plan and free market options. Select such criteria as cost, effectiveness in giving low-income persons choices, and social justice.
2. Score the options and decide which you prefer.
3. Can you think of other options, perhaps one that combined free market and guided plan options, that might have been considered?

**What You
Can Now Do**

CHAPTER SUMMARY

You are now equipped to do the following:

- Identify stakeholders and understand how their vantage point affects their perspectives
- Identify a range of policy options that often recur in policy advocacy work
- Diagram a proposal in the context of alternative options that occur with respect to specific issues
- Examine trade-offs using both quantitative and qualitative approaches
- Understand how analytic skills must often be coupled with political, interactional, and value-clarifying skills

Having discussed how we meld an array of options together to form a policy proposal, we discuss how we write policy proposals in the next chapter.

NOTES

1. For an overview of one effort to secure federal legislation to fund shelters for abused women, see the *Congressional Quarterly Almanac*, vol. 35 (Washington, DC: Congressional Quarterly Service, 1979), pp. 508–509. Also see Liane Davis and Jan Hagen, "Services for Battered Women: The Public Policy Response," *Social Service Review* 62 (December 1988): 649–667.

2. Bruce Jansson, "The History and Politics of Selected Children's Programs and Related Legislation" (Ph.D. dissertation, University of Chicago, 1975), pp. 66–67, 76–77.

3. See Paul Gorman, "Block Grants: Theoretical and Practical Issues in Federal/State/Local Revenue Sharing," *New England Journal of Human Services* 4 (Spring 1984): 19–23; Robert Fulton and Ray Scott, "What Happened to the Federal/State Partnerships?" *New England Journal of Human Services* 4 (Fall 1984): 38–39; and Allen Imersheim, "The Influence of Reagan's New Federalism on Human Services in Florida," *New England Journal of Human Services* 5 (Spring 1985): 17–24.

4. Some overview literature on auspices includes Ralph Kramer, *Voluntary Agencies in the Welfare State* (Berkeley and Los Angeles: University of California Press, 1981), and Bruce Jansson, "Public Monitoring of Contracts with Nonprofit Organizations: Organizational Mission in Two Sectors," *Journal of Sociology and Social Welfare* 6 (May 1979): 362–374.

5. For an overview of some criticisms of public agencies, see Ralph Kramer, "From Voluntarism to Vendorism: An Organizational Perspective on Contracting," in Harold Demone and Margaret Gibelman, eds., *Services for Sale* (New Brunswick, NJ: Rutgers University Press, 1989), pp. 101–102.

6. For a critical overview of the emergence and roles of nonprofit agencies in the federally funded welfare state, see Eleanor Brilliant, "Private or Public: A Model of Ambiguities," *Social Service Review* 47 (September 1973): 384–396.

7. For criticisms of voluntary agencies, see Kramer, "From Voluntarism to Vendorism," pp. 102–103.

8. For a defense of profit-oriented agencies, see Emanuel Savas, *Privatizing the Public Sector: How to Shrink Government* (Chatham, NJ: Chatham House, 1982).

9. For criticism of profit-oriented agencies, see Harold Demone and Margaret Gibelman, "Privatizing the Acute Care General Hospital," in Barry Carroll, Ralph Conant, and Thomas Easton, eds., *Private Means—Public Ends: Private Business and Social Service Delivery* (New York: Praeger, 1987), pp. 50–75.

10. Alice Rivlin, *Reviving the American Dream: The Economy, the States, and the Federal Government* (Washington, DC: Brookings Institution, 1992).

11. Bruce Jansson and Susan Smith, "Articulating a 'New Nationalism' in American Social Policy," *Social Work* 41 (September 1996): 441–451.

12. Paul Peterson, "State Response to Welfare Reform: A Race to the Bottom?" in Isabel Sawhill, ed., *Welfare Reform: An Analysis of the Issues* (Washington, DC: Urban Institute, 1995), pp. 7–10.

13. For an overview of funding options, see Paul Terrel, "Financing Social Welfare Services," in Neil Gilbert and Harry Specht, eds., *Handbook of the Social Services* (Englewood Cliffs, NJ: Prentice Hall, 1981), pp. 392–394.

14. Ibid., pp. 398–399.

15. Classic accounts of the authorizations and appropriations processes are found in Richard Fenno, *Power of the Purse* (Boston: Little, Brown, 1966), and Aaron Wildavsky, *Politics of the Budgetary Process* (Boston: Little, Brown, 1964).

16. See Demone and Gibelman, *Services for Sale.*

17. John Coons and Stephen Sugarman defend voucher and vendor payments in *Education by Choice: The Case for Family Control* (Berkeley and Los Angeles: University of California Press, 1978). Frederick Thayer criticizes them in "Privatization: Carnage, Chaos, and Corruption," in Carroll, Conant, and Easton, *Private Means—Public Ends*, pp. 146–170.

18. Various points of view on block grants appear in Richard Nathan and Fred Doolittle, "Federal Grants: Giving and Taking Away," *Political*

Science Quarterly 100 (Spring 1985): 53–74, and Richard Williamson, "The 1982 New Federalism Negotiations," *Publius* 13 (Spring 1983): 11–33.

19. Thayer, "Privatization."

20. Herman Leonard, *Checks Unbalanced: the Quiet Side of Public Spending* (New York: Basic Books, 1986).

21. Bruce Fretz and David Mills, *Licensing and Certification of Psychologists and Counselors* (San Francisco: Jossey-Bass, 1980).

22. David Hardcastle, "The Profession: Professional Organizations, Licensing, and Private Practice," in Neil Gilbert and Harry Specht, eds., *Handbook of the Social Services* (Englewood Cliffs, NJ: Prentice Hall, 1981), p. 677.

23. Ibid., pp. 679–683.

24. Ibid., pp. 666–687.

25. S. K. Khinduka, "Social Work and the Human Services," *Encyclopedia of Social Work,* 18th ed., vol. 2 (Silver Spring, MD: National Association of Social Workers, 1987), p. 691.

26. For a discussion of rationing, see Richard Frank, "Rationing of Mental Health Services: Simple Observations on the Current Approach and Future Prospects," *Administration in Mental Health* 13 (Fall 1985): 22–29.

27. A general discussion of means tests appears in Neil Gilbert and Harry Specht, *Dimensions of Social Welfare Policy,* 2nd ed. (Englewood Cliffs, NJ: Prentice Hall, 1986), pp. 82–84.

28. For a discussion of staff discretion, see Robert Goodin, *Reasons for Welfare: The Political Theory of the Welfare State* (Princeton, NJ: Princeton University Press, 1988), pp. 184–228.

29. For subtle forms of discrimination and rationing, see Sharon Sepulveda-Hassell, *An Assessment of the Mental Health Treatment Process: Eliminating Service Barriers to Mexican Americans* (San Antonio, TX: Intercultural Development Research Association, 1980), and David Ramirez, *A Review of Literature on Underutilization of Mental Health Services by Mexican Americans: Implications for Future Research and Service Delivery* (San Antonio, TX: Intercultural Development Research Association, 1980).

30. John Inglehart, "The Struggle between Managed Care and Fee-for-Service Practice," *New England Journal of Medicine* (July 7, 1994): 63–67.

31. Wes Shera, "Managed Care and People with Severe Mental Illness: Challenges and Opportunities for Social Work," *Health and Social Work* 21 (August 1996): 196–201, and Susan Rose and Sharon Keigher, "Managing Mental Health: Whose Responsibility?" *Health and Social Work* 21 (February 1996): 76–80.

32. Marc Rodwin, "Conflicts in Managed Care," *New England Journal of Medicine* (March 2, 1995), pp. 604–606.

33. John Fleishman et al., "Organizing AIDS Service Consortia: Lead Agency Identity and Consortium Cohesion," *Social Service Review* (December 1992): 547–560.

34. For a discussion of monitoring, see Bruce Jansson, "The Political Economy of Monitoring: A Contingency Perspective," in Demone and Gibelman, *Services for Sale,* pp. 343–359, and Kenneth Wedel and Nancy Chess, "Monitoring Strategies in Purchase of Service Contracting," in Demone and Gibelman, *Services for Sale,* pp. 360–370.

35. The analytic process of identifying and selecting options is discussed by Eugene Bardach, *The Eight-Step Path of Policy Analysis* (Berkeley, CA.: Berkeley Academic Press, 1996).

36. Ibid., p. 27.

37. See, for example, Robert Francoeur's "decision making matrix" in *Biomedical Ethics: A Guide to Decision Making* (New York: Wiley, 1983), pp. 127–137.

38. Bardach, the *Eight-Step Path,* pp. 49–54.

SUGGESTED READINGS

Federal, State, and Local Relationships

Bruce Jansson and Susan Smith, "Articulating a 'New Nationalism' in American Social Policy," *Social Work* 41 (September 1996): 441–451.

Paul Peterson, *The Price of Federalism* (Washington, DC: Brookings Institution, 1995).

Alice Rivlin, *Reviving the American Dream: The Economy, the States, and the Federal Government* (Washington, DC: Brookings Institution, 1992).

Profit-Oriented, Not-for-Profit, and Public Agency Relationships

Barry Carroll, Ralph Conant, and Thomas Easton, eds., *Private Means—Public Ends: Private Business and Social Service Delivery* (New York: Praeger, 1987).

Harold Demone and Margaret Gibelman, eds., *Services for Sale* (New Brunswick, NJ: Rutgers University Press, 1989).

Sheila Kamerman and Alfred Kahn, *Privatization and the American Welfare State* (Princeton, NJ: Princeton University Press, 1984).

Lester Salamon and Alan Abramson, *The Nonprofit Sector and the New Federal Budget* (Washington, DC: Urban Institute Press, 1986).

Stan Smith and Deborah Stone, "The Unexpected Consequences of Privatization," in Michael Brown, ed., *Remaking the Welfare State* (Philadelphia: Temple University Press, 1988), pp. 232–252.

Organizational Issues in the American Welfare State

Darlyne Bailey and Kelly Koney, "Interorganizational Community-Based Collectives: A Strategic Response to Shape the Social Work Agenda," *Social Work* 41 (November 1996): 602–611.

John Fleishman et al., "Organizing AIDS Service Consortia: Lead Agency Identity and Consortium Cohesion," *Social Service Review* (December 1992): 547–560.

John O'Looney, "Beyond Privatization and Service Integration," *Social Service Review* (December 1993): 501–534.

Fiscal Issues

Harold Demone and Margaret Gibelman, *Services for Sale* (New Brunswick, NJ: Rutgers University Press, 1989), pp. 101–102.

Herman Leonard, *Checks Unbalanced: The Quiet Side of Public Spending* (New York: Basic Books, 1986).

Paul Terrel, "Financing Social Welfare Services," in Neil Gilbert and Harry Specht, eds., *Handbook of the Social Services* (Englewood Cliffs, NJ: Prentice Hall, 1981), pp. 380–410.

Professional and Staffing Issues

Bruce Fretz and David Mills, *Licensing and Certification of Psychologists and Counselors* (San Francisco: Jossey-Bass, 1980), pp. 9–29.

David Hardcastle, "The Profession: Professional Organizations, Licensing, and Private Practice," in Gilbert and Specht, *Handbook of the Social Services*, pp. 666–688.

Allocation Issues

Richard Frank, "Rationing of Mental Health Services: Simple Observations on the Current Approach and Future Prospects," *Administration in Mental Health* 13 (Fall 1985): 22–29.

Prevention

Thomas Frieden et al., "Tuberculosis in New York City: Turning the Tide," *New England Journal of Medicine* (July 27, 1995): 229–233.

Dennis Poole, "Achieving National Health Goals in Prevention with Community Organization: The Bottom-Up Approach," *Journal of Community Practice* 4 (Nov. 2, 1997): 77–92.

P. J. Porter, "Ways and Means of Providing Primary and Preventive Health Services," *Journal of Health Care for the Poor* 6 (1991): 167–173.

Staff Discretion

Robert Goodin, *Reasons for Welfare: The Political Theory of the Welfare State* (Princeton, NJ: Princeton University Press, 1988), pp. 184–228.

Michael Lipsky, *Street-Level Bureaucracy* (New York: Russell Sage Foundation, 1980).

Policy Analysis

Eugene Bardach, *The Eight-Step Path of Policy Analysis* (Berkeley, CA.: Berkeley Academic Press, 1996).

C H A P T E R

9

Presenting and Defending Policy Proposals

We will help you become an effective policy advocate by discussing the following in this chapter:

- How to engage in combative persuasion like debates and hardball negotiations
- How to establish specific objectives with specific audiences
- How to diagnose audiences
- How to develop a persuading strategy
- How to devise tactics for apathetic, hostile, and expert audiences
- How to develop friendly communication strategies in debates and mediation
- How to write grant proposals

Having developed meritorious proposals, policy advocates also need to defend them, whether in one-on-one discussions, presentations to larger audiences, or debates. Without policy persuasion skills, they cannot attract sufficient support for their ideas to be effective. (See steps 5 and 6 of the policy analysis framework.)

POLICY ADVOCACY CHALLENGE 9.1

Reading About Persuasive Speaking

STEPHANIE DAVIS, RESEARCH LIBRARIAN, UNIVERSITY OF CALIFORNIA, IRVINE

The following books may be informative and helpful in learning more about persuasive speaking:

Aubuchon, Norbert. *The Anatomy of Persuasion.* (New York: Amacom, 1997).

Mutz, Diana C., Paul M. Sniderman, Richard A. Brody. *Political Persuasion and Attitude Change.* (Ann Arbor: University of Michigan Press, 1996).

Rybacki, Donald Jay, Karyn Charles Rybacki. *Advocacy and Opposition: an Introduction to Argumentation.* (Boston, MA: Allyn & Bacon, 1999).

Stettner, Morey. *The Art of Winning Conversation.* (Englewood Cliffs, NJ: Prentice Hall, 1995).

Tannen, Deborah. *The Argument Culture.* (New York: Random House, 1998).

We distinguish here between friendly and adversarial communications. In friendly communications, policy advocates try to decrease opposition to a proposal with conflict reducing techniques. For example, they stress commonalities with the audience or engage in win-win negotiations that emphasize shared interests. In adversarial communications, a policy advocate tries to *best* a person or group with opposing points of view through debates or hardball negotiations. Naturally, most of us would like to use friendly communications, but adversarial ones are sometimes needed. Communication that combines friendly and adversarial elements is often needed, as well.

It would be difficult to overstate the role persuasion plays in policy advocacy. In order to enact policies, advocates often face significant challenges from people who are deeply opposed to their position or who are apathetic. No matter how loudly persuaders shout or how articulately they make their case, their efforts will come to naught unless the audience sees merit in the message and decides to heed its prescriptions. People highly skilled in the art of persuasion tailor their messages to specific audiences and situations.[1]

Policy advocates try to influence people through interpersonal discussions, proposals, speeches to large audiences, memoranda, formal reports, debates or arguments, messages (such as editorials), or the mass media.

The social context is often important. One persuader may be successful in interacting with people in relative isolation. However, she may find her work frustrated by external noise, such as peer pressure or competing messages from other senders. For instance, political campaigners seldom have the luxury of engaging in extended personal discussion with voters. As they try to reach voters with *their* messages, they must compete with opposing candidates' messages, as well as messages from their families and friends. They must contend, as well, with voters' traditional political loyalties, such as when they have voted with an opposing candidate's political party in prior elections.[2]

Ideology and Policy Positions

Proposals and Ideology

Ideology powerfully shapes proposals in legislative settings, as well as the content and tenor of policy debates. As a general rule, policy debates are more likely to be adversarial if protagonists' positions are shaped by ideological differences. In 2000 through 2002, for example, Democrats and Republicans proposed markedly different versions of gun control legislation, patient-rights legislation, federal tax-cut legislation, and school-reform legislation; their different proposals emanated from their different ideologies and their different political constituencies.[3] Republicans tended to favor lower federal expenditures, corporate interests (in the case of gun manufacturers and HMOs), lower taxes, and greater consumer choice (school vouchers) whereas Democrats tended in the opposite direction in each of these areas. As they debated these issues, protagonists often made reference to the core values that they possessed—often contrasting them with ones held by their opponents.

The role of ideology ought not be overstated, however. In the 2006 elections, Democrats placed more emphasis upon criticizing the course of the war in Iraq as opposed to "staying the course" with no changes in military strategy. They chose an issue that was not directly linked to ideology partly because the incumbent president seemed politically vulnerable on military issues—and also to neutralize President Bush's contention that Republicans were better suited to wage the war on terrorism.

Legislators from both parties realize that the "devil is in the details." It is in legislative details that broader ideologies are often manifested. In the case of complex legislation, conservatives, moderates, and liberals may battle over scores of legislative details, as they did concerning welfare reform legislation of 1996—and as they will again in future years when this legislation is reauthorized. (Major legislation must not only be initially approved but must then be "reauthorized" periodically in future years to keep it in operation.)

When debating legislative details, policy debates are often less conflictual because protagonists focus on relatively small details of proposals that are less likely to involve basic values. Even here, however, conflict can be heated because protagonists understand that the way myriad details are resolved shapes the overall approach to welfare reform. Liberals realize, for example, that, if conservatives were to prevail with respect to many small details during the reauthorization of welfare reform, the overall nature of welfare reform programs would be conservative in nature. When discussing the reauthorization of welfare reform in coming years, these details may include the following:

- How much federal money to expend on the proposal
- How much child care, transportation funds, and health care to include
- How long to make the transition period during which former recipients can qualify for supplemental welfare payments, child care, transportation, and health care
- Whether to define many or few policies governing welfare-to-work at the federal level—or whether to let the states make most or all of these choices
- Whether to include federal monies for subsidizing employment of former recipients so their total wages bring them near or above poverty levels
- Whether to keep or relax the 5-year lifetime limits on welfare—and the kinds of exceptions that will be allowed if lifetime limits are established

The political context strongly influences the outcomes of grand debates like this one. If single mothers are mostly able to find jobs in the period just preceding reauthorization, even low paying ones, liberals will have more difficulty seeking liberal changes in welfare legislation. Were a deep recession to occur, however, leading to widespread loss of jobs by single mothers and a swelling of welfare rolls, liberals might find it easier to obtain funds for job training and child care for them, as well as relaxation of some time limits. Much would depend even in these circumstances on the public's perceptions of welfare: if they were generally hostile to recipients, liberals would still find it difficult to achieve reforms of welfare programs. If they viewed welfare recipients as victims of economic conditions, liberals would find more support for relatively liberal welfare-reform policies.

Unless one party has a huge majority in legislative chambers, compromise versions of legislation usually emerge in the course of negotiations. One party or faction will make concessions on specific points in return for concessions from another party or faction on other points. Each party or faction will want to convey the impression to their constituents that, on balance, they won or at least received major concessions from opponents. Sometimes a party or faction will want to delay the outcome if they think that delay will strengthen their position, such as when public opinion polls or trips to their home districts suggest widespread support for their positions. On other occasions, a party or faction may decide to resolve the conflict so they are not seen as sabotaging an eventual solution. They also may decide to do so if they think opponents are besting them in the polls or with their own constituents or with independent voters.

The effects of ideology on policy debates are sometimes muted by other factors. We should not forget that legislators often get tangible benefits from specific policies or programs. Even the most ardent conservative, for example, may favor certain big spending programs because her or his constituents benefit from them, such as when conservatives support major increases in food stamps because they benefit farmers in their districts. Similarly, many liberals vote for huge and sometimes unnecessary weapon systems because they provide jobs to their constituents. Personal experiences often assume a major role, such as when a conservative supports large increases for mental health programs because a close relative has a serious mental problem. So policy advocates should not assume that they cannot find allies even among legislators who they might expect to be ideologically opposed to specific proposals.

Electoral Politics and Proposals

Policy proposals and policy persuasion lie at the heart of political campaigns as opposing candidates try to assemble a winning strategy. Candidates need to identify which issues will resonate positively with their natural constituents, as well as with sufficient numbers of swing voters to give them a winning margin.

Various possibilities ensue. Candidates sometimes avoid issues they perceive as no-win, such as when some Democrats decided in 2006 not to criticize some elements of President Bush's treatment of terrorist detainees for fear they would be viewed as not sufficiently committed to anti-terrorism. They sometimes avoid issues that they think will polarize their potential supporters, such as when some Democrats in 2006, who wanted immediate withdrawal from Iraq, remained silent on the issue because they knew that some Democrats and many independent voters favored gradual withdrawal.

In other cases, candidates address issues but only take fuzzy positions, fearing that highly specific positions would antagonize key groups of their intended supporters. For this reason, debates between candidates are often disappointing to listeners who believe that no one took a strong position on major issues. Some Democrats in 2006 attacked President Bush's prosecution of the war in Iraq, but refrained from saying precisely what their strategy might be—an approach that allowed them to benefit from widespread uneasiness about the war but that did not expose them to the criticism that they wanted to "cut and run."

Candidates sometimes take contradictory positions on specific issues, emphasizing different points to different audiences. A Democrat might, for example, favor cuts in government spending with relatively conservative constituents, while favoring many new programs with more liberal ones. This tactic can backfire, of course, if opponents charged her with waffling on the issues.

Candidates often use combative persuasion where they try to best their opponents. By drawing distinctions between themselves and their opponents, they can build support for themselves. Their opponents, in turn, not only use the same tactic, but often contend that their opponents have distorted their positions or records. As the 2006 congressional elections approached, for example, Democrats often argued that Republican opponents had falsely accused them of not favoring counter-terrorism programs—and contended that Republicans had failed to support important counter-terrorism initiatives such as ones designed to make American ports safer from attack.

Combative Persuasion

In *combative persuasion*, presenters use confrontive strategies to modify the opinions and actions of those who oppose them.[4] Three kinds of combative situations exist. In the first type, persuaders *debate* an adversary hoping to convince observers to choose their point of view over that of the adversary. In a staff meeting, for example, a presenter might argue with another person to win over staff members, just as candidates for political office often debate their opponents on television. In the second type, persuaders use coercive, one-on-one confrontation to change an adversary's position. For example, the presenter might demand that an agency executive make the agency's services more responsive to a specific population's needs. In the third type, persons *negotiate* with other persons in a kind of extended debate where contending parties decide whether and when to make concessions to opponents—and when to accept ones that their opponents put forward. Negotiations often culminate with an agreement that represents the views of both participants—unless they stalemate with no resolution.

Adversarial Debates

Three parties exist in adversarial debates: the persuader, the adversary, and an audience of observers. Debates rarely follow a structured format (except when school debate teams meet), and arguments often arise.[5] For instance, a staff member presents a proposal in an agency meeting, one or more persons criticize it, and its initiator then defends it. Persuaders sometimes hope to change the minds of both their immediate adversary and the audience that hears their argument—or, if they cannot change the views of their immediate adversary, to secure the support of the audience or of influential persons within it.

To better understand adversarial debates, assume that Harry Johnson, a lobbyist for an AIDS advocacy group, is attacking a conservative legislator's proposal to require all testing services, both public and private, to give state public health officials the names of all persons who test positive for HIV. He is debating the legislator before a student audience in the mid 1990s before many states had anti-discrimination statutes outlawing discrimination against gays and against persons who were HIV positive or had AIDS. In this context, many AIDS advocates feared requiring testing centers to give state public health officials the names of all persons who tested positive for HIV (so they, in turn, could inform their sexual partners) could lead to discrimination against HIV-positive persons and persons with AIDS. With the so-called cocktail of drugs not yet widely used in the mid 1990s, many AIDS activists were less likely to believe that sexual partners who had become HIV positive *could* be medically helped. It was in this context, then, that Harry Johnson debated a conservative legislator to oppose his proposal. To illustrate the array of arguments that debaters can use, Policy Advocacy Challenge 9.2 presents 12 arguments Johnson used in his debate.

**POLICY
ADVOCACY
CHALLENGE 9.2**

Attacking
Someone Else's
Proposal

Bruce Jansson,
Ph.D.

Johnson can do the following:

- *Attack the values implicit or explicit in the proposal.* A debater can contrast any value premise with an alternative value premise. While the legislator values control to protect the public's health, Johnson favors protecting the privacy and freedom of people who test positive for HIV. Such privacy, he contends, conforms to traditions embedded in the Bill of Rights. Persons who are HIV positive but might remain free of AIDS symptoms for many years particularly need privacy to protect them from discrimination.

- *Attack the proposal's feasibility.* Public health departments would ask HIV-positive individuals to list persons with whom they have had sexual relations. Department officials would then alert each of those partners to their possible infection with HIV. However, it is extremely time-consuming to develop these lists and to contact the persons on them, and health departments lack sufficient staff. "If public health officials lack the staff to adequately accomplish their existing functions, how can we expect them to assume these added functions?" Johnson might ask.

- *Attack the legislator's motives* by saying, "He wants a witch hunt, not humanistic services for those who are HIV positive."

- *Attack some unanticipated or adverse consequences of the proposal.* People who fear they carry the virus may avoid testing if the results are not confidential. Many people would forgo testing, fearing that their identity would be revealed to employers, landlords, and others.

- *Attack the legislator's use of specific analogies.* The legislator contends that public health departments have long required divulging the names of persons with syphilis and gonorrhea. The legislator says this information has led to successful efforts to alert sexual partners to their possible infection. To attack this analogy to other sexually transmitted diseases, Johnson notes that syphilis and gonorrhea are currently epidemics despite these practices. Moreover, discrimination against people with these treatable diseases is not nearly as marked, he might argue, as against persons who are HIV positive. Unlike syphilis and gonorrhea, the initial infection with HIV is often followed by a lengthy period—sometimes more than 10 years—when the person has no serious symptoms, much less AIDS. "If we breach the confidentiality of persons with a disease of such duration," Johnson argues, "we risk extended damage to their careers and reputations that does not occur with treatable diseases, such as syphilis."

- *Attack the legislator's uses of data and analytic assumptions.* The legislator contends that such action has already been successful in Colorado. Johnson criticizes specific quantitative studies that the legislator uses to buttress this claim. Johnson attacks the methods used to collect the data, the applicability of the Colorado data to his state, and the way the legislator has interpreted the data. (We discuss methods of criticizing quantitative studies in more detail in Chapter Fourteen.)

- *Attack implicit models of human motivation* in the legislator's rationale for the proposal. Requiring that testing centers report HIV-positive persons' names to the

(continued)

public health department implies that most HIV-positive persons will not voluntarily cooperate with public health officials. This assumption suggests that most HIV-positive persons lack a strong sense of social responsibility. Johnson asserts that many HIV-positive individuals are (or can become) concerned about former and current sexual partners if given access to high-quality counseling that does not infringe on their confidentiality. When they receive their test results, for example, they can be told about voluntary counseling and the need to inform current and prior sexual partners of their risks. Johnson also reframes the issue, moving away from forcing HIV-positive persons to assume social responsibility to providing assistance to HIV-positive persons to help them arouse their inherent altruism. The gay men's community's remarkable generosity to people with AIDS and the proliferation of support networks they have established support this contention.

- *Attack the legislator's conception of the chain of events that would follow the enactment of his proposal.* The legislator assumes that testing centers will provide the names of HIV-positive people to the state's public health department; this department will contact HIV-positive people; HIV-positive people will agree to provide the names of previous sexual partners or persons with whom they shared needles when using drugs; public officials will contact these partners; and the partners will agree to be tested for HIV, will practice safe sex, and, if they test positive, will provide public officials with the names of their partners. Johnson contends that this chain of events will often be broken at one, two, or more points. We have noted that public health departments often lack the staff to make these contacts. When forced to divulge names, some HIV-positive persons may decline to be cooperative because of the violation of their privacy and the imposition of mandatory procedures. In the case of casual sexual encounters or needle sharing, HIV-positive persons may be unable to supply names. Because of the population's mobility, it will be difficult to locate some of the partners, even if authorities have their names.

- *Expose the vagueness in the legislator's proposal,* which may make it seem less attractive to other people. Perhaps his proposal fails to describe how the testing services, some of them private ones, will be linked to the state's public health department. Perhaps the proposal fails to discuss how the mandatory reporting policy will be evaluated for its effectiveness in slowing the spread of HIV.

- *Attack unacceptable trade-offs in the legislator's proposal.* Johnson commends the legislator for wanting to stem the spread of HIV (a desirable objective) but argues that, noble as it may be, this objective should not cost tens of thousands of individuals their privacy (a valued objective) or cost the government exorbitant amounts. When making this kind of argument, the lobbyist says, in effect, that we need to stem the spread of HIV with methods that do not violate personal privacy and that are not so costly.

- *Argue that the legislator's proposal will be rendered ineffective by other events.* Argue, for example, that technology that allows individuals to test themselves for HIV in the privacy of their homes renders moot the mandatory reporting law, because many people bypass public or private testing centers.

- *Offer a counterproposal.* Because tracking partners is expensive, Johnson argues that scarce public resources ought instead to be invested in public education projects, such as efforts to promote safe sex by the use of condoms. Perhaps scarce resources should be invested in teaching addicts and prostitutes how not to become infected and how not to spread the disease to other people. The lobbyist might conclude that the state will get a far better return on funds invested in an educational program than in a mandatory reporting program.

Participants in social policy debates can also use arguments drawn from the analysis of social problems that we discussed in Chapters Two and Seven. Recall from the discussion at the end of Chapter Two that the Claude Fischer and many of his sociologist colleagues at the University of California at Berkeley attacked the assertion by Richard Hernstein and Charles Murray that African Americans had lower intelligence than white non-Latinos as measured by a specific test (the AFQT test)—and that their lower intelligence scores caused them to have higher rates of such social problems as unwed pregnancies, dropping out of school, and crime. Had they debated Hernstein and Murray in person, they would have used arguments drawn from social science research and theory that would have included contentions that Hernstein and Murray had:

- not sufficiently considered the effects of various environmental factors that caused some persons to be more likely to have these social problems, including effects of school, their adolescent community environment, years of schooling, and academic track
- used a variable ("intelligence" as measured by the AFQT test) that did not measure intrinsic intelligence, but was deeply influenced by the schooling and social class of persons who took the test
- placed undue emphasis on a single alleged cause (AFQT test scores) of many social problems rather than a network of factors
- failed to test their theory with various populations, such as within Africa and with other marginalized groups in the United States
- failed sufficiently to test their theory with low-income persons who were *not* African American
- used erroneous statistical procedures to analyze their data

Social science research and theory, then, can and should be used extensively in social-policy debates. Such research and theory is not a panacea, however. Persons can differ about the quality of specific research projects when citing them or when attacking opponents' use of them. Research findings sometimes conflict as is amply illustrated in the field of medicine when conflicting results emerge from efforts to test the efficacy of specific medications or treatments. Yet social science theory and research can provide valuable clues about the kinds of social policies that will effectively prevent or address specific social problems. In some cases, evidence-based policies can be identified from existing research—and some policies can be attacked in policy debates on grounds that they conflict with this research.

As an exercise in attacking someone else's policy proposal, attack Harry Johnson's arguments in light of the extraordinary progress that had been made against AIDS by mid-1998. New drug therapies had appeared that markedly cut death rates from AIDS. Strong legal protections had lessened discrimination against people with AIDS. In early 1997, New York began a program to test newborns for AIDS and to tell mothers of the results, rather than (as previously) telling the mothers only when they asked. Many public health officials around the nation had begun to urge the reporting of persons who tested HIV positive to public health officials. Colorado and New York State had begun more aggressively to implement a partner notification system even in 1998 so that partners of persons with HIV could get testing. By 2002, many AIDS advocacy groups came to support partner notification systems.

To hone your debating skills, assume you now are debating against Johnson's position in the preceding debate—from the vantage point of someone deeply committed to eradicating this cruel disease and helping persons with it to get effective medical treatment. What arguments would you use—and where would you attack Johnson's positions?

Coercive Messages

Policy advocates may use coercive messages when they believe that decision makers will oppose their position and that cooperative messages will not work because of decision makers' political and ideological stance, discriminatory attitudes, vested interests, and traditions. In addition, decision makers may feel that existing resources are already so committed to other programs that they cannot support a new program.[6]

Coercive messages often begin when persons make a formal demand that includes a threat, for example, to take further steps, such as litigation, protests, sending delegations to even higher authorities, or publicizing the issue through the mass media.[7]

Persons who use coercive messages often try to use the social context in ways that will place additional coercive pressure on decision makers. They may insist that they listen to a delegation, rather than to one person. They may physically surround them with members of their group. They may inform the mass media of an encounter before it has occurred to place even more pressure on decision makers—or seek favorable media coverage in the wake of a specific confrontation.

Coercive messages are effective in those situations where decision makers capitulate—whether because they accept the merits of the arguments of persons who confront them or because they fear political or other costs to themselves if the confrontation is not quickly resolved.

But coercive messages also have drawbacks. Perhaps decision makers become so angered at the tactics of persons who use them that they dig in their heels. Perhaps they retaliate against them.[8] For example, staff in an agency that use coercive messages with their executive director may be fired or demoted. Moreover, once coercive messages have been initiated by one side in a dispute, a vicious circle of escalating intransigency and reprisal may begin that makes it increasingly difficult for the opposing sides to cooperate. Both sides then begin to view the conflict as win-lose, rather than win-win, so that any concession to the other side becomes a personal defeat.[9]

POLICY ADVOCACY CHALLENGE 9.4

Will a Coercive Message in New Orleans Work?

Bruce Jansson, Ph.D.

In the immediate aftermath of Hurricane Katrina, officials from different levels of government blamed one another for the botched response to the needs of the citizens of New Orleans, who remained stranded in homes, hospitals, and the Superdome for days, often with no or few supplies.

It was to be expected that federal, state, and local officials would compete for position as another hurricane season loomed in late July 2006—or nearly a year after Hurricane Katrina had hit. Michael Chertoff, the Secretary of the federal Homeland Security Agency, did not beat around the bush when he gave Louisiana Governor Kathleen Blanco just 10 days to repair "serious gaps" in the state's hurricane preparations in a 9-page letter he sent her on July 17, 2006. Contending that the federal government had taken unprecedented steps to help Louisiana should another major hurricane strike, he said that it had signed contracts with bus, rail, and air companies to evacuate 141,000 persons. But he said the state had not made sufficient plans to get evacuees to pickup points. Nor had they identified an additional 75,000 shelter beds—a deficiency that would force many of them to place an unfair burden on other states when they had to evacuate to them. Nor had the state devised a list of special-needs medical patients to be evacuated and sheltered in a hurricane.

Chertoff's letter was quickly made public by the mass media.[1] Even though he also praised Governor Blanco for its hurricane preparations, his letter must be considered coercive in nature, not just for its tone, but because he gave her only 10 days to comply. If it backfired, Governor Blanco would dig in her heels—and would demand that the federal government correct its own flaws in preparations within a specific time limit. She might, moreover, ask her top staff to withdraw from discussions with top federal officials.

Governor Blanco fired off an 18-page letter on July 26th identifying her own misgivings about planning preparations—and making some specific requests of the federal government. This letter, too, was released to the mass media. She asked the Federal Emergency Management Agency (FEMA) to take responsibility for evacuating group trailer parks. She asked the federal government to station its transportation officials in the Movement Control Center in the state's Department of Transportation and Development rather than in its FEMA headquarters in Baton Rouge. She sought more funds and staff from the federal government to help it develop more beds in shelters. She sought federal funds to allow hospitals to raise their generators off the floor and to obtain other supplies so that patients in precarious health could remain in them during and after a hurricane.

Please address these questions:

1. Why would Secretary Chertoff and Governor Blanco resort to coercive messages in this situation as opposed, say, to private phone calls or meetings?
2. Why did they believe that coercive messages would be more successful than friendly persuasion?
3. If you were a resident of New Orleans just as a new hurricane season loomed, would you be comforted or alarmed by these letters when you read accounts of them in the *Times-Picayune*?

---

[1] See Bill Walsh, *The Times-Picayune* (July 18, 2006): p. 1.

Negotiations: Hardball and Win-Win Options

We have discussed both friendly and adversarial approaches to communication. Either approach—or some combination of the two—can be used in negotiations where different participants engage in an extended discussion to try to reach an agreement that will resolve an issue under contention. Let's start with a friendly approach.[10] Directors of two different programs in an agency must decide which of them will administer a new program that will bring considerable prestige and revenue to the person who wins. Rather than staking out a position at the outset, Mary Jones (who wants an amicable solution) encourages mutual discussion of the situation.

She encourages Jack Hoopes, the other administrator, to acknowledge that he would benefit from the added revenues and the challenge of running a new program, just as she would. Rather than moving toward rapid closure and a hardening of positions, Mary moves the discussion toward brainstorming, in which each of them imagines alternative solutions:

1. The new program goes to only one director.
2. The two directors jointly administer the new program.
3. One director receives basic authority for the program but gives the other director key roles in the new program, while retaining the program's revenue for his or her unit.
4. A rotational system is devised to give each of the directors a chance to administer the program.

To Jones's delight, Hoopes's initial adversarial stance has diminished by their third meeting. Already overburdened by other programs, he wants responsibility for only one facet of the new program. To underscore her desire to reach a conciliatory solution, Jones offers to cede to Hoopes one of her current programs that closely resembles other programs that he directs—and she makes this concession without a request by Hoopes. After only five meetings, Jones and Hoopes have not only concluded this negotiation, but in a win-win style that heightens their sense of mutual respect.

This win-win approach can be contrasted with a hardball or win-lose approach.[11] Assume that Jones and Hoopes strongly dislike one another, have already had repeated battles over turf and revenue, and want jurisdiction over the new program. Both believe that they will lose significant prestige to the other party if he or she gets control of the new program. In their first meeting, both of them state that they want control of the new program because it fits in with their existing programs and, fearing to appear weak, stick to this position during the next four meetings. The agency director then tells them that she will decide if they cannot reach an agreement, and Jones reluctantly implies that she will consider ceding the program to Hoopes, but only if she receives some of his existing programs in return. Convinced he has Jones at a disadvantage, Hoopes makes no concessions during the next three meetings, finally agreeing to cede a small program. Unsatisfied with this concession, Jones demands a larger program instead. Only after several additional stalemated meetings and another threat by the agency director to intercede, Hoopes agrees to Jones's request. Both parties leave the negotiations with renewed animus toward one another, determined not to yield any ground in future negotiations.

Hardball negotiations usually begin with each side presenting an initial position. As the negotiations proceed, each side decides whether and when to grant concessions to the other side—as a means of testing their intentions, as a sign of good faith, or as a quid pro quo for a concession the other side has made. As the negotiations proceed, each side has to decide how tolerable a stalemate would be, whether the other side will match its concessions, and when to make concessions. If both sides believe it is necessary to resolve the conflict, each party will gradually reveal where it is willing to make concessions. The two sides often use delays, veiled or open threats, and inducements to persuade the other side to make concessions.

We should not forget the role of mediator, who operates between contending factions. Assume that two opposing factions in your agency have been embroiled in conflict for a sustained period. They want to resolve the conflict but do not know how to achieve this resolution. You approach both parties with an offer to mediate the dispute, and they accept. After talking with both sides to better understand their position, you set up a meeting where you will act as mediator. During this meeting, your role is not to suggest solutions, but to facilitate a discussion in which both sides state their concerns and wishes, brainstorm possible solutions, and move toward a settlement. Several meetings may be needed. In more complex mediations, such as between members of a union and those of management in a social service agency, the two parties may meet separately and communicate only through the mediator. For mediation to be successful, each party to a conflict has to believe that the mediator will not manipulate the situation to the other's advantage, but will merely help the two sides to come to a settlement.[12]

In both adversarial and friendly negotiations, a positive outcome is not guaranteed. Even after a friendly start, two parties may become sufficiently stalemated so that no solution emerges. Or a solution may have to be imposed by a higher-level person or by an official *arbitrator* who is appointed to reach a solution. Arbitrators are frequently used in stalemated negotiations between labor and management.

Adversarial or Friendly Communication: Which Is Preferable?

Let there be no doubt: friendly communications and negotiations are preferable to adversarial ones in many situations. Parties to conflict can usually settle issues more rapidly when they accommodate one another, are more likely to emerge from friendly communications with respect for one another, and are more likely to develop creative solutions. Indeed, an extensive literature urges policy practitioners to make greater use of collaborative techniques.[13]

Yet friendly communications are not always possible. The relations between Michael Chertoff and Governor Blanco, discussed in Policy Advocacy Challenge 9.4 on page 305, illustrate this. The tense relations between these two persons were linked to their partisan differences since Chertoff represents the Administration of George W. Bush whereas Governor Blanco is a Democrat. It illustrates, as well, the high political stakes with both sides wanting *not* to be blamed if the response to another hurricane was flawed. Their tense relations were linked, as well, to the magnitude of resources needed to protect Gulf Coast citizens from another large hurricane. Both Governor Blanco and Secretary Chertoff believed that, if they capitulated to the other or let the other off the hook, they would risk blame or having to find huge resources.

In Table 9.1, we identify some situations where friendly and adversarial approaches are used. Policy advocates should first attempt conciliation to see if the opposing party will engage in collaborative problem solving. But if their conciliation fails and their opponent tries to steamroller them, they may have to use hardball strategies. (See Policy Advocacy Challenge 9.5.)

TABLE 9.1
Situations favoring friendly and adversarial approaches

Situation	Friendly approaches	Adversarial approaches
Relations between parties	Amicable	Hostile
How this issue has been discussed in the past	With low conflict and mutual concessions	With high conflict and few concessions
Extent to which one or both parties have a rigid position based on ideology or self-interest	Neither party has a fixed position at the outset	Both parties have fixed positions at the outset
Extent to which parties attach symbolic importance to issue (e.g., view a loss or victory as having extra-ordinary consequences)	Neither party attaches symbolic meaning to the outcome	Both parties believe a victory is vital to their well-being, to advance their self-interest or their ideology
Role of onlookers or followers	Onlookers do not pressure the parties to best each other	Onlookers pressure each party to best the other side
Extent to which parties value conciliation	Both parties value conciliation	Both parties value hardball tactics
The effects of the negotiating style	Low conflict and mutual concessions reinforce a win-win style	High conflict fosters more conflict and reinforces a win-lose style

POLICY ADVOCACY CHALLENGE 9.5

Using Hardball and Softball Styles of Negotiation in Preparing for New Hurricanes in New Orleans

BRUCE JANSSON, PH.D.

Try out conciliatory and hardball negotiating strategies between Secretary Chertoff and Governor Blanco with respect to "who does what" in preparations for the hurricane season beginning in late summer 2006 after re-reading Policy Advocacy Challenge 9.4 on page 305.

Create the negotiating situation by assigning different persons to the two sides. Assume that the two sides have still not resolved how to get hospitals prepared to house very sick patients in New Orleans during a hurricane, how to get 30,000 additional shelter beds, and how to get potential evacuees to specific places where they can get on busses, railroads, or airplanes. Address these preparation issues first in a hardball manner and have the two sides negotiate for, say, 40 minutes. (You can begin with a period where both sides state their entering positions for 5 minutes each—and then negotiate across a table for another 30 minutes.) Ask whether these hardball negotiations were successful or not.

Then try negotiating these issues in a softball manner for 50 minutes. Have each side in its opening presentation during the first 10 minutes ask conciliatory or open-ended questions of the other side. Then have members of each side discuss the issues in a nonconfrontational manner *outside* the official negotiations, while seated in a circle, for 15 minutes. Then have the two sides re-convene in an official negotiation to see if a plan can be developed that is acceptable to both sides. Ask whether these soft ball negotiations were successful or not. What differences existed between the processes and outcomes associated with them as compared to the hardball negotiations?

Discuss which style works best in different situations. Was it difficult to shift styles in midstream? What interpersonal skills are needed for each style?

Persuading Specific Audiences

We have mostly emphasized combative persuasion thus far even though we discussed softball negotiations as an alternative to hardball ones. Now we turn to *friendly persuasion,* which rests on techniques for changing an audience's beliefs and actions by engaging it in a cooperative transaction rather than by confronting it. When such persuasion is used skillfully, audiences are hardly aware that their perspective has changed or that the persuader has been using a carefully developed strategy.

We discuss several kinds of persuasion: written, verbal, and PowerPoint presentations.

Determining Objectives

Before persuaders can decide how to fashion a message, they have to establish objectives. Objectives can be ranked on a continuum extending from ambitious to modest. At the most ambitious level, persuaders hope both to markedly modify the audience's beliefs and to convince them to take specific actions, such as helping change a policy, performing specific tasks, or pressuring decision makers to support a proposed policy. At a somewhat more modest level, a persuader may be content, at least in the short term, merely to modify others' beliefs, perhaps as a precursor to having them take action. (As we will discuss later, changing people's beliefs does not necessarily cause them to change their actions.) Hoping eventually to convince an agency executive to support a new policy, a staff member might send him information about an unmet need in the community or a promising pilot project in another agency.

At any even more modest level, a policy advocate may wish merely to maintain an audience's beliefs and actions. Assume that some agency staff fear that someone will soon question a favored program, and they want to head off this attack by maintaining, or even strengthening, their director's support for the program. Assume as well that the director has funded the program relatively generously in the past. These staff members need to send messages that reinforce the program's importance so the director will not be unduly influenced by the impending attack.[14]

At a similarly modest level, a policy advocate may wish merely to educate or sensitize other persons about an issue or problem—perhaps as a preliminary step so that they will support a policy proposal at a subsequent point.

We also need to distinguish between the short- and long-term objectives of persuasion. When planning a message on one occasion, a policy advocate may have a relatively modest objective, such as sensitizing an audience to an issue. However, he or she may anticipate relaying a series of messages to an audience that will ultimately change their beliefs and rally their support of a new policy. Indeed, policy advocates often hope to persuade people bit by bit. A campaign might consist of interpersonal discussions, a memorandum, and a formal presentation, each planned to move an audience toward support of a policy.

It is more difficult to develop a series of presentations, of course, than to make a single presentation. In a series of presentations, the policy advocate must decide when to proceed beyond educating the audience to seeking their support for new policies and beliefs. The policy advocate does not want to proceed too cautiously or too rapidly from modest to ambitious objectives.

Diagnosing Audiences

Policy advocates often try to diagnose audiences. They want to know the audience's beliefs, degree of motivation on an issue, fears and hopes, and the extent to which situational or historical factors may influence their response to a message.[15]

When examining audiences' beliefs, policy advocates gauge the degree of opposition to their message. Audiences are most hostile to a message when they oppose both its value premises and its fundamental argument. When policy advocates seek to persuade a conservative audience to support softening some of the deterrent provisions of welfare reforms, for example, the audience is likely to disagree with their value premises that society is obliged to help impoverished people, that it should expand its social welfare roles, and that unemployment and low-paying jobs, rather than the size of the existing welfare grants, are the primary causes of expanding welfare rolls.

Audiences are less hostile when the value premises and logic of the message approximate their own beliefs or when they have a flexible or undefined position. When an audience has a broad zone of tolerance, it is open to new ideas, values, or perspectives. Advocates encounter a difficult challenge when the audience's zone of tolerance is relatively narrow.[16]

When an audience is hostile to a policy, persuaders have to try to figure out why. Indeed, theorists suggest that audiences are most receptive to messages relevant to their own fears and hopes. When a new agency program is proposed, for example, some staff may fear it will jeopardize their current responsibilities; divert funds from favored projects; or cause new burdens that they do not wish to shoulder, such as learning new skills or working longer hours. Skillful persuaders try to allay these kinds of fears in their messages, such as by contending that the new program will increase agency revenues, increase the agency's prestige, and allow some staff to migrate to challenging and interesting positions in the new program.[17] They might also appeal to the staff's commitment to the well-being of community residents by showing how the new program will help the agency's clientele.[18]

Audiences also differ in their levels of involvement in specific topics. All of us have been part of audiences that are disinterested in a message. Perhaps we have been inundated with boring messages about the same subject or do not perceive its relevance to us. In such cases, a novel or unusual argument is sometimes effective. (See Policy Advocacy Challenge 9.6.)

POLICY ADVOCACY CHALLENGE 9.6

Using a Novel Message

Patsy Lane, MSW, Director, Department of Human Services, City of Pasadena

During the time I was a member of the statewide Child Development Policy Board, state legislators and administrators were considering "loosening" the regulations for licensing child-care centers, as a cost-saving measure. One proposed change was to reduce child-care licensing staff by decreasing the required number of licensing staff's on-site visits to child-care programs. Such site visits were already perceived as dangerously few by the social service and child-care providers—in many cases, only once every few years. Various child and family advocacy groups tried to educate state decision makers that any reduction in such regulations would be detrimental to the quality of child care and would place children at risk. It was a challenge to find an effective way to communicate to legislators how problematic such a regulatory change would be: Often, the objections were dismissed as overly protective of children.

Finally, a staff person of the Child Development Policy Board submitted a very effective one-page chart: a comparison of inspection requirements for child-care facilities with those for dog kennels. Dog kennels, it seemed, averaged a regulatory site visit every 6 months, while child-care facilities averaged one such visit every 2 years. This comparison created a dilemma for elected state officials and administrators: Would they be perceived as valuing the safety and care of dogs in kennels much higher than those of children in licensed child care?

Outcome   Shortly thereafter, the proposed reduction in regulatory visits to child-care facilities was dropped.

Lessons Learned   A key lesson in this case was the importance of how a message is communicated. Sometimes, the logical, professional, well-researched, well-documented approach (i.e., "regular site visits prevent problems and promote good child-care practice") does not succeed in advancing good policy and practice, so look for other creative ways to frame and illustrate the issue.

The social context may influence the audience's response to a particular measure. If a social agency is cutting costs, for example, its staff members are unlikely to support a costly new program. Audiences' responses also are influenced by prior events. If, for example, a specific issue has been presented previously to some members of an audience, their recollections of prior discussions, which they may communicate to those who were not present, can powerfully shape the whole audience's responses. If an issue was divisive, it may generate extensive conflict when it is reintroduced. By contrast, policy issues associated with positive traditions often have a good chance of being met with a positive audience response.[19]

Until now, we have assumed that audiences' viewpoints are relatively homogeneous. In fact, audiences usually contain a range of perspectives; one faction may support a new policy, while another faction may be opposed. Practitioners must identify a mixed audience's factions.[20] They should decide how to address the subgroups in their messages, perhaps appealing first to one segment of the audience ("Some of you fear that . . .") and then to another ("Others of you believe that . . ."). Even when audiences have divergent perspectives, policy advocates can identify and appeal to common values, hopes, or aspirations, saying, for example, "Despite our differences on this issue, we all agree that this agency needs to diversify its services."

Tailoring Objectives to the Audience   Policy advocates often establish objectives that are either too modest or too ambitious. Persuaders may falsely believe that an audience is so hostile to their message that they can hope to achieve only minor changes. By contrast, persuaders establish unrealistic expectations if they falsely believe that their audience is similar to themselves. Those with liberal perspectives, for example, may unrealistically expect to make an extremely conservative audience accept a policy that stems from liberal premises, only to find that the message merely unites the audience in its preexisting opposition to knee-jerk liberals.

Strategies of Persuasion

With objectives, audience, and situation in mind, policy advocates must develop a persuading strategy by selecting a medium, a sequence of presentations, a format, and a presentation style. After discussing these components, we will discuss tactics for specific audiences.

Selecting a Medium

Persuaders rely on symbols, such as words and visual aids, to influence audiences' ideas and actions, but they can present these symbols in many ways: through speech, documents, graphic aids, or some combination of these methods. Because these modes of communication are so familiar, we often do not consider their relative merits.

PowerPoint presentations have become ubiquitous in the United States. They couple verbal content with PowerPoint slides. They can also include video content and music in a format that can powerfully influence the views of an audience. We present an example of a PowerPoint presentation at this chapter's conclusion in Policy Advocacy Challenge 9.11.

Public speaking allows presenters to interact with the audience. Oral communication allows persuaders to be flexible; if they are skilled at thinking on their feet, they can change their message midway through to respond to perceived fears and hopes that will impede or facilitate a positive response. When persuaders want an audience to become emotionally involved in an issue, they often use arguments that culminate in a call to audience members to support a cause actively.[21]

Written communications, such as memoranda, letters, and reports, allow precision, unlike spoken communication, where definitions and details are often relatively vague. When presenters want audiences to commit themselves to a course of action, they can elicit relatively binding agreements with documents; a memo, for example, may ask people to check a specific category, such as "agree or support," "disagree," or "undecided." Written communications are useful in explaining technical subjects, such as the implementation details for a specific policy or a summary of existing research; it is difficult to convey technical subjects in brief addresses.[22]

Graphic materials, such as graphs and slides, simplify complex materials and often help capture the attention of a hostile or indifferent audience. Someone seeking support for vulnerable populations, for example, can use pictures or slides to promote sympathy or interest. If used to excess, however, graphic materials can lose an audience's attention.[23]

Certain rules should be observed when using PowerPoint slides or other graphic materials. The slides themselves must be relatively simple. Indeed, some persons contend they should contain no more than five or six words. If they are complex and contain too many words, members of the audience become so absorbed with reading them that they lose touch with the central themes that the presenter seeks to emphasize. If they contain too many words, moreover, the presenter often succumbs to the temptation to read them to the audience—often not even looking at members of the audience. Slides are merely *aids* for a presentation and should not divert the audience excessively from the presenter and her or his message. It is often fine to augment PowerPoint slides with pictures drawn from the Internet, diagrams, or audio effects such as music—but such augmentation must itself be done with caution so that the slides to not detract from the presenter or the presenter's message.

When using PowerPoint slides, then, considerable attention must be given to the text that the presenter gives as she or he displays the slides. The presenter should devote some or considerable time during the presentation to words *not* on the slides, even perhaps leaving the screen blank during portions of the presentation to reinforce her or his relationship with the audience.

These provisos should not suggest the PowerPoint slides cannot be highly effective—merely that they must be viewed as only a part of a larger message. Presenters want audiences to emerge from their presentation impressed by the slides—but, even more important, by them and their messages.

Using a Sequence of Presentations

When we envision presentations, we customarily think of one effort to convince an audience to take a specific position on an issue. In fact, skilled persuaders realize that they will be more effective if they use a sequence of persuasive encounters—a variety of written, interpersonal, and other communications, perhaps culminating in a formal presentation. A persuader might first use some informal personal encounters to discover where people stand on an issue and what they fear or dislike to initiate the process of changing the audience's knowledge or beliefs.[24] She might then plan a meeting to educate her audience about an issue as a prelude to a meeting to take action.

Selecting a Format

When you do a formal presentation to an audience, the format is critical. Every speech has a beginning, middle, and an end. Your challenge is to command your audience's attention at the outset, impart important substantive information in the middle, and conclude with the presentation's essential purpose (such as persuading the audience to take action, set up a committee, or take a specific problem seriously).

It is essential to decide what you want the audience to do as a result of your presentation, for example, to set up a committee to study an issue, to take a condition very seriously, or to gain new knowledge. Once you have decided on your objective, you can develop a format that will achieve it.

Do not lock yourself into a single format prematurely. Try different versions of your speech. Think about novel points you can make at the outset or in the conclusion that will appeal to your audience. Brainstorm to develop alternative outlines.

Skilled policy advocates use basic formats tailored to specific kinds of communications. These formats establish an integrating logic for a presentation. Seven such formats are given in Box 9.1.[25]

Our discussion suggests that policy presenters should tailor their outline to the subject they are discussing. While outlines can take different forms, they need to include a logical sequence of topics that structures the presentation for both the presenter and the audience.

Fine-Tuning a Presentation   Once presenters have developed a medium, analyzed the audience, and developed an outline, they can fine-tune the presentation in numerous ways and, in the process, revise the outline. Presenters often use specific techniques to make a presentation more interesting to the audience. They may add case examples to capture the audience's attention. They may elicit audience participation during part of the presentation by asking, "Which of these options do you prefer?" or "Can you think of an option I have not considered?" They may use a particular visual aid, such as a chart distributed to the audience or presented by overhead projector.

B O X   9 . 1 | Alternative Formats for Policy Advocates

To discuss how a problem developed, you can use a *time* structure of the sequence of events that caused the problem. Such a speech might begin, "I want to discuss how the problem with our agency's intake procedures developed by taking you through a sequence of events."

A. Intake procedures in 1985.
B. Revisions of intake procedures in 1986.
   1. Why revisions were made.
   2. The nature of the revisions.
C. Changes in the composition of our agency's clients between 1987 and 1991.
D. Intake problems caused by these changes in clientele.
E. Options we should consider in revising our intake procedures again.
   1. Option 1.
   2. Option 2.
F. Call for a task force or committee to make recommendations.

To explain a problem, you can use a *topical* structure that discusses a problem's components. Such a speech might begin, "I want to discuss operating problems in our agency as a prelude to some policy recommendations."

A. We are experiencing a number of problems in our agency's program for school dropouts.
   1. Problem 1.
   2. Problem 2.
   3. Problem 3.
B. Relationships among these three problems.
C. Options we should consider to address these problems.
   1. Option 1.
   2. Option 2.
   3. Option 3.

To establish that a problem exists and needs attention, you can use a *criticism* structure to describe the problem and the criteria for demonstrating that it is a problem. For example, you might say, "Our intake procedures are faulty because clients with serious problems do not receive prompt attention and because the procedures are unfair."

A. An overview of our intake procedures.
B. Why our intake procedures need to be overhauled.
   1. Problems of fairness.
   2. Problems encountered by clients who are denied immediate service.
   3. Administrative problems.
   4. Staffing problems.
C. The need to collect more information about Problems 2 and 4.
D. Call for a committee to collect the information and make some recommendations.

B O X   9 . 1   *(continued)*

To show a cause-effect relationship, use an *association* structure. Say, "I want to discuss how the problem with our intake procedures stems from the rapid increase in our waiting list."

A. Discuss problems with the intake policy.
B. Discuss specific changes in the nature of the clientele using the agency during the past five years.
C. Link the problems with the changes in clientele.
D. Discuss possible implications for changing intake policy.

To gain acceptance of a plan, use an *argument* structure, where you present the elements of the problem and the central features of your corrective plan. Begin, "I want to discuss why our intake policies are faulty and then present a five-part plan to deal with the situation."

A. Discuss problems with the intake policy.
B. Provide solutions.
C. Discuss how the solutions address specific criteria.
   1. Administrative feasibility.
   2. Fairness.
   3. Cost.

To criticize someone else's statement of a problem or plan, use a *refutation* structure, where you state his or her central tenets and then present your arguments about why they are flawed. Say, "I want to discuss why the plan Susan Smith offered to correct our intake system is flawed."

A. Provide an overview of the intake problems.
B. Describe the central elements of Smith's plan.
C. Discuss how it fails to address certain criteria.
   1. It is not administratively feasible.
   2. It is not fair to certain kinds of clients.
   3. It would be too costly.
D. Discuss an alternative approach and why it is better.

To influence people to take action, use a *directive* structure, where you state the reasons why immediate emergency action is needed. You might say, "This situation is urgent. We should send a delegation at once to see the head of the welfare agency."

A. Why this problem has taken on urgency.
   1. Effects on clients.
   2. Possible political ramifications.
   3. Implications for our funding.
B. Why a delay in addressing it would be calamitous.
C. Alternative courses of action.
   1. Write a letter.

(continued)

BOX 9.1 | *(continued)*

> 2. Contact the head of the welfare agency by telephone.
> 3. Send a delegation.
> 4. Other actions.
> D. A call to action.
>   1. Send a delegation.
>   2. Have the delegation make the following arguments.
>   3. Supplement the delegation with other actions.
>   a. Call the mayor.
>   b. Contact a member of the county board of supervisors.

The following is an illustrative presentation to the staff of an agency about its flawed intake procedures. The speech is based on an outline and uses a criticism structure.

- Initial statement, an overview of the presentation: "I will discuss three reasons why I think our intake policies are flawed."
- Supporting arguments: "Why do I think they are flawed?"
  - Certain clients with serious conditions have to wait long periods. (Discuss Client A as an example.)
  - Certain kinds of people drop off the waiting list disproportionately. (Discuss Client B as an example.)
  - Our waiting-list procedures frustrate certain clients. (Discuss Client C as an example.)
- Ask the audience to share any experiences they have had with the intake procedures.
- Recommendation: Establish a committee to find alternative ways to structure our intake procedures.

Developing an Effective Presentation Style

Your effectiveness as a presenter is based not only on the substantive content of your presentation, but also on your *delivery style,* including your relationship with the audience, your speech patterns, and your use of gestures.[26]

You have to feel comfortable with your basic outline before you begin your presentation, and you need to have rehearsed it so that you need only to look at the bold headings from time to time as you make the presentation. Most audiences like presenters to make eye contact with them.

To offset the fear that you will ramble, you may start by explaining the presentation's basic logic, that is, the basic points you will cover. Select an interesting case example, visual image, or analogy to gain the audience's attention at once. Make clear transitions as you move from topic to topic with statements like, "Having discussed why intake procedures are flawed, we can now move to possible remedies." Wrap things up with a thoughtful conclusion that draws on the preceding sections of your presentation.

Try to avoid distracting habits, such as fumbling with papers, using excessively rapid or slow speech patterns, or pacing back and forth. Some experts in presentation videotape themselves before making presentations to discern the unconscious, distracting mannerisms that all of us have.

What do you do if you are frightened about making speeches? Most important, try not to run away from public speaking opportunities, as difficult as they may seem. Some of us develop fright instincts when making speeches and we can break these patterns only with practice. Many people find it useful to pause momentarily before speaking to gain equilibrium, to collect their thoughts, and to remind themselves of the presentation's outline.

Tactics for Specific Audiences

You will want to modify your outline as you consider the likely nature of your audience, which may be hostile, apathetic, or expert.

Policy advocates sometimes encounter *hostile audiences* with values or beliefs that predispose them to oppose a specific message. Various techniques can decrease hostility. You can identify common values, perspectives, and practical concerns that link you to the audience. These links may be common group memberships, educational affiliations, or demographic traits. Or you can appeal to higher values that you share with the audience, by saying, for example, "All of us share concern for the homeless people we see on the streets." Some policy advocates seek conservatives' support for social programs by appealing to their patriotism; if Americans want the nation to remain competitive in international markets, these advocates may argue, they need to address the high dropout rate in schools.[27]

You can establish your credibility with hostile audiences by citing authorities or experts the audience is likely to respect and by discussing credentials or experiences of your own that increase your credibility. To seem reasonable, you can present both sides of complex issues and freely admit that alternative viewpoints are inevitable. Rather than beginning with your conclusion, you can build a case, hoping that your evidence will gradually change the audience's view of an issue. You might reach your eventual proposal only after rejecting or refuting alternative positions.[28]

Humor often defuses tense situations. Some persuaders make fun of themselves so the audience perceives them as unceremonious and unpretentious. If told with skill, anecdotes at the start of a presentation may ease audiences into subjects they find difficult or stressful.

Apathetic audiences present similar challenges. It is important not to overwhelm apathetic audiences with complex arguments or data, which will intensify their apathy. Nor is it wise to tell the audience that they should care about an issue, an intrusive technique likely to make them retreat even further into apathy. The skillful persuader makes the presentation interesting and lively, stresses few themes or arguments, presents a simple argument, and offers interesting and unusual evidence that the audience has not heard before.[29]

The members of *expert audiences* perceive themselves to be well versed in the presentation topic. Presenters need to offer an array of perspectives and evidence to such audiences, admitting that the existing knowledge is imperfect and that choices are difficult. They need to discuss the merits of alternative options and not move quickly to a single solution. The presenter should pay tribute to the audience's expertise by recognizing that they have thought extensively about the subject and, perhaps, by eliciting their opinions or suggestions.[30]

Other Tactical Choices

Additional tactics help presenters modify their outlines.

Single-sided or Two-sided Arguments?   Should persuaders present the strongest possible argument for a specific policy (a single-sided argument), or should they consider both sides of an issue (a two-sided argument)? Some social psychologists suggest two-sided arguments for critical or hostile audiences because the persuader anticipates and defuses some criticisms and therefore appears reasonable and open-minded. Single-sided arguments are more effective with audiences that share the values of the speaker.[31]

How Much Dissonance?   All persuaders want to change their audience's beliefs, but they have to decide how much dissonance, or discrepancy between the audience's beliefs and the proposal, to introduce. If they ask for massive changes, they risk alienating the audience. If they ask for minor changes, they risk undermining possible support for more extensive change.

When persuaders anticipate hostility, they should probably not begin by suggesting massive changes. Several presentations should be scheduled, the first one seeking to educate the audience, rather than to secure a commitment to major change. A sympathetic audience is more immediately open to a commitment to major change.[32]

Climax or Anticlimax?   Social psychologists' findings on whether the beginning of a presentation or the end makes the strongest impression are contradictory, but either the introductory or the concluding portion of a speech is the strongest, and the weakest points should be inserted in the middle sections.[33]

Who Should Present?   When a choice exists, persuaders need to ponder carefully who should present information to a specific audience. Presenters to hostile or apathetic audiences should have either high credibility with them or styles of communication suited to overcoming hostility and apathy. It is sometimes useful for multiple presenters to give different portions of a presentation.[34]

Adapting the Setting   Skillful persuaders sometimes find or create a setting conducive to reaching a specific audience. Intimate settings may be chosen over formal settings to increase rapport. Seating arrangements may be devised to facilitate exchanges between the presenter and the audience. Graphic aids, such as slides, may overcome an audience's apathy. Sometimes, an audience is broken into smaller groups that later reconvene to share their solutions to a specific problem.[35]

Honoring Protocols and Expectations   Audiences often have specific expectations about a presentation. Legislators, for example, expect testimony to legislative committees to be relatively brief—not more than 10 or 15 minutes.[36] (Detailed materials and the text of the presenter's comments are submitted separately.) An audience may have certain expectations regarding the formality, tenor, and style of a presentation. An audience of persons who consider themselves experts on a subject expect the presenter to offer alternative viewpoints, whereas an audience of activists often expects a call to action. To understand these expectations, presenters need to speak with audience members before their presentation or with people familiar with the audience.

Assembling a Strategy

To illustrate persuading strategy, let's examine how Harry Johnson, our lobbyist for an AIDS advocacy group who was introduced in Policy Advocacy Challenge 9.2, develops strategy to secure support for legislative reforms for people with AIDS.

The Hostile Audience

Suppose that Harry wants to convince some conservative Republicans—the people most likely to be critical of the gay community and to believe that people with AIDS "brought it on themselves"—to support a major legislative initiative. The legislation would expand the state's funding of home health care programs to serve people with AIDS. It would cover homemaker, visiting-nurse, and physical therapy services. Both Medicaid recipients and people considerably above the poverty line would receive these services. (Currently, counties fund most state home-health services, but only for individuals who meet restrictive income standards.) Admittedly, the new program will be expensive, because many people with AIDS who are not eligible for existing county programs will need extended home-health services.

Even before the presentation, Harry enlists the assistance of several sympathetic Republican legislators, who agree to moderate the sessions and expedite discussion. He wants his introduction to make at least some of the conservative legislators perceive the problem in human, personal terms rather than abstract, ideological ones. He decides to present several case histories of HIV-positive people who have encountered difficulty when seeking home-based services. To decrease the audience's perception of the problem as belonging only to gay radicals, he relates several cases of conservative Republicans who have contracted the disease. He also makes analogies with older people and people with disabilities to communicate that the AIDS population's home-health needs and problems are similar to those of other, more accepted populations. He concludes the first presentation with a question-and-answer session about the dimensions of the problem.

Johnson wants the audience to be favorable to a legislative proposal that a bipartisan group has tentatively drafted. He decides to use a format with a two-sided argument. He acknowledges that some persons in the audience may believe that existing policy is sufficient—and he does note that it is less expensive simply to use the home health services currently funded by Medicaid in his state. But he then discusses why an expanded home-health program, with broader eligibility criteria than Medicaid, would be worth considering. Even here, he discusses different options and their likely cost to the state—and their plusses and minuses. He wants to project an image of reasonableness and attentiveness to cost, since he knows that his conservative audience values these attributes. At the end of the presentation, he makes the best case possible for the legislative proposal that the bipartisan group has tentatively drafted. He encourages questions from the audience at the end of the presentation, showing how the bipartisan group considered them when drafting the legislation. He concludes by seeking the support of the group for the proposal, while also planning to seek some revisions in the proposal from the bipartisan group so that the proposal can be altered to make it more appealing to some conservative legislators.

In developing this plan for his presentation, Johnson rejects other alternatives, such as a call to action, a format that allows no give-and-take with the audience, and a discussion that does not focus on the likely cost of the proposal. He hopes later to re-convene this group of conservatives when he can show them that he has secured some changes in the bipartisan draft that will draws upon their comments.

The Sympathetic Audience with Some Hostile Members

The legislative proposal is introduced into a legislative committee with many sympathetic members but some hostile ones. Johnson, who hopes to intensify support for the proposal, encounters the dilemma of addressing a mixed audience. Should he write off the minority and direct his comments to the sympathetic members, or should he target his comments to the hostile minority because he already expects the majority to support the proposal?

Johnson decides to focus his comments on those who are sympathetic but to include points in his presentation that will attract some votes from those who are hostile. (The sympathetic do not need an extended argument and want only a brief, dramatic message to energize them to support the proposal.) Indeed, he focuses his presentation on a particularly poignant case. To appeal to the hostile members, however, he selects a case that illustrates how providing a homemaker and other services will allow some people with AIDS to remain productive workers (and hence taxpayers) for a longer period than if these services are unavailable.

The Expert Audience

Johnson also seeks support for the proposal from hospital administrators, whose professional association wields power within the state. Unlike most legislators, who have scant knowledge of the intricacies of health care programs, hospital administrators are familiar with the existing programs. Therefore, Johnson decides to emphasize practical cost and administrative issues, such as how the proposal will be implemented, how the state will monitor it, and how it will affect the duration of hospitalization of people with AIDS.

To enhance his rapport with this audience, Johnson cites evidence and arguments obtained from a hospital administrator and some hospital social workers who specialize in discharge planning. Because the proposal's funds will be funneled through nonprofit agencies, he discusses how these agencies will coordinate their services with hospitals. Throughout his presentation, Johnson elicits input from the experts, both to obtain their insights and to make it clear that he respects their expertise.

Interpersonal Discussions

As this legislation progresses from initial proposal to drafted legislation to (it is hoped) enacted legislation, Johnson will have countless discussions with foes and friends of the legislation, officials in the state's bureaucracies, local officials, and community activists. These discussions will take many forms. In some of them, Johnson will solicit information about people's positions, biases, and perspectives, thus maintaining a fact-finding posture. Of course, his patience will be tested when individuals are hostile toward people with AIDS, like the legislator who maintains that "persons who contract AIDS should bear all the costs of home health care even if it makes them destitute." As Lewis Dexter suggests, the lobbyist should remain "benevolently neutral" in some of these hostile discussions.[37] While he need not agree with these legislators, he need not attack them either. Indeed, he might say, "We share a desire to bring this epidemic under control. What are your ideas about how to help people with AIDS remain productive members of society in the interim?"

In some of these discussions, Johnson uses a directive format, seeking support for the proposal. He asks the leader of an advocacy group to mobilize support for the legislation by obtaining letters and phone calls from key legislators' constituents. He also uses a combination of flattery and emotional language: "We've turned to you many times in the past, and you have never let us down. How do you think we can place pressure on these five legislators who are possible swing votes?"

Other discussions follow a substantive format, such as those with health experts. In these conversations, Johnson seeks assistance in defining the home-health needs of people with AIDS, the potential cost of specific provisions in the legislation, and the administrative considerations.

We can often improve our presentation skills by studying the work of successful presenters. (See Policy Advocacy Challenge 9.7.)

POLICY ADVOCACY CHALLENGE 9.7

Diagnosing Why Specific Speeches Are Successful

Bruce Jansson, Ph.D.

For a compilation of the top 100 speeches in American history with persons ranging the full political spectrum from Martin Luther King and Jesse Jackson to Ronald Reagan and Richard Nixon, go to **http://www.americanrhetoric.com/top100speechesall.html**.

Select and listen to one of them (your computer will need audio capabilities). Ask:

- What goal or objective did the speechmaker seem to have?
- What audience did he or she address and how was the speech tailored to them?
- How was the speech organized?
    - What did the speechmaker emphasize at the beginning of the speech?
    - What middle-speech content did he/she have?
    - How did the speechmaker finish the speech?
- How did the speech maker's style of presentation enhance or detract from the speech
- Summarize briefly why you think this speech was ranked as one of the top 100 in recent American history?

Gaining Support for Grant Proposals

When constructing proposals, such as legislative proposals, proposals to establish new programs in agencies, and grant proposals, policy advocates find that specific strategies often make their proposals more enticing to decision makers and funders. We focus here on a grant proposal written from an agency site. At first glance, some readers may wonder whether grant proposals are policy proposals, since they do not involve legislation. In fact, grant proposals are part of policy advocacy. They seek resources, after all, to fund innovative policies of agencies and agency networks. In many cases, they allow expansion of services to underserved populations. They often establish new programs. They are, in fact, agency counterparts to legislative proposals. Let's return to our discussion from the preceding chapter of the social work intern who wanted resources to expand translation services for Latinos in the hospital where she had her internship.

Writing an Imaginative Title

Policy advocates should develop creative, eye-catching titles for their proposals—titles that will attract support from a wide range of persons. In naming her proposal in a foundation grant, for example, the student intern could select a purely descriptive title, such as "Increasing Translating Services to Latinos in XYZ Hospital." Alternatively, she could select a more imaginative title, such as "Linking the University with a Hospital to Help Latinos Navigate the Health System."

Giving a Compelling Rationale

Proposal writers have to provide a compelling rationale, or decision makers and funders will perceive their proposal as addressing trivial problems.[38] Bear in mind that most proposals must compete with many others, and in the winnowing process, proposals that are perceived to be unimportant are likely to be discarded.

The student intern should provide dramatic instances of harm to Latino patients caused by the lack of translation services. She should present data that show the desperate shortage of translating services, as well as the likelihood that this shortage will not be redressed by the hospital in the near term. She could provide quotations from physicians, nurses, and social workers that confirm the shortage of translators, as well as the adverse effects of this shortage on patients.

Drawing on Research Findings

Some innovative policies hinge on the research and conceptual work we discussed in Chapter Six. The student intern might find data demonstrating that Latino patients without adequate translation services suffer specific consequences in medical transactions. Or she might find data from a pilot project in another setting where student volunteers have successfully served as interpreters.

Setting Clear Objectives

Proposals fare best when they contain clear objectives.[39] The student intern ought to estimate the number of patients who would be helped annually by her student volunteers, both overall and on specific units. She should estimate how many students would be recruited to be volunteers. Objectives are often made clearer when they are linked to specific time lines. Perhaps the intern would allow 3 months to recruit and train her 40 students as a prelude to moving ahead with the translation services.

Including an Evaluation Component

Policy advocates often include an evaluation component in their proposals to gauge whether their innovation has been successful.[40] The student intern might propose gathering data directly from Latino patients who have used the volunteer students. Or she might propose gathering data from medical staff, nurses, and social workers. She might also ask the students to evaluate the project, asking whether they have received adequate training and whether they have expanded their knowledge of the health care system.

Demonstrating Feasibility

Laudatory as a proposal may be, decision makers and funders must believe that it is feasible.[41] The student intern would need to answer such questions as the following: Do top hospital and university administrators favor the proposal, and will they cooperate with it? Who will be in charge of the program's implementation? Has the student intern already located a competent coordinator whose qualifications are included in her proposal? Where will the project be housed? How will the volunteer students be trained? In what accounts will the project's funds be kept? Who will audit or oversee the budget? And how long will it take to get the program up and running?

Establishing Partnerships

Many policy innovations are not accepted by legislatures or private funding sources because they are not clearly linked to other programs, whether through joint planning, referral networks, joint programs, or shared facilities. These partnership links must be clearly articulated. The student intern should discuss how she would gain the cooperation of local colleges and hospital administrators in her project and how she would get these administrators to work together.

Demonstrating Support

Proposals rarely are approved if they lack substantial support.[42] The student intern should attach letters of support for her project from top college and hospital administrators, as well as from community leaders. When people introduce legislative proposals, they often try to get a range of legislators to be cosponsors.

Proposals are strengthened, moreover, if they demonstrate tangible support. Perhaps the hospital and university will agree to provide some funding for the project, and to make in-kind contributions such as donating office space, equipment, supplies, and staff time.

Many foundations also want evidence that other institutions will contribute to a project once foundation or government funding ceases. Perhaps the student intern could obtain assurances from university and hospital staff that they will assume a larger share of the project's funding after several years.

Developing a Realistic Budget

Policy advocates must develop realistic budgets that clearly state what magnitude of resources are needed and how they will be used. If advocates seek excessive funding, foundations and legislators may see their proposals as wasteful. If they seek funding that is clearly inadequate, funders may regard the proposal as unrealistic. The student intern would need to write a so-called line item budget that shows the precise funds needed for different categories of expenditures, such as salaries, supplies, transportation, rent, mailings, and telephone.[43]

Finding Funders

The student intern has to search for potential foundation funders for her proposal. These foundations include corporate foundations, small family foundations, large foundations, and community foundations. Corporate foundations typically give small grants to projects where their corporate headquarters (or major installations) are located. They are particularly fond of sponsoring events, like luncheons, and giving in-kind contributions, like supplies or copy machines. Small family foundations are established by wealthy individuals who typically give relatively few grants each year compared with large foundations. Some large foundations, like the Ford and Rockefeller Foundations, usually fund ambitious proposals with national implications, unlike other large foundations that emphasize grants to specific parts of the country. Community foundations, such as the Rhode Island Foundation, the Milwaukee Foundation, or the California Community Foundation, are quasi-public entities that have some public officials, as well as community leaders, on their boards. (See Policy Advocacy Challenge 9.8) Their charters require them to make grants exclusively in their local jurisdictions.[44]

POLICY ADVOCACY CHALLENGE 9.8

Finding Funders Via the Web

STEPHANIE DAVIS, REFERENCE LIBRARIAN

Following are some useful references for fundraising and grant writing in the human services:

Cheryl Clarke, *Storytelling for Grantseekers: The Guide to Creative Nonprofit Fundraising* (San Francisco: Jossey-Bass, 2001).

Kim Klein, *Fundraising for Social Change,* 4th ed. (San Francisco: Jossey-Bass, 2001).

Mal Marwick and Stephen Hitchcock, *Ten Steps to Fundraising Success: Choosing the Right Strategy for Your Organization* (San Francisco: Jossey Bass, 2002).

Mal Marwick, Ted Hart, and Nick Allen, eds., *Fundraising on the Internet: The e-Philanthropy Foundation.org's Guide to Success Online* (San Francisco: Jossey-Bass, 2002).

Flexibility is critical in finding funding sources, as discussed in Policy Advocacy Challenge 9.9.

POLICY ADVOCACY CHALLENGE 9.9

Creatively Seeking Funding Sources

PATSY LANE, MSW, DIRECTOR, DEPARTMENT OF HUMAN SERVICES OF THE CITY OF PASADENA

While serving as an administrator for VOALA (a large nonprofit organization), we were seeking funds to rehabilitate an old, deteriorated skid-row hotel and convert it to a new alcohol detoxification, recovery, and support service site. Funding specifically for such a project was very limited, but in our search, we learned that the federal Department of Housing and Urban Development had something called an Urban Development Action Grant (UDAG). At first glance, UDAG funding did not seem relevant to our proposed creation of an alcohol recovery and social service site, but as we reviewed the category called "Neighborhood Revitalization," we began to rethink our project. It seemed apparent that to rehab a deteriorated skid-row hotel and create a new hub offering a range of social and health services (including addressing local problems with public inebriates) would eliminate an area of "urban blight" and revitalize a neighborhood —key criteria for UDAG funding. We redesigned the concept, broadening the range of health, housing, and social services and including information and education activities to further enhance the neighborhood.

Outcome Our organization submitted the grant proposal, and the project was awarded $1.6 million in UDAG funds.

Lessons Learned Most human service programs have multiple outcomes, address multiple issues, and fit into more than one funding category. Flexibility and creative design are keys to making a project fundable by a variety of potential sources. If you view a potential project from a limited perspective, or as a single-category item, you may miss out on key opportunities for funding, partnerships, collaboration, and other resources.

Revising the Proposal

Proposals rarely emerge full-blown from first drafts; they are gradually developed in an evolutionary process. Amendments to bills are written in successive committee deliberations during the legislative process. Grant proposals to foundations, government authorities, and other funding bodies also are extensively revised as they are drafted.

In some cases, the framer will write a one-page version and circulate it to other persons, including a staff member in a foundation or a government agency. A later version, which may be four or five pages long, will be circulated for comments again as a prelude to a lengthier final version.

Translating complex ideas into fluent prose requires considerable skill. Excessive jargon, long-windedness, complex sentences, and poor syntax diminish interest in a proposal. Many decision makers, such as legislators, who lack technical understanding, are disinclined to read dense, lengthy materials. Policy practitioners sometimes err, of course, in the opposite direction; if their proposal is too brief and fails to address important issues, their work may be discarded as superficial.

We provide an example of a grant proposal in Policy Advocacy Challenge 9.10 that social worker Katrina Gould developed while she interned in an AIDS program.

POLICY ADVOCACY CHALLENGE 9.10

Writing a Grant Proposal: The AIDS Preventive Education Project

KATRINA GOULD, MSW

Problem Statement

The city council of Pasadena received a report from the City Health Officer on "The Status of AIDS in Pasadena." As a result, the city council appointed the Pasadena AIDS Strategic Planning Task Force. The task force was charged with developing a proactive plan to determine what Pasadena and public and private organizations could do to address the AIDS crisis.

The task force consisted of Pasadenans, including AIDS service providers, politicians, persons with HIV, doctors, school board members, religious leaders, and public health officials. They formulated the following mission statement: "No member of our community will be newly infected by HIV and those infected will get appropriate care."

To begin to assess AIDS-related needs in Pasadena, the task force developed a continuum-of-care model. It consisted of four major categories into which all educational and treatment services would fall. The continuum included preventive education, early intervention, symptomatic intervention, and extended care.

Recognizing that preventive education is the best "cure" we have for HIV, the task force focused much of their attention on it and dedicated nearly four times as many recommendations to it as to other sections of the continuum of care. Several recommendations focused on guidelines for HIV preventive education in relation to substance abuse, calling for educational materials and programs. The plan urged community groups and institutions to become involved in preventive education.

These recommendations gave rise to this proposal, which aims to train the staff of drug treatment facilities to teach its clients behaviors that will decrease their chances of becoming infected with HIV.

Agency Description

The mission of the All Saints AIDS Service Center (ASASC) is "to serve people whose lives are affected by HIV and AIDS by providing service, preventive education, and advocacy for an appropriate community and government response." It is a nondenominational, not-for-profit agency established in 1988 that has offered direct services to 750 persons with AIDS, as well as preventive outreach programs to thousands in the San Gabriel Valley region of Los Angeles County, including Pasadena. Currently registered with the

(continued)

center are 400 clients, and 60 new clients register for these services each month. More than 300 people attend one of the center's 13 support groups, which are conducted in English and Spanish. The center's health education team provides outreach services to public agencies, local corporations, prisons, parole officers, Head Start programs, Planned Parenthood, schools, colleges, and other health-care agencies. The staff has 25 members and 600 volunteers. ASASC implements its education and prevention programs in its education and prevention section. The programs mentioned in this section are described in an attached appendix.

Proposed Program

Goals   The primary goal of the preventive education plan is to teach the staffs of six to eight Pasadena agencies facts about HIV/AIDS, information about the relationship between addiction and HIV, and training in behaviors that reduce the risk of acquiring the disease. It is hoped that, by focusing on the staffs of these agencies rather than on their clients, community preventive education will continue, even after this grant's 12-month period.

Objectives   To achieve these goals, the proposed project will meet these objectives:

1. ASASC will develop a training curriculum in collaboration with a representative from the Public Health Department. This curriculum will build on ASASC's existing AIDS 101 curriculum to change the attitudes and behaviors that place the substance-abusing population at risk. This curriculum will be developed by the end of the first six weeks of the project.
2. ASASC will conduct four intensive sessions per agency for the staff of six to eight agencies. These sessions will occur between the 3rd and 9th months of the 12-month period.
3. Two months after the final education session, ASASC will conduct one follow-up session for each agency to address successes and challenges specific to that agency. ASASC will conduct two follow-up evaluative sessions during the 10th and 12th months for all involved agencies.
4. ASASC will seek specific levels of demonstrated competence from the staff of drug treatment centers at specific points in this project:
   - Of the trained drug treatment staff, 80 percent will meet specific criteria during teach-back presentations at each agency's fourth intensive session.
   - Of the trained drug treatment staff, 80 percent will exhibit a 90 percent rate of knowledge at the end of the project, imparted to them between the first and the final sessions.
   - Of the trained drug treatment staff, 50 percent will demonstrate that they have disseminated HIV/AIDS information by making formal presentations during the 12 months of the project.

Proposed Plan

ASASC will train the staff of at least six to eight Pasadena agencies that treat users of drugs, including alcohol and intravenous drugs. The training will include four intensive sessions with direct-service personnel the agency has chosen to participate in the training.

The training will consist of a pretest to gauge the level of knowledge with which participants enter the program; information addressing interconnections between low self-esteem, risky behavior, and substance abuse, and discussions of the possible origins of addictive and risky behavior; role playing about safe sex, in which drug treatment staff will deepen their understanding of the discomfort and difficulties in making behavior changes; basic information on HIV/AIDS, such as how infection occurs, how infection spreads, and the biology of AIDS; a list of community resources and discussion about how to access them; information about psychodynamic issues that emerge when substance abusers become aware that they have been at risk and want to be tested; and discussion of homophobia and how it shapes the views many persons have of HIV and AIDS.

Month-by-Month Time Line   The first 2 months of this 12-month project will focus on setup tasks, including recruiting a health educator to implement the program, having the health educator and Public Health Department collaborate to build a curriculum for training drug treatment center staff, contacting drug treatment agencies that might participate in the project, and assembling reading material for the educational project.

In the next 6 months (months 3 through 9), the health educator will conduct training, sometimes in conjunction with other staff of ASASC's education and prevention section.

The final 3 months (months 10 through 12) will emphasize discussions among the trainees of the various drug treatment centers. They will meet at ASASC offices to explore problems they have encountered in helping their substance abuse clients modify their risky behaviors. These meetings will provide ASASC with feedback about its training strategies. They will also help the trainees see ASASC as an ongoing resource.

Staffing and Evaluation   The health educator will be hired by and report to ASASC's coordinator of the education and prevention program. ASASC already has an Education Advisory Committee, including experts on immunology, psychology, child abuse prevention, nursing, legal issues specific to HIV and AIDS, social work, and education. Members of this committee, in liaison with the Public Health Department and the health educator, will develop instruments and materials to evaluate this project at various intervals. Methods of evaluating the "teach-backs," where trainees teach clients through role play, will also be developed.

Budget

Personnel Costs

Coordinator of Education and Training (1/5 FTE* @ $32,000)	$ 6,400
Health educator (1 FTE* @ $28,000)	28,000
Fringe benefits 18%	6,192
Subtotal for personnel	$ 40,592

Travel

100 miles per month of local travel (@ $ 28/mile for 12 months)	$ 336
Airfare to project meeting in Washington, DC	300
Conference costs	550
Subtotal for travel	$ 1,186

(continued)

Direct costs

Educational materials	$ 1,750
Printing/copying	575
Postage	75
Advertising	75
Supplies	75
Software support	75
Equipment repairs	75
Books and publications	125
Refreshments	50
Subtotal for direct costs	$ 2,875

Indirect costs

Rent	$ 5,750
Telephone	1,150
Insurance	500
Janitorial	1,300
Audit	375
Copier maintenance	250
Miscellaneous	125
Administration	840
Subtotal for indirect costs	$ 10,290
Total cost of project	$ 54,943

*Full-time equivalent

Source: This is part of a proposal prepared by Katrina Gould, MSW, in collaboration with staff at the All Saints AIDS Service Center, Pasadena, California.

❧ EXERCISE ❧

Pretend that you are a grant officer at a foundation that has just received this proposal. Imagine that you have a pile of 200 other grant proposals on your desk and that you can pick only 20 of them for funding. Having a skeptical orientation, ask tough questions about this proposal.

To get yourself into the mind-set of a foundation staff person, make a list of key questions that you would be likely to ask about all grant proposals. (*Hint:* Draw on the discussion of qualities of good policy proposals in the preceding section of this chapter—but feel free to add other questions that may be germane to your foundation.) How does this proposal stack up on these questions? Would you fund it?

PowerPoint presentations are widely used to provide audiences with an overview of a policy issue and to make policy recommendations. A PowerPoint presentation is discussed in Policy Advocacy Challenge 9.11 that was developed by MSW students to persuade a panel of public officials in Los Angeles County to support a "housing first" policy for homeless persons. (See Policy Advocacy Challenge 9.11.)

In the spring semester of 2006, 13 classes of policy advocacy students in the MSW Program at the School of Social Work of the University of Southern California addressed various aspects of the homelessness issue in Los Angeles County. A panel of city and county officials came to the School at the end of the semester to hear the findings and recommendations of each of the classes. I discuss here the presentation that my group made, composed of myself, Robert Hernandez, Ali Wagner, Laura Koonin, Carolyn Ryan, and Alicia Case.

My student group partnered with the not-for-profit advocacy group LAMP that favored a "no strings attached" policy that would seek *immediately* to give each homeless person a place to live regardless of whatever drug, mental health, health, or other issues that they might have. (Of course, many homeless persons are simply poor and unable to afford rent.) We wanted not just to *manage* homelessness but to *end* it.

We wanted to develop a presentation that had a clear message to *end* homelessness in Los Angeles County within the next 10 years by providing sufficient housing along with supportive services for those homeless persons needing them. We knew we had only a limited time slot of roughly 10 minutes.

We chose Bob Hernandez to make the presentation from our group, since we knew he could speak passionately without being overly emotional—and he was very versed in the issue because he had been an MSW intern at LAMP. We were certain he could connect on a personal level with members of the audience and yet provide them with the central ideas we wished to convey.

Our group also had a member, Ali Wagner, who had designed PowerPoint presentations professionally. She was skilled in making PowerPoint slides that focused on the major concepts we wished to present, while not being excessively cluttered.

With contributions from all members of our group, then, a presentation strategy emerged. We would start with an agenda for our presentation so the audience would know what to expect. We would then show them a map of LA's primary skid row in downtown Los Angeles. We would share our values with the group that led us to prioritize ending homelessness in the first place. We would then contrast the current punitive approach to dealing with homeless persons—and the cycle of homelessness—that it engendered with our housing-first strategy. We would demonstrate that our approach would cost no more per homeless person than the current policy. We would conclude with a piece of model legislation that could put "housing first" into place. To show the public officials that our ideas actually work, we decided to end the presentation with a specific example of a renovated apartment building with supportive services. We would urge the county and city to develop a unified single plan that would link public and private sectors.

We knew that public officials were often moved to action by specific case stories. So we selected "Nancy's Story" to move them to action before making a final plea for permanent supportive housing.

Here is our 10-minute presentation with our PowerPoint slides and the text that went with each of them.

(continued)

Slide 1

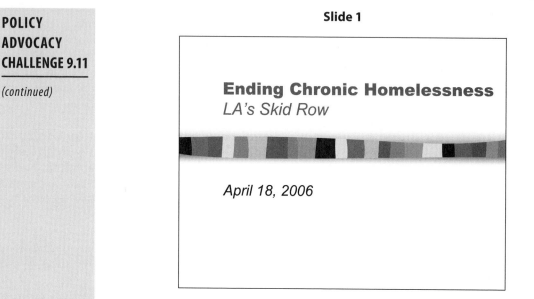

Text that Accompanies Slide 1

- Thanks to the panel.
- Our role as social workers is to create awareness, educate, and advocate on behalf of our clients.
- Our goal, today, is to provide a voice for the chronically homeless on skid row in downtown Los Angeles. The chronically homeless are defined as individuals who have one disability, or more, and have been homeless for a year.
- We want to express concerns and advocate on their behalf.

(next slide)

Slide 2

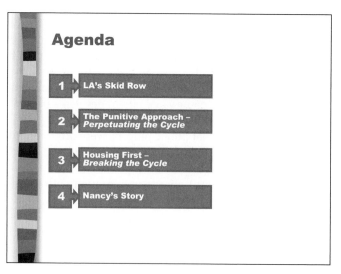

Text that Accompanies Slide 2

- First, we would like to explain the characteristics of the skid row population.
- Second, we would like to express concerns about the cycle of homelessness and how, we believe, the criminalization of the homeless is not the solution to ending homelessness.
- Next, we would like to offer insight on possible solutions to ending the cycle of homelessness.
- Our closing thoughts will offer hope that we can end homelessness.
- For references, we have included the names of specific studies on the relevant slides and we would like to note that we are highlighting several points made in the recent report issued by Bring LA Home report, "The Campaign to End Homelessness."

(next slide)

Slide 3

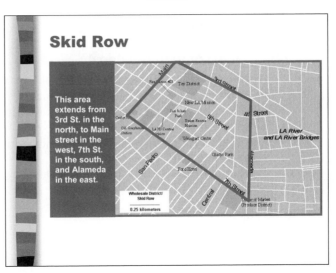

Text that Accompanies Slide 3

- Today we are focused on the homeless population on skid row in downtown Los Angeles.
- Skid row is a 50 square block area on the eastern side of downtown. On any given night, approximately 10,000–12,000 people call Skid Row home. These individuals are either living in shelters, jail, hospitals, or literally on the streets.

(next slide)

(continued)

Slide 4

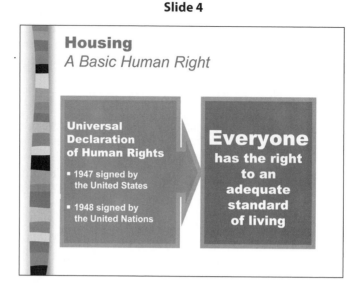

Text that Accompanies Slide 4

- Article 25 of The Universal Declaration of Human Rights states in part, "Everyone has the right to a standard of living adequate for the health and well-being of himself and of his family, including food, clothing, housing and medical care, and necessary social services."
- Our work is to ensure that the chronically homeless population on skid row are afforded this right.
- Our belief is that everyone wants to end homelessness, but not everyone agrees on how to end it.

(next slide)

Slide 5

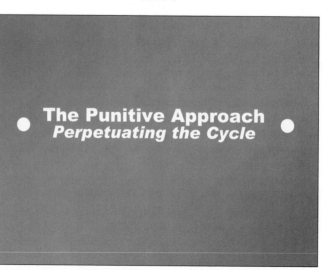

Text that Accompanies Slide 5

There are those that support the punitive approach, or the criminalization of the homeless, which we suggest perpetuates the cycle of homelessness.

(next slide)

Slide 6

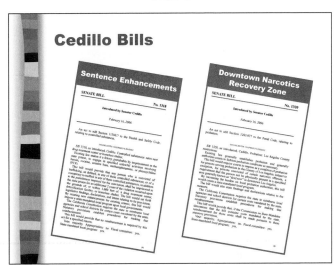

Text that Accompanies Slide 6

- We are concerned about the pending legislation put forth by Senator Gil Cedillo. Although well-intended, we believe the bills supporting sentence enhancements and a downtown narcotics recovery zone will:
- Not deter crime, but will enhance the number of people caught in the cycle of homelessness.
- We believe this bill create an opportunity for racial profiling.
- Will further contribute to the overcrowding in jails.
- We are concerned that homeless individuals convicted of drug crimes, once released, will not be allowed to return to skid row, the area in which they are arrested, which is the very area that provides them with the housing and services they need. Thus, setting them up for homelessness again, in another city.
- Both of these bills, we believe, trap individuals in the cycle of homelessness.

(next slide)

(continued)

**POLICY
ADVOCACY
CHALLENGE 9.11**

(continued)

Slide 7

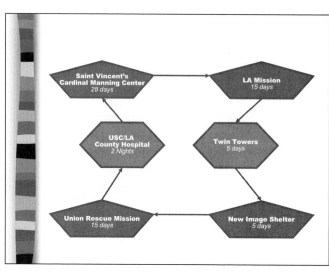

Text that Accompanies Slide 7

- For these people, it is a revolving door as they cycle from the streets to costly acute care services such as hospitals, city shelters and jail, and then back to the streets.
- We suggest that the cost of doing nothing to stop this cycle is, in reality, quite costly.

(next slide)

Slide 8

Text that Accompanies Slide 8

- Using city and county services such as jail, hospitals, and shelters to house the mentally ill homeless is not cost effective.
- For these homeless individuals caught in this cycle, the total cost per person per year is $40,449.

- This cycle is costly, ineffective, and it perpetuates homelessness.
- We believe it is time to break that cycle.

Cite: Bring LA Home

(next slide)

Slide 9

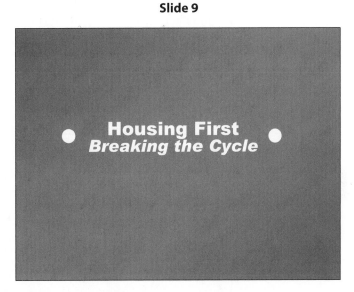

Text that Accompanies Slide 9

The way to break that cycle is to provide housing first.

(next slide)

Slide 10

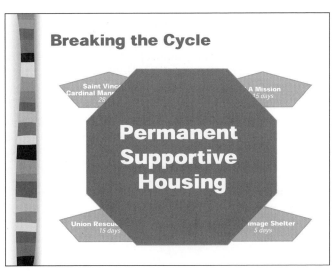

(continued)

Text that Accompanies Slide 10

The housing first approach provides permanent, affordable housing that is linked to services to enable tenants with special needs to live as independently as possible.

Providing permanent supportive housing for the homeless is a proven model that:

- Provides stable housing with services that support the individual and help prevent them from returning to the street.
- Creates a foundation on which the process of recovery can begin. Having a place of one's own may—in and of itself—serve as a motivator for consumers to seek counseling, job training, and refrain from drug and alcohol abuse. Having a home motivates a potential homeless person in doing whatever it takes to keep a home.

(next slide)

Slide 11

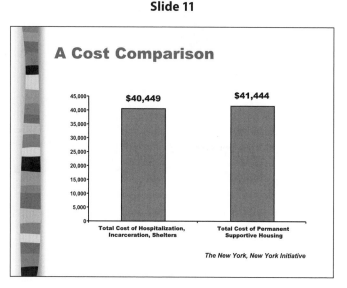

Text that Accompanies Slide 11

- These totals are taken from a New York study that compares the costs of acute services to the costs of permanent supportive housing. As you can see, the cost for acute services (or doing nothing) is roughly $40,000 per person per year.
- The cost of providing housing with supportive services is only about $1000 more per person per year—essentially, we break even.
- The critical point to remember here is that over the course of time, the cost of acute services will rise while the cost of permanent supportive housing will decrease. Once we have individuals, in housing, with services, the costs per person per year will decrease to almost half of the cost of acute services.

(next slide)

Slide 12

Text that Accompanies Slide 12

In comparison, housing the homeless through the permanent supportive housing approach is less costly than using city and county services.

- Hospitalization is 49 times more costly than supportive housing.
- Jail is 47% more costly than supportive housing.
- One month's stay in a mental hospital could pay for about 20 months in supportive housing.
- One day in the hospital could pay for more than 45 days in supportive housing.

Cite Bring LA Home

(next slide)

Slide 13

(continued)

Text that Accompanies Slide 13

Another example of how we can end chronic homelessness is the St. George model—an effective and creative approach to housing:

- A renovated 88 unit apartment building on the edge of skid row owned by skid row housing trust (SRHT).
- Tenants all have a mental illness and were chronically homeless.
- Wrap around supportive services provided by Lamp community, SRHT, and other skid row collaborative partners in the basement of the building.

There are other creative strategies that provide housing. For example:

- Master leasing
- Informal agreements with landlords
- Purchasing and rehabilitating existing units and working with developers to create new ones.

(next slide)

Slide 14

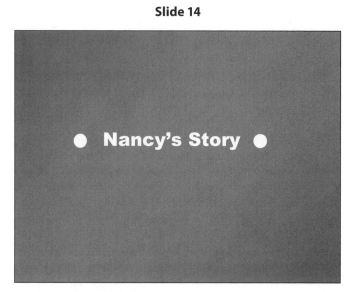

Text that Accompanies Slide 14

I have a letter here from a client whose life has been changed by the model we are suggesting. I would like to highlight parts of her story that speak to what we are discussing here today.

Nancy . . .

(next slide)

Slide 15

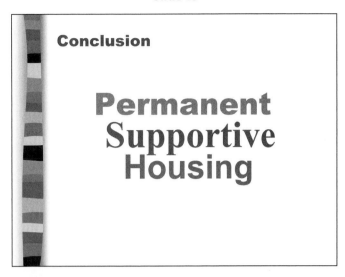

Text that Accompanies Slide 15

In conclusion, we hope that the numbers speak for themselves. We propose that the permanent supportive housing approach is the most cost-effective way to end the cycle of homelessness. This approach gets the homeless individual off of the street, into housing, with services that support their effort to remain in housing and off of the streets.

Thanks to panel.

The end.

Our presentation received a standing ovation due to the combination of a very convincing delivery, impactful visuals, a clear policy message, use of data, a case study of Nancy who represented a pathway for a better future, and a strong conclusion. We succeeded in showing that social workers can offer practical solutions by connecting needs and services with stakeholders. We learned that social workers can influence policy even as they offer clinical and other services. We learned that presentations are a critical component of policy practice and policy advocacy.

Some questions to ponder as you view the PowerPoint presentation:

- Why is it important to have relatively little text on PowerPoint slides?
- Why is it important for presenters of PowerPoint presentation not to look excessively at the screen and to focus mostly on the audience?
- Why is it important not to mechanically read the text on the slides to the audience, but, rather, to have "fresh" text that is not identical to the text on the slides?
- What other positive attributes of this PowerPoint presentation can you identify?

What You Can Now Do

CHAPTER SUMMARY

Our discussion in this chapter suggests that communication skills are a key part of policy advocacy—whether oral presentations (such as debates, negotiations, or speeches) or written presentations (such as succinct policy memos or grant proposals). You are now equipped to do the following:

- Engage in debates on affirmative or negative sides
- Use hardball and win-win options in negotiations
- Develop strategy for making presentations to audiences, such as diagnosing them, setting objectives, selecting a medium, and developing a format
- Improve your presentation style
- Write grant proposals

In the next three chapters we turn to tactics for developing and using power resources in policy advocacy—as well as tactics for participating in electoral politics.

NOTES

1. Willard Richan, "A Common Language for Social Work," *Social Work* 17 (November 1972): 14–22.
2. Herbert Simons, *Persuasion*, 2nd ed. (New York: Random House, 1986), pp. 18–21, and Donald Cegala, *Persuasive Communication: Theory and Practice*, 3rd ed. (Edina, MN: Bellwether, 1987), pp. 13–15.
3. Michael Barone, "The 49 Percent Nation," *National Journal* (June 9, 2001): 1710–1716.
4. Simons, *Persuasion*, pp. 253–254.
5. Ibid., pp. 190–192.
6. George Brager, Harry Specht, and James Torczyner, *Community Organizing*, 2nd ed. (New York: Columbia University Press), pp. 355–357.
7. Simons, *Persuasion*, pp. 253–256.
8. Ibid., pp. 259–261.
9. Ibid., pp. 253–256.
10. Roger Fisher and William Ury, *Getting to Yes: Negotiating Agreement without Giving In* (New York: Penguin Books, 1991).
11. Ibid. Also see Herb Bisno, *Managing Conflict* (Newbury Park, CA: Sage, 1988), pp. 99–147.
12. See Jay Folberg and Alison Taylor, *Mediation* (San Francisco: Jossey-Bass, 1984).
13. Fisher and Ury, *Getting to Yes.*
14. Simons, *Persuasion*, pp. 23–24, 141–142.
15. Karlyn Campbell, *The Rhetorical Act* (Belmont, CA: Wadsworth, 1982), pp. 69–118.
16. Ibid., pp. 101–116.
17. Ibid., pp. 69–118.
18. Stan Paine, G. Thomas Bellamy, and Barbara Wilcox, *Human Services That Work* (Baltimore: Paul Brooks, 1984), pp. 42–44.
19. Morton Deutsch, *The Resolution of Conflict: Constructive and Destructive Processes* (New Haven, CT: Yale University Press, 1973), pp. 124–152.
20. Segmentation is discussed extensively in marketing literature; see Phillip Kotler, *Principles of Marketing*, 4th ed. (Englewood Cliffs, NJ: Prentice Hall, 1989), pp. 42–46. Also see Simons, *Persuasion*, pp. 143–146.
21. George Brager and Stephen Holloway, *Changing Human Service Organizations* (New York: Free Press, 1978), pp. 199–203.
22. Ibid.
23. See Marya Holcombe and Judith Stein, *Presentations for Decision Makers* (New York: Van Nostrand Reinhold, 1983).
24. Ibid., pp. 16–25.
25. Ibid., pp. 11–13.
26. Simons, *Persuasion*, pp. 124–129, and Robert Reid, *Work of Nations: Preparing Ourselves for the 21st Century* (New York: Knopf, 1991), pp. 154–168.
27. Hedrick Smith, *Rethinking America* (New York: Random House, 1995).
28. Simons, *Persuasion*, pp. 148–154.

29. Ibid., pp. 153–154.
30. Ibid., p. 153.
31. Cegala, *Persuasive Communication*, p. 136.
32. Simons, *Persuasion*, p. 153.
33. Cegala, *Persuasive Communication*, p. 134.
34. See Brager et al., *Community Organizing*, pp. 342–343.
35. Paul Ephross and Thomas Vassil, *Groups That Work* (New York: Columbia University Press, 1988), p. 157.
36. George Sharwell, "How to Testify before a Legislative Committee," in Maryann Mahaffey and John Hanks, eds., *Practical Politics: Social Work and Political Response* (Silver Spring, MD: National Association of Social Workers, 1982), pp. 85–98.

37. Lewis Dexter, "Role Relationships and Conception of Neutrality in Interviewing," *American Journal of Sociology* 62 (September 1956): 153–157.
38. Craig Smith and Eric Skjei, *Getting Grants* (New York: Harper & Row, 1980), pp. 173–181.
39. Armand Lauffer, *Grantsmanship and fund raising* (Beverly Hills, CA: Sage, 1983), pp. 238–246.
40. Ibid., pp. 80–84.
41. Ibid., pp. 236–246.
42. Smith and Skjei, Getting Grants, p. 152.
43. Soraya Coley and Cynthia Scheinberg, *Proposal Writing* (Newbury Park, CA: Sage, 1992).
44. Ibid.

SUGGESTED READINGS

Policy-Persuading Strategies

Austin Freeley, *Argumentation and Debate*, 6th ed. (Belmont, CA: Wadsworth, 1986).

Willard Richan, "A Common Language for Social Work," *Social Work* 17 (November 1972): 14–22.

Herbert Simons, *Persuasion*, 2nd ed. (New York: Random House, 1986).

Negotiations and Mediation

Herb Bisno, *Managing Conflict* (Newbury Park, CA: Sage, 1988), pp. 98–147.

Roger Fisher and William Ury, *Getting to Yes: Negotiating Agreement Without Giving In* (New York: Penguin Books, 1991).

Jay Folberg and Alison Taylor, *Mediation* (San Francisco: Jossey-Bass, 1984).

Margaret Gibelman and Harold Demone, "Negotiating a Contract: Practical Considerations," in Harold Demone and Margaret Gibelman, eds., *Services for Sale* (New Brunswick, NJ: Rutgers University Press, 1989), pp. 131–148.

Developing Grant Proposals

Soraya Coley and Cynthia Scheinberg, *Proposal Writing* (Newbury Park, CA: Sage, 1992).

Jean Potuchek, "The Context of Social Service Funding: The Funding Relationship," *Social Service Review* (September 1986): 421–436.

P A R T

5

ADVOCATING FOR CHANGE

No matter how skilled policy advocates are in accomplishing agenda building, problem analyzing, and proposal writing, their work comes to naught if they cannot get their recommendations enacted, whether in agencies, communities, or legislatures. Therefore the discussions of power and strategy in the next four chapters are critically important to policy advocates.

Chapter Ten discusses how to develop and use power. **Chapter Eleven** covers how to develop political strategy. **Chapter Twelve** addresses how to develop and implement political strategy in legislative, community, and agency settings. **Chapter Thirteen** discusses how to change the composition of government by participating in electoral politics.

C H A P T E R

10

Developing and Using Power

POLICY PREDICAMENT

A social work intern in a mental health agency discovers that no mental health services are provided to children whose parents have been institutionalized for psychiatric problems. She soon discovers numerous political obstacles to the development of such services. What political tactics would she devise? We present this case in Policy Advocacy Challenge 10.2 after briefly discussing politics. At the chapter's end, we discuss a portion of Governor Kathleen Blanco's strategy to secure resources for New Orleans from a sometimes reluctant administration and Congress.

Power and politics have a bad reputation among some professionals, who regard them as unseemly—even unethical. However, power and politics can often be used for ethical purposes, and each of us can develop and use power resources to help stigmatized groups and unpopular causes. To help you become an effective policy advocate, this chapter discusses the following:

1. The positive functions of politics in policy deliberations
2. The transactional nature of power relationships
3. Person-to-person and substantive power resources
4. Ways to shape policy outcomes indirectly by using decision-making procedures, processes, and contexts
5. Personal characteristics that enhance political effectiveness
6. Issues of autonomy, discretion, compliance, and whistle-blowing
7. The importance of power differentials
8. External and internal vantage points when making policy changes
9. Ways that policy practitioners develop power resources, including use of the Internet
10. Ways that members of vulnerable groups or out-groups encounter challenges when seeking and using power

11. The psychology of power as illustrated by intimidation and assertiveness
12. The dynamics of task groups, including coalitions and networks

In Defense of Politics

People sometimes call those who are preoccupied with political realities opportunistic, power-hungry, or wedded to special interests. Some truth exists in these assertions, but they obscure how important politics are to policy advocacy. Before discussing some of these functions, we define the word *politics* more precisely. Some people equate politics with government policy making; indeed, one part of Webster's definition declares it "the politics and aims of a government [and] the conduct and contests of political parties."[1] Certainly, these government and party functions belong in a definition of politics, but what about politics in other settings, such as social agencies, professional associations, and communities? Webster's comes to our aid by including in its definition, "the political connections or beliefs of a person [and] the plotting or scheming of those seeking personal power, glory, position, or the like."[2] Webster's choice of *plotting* and *scheming* suggests a disdain for political activity, though the definition includes power-related struggles in any setting. We need a definition that does not cast aspersions on persons who develop and use power, because leaders such as Franklin Roosevelt, Robert Kennedy, and Marian Wright Edelman have used power for noble ends.

At the risk of rewriting the dictionary, let us hazard our own definition. Politics represents efforts by people in governmental and nongovernmental settings to secure their policy wishes by developing and using power resources. When defined in this manner, politics becomes relevant not only to highly placed officials, but to anyone who tries to influence policy making.

It is difficult to imagine a world where politics does not exist, because political processes are endemic in social interactions. (See Policy Advocacy Challenge 10.1.) Without political recourse, people who lack formal authority would have to obey existing policies or seek remedies through other means, such as force.

POLICY ADVOCACY CHALLENGE 10.1

Familiarizing Yourself with Political Institutions

STEPHANIE DAVIS, RESEARCH LIBRARIAN

Information about politics can be found in many places, such as C-SPAN on cable television, on the Web, and the Internet at an array of Web sites like the following:

The U.S. Senate   This site gives the name and state of all U.S. senators, along with links to their offices to view what issues they are currently focused on. It details what the Senate as a whole is working on, and it offers an opportunity to contact your state's senators via e-mail to voice your own opinion.
http://www.senate.gov

The U.S. House of Representatives   This site gives the name and state of all U.S. representatives, along with links to their offices to view what issues they are currently working on. It also details what the House as a whole is considering. It offers an opportunity to contact your representative via e-mail to voice your own opinions.
http://www.house.gov

(continued)

The White House   Home page for the president and the vice president. This site gives you the opportunity to visit the press room and see what daily activities are occurring at the White House. It also offers an e-mail link for writing to the president or the vice president on issues of importance to you.
http://www.whitehouse.gov
   To access information about your state legislature and your governor, you need to find Web sites specific to your state by consulting your librarian or using a search engine like Google.

The political process in a democracy provides a way for people with conflicting values or opposing positions to resolve their differences. Some policy analysts claim to be purely objective and scientific in their approach, but even they make many value-laden choices in their analyses.[3] Therefore, even an analytic position often requires negotiation through the political process.

Analytic and Political Approaches to Policy Advocacy

The political model differs markedly from the analytic approaches we discussed in the preceding chapters. If the analyst wants to discover technically superior solutions to a problem by using quantitative and qualitative techniques, the adherent of the political approach wants to understand existing political realities to select feasible options and develop an effective political strategy to outmaneuver likely opponents.[4] If the analyst assumes that the truth will win out, the politician assumes that might will prevail. If analysts devote most of their time to technical tasks, political practitioners devote their time to gauging patterns of support for and opposition to specific issues, to developing power, and to implementing political strategy. (Of course, sophisticated policy practitioners can creatively couple analytic and political approaches in specific situations, as we discussed in Chapter Three.) Policy advocates who use a political approach ask questions like those presented in Box 10.1.
   Let us now consider the policy predicament encountered by the social work intern who wanted to develop innovative services for the children of parents who have been institutionalized for psychiatric reasons. (See Policy Advocacy Challenge 10.2.)

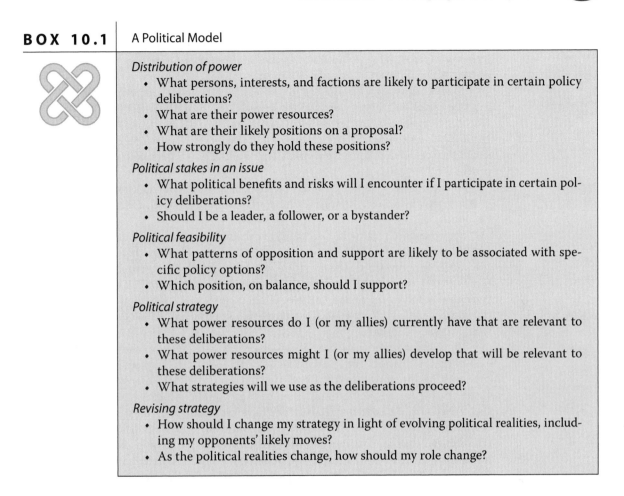

B O X   1 0 . 1 | A Political Model

Distribution of power
- What persons, interests, and factions are likely to participate in certain policy deliberations?
- What are their power resources?
- What are their likely positions on a proposal?
- How strongly do they hold these positions?

Political stakes in an issue
- What political benefits and risks will I encounter if I participate in certain policy deliberations?
- Should I be a leader, a follower, or a bystander?

Political feasibility
- What patterns of opposition and support are likely to be associated with specific policy options?
- Which position, on balance, should I support?

Political strategy
- What power resources do I (or my allies) currently have that are relevant to these deliberations?
- What power resources might I (or my allies) develop that will be relevant to these deliberations?
- What strategies will we use as the deliberations proceed?

Revising strategy
- How should I change my strategy in light of evolving political realities, including my opponents' likely moves?
- As the political realities change, how should my role change?

POLICY ADVOCACY CHALLENGE 10.2

Developing an Innovative Program in an Inhospitable Setting

Stacy Stern, MSW

In this case, a social work intern tries to develop an innovative program in a mental health agency. She notes that the agency, which considers itself an advocate for children's mental health needs, lacks a program to help children whose parents have been institutionalized for psychiatric problems. She hopes to obtain approval for an eight-week crisis model of services to these children but soon realizes that she has encountered numerous political barriers.

It is curious that the Mountain View Child Guidance Clinic considers itself an advocate for children's mental health needs when it neglects children of the psychiatrically hospitalized parent. Such children are in crisis and experiencing extreme family disequilibrium. They need immediate assistance in understanding and dealing constructively with feelings and thoughts associated with this experience. It is preferable

(continued)

that this intervention occur at or near the time of the crisis, when defenses are most fluid and before maladaptive patterns of functioning have solidified. To meet this need, I am trying to develop, in addition to the brief services offered by the clinic, a crisis group for the children of psychiatrically hospitalized parents.

The coordination and cooperation necessary for such a program would be a landmark in the clinic's history. Its success would depend on the referrals of psychiatrists who assist patients admitted to local public and private psychiatric hospitals. If the clinic bypasses the physician's authority and accepts referrals directly from hospitals' social service departments, we would alienate some physicians, who might imperil the program by boycotting it.

Announcements could be sent to the hospitals, their social service departments, and specific physicians. The service must offer support to both the physician and the hospital.

The politics of this agency dictates that the new program not be called preventive, lest funders and policy makers not favor it. Because they believe that no room exists in the budget for prevention, this program will be called crisis intervention.

We could approach four local hospitals with announcements of the new clinic program. A follow-up phone call would add a personal touch and hopefully clinch the process. As a staff member, I would persuade physician friends of its merit, while soliciting their support.

There are a number of barriers to change in this agency. The clinic focuses its energy on the quantity rather than the quality of services. Of primary importance to the executive director is avoiding a waiting list. To this end, he mobilizes all forces and automatically shelves any program change that would conflict with this aim. Further, staff are usually inundated with work and have little time to create innovative services. Similarly, the agency values efficiency in programming and expenditures. Clinic executives believe that they cannot afford to risk any revenue by applying funds to areas other than those directly funded and approved. Another barrier to innovation is the agency staff's disinclination to participate in program development, which deprives the agency of new program ideas. Staff members seek what fulfillment is available through the clients themselves and leave the business of the clinic to the bureaucracy.

I am only a student intern in this agency, but I want to get this innovation off the ground before my field experience ends. Considering the nature of the agency, it is essential to introduce the change in an administratively sanctioned way through approved channels. Therefore, I initially broached the idea of the innovation to the director of outpatient services, Mr. Jones, who is my preceptor for short-term and intake cases. On first mentioning the plan, I was careful to make it appear to be an idea that I had developed in the course of discussions with him. I told him I saw the idea as consistent with comprehensive mental health care for children, an ideal he often espouses. Underscoring that the services would take only eight weeks, which he likes, and stressing its efficiency in terms of the waiting list, I ventured to actually propose a pilot plan. He groaned and suggested that I "write it up," with no explanation of what that meant. Rather than irritate him further, I did not mention the project for several weeks. I then told my regular field instructor that I was discussing with Mr. Jones a new program for the children of hospitalized patients, and I received her approval to use this project as a learning experience in program design.

Several weeks later, I found that Mr. Jones had completely forgotten my plan. But in further discussion, he expressed strong interest and even brainstormed an initial strategy with me that would help the innovation gain gradual support in the Mountain View Child Guidance Clinic. He argued that we should develop a two-phase strategy. In phase one, I would develop a pilot project. Because I am a student intern, it would not need formal clearance by high-level executives or the agency board. He would simply notify the executive that a student intern was establishing a pilot group for children of institutionalized parents. He urged a low profile during this initial period. After we initiated the project, he would develop a strategy for a formal proposal that would go to the executive director and hopefully eventually to the board. That would be phase two. If all went well, the agency would formally earmark funds for the program. He hoped that my experience with the pilot project would provide useful information for writing the formal proposal and presenting it orally to the executive and the board. He concluded our meeting by saying, "You know you will have to do the entire program in the pilot phase. All the screening and everything." He seemed tantalized by the idea of obtaining increased service with no additional expenditure of staff time.

To date, I have succeeded in involving Mr. Jones in planning sufficiently to encourage his sense of investment in the program. I have abided by the rules in recognizing his authority and decision-making powers and deemphasizing my own initiative. My short-term strategy, then, is to begin the program myself. But a number of obstacles could still interfere with program acceptance by key decision makers, even during the pilot phase.

One obstacle is the issue of community coordination. Currently, the clinic has superficial coordination with local mental health agencies, exchanging cases only sporadically. No clear plan exists for coordination of services. This program necessitates an intermediate type of coordination, a case-planning coordination organized into a whole-family approach. The current fragmentation in the treatment of families with a disturbed member would be a danger to this program, because it would undermine the purpose of comprehensive care. What factors are involved in this coordination process?

First, there is the issue of goal conflict. On the surface, there appears to be little; both the psychiatric hospitals and the clinic serve and are concerned with families' mental health needs. But is that really the case? In fact, the hospitals view the treatment of the parent-patient from a pathology rather than a family systems perspective. Therefore, they may choose to refer the child not for group, but for individual treatment as an "impaired" family member. It will be important to impress on these staff members that the groups help the child in crisis, rather than provide long-term therapy. With regard to the power relationships between agencies, the major snare seems to be the physicians' autonomy. The administrators of local psychiatric hospitals may perceive the children's group as highlighting their own program deficiencies and therefore may choose to provide a similar service themselves.

At present, the agencies do not consider themselves interdependent. Instead, they coexist in separate realms of the psychiatric community and rarely communicate. More positively, though, they may cooperate with this project, not only because of the children's emotional needs, but also because child and adult agencies are complementary community services that do not usually compete for the same clientele.

To alleviate some of the tension between agencies and to facilitate the common goal of improved community mental health, I will plan individual visits to each hospital's social services department. I may be invited to present this program to the monthly meeting of hospital psychiatrists, an opportunity for a direct encounter with most of the staff physicians. In addition, I will invite representatives of each hospital to the clinic for an orientation and open house, which should improve relationships between clinic and hospital and emphasize the community nature of the project.

Within the clinic itself, a political process will follow the initiation of this program. When Mr. Jones seeks its official approval, he must submit it to the medical director for confirmation; he in turn will take it to the executive committee for approval, and they will then present it to the board of directors for final approval. However, because Mr. Jones is the most powerful person in the agency, his approval should lead to its acceptance.

A complicating factor is the director of training, Ida Brown. To be candid, she does not particularly like Mr. Jones and often opposes any proposals he initiates. She may interfere in the decision-making process by pushing for a nondecision; that is, she may suggest that the plan be initiated only after lengthy study or pending the location of special sources of external funding. Another problem may arise because many in the agency focus on the child of an institutionalized adult as a patient, a view that clashes with the program's preventive mission.

I also see several other groups developing in relation to the program. One consists of the senior administrator and the chief of program development (also the director of support services). These two men are allied in their unstated mission to increase clinic prestige and influence in the community. They will probably support the program from their stated position of commitment to enriching the quality of the services available to the community. This position would appear reasonable and would underscore the senior administrator's interest in the efficient business operation of the clinic.

The executive director himself will probably support the program in deference to Mr. Jones, to whom he defers on all issues pertaining to the outpatient services of the agency. The outpatient service functions virtually independently of the day-treatment and other components of the agency.

The medical director is also a figurehead, whose medical degree is valued by the agency. He will most assuredly remain neutral lest he find himself in the middle of a political battle. He appears to have little power in the agency.

The board of directors also has little power in this agency. The members are most concerned about what mural is painted on which wall and how chairs are grouped in the waiting room. Program development is not their expertise, and they usually abide agreeably by decisions made by the executive director.

In the future, I see this program as an integral part of the clinic's services, if it can survive the pilot and approval stages. The children served during their first experience with a parent's hospitalization may choose to return to us if the parent is rehospitalized. Children who have experienced numerous parental hospitalizations will be able to compare previous episodes with the one eased by clinic services. We may then see self-referrals by children and families, reducing the need for physician referrals.

Mr. Jones wants me to assist him in writing the formal proposal after my pilot project has been in operation for five months. The project has made me realize that good clinical skills need to be supplemented by program design and political skills. How else can social workers develop and institute innovative services?

∽ EXERCISE ∾

List both barriers to this innovation and potential sources of support. Remember, of course, that some barriers can be eliminated or partly addressed by the strategy of the social work intern.

If you had encountered this situation and had wanted to obtain this mental health innovation, would you have persevered, or would you have decided not to proceed because too many political barriers existed? Does a danger exist of prematurely deciding that the "glass is half empty?" In the case of the children who needed help while a parent was institutionalized, what ethical implications might the intern have faced had she decided to discontinue her effort?

How does this case illustrate the adage that many people fail to secure their policy objectives because they prematurely discount their power resources? What power resources did this intern have?

Source: This case is adapted from one by Stacy Stern, MSW. Names and locations have been altered.

The Nature of Power

If politics is both inevitable and, at least in some cases, beneficial, policy advocates have to understand political power and develop skill in using it. We will first discuss the transactional nature of power relationships and then analyze the power resources that people use in these relationships. We will also discuss other kinds of power that use decision-making procedures, processes, and contexts. We will use the case presented in Policy Advocacy Challenge 10.2 to illustrate power and how it is used.

When the social work intern wanted to develop an innovative program to help children, she realized at once that various barriers to preventive programs existed in the agency. In this simple two-person situation, where X "sends" power and Y "receives" it, X succeeds in exercising power by convincing Y to take an action that he would not otherwise have taken. The social work intern has exercised power with her preceptor, Mr. Jones, if he assents to a program that he would not otherwise have supported.[5] (The intern has not exercised power if Mr. Jones would have initiated the innovation anyway.)

If X uses physical coercion, Y has virtually no choice—for example, when a criminal suspect is forced to enter a police car at gunpoint. In some situations, it is difficult to determine the line between voluntariness and coercion; for example, people in desperate economic straits may feel forced to accede to requests if they fear the loss of their jobs. However, some people do leave jobs to follow the dictates of their conscience.[6] Were the intern to make Mr. Jones support the innovation by holding a gun to his head, she would be forcing him to make this decision. We agree with Peter Bachrach and Morton Baratz that force is not power, because it gives people little or no choice.[7]

Real power involves transactional rather than unilateral relationships and choices.[8] The receiver in a power transaction (Y) can choose whether to accede to the sender's (X's) suggestions. Y has many options; for example, he or she could refuse to follow X's suggestions, voice indecision, agree but not really mean it, agree enthusiastically, or respond ambiguously. The social work intern had to discuss the program innovation with Mr. Jones on two occasions before he formally committed himself to her project. He gave only symbolic support on the first occasion (probably not wishing to discourage the intern), and had completely forgotten the plan when the intern reintroduced the idea several weeks later. However, he seemed to support the idea enthusiastically

FIGURE 10.1
Direct power
transactions

on the second occasion, even initiating ideas about strategy. If the exercise of power is transactional, the actions of both partners must be examined. We can portray power relationships graphically by placing arrows between X and Y, as in Figure 10.1.

Power's transactional nature has important consequences for political strategy. Even in this simple two-person example, success in using power hinges on a number of considerations. X first has to decide that a particular issue warrants the expenditure of power. The intern's commitment to children's well-being, as well as to preventive mental health, led her to put effort into securing the innovation. (We discuss the intern's power resources later.)

Power often enters into transactions that involve more than two persons. (See Figure 10.2.) We first discuss the transactional nature of power to provide an overview and then move on to power resources. As a person with little formal power, the intern realized that officials in the upper reaches of the organization ultimately would have to approve the plan. Because she could not shape their actions directly, she had to work through Mr. Jones, hoping that he would convince them to support the innovation.[9] In this case, two sets of transactional relationships exist; the intern (X) tries to convince Mr. Jones (now Z) so that he will persuade, say, the director of medical services (Y). See Figure 10.2, where the dashed line signifies the intern's exerting power over the medical director by using Mr. Jones as an intermediary. (Intermediaries are commonly used in legislatures and agencies.) We will now discuss the various power resources people use with other people in power relationships, including person-to-person power, substantive power, and indirect power.

Person-to-Person Power

Policy advocates sometimes exert power in personal discussions with others. We call this *person-to-person power.* In their classic article, John French and Bertram Raven discuss expert, coercive, reward, referent (including charisma), and authority (or legitimate) power resources.[10] Other theorists have identified yet other kinds of power resources. We discuss nine kinds of these power resources, which include expert, coercive, reward, referent, authority-based (or legitimation), position, information, connections, and value-based ones.

When using *expertise* senders display their personal credentials and knowledge to convince others. They might, for example, argue that a specific policy recommendation that they make is supported by empirical evaluations, i.e., is an evidence-based policy. Or they might suggest that they have expertise that led them to select this policy. For such entreaties to be effective, of course, the receivers have to believe that the senders *are* experts. The student intern in Policy Advocacy Challenge 10.2 realized that high-level officials would be more likely to approve her innovation after its successful implementation as a pilot project. After this success, they could argue, as experts, "We know how to implement this kind of innovation."

FIGURE 10.2
Indirect power
transactions

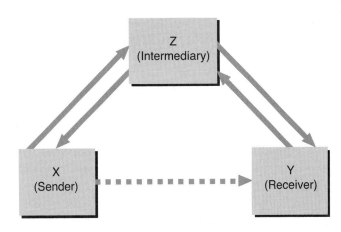

Policy advocates use *coercive power* when they threaten penalties, for instance, by hinting at the loss of a job, a promotion, or a desirable position if another person does not support a specific policy. Politicians may threaten to punish opponents by opposing legislation they want, cutting programs or funds from their districts, or not granting them positions on key committees. Threats may backfire as well, because they may alienate people—and the recipient of a threat must believe its sender can actually implement the threat.

When using *reward power,* policy advocates promise inducements, such as promotions, pay increases, financial or other support in upcoming campaigns, and bribes. They may also promise a quid pro quo: They will support someone's policy request in return for that person's support.[11] Like coercive power, reward power backfires if people believe they have been offered a bribe or other unethical inducement. Here, too, the receivers must believe the sender can and will give them the promised reward when they have taken the actions she requests.

Referent power "originates from being seen as someone associated with people or groups that other people identify with or want to belong to."[12] Members of specific professions or specific racial or ethnic groups often respect the views, for example, of members of their own profession or group. *Charismatic power* can be viewed as a subset of referent power.[13] Persons who possess personal qualities of leadership, moral authority, and persuasiveness can often stimulate others who admire these qualities to follow their policy wishes.

The *power of authority (or legitimation)* stems from one's position in an organization's hierarchy: Followers hope to receive rewards and avoid sanctions by following their superiors' suggestions. Persons who use the power of authority try to influence the actions of subordinates in several ways. They may imply that it is the duty of employees to follow the wishes of persons with higher rank. They may suggest that persons who deviate from their wishes will suffer repercussions, such as demotion or loss of employment. Or they may reward persons who accede to their wishes. In practice, then, power that derives from the organizational hierarchy is often coupled with coercive and reward power.

The power of *position* gives certain persons power resources due to their strategic location in an agency or legislature with respect to its workflow. As Sager notes, for example, intake workers in social agencies possess power by virtue of their ability to create rules and procedures for intake, as well as their implementation of these rules. These rules and procedures must often be honored by others in their agencies—and, because flows of clients into an organization is vital to its survival and (in some cases) revenues, intake workers possess considerable power resources. Others view them as indispensable to the organization and will listen to their perspectives because of this.[14]

Information power derives from persons' control of critical information in specific situations.[15] As an example, take a so-called majority (or minority) whip in the U.S. House of Representatives. This person not only has records about how legislators have voted in the past, but keeps tabs on their current policy preferences. A policy advocate who wanted to get legislation through the House might consult the whip—and his or her advice about the feasibility of getting a specific measure enacted might influence whether and how the policy advocate chose to proceed. In similar fashion, intake workers in agencies possess important knowledge about why specific persons come to the agency and what they need—information that could be used by higher-level staff to decide whether to initiate a specific new program.

Connections power derives from the particular networks or key contacts of specific persons.[16] Assume, for example, that a policy advocate wanted to get a policy enacted in a specific legislature, but had no key contacts among its legislators or legislative staff—and contrast this person with another policy advocate who had devoted the past 20 years to mixing and dealing with legislators and staff on myriad issues. The latter policy advocate would likely be more effective in getting the policy enacted—unless the former advocate, realizing she lacked such networks, compensated for this disadvantage by drawing into her coalition some key persons who *did* possess them.

Value-based power derives from a person's ability to appeal to others based upon their shared ethical commitments. (Sager called this "commitment to purpose.")[17] We discussed in Chapter Two a variety of ethical principles, as well as the use of utilitarian ethical arguments for supporting specific policies. We also discussed different ideologies that emphasize specific values such as equality or fairness (in the case of liberals) or liberty and autonomy (in the case of conservatives and libertarians). Persons will often heed the advice of those people who share their values and ideologies.

We have discussed nine kinds of person-to-person power. Our discussion suggests that policy advocates can draw upon many kinds of power resources when seeking policy changes—or can draw into their coalitions persons who possess power resources that they personally lack.

We have discussed person-to-person power in dyads and triads, but it is also used when a sender gives presentations to groups. An executive might say to his or her whole staff, for example, "Support this policy or our agency will suffer severe financial repercussions" (coercive power), or a politician might say to a neighborhood group, "Have people vote for me if you want this proposed neighborhood project to be funded" (reward power).

Person-to-person power is most effective when the sender selects the kind of power that the receiver is likely to honor. The receiver may respond to expertise, for example, but not to coercion. Effective users of power learn as much as they can about the predispositions of the people they seek to influence. It is also most effective when it is applied skillfully. Practitioners who use expertise as a power resource, for example, have to marshal persuasive evidence sufficiently skillfully that the receiver believes that the *expert* is an expert.[18]

Power resources can be used singly or in tandem. (See Policy Advocacy Challenge 10.3 that discusses how lobbyists for New Orleans would need to use many of these various person-to-person power resources.) An advocate may use both a carrot (reward power) and a stick (coercive power) in persuasion. A policy advocate might use one power resource a specific point in time, only to use another one at a later point in time. When viewed in tandem, the use of power resources constitutes a policy advocates *strategy*, which we discuss in the next three chapters.

POLICY ADVOCACY CHALLENGE 10.3

How Lobbyists for New Orleans and Louisiana Need Many Kinds of Power

BRUCE JANSSON, PH.D.

New Orleans—not to mention many other cities and towns in the Gulf Coast—needs lobbyists in Baton Rouge and Washington, DC that use multiple power resources to get the resources and programs it would need to rebuild itself and to meet the urgent needs of its citizens.

Take as an example the small city of Treasure Island, Florida to show what lobbying can accomplish.[1] Its leaders had tried for years to obtain funds to rebuild a major bridge, but succeeded only when they hired a lobbyist who had known their Congressman for decades. They soon learned from the Congressman that he had obtained a $50 million appropriation by slipping an earmark into a larger piece of legislation. Paying $5,000 per month for a lobbying firm, they received in the next three years $500,000 to fix a sewage plant, $625,000 to repair wooden walkways over the dunes, and $450,000 for pedestrian crosswalks.

New Orleans was not alone, then, even if it had needs far greater than any other city. Indeed, the number of public entities hiring private firms to lobby for them increased from 763 in 1998 to 1,421 in 2006.

To be successful, lobbyists astutely use a variety of power resources in combination. They possess expertise on the issues that are of concern to the clients. They donate resources liberally to the campaign funds of those Congresspersons who help them. They have connections with influential legislators and their staff. They know the staff of important Congressional committees, including the appropriations committees.

Lobbyists are also well versed in the legislative processes used by Congress to determine who gets what resources and when. They know how to obtain so-called earmarks, which are funds for specific projects that are inserted in larger pieces of legislation that have little to do with the city or town where those projects exist. This is "subterranean work," outside the scrutiny of the mass media and often not even debated on the floor of the Senate and the House.

These power resources are particularly effective with legislators. They lack the time to gain expertise in the issues that the lobbyists represent due to the many pieces of legislation and the many claimants for public resources. Because the cost of political campaigns has greatly risen, they need campaign contributions. They want to be able to boast in the next round of elections that they obtained key resources for cities and towns in their jurisdiction. They are, in short, as dependent on lobbyists as the lobbyists are upon them.

---

[1] Jodi Rudoren and Aron Pilhofer, "Hiring Lobbyists for Federal Aid, Towns Learn that Money Talks," *New York Times*, July 2, 2006, pp. 1, 14.

(continued)

To get the resources it needed, New Orleans would need a cadre of effective lobbyists. It would need, moreover, to link its lobbying to the lobbying of the state of Louisiana, as well as other cities and towns in the Gulf Coast. These behind-the-scenes lobbying activities, more than any speeches that Mayor Nagin or Governor Blanco would give, would determine in considerable measure how rapidly New Orleans was rebuilt.

Some questions to ponder:

• Why do many legislators depend heavily on lobbyists?
• Is it ethically correct for cities to hire lobbyists that they fund with taxpayers' dollars?
• Why do many chapters of the National Association of Social Workers hire their own lobbyists?

Power Resources that Stem from Policy Maneuvering

If we stopped with person-to-person power resources, we would ignore a wide range of other power resources that policy advocates develop and use during policy maneuvering. These power resources develop from specific actions that policy advocates take during policy deliberations—often in response to the actions of other persons. They stem less from the specific characteristics of power users themselves, as in the case of person-to-person power resources, and more from give-and-take with other persons in the policy-making process.

Substantive Power

People often form opinions about a policy, not because they have been encouraged to support or oppose it, but because of how they view its substantive content. Policy practitioners exercise *substantive power* when they shape the content of policies to elicit support from specific persons. For example, two persons favor providing low-income housing subsidies in a government program, but one wants the subsidies to go only to people below poverty standards, while the other also wants the subsidies to go to people with moderate incomes. The initiator of the housing-subsidy proposal might decide against a precise definition of the income levels, hoping that both persons will vote for it. Indeed, the use of *vagueness* is often an effective tactic when persons disagree about the specific details of a proposal.[19] Of course, vagueness also can be counterproductive because an excessively vague proposal will arouse the opposition of those who strongly favor specific measures. Moreover, when key points of legislation are not defined, the implementers of the legislation have more leeway. If one party believes the other party will control the presidency (and thus the top appointive positions in implementing agencies), they will want to make key points specific so their political foes cannot implement the legislation contrary to their wishes. For example, in 1988, some Democrats, fearing that Republicans would not insist on minimum child-to-staff ratios when implementing a national day-care proposal, tried to place specific ratios in the federal legislation.[20]

Policy advocates exercise substantive power when they change a policy's content to enhance specific decision makers' support for it. In the aforementioned day-care proposal, its advocates inserted many provisions to counter conservatives' opposition, such as putting a modest ceiling on the program's costs and giving the states a significant role in shaping the programs within their boundaries. These changes may be made when a proposal is initially drafted, during deliberations, or when the proposal goes before a legislature or other decision-making body. Substantive power often involves compromises; one faction may modify one provision in exchange for another faction's changing another provision.

Policy advocates encounter dilemmas when using substantive power. They may change a policy proposal to obtain one person's support, only to find that they have alienated someone else. When they make numerous concessions to obtain opponents' support, proposals may become so diluted as to be, in the words of Bachrach and Baratz, "decisionless decisions" or merely symbolic measures.[21]

For example, Senator Hubert Humphrey and Representative Augustus Hawkins initiated a legislative proposal in the 1970s requiring the federal government to create jobs whenever the national unemployment rate exceeded 3 percent. By the time the legislation was enacted, it was only a vague statement that the federal government would seek full employment. It required no specific actions, such as developing public works when considerable unemployment existed.[22] Skillful policy practitioners often refrain from offering changes in a proposal until they are certain that compromises are needed for its passage.

A policy advocate using substantive power also may couple a relatively unpopular proposal with more popular ones. In "Christmas-tree legislation" (so named because of the "gifts" many legislators place in it for certain persons or interest groups) in Congress, politicians insert various previously unenacted proposals in a larger piece of legislation just before the yearly congressional session finishes at the end of December. Politicians who oppose these inserted measures nonetheless vote for the legislation because it contains some of their own measures.[23] A controversial proposal may be swept to victory when it is attached to a popular proposal. Foes of abortion, for example, won prohibition of the use of Medicaid funds for abortions when they attached it to the appropriations bill for the Department of Health and Human Services.[24]

Proponents have many ways to shape a proposal so that it is nonthreatening to potential opponents. A program may be designed and portrayed as a pilot project to defuse opposition.[25] Proponents may place a proposed program under a specific government unit's jurisdiction to make it more appealing to potential opponents. Proponents enhanced support for the Supplementary Security Income (SSI) program, which provides income to destitute older people and people who are disabled, by proposing that it be placed under the jurisdiction of the Social Security Administration, because that unit of government was more acceptable to conservatives than units that administer welfare programs.[26] Proposals' titles are often selected to make them more acceptable to conservative politicians. Senator Moynihan emphasized family support payments rather than welfare payments when discussing a welfare reform initiative in 1988.[27]

Christopher Matthews contends that many successful politicians avoid discussing basic principles when considering legislation.[28] Realizing that mentioning fundamental principles often alienates valuable allies with different perspectives from their own, they focus instead on the precise details of the legislation. It is better, they reason, to win battles over the content of legislation than to have shouting matches about ultimate purposes. On the other hand, an enunciation of basic principles is needed in some cases to rally support for a measure.

We discussed negotiations—both softball and hardball ones—in the last chapter. In fact, negotiations and bargaining also illustrate the use of substantive power resources. Advocates yield on some points while insisting on others in a give-and-take process with opponents—hoping that such bargaining will convince many persons to support specific legislation or policies.

Power in Decision-Making Procedures

Policy is often fashioned by *decision-making* or *procedural power* during deliberations. In legislatures, for example, numerous people and committees, and finally the full body must assent to a policy before it can be enacted.[29] (Recall Figure 4.3 depicting the normal course of legislation through both chambers of the Congress.)

There are many parliamentary techniques and strategies for increasing a proposal's chances of enactment, or for blocking a proposal: bypassing persons, committees, and meetings unfavorable to the proposal, while routing the proposal to those more favorable; persuading party officials to steer a proposal to the committee most favorably disposed or to leapfrog a meeting or procedure; and using person-to-person power with key decision makers, such as chairs of important committees, not only to obtain their support, but also to secure their assistance with logistic details. A committee chair can place a proposal in a preferred position on a meeting agenda, insist that policies undergo further subcommittee deliberations, or abbreviate lengthy deliberations to help or prevent a specific measure's enactment. Clever strategists are well versed in such tactics.[30]

Procedural tactics are sometimes counterproductive, however, provoking accusations of unfairly stifling dissent by rushing a proposal through a legislature, stacking the cards for or against a proposal, or bypassing normal channels. Ethical objections may also be raised when concerned persons are excluded from policy deliberations.

When initiating proposals, it is necessary to know who the key decision makers are, whether they favor a proposal, and whether the opposition can be overcome. During the first six years of the administration of George W. Bush, Republicans chaired the committees of both the House and the Senate because they had majorities in both chambers. White House staff members and these Republican chairs mobilized party support for bills that Republicans favored. Disgruntled Democrats discovered that many of their legislative initiatives never made it beyond these committee chairs. So they hoped that they could regain majorities in either or both the Senate and the House in the elections of 2006 in hopes that their policy proposals would receive more attention. (See Policy Advocacy Challenge 10.4.)

POLICY ADVOCACY CHALLENGE 10.4

How National Politics Works—the Wrong Way

BRUCE JANSSON, PH.D.

It is sometimes instructive to study how politics works—the wrong way. In the eyes of Norman Ornstein, a person who had studied Congress for 25 years, a "culture of corruption" had established itself in Washington—a culture that manifested itself in relationships between lobbyist Jack Abramhoff, House Majority Leader Tom Delay, Congressman Bob Ney, and others. View the documentary "Capitol Crimes" that was narrated by Bill Moyers on PBS at **http://www.pbs.org/moyers/moyersonamerica/capitol/index.html**. (It lasts about one and one-half hours—time well spent because it so graphically discusses how Congress and other political institutions work—at their worst.) The documentary traces how Abramhoff used a variety of power resources—many of them illegal—to get favors for his clients, including owners of sweatshops abroad. At the time of the documentary, Abramhoff had been indicted for various crimes, but chose to cooperate with federal investigators by giving them information about his dealings with various Congressmen. Congressmen Delay had been indicted for illegal funneling of corporate funds into Texas legislative contests. Congressman Ney had been indicted for bribery.

As you watch this documentary, ask these questions:

- What power resources did Abramhoff use to secure assistance for his clients?
- Why did it take so long for federal investigators to uncover his—and the others'— illegal activities?
- How does the documentary prove the saying, "money corrupts, but power corrupts absolutely?" Also ask whether many persons use power ethically—and cite some examples.
- What makes some power transactions unethical?

Decision-making procedures also exist in agencies. A staff member, committee, or executive may propose a new agency program, which is then developed by a staff committee and brought to the full staff for consideration. The executive then may take it to the board of directors, which may refer it to a board committee before taking a final vote. Or simpler procedures might be used: A hospital social services director wants to develop social work services on the neurology ward and only seeks the agreement of the medical director of neurology. After the services have been in effect for some time, the staff member obtains formal approval from a higher hospital official, perhaps when he needs additional funding from the hospital's budget.

In Policy Advocacy Challenge 10.2, the social work intern carefully considered procedural options as she developed a strategy for her program innovation. Because of barriers to this innovation in the agency, such as tight budgets, the intern and her preceptor decided the innovation would be doomed if they began with a formal proposal to the executive director. Therefore, they planned a two-phase strategy: first to develop a pilot project without securing formal high-level clearance, and then, after proving the program workable, to develop a formal program proposal that would go through the executive director to the board for approval. The intern and the preceptor improved their proposal's chances not through efforts to convince other people of its merits, but by shaping the decision-making process.

Process Power

Policies are shaped in the give-and-take of deliberations, which are characterized by their tenor, tempo, and scope of conflict. The *tenor* is the level of conflict; the *tempo* is the timing, pace, and duration of deliberations; and the *scope of conflict* is the number and kind of people who participate in them. Policy advocates use *process power* when they influence the tenor, tempo, or scope of conflict of deliberations in order to get a specific proposal enacted.

Let's begin with the crude analogy of a schoolyard dispute to illustrate tenor, tempo, and scope of conflict. After the two parties have developed their positions in the dispute, they must decide how to resolve it. First, they shape the tenor of deliberations: Will they use brute strength (a fight), have an amicable discussion, or take some middle course in which they shout at each other but do not fight? Next, each must decide what tempo of deliberations will help their cause: Will they seek a speedy settlement or protracted deliberations? Finally, they determine who should participate in the conflict: Do they want a narrow scope of conflict that will exclude outsiders from their interaction or will they invite others to join the fray, in the belief that a broad scope of conflict will help their cause?[31]

A bully with physical superiority might decide to initiate a fight that involved only himself and a proverbial 90-pound weakling, whereas the weakling might want to enlarge the scope of conflict to include powerful allies, including some bystanders. The bully might want to resolve the issue speedily so the weakling would not have time to organize an attack—favoring a rapid tempo. The weakling, realizing he had no chance in the event of actual combat, might wish to convert the impending battle to a lower tenor, such as "settling our differences by talking things out."

The social work intern in Policy Advocacy Challenge 10.2 used process power to increase her chances of getting her innovation accepted. She wanted to keep it low profile during its pilot phase so it would not create controversy because she feared that it would otherwise be rejected by agency staff. She wanted to wait until she had initiated the pilot project before even developing a formal proposal with Mr. Jones that might be forwarded to the Executive Director and the Board. Contrast this strategy with one that emphasized confrontation, a rapid tempo, and a broad scope of conflict.

We can usefully contrast win-lose politics with win-win politics. In win-lose politics, each side in the contest believes that it loses each time the other side wins and therefore wants to contest every point. In win-win politics, the two sides believe they will obtain mutually beneficial concessions. While they do not want to concede all points, they are open to compromise so they will both emerge better off than before deliberations. It would be a more pleasant world if people perceived win-win possibilities in more conflicts and transformed these conflicts into win-win situations. In many cases, however, this approach is not feasible. Parties may have conflicting values, may not trust their opponents, and may believe they will suffer severe losses if they make concessions.

Individuals can sometimes influence the level of conflict. People who wish to intensify discord, for example, can use emotion-laden words; refer to conflicts in the fundamental values at stake; enlarge the scope of conflict by publicizing the issue; use unusual tactics, such as the filibuster in the U.S. Senate; or clearly state that they do not want amicable resolution: "We plan to fight to the finish," or "We will accept no significant changes in our proposal!"[32] People who believe that conflict will be detrimental to their cause will try to diminish conflict, for example, by emphasizing a proposal's technical features, identifying the common interests of all the parties, and discouraging the participation of those who will raise the level of conflict.

Timing is another kind of process power. The timing of a disputed proposal often favors a specific side. If someone introduces a proposal at an inopportune moment, its chances may be imperiled, no matter how skillful its defenders or how great its merits. Whether in agency or legislative settings, such background factors as budgetary deficits, a crowded agenda, or an unsympathetic executive provide a harsh environment for a policy proposal. When a favorable context exists, a proposal defeated earlier may suddenly sail through the political process.[33]

In the give-and-take of policy deliberations, policy advocates use other power resources to increase their odds of success. They may try to coopt other persons by giving them credit or by involving them in key tasks. In the case of Policy Advocacy Challenge 10.2, for example, the intern coopted Mr. Jones by giving him credit for developing the innovation even when she had first thought of it. Policy advocates may try to intimidate opponents by giving the impression that they have the momentum and are certain to prevail.

Unfortunately, policy advocates sometimes have limited power to influence the political process because of limited control over the actions of their opponents. Someone who wants to limit conflict, for example, may find that goal sabotaged by opponents who succeed in escalating conflict or enlarging the scope of conflict by publicizing it in the mass media—as the frequent leaks to the press about government business suggest. Even skillful policy advocates miscalculate. Someone who introduces a proposal at a seemingly opportune moment may later become aware of background factors that will scuttle it. Moreover, policy processes often develop a momentum that cannot be slowed, no matter what advocates do.[34] Tradition also frustrates policy advocacy: Issues that have previously generated high conflict, such as national health insurance, are sure to stir up conflict if reintroduced.[35] The dimensions of a proposed change also shape the course of conflict; proposals for massive changes are more likely to polarize liberals and conservatives than more modest proposals.[36]

Shaping Contexts Including Use of the Internet

We have already noted that power transactions occur within a context that includes public opinion and interest groups. Policy advocates can increase their odds of success in many situations if they place pressure on decision makers from external sources, such as by involving interest groups, forming coalitions, or by using the internet to solicit support from persons likely to be sympathetic with their policy initiative.

The Internet has become a powerful tool for mobilizing constituencies to support specific causes or policies. Policy advocates can vastly increase their ability to shape decisions of public officials by mobilizing large numbers of persons to participate in specific policy projects through the Internet as is discussed in Policy Advocacy Challenge 10.5.

POLICY ADVOCACY CHALLENGE 10.5

Using the Internet to Organize Pressure on Decision Makers

CONVIO CORPORATION

The Convio Corporation (**http//:www.convio.com**) has developed software that is used by many NGOs to help them develop and manage advocacy campaigns for specific issues. We include an excerpt from their publication, "Using the Internet for Effective Grassroots Advocacy" to illustrate how the Internet can be used in Web-based advocacy efforts.

Getting Started: Outreach and Engagement

The first step in any online advocacy program is building a base of supporters with whom you can develop a strong online relationship. This means gathering new e-mail addresses, promoting advocacy among current online constituents, learning about constituents' interests, and keeping them informed and engaged. Using the following techniques will help you get your online advocacy program off the ground, or help to improve your existing program.

Recruit New Activists   To build online relationships with constituents and convert them to activists, you must first get e-mail addresses. Consider this: Every time you communicate with constituents, you have the opportunity to collect e-mail addresses. Try the following approaches to develop your e-mail file.

(continued)

Gather E-mail Addresses Offline   Planned interactions such as donor appeals, membership drives, and event invitations are perfect times to ask for e-mail addresses. Simply add a field for e-mail collection to all response forms. At events where you will interact with a large number of constituents, consider setting out a newsletter sign-up sheet, or offer a giveaway for attendees who drop in a card with their name and e-mail address.

When asking for e-mail addresses, emphasize the benefits your constituents will receive by providing you with this information. Remind supporters that by communicating with them online, your organization can save money and administrative work, allowing you to more effectively serve your mission. Also, emphasize the benefit of timely communication: With e-mail communications, you are better equipped to respond to compelling events and inform them quickly of important news, developments, events, and programs.

Gather E-mail Addresses Online   Your Web site is the best source for reaching new prospects and existing constituents and collecting their e-mail addresses. Visitors to your Web site have sought you out because they are interested in your organization. This existing affinity is a powerful incentive for online visitors to provide you with the information you need to build relationships with them online.

TIP: When collecting e-mail addresses, be sure to let people know that the organization is collecting this information and how it will be used. Always give people a chance to opt out of receiving e-mail by providing a check box that says something like, "I'd like to receive future mailings," which they can uncheck.

Mobilizing Activists Through Online Campaigns

Once you have built a file of e-mail addresses and started to create e-relationships, it's time to begin online campaigns that motivate people to take action. While e-mail is the cornerstone of any online campaign, Web site content is a key consideration as well. The approaches in this section will help you to create effective e-mail messages as well as successful multi-phased online campaigns.

Create Compelling E-mail Messages that Inspire Action   E-mail is the most efficient and cost-effective way to reach activists immediately. There are many things you can do to increase the effectiveness of each message you send. Keep subject lines short and use them to convey urgency and compel recipients to open the e-mail immediately. Personalize the message by including the recipient's name and noting that he or she is receiving the e-mail as a result of having indicated an interest in the topic at hand. Make the e-mail brief, but provide enough background to trigger action.

Test Your Message   Prior to sending your e-mail to hundreds or thousands of supporters, you should thoroughly test your communication. This important process prevents distribution of e-mails containing costly and/or potentially embarrassing mistakes. Designate and train a few people within your department or organization and send test messages to this group to maintain consistent quality standards.

You also should take advantage of the inherent benefits of the Internet by sending test messages to a sub-set of target recipients prior to sending it to your entire e-mail file. Because the Internet allows you to send messages and receive responses quickly, you can compare response rates of different messages and subject lines, then refine your e-mail message before sending it to the entire constituent base—ensuring the maximum response for each e-mail campaign.

Include Landing Pages or Micro Sites   While e-mail is the cornerstone of your online advocacy efforts, it is also important to include a link to a landing page for each campaign. A landing page is a Web page where constituents can go to find out more about your action alert and where they can take action. Another way to extend the reach of your advocacy campaign is to promote it on pages throughout your Web site to capture the interest of new site visitors and those who do not receive your e-mail communications. Also consider creating a micro site. This can be a section on your Web site with its own Web address and that has its own campaign branding. Similar to a landing page, a micro site has a very tight focus on a specific campaign to drive people to act immediately.

Use Vote Data   Using the Internet to influence public policy makers before a vote is critical. But, continuing grassroots efforts after votes have taken place also can help ensure ongoing support for the issues most important to your organization. Your online advocacy software should allow you to use legislator vote data to:

- Develop scorecards that rate legislators based on how they voted with respect to your organization's position on an issue.
- Create vote pages with a description of an issue, vote date, your organization's position on the issue, how constituents' legislators voted on the matter, and the legislators' scorecards.
- Provide an option for a constituent to send a "thank" or "spank" message to his/her legislators based on their vote.
- Target action alerts to a subset of your e-mail file based on how individuals' legislators voted on a specific issue, as well as by state, congressional district, or interest.

Give Activists Multiple Options for Taking Action   After you've spread the word about your latest advocacy effort, it's critical to give activists a convenient way to make their voices heard. Remember, not everyone wants to take action in the same way.

Provide pre-formatted letters on your Web site that constituents can easily customize and automatically send to the correct decision makers. Populate any form fields automatically for returning advocates for their convenience. Give activists the option to send messages via e-mail, fax, or mail. Your activists will appreciate these conveniences to making their voices heard.

Ensure Message Delivery   Your online advocacy campaign's success will depend largely on getting your activists' messages to the right decision makers. But, with the growing volume of e-mail aimed at decision makers today, reaching the right people at the right time has become a challenge. Messages might not get delivered or, if they do, might go unread because staffers cannot keep up with the volume.

To manage the flood of messages, many legislators' offices only accept constituents' input through Web-based forms on the legislators' Web sites. At the same time, an increasing number of advocacy groups are realizing that general e-mail blasts are

(continued)

POLICY
ADVOCACY
CHALLENGE 10.5

(continued)

not always effective, and they are looking for alternatives to ensure their messages get through. The right online tools can help.

Look for Flexibility in Targeting   Invest in online tools that provide the flexibility to easily and quickly create target groups of the exact decision makers and influencers required for each campaign. You should be able to organize targets in a variety of ways (legislators, cabinet secretaries, and media, for example) to build a rich database for future use.

Offer Multiple Delivery Options   Don't rely entirely on e-mail to get your message across to decision makers. With e-mail volume increasing so dramatically, a multi-channel approach that also includes personal letters, faxes, and phone calls will help ensure that the message gets through. Look for online tools that will automatically try an alternative means of delivery if a message fails to get through. For example, if an e-mail bounces back repeatedly, your online advocacy software should automatically send a fax as a back-up. When you do use e-mail, be sure to have online tools that can automatically route constituents' messages through Web forms or other technology-based filters, if necessary.

We discussed the Convio Corporation's software for managing policy-advocacy campaigns using the Internet, but other kinds also exist that can be used in tandem to develop an advocacy campaign. (See Policy Advocacy Challenge 10.6.)

POLICY
ADVOCACY
CHALLENGE 10.6

Integrating
Software
to Develop
an Advocacy
Campaign

BRUCE JANSSON,
PH.D.

In addition to the Convio Corporation's software discussed in Policy Advocacy Challenge 10.5, other software exists that assists policy advocates in developing campaigns to change policies, including such free ones as CitizenSpeak and CivicSpace Labs where advocates can create their own online campaigns. Wanting to develop the Free Schuylkill River Coalition to create a pedestrian pathway along Philadelphia's Schuylkill River, policy advocates used a free e-mail advocacy service for grassroots organizations (**http://www.citizenspeak.org**) that created a web address for their campaign and sent it to an initial cadre of 50 persons via e-mail.[1] Using CitizenSpeaks' "Tell-a-Friend" feature, the group not only greatly enlarged its e-mail address list but refined the group's message and goals by viewing members' online comments. Then the coalition invited readers to its newly created blog that gave additional information about their campaign by using the low-cost and easy-to-use TypePad software (**http://www.typepad.com**). This software allowed the coalition to include photo albums, invite and manage comments, add track backs, and monitor weblog statistics. Then the Free Schuylkill River Coalition signed up for Constituent Mail (**http://www.constituentmail.com**), which is an easy-to-use and low-cost online e-mail management service that lets organizations maintain and segment a database of personalized HTML e-mail communications. It used this software to invite supporters to a rally that was attended by the media, which brought additional attention to their project.[2]

[1] For a detailed account of this campaign, see Allison H. Fine, *Momentum: Igniting Social Change in the Connected Age*, San Francisco, Jossey-Bass, 2006, pp. 179–181.
[2] Ibid., p. 181.

By integrating various Internet tools, policy advocates can develop a campaign that increases their supporters many times over, helps them keep in touch with members, and helps them to organize key events. In this particular case, the Coalition won a key victory over a railroad company that wanted to block their pedestrian walkway by not allowing pedestrians to cross their tracks.[3]

Some questions to ponder:

- How do these kinds of software packages save the organizers of policy advocacy projects considerable time?
- Can such software supplant the need for traditional organizing—or must the software be supplemented by considerable in-person contacts by the organizers of policy advocacy projects?

---

[3] Ibid., p. 181.

Politicians are also more likely to take the advice of an advocate who is backed up by affiliation with a recognized group or coalition. Such affiliations give advocates several advantages. Recognized groups or coalitions can mobilize external pressure by activating their members and those of affiliated organizations. As a result, they are more likely than solo advocates to get attention from the mass media, particularly as they develop long-standing associations with reporters and officials in television and the print media. Because they can obtain funds from foundations and other sources more easily than solo advocates can, advocacy groups and coalitions can conduct more sophisticated research than solo advocates—research that enhances their standing with legislators and government officials. And because advocacy groups are long-standing organizations, their staff can develop ongoing associations with government officials and legislators, as well as close working relationships with the staff of other advocacy groups that allow them to pool resources, share contacts, and form coalitions around specific issues. It is not sufficient only to develop advocacy groups and coalitions, however; policy advocates need also to enlist them in well-conceived campaigns to secure policy reforms.

Sometimes policy advocates can use a low scope of conflict, relying on personal relationships with policy makers to bring policy changes. In such cases, advocates do not mobilize external pressure on legislators because they believe they can secure policy reforms without it. In other cases, however, they do need to mobilize external pressure in a well-coordinated campaign that includes letter writing, coverage by the mass media, and even demonstrations.

Policy advocates should try, then, to work with and through advocacy groups and coalitions whenever possible. If such groups do not exist, policy advocates should form them. (We discuss strategies for organizing coalitions in the next chapter.)

External pressure can also be placed on social agencies. As Yeheskel Hasenfeld and other organizational theorists with a political economy perspective note, organizational policies are shaped by many forces.[37] Funders, courts, community groups, and community leaders all can shape organizations' internal policies. Just as policy advocates sometimes pressure legislators, they sometimes pressure social agencies to modify specific policies or to consider program innovations.

Hedrick Smith argues that television has revolutionized political tactics in Congress, especially since the decline in power of political party leaders and legislative committees. The committees have lost power because of procedural changes and an increase in party members' power to choose their committee memberships.[38] Viewing themselves as quasi-independent of their party and seeking a national as well as a local constituency, many politicians regularly make videotapes that they forward to the media in their constituencies. Through the mass media, then, politicians increase public support for issues they believe will enhance their popularity. Advocacy groups and coalitions also need to make skillful use of the mass media, as we discuss in Chapter Thirteen, by having press conferences, writing editorials, briefing reporters, and staging media events.

Successful Power Users

Personal characteristics—*persistence*, for example—increase some persons' ability to shape policy outcomes. Jane Addams and Martin Luther King, Jr. persevered over decades despite repeated failures in their quest for social justice. Even our student intern, who might have been discouraged by her preceptor's initial irritation about her proposed innovation, brought up the issue again several weeks later and secured a positive response. As we noted in Chapter Six when discussing agenda building, some issues float for years and then resurface when someone is sufficiently persistent to reintroduce the measure.

Policy advocates who focus on an issue's content and avoid attacking the motivations or character of their opponents are often viewed more positively than those who make personal attacks.[39] As we point out in the next chapter, even though we often have to respond to unfair attacks on our intentions or motivations, we do not usually enhance our personal power by initiating such attacks.

Although skillful policy advocates are flexible, they do not bend with every breeze. Personal credibility, which is essential to the effective use of power, will be eroded if they seem excessively opportunistic. They must be able to stick to their basic convictions, even in the face of opposition.

However, successful policy advocates also are skilled in fashioning compromises, which are frequently needed to obtain support in agency and legislative settings.[40] A fine line sometimes exists between having convictions and being able to compromise.

Power in Organizations

We have discussed power relationships and power resources, using many examples from legislative settings. As our example of the social work intern suggests, power relationships and power resources also are used extensively in social agencies as advocates try to improve services for clients. We now discuss a special kind of policy issue that many social workers confront at some point in their professional work: when to challenge policies or practices that they believe to be unethical and that are supported by higher level staff and officials.

Discretion, Compliance, and Whistle-Blowing

The interrelationship of discretion, compliance, and whistle-blowing confronts direct service and other social service staff throughout their careers. Considerable controversy may exist in an agency about how much discretion, or autonomy, policy makers and administrators should grant human service workers. Under what circumstances should social workers be able to disobey policies they believe are unethical? When should social workers take their disagreements about internal agency matters to external parties, such as the mass media?

Defining Zones of Discretion

When analyzing policy implementation, we often think in broad terms, such as agency budgets and leadership, taking a top-down perspective. We also can take a bottom-up perspective by beginning with the line worker, who translates policy into action.

High-level policies may seem to dictate virtually all the actions of direct-service staff. However, much of their work occurs within zones of discretion, where their own judgments and choices shape their actions.[41]

Why do agencies cede so much discretion to their direct-service staff? Assume that you are a high-level administrator and are quite certain about the intake policies you want in your agency's program for children with learning disorders. You can write some definitive admission standards, such as "Only children from families with XYZ income shall obtain admittance to this program." Because this kind of policy is quantitative, it is clear-cut and allows no exceptions. However, when you come to "learning disorders," you despair of writing an exact definition, and you must cede to those who will implement this policy considerable discretion in selecting children with learning disorders. Moreover, you must let professional workers determine when a child has reached sufficient learning competence to make her or him ineligible for continuing service. Realizing that some people will need extended help and others may overcome their problems quickly, you decide against a blanket rule that establishes a maximum period of service.

Our discussion suggests that professionals are given so much discretion because they often are required to use their own judgment on complex social problems, human motivation, and clients' progress. High-level officials may also decide that professionals need the latitude to make exceptions to policies. Assume, for example, that legislators are aware that some psychotic patients need to be committed to institutions even though they are not suicidal and have not physically threatened other persons, the criteria usually used for involuntary commitment. Legislators may add professional judgment to those criteria, even though such discretion may sometimes lead to unnecessary commitment.

In connection with the autonomy of direct-service workers, we must note as well that the location and nature of their work precludes detailed oversight. Direct-service workers conduct much of their work in private interactions with clients. Moreover, many human services agencies do not conform to the bureaucratic models discussed by Max Weber; rather than having tight controls in centralized structures, many of them are "loosely coupled" organizations with several quasi-independent programs, units, and branches. In such organizations, it is difficult for top administrators to regulate the work of direct-service staff.[42]

Ceding discretion to professionals bears some risks and may lead to discrimination against certain clients in the name of professional judgment. A professional may decide that people with specific learning disorders should not be allowed into a program, because he or she is prejudiced against them and has erroneous perceptions of their condition.[43]

Some professionals take advantage of the discretion allowed them to further their own material interests or their own narrow approach to service delivery. Franklin Chu and Sharland Trotter discovered that many mental health professionals failed to implement federally legislated policies because they were uninterested in working with psychotic or low-income persons.[44] A few social workers have even siphoned clients from their public agency for their private practice, despite the widely held ethical norms that prohibit this practice.

There is a constant tension between maximizing professional discretion and making binding rules to prevent discrimination against particular clients and to protect the public interest. If professionals often want to expand their discretion, policy makers often want to constrict it.

Issues of Compliance

A social worker in a public welfare setting dislikes specific, punitive policies. A social worker in a child welfare office objects to pressures to reunify families that have not been adequately analyzed or helped. Social workers who do not want to implement specific policies can adopt several strategies. First, they can keep their noncompliance secret even from their supervisors by bending or ignoring rules, by enforcing rules half-heartedly, or by counseling clients in ways that circumvent specific policies. Second, they can comply with official policy but use every available means to seek exemptions for specific persons. For example, to help an older person avoid early discharge from a hospital, they might claim that no nursing home beds can be found, after a half-hearted look for a bed, or they may even lie about a bed's availability. (Such deception returns us to the first strategy.) Third, they may comply with official policy in every respect, even while believing it to be defective. Fourth, they may comply with official policies while trying to change them.

No easy answers exist for such dilemmas. The duty to obey official policy cannot be dismissed lightly; professionals' credibility would be severely jeopardized if they routinely flouted the rules. Yet some policies are unethical or harmful to clients, whether to all clients or just to those with idiosyncratic needs. Beneficence requires us to consider disobeying policies that appear to be inimical to clients' needs or to be in violation of professional ethics. However, it is difficult to protest policies when high-level officials strongly promote them or when agency officials fear that higher authorities, such as legislators, will retaliate if they discover noncompliance.

By the same token, direct-service social workers sometimes find that their colleagues do not implement good policies. (Social workers may fail to implement meritorious policies because they have narrow helping philosophies that deemphasize such activities as outreach, they believe they lack the necessary expertise or resources, they feel burned out, or they are prejudiced against certain kinds of clients.) In such cases, social workers should try to change their colleagues' behavior through educational techniques or technical assistance, or even by alerting higher management to the noncompliance.

Changing peers' behavior can pose a formidable challenge, however, particularly when the agency atmosphere is not conducive to challenging the norms.

Whistle-Blowing

Individual staff members should try to work through normal channels, but what if they find specific policies or other staff members' actions (such as corruption) so morally flawed that they cannot abide their continuation? And what if they fear that open opposition will cause their dismissal or other penalties? An emerging literature suggests that staff members can ethically publicize flawed policies and actions by divulging informa-tion to persons outside the organization, such as members of the mass media, legis-lators, state authorities, regulators, or funders.[45] They can reveal this information to outsiders, either using their own names or speaking on condition of anonymity in order to prevent personal reprisals. However, whistle-blowers who make their names public are sometimes perceived as more credible than those who leak charges anonymously. They also can give the information to the National Association of Social Workers (NASW), which will protect their identity while making the information public.

Whistle-blowing is an attempt to correct lapses by calling external parties into the conflict. It is ethical if the policies or actions are major, not trivial, violations of ethics or professional standards; if the whistle-blower has extremely good evidence that he or she cannot modify policies by conventional means; and if the whistle-blower has excellent evidence that he or she will be subjected to serious penalties as a result of raising questions about the policies or conduct. (Despite recent legislation in some states that protects whistle-blowers, as well as sanctions that the NASW can exact against employers who fire whistle-blowers, persons sometimes have justifiable rea-son to believe that they will be in jeopardy if they engage in whistle-blowing.) At the same time, whistle-blowing is abused when persons raise trivial issues, such as minor indiscretions in an agency, or when they have not fully considered alternative means of changing policies.[46]

Our prior discussion of discretion suggests that social workers often encounter not objectionable high-level policies, but vague policies that require them to develop means of filling the policy vacuum.

Power Differentials

So far, our discussion may falsely suggest that all of us have an equal opportunity to wield power, and that if we just put our minds to the task, we will succeed in having policy proposals enacted. This optimistic conclusion ignores harsh realities, such as the power differentials that give some people a significant advantage over others.

Legislators and high-level government officials have *formal authority*, which gives them the power to approve or disapprove certain policy initiatives; to make proposals; and to obtain access to program, budget, and technical information. They have access to other highly placed people who yield information and assistance that are not avail-able to others, and they often command obedience from others when they issue direc-tives or make recommendations. Executives of agencies and government bureaucracies have considerable power over their subordinates, as well as experience and knowledge. Technical experts on specific topics often have extraordinary power in governmental and agency settings.

The leaders, staff members, and lobbyists of groups that have large constituencies, such as interest groups, professional associations, and social movements, derive power from these constituencies that can exert influence on decision makers who do not heed policy suggestions. These leaders, staff members, and lobbyists also have useful exper-tise that helps them cultivate personal relationships with decision makers that further enhance their power. Some interest groups increase their power by making large cam-paign contributions to politicians who support their position. In a compelling account of how the mass media and large interest groups (such as the American Association of Retired Persons and political action committees) influence policies, Hedrick Smith contends that well-organized, grass-roots constituencies with extraordinary resources and access to the mass media are wielding increasing power in legislative settings.[47]

Individuals who help shape and enact budgets, such as legislators on appropriations committees and officials who control budgets in bureaucracies, often have extraordinary power because "those who pay the piper call the tune." A professor of mine once lamented social workers' tendency to seek jobs in organizations' personnel sections when the staff in the fiscal departments usually have more power to shape the policies and programs of bureaucracies. Officials in the federal Office of Management and Budget (OMB) are key players in establishing the nation's domestic policy because they shape the president's budgetary recommendations.

In some cases, authority figures command obedience even when their suggestions are ethically flawed.[48] The impulse to obey authority figures may stem from peer pressure, loyalty to the organization, lack of information about specific issues, or fear of sanctions.

We should not overlook the role cultural symbols play in giving certain persons and groups more power than others. Officials affiliated with socially acceptable issues, such as children, health, and education, are often more influential than people associated with socially stigmatized groups, such as people who are mentally ill, welfare recipients, or ex-offenders.[49]

Discrimination patterns in the broader society influence power transactions. Rosabeth Kanter suggests that women are often excluded from decision making in large organizations because of gender-based prejudice and because they lack access to old-boy networks. Members of minority groups often encounter similar problems.[50]

Although few people would deny that power differentials exist, some theorists, such as C. Wright Mills, have suggested the existence of a power elite, such as the leaders of well-financed interest groups, that monopolizes power and consigns other people and interests to marginal roles.[51] On the other hand, "pluralist" theorists, such as Robert Dahl, have suggested that many interests and people shape policy choices.[52] These theorists point to the multiple interest groups that shape policies in municipal, county, state, and federal jurisdictions.

Who is right? Each theory applies in some situations. In some areas, specific people and interests have the power to dominate policy making, whereas in others, policy choices stem from a political process in which almost anyone can participate. In still other situations, certain people and interests have the power to set agendas and shape choices, but determined and well-organized groups can force them into important concessions. As we discuss in the next chapter, policy practitioners need to be realistic in assessing the distribution of power in specific settings.

The case of the student intern illustrates how persons with little formal power can be surprisingly successful. By taking the initiative, working through an intermediary (Mr. Jones), developing an effective innovation, and securing support for the innovation from psychiatric hospitals, the intern mapped a sophisticated strategy to secure a major policy change in her agency.

Ethical Issues

Some social workers believe that developing and using power is unprofessional. We argued in Chapter Three, however, that although they may be unaware of it, social workers use power frequently in their work, including their direct-service work.

Whenever they guide, direct, or suggest options to clients, they use power. When they make recommendations to supervisors or external authorities, such as the courts, they use power. Indeed, we argued in Chapter Two that it may be unethical not to use power in certain situations, such as questioning defective policies or seeking policy changes. In such cases, we said, social workers (and other professionals, such as teachers, attorneys, and physicians) may fail to advance beneficence, social justice, and fairness.

Power can be used unethically—dishonestly or manipulatively—but we cannot make simple, easy-to-follow ethical rules. Someone who is blatantly dishonest to gain a strategic advantage is clearly behaving unethically, but there are grayer areas in ethics. For example, should someone volunteer to an opponent that she will attack his position in a forthcoming meeting? Is withholding this information the same as lying? As discussed in Chapter Two, we may also encounter ethical dilemmas when we use power, as when honesty and social justice conflict. For example, what if enacting a measure to help low-income persons hinges on your telling a falsehood to an opponent of that measure? Faced with this ethical dilemma, you would certainly want to reflect carefully and seek consultation before acting.

The use of manipulation is also an ethical issue. Assume that you want to win and are convinced that you cannot win unless you use a devious parliamentary maneuver that will place your opponent at a disadvantage, use a threat to gain an opponent's support, or suppress data that would make your position appear less tenable. All of these behaviors are manipulative because they will give you an advantage at the expense of open discourse and free choices Such tactics are usually unethical and even counterproductive because they may cause others to distrust you and even oppose your position.

However, certain manipulative behaviors, like some forms of dishonesty, can be justified in limited situations. You might rightly decide that ethical principles, such as social justice and beneficence, are at stake; that your opponents are using hardball tactics, so you must use them, too; and that you will lose without some form of manipulation. Here, too, you will want to reflect and seek consultation. (See Policy Advocacy Challenge 10.7. for discussion of manipulation in political communication.)

POLICY ADVOCACY CHALLENGE 10.7
 	
The Use of Manipulation in Political Communication
 	
BRUCE JANSSON, PH.D.
	Democrats contend that the President George W. Bush engaged in manipulative rhetoric on the eve of the 2006 Congressional elections. The stakes for this election were high for both sides: if the Democrats prevailed, they might regain control of both the House and the Senate for the first time in decades.
	
	    Background political conditions seemed to favor the Democrats. Widespread discontent existed with respect to the war in Iraq. A scandal occurred in early October involving a Republican Congressman alleged to have made suggestive advances on male pages in the Congress.
	
	    Following Republican strategies in the presidential election of 2004, however, Republican strategists wanted to portray Democrats as soft on terrorism. It was difficult to do this on a factual basis because Democrats had supported huge budgets for the Homeland Security Agency—and had even challenged Republicans to approve more funds for protection of the nation's ports and its chemical factories, as well as to screen baggage on airlines.

(continued)

But Republicans *could* use manipulative rhetoric to make it appear that the Democrats *were* soft on terrorism. The president had recently told an interviewer, for example, that "Most people want us to win."[1] He had said at a fund-raising event, "I need members of Congress who understand that you can't negotiate with these folks." He had characterized Democrats as "cut and run" and "defeatocrats." He had said that he needed help from lawmakers who "understand you can't negotiate with terrorists."

What made these words manipulative, Democrats contended, was that they failed to say to whom they applied. Nor did they give specific examples. So the statements left impressions that a large group of unnamed persons—implied to be Democrats—were not concerned about terrorism or wanted to leave Iraq on a moment's notice. The statements often took Democrats criticisms of the war in Iraq to their logical and extreme conclusion—or far more extreme than Democrats arguments had actually been.

In turn, some Republicans claimed that Democrats had sometimes used manipulative rhetoric, such as when President Clinton called Republicans "partisan"—as if that statement was not itself partisan.

Some questions to ponder:

- When is rhetoric "manipulative?"
- What remedies do persons possess who believe they are unfairly attacked?

[1] Quotes in this Policy Advocacy Challenge can be found in Jim Rutenberg, "For the White House, War of Words, at Least, Is Battle Where It Excels," September 26, 2006, p. A 21

Developing and Using Power in Situations Where Advocates Are Disadvantaged as Compared to More Powerful Players

In some situations, policy advocates have less power than more advantaged players. Members of oppressed out-groups, such as women, gay men and lesbians, and racial minorities, may be challenged to obtain and use power in specific settings. Yet we should not assume that they cannot achieve significant successes as is illustrated by tactics of low-budget lobbyists in Policy Advocacy Challenge 10.8. Indeed, it is remarkable how much can sometimes be achieved with minimal power resources.

**POLICY
ADVOCACY
CHALLENGE 10.8**

How Low-Budget
Lobbyists Get
Power

KATHY BEASLEY
CALIFORNIA JOURNAL

The phone rang a dozen times before a harried Rand Martin could grab it. He disconnected the caller when he tried to put the line on hold so he could finish another call. Such is life when you are between secretaries and cursed with a cheap, quirky phone system.

He would probably receive little sympathy from Sherry Skelly, who lacks not only a secretary but, until recently, a desk, a typewriter, and an office. Until she managed to scrape up the money, she had been using a donated hallway as her headquarters. She still makes do with a single phone line and an answering machine.

Martin and Skelly are lobbyists, Martin for the AIDS-oriented Lobby for Individual Freedom and Equality (LIFE), and Skelly for the California Children's Lobby. You can tell they are lobbyists because they work bills, meet with legislators and consultants, and testify at hearings. Their pictures are also in the Secretary of State's *Directory of Lobbyists*.

But if you look for other signs that signify "lobbyist" to most of the public, you will not find any. The organizations they represent never show up on the lists of heavy campaign contributors. They keep their fingers crossed when they send their cards to legislators on the floor, hoping to speak with them, for, unlike their heavyweight counterparts, Martin and Skelly are unable to command an audience. They do not have legions of staff to keep them posted on the dozens of bills they must track. If they hit the Sacramento hot spots at night, it is to relax and enjoy themselves; their budgets do not allow for the drinks or dinner that might further connections with lawmakers and legislative staff. In short, what these two lack is money.

Of course, they are not alone. The Fair Political Practices Commission lists 762 registered lobbyists. Ranking lobbyists by affluence, there are only eleven big operators at the top. Those 11 receive in excess of $500,000 in client fees and spread around hundreds of thousands of dollars more in campaign contributions.

Much lower in the rankings are the lobbyists for public interest groups—California Common Cause, Consumers Union, American Civil Liberties Union—along with lobbyists for state agencies, departments, and commissions. Although they have no money to grease the wheels of power, they usually have enough resources to track bills, produce position papers, and rally the public.

Scraping dead bottom are a subgroup of public interest entities, such as LIFE and California Children's Lobby, whose annual budgets detail how many stamps may be used and how many photocopies may be made in one month. Martin runs his operation on a budget of $80,000, including office rent, his salary and that of a secretary. Skelly makes it on $63,000. Clearly neither of them is in it for the money. If it is true that money turns the wheels in the capital, then one would expect Martin's and Skelly's work to be mostly futile. So who are these penny-pinching lobbyists, how do they get by, and what can they possibly accomplish?

"A lobbyist is a be-all," says the 27-year-old Skelly. "I feel like I'm a mediator and a resource who can provide expertise on an issue. If you have no money, you end up working closely with consultants, and consultants are very detail-oriented."

Expertise, a flair for detail, credibility—these are the tools a low-budget lobbyist brings to work every day. Some of the weight such a lobbyist carries is personal, earned over years of consistently giving good advice and testimony; some of it comes from the organization he or she represents.

California Children's Lobby, for instance, is an umbrella group for child-care providers, child-care educators, and parent groups around the state. Skelly says the lobby has a twenty-year track record of grass-roots activism that makes it an effective advocate on children's issues.

"It's a very sophisticated network," she says. "With the phone tree we have, we can get forty calls into a member's office on a particular bill within an hour. These people know the [legislative] members in their areas; they write letters, make phone calls, and involve the parent groups. This committed network has been developing for the past ten or twenty years, and now it's primed and ready to go."

Skelly, who has been with California Children's Lobby for almost a year, says she is the only full-time lobbyist for children's issues in Sacramento. Although that has the drawback of spreading one person too thinly over hundreds of bills, it does mean that Skelly has become a focal point for children's issues and a natural funnel for information, studies, and trends.

(continued)

But beyond the clout of her organization, Skelly works on developing her own ties and credibility. She knows about one-quarter of the members of both houses. "When I meet a member, I don't just talk about my bills," she says. "Education bills, minimum wage—if I know a certain member is interested in something this year, then I talk about that. Then they know I'm interested in their concerns and views and not just pushing my agenda." Just as important are her consultant contacts. "Consultants tap into [lobbyists] as a resource. You have to prepare good amendments for bills and make good suggestions well in advance of hearings if you are going to influence the outcome."

The 34-year-old Martin, who has been a lobbyist on health issues for 3 years, says he is always working on his recognition and credibility with both legislators and consultants. Unlike Skelly's organization, Martin's group is still learning to flex its political muscles.

While children's issues may be simmering on a front burner this year, Martin's issue has been boiling at high speed for a couple of years.

Martin was instrumental in forming the Lobby for Individual Freedom and Equality, an umbrella organization for 42 California organizations concerned about AIDS. He has been its sole lobbyist since it began.

The first full year of operation, he felt swamped, working out of his living room to track 65 bills. Confronted with 142 bills this year, last year is beginning to look calm in retrospect.

"The number of bills, so many legislators and staff to get to know, plus keeping a fledgling organization afloat—it's been difficult," Martin says.

The difficulties are not just in the part of the job that deals with bills. He has learned quickly that a discount lobbyist not only needs to keep an eye on developments in the capital but also needs to educate, guide, and cajole the groups he represents. One of his biggest tasks is forming his backers into a cohesive, effective voice.

"Gays and lesbians have always been very adept at turning people out on a single issue, but they've been unable to do it on a consistent basis," Martin says. "LIFE has been working to build that kind of network. LIFE illustrates a new political maturity that acknowledges the need for a group to have continuous visibility."

Networking and consensus-building are slow processes, however, and the AIDS epidemic is moving very quickly. "Building a network takes longer than gaining personal access to an individual legislator, but it's every bit as important," Martin says.

Important, yes; comfortable, no. Martin is often caught between a legislative agenda that threatens to move ahead without LIFE and purists on his board who believe compromise is synonymous with evil. "It puts us in a tough position, because we have liberal legislators who want to side with us telling us we have to give on some things," Martin says. "But then we have those who believe LIFE needs to maintain a pure image in the gay-lesbian community. And there's a need for those kinds of people: they create such a pure position, we look like moderates in comparison."

So Martin frequently finds himself in the role of an educator, not just to consultants and legislators, but to his own group members, who need to understand how the process works and what is probable, feasible, and impossible.

Skelly agrees with the vision of a lobbyist as an educator. She conducts seminars and attends the monthly meetings of a half-dozen child-oriented organizations. It's important for the folks back home to understand how Sacramento works and how they can affect what comes out of the capital.

"The Children's Lobby network can produce a teen parent and her partner, holding a baby, to give testimony at a hearing," Skelly says. "We can call on experts in the field and find out anything a legislator might want to know. These people are on the scene where state programs are actually working, so they are in a good position to know what's wrong and what needs to be done. They need to be able to convey that information to the legislature."

Skelly says that such personal testimony at hearings can have a "significance beyond dollars."

But dollars do count, no matter how optimistic or well-armed with statistics a lobbyist may be.

"A lobbyist without money just doesn't have the access," Martin says. "It's most visible when lobbyists are giving testimony. The committee members sit up and listen when it's someone with clout or money; they pay attention."

Martin says this matter-of-factly, with little bitterness in his voice. He regretfully accepts reality; lobbyists without the big bucks have to be more diligent in preparing arguments, supplying statistics, and proposing improvements—sometimes to no avail.

"You take a lot of frustration home. But then there have been people we've turned around on a particular issue," Martin says. "I think we've had a lot of impact on Dr. Filante (Assemblyman William Filante) and helped build his leadership on the AIDS issue among Republicans."

Skelly says her biggest victory came last year when she helped secure $500,000 in the state budget for California State University child care. The governor had already vetoed a $1.2 million expenditure, so getting the partial funding past his blue pencil was a plus. "These campus centers had been struggling along for twenty years without any state funding, and many of them were on the verge of closing," she says. "So this was the first time general-fund money was ever committed to campus child care, and I was very excited about it."

The upbeat Skelly cannot remember a defeat that left her depressed in the past, but even an optimistic nature will not block reality this year. California Children's Lobby's top priority is a statutory cost-of-living adjustment for child care. The governor has already vetoed similar legislation in the past. The governor also placed an equitable cost-of- living adjustment in his budget proposal this year, cutting the ground out from under Skelly's arguments by removing the need for immediate action. "I have to admit I'm beginning to anticipate a problem," she says.

Like all lobbyists, Martin has experienced both victories and defeats. His biggest victories have been killing two of GOP State Senator John Doolittle's ten-bill AIDS packages, and his worst defeat was the passage of a bill to test prostitutes for AIDS.

Victories that come by defeating bills are often fleeting. One of Doolittle's bills would have substantially relaxed AIDS test confidentiality laws, including turning results over to public health officials, and the other would have allowed widespread testing in psychiatric institutions. Those two are dead, but other measures this year are likely to accomplish at least some of Doolittle's goals.

The prostitute bill's passage was the type of fluke that leaves lobbyists with nightmares. The bill swept out of the Assembly, not as a well-reasoned policy decision,

(continued)

but on a Gang-of-Five tidal wave while Martin watched helplessly. "It happened so fast, and most of it was behind closed doors," Martin says, "so we really couldn't do much about it."

Had the Gang of Five, a group of dissident Democrats, not been trying to find common ground with Republicans so they could successfully challenge Speaker Willie Brown, the prostitute bill would have stayed buried or at least could have been modified to be less objectionable to LIFE, Martin says. But it is just one of several bills on which Martin expects defeat, leaving him feeling stressed and making his shoestring-budget operation all the more depressing.

"Burnout is common with public interest lobbyists," Martin says. "The ones you see around the building who have been here for 20 or 30 years work for industries, big-buck clients."

So if Martin received an offer from a big-time lobbying firm, would he switch?

"I couldn't leave LIFE dangling in midsession," says Martin, who is gay and deeply committed to the fight against AIDS. "But in the longer term, yes, I'd probably move on. You can have a deep personal commitment to an issue, but it only lasts until burnout hits."

Martin, whose father is a Washington, DC, lobbyist, is already well sidetracked from the theater career he had planned. He keeps his hand in acting and directing with a Davis community theater group, but his future is in the capital. "It's in my blood," he says simply. "The more I've been involved in government activities, the more I've been fascinated with what is going on in Sacramento."

The fascination is still there for Skelly, as well. "I really enjoy lobbying. It's exciting and stimulating."

Skelly didn't start out as a lobbyist. An active role in starting a child-care program at UC Santa Barbara put her in the limelight when the university's student association needed a lobbyist. Two years there and another year with the Children's Lobby have satisfied her itch to do something professionally that focuses on children.

"I have a bottom-line commitment to education and children's issues. I might move on to something else in the future. But I'm pretty dedicated to children's issues and, right now, I couldn't imagine doing anything else."

Some questions to ponder:

- How do policy advocates compensate for their meager resources in state capitals, where well-heeled lobbyists, with many times their resources, compete with them for the attention of legislators?
- What kinds of power resources do they have?
- How can they achieve some successes even when they cannot wine-and-dine legislators extravagantly?
- Do they have any advantages when contrasted with well-heeled lobbyists?

Obtaining Power Resources

To this point, we have discussed the kinds of power resources that policy advocates use in agency, community, and legislative settings. We now turn to tactics for developing power resources in the first instance. To do this, policy advocates must build their personal credibility, learn how to network, and create links with groups that can help them in their policy practice.

Building Personal Credibility

Whether they are attorneys, physicians, or social workers, professionals require personal credibility to be effective with their clients. Similarly, the personal credibility of policy advocates influences the degree to which others will listen to them.[53] (See Policy Advocacy Challenge 10.5.)

Several tactics can enhance individuals' personal credibility. They can emphasize that they are reasonable and pragmatic team players affiliated with successful institutions, who have integrity and authoritativeness and a positive track record. People often use Machiavellian tactics as well to enhance their personal credibility, although not without ethical and practical risks.

Appearing Reasonable and Pragmatic   Policy advocates sometimes increase their credibility with decision makers who have different values by not emphasizing a proposal's underlying principles and by focusing instead on its substantive provisions.[54] Assume, for example, that a policy advocate who has a radical perspective wants to redistribute resources to poor people by substantially increasing the benefits of the food stamp program. When dealing with the aide of a conservative legislator, this policy advocate will downplay his radical ideology and emphasize instead both the details of the reform and the objective of increasing distressed farmers' revenues. By downplaying his ideology, which is dissonant with the ideology of conservative politicians, the policy advocate will seem more credible to the aide.[55]

Policy advocates who sacrifice their preferences excessively in their zeal to appear reasonable and pragmatic may find this strategy counterproductive if other people perceive them as disingenuous.

Appearing To Be a Team Player   Adherents of power-dependence theory suggest that others view us as credible when they depend on us.[56] Let us consider the social work units in two hospitals. The unit in Hospital 1 contents itself with providing crisis intervention services to patients, whereas the unit in Hospital 2 fills several functions besides traditional counseling. The staff members assume a highly visible role in discharge planning, providing financial counseling for patients, providing social services to rape victims, serving as intermediaries between the hospital and the state's department of children's services in suspected cases of child abuse and neglect, operating a substance abuse clinic, and providing home-based services to frail, older persons. Top decision makers in Hospital 2 depend on the social work staff for these services. Indeed, they cannot imagine how their hospital would function without this unit. By contrast, top decision makers in Hospital 1 hardly know that the social work unit exists, much less that it is vital to the hospital. According to power-dependence theory, decision makers are more likely to heed suggestions of the director or other staff of the expansive social work unit at Hospital 2 than at Hospital 1.[57]

Power-dependence theory suggests, then, that policy advocates can increase their stature by assuming multiple functions beyond their narrow job descriptions. As the director of a social work unit once said to me, "I might even consider washing windows!" These expanded functions serve several purposes; they make high-level administrators feel beholden to the units and individuals who perform these many positive tasks for the institution, and they make these units and individuals appear to be team players who care about the institution's broader interests.

Policy advocates also can enhance their credibility by taking the initiative to make changes within an organization. Assume, for example, that in a casual conversation with a social worker, a hospital administrator remarks on "the turnover of nursing and social work staff in the pediatrics unit during the past five years, which has severely jeopardized the quality of services and staff morale." If the social worker seizes the initiative and offers to survey the staff before discussing possible causes of the turnover, she makes the administrator dependent on her by performing a necessary task. Volunteering this service makes her appear to be a team player. If she assumes additional roles on this project, such as chairing a committee, she continues this proactive and positive role. We can imagine that these assertive actions would enhance her credibility on this issue.

People can also increase their image as team players, and thus their credibility, by shaping policy proposals germane to an organization's mission.[58] Of course, ethical concerns limit the use of this tactic because we should not make proposals based on morally objectionable values. If a hospital does not wish to serve any poor patients who lack insurance, even those with emergency conditions, a social work unit should not seek funds for additional staff to screen out such people.[59]

Personal Integrity
Some people may rightly wonder whether some of these tactics for increasing personal credibility will imperil practitioners' integrity. If we constantly appear to be reasonable and to be team players, when should we speak out for specific causes or not be team players when we think the team needs fundamental reforms?

Policy advocates may take as models many effective legislators who have combined moderate approaches with principled and outspoken positions on certain issues. When he was president, Bill Clinton often hewed to a moderate course, yet he often tangled with such conservative opponents as Representative Newt Gingrich, refusing to back down when challenged at key points. Yet he enjoyed considerable popularity and was overwhelmingly re-elected in 1996. Perhaps one reason for his credibility in the area of budget politics—despite his personal scandals—was that many people perceived him as having integrity on budget issues, such as not making sweeping cuts in entitlements, and as being able to draw the line when his most fundamental beliefs were challenged.[60]

Authoritativeness
When we want to change a policy in an agency, community, or legislative setting, opposition may arise from people who say the change is not warranted. The policy advocate often can diminish such inertia by demonstrating authoritativeness on the subject and offering evidence that supports the policy change, whether by citing important research, documenting similar changes in other settings, or quoting reputable experts.[61] In the case mentioned previously of the high rate of staff turnover in the hospital's pediatrics service, the social worker might conduct her survey of the situation by using a well-known standardized instrument that measures staff morale. As individuals appear to be authoritative on a specific issue, they increase the likelihood that they will be perceived as authoritative on future occasions.

Developing a Positive Track Record
One cannot develop credibility merely by using rhetoric; people have to observe firsthand, or hear secondhand, that someone is competent, trustworthy, or authoritative, or that a department performs indispensable services.

Secondhand reports may be quite helpful in establishing credibility. As people initiate useful policies and try to change existing policies, they obtain a good reputation not only with those they encounter directly but also with those who hear positive feedback about them.

Affiliating Oneself with Successful Institutions   Credibility stems not only from individuals' actions and attributes, but also from their affiliations. Assume that a hospital administrator receives requests for additional funding from the directors of two units. The first director's unit has been marked by chronic and repeated turmoil, and the administrator does not perceive it as providing quality services. The second director's unit is widely viewed as outstanding; the hospital administrator has received many positive reports about its services and staff. Although the directors may have similar personal characteristics, we can guess whose request the hospital administrator is more likely to heed.

The lesson for social workers who work in bureaucracies is simple. Personal credibility stems in part from being associated with a well-regarded and effective unit. That unit, in turn, derives its reputation from the quality of its work and its staff.[62] Practitioners can enhance their credibility indirectly by improving the services of the unit that employs them.

Using Machiavellian Tactics   Some individuals try to enhance their credibility by using negative tactics, such as harming others' reputations, buck-passing, sandbagging, and turf or empire building. Those who use Machiavellian tactics often assume that they can enhance their own reputation only by diminishing the reputations of their colleagues. Buck-passing means blaming others for one's own failures,[63] and sandbagging means diminishing another's accomplishment by contending that others, perhaps even oneself, were really responsible for it.[64] As any participant in bureaucratic politics can confirm, many people excel in turf or empire building, which means accumulating power and responsibility by wrestling them from others.[65] People malign colleagues to diminish their initiatives by suggesting that the proposals reflect ulterior and evil motivations, such as a desire for status or power.[66]

These negative tactics are quite effective in some political campaigns, and some administrators obtain power by using them. But the credibility of those who use them can suffer, because they can be perceived as immoral.

Illustrations from Policy Advocacy Challenge 10.5   Policy Advocacy Challenge 10.5 illustrates how many interactional skills low-budget lobbyists need to develop power resources. Rand Martin tells us that his power depends on his being reasonable and pragmatic in dealing with legislators, though he finds it is difficult to make concessions that he and his allies do not want to make. He discusses building a reputation for personal integrity and authoritativeness by providing well-researched, accurate information to legislators. Both he and Sherry Skelly mention the need to develop a track record of timely and responsible contributions to legislators.

Networking

A network is the number and range of supportive relationships a person has.[67] Networks are important to policy practitioners in several ways. Individuals with broad networks develop early-information systems through which they learn about issues, problems, and trends relevant to their work, and they have many sources of advice as they develop policies and strategies.

There are many kinds of networks. *Lateral networks* consist of relationships with colleagues; *vertical* and *subordinate networks* consist, respectively, of persons who are superior to and beneath a person in an organization's hierarchy. People have *heterogeneous networks* when they have supportive relationships with others in a range of positions both within and outside their work. A social worker in a hospital has a heterogeneous network, for example, when it includes members of different units or departments and different professions. Some relationships in networks are short-term, perhaps fashioned in response to a specific problem, while others are long-standing.

Strategies that help expand a person's networks include enhancing visibility, seeking inclusion in decision-making bodies, cultivating mentors, obtaining access to informal groups, and developing links with social movements.

Enhancing Personal Visibility

Some people develop networks by increasing their visibility in bureaucratic, community, legislative, and social settings.[68] An example is the young Lyndon Johnson, who lived in a boardinghouse when he first arrived in Washington, DC, as an aide to a legislator. To meet other aides who lived in the same boardinghouse, he brushed his teeth three or four times each morning and took several showers. In these encounters, he asked the other aides about their jobs and their interests, a tactic that convinced each aide that Johnson cared about him.[69]

Indeed, politicians often employ a tactic that others can use. Although exchanging information is important, both as an end in itself and as a method of establishing a relationship, it should be supplemented by actively seeking advice, support, or suggestions from others. As Christopher Matthews notes, people like to be asked for advice; it makes them feel important and wanted.[70]

Obtaining Inclusion in Decision-Making Bodies

To examine specific problems, agencies often establish either ongoing committees or time-limited ad hoc committees.

Membership on these committees is sometimes controlled by top officials in the organization. However, individuals can seek membership by showing interest or by suggesting the formation of a committee to examine a problem. Committee membership is an excellent opportunity to obtain an inside position on important issues, improve one's credibility, and extend one's network.

Seeking Mentors and Inclusion in Informal Groups

In her research on why women have difficulty obtaining promotions in corporations, Rosabeth Kanter implicates their exclusion from mentoring relationships and old-boy networks.[71] Males, she observes, develop informal relationships with high-level male officials, who become their mentors, giving advice and information about the internal workings of the corporation, its politics, taboo subjects, informal factions, upcoming policy issues, and strategies for obtaining promotion. Mentors also introduce these neophytes to important officers of the corporation and into informal cliques and relationships, and go to bat for them when they need high-level assistance.

As J. McIver Weatherford notes with respect to legislatures, old-boy networks span the legislative, bureaucratic, and lobbying spheres of government as people move among them in their employment.[72] In both state and federal capitals, powerful legislators have an intricate network of acquaintances, many of them former aides, in lobbying and the bureaucracy. They tap into these rich networks at many points in their work—when contemplating whether to introduce legislation, when seeking to help a constituent with a specific problem, and when searching for issues that will enhance their reputation as initiators of new legislation.

These old-boy networks contain a wide-ranging set of contacts that provide their members with assistance, information, business connections, and job possibilities. Many high-level decisions are made during social encounters among the people in these networks; those outside such networks are not consulted about these decisions and therefore have no advance notice of future policy changes.[73]

The workings of the mentor system and the old-boy network are manifestly unfair to those not included in them. Lacking allies within such networks, many women and racial minorities are excluded, as are loners, or those disinclined to maintain a network of relationships.[74] Declarations about the evil nature of these networks, however, will not make them disappear, nor will the moral victories of those who avoid them erase the disadvantages this exclusion brings.

Illustrations from Policy Advocacy Challenge 10.5   Both Rand Martin and Sherry Skelly make clear that low-budget lobbyists depend on contacts within the state's legislature and governmental agencies. While lacking money to entertain legislators and their aides, they can nonetheless develop a range of connections by increasing their visibility in an arena filled with other lobbyists with greater resources.

Developing Links with Social Movements   Some policy advocates develop links with groups that take interest in issues such as AIDS, reforms for children, and persons with physical or mental disabilities. The members of such groups, who often have minimal resources, are highly knowledgeable about specific issues and deeply committed to them. Other people become active in local chapters of professional organizations, such as the National Association of Social Workers, or form relationships with politicians or civil servants.

Such connections increase a person's power within her or his own organizations because those who have them are often viewed as more credible than those who lack them. They bring into an organization ideas and information from these external contacts.[75] In turn, to help these external groups or movements, the members sometimes recruit other staff or even clients as volunteers, though they must be certain that their clients do not believe they must participate to receive services.[76]

Illustration from Policy Advocacy Challenge 10.5   Sherry Skelly tells us that maintaining external allies is critical to a low-budget lobbyist's success. She inherited and helped maintain a sophisticated network of children's advocates throughout the state. She uses the network to increase her expertise on myriad issues and to place pressure on legislators at pivotal points.

Power Challenges Encountered by Members of Vulnerable Populations

We have already alluded to Rosabeth Kanter's pioneering work on problems that female executives confront when seeking power in organizations. Her observations apply as well to persons of color, gay men and lesbians, people with disabilities, and members of any groups that confront prejudice.[77]

Members of these groups use the techniques we have already discussed, such as networking, but they must be even more diligent and persistent. They can also develop relationships with other members of their own group in their workplace, such as women who have attained positions of power, to provide special assistance, support, and advice. When such contacts are lacking, they should seek help from mentors outside the organization, in similar or related organizations.

Members of vulnerable populations can also find allies among mainstream persons, who may, for example, take the lead in diversifying an agency's staff or including a broader range of staff in supervisory positions.

The case of the low-budget lobbyists illustrates how persons with marginal power resources can gain significant power with careful strategy. (See Policy Advocacy Challenge 10.9.)

POLICY ADVOCACY CHALLENGE 10.9

Developing and Using Power Post-Katrina Louisiana

NORMA RUTLEDGE, M.ED., B.C.P.S

Go to **academic.cengage.com/ social_work/jansson** to watch this video clip

Norma Rutledge, the Executive Director of the Baton Rouge Crisis Intervention Center, was herself in the eye of a hurricane in the weeks and months following Hurricane Katrina. She had been a counselor for youth for 20 years with a school-based alcohol and drug abuse prevention program. In the days following the hurricane, she worked around the clock to help organize Baton Rouge's services to address the needs of the 250,000 evacuees who fled New Orleans and its surroundings for her city. She had to develop collaborations between different agencies and interact with state officials.

Listen to Policy Advocacy Challenge Video 10.9 where she discusses how she developed power resources in the years preceding Hurricane Katrina that stood her in good stead in the hurricane's wake.

Questions to ponder:

- What strategies did she use before Katrina to build power resources?
- How did these help her in the weeks and months following Hurricane Katrina to help evacuees who fled to Baton Rouge?
- How does her discussion dispute the assertion that clinical persons cannot develop power resources?

Developing Assertiveness

Policy advocates sometimes fail to seize strategic opportunities to shape policies because they assume they cannot win. In some cases, as our discussion of power differentials suggests, the deck is stacked against them. In many other cases, however, individuals undermine their own effectiveness by becoming fatalistic.

To use power effectively, people must first decide that they possess power resources, that they can use them successfully, and that they want to use them. The word *assertiveness* describes this proclivity to test the waters, rather than to be excessively fatalistic.

Assertiveness is undermined, however, by two dispositions. The first is a victim mentality that disposes people to believe that others will conspire to defeat their preferences.[78] A director of a hospital's social work department might believe, for example, that the nurses and physicians will systematically oppose any proposals by social work-ers. The second is fatalism about using power in a more general sense; some people believe that only high-level persons or powerful interests can wield power successfully, and that people outside these exalted categories cannot effectively participate in policy deliberations.

Both the victim mentality and fatalism create self-fulfilling prophecies. People who believe that others will conspire against them and that only a restricted group can use power effectively will fail to use their personal power resources; those who see them as disinclined to participate in policy deliberations are likely to ignore their occasional suggestions and to exclude them from policy deliberations, further reinforcing the vic-tim mentality and fatalism.[79] Fatalistic practitioners ignore the diversity of potential power resources and assume that they cannot increase theirs even by enhancing their credibility, finding allies, establishing networks, developing expertise, and obtaining information.

To understand this problem, recall our discussion of the sender of power (X) and the receiver of power (Y), as illustrated in Figure 10.1. Assume that you are Y, that you work in an agency, and that your program director intimidates you. Through his demeanor toward you, his intimidating remarks, and even his veiled threats, your director seeks to dissuade you from trying to make changes in the program.

What can you do? You can realistically assess both the risks and the benefits of trying to change defective policies. Those who intimidate others derive power from convincing them that they have no recourse but to follow the intimidator's suggestions that he or she has won. Ask yourself, "Is my program director's power as extensive as he suggests, or can I use my own power resources without incurring unacceptable penalties, such as losing my job?" Ask other people how they perceive a specific policy to see if your perceptions have merit, and find out whether they also feel intimidated or whether your director is singling you out. You can try direct communication with your program director, focusing on substantive issues and the specific issues on which you differ with him to see if he is more bark than bite. Accusing someone of seeking to intimidate you usually makes the situation even worse.[80]

If you are truly subject to intimidation, you should not expect easy answers. An assertive person does not passively accept a situation but tries to diagnose it, identify-ing possible strategies and then trying several options in search of one that works.

Here is an example of assertiveness. The director of a hospital's social work depart-ment requested a budgetary increase for her department but was denied. She noticed, however, that even unsuccessful entreaties served to educate top officials about social work programs and that some officials actually felt guilty about denying well-presented and justified requests. She decided not to be intimidated and to make further requests for funds for her department. She discovered that skillfully and frequently request-ing funds brought increases in her unit's budget. Unlike departments with more timid executives, her department gained size and stature as she assertively sought resources, even after a number of unsuccessful requests.[81]

Illustration from Policy Advocacy Challenge 10.5   Policy advocates with minimal resources must combat burnout and fatalism. Despite the overwhelming advantage of the lobbyists with munificent resources, these two low-budget lobbyists have asserted themselves, persevered, and obtained notable successes.

Can Direct-Service Staff Use Power Resources?

Our discussion of out-group members' special problems and of assertiveness leads naturally to the question: Can people at the bottom of the heap, like direct-service staff members, use power resources, or does their subordinate position in the organizational hierarchy make them powerless? Organizations vary considerably; some executives elicit and even expect input from direct-service staff, and other executives are authoritarian.[82]

Direct-service staff already have considerable power stemming from their personal knowledge of an agency's problems. Many supervisors and executives value suggestions from direct-service staff about a range of agency matters and respond readily to well-conceived suggestions for changing existing services. Executives depend on direct-service staff for the agency's reputation, efficiency, revenues (when the agency charges for services), and public relations with clients and other agencies. Most agencies would cease to exist if they lacked competent front-line staff.

Direct-service staff members who belong to unions can imply or state that their work will be disrupted if certain demands are not met; such demands usually involve salary and workload, but unions sometimes also seek changes in policy. Even without union backing, direct-service staff can vigorously protest some policies by taking their case directly to high-level staff.

Direct-service staff often have access to at least some agency decision-making processes, such as staff meetings, retreats, unit meetings, and meetings with supervisors. Developing their power through the strategies we discussed earlier in this chapter (such as enhancing personal credibility and visibility, networking, and developing relationships with external groups) is likely to increase their power in these agency deliberations. Moreover, they can seek membership on specific agency committees or even suggest that a committee be formed to examine a specific issue.

Direct-service staff can also wield power indirectly as in Policy Advocacy Challenge 10.1 by influencing a supervisor to initiate a suggestion. They can also form coalitions within the agency to pressure administrators to modify specific policies. However, staff members should be realistic about the limits on such power.

Direct-service staff members often derive power from their autonomy.[83] Although regulations may govern the length and intensity of services, recommend procedures, and establish priorities, they are difficult to enforce because the details of direct-service work are hard to supervise. Moreover, it is possible to bend some rules without technically violating them. Carried to an extreme, autonomy brings anarchy, but in moderation, represents an important kind of power.

In addition to their participation in decision making, direct-service staff members can shape outcomes by helping to build agendas, define problems, and construct proposals, as discussed in Chapters Six through Nine.

Direct-service staff do not, of course, have the power resources of executives, funders, or legislators, so they must enhance their power resources imaginatively and select the issues on which they will use their influence.

Returning to New Orleans

We can use the discussion of this chapter to better understand a key part of Governor Kathleen Blanco's political strategy to secure resources from the federal government for the rebuilding of New Orleans, as well as other storm-devastated communities in Louisiana. (See Policy Advocacy Challenge 10.10.)

POLICY ADVOCACY CHALLENGE 10.10

Governor Blanco's Key Political Move in Louisiana Post-Katrina

BRUCE JANSSON, PH.D.

It seemed an unlikely decision by Governor Kathleen Blanco when she asked John Breaux to be her point man in Washington, DC with Congress and the Bush administration to get resources for New Orleans and other storm-ravaged towns and cities in Louisiana. (He accepted this invitation in late October 2005.) After all, Breaux had retired in early 2005 after 18 years as a U.S. senator from Louisiana.[1]

It was a politically cunning decision. Almost uniquely among high-level Democrats, Breaux had close links with the Bush administration. Bush had named him as vice chairman of a bipartisan commission to find ways to change the nation's tax system. He had worked closely with the administration to design the Medicare drug prescription benefit for seniors. Bush had even hoped to entice him to join his cabinet after his 2000 presidential victory, but Breaux had declined. Yet Breaux also knew all of the top Democratic leaders in Congress.

Working out of the Washington, DC lobbyist firm of Patton Boggs, Breaux agreed to work for the governor without charging a fee—and indeed was barred by federal law from lobbying Congress until January. His political challenges were many. He had to work quietly in order not to antagonize the Bush administration. He had to help to coordinate a statewide lobbying effort that was relatively chaotic with many lobbyists representing the state, cities, and towns of Louisiana. He had to surmount rivalries and jealousies between the governor and Mayor Nagin of New Orleans, as well as between Louisiana Senators Mary Landrieu (a Democrat) and David Vitter (a Republican). He had to negotiate between the administration, which wanted to cut spending, and the governor and the Louisiana delegation of Congresspersons. He had to help state officials and the state's delegation to Congress to be realistic: their request for $250 billion from Congress for hurricane damage had been widely ridiculed by the Bush Administration and some Congressional Republican leaders as excessive. He had to work closely with Governor Blanco's legislative liaison in Washington, DC, Stephanie Leger.

Widely respected on both sides of the aisle and with a large network of legislative and congressional staff acquaintances, Breaux also had a low-key personality that was well-suited to behind-the-scenes negotiations.

Perhaps his most significant challenge, however, was to not allow the administration to place Louisiana and New Orleans on a back burner when other national issues, such as the war in Iraq, often distracted them. Almost from the start of his assignment, he demonstrated that he had high-level access, getting White House Chief of Staff Andrew Card to call a White House meeting to discuss how to rebuild the state's health care system.

Questions to ponder:

- What power resources would be most central to Breaux's challenge?
- Discuss how this assignment would require the use of multiple power resources.
- Would Governor Blanco gain or lose personal power by turning to Breaux in this situation?

---

[1] I rely heavily on the following article to write this Policy Advocacy Challenge: Joseph Schatz, "Dealmaker Takes on Strategies to Rebuild," *Congressional Quarterly Weekly*, December 5, 2005: 3251–53.

What You Can Now Do	# CHAPTER SUMMARY

You are now equipped to do the following:

- Define power and politics
- Engage in power relationships
- Use an array of power resources including direct and indirect ones
- Use power in organizational settings through normal channels and, rarely, through whistle-blowing
- Surmount power differentials in certain circumstances
- Grapple with ethical issues when using power resources, understanding that power can be used both ethically and unethically
- Develop power resources
- Network
- Develop skills in assertiveness

In the succeeding chapter, we discuss how we use our power resources to develop political strategy, whether in legislative, agency, or community settings.

NOTES

1. *Living Webster Encyclopedic Dictionary of the English Language* (Chicago: English Language Institute of America, 1977), p. 737.
2. Ibid., p. 737.
3. Martin Rein, "Value-Critical Policy Analysis," in Daniel Callahan and Bruce Jennings, eds., *Ethics, the Social Sciences, and Policy Analysis* (New York: Plenum Press, 1983), pp. 96–100.
4. William Coplin and Michael O'Leary, *Everyman's Prince* (North Scituate, MA: Duxbury, 1976).
5. Peter Bachrach and Morton Baratz, *Power and Poverty* (New York: Oxford University Press, 1970), pp. 17–38.
6. For a discussion of the dilemmas of those who receive power resources, see Stanley Milgram, *Obedience to Authority* (New York: Harper & Row, 1975).
7. Bachrach and Baratz, *Power and Poverty*, pp. 17–38.
8. Ibid.
9. Edward Banfield, *Political Influence* (New York: Free Press, 1961), pp. 307–314.
10. John French and Bertram Raven, "The Bases of Social Power," in Dorwin Cartwright and Alvin Zander, eds., *Group Dynamics: Research and Theory* (New York: Harper & Row, 1968), pp. 259–269.

11. Doris Kearns, *Lyndon Johnson and the American Dream* (New York: Harper & Row, 1976), pp. 190, 224–227.
12. Jon Sager, "Sources of Power," in Jack Rothman, John Erlich, and John Tropman, eds., forthcoming 7th edition of *Strategies of Community Intervention*, Wadsworth, 2007.
13. Sager, "Sources of Power," p. 24.
14. Sager, "Sources of Power," p. 7.
15. Sager, "Sources of Power," p. 16.
16. Sager, "Sources of Power," p. 21.
17. Sager, "Sources of Power," p. 24.
18. See Christopher Matthews, *Hardball: How Politics Is Played* (New York: Summit Books, 1988), pp. 21–43.
19. Bruce Jansson, *Theory and Practice of Social Welfare Policy: Analysis, Processes, and Current Issues* (Belmont, CA: Wadsworth, 1984), p. 184.
20. Julie Rovner, "Daycare Package Clears First Hurdle in House," *Congressional Quarterly Weekly Report* 46 (July 2, 1988): 1833–1836.
21. See Bachrach and Baratz, *Power and Poverty*, pp. 17–38.
22. *Congressional Quarterly Almanac*, vol. 34 (Washington, DC: Congressional Quarterly Service, 1978), pp. 272–279.
23. Jansson, *Theory and Practice*, p. 184.

24. Joseph Califano, *Governing America* (New York: Simon & Schuster, 1971), p. 67.

25. Gerald Zaltman and Robert Duncan, *Strategies for Planned Change* (New York: Wiley Interscience, 1977), p. 100.

26. Vincent Burke and Vee Burke, *Nixon's Good Deed: Welfare Reform* (New York: Columbia University Press, 1974), pp. 195–204.

27. Congress, Senate, Committee on Finance, *Hearings before the Subcommittee on Social Security and Family Policy* (January 23, 1987), pp. 2–14.

28. Matthews, *Hardball*, pp. 144–154.

29. Lewis Froman, *The Congressional Process: Strategies, Rules, and Procedures* (Boston: Little, Brown, 1967).

30. Eugene Bardach, *The Skill Factor in Politics* (Berkeley and Los Angeles: University of California Press, 1972), pp. 234–240.

31. Eric Schattschneider, *The Semisovereign People* (New York: Holt, Rinehart & Winston, 1980), pp. 20–46.

32. Morton Deutsch, *The Resolution of Conflict: Constructive and Destructive Processes* (New Haven, CT: Yale University Press, 1973), pp. 124–152.

33. John Kingdon, *Agendas, Alternatives, and Public Policies* (Boston: Little, Brown, 1984), pp. 1–22.

34. Deutsch, *The Resolution of Conflict*, pp. 124–152.

35. Ibid., p. 368.

36. See Theodore Lowi's discussion of the politics of redistributive measures in "American Business, Public Policy, Case Studies, and Political Theory," *World Politics* 16 (July 1964): 677–715.

37. Yeheskel Hasenfeld, *Human Service Organizations* (Englewood Cliffs, NJ: Prentice Hall, 1983).

38. Hedrick Smith, *The Power Game: How Washington Works* (New York: Ballantine Books, 1988), pp. 388–444.

39. Matthews, *Hardball*, pp. 144–154.

40. Ron Dear and Rino Patti, "Legislative Advocacy," in *Encyclopedia of Social Workers*, vol. 2 (Silver Spring, MD: National Association of Social Workers, 1987), p. 37.

41. Michael Lipsky, *Street-Level Bureaucrats: Dilemmas of the Individual and Public Service* (New York: Russell Sage Foundation, 1980), pp. 16–18.

42. Kenneth Weick, "Educational Organizations as Loosely Coupled Systems," *Administrative Science Quarterly* 21 (March 1976): 1–9.

43. Robert Goodin, *Reasons for Welfare* (Princeton, NJ: Princeton University Press, 1988), pp. 184–228.

44. Franklin Chu and Sharland Trotter, *The Madness Establishment* (New York: Grossman, 1974).

45. Sissela Bok, "Blowing the Whistle," in Joel Fleishman, Lance Liebman, and Mark Moore, eds., *Public Duties: The Moral Obligations of Government Officials* (Cambridge: Harvard University Press, 1981), pp. 200–215.

46. Ibid.

47. Smith, *The Power Game*.

48. Milgram, *Obedience to Authority*.

49. Richard Fenno, *The Power of the Purse* (Boston: Little, Brown, 1966), pp. 366–390.

50. Rosabeth Kanter, *Men and Women of the Corporation* (New York: Basic Books, 1977), pp. 129–163.

51. C. Wright Mills, *The Power Elite* (New York: Oxford University Press, 1956).

52. Robert Dahl, *Pluralist Democracy in the United States* (Chicago: Rand McNally, 1967).

53. See Herbert Simons, *Persuasion*, 2nd ed. (New York: Random House, 1986), p. 130. Also see discussion of credibility by George Brager, Harry Specht, and James Torczyner, *Community Organizing*, 2nd ed. (New York: Columbia University Press, 1987), pp. 342–347.

54. Matthews, *Hardball*, pp. 144–352.

55. Rochelle Stanford, "Beleaguered Lobbyists for the Poor—Taking Allies Where They Can Find Them," *National Journal* 12 (September 20, 1980): 1556–1560.

56. Richard Emerson, "Power-Dependence Relations," *American Sociological Review* 27 (February 1962): 31–40, and D. J. Hickson et al., "A Strategic Contingencies Theory of Organizational Power," *Administrative Science Quarterly* 16 (June 1971): 216–229.

57. For research findings on power-dependence theory in hospital settings with social work departments, see Bruce Jansson and June Simmons, "Building Department or Unit Power within Human Service Organizations: Empirical Findings and Theory Building,"

Administration in Social Work 8 (Fall 1984): 41–44, 49–50.

58. See Bruce Jansson and June Simmons, "The Ecology of Social Work Departments: Empirical Findings and Strategy Implications," *Social Work in Health Care* 11 (Winter 1985): 1–16.

59. Bruce Jansson and June Simmons, "The Survival of Social Work Units in Host Organizations," *Social Work* 31 (September 1986): 342.

60. Joel Fleishman, "Self-Interest and Political Integrity," in Joel Fleishman, Lance Leibman, and Mark Moore, eds., *Public Duties: The Moral Obligations of Government Officials* (Cambridge: Harvard University Press, 1981), pp. 67–77.

61. Eugene Bardach, *The Skill Factor in Politics,* pp. 204–206, 216–220.

62. Jansson and Simmons, "Survival of Social Work Units," p. 341.

63. Matthews, *Hardball,* pp. 207–209.

64. Ibid., pp. 203–204.

65. J. McIver Weatherford, *Tribes on the Hill* (New York: Rawson, Wade, 1981), pp. 87–111.

66. Matthews, *Hardball,* pp. 194–211.

67. Noel Tichy, *Strategic Change: Technology, Politics, and Culture* (New York: Wiley, 1983), pp. 69–94.

68. Weatherford, *Tribes on the Hill,* pp. 20–24. Also see Tom Peters and Nancy Austin, "MBWA(Managing by Walking Around)," *California Management Review* 28 (Fall 1985): 9–34.

69. Matthews, *Hardball,* pp. 21–33.

70. Ibid., pp. 59–73.

71. Kanter, *Men and Women of the Corporation,* pp. 181–184.

72. Weatherford, *Tribes on the Hill,* pp. 87–111.

73. Ibid.

74. Ibid., pp. 250–253.

75. See how a social movement led to legislative reform in Wyoming in William Whitaker, "Organizing Social Action Coalitions: WIC Comes to Wyoming," in Maryann Mahaffey and John Hanks, eds., *Practical Politics: Social Work and Political Response* (Silver Spring, MD: National Association of Social Workers, 1982), pp. 136–158.

76. See Frances Piven and Richard Cloward, "New Prospects for Voter Registration Reform," *Social Policy* 18 (Winter 1988): 2–15.

77. Kanter, *Men and Women of the Corporation.*

78. Ibid., pp. 158–160, 196–197.

79. Ibid., pp. 196–197.

80. Linda MacNeilage and Kathleen Adams discuss various strategies in *Assertiveness at Work* (Englewood Cliffs, NJ: Prentice Hall, 1982).

81. Jansson and Simmons, "Survival of Social Work Units," pp. 339–340.

82. David Mechanic, "Sources of Power of Lower Participants in Complex Organizations," *Administrative Science Quarterly* 7 (December 1962): 349–364.

83. Michael Lipsky, *Street-Level Bureaucrats: Dilemmas of the Individual and Public Service* (New York: Russell Sage Foundation, 1980), pp. 13–18.

SUGGESTED READINGS

Building Personal Credibility

Richard Emerson, "Power-Dependence Relations," *American Sociological Review* 27 (February 1962): 31–40.

Bruce Jansson and June Simmons, "Building Department or Unit Power within Human Service Organizations: Empirical Findings and Theory Building," *Administration in Social Work* 8 (Fall 1984): 41–50.

Bruce Jansson and June Simmons, "The Ecology of Social Work Departments: Empirical Findings and Strategy Implications," *Social Work in Health Care* 11 (Winter 1985): 1–16.

Christopher Matthews, *Hardball: How Politics Is Played* (New York: Summit Books, 1988).

Networking

Rosabeth Kanter, *Men and Women of the Corporation* (New York: Basic Books, 1977), pp. 129–163, 181–197.

Noel Tichy, *Strategic Change: Technology, Politics, and Culture* (New York: Wiley, 1983), pp. 69–94.

J. McIver Weatherford, *Tribes on the Hill* (New York: Rawson, Wade, 1981), pp. 87–111, 250–253.

Working with Task Groups

Milan Dluhy, *Building Coalitions in the Human Services* (Newbury Park, CA: Sage, 1990).

Paul Ephross and Thomas Vassil, *Groups That Work* (New York: Columbia University Press, 1988).

Irving Janis, *Victims of Groupthink* (Boston: Houghton Mifflin, 1972).

John Tropman, Harold Johnson, and Elmer Tropman, *The Essentials of Committee Management* (Chicago: Nelson-Hall, 1979).

The Nature of Power

Peter Bachrach and Morton Baratz, *Power and Poverty* (New York: Oxford University Press, 1970).

Varieties of Power

John French and Bertram Craven, "The Bases of Social Power," in Dorwin Cartwright and Alvin Zander, eds., *Group Dynamics: Research and Theory* (New York: Harper & Row, 1968), pp. 259–269.

Lewis Froman, *The Congressional Process: Strategies, Rules, and Procedures* (Boston: Little, Brown, 1967).

Christopher Matthews, *Hardball: How Politics Is Played* (New York: Summit Books, 1988).

Hedrick Smith, *The Power Game: How Washington Works* (New York: Ballantine Books, 1988).

A Defense of Politics

Eric Schattschneider, *The Semisovereign People* (New York: Holt, Rinehart & Winston, 1960).

Using Power from Internal Vantage Points

Burton Gummer, *The Politics of Social Administration: Managing Organizational Politics in Social Agencies* (Englewood Cliffs, NJ: Prentice Hall, 1990).

Bruce Jansson and June Simmons, "The Survival of Social Work Units in Host Organizations," *Social Work* 31 (September 1986): 339–344.

Using Power from External Vantage Points

Donald deKieffer, *The Citizen's Guide to Lobbying Congress* (Chicago: Chicago Review Press, 1997).

Power Resources of Direct-Service Staff

Michael Lipsky, *Street-Level Bureaucrats: Dilemmas of the Individual and Public Service* (New York: Russell Sage Foundation, 1980).

David Mechanic, "Sources of Power of Lower Participants in Complex Organizations," *Administrative Science Quarterly* 7 (December 1962): 349–364.

The Problem of Assertiveness

Rosabeth Kanter, *Men and Women of the Corporation* (New York: Basic Books, 1977), pp. 158–197.

Linda MacNeilage and Kathleen Adams, *Assertiveness at Work* (Englewood Cliffs, NJ: Prentice Hall, 1982).

Stanley Milgram, *Obedience to Authority* (New York: Harper & Row, 1975).

Ethical Issues in Politics

Chauncey Alexander, "Professional Social Workers and Political Responsibility," in Maryann Mahaffey and John Hanks, *Practical Politics: Social Work and Political Responsibility* (Silver Spring, MD: National Association of Social Workers, 1982), pp. 22–25.

George Brager, Harry Specht, and James Torczyner, *Community Organizing*, 2nd ed. (New York: Columbia University Press, 1987), pp. 316–339.

Joel Fleishman, "Self-Interest and Political Integrity," in Joel Fleishman, Lance Liebman, and Mark Moore, eds., *Public Duties: The Moral Obligations of Government Officials* (Cambridge: Harvard University Press, 1981), pp. 52–92.

C H A P T E R
11

Developing Political Strategy

We have discussed the nature and varieties of power. Now we turn to how policy advocates use their power resources to create political strategy in agency, community, and legislative settings. *Political strategy* is a sequence of actions and verbal exchanges that advocates believe will increase the likelihood that a proposal will be enacted. We discuss the following in this chapter:

1. How to establish objectives and positions
2. How to gauge who supports and opposes specific policies
3. The importance of situational and contextual factors to policy strategy
4. How we build alternative scenarios to select and revise political strategy
5. Seven recurring steps in strategy building

Establishing Some Objectives

To develop intelligent strategy, policy advocates first have to answer this question: Why am I participating in the political process? Then they must decide which side they are taking and the degree and kind of policy changes they seek.

Determining a Position

Strategists must first decide whether to do the following:

1. Initiate their own proposal (an affirmative position)
2. Change others' proposals (an amending position)
3. Oppose others' initiatives (an opposing or blocking position)
4. Assume no role (a bystander position)

These choices are important because they commit the strategist to certain obligations and risks. People who *initiate* their own proposals have to invest considerable time in research, discussion, meetings, and negotiations. They have an advantage, however: Their ideas are likely to figure prominently in ensuing policy deliberations. By taking the initiative, they can shape discussion at the outset by giving prominence to their analysis of a specific problem and their policy proposals. Were they *not* to take the initiative, they realize that some important problems or proposals would never be addressed. By taking the initiative, policy practitioners exercise leadership in agency, community, and legislative settings.

Yet initiators expose themselves to criticism by placing their ideas in front of a larger audience. Opponents may question their motives, such as contending they seek to further their own interests. Or they may attack their analysis of a problem or their policy proposals. For many initiators, however, these perils pale beside the benefits of initiating proposals.

Unlike those who initiate proposals, policy advocates who agree generally with the initiators' position confine themselves to *amending* a proposal to advance their preferences for specific changes. Amenders often play a key role in policy deliberations. If they do not like a policy proposal, they can change its direction in fundamental ways by changing its details—even gutting it. If someone dislikes a policy, for example, they can try to get others to cut the amount of resources devoted to it. If amenders like a policy proposal but want to make it even better, they can change specific provisions to seek this result, such as increasing the amount of resources devoted to it.

It is easier in some respects to *block* proposals than to develop them, because opposers need only pinpoint their flaws or use procedural maneuvers to defeat them. Because of the sheer number of sequential points through which legislative proposals must pass, blockers need only defeat them at a single point to prevail. They can also block them by cutting off their funding, obtaining a legal injunction against them through litigation, or not renewing them in the case of policies that must be periodically reauthorized.

Yet blockers may be perceived merely as naysayers who lack constructive alternatives. They may be accused of inciting "gridlock" rather than being responsible contributors to policy deliberations. Acutely aware that his father had been perceived as a naysayer when he vetoed a record number of congressional initiatives during his tenure, President George W. Bush had not vetoed a single major piece of legislation as he neared the end of his sixth year in office, even though he sometimes threatened vetoes if Congress enacted specific policies that he disliked. To the extent they are perceived to have the power to block specific initiatives, factions that might block them often intimidate initiators who decide it is folly even to try to get a specific policy enacted.

Strategists may adopt a *bystander* role because they believe they lack the power to influence the outcome, because they want to save their political resources for a future issue, because they believe their involvement in deliberations will antagonize one or both sides in the controversy, or because they expect to assume a mediating role later. Bystanders are not truly neutral in many situations, however, because their non-participation often tilts power toward one or another faction in policy deliberations. Those legislators who absent themselves from key votes often shape outcomes as much as those legislators who *do* vote, particularly when votes are closely divided. Bystanders also can be accused of lacking courage of their convictions.

Strategists' roles often depend on their analysis of a proposal's prospects. If they believe them to be extremely bleak, for example, advocates may be reluctant to initiate a proposal. If they believe a policy will be enacted, they may be reluctant to try to block it. However, policy advocates sometimes oppose objectionable policies or initiate proposals in the face of overwhelming odds, because they believe fundamental principles are at stake, because they want to educate voters about the issue, or because they want to please some segment of their supporters who are deeply committed to a specific proposal.

At national and state levels of government, the leaders of the two major parties must frequently decide which issues to champion, which ones to oppose, and which ones to leave alone. They realize, of course, that the leaders of the opposing party must make the same kinds of choices, because both parties want a competitive advantage in forthcoming elections. (See Policy Advocacy Challenge 11.1.)

POLICY ADVOCACY CHALLENGE 11.1

Finding Information about National Political Strategy

STEPHANIE DAVIS, RESEARCH LIBRARIAN, UNIVERSITY OF CALIFORNIA, IRVINE

Political parties must strategize constantly to make their stance on issues known to the population in order to gain votes and win elections. One strategy is to gain endorsements from an organization, a specific political party, or other politicians in order to swing supporters' votes to a certain candidate. Take any important political race in congressional or presidential elections. Find out from opposing candidates' Web sites which community organizations, state officials, trade unions, public officials, and professional organizations endorsed which candidates—and then speculate why they made these endorsements. Which policies did the candidate support that contributed to support for his or her candidacy from specific groups or persons? Candidates use Web sites, political advertisements, and speeches to gain votes. Candidates also often publicize how they tried to *block* certain proposals, such as when a candidate brags that she opposed "big oil interests" when she seeks the votes of environmentalists or persons troubled by the high cost of gasoline.

More can be learned about political strategy in the form of party platforms, agendas, policy issues, and educational information on the following Web sites of political parties in the United States. While there traditionally have been two major parties in the United States, others are gaining ground.

1. Democratic National Committee **http://www.democrats.org/index.html**
2. Republican Party **http://www.rnc.org**
3. Green Party **http://www.greenpartyus.org**
4. Libertarian Party **http://www.lp.org/organization**
5. Reform Party **http://www.reformparty.org**

◠ EXERCISE ◠

Visit the Web sites above and compare each party's stance on your research topic.

Selecting the Extent of Policy Changes

Policy advocates must decide whether to seek major or incremental changes, a choice that is often difficult. Policy advocates sometimes want major changes in those policies that they believe are fundamentally flawed, or when they want to appeal to a segment of the population or key interest groups that dislike it. They may seek only incremental changes when they believe that major changes are not politically feasible, require large investments of time and energy, or will antagonize key supporters.[1]

Selecting a Time Frame

Policy advocates often ask the following: Do we want specific changes to be enacted in the short term (during an upcoming meeting, the present year, or the present session of a legislature), or will we accept an extended time frame?[2] They sometimes want immediate results because they believe urgent action is needed, because they want to be able to claim a specific policy victory in an upcoming election, or because they believe it will be more difficult to get them enacted at a later point in time, such as after a specific election. Policy advocates realize that it is more difficult to get a policy enacted when they lose momentum, since other issues may intrude. In other cases, however, policy advocates select a longer time frame, deferring action on a policy proposal until times are more propitious. They may believe they will have greater support for a policy after a specific election. They may not want to defer action on a proposal until other issues are resolved. It is often difficult to maintain interest in a specific issue over a long period of time, however.

Grounding Strategy in Current Realities

Political strategy must be firmly linked to existing realities, including power distribution, contextual factors, past stances, vested interests, cohesion of likely opponents and proponents, situational realities, and the setting.

The Power Distribution

Kurt Lewin, the noted social psychologist, pioneered the concept of force field analysis to assess the distribution of power in specific situations.[3] To obtain a rough estimate of the support for a proposal, Lewin suggests enumerating persons by name and indicating the strength of their support or opposition in a diagram where the line lengths correspond to the level of their opposition or support. Figure 11.1 depicts a power distribution that is relatively evenly balanced between supporters and opposers.

Useful as a force field diagram is, it lacks key information. It does not tell us the relative power of a person to shape policy on a specific issue. The chair of a committee that is considering a proposal, for example, often has more power than any other member of the committee. It does not tell us the salience (or importance) that specific individuals attach to an issue. Someone who has strong convictions about an issue and is well positioned to affect policy, for example, may not see it as very important. Perhaps he is more interested in other issues, does not think it can be enacted, or lacks the time to invest in it.

Nor does force field analysis tell us to what extent advocates can mobilize persons who will support a policy initiative—not just persons who are decision makers but persons external to them. As we discuss in many chapters, for example, the Internet is an important tool in mobilizing persons to participate in advocacy coalitions around

FIGURE 11.1
Support of and
opposition to a
measure

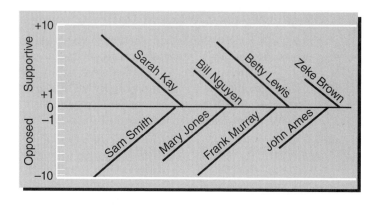

key issues. So we could add to Figure 11.1 another line not with the name of a specific person, but a category called "potential supporters" of a measure, i.e., persons and
advocacy groups that might be enlisted in a particular advocacy project through the
Internet or by other means.

William Coplin and Michael O'Leary have developed a simple system for scoring the distribution of sentiment, salience, and power on specific issues.[4] To illustrate
their approach, let's take a simple situation—a family of four that must consider two
issues: whether to ask Grandmother to move into the house after a recent illness and
whether to allow the 18-year-old son, Sam, to own his own car. The two parents (Mary
and Frank) and the two children (Sam and Diane) have decided to reach these decisions democratically but, as we know, policy making does not usually occur on a level
playing field. Assume that we know the family well enough to construct Table 11.1,
which represents the sentiment, salience, and power of each of the family members.
(The initials *M, F, S,* and *D* stand for the mother, Mary; the father, Frank; the son, Sam;
and the daughter, Diane.)

First, we give each person a score for his or her sentiment on the two issues
(extending from –10, very negative, to +10, very favorable). Table 11.1 shows that Mary
strongly favors allowing her mother to live in their home (her score is 10), whereas
Frank opposes the move (his score is –5). The children are mildly supportive (their
scores are 2 and 4). All family members support allowing Sam to have a car, having
scores of 4, 2, 10, and 8; predictably, the two children support this policy more strongly
than either of their parents.

Second, we score each person with respect to the salience, or importance, that
they give each issue on a scale from 1 (low salience) to 10 (high salience). Both parents
attach considerable importance to each of the issues; hence, their scores of 8 on the
issue of Grandmother and 7 on the issue of Sam's car. The children attach much more
importance to the issue of the car (they both score a 7), while attaching less importance
to Grandmother's residence in their home (their scores are 3 and 4).

Third, we estimate the family members' relative power to influence choices on a scale
from 1 (low power) to 4 (high power). The parents have far more power than the children;
thus, they score a 3 on each issue, while the children score a 1 or 2 on each issue.

To obtain an overall reading of the distribution of sentiment, salience, and power, we
multiply each person's scores on each issue. Mary's score is 240 (10 × 8 × 3) on Issue 1 and
84 (4 × 7 × 3) on Issue 2; Frank's scores are –120 (–5 × 8 × 3) on Issue 1 and 42 (2 × 7 × 3)

TABLE 11.1
Estimating the distribution of sentiments, salience, and power

	Issue 1: Grandmother					Issue 2: Car			
	M	F	S	D		M	F	S	D
Positions on the issues (−10 to +10)	10	−5	2	4		4	2	10	8
Salience (1 to 10)	8	8	3	4		7	7	7	7
Power to influence the outcome of this issue (1 to 4)	3	3	1	1		3	3	2	1
Totals for each participant (multiply the numbers down each column)	240	−120	6	16		84	42	140	56
Grand total for each issue (add the totals for each person)		142					322		

on Issue 2. The two children have considerably higher (more favorable) scores of 140 and 56 on Issue 2 than on Issue 1, where their scores are 6 and 16.

Now, we total the participants' scores on each issue. Because a higher score indicates a more favorable prognosis for a proposal, it appears that Sam is more likely to have a car (84 + 42 + 140 + 56 = 322) than is Grandmother to be asked to move into the family home (240 + −120 + 6 + 16 =142). Table 11.1 shows that a single negative score for a powerful participant (father or mother) markedly decreases the likelihood that a specific proposal will be approved.

A numbers approach to force field analysis may seem far-fetched, but politicians in legislative bodies sometimes use this kind of numeric analysis, crude and imperfect as it may be, to determine the prognosis for pieces of legislation.[5] If a proposal has an extremely low or unfavorable score, policy practitioners may decide the situation is hopeless, unless they can develop strategy that will enable them to change the sentiment, alter the salience, or modify the power of those who oppose their proposal.

Moreover, identifying the important participants, as well as their sentiment, salience, and power, helps policy practitioners develop strategy.[6] The data in Table 11.1 suggest several strategy options. Assume that Mary wants Grandmother to move into her home. She may try to bring Frank to at least a neutral sentiment, she may hope to reduce the salience he attaches to the issue, or she may try to isolate him from the decision-making process, thus reducing his power to influence the outcome. She may also seek to alter the children's sentiment, salience, and power, perhaps by promising them support for the car in return for their support on the Grandmother issue.

Table 11.1 does not include coalitional power where advocates augment their power by teaming with others. Mary may increase her power by forming a coalition with her children. She may also try to add new participants to the struggle such as by getting other relatives to become participants or by securing the family physicians' support.[7]

We have already mentioned, moreover, that force field analysis must include a category of persons and groups called "potential supporters" of a specific measure—persons and groups that might be enlisted to a cause through the Internet using techniques that we discussed in Policy Advocacy Challenge 10.4 on page 358. We should realize that policy advocates rarely achieve policy victories acting by themselves. They must usually work with others to get progressive changes because individuals usually lack sufficient power to obtain them.

With respect to the Internet, consider these realities. More than 75 percent of Americans had Internet access at home in 2006; 29 percent of American adults used the Internet in the 2004 election to get political news (up from 4 percent in 1996), and young persons especially use cell phones, wireless e-mails, the Internet, Web sites, and instant messaging. We are entering an era of "connected activism" where technology helps advocates form networks that provide information to large numbers of persons and involve them in specific advocacy projects. Technology is not a panacea—for example, opponents of policy advocates can also use it—but it can be hugely helpful to specific advocacy projects as is illustrated by use of the Internet to save animals left homeless in Hurricane Katrina's wake. (See Policy Advocacy Challenge 11.2; also see discussion of other free or low-cost software packages useful in organizing policy advocacy campaigns in Policy Advocacy Challenge 10.6 on page 364.)

POLICY ADVOCACY CHALLENGE 11.2

Using the Internet to Save Animals in Katrina's Wake

JONATHAN LACKLAND, FORMERLY WITH THE AMERICAN SOCIETY FOR THE PREVENTION OF CRUELTY TO ANIMALS

Internet advocacy has revolutionized many causes including, but not limited to, drugs and alcohol, welfare reform, mental health, child welfare, gun violence prevention, wildlife, and companion-animal-related issues. The American Society for the Prevention of Cruelty to Animals (ASPCA) uses its Advocacy Brigade, i.e., Internet advocacy, as a way to educate the public about those issues affecting companion animals.

All of us saw heartbreaking images of animals being swept away by heavy floods in Hurricane Katrina's wake while residents pleaded for their animals' lives to be saved. To make animals a priority, the ASPCA waged an aggressive, collaborative Internet advocacy campaign, using software by Convio Corporation, to inform the public of the devastation that animals suffered. The Advocacy Brigade included 82,000 persons not only to support relief efforts, but to contact their respective legislators to take action and provide support to the relief efforts to save animals. The Advocacy Brigade also helped raise more than $13 million that was used to offer animals vital services, help shelters rebuild their facilities, rescue animals, reunite animals with their owners, and help animals be adopted by reliable and loving households.

Some questions to ponder:

- Can you think of ways the Internet could be used to improve funding for child welfare services?
- How could policy advocates interested in improving child welfare services develop a roster of 82,000 persons, complete with their e-mail addresses, in a large city?
- How might policy advocates wanting to improve child welfare services engage these 82,000 persons in policy reforms?

Force field analysis is not a panacea, even though it is often highly useful to policy advocates. Others' positions might be falsely judged. Persons may change their positions abruptly. Some persons may become bystanders when an advocate thought they scored high on salience. Someone who the advocate thought was well positioned to shape outcomes with respect to an issue might be unable to influence the course of policy deliberations.

Force field analysis can, then, lead advocates to commit two kinds of errors: refraining from pursuing a proposal that could be enacted when they predicted it could not—and supporting a policy only to find that it cannot be enacted. Predicting policy outcomes is often frustrated by the fluid nature of many policy deliberations as persons change their positions or take actions that were not predicted by the policy advocate in advance.

Despite these cautionary notes, force field analysis is often very helpful. Without efforts to gauge our support and opposition, we may blindly commit ourselves to proposals that are not politically feasible. Or we may fail to take actions that can change the positions of participants in policy deliberations. Force field analysis also helps us to estimate the time and political resources required to get a specific policy enacted. If we face a difficult battle, better to know that up front so that we can be prepared for likely realities that we will confront. (See Policy Advocacy Challenge 11.3, where Bob Erlenbusch discusses how he used force field analysis on many occasions.)

POLICY ADVOCACY CHALLENGE 11.3

How I Used Force Field Analysis in Helping Develop a Plan to End Homelessness

BOB ERLENBUSCH, PH.D.

Go to **academic.cengage.com/ social_work/jansson** to watch this video clip

In the real world, policy advocates must frequently determine what positions persons hold prior to key meetings. They need to know, for example, if a large number of attendees will agree or disagree with specific proposals that will be discussed in the meeting. In some cases, they may try to change their views prior to the meeting. See Policy Advocacy Video 11.3 where Bob Erlenbusch, Chairman of the Board of the National Coalition on Homelessness and Executive Director of the Los Angeles Coalition Against Homelessness and Hunger, discusses his use of force field analysis before key meetings of a Blue Ribbon Commission on Homelessness that developed a plan to end homelessness in Los Angeles County.

Some questions to ponder:

- Why did Bob Erlenbusch need to know the positions of persons prior to key planning meetings of the Blue Ribbon Commission?
- Did he try to change some persons' views prior to the meeting?
- Why are "one-on-one" meetings often critical when conducting force field analysis?

Identifying Contextual Factors

Although knowing a policy's relative support and opposition is useful, we need to know also why people take certain positions and how they are likely to act when an issue enters policy deliberations. Analyzing participants' past stances during deliberation, vested interests, and cohesion of likely opponents and proponents allows a more accurate prediction of people's likely actions than does merely estimating their current position.

Past Stances

Many issues may have been deliberated previously. The responses of decision makers, interest groups, and the general public to policies depend on their recollections or accounts of the prior deliberations.[9] Deliberations are more likely to be conflictual, for example, when an issue has previously been associated with ideological polarization, as illustrated by the controversy that arises whenever Congress considers national health insurance, gun control, or abortion. Indeed, many politicians avoid such issues because they do not want to become embroiled in controversies among their constituents or in an extended legislative battle with an uncertain outcome. In other organizations, too, participants may avoid reintroducing issues or policies that are associated with prior controversy.

Policy advocates sometimes erroneously conclude that the controversies associated with an issue will continue. After Congress defeated President Clinton's national health measure in 1994, many people thought no health reforms could be enacted for years, but Clinton managed to get Congress to approve a measure to fund health coverage for more than 5 million uninsured children in 1997. Indeed, skillful policy advocates try to offset the negative effects of past stances by emphasizing developments that now make a change more feasible. Clinton's proposal was strengthened, for example, by his argument that, with the exodus of hundreds of thousands of single-headed families from the welfare rolls after the welfare reforms of 1996, many children would need to be medically insured since many mothers would no longer be eligible for Medicaid once they had left welfare—and many of their employers would not offer health insurance to them.

Vested Interests

People often base their position on an issue on their own interests.[10] Politicians may worry, for example, that a certain policy will antagonize some of their constituents or enable the other party to expand its constituency or obtain an electoral advantage. An executive of a social agency or a government bureaucracy may fear that a proposal will shift resources or program responsibilities to rival agencies, impose controls or regulations on their activities, or diminish their revenues. Alternatively, people may support a policy because they believe it will enhance their power, prestige, or resources. It is no secret that many politicians support some policy proposals to obtain campaign contributions from special interests that will benefit from them. If Democrats are more likely to receive contributions from trade unions, Republicans are more likely to receive resources from corporations. If Democrats are more likely to seek votes from women and persons of color,[11] Republicans are more likely to seek them from relatively affluent persons. Both parties cater to independent voters and moderates because they realize they often are swing voters who can determine the outcome of pivotal elections.

Cohesion of Likely Opponents and Proponents

Although we can sometimes calculate with considerable precision specific individuals' positions on an issue or policy, our analysis is incomplete if we fail to examine their relationships. For example, evenly balanced support of and opposition to a proposed policy should end in a stalemate. The proponents may still win, however, if their close working relationship allows them to evolve a strategy and to work together to implement it, while their opponents remain disunified. Moreover, if leaders with knowledge, commitment, political expertise, and considerable power support a specific proposal, it is more likely to be successful because they are often adept at assembling and maintaining supportive coalitions.

Situational Realities

Situational realities often shape the course of policy deliberations. In legislative settings, for example, the success of proposals is often influenced by coming elections, the balance of power between the contending parties, rivalries among powerful legislators and among members of the two legislative chambers, the budget, changes in leadership, the other proposals vying for attention, and the time remaining in a legislative session.[12]

These kinds of situational factors influence decision makers' interest in a proposal and the extent of the conflict associated with it. When national elections are imminent, for example, politicians of both parties begin to jockey for position; they want to take conspicuous positions that will consolidate their existing support and also draw some of their opponents' constituents to their side. Liberal Democrats from northern cities may support social programs and publicly oppose conservative initiatives, such as efforts to rescind regulations that promote affirmative action. Conservatives not only promote issues that will solidify their traditional support but also advance social measures that will attract some Democrats to their cause. By the same token, impending elections may make all politicians avoid issues offering no advantage or that are fraught with significant political risks. For example, some liberal Democrats who normally support the federal financing of abortions may avoid this divisive issue in an election year.

Personal and institutional rivalries also influence efforts to initiate proposals. Legislative committees may jealously guard their jurisdiction over certain issues; and, when they hear rumors that another committee is developing a proposal, may hurriedly frame their own proposal. This kind of rivalry may exist between committees within a legislative chamber or between rival committees in the two chambers. As one example, the House Economic and Educational Opportunities Committee and the Senate Committee on Labor and Human Resources each developed rival versions of national health reform early in the Clinton administration.

Situational factors also influence the political process social agencies. Some policy proposals fare well when a new leader is selected who favors them.[13] Just as in legislatures, internal institutional and personal rivalries sometimes determine who will support or initiate a specific policy proposal. Budget realities and external funding can significantly influence the politics of specific proposals, such as favoring ones that enhance funding.[14]

Adapting Strategy to the Setting

Skillful policy advocates realize that they have to adapt their strategy to the setting. We discuss later in this chapter, for example, how agency politics differ from legislative politics. However, there are many types of agencies, including those with a win-win and team-building atmosphere, and others with more conflictual relationships among staff or units. Two legislative committees may have entirely different norms and operating procedures. If the members of the House Economic and Educational Opportunities Committee are accustomed to wide-open conflict between liberals and conservatives, for instance, the members of the House and Senate Appropriations Committees have traditionally prided themselves on quiet, private deliberations, in which they seek behind-the-scenes solutions to budgetary issues.[15] Policy practitioners must adapt their tactics to such idiosyncrasies.

Developing Alternative Scenarios

We have discussed to this point a variety of considerations that policy advocates may consider as they move toward developing political strategies to secure the enactment of specific policy proposals. We have discussed not only force field analysis, but other situational, institutional, and historical factors that can give us clues about how to proceed to get support for a specific policy.

Policy advocates sort through a series of political options much as a quarterback considers the possible plays to use in a tight situation. Indeed, creative strategists run through successive what-if scenarios in which they explore whether various actions or statements may help them obtain their policy preferences.[16] Imagine three what-if scenarios. In Scenario 1, the policy advocate asks, "What would happen if I made a *single* presentation to a decision maker, suggesting a course of action?" This presentation might involve a request that a problem be taken seriously enough to be placed on a committee agenda, or a suggestion that a policy option be seriously considered. In some cases, this single presentation (a modest strategy) will suffice, particularly if the practitioner correctly assesses the current environment as supportive.

Policy advocates often develop at least two additional scenarios. Scenario 2's strategy is somewhat more ambitious; perhaps the single presentation will be coupled with discussions with key decision makers to make them more sympathetic to a proposal. Scenario 3 is even more ambitious; it may involve creating a coalition, cultivating a constituency, coupling presentations with many personal discussions, allocating specific roles and tasks to a range of people, and mixing internal pressure with external pressure. An example of an ambitious strategy occurred in the early 1990s. A coalition of organizations, in which the National Organization for Women was a central participant, developed a legislative proposal that would allow employees to obtain unpaid leave from work following the birth of a child, because of a parent's illness, or because of the death of a family member or close relative. NOW's members not only had personal liaisons with legislators and government officials but also exerted extensive external pressures on congressional members through letter writing and articles in the mass media.

We contrast the three preceding scenarios with an improvised one. In some cases, policy advocates decide not to formulate a strategy, but to seize opportunities as they arise.[17] At an opportune moment, they may inject an idea into committee discussions, a staff meeting, or a conversation with an official in their organization. Improvisational strategies are sometimes useful when policy advocates lack the time or knowledge of the situation to develop more refined strategies. However, unlike the three preceding strategy scenarios, improvisational strategies do not enable the policy advocate to mobilize and use power resources systematically.

Policy advocates need not invest major resources in this preliminary development of strategy scenarios because they need only the broad outlines of strategy at this point. In effect, they ask: Does this issue now require a major investment of resources and time, or should we address this issue with a modest or improvisational strategy?

Selecting a Strategy

Pragmatic considerations and stylistic preferences shape the selection of strategy. Policy advocates review strategy options in light of the realities we have discussed in this chapter. If their force field analysis suggests that there is extraordinary opposition to their proposal, for example, they may select an ambitious, complex strategy that requires a significant investment of time and energy. However, they must also consider the limits of their resources and time. If a proposal can be enacted with a relatively simple strategy that requires few resources and little time, most policy practitioners will select it.[18] Even when they fear a more ambitious one is needed, they may select a relatively modest strategy because they lack time or they place a higher priority on another issue.

Policy advocates' strategy choices are also influenced by their stylistic preferences. Some of us state our positions directly, whereas others discuss them in private deliberations. Some people like to precipitate conflict by advancing controversial positions, and others serve as mediators. Some initiate policies; others prefer to amend or oppose proposals.

Different styles have advantages and disadvantages. Mediators facilitate compromises, but are sometimes accused of failing to take a solid position. Champions of ideological positions initiate proposals for bold changes but sometimes lack the compromise skills necessary for enactment. Persons who select only sure winners or who avoid controversial issues can be seen as lacking courage or leadership.

Revising the Strategy

Strategies often need to be revised. Perhaps a policy proposal attracts far greater support—or opposition—than advocates anticipated. Perhaps opponents developed an effective coalition to oppose a specific proposal—or supporters were far more cohesive than was anticipated. Perhaps new situational factors arise, such as an improvement in the finances of an agency or a state. Perhaps new leaders arise in the wake of elections, or there is a leadership succession in an agency that either hinders or promotes the enactment of a specific policy proposal.

Seven Recurring Steps in Strategy

We have discussed various factors that policy advocates must consider when they develop strategy, such as the need to establish objectives, to select the extent of policy changes, to select a time frame, to examine the distribution of power, to identify contextual factors, to examine situational factors, to construct alternative scenarios, and to develop strategy. With this as a backdrop, we can now discuss seven recurring steps (see Box 11.1) that policy advocates take when they develop strategy, even if they do not take these steps in any particular order. (In Chapter Twelve, we illustrate these steps in legislative, organizational, and community settings.)

Specific policy advocates must also decide what role they wish to assume in a policy-advocacy project. Do they wish to be part of the leadership team? Do they wish to be volunteers to the project, such as engaging in fund raising, hosting events, organizing e-mail or letter-writing campaigns, or undertaking other activities? These decisions hinge on the time and resources of specific policy advocates.

Organizing a Team or Coalition

Particularly in an ambitious project, policy advocates need to organize themselves into a coherent unit. As events unfold and opposition emerges, it is important that a proposal's proponents develop a common strategy so they will not disintegrate in the face of conflict or give out contradictory messages, and they will implement strategy effectively. They can either establish a new group or work with an existing advocacy group. Whatever approach they take, policy advocates have to devote time and skill to keeping their team or coalition functioning effectively (See Policy Advocacy Challenge 11.4).

BOX 11.1 | Seven Steps in Formulating and Implementing Strategy

Organizing a team or coalition
- How will proponents organize a leadership team that will develop and coordinate strategy?
- To the extent resources are needed, whether money or supplies, how will they be obtained?
- To the extent a division of labor is required, such as committees or leaders focusing on specific tasks, how will it be worked out?

Establishing policy goals
- What do proponents wish to achieve?

Specifying a proposal's content and getting early sponsors
- What minimal features or content should the policy proposal contain?
- On what points can proponents negotiate or compromise?
- Can early sponsors be found, such as key legislators, who will support the proposal?

Establishing a style
- What level and scope of conflict will proponents seek?

Selecting power resources and framing strategy
- What kinds of person-to-person, substantive, decision-making process and context-shaping power resources will be used? To what extent can the Internet be used to mobilize support?
- Who will use these power resources and in what situations?

Implementing strategy
- How is the strategy to be put into action?
- When might it be necessary to improvise?

Revising the strategy
- How should the game plan be revised in light of the opponents' strategies?
- What new events or background factors suggest a change in strategy?

POLICY ADVOCACY CHALLENGE 11.4

Keeping a Coalition Together in New Orleans

RUSSELL HENDERSON, MSW, LCSW

Go to **academic.cengage.com/ social_work/jansson** to watch this video clip

It is often challenging to keep coalitions functioning once they have been established. Yet coalitions are often critical to the success of policy advocates, because they allow them to pool power resources and financial resources in a common cause. Listen to Policy Advocacy Challenge Video 11.4 with Russell Henderson, Organizer of the Rebuilding Louisiana Coalition and faculty member who teaches social policy at Dillard University in New Orleans, to hear him talk about challenges in building coalitions.

As we discuss in Chapter Twelve with respect to task groups, coalitions, and networks, proponents need to address at the outset issues of coordination, leadership, building constituencies, resolving conflict, dividing labor, and communication. They must continue to attend to these issues as events unfold. People may lose interest or become disenchanted with the cause, disagreements may develop about strategy, some people may think others are seeking the limelight, and some may become restive after setbacks.

Establishing Policy Goals

Early in the process, policy advocates have to establish policy goals within the context that they encounter. Do they want basic change or incremental change? Who are the likely proponents and opponents? Will the proposal meet major resistance or be widely accepted?

Policy advocates often align themselves with existing advocacy groups and volunteer to help them as they can. In such situations, fundamental decisions about policy goals, as well as some of the other seven steps in political strategy, are made by others. Volunteers often ask what they can contribute to this larger effort, such as by fund raising, hosting events, helping to organize letter-writing and e-mail campaigns, and visiting legislators from their hometown districts.

Specifying a Proposal's Content and Getting Early Sponsors

Policy advocates aim ultimately to have their proposal enacted, but they often must ask: Precisely what proposal? They have to decide what points of a proposal are most important to them and resist efforts to change or delete them. If they are willing to compromise excessively, they risk ending up with nothing, but if they are too rigid or dogmatic, no proposal at all may be enacted.

Early in the process, policy advocates need to find sponsors who will agree to support the proposal. If possible, such sponsors should include some influential people who sit on key committees or hold important positions.

Establishing a Style

To be effective, a strategy needs an overarching style. Will behind-the-scenes and nonconflictual deliberations suffice, or is more conflictual and publicized interaction advisable? Of course, the style may change: If a low-conflict approach is unsuccessful, policy practitioners may wish to use a higher-conflict approach. For an example of a policy advocate who selected a conflictual strategy at a specific point in time, (see Policy Advocacy Challenge 11.5).

POLICY ADVOCACY CHALLENGE 11.5

A High-Level Public Official "Goes Public" in Post-Katrina Louisiana

BRUCE JANSSON, PH.D.

Walter Isaacson, the former chief executive of CNN and managing editor of *Time Magazine* was persuaded by Governor Kathleen Blanco of Louisiana to assume a high-level position in the Louisiana Recovery Authority (LRA), which was created by the state of Louisiana in Hurricane Katrina's wake to serve as a conduit for federal money that would help New Orleans and other Gulf Coast communities rebuild. He agreed to be a Washington-based lobbyist and strategist for the LRA in late fall 2005.

Isaacson soon realized that his job would be a delicate one. The Louisiana delegation, composed of senators and representatives elected to Congress, had already chosen an aggressive strategy, demanding the Bush administration to ante up $250 billion both for relief of citizens and for rebuilding of communities. Many officials

(continued)

in the administration and conservative Republicans in the Congress were offended by the audacity of this demand—and were determined not to heed it.

Isaacson was by nature a blunt-speaking individual widely known for his assertiveness. As he said, "I came out of CNN where there were times we treated every issue as grist for _Crossfire_.[1] A native of New Orleans, he wanted very much to see it get the huge resources it desperately needed.

Yet he knew that a soft-sell, low-profile posture might be more effective than a confrontational one. Indeed, Blanco had taken care to name persons from the left, center, and right to the Board of the LRA, including Donna Brazile (a Democratic Party activist) and Mary Matalin (an advisor to President George Bush, Sr. and to Vice President Dick Cheney).

A key policy challenge that Isaacson faced was to secure support from the Bush administration for a "Louisiana Recovery Corporation" (separate from the LRA) that would use federal resources to tackle a central challenge facing New Orleans: helping citizens rebuild their homes, demolish them, or buy new homes. Minus huge resources for this task, New Orleans would remain cluttered for decades with destroyed homes.

Isaacson learned in January 2006, however, that President Bush would not support funding for the Louisiana Recovery Corporation. He feared its high cost. He did not want additional federal bureaucracy. He feared the federal government might have to purchase homes that citizens had abandoned, making it a larger holder of real estate.[2]

Frustrated by Bush's inaction, Isaacson chose to go public with criticism of the president, saying his opposition to creation of the Louisiana Recovery Corporation "undercuts the credibility of a president when he says he wants New Orleans to be able to rebuild itself." Administration officials were furious with Isaacson for this public criticism, but soon decided to cooperate with him by dispatching Donald Powell, who he had named to be his coordinator for the Gulf Coast rebuilding effort.

Powell assured Isaacson that he would open communications with him and Congress to facilitate reaching an agreement. The White House soon announced it would request $4.2 billion from Congress to help redevelop New Orleans—with Blanco saying the state would use the funds to pay homeowners to repair, rebuild, or relocate up to $150,000 each.

Some questions to ponder:

- Was Isaacson's "going public" a sensible move in these circumstances?
- Does policy advocacy require risk taking?

---

[1] Joseph Schatz, "Navigating Crossfire on the Gulf Coast," _Congressional Quarterly Weekly_, March 6, 2006: 583.
[2] Ibid, p. 584.

Selecting Power Resources and Framing Strategy

Decisions must be made about who will use which power resources in which situations. If several people are involved in a project, they may divide the responsibilities for talking with specific people, making presentations, doing research, compiling lists of supporters, and other functions. For example, people seeking policy changes in an agency may decide the following: Joe will propose a place on the next staff meeting agenda to discuss modifying the intake procedure; Mary will comment on the inadequacies of the existing procedure at the staff meeting; Tom will make some comments that support Joe and Mary; Elise will suggest forming a task force to devise a new policy. Moreover, this group might decide to approach some staff members before the meeting to get support for the policy change. Similarly, a coalition of groups seeking a change in legislative policy might assign specific research to one group, ask another group to approach important legislators, and ask still another to compile a mailing list that can be used later in a letter-writing campaign.

Decisions need to be made, as well, about whether and how to use the Internet to mobilize support for a specific campaign or issue, and how to use it to influence decision makers.

Implementing Strategy

Having devised a strategy, policy advocates must implement it skillfully. They must use the full range of policy practice skills (interactional, political, and analytic) to carry out their strategy over an extended period. Skillful advocates sometimes have to deviate from their planned strategy when circumstances require improvisation.

Revising the Strategy

Policy advocates who hold rigidly to a strategy often imperil their success. They may have made miscalculations in devising their strategy, such as underestimating the strength of the opposition or the opponents' counter strategy. Unanticipated events also shape deliberations and may require a modification of strategy.

A Policy Advocacy Challenge: How to Block Ill-Advised Policy Proposals

The *blocking* of policies can be as important as initiating them, as the presidencies of Ronald Reagan, Bill Clinton, and George W. Bush suggest. Both presidents Reagan and Bush took aim at a variety of existing social programs, seeking deep cuts in them or even their termination. After the initial success of Reagan and conservative Republicans in cutting many domestic programs by one-fourth or more in 1981, coalitions of advocacy groups in Washington, DC, as well as in many states, developed a campaign to stop further cuts. They were assisted by a deep recession that began in 1982 and extended into 1984—a situational factor that made Americans more sympathetic with the plight of low-income groups that were the primary users of the programs that Reagan had cut. Due to their efforts, most further cuts were averted. They supplemented work by congressional legislators with lobbyists and advocacy groups, with the latter groups orchestrating many demonstrations against further cuts around the nation.

Similarly, a combination of Democrats and moderate Republicans defeated a variety of initiatives put forward by conservative Republicans during the presidency of George W. Bush. They defeated proposals to privatize Social Security, to enact large educational voucher programs, to enact national legislation to ban gay marriages, and to make even deeper tax cuts at a time when the nation's deficits soared. Here, too, they linked relatively liberal legislators with advocacy groups to build opposition to these policies and eventually to defeat them.

President Clinton and an array of advocacy groups, in turn, defeated the quest by conservatives to divest Medicaid of its entitlement status and to devolve it to the states. Clinton and advocates contended that such policies could gut the major health safety-net program on which millions of low-income and uninsured persons depended. Advocates argued that some states and Congress would decide not to fund it, or to severely cut its funding, if its federal entitlement status was removed. (Federal entitlements' annual funding is currently guaranteed by law up to the level of claimed benefits, so they cannot be cut beneath this level.) In an epic battle waged in 1995 and 1996, Clinton defeated this proposal that was championed by Newt Gingrich, the conservative Speaker of the House. Less than a decade later, congressional liberals and moderate Republicans, as well as advocacy groups, defeated a similar attempt by congressional Republicans to disentitle Medicaid.

For an example of a blocking campaign, see Policy Advocacy Challenge 11.6 authored by Professor Robert Schneider.

POLICY ADVOCACY CHALLENGE 11.6

Blocking the Governor's Abolition of the Department of Aging

ROBERT SCHNEIDER, DSW, PROFESSOR, SCHOOL OF SOCIAL WORK, VIRGINIA COMMONWEALTH UNIVERSITY

In 1994, the conservative governor of Virginia, George Allen, was implementing with a vengeance his promise to taxpayers to reduce the size of state government. One particular target was the Virginia Department for the Aging (VDA), which was a freestanding agency with its own commissioner and board of advisors. The governor and his Secretary of Health and Human Services (HHS), Kay Cole James, announced in September that by the end of the year, they would transfer this department into another department, the Department of Medical Assistance Services (Medicaid), all in the name of efficiency and eliminating duplication, of course. The VDA would lose its freestanding status, its commissioner would be reduced to an assistant director, the advisory board would be gone, control of the budget would shift to the Medicaid commissioner, and decision making on behalf of the aging would be buried deeper in the state bureaucracy.

As a 10-year member of VDA's board and its chairperson from 1985 to 1987, I read this announcement with grim uneasiness. Governors have every prerogative to make administrative shifts to improve state service delivery, and political pressure can be largely ignored. But this action was going to reverse years of effort to improve the status of the VDA. Several of us had worked perseveringly to upgrade this unit from an office on aging in another department to an independent department with its own budget, decision making, commissioner, and board. It would disappear, for the most part, with this plan. But what could I do? How could we stop this highly popular governor? The odds seemed slim to zero.

After a day or two of pondering and stewing, I got on the phone and called four other former chairpersons of the VDA's Governor's Advisory Board. Saying that there must "surely be something we can do," I suggested a meeting in Richmond the next week. When we met, we all agreed that we had to take action to at least delay this decision. A certain spirit of shared concern and determination evolved, and from then on, we became known as the Gang of Five.

Remember now, that this meeting was in early September, and a final recommendation from the governor was going to be made in November. How should we proceed? Here is what we did. First, we called on two very experienced veterans of state politics and human services administration to ask for advice. We met with them the following week, and from this meeting, we decided to delay the decision by insisting that some public comment period be allowed for citizen input. Public feedback is a very crucial process in Virginia, but this governor ignored it whenever possible. But the chances he would stop his decision were still unlikely, so we devised a backup plan. This strategy would go to the heart of the issue; that is, it would kill the decision in November by influencing the panel of decision makers, the Virginia Joint Commission on Health Care (JCHC), a legislative committee of the General Assembly of Virginia that made recommendations on all matters pertaining to health. The governor's proposal would first have to pass this group, and we believed that if we had any chance at all, this was the place not only to delay, but to kill the proposal.

While writing to the governor and his secretary to delay the proposal for public comment, we began other tactics. Those of the Gang of Five who knew members of the JCHC were asked to contact them and explain the consequences of the governor's proposals. One of us was an extremely close friend of the commission's senior Democrat. The Gang called on me to write our concerns into a statement that we could circulate far and wide. After consulting with the other four members, I drafted a two-page document outlining the issues, the potential effects of the new proposal, and some action steps that individuals or groups could take. I also began organizing a communication system so that we could write or phone all of the members of the JCHC, the key leaders of the Aging Network (a loosely organized group of policy advocates), the area agencies on aging, and the media.

We quickly discovered that there was little enthusiasm for the governor's proposal among the members of the JCHC. The Secretary of Health and Human Services also found out, and asked us to meet with the commissioner of the Medicaid department. In mid-October, the Gang of Five walked into the commissioner's office armed with the written analysis and other research, particularly around budget issues, and met with him and his well-prepared staff for two hours. They offered us some minor changes, such as retaining *aging* in the name of the agency, and promised us that the new assistant director would have full access to all decision making. We insisted that they show us how their proposal would improve the services for the older people of Virginia. Our argument was based on an opposite view, that, at no cost savings for taxpayers, much of the progress and the improvement of services for the aging would suffer significantly. At that meeting, we sensed that they were afraid of us and what we might be able to do, since there was already a rumor (not unfounded) that we were organizing a mass rally of older Virginians for the November JCHC meeting. We declined their offers and left our documents with them to study.

By this time, our confidence was rising, and support from the Aging Network was in evidence, even though much of it was quiet and almost secretive since many feared retribution. We wrote letters to the JCHC members and outlined the dangers of the shift. We called and met with them. Several regional agencies organized vans and buses of their clients to come to Richmond in November. However, we discovered that at the JCHC meeting, there would be time for comments only from commission members, not from others in attendance.

Through contacts with friends of the commission's chair, the night before the meeting I asked for the opportunity to speak to the commission. The next morning, in a room filled with older Virginians, the discussion opened with the Secretary of HHS outlining the reasons for the governor's proposal. The chairman of the commission, asking for clarification, caught my eye and asked if I would be kind enough to explain

(continued)

the point. This gave me the chance to make my speech and outline our Gang of Five's contentions. Interestingly, I was the only speaker from the gallery that morning. The commission wanted other points clarified and delayed a decision until its December 27, 1994, meeting.

While we had at least won a delay, we were not overconfident. We would be prepared for the December 27 meeting and also decided to go on with planning a mass rally in mid-January, just after the opening of the annual session of the General Assembly. The lieutenant governor, unlike the governor, agreed to speak at noon at our rally on the Capitol grounds. Our efforts turned to mobilizing hundreds of seniors to come to Richmond in the winter. We decided to piggyback on an already scheduled Senior Day planned by the VDA to begin at 10 a.m. We sent invitations to agencies, individuals, associations, groups, legislators, and others to meet with us at noon *after* their earlier session in a nearby church, St. Paul's. We designed bright orange, three-inch stickers saying "SOS" (Support Our Seniors) and distributed about 4,000 of them. We also planned for many to come to the December 27 meeting.

However, the JCHC canceled its meeting on December 27 and rescheduled it for a week before our planned rally in January. Consequently, we had to alert all of our contacts of this change and hope that they would make the difficult adjustments in transportation and preparation. In early January, the JCHC met, facing a sea of bright orange dots in the gallery and changed the agenda to deal first with the governor's proposal. Saying, "I see many of you are here for the obvious—let's get this item finished first," the chairman asked the commission members for comment. A few minor questions later, a nearly unanimous vote rejected the proposal. The secretary then spoke and acknowledged the vote, saying that she disagreed with it but would respect the decision. The chairman then suggested to the audience that those who wished to leave could do so. Orange dots began disappearing through the doors.

We followed up a few days later with our mass rally. It was great fun to see another sea of orange dots come out of St. Paul's church and the VDA's morning meeting, where the secretary again spoke and acknowledged the defeat of the governor's proposal. They all headed across the street to the Bell Tower, where the Gang of Five held its rally with 500 to 600 older Virginians. The lieutenant governor spoke eloquently about services to the aging. We were thrilled and amazed at what had happened, remembering our bleak prospects only three months before.

Much happened between 1994 and 2006 illustrating how fluid the context is. Virginia Governor George Allen became U.S. Senator George Allen only to be defeated in 2006 by Jim Webb. Virginia Secretary of Health and Human Services Kay Cole James became Director of the Office of Personnel under President George W. Bush. The Governor's Advisory Board to the Department for the Aging became the Virginia Council on Aging with half the previous membership. The Virginia Department for the Aging got a new commissioner, Dr. Ann McGehee, who was then replaced by Julie Christopher. The department lost its responsibility for long-term care policy development and planning to the staff of the Joint Commission on Health Care. Republicans took control of the House and Senate for the first time in more than 100 years. The Gang of Five keeps an eye on the department and stands ready to act.

∽ EXERCISE ∽

After reading this case, discuss the following questions:

- What objectives did Robert Schneider and his allies establish early in their crusade?
- What group or coalition took the lead in fighting the governor?
- What initial strategy, as well as backup strategy, did the Gang of Five develop?
- How did Robert Schneider get the chance to speak at the commission meeting?
- Why was securing a delay important?
- How did the Gang of Five mobilize pressure from multiple sources?

Policy initiatives to secure the enactment of new policies—as opposed to efforts to block policies—also lie at the heart of policy advocacy. Insufficient as it may be, the American welfare state—with its thousands of social programs, civil rights regulations, and budget items—would not exist save for the determined efforts of policy advocates *both* to block and to initiate policies. It is the *combination* of blocking and initiating strategies by policy advocates that have made the United States, its states, and its communities more humane places.

What You Can Now Do

CHAPTER SUMMARY

Political strategy puts power resources to use. You are now equipped to do the following:

- Develop objectives and positions at the outset
- Ground strategy in current realities by doing a force field analysis that includes persons' positions, contextual factors, situational realities, and likely future developments
- Build alternative scenarios to select and revise strategy
- Use seven steps in building strategy including organizing a team or coalition, or working through an existing advocacy group, establishing policy goals within a context, specifying a proposal's content and getting early sponsors, establishing a style, selecting power resources and framing strategy, implementing strategy, and revising the strategy

We are now prepared to see in the next chapter how policy advocates put political strategy into action in legislative, agency, and community settings.

NOTES

1. Ron Dear and Rino Patti discuss the need for compromises in policy making in "Legislative Advocacy," *Encyclopedia of Social Work,* 18th ed., vol. 2 (Silver Spring, MD: National Association of Social Workers, 1987), p. 37.

2. George Brager and Stephen Holloway, *Changing Human Service Organizations* (New York: Free Press, 1978), pp. 107–128.

3. Kurt Lewin, *Field Theory in Social Science* (New York: Harper & Row, 1951).

4. William Coplin and Michael O'Leary, *Everyman's Prince* (North Scituate, MA: Duxbury, 1976), pp. 7–25.

5. Stephen Frantzich, *Computers in Congress* (Beverly Hills, CA: Sage, 1982), pp. 248–250.

6. Coplin and O'Leary, *Everyman's Prince*, pp. 20–25, 170–175.

7. Eric Schattschneider, *The Semisovereign People* (New York: Holt, Rinehart & Winston, 1960), pp. 1–19.

8. Allison Fine, *Momentum*, San Francisco, Jossey-Bass, 2006, p. 7.

9. See the discussion of organizations' traditions, objectives, and ideology in Brager and Holloway, *Changing Human Service Organizations*, pp. 57–66.

10. Brager and Holloway discuss the role of persons' tangible interests in shaping their position in *Changing Human Service Organizations*, pp. 85–92.

11. Julie Kosterlitz discusses feminist pressure in "Not Just Kid Stuff," *National Journal* 20 (November 19, 1988): 2934–2939.

12. See John Kingdon, *Agendas, Alternatives, and Public Choices* (Boston: Little, Brown, 1984), pp. 152–170.

13. See Perry Smith, *Taking Charge* (Washington, DC: National Defense University Press, 1986), pp. 17–26.

14. See Yeheskel Hasenfeld, *Human Service Organizations* (Englewood Cliffs, NJ: Prentice Hall, 1983), pp. 43–49.

15. Richard Fenno, *The Power of the Purse* (Boston: Little, Brown, 1966), pp. 193–195.

16. See Schelling, *The Strategy of Conflict.*

17. Eugene Bardach, *The Skill Factor in Politics* (Berkeley and Los Angeles: University of California Press, 1972), pp. 188–189.

18. Brager and Holloway, *Changing Human Service Organizations*, pp. 140–141.

SUGGESTED READINGS

Gauging Political Feasibility

William Coplin and Michael O'Leary, *Everyman's Prince* (North Scituate, MA: Duxbury, 1976).

Understanding and Predicting Conflict

Morton Deutsch, *The Resolution of Conflict: Constructive and Destructive Processes* (New Haven, CT: Yale University Press, 1973), pp. 124–152.

Developing and Implementing Political Strategy

Eugene Bardach, *The Skill Factor in Politics* (Berkeley and Los Angeles: University of California Press, 1972), pp. 183–240.

Ron Dear and Rino Patti, "Legislative Advocacy: Seven Effective Tactics," *Social Work* 26 (July 1981): 289–297.

Case Studies of Legislative Politics

Jeffrey Birnbaum and Alan Murray, *Showdown at Gucci Gulch* (New York: Random House, 1987).

Eric Redman, *The Dance of Legislation* (New York: Simon & Schuster, 1973).

Policy Practice in Legislative Settings

Donald deKieffer, *The Citizen's Guide to Lobbying Congress* (Chicago: Chicago Review Press, 1997).

Willard Richan, *Lobbying for Social Change* (New York: Haworth Press, 1996).

Politics in Agency Settings

Burton Gummer, *The Politics of Social Administration: Managing Organizational Politics in Social Agencies* (Englewood Cliffs, NJ: Prentice Hall, 1990).

Politics in Community Settings

Kimberly Bobo, Jackie Kendall, and Steve Max, *Organizing for Social Change: A Manual for Activists in the 1990s* (Washington, DC: Seven Locks Press, 1991).

12

Putting Political Strategy Into Action

POLICY PREDICAMENT	Millions of workers across the nation constitute the so-called working poor. Often working near and just above the minimum wage, they lack resources to escape poverty. To remedy this situation for some workers, policy advocates across the nation decided to launch a grass-roots campaign in scores of cities to persuade city councils and mayors to require a "living wage" for persons hired by firms that were reimbursed by public contracts. Professor Manny Gale, Emeritus Professor of Social Work and Gerontology at California State University in Sacramento, helped develop such a campaign in Sacramento. (See Policy Advocacy Challenge 12.8 on page 442.)

We have provided, thus far, an overview of strategy no matter what the setting. Whether policy advocates work in legislative, community, or agency settings, they have to take the seven strategy steps described in Box 11.1 on page 402. They have to organize a team or coalition (or tap into an existing one), establish policy goals within the context of a specific setting, specify a proposal's content, establish a style, select power resources and framing strategy, implement strategy, and revise strategy. Yet different settings also provide specific challenges, so we now discuss how to develop and implement political strategy in legislative, agency, and community settings.

We discuss in this chapter how policy advocates can do the following:

- Organize a campaign to secure the enactment of a specific legislative proposal
- Use an array of interventions that puts pressure on legislators including use of the Internet
- Organize or participate in an effort to change an agency policy
- Organize or participate in a community-based effort to change a community policy
- Work with task groups to seek policy changes in legislatures, agencies, or communities

BOX 12.1 | Specific Activities That Policy Advocates Can Undertake within Larger Projects

Testifying before a legislative committee
Lobbying specific legislators in person
Writing a letter to a legislator as part of a larger campaign
Telephoning a legislator's office about a specific measure (or organizing a phone tree)
Writing a letter to a newspaper about a specific measure
Participating in a demonstration about a specific measure
Alerting a legislator to a specific issue or problem in the human services
Raising funds for a specific advocacy project

Strategy in Legislative Settings

Policy advocates sometimes work to get a specific piece of legislation enacted—an ambitious undertaking in light of the sheer number of measures that legislators consider during any given session.[1] Policy advocates can develop their own action system to get legislation enacted, or they can be part of a larger coalition or network. No matter who takes the lead, policy advocates must undertake the tasks enumerated in Box 12.1.

Organizing Legislative Advocacy Projects

Organizing a Team or Coalition

Policy advocates need an organized group that will spearhead the drive toward enactment of a legislative proposal. It may be an existing group, such as an advocacy group; a coalition of groups established to secure legislation; or the NASW. This group needs leadership, such as a strategy committee that will pull together research materials and devise a master strategy. If an advocacy group is leaderless, its members will probably march in different directions and give out conflicting messages, undermining the group's effectiveness.[2]

An organized group is needed especially in legislative settings because legislatures are complex organizations with participants who make their living by supporting *and* opposing legislative proposals. To succeed in this environment, an advocacy team must operate with considerable efficiency. The team has to create a unified and effective strategy to keep its proposal from being lost among the hundreds of measures on the legislative agenda. If the proposal is controversial, like many that would redistribute resources or services to oppressed populations, it is likely to encounter opposition that can be overcome only by effective strategy. (See Policy Advocacy Challenge 12.1.)

POLICY ADVOCACY CHALLENGE 12.1

Managing a Legislative Advocacy Network

JULIE STEEN, PH.D., ASSISTANT PROFESSOR, SOUTHERN ILLINOIS UNIVERSITY AT CARBONDALE

After I earned my MSW, I began work as a legislative advocate at a statewide child abuse prevention agency in Florida. I was responsible for creating and coordinating a network of advocates committed to the well-being of children. We began with a group of social workers from child abuse prevention and treatment agencies. A number of adult survivors of abuse also jointed the network after hearing about the cause. This network consisted of approximately 100 members and was aptly named *STAND UP AND SHOUT*. In coordinating the network efforts, I met with child advocates from other fields, including child health, early education and care, and developmental disabilities. These child advocates came together to form a broad coalition that was named ONE VOICE FOR CHILDREN. The advocates brought their own networks and merged them into one entity, allowing us to reach many more people and consequently to increase the impact of our advocacy efforts.

As the coordinator of the STAND UP AND SHOUT network, I was responsible for informing advocates across the state about the child welfare issues that were subjects of legislative proposals, I tracked the status of every bill during the legislative session. I created legislative updates and mailed these to the network members every week. I guided the advocates through the legislative process and encouraged them to make calls to legislators, meet with their local legislative delegations, and write letters to the editors of local newspapers.

Policy analysis was central to this work. Advocates must be fully aware of the details of each bill they are supporting or opposing. I analyzed the bills on our legislative agenda with special attention to the impact of the bills on children's well-being. The results of my analyses and legislative committee analyses became the source of messages for advocacy efforts that were used by members of the network in their communications with legislators—including whether to support or oppose specific pieces of legislation. For example, I recommended that members of STAND UP AND SHOUT oppose a bill that would have placed our state in violation of federal law and that would have therefore threatened our state's ability to draw down federal funds.

I also recommended that network members oppose a bill called the Family Bill of Rights, which was designed by its authors to limit the power of child protection agencies to remove children from homes that they believed neglected or abused them. The bill required a court order *before* children could be removed from their homes—a delay that might have led to serious injury to, or even the death of, some abused children. We placed an enormous amount of time and energy into defeating this bill, flooding legislators' offices with calls urging opposition to the bill. We succeeding in defeating the provision mandating a court order.

I saw many important issues enacted by the legislature during my time as a legislative advocate in Florida. We helped enact children's health insurance, mental health parity, and school readiness programs.

I was one of few social workers practicing as a policy advocate—most others were lawyers, public health professionals, and political scientists. My hope is that social workers will join the field of legislative advocacy in increasing numbers so that we can become formidable participants in improving the lives of children by getting legislation

(continued)

enacted that improves their lives. Legislative advocacy requires expertise, skills, passion, and idealism—but it allows us to advance social justice.

Some questions to ponder:

- Does the Internet make even more feasible the development of networks of policy advocates who influence legislative enactments?
- Should the staff of many social agencies become part of networks like STAND UP AND SHOUT?

A stifling or overly centralized team will be counterproductive because the collaborators need the freedom to be innovative and to use their distinctive strengths. Yet many good projects founder because proponents fail to set up a central leadership that will identify the key tasks, allocate these tasks to team members, and monitor the expeditious completion of the tasks.

Early in the process, proponents need to identify their allies without ruling out possible allies too aggressively; strange bedfellows often rally to an issue. Advocates should have a big-tent philosophy, to the extent this is possible, while also recognizing likely foes from their past records and prior statements.[3] (Remember that persons and groups do not become *actual* foes until they have taken action against a specific proposal.) Some groups or persons may agree to participate, but only on terms that are unacceptable to the proponents, such as demanding unacceptable provisions in the proposal.

Early in the process, policy advocates also should compile a *resource book* that includes the existing law, legal memoranda from attorneys who have been consulted, likely opponents, likely allies, congressional contacts on key committees (both aides and legislators in both supporting and opposing camps), civil servants from administrative agencies that will be affected by the proposal, and a set of key issues.[4] The organization's team has to know who the key players are. Once proposed legislation is introduced, it is immediately referred to a committee, and based on tradition, advocates should be able to predict how their proposal is likely to be routed. Then they need to analyze which members of the committee are likely to support and oppose the proposal.

Because it contains sensitive information, this resource book (actually, a spiral notebook divided into sections) should not be disseminated beyond the key leaders of the coalition. (If a list of likely foes is widely seen, for example, they may become real foes.)

Establishing Policy Goals in a Legislative Context

At the inception of their work, policy advocates must decide what kinds of policy changes they seek. Do they want to develop new legislation or amend an existing piece of legislation? Do they want to increase funding for a specific program, or do they want to change the administrative regulations that guide the implementation of an existing program? (We discuss implementing issues in more detail in Chapter Fourteen.) Do they seek relatively modest changes or more ambitious reforms? To what extent are they willing to compromise with likely opponents of their proposal to increase the likelihood of its enactment?

Writing a Policy Brief: Specifying a Proposal's Content and Getting Early Sponsors

The first rule of legislative lobbying is to do your homework. Advocates have to write a *policy brief,* which comprises an analysis of the existing law, their proposal, why they want to change the existing policy, and the likely objections to their proposal (with rebutting responses).[5] (This policy brief should also be kept in a spiral notebook, separated into sections.) Advocates must know their issue so that they can state concisely (1) what they are concerned about; (2) how their issue affects other areas, such as likely costs and effects on other programs or laws; (3) an array of possible remedies with their likely costs and implementation problems; (4) an initial proposal (not yet in the form of a legislative bill) that addresses the problem; and (5) the likely arguments of opponents. (See Policy Advocacy Challenge 12.2.)

POLICY ADVOCACY CHALLENGE 12.2

An Example of a Policy Brief

MARCIA MABEE

Memorandum to the Commissioner

1. Policy Issue   In the context of the next five-year plan, what should be the role of state hospitals for people with mental illness? Specifically, should DMH care for its remaining institutionalized clients completely within existing institutions, completely within the community by purchase of services (POS), or somewhere in between? How can the department shape its personnel policy accordingly?

Recommendations: The goal for clients who are mentally ill should be to liquidate existing state hospitals, leaving one small institution in each of the seven regions to serve violent patients. The proposed facilities would be operated under private auspices under state contract. Community care services should be completely POS. DMH's personnel policy should be, implicitly, one of attrition, where civil servants in DMH are trained and transferred to other state positions and to community service settings under public auspices in settings like municipal hospitals. Explicitly, DMH should work closely with unions to arrange for three options: early retirement, training and transfer to other state positions, and training and transfer to community service settings under public auspices to preserve vesting but not civil service protections. These places might be municipal hospitals, state-university-sponsored settings, and so forth.

2. Summary and Analysis of Issues   The impetus for deinstitutionalization stems from a belief, buttressed by research findings, that large institutions inhibit and discourage the potential of those who are mentally ill to function independently. Prevalent in the past 20 years, this belief underlies passage of the Community Mental Health Centers Act of 1963. Legal developments, especially several Supreme Court decisions, have hastened deinstitutionalization by prohibiting involuntary commitment without provision of treatment. Social programs, such as Medicaid, Medicare, Title XX, and SSI, have provided heretofore absent funding for community services. These developments took 370,000 people out of public mental hospitals from 1955 to 1975. In Massachusetts, 7,000 people left state hospitals between 1971 and 1978.

(continued)

Current situation: These deinstitutionalized clients have frequently been placed in nursing homes that lack the resources and the inclination to meet the needs of residents who are mentally ill. Many other individuals reside in substandard boarding houses, do not receive rehabilitation or treatment services, frequently decompensate, and are readmitted to state hospitals. Still other individuals are simply lost to follow-up treatment.

This situation stems from gaps in community services for the deinstitutionalized population, the availability of services not tailored to the needs of the individual who is mentally ill but offering a protective environment, and pressure to deinstitutionalize quickly because of mounting costs and a desire to avoid legal suits. This urgency precludes planning to fill service gaps and to foster receptive community attitudes.

What should the optimal community care system look like? What is needed? The literature abounds in descriptions of successful and unsuccessful community care programs for deinstitutionalized people who are mentally ill. The same essential program elements emerge again and again as keys to success or failure. They are targeting patients who are chronic, which is a priority; links to other resources, for example, vocational rehabilitation; community provision of the full range of functions associated with institutional care; individually tailored treatment; culturally relevant programs tailored to local communities; specially trained staff attuned to the survival problems of clients who are mentally ill and living in noninstitutional settings; public or private beds; and internal evaluation of these resources.

The problem at hand is how to move states such as Massachusetts from having half-filled institutions and underserved deinstitutionalized clients to a fully community-based model that incorporates these eight program elements.

3. Available Options   The following options are available to us:

Option 1: Discontinue deinstitutionalization. Devote scarce resources to upgrading institutions.

- Pro: This option appeals to those who doubt the potential of individuals who are mentally ill for growth and who, because of concern or contempt, want them off community streets. It is administratively simpler, leaving the state in complete control. However, it is likely to be more costly than using community services, because community-based programs have federal funding sources, such as SSI and Medicaid.
- Con: Research offers strong evidence that large institutions reduce individualization, thereby discouraging the ego development necessary for independent functioning. Current concern for civil liberties will not tolerate this option, particularly with regard to those who are mentally ill.

Option 2: Develop a complete community care system, incorporating the eight program elements. Fund the services with POS.

- Pro: Critics of POS say that providers dominate the state, which loses control. However, this has been due largely to a lack of state planning; an abundance of personnel trained in direct service, rather than management; and a state inferiority complex. These deficiencies can be altered. State legislatures must be persuaded to keep providing funds to support institutional care and new funds to develop community services. Once community settings are in place, institutional expenditures can be converted to community expenditures, and new funds can be discontinued. This interim support of two systems is vital to planning efforts. Administrative personnel can be retrained and direct-service personnel phased out. Liquidating property assets and converting direct-service expenditures into POS money provide the state with buying power it need not be afraid to exercise. Community mental health centers and other financially distressed community service settings will welcome state funding.

- Con: As exemplified by community mental health centers, community programs reject people who are mentally ill as "unrewarding." Community residents reject people who are mentally ill out of fear, disgust, and concerns about property devaluation. Although some programs may welcome state funding, delayed payment creates prohibitive cash flow problems.

Option 3: Develop a community care system incorporating the eight key elements using POS, but maintain small, regionally located state institutions to treat people who are mentally ill and violent. The proposed facilities would be privately managed and staffed. Develop a limited number of direct-service community programs under other public auspices, such as municipal hospitals and state-university-sponsored settings. Staff them with transferred institutional personnel.

- Pro: This option is particularly suited to people who are mentally ill. Patients who are violent frequently cannot be treated safely in community hospital settings. Small, secure institutions in each region will provide more humane, cost-effective care than will large institutions preserved for this purpose. The rationale for private administration, as for POS versus direct services, rests on the assumption that personnel currently serving in state institutions would re-create in the proposed small institutions the negative institutional practices that suppress client development. As institutional personnel are moved into community settings, they can be purged of their institutional ways; the literature describes how this has been done successfully. Most of the best personnel have now left the state systems. Private community programs are fiercely resisting incorporating the remaining state personnel, even the professionals. However, because unions are strong and influence state legislators, and out of a sense of fairness, employee concerns about jobs and retirement benefits must be considered. Three options may meet state personnel's needs, while preserving the state's policy of attrition: early retirement benefits, training and transfer to other state positions, and training and transfer to community settings under other public auspices.
- Con: Any residual institutional role is dangerous, because it will be overutilized. The incentives needed to attract private management and professional staff for the proposed facilities would outweigh any cost-effectiveness the facilities would provide.

4. Recommendation: Choose Option 3   *Rationale:* People who are mentally ill have few, if any, advocates (families are often nonexistent for one reason or another) and suffer from a fluctuating disease requiring several treatment methods. As a result, inpatient beds must be available, and some of these beds must be in a secure setting to protect others from patients who are violent and patients who are suicidal from themselves.

(continued)

5. *Implementation Factors* *How can legislators be persuaded both to keep supporting an institutional system and to develop community-based services?* They must be impressed with the horrors of a poorly planned deinstitutionalization process. Plenty of examples exist, probably even locally. Use them to gain crucial planning time.

How can unions be persuaded to comply with an implicit attrition policy that will no doubt be perfectly explicit to them? The state administration must convince local legislators—that is, those whose areas are most affected by deinstitutionalization—that institutions are inhumane, anachronistic relics that must be abolished (the state can point out that Senator Backman has been vocal in this regard), but that the state wishes to be fair to employees caught in the middle.

DMH management should be sure to broaden the base when dealing with unions. They should meet not only with union leaders but also with the rank and file and with respected professionals. DMH should be sensitive to employee anxieties and committed to retraining and relocation efforts. New York State has been successful in this area and offers a good model.

What about the future? Should the state aim to dismantle all direct-care services permanently? No. Once the current system has been dismantled and POS has been in operation for a while, DMH should evaluate the cost-effectiveness of direct-care services versus POS, especially for outpatient services.

∽ EXERCISE ∾

As you read this case, try outlining a memo on another issue. If you want practice in writing succinct policy memos, also try making this memo even more concise, such as by reducing its length by one-half. Sometimes, even one- or two-page memos can be highly effective in generating interest in a policy issue.

Source: This case is a modified version of one by Dr. Marcia Mabee.

The policy brief states the policy advocate's recommendations, but does it in the context of alternative policy options that opponents are likely to raise. It places the issue in its context. It states likely opponents and their positions. The policy brief serves as an orienting tool for policy advocates. It often is not shared with other persons, although it may be shared with legislative allies to give them an overview of the advocate's position. It states likely objections or opposition to the advocate's position—and ways to rebut it. As a project unfolds, advocates and their allies have to stand together behind clearly formulated positions—not wanting allies to use different arguments and data when the proposal reaches the legislative process. Of course, an advocate may choose to modify a position as the legislative process unfolds in the context of political realities.

We can distinguish between the policy brief that advocates have developed for their own internal use, and proposals they subsequently present to legislators and others, which are often one- or two-page documents that state very succinctly the purpose, rationale, and content of a proposal. Since legislators and others are very busy, it is essential that documents that reach them be brief.

Most legislators are lawyers, so advocates need to have expert legal opinions early in the advocacy process. Sometimes, they commission a legal memorandum from an experienced law firm (for a fee that is negotiated in advance) to outline the existing law as interpreted by the courts and to tell them how other laws would be affected by the implementation of their proposal.[6] Alternatively, as we discuss later, advocates can get expert advice from staff assistants to legislators, members of legislative committees, or civil servants. The extent they need legal consultation depends, of course, upon the nature of the issue that they address.

Advocates must make key contacts early in the policy process to secure commitments to the general thrust of their project, even though they have not yet drafted a specific piece of legislation. Later, they will try to get some legislators to sponsor their legislation by agreeing to put their names at the top of the legislative proposal.

Establishing a Style

Legislative advocates usually have an out-front, assertive style. They have to draw attention to their proposal by making contact with many legislators, including those who are on the committees that will consider their proposal.

Personal lobbying, letter writing, and press coverage are often more effective than demonstrations.[7] Protests sometimes incite the opponents of a measure or lead to incidents that make the change effort controversial. Yet demonstrations and protests are sometimes essential to educating the public and making legislators aware that many people want them to take action with respect to s specific policy—as was illustrated by the Civil Rights Movement in the 1950s and 1960s, as well as huge demonstrations in 2005 and 2006 for immigration reforms at the federal level. To be effective, demonstrations and protests must be supplemented by legislative lobbying where policy advocates develop specific legislative proposals and seek support for them.

The Internet provides powerful tools for influencing public officials as we discussed in Chapters Ten and Eleven. A policy advocate who has access to e-mail addresses of a broad audience—or who possesses a widely used Web site—can ask persons to take specific actions at specific times, such as e-mailing key legislators or other public officials. E-mails and Web sites can be used, as well, to mobilize audiences at key points in time, such as getting persons to attend important legislative hearings.

Policy advocates must decide whether or not they want to assume a relatively nonconflictual style. If they seek only modest changes in existing policy that they believe will attract widespread support, they might seek a relatively nonconflictual political process and a narrow scope of conflict. By contrast, some policy advocates might decide that considerable conflict is necessary to secure the enactment of a controversial reform that pits conservative legislators against liberal ones. In such a situation, they might broaden the scope of the conflict by seeking media coverage and by encouraging many groups to pressure legislators.

Selecting Power Resources and Framing Strategy

Once advocates have finished their research and put together a resource book, they have to develop a *strategy book* that lays out their tactics for the entire campaign. Like the resource book, this material should be kept confidential.[8] It should specify the following:

1. *Press representation.* This task should be done by people who can effectively speak for the legislative proposal. Also to be decided are who will issue press releases and who will be the contact persons if the press need additional information.

2. *Legislators to be contacted,* particularly on the committees likely to hear the legislative proposal. Advocates should also list the key aides of legislators and their personal phone numbers, as well as legislators who are likely to be friendly to the legislative proposal even if they are not on the key committees. Advocates should do a complete analysis of the voting records of these legislators on similar pieces of legislation; this information is available from such lobbying organizations as Americans for Democratic Action and the AFL-CIO's Committee on Political Education. They also should do an analysis of their home districts, making a page for each legislator that will later serve as briefing material for the advocates who lobby the legislators. For each legislator, advocates should note whether they or their allies have special links with them, whether they know people who live within their constituencies, and whether specific arguments are likely to be particularly persuasive with them. Advocates should decide how to use the Internet to elicit e-mails or other personal actions, such as attending key events that can be part of the advocacy project.

3. *A committee to spearhead a letter-writing or e-mail campaign,* to decide when letters or e-mails will be sent, what their substantive content will be, and who will send them. As with legislative testimony, the advocates need to put forth a consistent argument with legislators. Letter writing and e-mail campaigns must be carefully planned, since legislators can be "turned off" by communications that are mass produced rather than written by individuals who say in their own words why they want a specific piece of legislation to be enacted (or blocked).

4. *An initial plan for a blitz of the legislature.* A large group will make appointments with an array of legislators and their staff to push the issue on specific prearranged days. The plan should discuss when this will occur, who will participate, and which key legislators should be targeted.

So far, the advocates have only identified a specific problem and a proposed remedy, but they haven't drafted a specific legislative proposal. Nor have they lined up legislative sponsors.

The Internet allows advocacy organizations to develop a reservoir of persons who can be called upon during advocacy projects to undertake some of the tasks enumerated in the resource book. (See Policy Advocacy Challenge 12.3.)

POLICY ADVOCACY CHALLENGE 12.3

Using the Internet to Develop an Action System Using Volunteers

JEFF MARTIN, AMERICAN ASSOCIATION OF DIABETES

The American Diabetes Association (ADA) has been using Convio's © Advocacy tool since May 2003 to maintain a strong advocacy program that relies on our volunteers at both the state and national level. One focus has been to get different states to enact SAFE AT SCHOOL (SAS) legislation to fund staff and programs needed to keep diabetic children safe while they are at school. For example, each school should have programs in place to maintain diabetic children through programs that test blood sugar, allow children to keep and eat snacks if they have low blood sugar, and allow children to carry and administer insulin (if blood sugar is high. They should have a nurse or other staff person who has the requisite knowledge to help children maintain their blood sugar at healthy levels. Given the current epidemic of diabetes among American youth, SAS legislation is vitally needed.

The Internet allows us to collect and use information that is key to our advocacy efforts. It allows us to have lists of ADA volunteers in each state with their e-mail addresses. It allows us to conduct need surveys in different states. For example, when we learn that advocates have been unable to educate and negotiate with some local school districts in a specific state so that they implement needed safety programs, we can survey ADA volunteers in that state to see if they agree to support the introduction of SAFE AT SCHOOL legislation in their state. We can then share information regarding volunteers' interest in participating with their local ADA office—so that it can then call on their assistance in a campaign that they develop to get SAFE AT SCHOOL legislation enacted in a specific state. For most organizations, but particularly for those in the non-for-profit arena, the importance of this "force multiplier" capability cannot be overstated.

When we develop a campaign for SAS legislation in a specific state, we can use the Internet to enlist volunteers in it. We give them background information on legislation. We identify which legislators we are targeting. We given them specific messages about our position on the legislation that we wish them to send to legislators—and the mechanism to send that message. We can do all of this centrally, removing the need for any extra work by volunteers to orchestrate this. (We have learned that we increase the likelihood of volunteers' participation if we remove the need for them to do extra work.)

By having information at both state and federal levels and by sharing it back and forth, the ADA has had remarkable success in getting SAS legislation enacted—at last count in 16 states.

Some questions to ponder:

- In the case of the ADA, how might it recruit volunteers from the huge number of families that have diabetic children?
- How might the ADA assign volunteers to specific tasks in a campaign to get SAS legislation in a specific legislature?
- How might information about ADA volunteers in many different states help the ADA get needed legislation in Washington, DC?

Implementing Strategy

Implementing a strategy skillfully requires adherence to the conventions or protocols of legislative politics regarding lobbying, testifying, using the mass media, and writing letters.

Approaching Legislative Staff   At numerous points during their work, policy advocates talk with legislative committee staff that number roughly 7,500 in the Congress alone.

They must devote considerable time to discussions with legislative staff; indeed, they will probably spend more time with them than with the legislators themselves. Most legislators rely on their staff to make recommendations about key issues—and often scuttle measures when lobbyists have failed to brief their staff.[9] In light of the sheer number of bills submitted to legislatures (20,000 are submitted to the Congress each year), legislators must depend on their staff in this way.

We have already discussed that the policy brief developed for internal use by advocates must be condensed into a brief format so that legislators and others can quickly understand its rationale and substance. For example, a two- to three-page document that also might contain appendix materials is useful.

Advocates should realize that each legislator's office is like a small agency. The legislator often has a personal secretary who makes appointments; an administrative assistant; legislative assistants who specialize in such areas as domestic policy, foreign policy (in the case of the Congress), and liaison to committees on which the legislator sits; a press aide; and so-called case workers who manage constituent relations.

Advocates usually approach the chief staff person first, sometimes known as an administrative assistant or a senior legislative assistant. These aides are gatekeepers for legislators and political strategists, and they are usually more interested in a proposal's political merits than in its substantive merits. Advocates must convince this aide that the legislator's support of their issue will bring him or her substantial political gain, through positive public relations, press releases welcoming the legislator's support, and well-publicized events in the legislator's district to show his or her support for the proposal and the support of key constituency groups. Advocates should be even-tempered but appropriately assertive in their discussions, and they should not oversell their proposal by making inflated claims. (Advocates should remember that in most cases, they are talking with seasoned political professionals who are very well versed in legislative politics.) If the administrative assistant likes their proposal, a legislator's support is often likely, though details are often worked out with lower-level staff that have substantive expertise in the proposal area. These aides are called legislative assistants.

In discussions with legislative assistants, advocates can focus more on the substance of their proposal than on its political merits. In these discussions, advocates give information about the proposal and its merits, and ask for advice. If legislative assistants like the proposal, they can often convince the administrative assistants—and the legislators themselves—to support the proposal.

At some point, advocates will work with a legislator's press aides, such as by drafting a press release for them that announces the legislator's support for the proposal.

(Advocates usually schedule appointments with administrative assistants or press aides, through the legislator's personal secretary.)

Working with Committee Staff Proposals are processed by legislative committees, which have their own staff, usually appointed by the senior members of the committee. (Nearly 7,500 committee staffers work in the federal legislature; they are powerful participants in the legislative process.) Some of these staff are appointed by members of the majority party and some by members of the minority party. Since they are technically versed in specific areas, advocates should focus with them on the actual provisions of a proposal.[10] Advocates should seek meetings, perhaps over lunch, with committee staff who are responsible for the topic of the proposal; they should brief them and ask them what further information they need, offering to get it for them promptly. Advocates will probably need to keep in touch with key committee staff on a weekly basis or more frequently. They should also consult with staff members from the opposing party. Legislators' personal staff often defer to committee staff members' expertise.

Thus far, advocates probably do not have an actual legislative proposal, but simply a general position or a rough draft of a legislative proposal. At this point, to get help with the proper wording of the proposed legislation, advocates should ask for expert advice from the legal counsel of the legislative committee, the committee staff, or a legislative assistant of a friendly legislator who has sufficient expertise to help them in the drafting effort.

Policy advocates need sponsorship and support if their bills are to be enacted. They must find legislators who will agree to place their names as sponsors (or introducers) at the top of the legislation. Advocates should seek numerous sponsors from both political parties and sponsors who are highly placed in the legislative chambers, such as the presiding office, the majority whip, and the chairpersons of the committees that will examine the proposed legislation.[11] Of course, as we have already discussed, a legislator's agreement to sponsor a bill is not an agreement to invest considerable energy in its enactment, although advocates hope that their discussions with legislators and their aides will convince them to commit their personal resources to it.

Advocates also should seek formal support from the head of government—the governor, president, or mayor—and from the director of the department or agency that will implement the legislation. Of course, their support cannot always be obtained, as many liberal advocates have discovered when they confronted conservative administrations.

Lobbying Legislators   *Lobbying* legislators is having personal discussions with them or their aides to elicit support for a bill. In this effort, advocates should use the background material on legislators in their resource book and their strategy book. (See Policy Advocacy Challenge 12.4.)

POLICY ADVOCACY CHALLENGE 12.4

How to Lobby Legislators

RON DEAR, DSW

Go to **academic.cengage.com/ social_work/jansson** to watch this video clip

Listen to the Policy Advocacy Video 12.4 where Ron Dear, Associate Professor Emeritus from the School of Social Work of the University of Washington, discusses strategies he has found useful from years of lobbying for the University of Washington and other causes in Olympia—the capital of the state of Washington.

Some questions to ponder:

• Why are legislators often dependent on lobbyists?
• What characteristics of lobbyists make them more effective in their work—and what should they avoid doing?
• What skills do many social workers possess that would make them excellent lobbyists?

Through the legislator's appointment secretary, an advocate makes an appointment at least a week in advance for no more than 15 minutes. Advocates should be certain that legislative assistants are also asked to be present, to avoid the appearance of going over their heads. The legislative assistant should be briefed before the meeting. (As we noted earlier, some legislators will dismiss a project if their legislative assistants have not been briefed—and they themselves usually expect to have been briefed by their legislative assistants before they meet with an advocate.[12]) If possible, advocates should include in their delegation someone from the legislator's home district.

On their arrival, advocates should first talk with the legislative assistant, introducing him or her to their delegation and bringing additional briefing materials. When advocates enter the legislator's office, they should cordially introduce their delegation, praising the help they have received from the legislative assistant even if they have received little assistance. (They may need the assistant's further help later.) They should give the legislator a one- or two-page summary of their issue and briefly go over its main points, stressing the political gains the legislator will receive in his or her constituency from his or her support. Appendix materials can accompany the summary or can be provided later on request. Advocates should never bully legislators or make outlandish claims; they should present their case succinctly and with appropriate assertiveness.[13] Advocates should specifically ask the legislator to support their proposal and should keep their comments short, not exceeding 15 minutes unless the legislator lengthens the session. Do not get sidetracked by extraneous issues, and keep the legislator on the topic if he or she tries to shift the subject. Each member of the delegation should leave a business card. If the legislator asks questions to which they do not know the answer, the advocates should offer to get the answers to him or her promptly.[14] Remember, your reputation for honesty is one of your most important power resources in legislative settings—even though many people think most legislators are double-dealers, and not to be trusted.

The follow-up to the meeting should include short thank you notes to the legislator and to individual staff members, briefly restating the basic points made in the meeting.

Advocates should not be awed by legislators, even those with considerable reputations. Instead they should view the meeting as a service because it gives the legislator a chance to enhance his or her reputation by supporting their issue, and provides the legislator with facts and arguments that can be used to support the issue.

Branching Out to Reach Allies

Advocates need an array of allies to support their projects,[15] including government agencies and other interest groups. Most government agencies have their own lobbyists, so their support of an advocacy proposal often means added clout with the legislature. Advocates should ascertain which agencies are most likely to help them by gauging which agencies' budgets, responsibilities, or prestige will be enhanced by the proposal, and which agencies are currently working in the area of the proposal. In their discussions with civil servants or politically appointed agency staff, advocates should emphasize that their proposal is intended to help the agency do its job even better. At some point in the legislative process, some agencies may issue a formal position on the advocates' proposal; if this position is supportive, the advocates should work closely with the agency's legislative liaison office to enlist its aid.

Advocates establish some allies when they form their team or coalition. They should then approach other interest groups that share the objectives of their project. Careful ground rules must be established: Advocates want the support of other groups, but they do not want loose cannons that take positions, make arguments, and use tactics that are divergent from those of the original team. The team cannot excessively muzzle or restrain its allies, but establishing some clearance and review methods will coordinate the collaboration. While endorsement by myriad groups looks impressive, advocates most want as allies groups that will commit time, resources, and public support. Endorsements should include permission to use allies' names publicly.

Advocates can sometimes persuade legislators to write letters to their colleagues supporting the advocates' position. These letters may be very effective, especially when they come from respected or powerful legislators. (Several letters can be written or a number of legislators can sign a single letter.)

The Blitz   Policy advocates often decide to invade the legislature with a concentrated all-out mobilization of resources. A blitz takes many weeks of planning. Appointments for three- or four-person delegations to crucial legislators must be made weeks in advance; a master schedule of the visits must be devised; and delegations must have fact sheets on the proposal as well as information on the legislators they will visit.[16] At the appointment, the delegation presents arguments for its proposal and asks the legislator about his or her questions or concerns. After the blitz, the legislators' questions must be answered promptly—and members of delegations must send personal thank you notes to the legislators. The leadership team reviews the feedback received by the delegations to gauge which legislators are supportive, uncertain, or opposed.

Getting Legislation Introduced   A sponsoring legislator introduces the advocates' proposal into the legislative process, so it is referred to a legislative committee. The chairperson of that committee then refers it to a subcommittee that schedules hearings on the proposal. Whether these hearings are scheduled at all, as well as their timing, is critical. Hearings on a proposal that are delayed to the end of a legislative session receive the required committee report so late that action cannot be taken by the full legislature.[17] Roughly two-thirds of bills introduced in Congress receive no hearings at all. The chances that early hearings will be held on a bill increases when the committee chairperson cosponsors it or when it is actually introduced by the incumbent administration. So advocates need to approach the chairperson of the legislative committee immediately after their proposal has been introduced. They can also ask their other congressional supporters to request that the chairperson schedule early hearings. In a few cases, their congressional supporters will decide that their measure should be reassigned to another committee or should even be reported from the committee by means of unusual parliamentary tactics that will bypass committee members who oppose it.

Testifying   Once hearings are scheduled, advocates should make certain that representatives of their group or coalition are invited to testify, by getting friendly committee staff or staff of legislators to recommend them. Advocates should make clear that they want to testify and that they will keep their testimony brief. Sometimes they ensure a chance at testifying by offering a well-known person, but they should be certain that celebrities are well briefed and use arguments that the advocates' team has assembled.

The protocol for legislative testimony is simple. Advocates submit a brief written statement several days before their testimony. In the first two pages or so, the rationale, focus, and substance of the proposal is presented so legislators can quickly understand it. (Appendix materials that provide further detail can be attached.) This statement must be carefully written so that it reads well and also contains detailed information and data, often in the appendix, that cannot easily be given in a speech. It gives a fuller exposition of the advocate's position and is intended to be read by legislators and their aides.

However, the statement cannot be read at legislative hearings, where testifiers are expected to speak only for about 10 minutes. Advocates should list their main points, making their testimony dramatic and spontaneous so that it captures the committee's attention, perhaps by using specific cases as illustrations. Friendly legislators may prompt some committee members to ask questions that will elicit the strong points of the proposal or that will undermine the arguments of opponents. Advocates should be prepared for friendly as well as hostile questions from legislators; ideology and political interests often shape legislators' responses. If asked hostile questions, advocates should stand their ground, stick to their key arguments and data, and not volunteer information that goes beyond the questions asked. Advocates want to be seen as principled people with a well-reasoned case.[18]

Candor and honesty are highly valued in legislative hearings. If advocates do not know the answer to a question, rather than bluffing, they should say they will find the answer and send it in writing to the committee.

Using the Mass Media   The mass media can often help policy advocates reach a broad audience that will, in turn, place pressure on politicians to take action. Advocates have several options.[19] A press conference that makes their case for a proposal may be scheduled on the same day as a blitz or the first legislative committee hearing.

Of course, advocates must first get the attention of the mass media, which are besieged by people who want coverage. Advocates must make their story appear dramatic and relevant to larger social issues. They should establish personal links with key reporters in the print media, radio, and television, giving them full information about their issue and why it is important.[20] (Some reporters will be less friendly than others, and some critical stories about their project may appear if their issue is controversial.) To get reporters to come to a news conference, send written materials announcing it to reporters with whom you have established contacts and to others. You can also target the mass media in pivotal politicians' districts. If, for example, the chair of a legislative committee has bottlenecked a proposal, allies from an advocacy group in her district might call a press conference to pressure her into supporting the legislation.

Policy advocates sometimes use demonstrations to pressure legislators and to get coverage from the mass media. This tactic may not be as effective as lobbying legislators directly, but it will dramatize an issue and make clear that a substantial group is interested in it. Like legislative blitzes, demonstrations must be organized with care to prevent unnecessary altercations with police and to achieve maximum effect.[21]

Another tactic is writing guest editorials to be sent to the editorial offices of newspapers, radio stations, and television stations. Such editorials should not exceed 800 words and are more likely to be published if well-known persons write them and if they convey a dramatic, well-written message. Advocates can also write letters to the editors of periodicals, stating their central points briefly and dramatically. (See Policy Advocacy Challenge 12.4.)

Orchestrating Telephone and Letter-Writing Campaigns and E-mail Campaigns   Campaigns to call or write the offices of legislators may use the membership lists of community or professional groups. Letter writers should be provided with suggested themes, but not with form letters: legislators consider individualized letters more credible than standardized letters.[22] (See Policy Advocacy Challenge 12.5.)

POLICY ADVOCACY CHALLENGE 12.5

Writing Effective "Letters to the Editor"

RONALD B. DEAR, DSW, ASSOCIATE PROFESSOR EMERITUS, SCHOOL OF SOCIAL WORK, UNIVERSITY OF WASHINGTON

These are the 10 tips I offer my students when I give them the assignment of writing a letter to the editor of a newspaper or other periodical. These tips can also prove useful when writing letters to legislators and other public officials.

1. *Start with your reason for writing.* Be specific about the issue to which you are responding; for example: "I agree with your editorial of October 15 on the necessity of family leave policy, but you seem to have concluded. . . ." You do not need to state the name of the periodical or, if you are writing to a newspaper, the section in which the article or editorial appeared—the editor will know.

2. *Be timely.* Write immediately when you see something to which you wish to respond. You are most excited and concerned at that point. Also, people quickly forget editorials, columns, and letters. Don't respond to yesterday's news or issues. A fine letter, sent too late, will never get published.

3. *Brevity is important.* Your letter should be no longer than one page, 200 to 250 words. Longer letters do, of course, get published occasionally, but they are the exception rather than the rule. To make your letter more readable, divide it into several short paragraphs rather than one long one.

4. *Get to your point right away.* Don't ramble. This is no time for a mystery. You are responding to something. Why? Make it clear.

5. *Address only one issue or topic.* Too many issues and topics make the letter confusing and raise the question about what it is, exactly, you are writing about.

6. *Tone.* Make it terse. Punchy. Humorous, if possible. Be provocative, but always be civil. Give strong opinions. Use logical, lively writing. Editors look for challenge, especially of their views. They like differences of opinion to be well stated.

7. *Give reasons for your views.* Be very specific and, when appropriate, use factual information. However, when you cite dates and facts make sure they are correct; for example: "Recent poverty data, as cited in the New York. *Times* on October 2 . . ." or "The *U.S. Statistical Abstract* 1996, p. 412, shows that most elderly are not poor."

8. *If you have expertise on the subject, say that you do*—for example, "I have been a CPS worker for the past 12 years and. . . ."

9. *If you have personal (as opposed to professional) experience that is relevant, state it*—for example: "I am a mother with three children, all in Seattle public schools, and I was appalled by the recent article on the upcoming levy."

10. *Be constructive as to what you think should be done.* You have commented and perhaps criticized. What would you do?

Finally, make sure you include your work and home phone numbers. Editors will always verify a letter before they publish it.

Effective letters are short, rarely exceeding two pages that quickly get to the point; they describe the issue and the advocate's organization or interest in it, discuss the current law and the proposed changes in it, urge positive action, and make clear that the legislator's position will be closely followed in their home district. (See Policy Advocacy Challenge 12.6.)

**POLICY
ADVOCACY
CHALLENGE 12.6**

A Letter to the
Editor Written
in New Orleans
Post-Katrina

Rebecca Kendig

This letter was sent to the Times-Picayune in New Orleans on June 21, 2006 and subsequently published. Rebecca Kendig was responding to an article written on June 19, 2006 titled "Police Seek Leads in 5 Killings," p. 1

New Orleans needs to ensure that "rebuilding our city" encompasses much more than physically constructing homes; repairing and strengthening levees, and opening and ameliorating public schools and hospitals. We need to finally acknowledge that our neediest and most vulnerable children need help—real help—if they are going to live positive and productive lives and reject drugs, guns, and violence.

Katrina did not wash away the inequities that plague our city; she did not eradicate crime; and she didn't "fix" the problems that we faced before her. In fact, she exacerbated these issues—leaving those with the least to live for—even more hopeless and with even less to lose. As sad as it is, many of our youth fall into this category—and although their lives have just started—they feel as though their days are already numbered—and in many cases, they are right.

One of the youth who was killed this past weekend was interviewed by our organization while he was housed at a juvenile prison. When asked what he wanted to do upon his release from prison, he responded, "If I had a choice, I would get out of the game and get an education." This young man, like so many of our neediest youth, did not feel that he had choices, nor did he believe that there was a way for him to escape the dangerous lifestyle that he was caught up in.

We need to come together as a community to provide all of our youth with real choices. We need to work patiently with these youth—whose short lives have been plagued by disconnectedness, violence, and hopelessness—and let them know that their lives have meaning beyond the streets. If these youth are ever going to enjoy a future that so many of us take for granted—one that involves education, employment and a stable family life—they need all of our help.

It is not until we come together as a community and provide our neediest youth with the quality services, education, employment training, and consistent support and involvement of caring adults that these young people will begin to make healthier decisions—decisions that unfortunately have impacts far beyond their own lives. Until we assist this "lost generation" to find a positive sense of purpose and self-worth—we will never see these youth become the wonderful adults they are capable of being, nor will we see a real reduction of crime in this city—not now or for years to come.

Sincerely,
The Youth Empowerment Project
Melissa Sawyer, Director
Rebecca Kendig, Director of Case Management Services
Angela Conyers, Legal Director
Sheldon Escher, Youth Advocate

Some questions to ponder:

- How did the letter begin with a clear point of view even in its first sentence?
- How did the authors give the issue a sense of urgency that would appeal to the wider community?
- Was the use of a case example effective?

E-mail campaigns have emerged as an important advocacy tactic, with large numbers of e-mails going to key legislators at key points as advocates develop substantial e-mail lists of persons who support their cause. (Refer back to Policy Advocacy Challenge 10.4 on page 358, as well as Policy Advocacy Challenge 12.3 on page 420, which discuss how advocates can develop and use lists of volunteers who can be brought into an advocacy campaign at strategic points.) Of course, e-mails cannot be used as an exclusive tactic, but must be supplemented by personalized letters and other communications. They need to be one tactic in a larger campaign to be effective.

Revising the Strategy

Advocates must revise their initial strategy at various points during their campaign because a campaign for an issue is an evolving phenomenon shaped by changing events.

For example, other groups and politicians often advocate rival measures. In such cases, policy advocates must try to influence the rival measures when their own measures are stymied. Many other factors can also necessitate changes in strategy. For example, expected opposition or support might not materialize or might increase, external events (such as a budget shortfall) might intrude, or a parliamentary obstacle might emerge or be removed.

Strategy in Agency Settings

The seven strategy steps listed in Box 11.1 also are relevant to organizational settings. Here, too, policy advocates must develop a strategy that will enhance the achievement of their policy objectives.

Organizing a Team or Coalition

Policy advocates often want to obtain changes in agencies' policies as they work within them or as they monitor them from a funding agency. As in legislative settings, policy advocates need to assemble a team or coalition, even if it is loosely constructed, from among people with similar values, people from specific units or programs, members of informal groups or associations, union leaders, or people from different levels in the agency's formal organization.

Establishing Policy Goals in the Organizational Context

Policy advocates are involved in an array of policy goals. One is the extent to which they will respond to policies that descend on them from external sources, such as legislatures, government agencies, insurance companies, and the courts. Their responses include deciding not to seek funds from certain sources (thus avoiding specific policies), seeking external funding from programs whose policies they enthusiastically support, and seeking external funding from programs whose policies they partially accept. When they do accept funds, agency staff has to decide whether to comply with the policies that accompany the funds. They may have various amounts of discretion. For example, a not-for-profit agency that accepts funds for services to teenage mothers who receive welfare may strictly enforce the coercive policies of the welfare authorities or may soften the edges of these policies by not reporting some information to the welfare authorities or by taking other evasive actions.

Shaping informal policies is an important activity in social agencies. (In Chapter One, we stated that the shared beliefs and norms of staff constitute one form of social policy.) When they believe that current informal policies are having a negative effect, staff members can modify them by trying to modify the organization's culture through educational techniques, the use of consultants, and direct interventions with colleagues. They can also shape informal policies by promoting the hiring of people whose policy preferences concur with their own.

Policy advocates may also try to influence who oversees specific programs, where services are provided, what budget allocations specific programs receive, and what kinds of funds the agency seeks from external funders. In each of these cases, a policy advocate shapes the agency's policies by influencing their implementation and budget choices rather than by trying to change official agency policies.

Agency staff can try to shape official policy at the highest levels of the agency, such as its mission, formal policies, and budgets, or they can concentrate on policies in specific agency units or programs, even bypassing higher-level staff when they believe they will receive more favorable responses at the unit or program level. (Recall that the student intern in Policy Advocacy Challenge 10.2 decided with her preceptor not to bring her innovation to high-level staff until it had been implemented as a pilot program.)

Astute tacticians analyze an issue's political economy. When doing force field analysis, they ask whether a specific policy will deter clients or attract a steady stream of clients and resources to the organization. They also note how it will enhance the agency's reputation, flow of clients, support from funding sources, or support from accrediting agencies. Because executives often favor maintaining staff morale, reducing internal conflict, and providing quality services, tacticians can also emphasize these kinds of positive consequences of a specific policy proposal.[23] Recall how the student intern in Policy Advocacy Challenge 10.2 planned to argue that developing group services for the children of institutionalized parents would increase referrals to the clinic and its prestige in the community.

Skillful tacticians view an organization's *formal attributes*—meaning its hierarchy and division of labor—as both constraints and opportunities. As a constraint, hierarchy intimidates persons who believe that their superiors will oppose a policy change. In organizations that lack a team-building atmosphere, some persons understandably fear that they may lose a promotion, a pay increase, or even the job by supporting even relatively small changes that top officials do not favor. Where intimidation and fear exist, support for proposed policy changes may be significantly reduced. When social service organizations are unionized (many public and nongovernmental agencies have unions), lower-level staff may be emboldened to support policy changes, though many unions restrict themselves to bread-and-butter issues, such as employees' wages and working conditions.

Hierarchy also provides opportunities. Astute tacticians can defuse the formal organization's negative aspects by finding allies for a proposed change within the higher ranks of administration. (The student intern in Policy Advocacy Challenge 10.2 hoped to defuse opposition to her proposal by obtaining Mr. Jones's support, since other staff deferred to him on issues relating to outpatient services.) In rarer instances, they can use top officials' opposition to a suggested change to rally lower-level staff against these top officials, a tactic trade unions often use. This tactic must be used with caution, however, because it may merely entrench higher-level officials' opposition to a proposal and may lead to recriminations.

The division of labor is a constraint when it fragments organizations into competing units, causing members of one unit to oppose policy reforms that may benefit other units. When this win-lose ethos prevails, a policy practitioner may find it difficult to establish broad-based support for a change in existing policies. Indeed, the student intern in Policy Advocacy Challenge 10.2 feared that the director of training, Ida Brown, would oppose the innovation because it had come from Mr. Jones, a person she viewed as a rival. Divisions into separate units also can provide rich opportunities for coalitions if policy advocates can devise proposals that appeal to persons with different perspectives and interests, perhaps framing a proposal so that various units will have part of the action. The staff members of the unit that initiates a proposal might agree to a concession to another unit in return for its support.

Because organizations tend to have scarce resources, policy reformers must usually place *budget implications* at the fore in their force field analyses. A policy proposal's prognosis is usually bleak if it will cost the organization considerable funds and has little long-term prospect of generating offsetting funds from fees or external funders. Since it was unclear whether the student intern's innovation in Policy Advocacy Challenge 10.2 would generate fees or resources from funders, she probably should have devoted more energy to examining its fiscal implications.

When examining a proposal's budgetary implications, policy advocates need to consider fee-generating possibilities: whether external funders may be interested in funding it, whether the start-up costs will be offset by revenues once the innovation is institutionalized, and whether an inexpensive pilot phase is possible.

Policy changes that advance the important central goals of the agency (i.e., the *agency mission*)—or at least goals that the top management values—probably have a better chance than changes that are seen as irrelevant to these goals.[24] The student intern's innovation appealed to Mr. Jones in Policy Advocacy Challenge 10.2 precisely because he viewed it as furthering his commitments to community mental health and to outpatient services. When considering an issue's relationship to the agency's mission, policy advocates should refer also to the agency's context: Perhaps a proposal is not congruent with an agency's current mission, but it represents an innovation that addresses emerging community needs or issues that specific funders have prioritized.

It is easy to forget that policy advocates can obtain support for some proposals simply by emphasizing their relevance to beneficence or clients' well-being. As we discussed in Chapter Two, the hallmark of professions is their expressed ethical interest in helping clients. When conducting force field analyses, then, a policy advocate should ask what kinds of evidence will show that a specific proposal advances clients' well-being. Expert opinions, feedback from clients, evaluators' findings, and social scientists' work can buttress the case that a proposal will help clients. (The student intern could have strengthened her case for her innovation by finding evaluative or theoretical literature showing that her innovation would significantly help children.)

Recall our discussion in Chapter Four of *boundary spanners,* who derive power from their ability to lead an agency to sources of funds and referrals that will enhance its survival. Strategists strengthen support for a proposal when they can show that it will bring new funds and referrals or will enhance the agency's prestige in the wider community.

An advocate must gauge the *informal relationships* among organizational participants when assessing a proposal's potential support. When we conduct force field analyses to examine agency employees' separate opinions, we may ignore important relationships among agency staff members. People often take cues from others whom they respect, so convincing a single pivotal person often brings many other persons' support. Policy advocates need to be able to understand long-standing patterns of association and deference in their agency when they try to predict a proposal's outcome.[25]

Using *intermediaries*, which we discussed in Chapter Ten, is particularly important in the politics of organizations. A policy advocate who is a direct-service worker often seeks higher-level intermediaries' support for a proposal, so that other employees will follow their superiors' leads. It also is useful to seek the support of intermediaries in other units of the organization, because some people defer only to the superiors in their own units.

Policy advocates should not reach premature conclusions about the feasibility of a specific policy proposal; even when the outlook is bleak, support may be gained for a proposal if it is framed correctly and if process tactics (such as timing and the use of intermediaries) are chosen well.

Specifying a Proposal's Content

Policy advocates have to frame a proposal that specifies what they want to change in light of their objectives and the political realities—and whether they want merely incremental or larger shifts in policy. They can work on many fronts when participating in their agency's politics—changing official or informal policy, policy on implementing and budget choices, policy at higher levels of an organization, or policy in specific units.

Establishing a Style

Legislators are used to open, protracted, and public conflict among the members of different parties and persons with different ideologies. Indeed, they use conflict over specific issues to prove that they represent their constituents' interests better than the members of opposing parties do. In contrast, organizations' staff members tend not to want ongoing, protracted conflict, partly because staff members have to work together every day to implement agency programs. (Some leaders of organizations actively quell conflict to preserve their own power and preferences, to emphasize win-win decision-making processes, or to enhance the implementation of agency programs.)

If the politics of organizations tend to be more muted than the politics of legislatures, they can still be highly conflictual. Burton Gummer speculates that organizations are most likely to be politicized when they have scarce resources; when there is considerable internal conflict over the priority of different programs; when staff members have different service approaches or philosophies, such as different treatment methods; and when there is conflict between units, programs, or departments. He also notes that most organizations have at least some of these features.[26]

Style must be tailored to the setting and the issue. A frontal attack that polarizes the agency should be chosen only after all other alternatives have been weighed. Of course, conflict is usually unavoidable when major changes are sought that will infringe on the values and interests of key members of the organization.

Consensus-building efforts such as retreats, the use of external consultants who devise collaborative strategies, or group exercises that encourage full discussion of specific issues, frequently meet with considerable success. These devices are also used, however, to promote the views of a specific faction, as when executives use external consultants as "hired guns."

Selecting Power Resources and Framing Strategy

An array of strategy options exists in organizations:

Option 1. A direct-service worker decides to implement (or not to implement) a policy without consulting anyone. (We discussed issues of autonomy in Chapter Ten.)

Option 2. A social worker decides, much like the student intern in Policy Advocacy Challenge 10.2, to begin a pilot program with the support of her supervisor before seeking high-level policy clearance.

Option 3. A social worker decides to organize a broad-based coalition within his organization to seek a specific policy change. He decides to use a confrontive, polarizing style of politics, even though he realizes that the outcome is uncertain and that he risks alienating high-level officials.

Option 4. A social worker decides to develop a program innovation, but only after consulting extensively and striking deals with several people that result in extensive modifications of her original proposal.

Option 5. A social worker decides to change staff members' informal norms because she decides that they harm certain kinds of clients by giving them misdirected services. She persuades a high-level official to bring in an external consultant to give the staff technical training in new approaches to service delivery.

Option 6. A social worker sets up a task force to seek a collaborative win-win solution to a problem in an agency. She believes that a collaborative planning project will produce a better solution than a conflictual approach.

Option 7. Convinced that a proposal will be accepted only if it has the executive director's support, a social worker uses her supervisor as an intermediary to seek the executive director's approval for her proposal.

Option 8. Despairing of any other approach, a social worker settles on whistleblowing, taking an issue directly to the mass media in hopes that external pressure on the agency will make its officials remedy some of its staff members' unethical behavior.

Option 9. A policy advocate does not take an active role in developing a proposal but waits until a strategic moment to place pressure on people to modify the proposal. She uses her negotiating and mediating skills to develop a compromise proposal.

Revising the Strategy

As in legislative settings, strategists must often change their strategy as events unfold, investing greater political resources when they encounter more opposition than they had predicted, revising a proposal in response to a budget shortfall, or taking advantage of the fact that the expected opposition has not materialized.

Developing Strategy in Community Settings

Policy advocates in community settings try to change policies of community institutions or governmental agencies.

Establishing Policy Goals in the Community Context

As in legislative settings, policy advocates must decide whether they will settle for incremental policy changes or whether they want major changes. This choice is, in turn, linked to estimates of likely support or opposition to the policy change. In some cases, an entire community will rally together for or against specific policies—and encounter scant opposition from the institutions they are challenging. In other cases, the community is polarized into competing groups. In still other cases, community groups encounter powerful entrenched interests that will not easily yield.

Specifying a Proposal's Content

Policy advocates can address an array of community issues: They may want a school to help dropouts or provide condoms to students; a zoning board to approve a halfway house for mental patients in a specific neighborhood; the city to fund an innovative program; an agency to establish a new program to serve a population that is underserved; or the community to help in an agency's operations, as through adding community residents to its board.

Community-based policy advocates may create community forums or community planning projects to solicit ideas from residents about community improvements. In one instance, a social worker helped a community group obtain volunteer architects who, after many community meetings, developed a housing plan for the neighborhood. As this community group met with city officials, it persuaded them to allocate substantial funds to a housing-development project in liaison with federal officials.

Establishing a Style

Changes in community policies can sometimes be achieved without extensive conflict, such as when city officials concur with a recommendation by a community group. On less contentious issues, a policy advocate might develop a collaborative win-win process. To assuage community residents, for example, she might initiate certain safeguards to gain their support for a proposed halfway house. She might convene a meeting of the community residents to develop these safeguards, such as establishing a 10 p.m. curfew for the residents of the halfway house.

Controversies arise when the interests of institutions or powerful officials are threatened, or when a community is divided into competing factions. When a coalition supported the placement of a welfare office in its neighborhood, for instance, it was countered by a powerful group that opposed the office on the grounds that it would lower property values and bring criminal elements into the community. When a community is polarized or when advocates encounter entrenched interests, advocates need skill in mobilizing community groups, developing coalitions, and working with the mass media.

Selecting Power Resources and Framing Strategy

As in legislative settings, policy advocates in communities have to create a campaign to achieve their policy goals. (See Policy Advocacy Challenge 12.7.) Their strategy may include delegations to community leaders and administrators, petitions, letter-writing campaigns to local officials, demonstrations, stories in the mass media, community forums, and litigation. As it takes these actions, the campaign's leadership must try to sustain and build community support for its position.

When policy advocates seek to place a residential or half-way facility in a community, such as a shelter for homeless persons, they sometimes encounter virulent opposition from local residents. This opposition is often called Not-In-My-Back-Yard or NIMBY. Assume that you encountered such opposition in a community. What strategies might you consider to surmount it? Listen to Bob Erlenbusch, Ph.D., Chairman of the Board of the National Coalition on Homelessness and Executive Director of the Los Angeles Coalition Against Homelessness and Hunger, as he discusses strategies for averting opposition to shelters in specific communities on Policy Advocacy Video 12.7.

Revising the Strategy

Relatively minor and noncontroversial policy changes can sometimes be achieved with modest effort. When a community campaign runs into significant and unexpected opposition, the leadership team has to review its options and perhaps embark on a more extended and ambitious effort.

A Primer on Task Groups

I discuss at this point some challenges in working with task groups. No matter whether a policy advocacy project takes place in legislative, agency, or community arenas, policy advocates need skills in working with *task groups*, which focus on producing or influencing something external to the group itself. *Political strategy can only be effectively implemented in virtually any setting if effective task groups are established and maintained, so policy advocates must be familiar with them and skilled in working with them.* In contrast to groups for treatment, therapy, and education, task groups do not emphasize members' personal growth or learning.[27] Among the remarkable range of policy-related task groups[28] are those that concentrate on making and enacting policies, including the boards of agencies, legislative committees, and legislatures.[29] These groups often rely on policy recommendations from feeder groups, such as deliberative committees, subcommittees, study groups, or commissions that develop recommendations and forward them to decision-making entities.[30] Some of these groups are ongoing, such as an agency's program committee or the Select Subcommittee on Children and Youth in Congress. Executives and political leaders also establish ad hoc groups to study specific problems and make recommendations.

Other task groups specialize in implementing policies.[31] Assume, for example, that a county mental health and substance abuse agency develops a new program for students in the school district and establishes an ongoing oversight committee to suggest policy changes when the new program is not realizing its objectives. Ongoing coordinating committees are created as well to promote the communication and policy development of various agencies.

Additional groups are set up for a variety of purposes. Many committees that staff can and should join exist in agencies to examine specific issues. Unions have become a potent power source in the human services system by mobilizing vast numbers of employees in public and nonprofit agencies.[32] Community organizations, like those modeled on the theories of Saul Alinsky, represent specific neighborhoods.[33] Many groups with varying amounts of power and resources serve as advocates for specific populations and institutions. Social movements spawn many groups with an over-arching purpose, usually to advance the needs of a specific segment of the population, including advocacy groups for people who are homeless or people with AIDS.[34] Many national social movements have local affiliates, such as chapters of NOW or civil rights organizations. As we discuss later, coalitions merge the resources and power of member groups.[35]

Why Develop Task Groups? Task groups are more effective than individuals who try to shape policy on their own.[36] For example, individuals who pool their ideas are apt to reach more well-considered solutions. Pooled resources, effective leadership, and pooled policy practice skills also result in more effective efforts to mobilize pressure for reform.[37] Highly placed officials often form task groups to avoid accusations of excluding various interests from their deliberations. (Sometimes, they control the membership of such a task group to be sure it approves only their preferred options.) Some executives also try to increase political support for specific measures by appointing blue ribbon committees; such groups can give legitimacy to a policy because their members are influential persons.

Policy Advocates' Roles in Task Groups

Advocates participate in task groups as leaders, staff, or members. A *leader* is comparable to an orchestra's conductor or a football team's coach. The leader facilitates the group's work by helping to define its mission and acquire resources like funds and staff. He or she expedites the group's ongoing work by developing agendas and presiding at meetings, and helps shape the group's structure and membership by setting up subcommittees and a nominating process and by intervening at specific points to promote members' participation and decision making. As facilitators, leaders prevent or diminish excessive internal conflict and dysfunctional processes, such as scapegoating specific members. Besides the president or chair of a group, other leaders, such as treasurers and secretaries, perform important logistical tasks.

Staff expedite the work of the group. As expediters, they collect information, assemble materials, perform secretarial functions, and attend to logistical details to allow others to concentrate on developing ideas and taking specific actions. Between meetings, they often help the group's leaders plan upcoming sessions and accomplish specific tasks.[38]

The staff's role, however, places limits on their interventions within a group. Because they are background facilitators and expediters, rather than members or leaders, they must exercise considerable circumspection and restraint. They are apt to refrain from speaking when they disagree with the group's decisions, preferring to influence decisions more discreetly.[39]

Members of task groups provide ideas, perform specific tasks, give the group power by linking it to other interests, lead subgroups, provide resources, and sometimes assume leadership after a period of apprenticeship. While leadership is crucial, few task groups are successful without motivated and active members.[40]

What Successful Task Groups Need

Many task groups are highly successful in establishing and realizing their objectives through their deliberations and activities. Other groups flounder, split, procrastinate, or dwindle to nothingness, as many of us know from experience.

Theorists and researchers have identified several factors that contribute to a task group's success: the group's mission, leadership, developmental needs, procedures, structure, deliberative and interactional processes, and staff and resources.

The Task Group's Mission

Successful groups develop a mission that defines their objectives or goals. Although the mission often changes later on, the members should decide what they want to accomplish during the early stages of the group's existence. Several dangers exist. A group may establish unrealistic expectations, such as hoping to enact a major piece of legislation quickly. When it cannot accomplish this objective, the members' morale and the leaders' reputation may suffer. Another danger is that the group may fail to reach a consensus about its objectives, so that different factions and members have different expectations. In some cases, overt expectations clash with hidden ones, as when leaders possess personal agendas that they do not share with members.

The mission also includes agreements about procedural matters, such as the frequency of meetings, the way leaders are selected, and the group's size and its relationship to external bodies. Groups that do not agree on these matters and their major goals encounter controversies and misunderstandings.

The Task Group's Leadership

Skilled group leaders walk a tightrope. They should be directive and assertive, but should not dominate; they should encourage dissenting perspectives, yet prevent excessive or destructive conflict; they should perform tasks well, but be able to delegate; they should represent the group to the external world, yet not seek excessive personal credit; and they should emphasize the group's objectives, but not neglect the group members' social and emotional needs. Unskilled leaders may be domineering, passive, confrontational, dictatorial, or self-promoting.

A skilled leader understands the group's developmental, structural, and process needs and develops strategies to address them. At one point, a leader might encourage the group to engage in relatively unstructured brainstorming and, at another, to reach closure on a topic.

Effective leaders value democracy. They give members a considerable role in shaping the group's decisions, and they keep the group from engaging in the scapegoating of members who legitimately dissent.

The Task Group's Developmental Needs

Groups evolve through time as they strengthen their mission, engage in deliberations, and accomplish tasks. In early phases, they must agree on their mission, leadership, and procedures and form realistic expectations. During the middle phase, they update their mission, develop and implement procedures, experience successes that give them a sense of momentum, and set up a division of labor that involves the members fully in the group's activities. In later phases, some groups should disband when they are no longer needed, whereas others should regenerate by revising their mission and seeking new members. Some groups do not progress through these stages of development. For example, not having established a mission, some groups keep returning to the question: Why do we exist? Other groups fail to change their mission as events unfold. Some groups continue to exist after accomplishing their original mission.

The Task Group's Procedures

Some people falsely equate leadership and group effectiveness with agendas, minutes, and bylaws, which are merely procedures. Procedures do serve a useful purpose.[41] Agendas allow anticipation of and planning for the future. Minutes provide a history that the group can review to ascertain how it has evolved and what new tasks it might undertake. Bylaws provide mechanisms for selecting leaders, replenishing membership, dividing tasks among officers and subcommittees, and handling funds.

The Task Group's Structure

Task groups must organize internally, establishing subcommittees or ad hoc groups to facilitate a division of labor. They have to decide how large they should be to accomplish their mission and to increase their political clout. They have to examine their relationships with other groups: Do they wish to merge with them, participate in coalitions, or maintain independence?

These kinds of structural issues pose significant challenges. A group that splinters into numerous committees, for example, may lack direction, but a group that is too centralized may fail to delegate responsibilities to its members. A group may lose its identity if it merges with other groups or joins coalitions, but it may lack clout if it remains isolated.[42]

The Task Group's Deliberative and Interactional Processes

To be productive, groups need modes of interaction that allow their members to examine options, to assess the group's strengths and weaknesses, and to make informed choices and develop strategies to implement them. Positive interaction occurs in an open atmosphere where members believe that they are free to contribute ideas, that dissent is permissible, and that their ideas will be taken seriously, and where brainstorming precedes final decisions.[43] Moreover, group members need to respect each other and the deliberative process and to honor the group's decisions.

Deliberations are stifled or abbreviated when leadership and group processes do not favor dissent, brainstorming, and democratic procedures. Social psychologist Irving Janis suggests that groups succumb to "groupthink" when they move too rapidly to unanimous positions, scapegoat dissenters, and do not fully consider the strengths and weaknesses of their positions.[44] Intolerant leaders, membership that fails to represent a variety of perspectives, and truncated deliberations contribute to groupthink.

Janis, Robert Bales, and other researchers suggest that a group should progress through a series of stages when considering issues: (1) brainstorming options in a risk-taking and tolerant atmosphere,[45] (2) carefully and gradually reducing these options to a revised list, and (3) only after extensive consideration of the options' strengths and weaknesses, formulating a final position. This movement from large numbers of options to final choices occurs only when group members feel free to take risks and when the group tolerates internal dissent.

The Task Group's Staff and Resources

Groups that engage in complex work need staff and resources to accomplish logistical tasks, provide technical assistance, and facilitate the group's work. Staff may come from institutions, such as agencies, or may be volunteers. Resources may come from institutions, the membership, special events, private donors, or corporations or foundations.

Just like low-budget lobbyists, groups that lack resources or staff are at a marked disadvantage compared with richer groups. Of course, resources and staff do not guarantee success, and groups with few resources may accomplish a great deal.

Forming Coalitions

Coalitions are temporary associations created to consolidate power in support of a specific issue, such as a piece of legislation. (We discuss ongoing associations, called *networks,* in the next section.)

Why are coalitions needed by policy practitioners seeking policy reforms for oppressed populations? Those who represent the poor, the powerless, or the stigmatized have an uphill battle; powerful interests and public apathy or opposition often impede social reforms. Moreover, powerful groups have coalitions of their own, such as coalitions of trade associations, agricultural interests, and tax-cutting groups.

Coalitions are different from many task groups, bringing together representatives of separate organizations to seek common action. The representatives agree to share the costs and labor of their common endeavor in a form of division of labor. When seeking the enactment of a piece of legislation, for example, one member group of a coalition may handle mailings, another the lobbying effort, and another the organization of a phone bank to telephone legislators at critical intervals.[46]

The success of a coalition depends on some of the same elements discussed under "What successful task groups need." As Milan Dluhy suggests, for example, successful coalitions need the leadership of a small executive council that meets frequently and invests considerable energy in planning and overseeing the activities of the coalition. A single person can spearhead a coalition, but a coalition obtains power through the combined efforts of its member organizations. Coalitions must share the credit for their work, or the members will resent the publicity that a single person or organization receives.[47]

The members of a coalition must define its goals and mission at the outset. Do they seek the enactment of a single piece of legislation, continuing pressure on legislators (or agencies), the education of the public about a social problem or the needs of a population, the development of innovative programs, or some combination of these and other goals? They have to decide as well when to disband the coalition or whether to transform it into an ongoing association. (See the following discussion of networks.)

Having developed a mission, the coalition's leadership needs to divide the labor. The leading group should establish subcommittees to focus on tasks such as research, lobbying, developing a phone bank, obtaining funds, and doing public relations (including creating a newsletter and reporting events to the mass media). The central leadership group could perform the coalition's real work, but establishing committees encourages broader participation. (The chairpersons of the committees often sit on the central leadership council.) With a division of labor established, the leadership council meets regularly to monitor the committees' work and to coordinate a strategy for accomplishing the coalition's work.[48]

The leaders of coalitions have to decide what groups to enlist. It is easier to form coalitions of like-minded persons and groups because they are more apt to agree on policy and strategy. An advocate who wants to get more funding for child welfare in a local jurisdiction, for example, can form a relatively homogeneous coalition of children's advocates, social work leaders, and children's institutions. Coalitions that represent more heterogeneous perspectives are more challenging to form and maintain because they find it more difficult to arrive at a consensus on goals and strategy, but they sometimes have more clout because their members can appeal to different kinds of legislators, agencies, and citizens. For example, if the local chamber of commerce joins the child welfare coalition, although its leaders may not share some of the assumptions of children's advocates, they may be able to convince some moderate or conservative politicians to support the funding increases sought.

Establishing Networks

While coalitions are usually temporary alliances that end when they have accomplished their purpose, policy practitioners also establish ongoing networks of persons and organizations. These networks regularly inform their members of pertinent legislation, increase their members' political awareness, and foster the members' participation in the political process.[49] Indeed, Rand Martin's organization, the AIDS-oriented Lobby for Individual Freedom and Equality, is a network, an ongoing organization with a governing council.

Assume that persons interested in state child welfare reform want a mechanism for sharing information about legislation, hearing about program innovations in different counties, and keeping abreast of national legislation. Envisioning their network as an ongoing organization with agency affiliates and individual members, they set up an executive council that establishes a division of labor, central offices, and a newsletter. This committee would schedule occasional meetings and workshops to supplement the newsletter. Like a coalition, this executive council also mobilizes the pooled efforts of its membership to support or oppose important pieces of legislation.[50]

Addressing Dysfunctional Group Processes

Some task groups are highly productive and others are less effective. Indeed, policy advocates sometimes have to use group process skills to improve a task group's functioning.

The degree to which advocates can intervene depends on the position they hold in the group, that is, whether they are staff members, leaders, or group members, whose different roles were described earlier.

Despite the constraints and opportunities that are provided by these different roles, all participants can diagnose or anticipate specific problems. When a task group or coalition loses momentum, the problem usually lies with a failure to develop a coherent mission, inadequate leadership, flawed internal processes, inadequate procedures, flawed structures, an inadequate process of deliberations, or insufficient resources. To diagnose which of these is the problem, we observe the group's operations from the vantage point of our role in the group. We often form our judgments as well from the complaints of other participants. We may also base a diagnosis on such developments as poor attendance and failure to achieve specific tasks.

Having diagnosed the problem, a participant in a task group, often along with others, needs to evolve a corrective strategy, such as having behind-the-scenes discussions, developing ideas during group deliberations, assuming some leadership functions, using power, mediating, directly assuming specific tasks, using humor, and seeking the advice of persons outside the group.

In meetings, members can promote more efficient deliberation in many ways, for example, by asking, "Don't we need to spend more time discussing this idea?" "Isn't it time to reach closure?" "Can we couple this idea with one that was suggested earlier?" or "Is there a different way to look at this problem?" They can also suggest procedures for considering ideas, such as breaking up into smaller groups to seek solutions to a problem.[51]

Even group members who are not leaders can sometimes assume leadership functions. For example, when a leader appears to be pressuring the group toward premature closure on an issue, a group member or a staff member can keep the discussion open by asking to hear more on the subject. Persons adept at parliamentary tactics sometimes use them to inject new perspectives and delay decisions. And between meetings, members may contact leaders directly to add issues to the agenda or to give their opinions on procedural, process, or structural matters. Of course, members and staff risk alienating leaders or erroneously usurping the leaders' functions if they do not use discretion.[52]

As in any collectivity, participants in groups have power resources, like expertise. When disagreements arise about specific issues or even about the group's leadership, processes, or structure, participants may use these power resources to shape decisions.[53] Group members also sometimes try to influence other members between meetings.

Group members need to use their power resources with discretion and without overriding the normal deliberative group processes. Excessive use of power resources can turn a group into a miniature legislative body whose members substitute threats, coercion, and parliamentary maneuvers for deliberation. At the same time, however, the use of power resources sometimes overcomes stalemates, stops destructive activities such as scapegoating, or makes beneficial changes in the group's leadership.

We discussed the use of mediation in Chapter Eight. Mediation may be the best solution when groups become polarized into competing factions.[54] Mediators can help group members identify their common values and can suggest structural or process strategies that will diminish conflict, such as bringing in a neutral facilitator. They also can identify compromises that will appease both parties to a conflict.

Effective persuaders often inject humor into their deliberations to ease tension, relax group members, and encourage the group not to take itself too seriously.[55] Humor can sometimes help in discussing specific group problems, as when a leader says, "At the rate we're proceeding, all the legislators we know will be dead before we come up with a bill."

Participants in groups or subcommittees sometimes take the bull by the horns and volunteer to do difficult or conflict-producing tasks that other members have shunned. When a subcommittee completes a task or develops a position on a difficult issue, for example, all its members have a sense of accomplishment and momentum.

An Advocacy Campaign in Sacramento, California

Policy Advocacy Challenge 12.8 provides an interesting model of policy advocacy because it spans communities and legislatures—in this case Sacramento's city council. It also links the domestic economy with global issues, such as migration from developing nations as well as exporting of jobs abroad. As you read it, ask how its organizers resolved the seven steps that advocates confront when they develop policy advocacy campaigns.

POLICY ADVOCACY CHALLENGE 12.8

The Sacramento Living Wage Campaign

EMANUEL GALE, EMERITUS PROFESSOR OF SOCIAL WORK AND GERONTOLOGY, CALIFORNIA STATE UNIVERSITY AT SACRAMENTO

The Sacramento campaign is part of a national movement addressing issues of low-wage workers who are struggling for economic survival at below Federal poverty guidelines.

The dramatic changes during the past 25 years, including globalization, mega-mergers, de-industrialization, exporting of jobs, the increase in temporary jobs, the necessity of mothers to work, and the decline in incomes—have negatively affected the economic security of working families.

"Free Trade" agreements, NAFTA, WTO, and IMF, are exploiting developing nations and enriching corporations and banks, at the expense of working families at home and abroad.

The widening gaps in incomes since 1975 have been documented by federal and state sources. The U.S. Bureau of Labor Statistics data, analyzing real wages in the United States, demonstrate that average hourly wages peaked in 1973. Despite economic expansion, wages in 1998 were 13 percent below 1973.

A report of the Legislative Analyst's Office, "California's Changing Income Distribution" (Aug. 2000) reviewed the average adjusted gross income by percentile of taxpayers—1975–1998. The report documented that the bottom quintile lost 24.8 percent in purchasing power while the top quintile gained 66.3 percent.

Living Wage Campaigns

The first living wage ordinance was enacted in Baltimore in 1994. Since then, 65 communities have adopted similar ordinances. In California, 14 cities have joined the movement, including Los Angeles, San Francisco, San Jose, Oakland, Santa Cruz, and Santa Monica.

The ordinances apply to entities receiving financial assistance, e.g. service contracts, tax breaks, loans, grants or land. Included generally, are contracts over $25,000 per year, or city assistance over $100,000 per year.

The central provisions incorporate wages, benefits, worker retention, responsible bidders, temporary workers, and super-session by collective bargaining agreements.

While it is recognized that the ordinances cover a relatively small number of workers, campaigns are important to establish a community precedent regarding wages and benefits.

The Sacramento Campaign

1. *Planning:* Several key individuals, representing labor, community organizations and key faculty from CSU Sacramento, met early in 2000, to review issues in Sacramento. There was general agreement that there were serious economic problems for working families in Sacramento, the capital of the largest and wealthiest state in the nation. There was also agreement to explore the concept of a living wage campaign.

The planning for the campaign included identification of key areas of work—research, mobilizing a broad coalition of organizations, planned community events, a draft ordinance, and contacts with elected city officials.

A Steering Committee has met regularly to plan and coordinate the living wage campaign.

2. *Research:* Original research was not necessary because of extensive information that was already available. The essential task was to pull together information about Sacramento that presents an accurate picture of the city and California.

This included data of household incomes, rentals, health insurance, child care, and transportation. Also available was the meaning of low wages, including Federal Poverty Guidelines ($7.03/hr mom and two kids, $8.50/hr for a family of four) and the state's minimum wage. The California Budget Project, the Sacramento County Children's Report Card, and the Self-Sufficiency Standard, documented the income necessary for a mother and two children to maintain a basic standard of living.

3. *Organizing:* People volunteered to target organizations in the community for support of the campaign. These organizations included labor, community groups, and the faith communities. Materials were developed describing the movement across the nation, the general concept of the living wage, and data about Sacramento.

During a 6-month period from 2000–2001, more than 60 organizations had endorsed the campaign, including key representatives from the faith communities.

4. *Community Events:* The kickoff of the campaign was a Forum on Poverty in Sacramento in November 2000, attended by 325 people. The panel included three committed city council persons, and religious and community leaders. The program included presentation of data, testimony from working people, and responses from the panel.

The next planned events were similar forums targeted in key city council districts.

The local council persons were invited to attend and most did. The focus was to demonstrate that there was community support for the living wage campaign.

In May 2001, a major community rally was held in Cesar Chavez Plaza, across the street from the City Hall. More than 500 people attended, and called upon the city council to endorse the living wage.

In September 2001, a fundraising dinner attended by 300 people, generated $7,000.

5. *Draft Ordinance:* A small group, including several volunteer attorneys, reviewed ordinances from around the country and California, and agreed upon the central principles to be included in the Sacramento ordinance. The central feature designated the living wage to be $10/hr, including family health benefits or $12.84/hr, without benefits.

The health proposal is unique to Sacramento since ordinances around the nation and California only include the worker. Data to determine the cost of health insurance was derived from the recent Kaiser Family Foundation survey of California employers.

The attorneys have drafted the ordinance which has been submitted to the city manager and his staff for review.

(continued)

6. ***Political Process:*** Initial meetings were held with two city council persons who, it was believed, would support the Sacramento Living Wage Campaign. They were receptive and agreed to provide leadership.

Meetings were also held with the city manager, who is a key player in the city. The mayor and city council members are all part-timers, which gives the manager power on policy decisions.

The city manager also raised concerns about surrounding cities in the metropolitan area. With sales tax revenues an important revenue source, there is bitter competition among cities. Assemblyman Darrell Steinberg has introduced AB 680 to address the issue of revenue sharing.

Materials were developed for the city council. Contacts were made with each of the other council persons to present the proposal. A meeting was scheduled with the mayor's chief of staff, preparatory to a meeting with the mayor. Regrettably, despite 12 formal and informal requests, the Mayor has refused to meet. The conclusion is that she harbors strong feelings against the Labor Council, because of its support of her opponent in the last election.

As of this date, there are three committed council persons and two likely supporters. Five votes are necessary to pass the ordinance.

There have been several meetings with members of the Sacramento Chamber of Commerce to inform them of the effort. While they have not adopted a negative position, their view is that the living wage would be a job killer.

There has been a delay in the process because of resistance by the mayor and the city manager. It has taken almost a year, to get agreement to have an independent study of the potential financial impact of the ordinance.

Conclusion

The Sacramento Living Wage Campaign has been a significant effort because it has:

1. Focused attention on addressing the struggles of working families.
2. Been effective in organizing a broad coalition of more than 60 organizations, supporting the campaign. It has also involved key faculty and students in a significant community campaign.
3. Enabled the spotlight to focus on the problems in Sacramento, i.e., wages, poverty, child care, affordable housing, and transportation.
4. Focused attention on the political process and challenges, in enacting a living wage ordinance.

There is an invalid assumption that research, data and logic will determine social policy by themselves. What's needed is effective organizing so policy advocates can pressure policy makers to make humane policies!

ᴄᴐ EXERCISE ᴄᴐ

1. How does this case illustrate how policy advocates often need grassroots organizing skills?
2. What challenges did the policy advocates encounter when forming a coalition?
3. How did the organizers "co-opt" and involve public officials?
4. What interests do you think would likely oppose enactment of living-wage legislation at the city or county level?

What You Can Now Do

CHAPTER SUMMARY

You are now equipped to do the following:

- Use the seven steps in political strategy in legislative, agency, and community settings, including organizing a team or coalition, establishing policy goals, specifying a proposal's content, establishing a style, using selection power resources and framing strategy, implementing strategy, and revising strategy
- Participate in advocacy to secure enactment of policy proposals, such as by helping to devise a resource book, policy brief, or strategy book; working with staff of legislators or legislative committees; getting sponsors; getting, legislation introduced, testifying, and raising funds
- Participate in advocacy to put external pressure on legislators, such as by helping to organize blitzes or demonstrations, using the mass media, organizing letter-writing campaigns, using the Internet to generate support and actions, and lobbying
- Work with or organize advocacy projects in specific agencies to secure approval of specific policies
- Work with or organize advocacy projects in communities to secure approval of specific policies
- Work with or organize such task groups as coalitions, committees, task forces, and networks

Having discussed how we implement political strategy in specific settings, we turn in the next chapter to tactics to change the composition of government, since it is difficult for even the most skillful policy advocates to secure policy changes if they cannot find responsive legislators, heads of government, or civil service appointees. We shall note, as well, that some social workers also run for political office.

NOTES

1. My discussion of strategy in legislative settings relies heavily on Donald E. deKieffer, *The Citizen's Guide to Lobbying Congress* (Chicago: Chicago Review Press, 1997). While former Congresswoman Pat Schroeder praises the book in her preface, she adds a cautionary note that strategy prescriptions must be made with care because "members of Congress don't all react the same way."
2. deKieffer, *The Citizen's Guide,* p. 24.
3. Ibid., pp. 17–20.
4. Ibid., pp. 21–23.
5. I draw the term *policy brief* from Willard Richan, *Lobbying for Social Change* (New York: Haworth Press, 1996), pp. 155–182.
6. deKieffer, *The Citizen's Guide,* pp. 20–21.
7. Ibid., p. 31.

8. Ibid., pp. 27–35.
9. Ibid., pp. 89–103.
10. Ibid., pp. 105–113.
11. Ron Dear and Rino Patti, "Legislative Advocacy: Seven Effective Tactics," *Social Work* 26 (July 1981): 289–297.
12. deKieffer, *The Citizen's Guide,* pp. 105–113.
13. Marilyn Bagwell and Sallee Clements, *Political Handbook for Health Professionals* (Boston: Little, Brown, 1985), pp. 136–156.
14. Ibid., pp. 136–156.
15. deKieffer, *The Citizen's Guide,* pp. 115–121.
16. Ibid., pp. 147–155.
17. Ibid., p. 75.
18. Karen Haynes and James Mickelson, *Affecting Change: Social Workers in the Political Arena,* 2nd ed. (New York: Longman, 1986), pp. 76–78.

19. Bagwell and Clements, *Political Handbook*, pp. 216–234. Also deKieffer, *The Citizen's Guide*, pp. 37–49.

20. deKieffer, *The Citizen's Guide*, pp. 39–40.

21. Ibid., pp. 63–71.

22. Bagwell and Clements, *Political Handbook*, pp. 189–194.

23. D. J. Hickson et al., "A Strategic Contingencies Theory of Organizational Power," *Administrative Science Quarterly* 16 (June 1971): 216–229.

24. Ibid.

25. Rosabeth Kanter, *Men and Women of the Corporation* (New York: Basic Books, 1977), pp. 129–163.

26. Burton Gummer, *The Politics of Social Administration* (Englewood Cliffs, NJ: Prentice Hall, 1990), pp. 25–26.

27. Paul Ephross and Thomas Vassil, *Groups That Work* (New York: Columbia University Press, 1988), p. 1.

28. Tropman, Johnson, and Tropman, *Essentials of Committee Management*, pp. xiii–xiv.

29. Ibid., pp. 179–186.

30. Ephross and Vassil, *Groups That Work*, pp. 16–18, 22–24.

31. Tropman, Johnson, and Tropman, *Essentials of Committee Management*, pp. 196–203.

32. Dennis Chamot, "Professional Employees Turn to Unions," *Harvard Business Review* 54 (May 1976): 119–127.

33. Saul Alinsky, *Reveille for Radicals* (New York: Vintage Books, 1969).

34. Herbert Simons, *Persuasion*, 2nd ed. (New York: Random House, 1986), pp. 253–261.

35. Samuel Bacharach and Edward Lawler, *Power and Politics in Organizations* (San Francisco: Jossey-Bass, 1980), pp. 48–69, and George Brager, Harry Specht, and James Torczyner, *Community Organizing*, 2nd ed. (New York: Columbia University Press, 1987), pp. 193–200.

36. Robert Bales and Fred Strodtbeck, "Phases in Group Problem Solving," in Dorwin Cartwright and Alvin Zander, eds., *Group Dynamics: Research and Theory* (New York: Harper & Row, 1968), pp. 380–398. Also see David Sink, "Success and Failure in Voluntary Community Networks," *New England Journal of Human Services* 7 (1987): 25–30.

37. See Bacharach and Lawler, *Power and Politics in Organizations*, pp. 48–69; Brager, Specht, and Torczyner, *Community Organizing*, pp. 193–200; and Eugene Bardach, *The Skill Factor in Politics* (Berkeley and Los Angeles: University of California Press, 1972), pp. 215–230.

38. Tropman, Johnson, and Tropman, *Essentials of Committee Management*, pp. 5–23. For a compilation of literature on leadership, see Ralph Stogdill, ed., *Handbook of Leadership: A Survey of Theory and Research* (New York: Free Press, 1974).

39. Tropman, Johnson, and Tropman, *Essentials of Committee Management*, pp. 38–48.

40. Ibid., pp. 24–37.

41. Ibid., pp. 63–139.

42. Ephross and Vassil, *Groups That Work*, pp. 84–87, 166–183.

43. Irving Janis, *Victims of Groupthink* (Boston: Houghton Mifflin, 1972).

44. Ibid.

45. Bales and Strodtbeck, "Phases in Group Problem Solving," 47.

46. Milan Dluhy, *Building Coalitions in the Human Services* (Newbury Park, CA: Sage, 1990), pp. 53–57.

47. Ibid., pp. 59–63.

48. Ibid., p. 62.

49. Ibid., p. 52.

50. Marilyn Bagwell and Sallee Clements, *A Political Handbook for Health Professionals* (Boston: Little, Brown, 1985), pp. 189–194.

51. Ephross and Vassil, *Groups That Work*, p. 164.

52. Tropman, Johnson, and Tropman, *Essentials of Committee Management*, p. 45.

53. There is surprisingly little discussion of the positive uses of power in committees and task groups. Power is usually viewed as destructive of group processes.

54. Jay Folberg and Alison Taylor, *Mediation* (San Francisco: Jossey-Bass, 1984).

55. Ephross and Vassil, *Groups That Work*, pp. 158–159.

CHAPTER

13

Engaging in Ballot-Based Policy Advocacy

POLICY PREDICAMENT

The make-up of local, state, and federal legislatures, as well as the mayors, governors, and presidents that are elected, greatly influence what kinds of social policies are enacted. No matter how skillful policy advocates may be, their challenges in securing policies that help vulnerable populations are more difficult if they confront relatively conservative elected officials. We discuss at this chapter's end the vital significance of the Congressional elections of 2006 in shaping policies of the nation, as well as particular ballot-based advocacy challenges encountered by policy advocates in New Orleans in the wake of Hurricane Katrina. (See Policy Advocacy Challenge 13.11 at the end of this chapter.)

We discussed in the previous chapter how policy advocates influence the positions and votes of incumbent legislators and heads of government by lobbying or pressuring them. In this chapter, we discuss how policy advocates help determine who gets elected in the first place, because it stands to reason that advocates will have greater success if more public officials possess ideologies and perspectives that favor social justice. Ballot-based policy advocacy seeks to change the composition of government so more public officials will want to advance social justice. Policy advocates also want to influence the electorate to support (or oppose) specific propositions that are placed on the ballot by others or by themselves. We discuss the following in this chapter:

- Why ballot-based policy advocacy is so important to policy advocates
- How political campaigns are waged and the roles policy advocates can play
- How some policy advocates can run for office themselves
- How policy advocates can indirectly help progressive candidates
- How policy advocates can influence outcomes of elections
- How policy advocates can seek the enactment or the defeat of propositions

Why Ballot-Based Policy Advocacy Is Important

Persons who are interested in social justice must often turn for assistance to public policies enacted by municipal, county, state, and federal jurisdictions—and therefore must depend on the legislatures and heads of government (such as mayors, governors, and presidents) to enact enlightened ones. Public officials possess extraordinary resources and power compared with the private sector. (See Policy Advocacy Challenge 13.1.)

POLICY ADVOCACY CHALLENGE 13.1

Voting and Electoral Politics

STEPHANIE DAVIS, RESEARCH LIBRARIAN, UNIVERSITY OF CALIFORNIA, IRVINE

The outcome of elections often determines what kind of policies will even be placed on the agendas of public officials, not to mention which ones will be enacted. When Republicans won both branches of the Congress and the Presidency in 2000, for example, the likelihood of the federal minimum wage being raised was greatly reduced during the next eight years—unless Democrats, who were more likely to favor it, were able either to win the presidency back in 2004 or 2008 or win back one or both chambers of Congress in 2002, 2004, 2006 and 2008.

∽ EXERCISE ∽

Using the sites below, investigate how your state voted in the last two or three presidential elections or a past congressional election and answer the following questions:

- Which political party had the majority of votes in your state?
- What was the gender and age breakdown of votes?
- What kind of funding did the candidates receive?
- How does the winning candidate/political party impact your research topic?

United States Electoral College
http://www.nara.gov/fedreg/elctcoll

Project Vote-Smart
http://www.vote-smart.org

OpenSecrets.Org
http://www.opensecrets.org

Center for Voting and Democracy
http://www.fairvote.org

U.S. Census Bureau: Voting and Registration
http://www.census.gov/population/www/socdemo/voting.html

An excellent print source can be found in your library: *America Votes: A Handbook of Contemporary American Election Statistics*. (CQ Press, published annually since 1956.)

From 1931 to 2000 for example, the federal government spent roughly $56 trillion in direct outlays and another $12.8 trillion just since 1968 in indirect spending through tax concessions to individuals and corporations. Federal and state authorities have enacted an enormous number of regulations in recent decades that protect vulnerable populations from discrimination, prohibit specific unsafe working conditions, redistribute monies from more affluent to less affluent groups such as through the Earned Income Tax Credit and the food stamps program, and finance the bulk of secondary education and a large part of postsecondary education. Countless other victories were achieved by advocates who pressured high-level public administrators, like the heads of human service agencies in state and federal governments, to issue administrative regulations that precluded discrimination against out-groups in specific programs or that increased outreach to eligible persons not using important programs.

Policy advocates were able to achieve these policy victories only because they found key legislators, heads of government, and high-level public administrators sympathetic to their causes—or willing to be persuaded. Imagine working for social justice measures pertaining to African Americans, for example, in southern jurisdictions in eras preceding the enactment of federal civil rights legislation in the mid 1960s when few sympathetic legislators even existed—or working for legislation affirming the right of women to have access to birth control in the era preceding the heroic work of Margaret Sanger at the beginning of the 20th century when no female legislators existed because women did not even have the right to vote in federal elections. Sanger was jailed on numerous occasions merely for speaking publicly about birth control.

Yet even in the modern era, policy advocates have to battle to increase the number of persons in public office who really care about the plight of oppressed populations.

When Republicans swept both chambers of Congress in 1994 under the leadership of Newt Gingrich, for example, policy advocates found their access to political leaders to be severely limited compared with preceding years. With Congressional Republican leaders pledging to downsize the federal government radically and to rescind a host of government regulations, supporters of pro-choice, affirmative action, and scores of other issues found it difficult to get their measures before legislative committees—much less approved by legislative chambers. (Although a large cadre of relatively liberal Republicans had existed in the Congresses of the 1960s and 1970s, they had been largely replaced by conservative Republicans by the 1994 Republican landslide.)

Policy advocates also find their success diminished when relatively conservative heads of government are elected, as illustrated by the presidential election of 2000 when Republican George W. Bush bested Democrat Al Gore. Bush quickly translated his campaign promises into legislative proposals, such as getting a $1.35 trillion tax cut enacted, proposing significant increases in military spending, and favoring "faith-based" social programs—not initiatives that many policy advocates favored. (While Gore was relatively moderate, he had sought a tax cut of only $250 billion, which would have left considerable funds in government coffers for improvements in Medicare, public school reforms, and other domestic reforms—funds that no longer existed when Congress slashed taxes so deeply.) Bush's appointees to high-level administrative posts, moreover, meant that policy advocates were less likely to obtain administrative regulations to their liking. Instead of the relatively liberal Donna Shalala (Clinton's Secretary of Health and Human Services), they now dealt with the relatively conservative Tommy Thompson, the former Republican governor of Wisconsin, who became Bush's Secretary of Health and Human Services.

The election of Bush over Gore also had major consequences for the federal judiciary. By appointing scores of relatively conservative attorneys to judicial posts, Bush hoped to influence judicial rulings for decades to come on such issues as abortion rights, affirmative action, separation of church and state, gay rights, and devolution of federal powers to the states.

We need to be careful about overstating the effects of elections on policy choices. Politicians often vote for measures that seem dissonant with their ideological views. Those who strongly oppose big government, often support, for example, such popular programs as Medicare and Medicaid, because many of their constituents benefit from them. Presidents and governors sometimes appoint justices who they think will make certain kinds of rulings only to find they go in contrary directions.

By the same token, however, we should not understate the importance of the composition of legislatures and heads of government to the policy-making process. In a two-party system, the party that wins a majority in a state or federal legislative chamber has an extraordinary advantage over the other party. If it can persuade its members to vote as a bloc (or if it can attract some votes from the other party), it wins many majority votes. The majority party in a chamber controls the chairs of legislative committees and a majority of the committees' members—so it can determine which bills get onto committees' agendas and which bills are approved by committees. The party that wins governorships and the presidency also has an extraordinary advantage. Heads of government often control or shape what issues are placed on legislatures' agendas. They can veto measures they do not like and can shape public opinion through their access to the mass media.

The two major parties differ significantly in the modern era in their positions on social reforms. At the federal level, for example, a majority of Democratic legislators are far more likely than a majority of Republican legislators to support an array of social-reform issues. In 1992, for example, Congressional Democrats supported packages of liberal issues 75 percent of the time, compared with only 18 percent of the time by Congressional Republicans. This ideological schism between the two parties stems in part from their different constituencies. Democrats are more likely than Republicans to come from urban districts, the east and west coasts of the nation, eastern and middle-west northern industrial states, inner-city districts, and relatively liberal suburban districts whereas Republicans are more likely to represent rural areas, western states, southern states, and relatively conservative suburban districts. Republicans are more likely to represent relatively affluent voters.[1] (So-called blue states, such as California and New York, are dominated by Democrats, whereas so-called red states, such as many rural and Southern states, are dominated by Republicans. Democrats receive a higher percentage of votes from female, African-American, Latino, gay men, lesbians, and disabled voters than Republicans. Although both parties contain liberal, moderate, and conservative legislators and voters, the Democratic Party has had larger liberal and moderate contingents than the Republican Party, particularly from the early 1980s onward. Moreover, while both parties get huge contributions from special interests, Democrats are far more likely to receive funds from trade unions and Republicans get more from corporations. (Trade unions tend to favor more social-reform measures than corporations.)[2] It is accurate, then, to say that significant differences exist in parties' ideology, constituencies, sources of money, and positions on issues. Persons who say they attend church once a week or more frequently are far more likely to vote Republican than Democratic.

These group differences, which predispose Democrats to be somewhat more supportive of social-justice issues than Republicans, ought not to blind us, however, to certain political realities. Specific Democratic or Republican legislators often deviate from party norms, so some Democrats are very conservative and some Republicans are moderate or quite liberal in their voting patterns. Individual Democrats or Republicans can deviate from party positions on specific issues, such as a Republican who champions the right to abortion or a Democrat who opposes this position. (These deviations can be caused by personal experiences, fear that they will otherwise alienate important blocks of voters, or contributions from special interests.) Contributions from special interests influence the votes of members of both parties, so some Democrats vote against relatively liberal measures because they received campaign contributions from corporate or other sources.[3]

We should not overstate the extent the Democratic Party is committed to social justice, even if Democrats as a group are more likely to support a policy-advocacy agenda. The party has always had a big tent that included liberal, moderate, and conservative voters and public officials. Even in the heyday of the 1960s, when President Lyndon Johnson developed the Great Society with strong Democratic majorities in both chambers, many southern Democrats opposed civil rights measures and other reforms. Its liberal base of support eroded somewhat in the three and one-half decades following 1968 as populations expanded in Sunbelt states and in the suburbs where voters tended to be more conservative than in the traditional liberal base of big-city enclaves and northern industrial states. A majority of U.S. voters resided in suburbs by the late 1990s. Wanting to contest Republicans for southern states and suburbs, Democratic leaders increasingly endorsed the argument that the party had to swing to the middle to be successful—with less emphasis on positions favored by trade unions and persons of color. This movement toward the center occurred dramatically during the two-term presidency of Bill Clinton, who favored co-opting many Republican issues such as fighting crime, "ending welfare as we know it," cutting federal deficits and debt, protecting military spending, and placing less emphasis on traditional liberal issues like affirmative action. Critics contend that this swing toward the middle, while sometimes enhancing Democrats' political fortunes, has also diminished their commitment to social justice on key issues.[4]

Critics of the two major parties, such as Ralph Nader, the Green Party's presidential candidate in 2000, contend that both parties have been corrupted by the influence of monies contributed to them and their candidates by special interests. Members of both parties have been showered with contributions from corporations, pharmaceutical companies, HMOs, highway contractors, military contractors, the mass media, and many other groups.[5] If some of these funds have gone directly to candidates, others of them—so called soft money—have gone to the parties, who use them to support issue-based ads in particular races. These issue-based ads, in turn, are usually used by the two parties to support their candidates, such as by saying "support the candidate in this race who wants to raise the minimum wage" (a Democratic issue) or who "doesn't favor excessive gun control" (often a Republican issue).[6] While neither of the two major parties assertively backed campaign finance reform to curtail soft-money contributions to political parties, its prospects suddenly improved in 2002 when Enron, the huge energy corporation, filed for bankruptcy after giving huge resources to politicians. Campaign finance legislation was finally enacted in March 2002.

We have discussed the importance of the run-off or culminating elections for candidates, but we should not forget the importance of primary elections.[7] Each of the major parties has a primary election to determine which candidate will represent it in the ensuing partisan election. (In nonpartisan elections, such as for school boards, a first vote for all the candidates who seek a specific seat is followed by a run-off between the two candidates who received the most votes—assuming no one got a majority of the votes in the initial election.) Primary or first elections are very important to policy advocates because the initial batch of candidates in both partisan and nonpartisan elections often differ markedly from one another. A relatively conservative Democrat might, for example, oppose a relatively liberal Democrat in a primary election—just as two Republican candidates might differ markedly from one another in their views on social policy.

Policy advocates sometimes support so-called third parties, such as the candidates endorsed by the Green Party in congressional and presidential elections of 2000. Green Party candidates were considerably more radical than candidates from the major parties on domestic, environmental, and international fronts. By providing an alternative to the existing parties, third parties have the potential to push established parties to become more progressive. And some progressives hope that a third party might displace one of the major parties, providing voters with a truly progressive alternative.

Third parties also present a dilemma for policy advocates because the United States has a winner-take-all system rather than a system of proportional representation as in many European nations. In winner-take-all elections, only the party that gets a majority vote wins an election; in proportional representation seats are allocated on the basis of the percentage of votes that a party receives. So third parties in the United States get seats only when their candidate gets more votes than either of the candidates from the major parties—a daunting task because the third-party candidate has to convince huge numbers of Republicans and/or Democrats to shift parties. A Green Party in Italy would get 10 percent of the seats in a legislature if it got this share of the vote in parliamentary elections —rather than no seats, which would be the case in the United States if Green Party candidates got 10 percent of the vote nationally but failed to get more votes from other parties in specific elections.

The history of third parties in the United States is not encouraging to them. The last time a third party supplanted one of the two major parties occurred in the late 1850s when the Republican Party, under the leadership of Abraham Lincoln, took the place of the Whig Party. Relatively liberal third parties, such as the Green Party, also risk diverting votes from Democratic candidates—thus making the victory of Republican candidates more likely. (Far fewer Republicans than Democrats voted for Green Party candidates in the elections of 2000.) So a major debate took place among progressives in the 2000 elections—one that pitted natural allies against one another. (See Policy Advocacy Challenge 13.2.)

POLICY ADVOCACY CHALLENGE 13.2

When to Vote for Third Party Candidates?

BRUCE JANSSON, PH.D.

Al Gore and George W. Bush were selected as presidential candidates by the Democratic and Republican Parties, respectively, in summer 2000. It seemed a classic face-off between a relatively liberal and a quite conservative candidate. Having been vice president under President Bill Clinton for eight years and running for the presidency during a period of economic growth, many prognosticators believed Gore would win this election.

Ralph Nader complicated matters for Gore, however. A longtime consumer advocate with impeccable reformist credentials, Nader accepted the nomination of the fledgling Green Party—a party clearly to the left of the Democratic Party and far to the left of the Republican Party. On a host of issues, Nader took positions to the left of Gore. He championed living wage legislation, cuts in military spending, efforts to end slave labor in third-world countries, and massive increases in spending to avert pollution.

Clear differences existed, as well, between Gore and Bush. Bush wanted massive tax cuts at a time when budgetary surpluses were appearing after nearly 20 years of government deficits. Gore wanted only modest ones to allow greater domestic spending and to preserve the fiscal integrity of Medicare and Social Security. Bush wanted modest increases in federal spending on education, and Gore wanted greater spending. Bush wanted no campaign finance reform; Gore favored new limits on contributions. Bush wanted only modest measures to increase patient rights, but Gore wanted substantial measures.

Liberals faced a dilemma. If they voted for Nader in states that were closely contested by Gore and Bush, they risked inadvertently giving Bush a victory he would not otherwise have had. If the national race was close—and it was widely predicted to be razor thin—Nader votes might allow Bush to gain a majority of Electoral College votes that he would not otherwise receive.

What should liberals have done under these circumstances? When are votes for third party candidates advisable?

Policy Advocacy in the Electoral Process

The composition of legislatures and the selection of heads of government are determined by tens of thousands of political races each year in local, state, and federal jurisdictions. These include both partisan races, usually dominated by members of the two major parties, and nonpartisan races, such as in many city council, mayoral, school board, and judicial contests.

If Luciano Pavarotti described opera singing as "controlled screaming," electoral contests can be called "controlled conflict." Elections are conflicts that result in winners and losers based on vote tallies—conflicts where candidates use a variety of power resources to influence members of the electorate. Candidates know this is a win-lose conflict waged in a relatively brief time period. They know the final arbiters of these conflicts are voters and their votes. Yet elections represent controlled conflict because they are fought according to rules established by local, state, and federal authorities—rules that govern campaign finance and ballot procedures.

Developing Population Profiles

Astute candidates carefully analyze the voters in their districts long before ballots are cast.[8] Drawing upon data from previous elections, as well as polling data of their own, candidates estimate at the outset how close the election is likely to be. Some candidates realize they have little chance of winning, for example when they encounter a popular incumbent or when they run in a district where political opinion runs counter to their own beliefs and record. (A Democrat running in a strongly Republican district may realize she has an uphill battle at best.) In other cases, candidates may decide at the outset that they have a chance of winning, but that their races are likely to be closely fought. In still other cases, candidates may decide that they are favorites to win—or even that the election is theirs to lose. And in some cases, outcomes are exceedingly difficult to estimate.

When gauging their chances, candidates' odds of winning increase in the following circumstances:

- They are incumbents rather than challengers because incumbents have many advantages, including name recognition, support from persons and groups who have benefited from policy actions they have taken in prior years, and an ability to raise money from those persons and groups who like to back a likely winner.[9]
- They have considerable name recognition in their electoral district, quite apart from whether they are incumbents.
- They run in a district where a strong majority of voters share their political and ideological preferences. Democrats who face Republicans in districts with strong Democratic tendencies are far more likely to prevail than Democrats in strong Republican or conservative districts.
- They can find early endorsers who have considerable standing in the district, whether influential people, newspapers, or other public officials.
- They can anticipate support from relatively large blocs of voters because of their ethnicity or race, their occupation (such as being an auto worker in a district with large numbers of blue-collar workers), their religion (such as being Catholic in a district with many Catholics), or their gender (such as being a female candidate who can strongly appeal to large numbers of female voters).
- They are able to raise significant resources compared with likely opponents, whether monetary resources or help from volunteers. The mass media, mailings, and campaign research—which cost money—are invaluable to candidates.[10]
- They are fairly certain they can turn out specific blocs of voters in a contest that will probably have a low turnout, such as an election for a school board seat. If a contestant in a school board election has the support of the teachers' union—and opposing contestants do not—her chances increase because the union will probably help turn out school personnel and contribute volunteers who will persuade other voters to turn out.

Of course, it is important that candidates not be excessively fatalistic even if they lack some of these advantages. Underdogs do win electoral contests. Favored candidates often make mistakes or take their reelection for granted. As many candidates have discovered, a defeat in a specific election is often followed by victories in subsequent contests for the same seat or for other seats.

Candidates often develop voter profiles of their districts that identify blocs of voters who fall into at least four categories: probable strong supporters, probable strong opponents, probable swing voters whose support may be gained relatively easily, and probable swing voters who are tough prospects.[11] To these groups, we can add voters whose voting patterns are virtually impossible to predict. They also need to decide the likelihood that members of these various groups will actually vote, since it does no good to have strong support from voters who fail to turn out.

In developing voter profiles of their districts, candidates often make informed guesses based on party affiliations, demographics, and group affiliations.

POLICY ADVOCACY CHALLENGE 13.3

Developing Political Strategy for a Campaign

RAMON SALCIDO, DSW

Go to **academic.cengage.com/ social_work/jansson** to watch this video clip

Some social workers, such as Professor Ramon Salcido, have worked in many political campaigns and served as consultants for them. Listen to Policy Advocacy Challenge Video 13.3 where he discusses his role in advising the campaign of Representative Esteben Torres.

African-American or Latino candidates often can assume, for example, that voters with their ethnicity will favor them over other candidates, though they cannot assume complete support or that these voters will turn out to vote. Candidates of major political parties usually can assume that they will receive an edge from voters in their parties. Male and female voters may receive additional support from their gender groups. Other affiliations also can help some candidates, such as their religion, occupational group, and age.

Challengers can make informed estimates about incumbents by dissecting voting patterns from prior elections. Using census and voting data, they can discover in which precincts and with what demographic, racial, and political groups they ran strong or weak. Armed with this information, they can pinpoint their opponents' areas of strength and vulnerability.[12]

This population profile—which can be refined using poll and focus-group data—is vital to candidates. It allows them to estimate whether the election is likely to be closely contended, a landslide, or somewhere in between. If the election looks like it will be closely contended, candidates realize that they will have to invest great effort and resources in the election. The prospect of a landslide election is heartening to candidates who believe they will prevail, but disheartening to candidates who fear they will be on the losing end. In some cases, so many uncertainties exist in the population profile that candidates cannot make even tentative predictions—meaning they must gather more information as the race proceeds so they can devise intelligent strategy.

The population profile also is critical to candidates because it tells them where to channel their scarce resources. Candidates will not want to spend a lot of time speaking to voters who are certain to oppose them. Although they want to devote sufficient time and resources to encourage likely supporters to vote on Election Day, they do not want to allocate too many resources to them as compared with swing voters who might be converted through advertisements and personal outreach. (If they dissipate their scarce resources on certain supporters and opponents, they risk losing closely fought elections if opponents capture most of these swing voters.)[13]

Even if the prognosis is bleak or uncertain, candidates still may decide to run. Perhaps they want to gain name recognition for a future run for the same post or another one. Maybe they want to educate voters about a specific issue. Or they may want community recognition to advance personal business or professional interests.

As candidates proceed with their analysis of likely voting behaviors of specific groups, they place this analysis over a precinct-by-precinct map of the electoral district. This allows them to decide where to target their mailings, precinct walking, advertisements, and telephone banks. If a candidate wants to reach Latino voters in specific communities, for example, she might seek endorsements from Hispanic leaders; run media spots on radio and television, and in newspapers likely to be heard or read by Hispanic persons in these precincts; and recruit Hispanic volunteers to help with door-to-door visits and distribution of leaflets at local supermarkets. She also might try to get party officials to fund voter registration projects in these precincts.

Using Power Resources to Persuade Voters

Having identified the kinds of voters they want to prioritize—and even their geographic location—candidates need to convince voters to support them and to turn out on Election Day. They have numerous tools at their disposal. (See Table 13.1.) Indeed, astute candidates use all of these resources as part of their strategy.

POLICY ADVOCACY CHALLENGE 13.4

Why Social Workers Make Good Candidates

LAURA CHICK, MSW, CONTROLLER OF THE CITY OF LOS ANGELES

Go to
**academic.cengage.com/
social_work/jansson**
to watch this video clip

View Policy Advocacy Challenge Video 13.4 where Laura Chick, MSW, discusses why social workers possess skills that make them good campaigners. Chick won several races for the city council of Los Angeles and became the first woman to win a seat in a city-wide race in the history of Los Angeles when she became the Controller of Los Angeles in 2000. She still held this post in 2006 and received extensive coverage in the mass media for her many successes in locating fraud and inefficiencies in County government.

Using One-on-One Power Resources

Candidates need to make personal contact with many voters in a laborious one-on-one strategy. Through these contacts, candidates make voters believe that they have positive personal traits such as a concern for the voters' problems, high levels of energy, and an ability to listen. They can elicit suggestions or input about specific problems or policies. They can share their positions with voters to assure them that they care about their

TABLE 13.1
Power resources for influencing voters' views and actions

1. Using One-by-One Retail Power Resources
   a. Personal door-to-door visits in precincts or at special events
   b. Visits by surrogate volunteers door to door or at special events
   c. Distribution of leaflets to voters at neighborhoods or other locations
   d. Working the crowd at local or other events
2. Using the Media
   a. Political advertisements in radio, television, and newspaper outlets
   b. Appearances on radio and television outlets
3. Interacting with Opposing Candidates
   a. Participation in organized debates
   b. Participation in organized forums for candidates
   c. Responses to opponents' positions in media advertisements
4. Developing Positions on Issues
   a. Articulation of a set of campaign promises that tell voters what policies a candidate will use in forthcoming elections
   b. Positions on specific issues
   c. Introduction of new issues
5. Demonstrating Positive Personal Characteristics
   a. Convincing voters through personal conduct and by citing one's past resume that a candidate possesses such desirable characteristics as integrity, diligence, fiscal discipline, and compassion
6. Conducting Negative Attacks on Opponents
   a. Attacking their positions on specific issues
   b. Attacking their personal qualities, such as by citing their prior activities
7. Getting Out the Vote
   a. Convincing supporters that they will suffer negative consequences if they fail to vote
   b. Election Day visits by campaign volunteers to voters to persuade them to vote (and even to provide them with transportation to the polls)
8. Securing Endorsements
   a. Getting endorsements from influential citizens, groups, and public officials from the electoral district
   b. Getting endorsements from influential citizens, groups, and public officials from outside the electoral district
   c. Getting endorsements from newspapers, radio stations, and television stations
9. Convincing Other Potential Candidates Not to Run
   a. Talking up one's campaign before it begins to convince other potential candidates not to run
10. Seeking Support from Party, Trade Union, and Other Organizations

concerns. They can organize a sequence of local meetings in homes, churches, and community agencies that allow them to present positions and solicit inputs from voters. When supplemented by campaign literature that highlights their accomplishments, positive personal traits, and campaign promises, candidates build grassroots momentum.

Using the Media

Name recognition is an extraordinarily valuable asset in political campaigns because many voters select names on ballots that are familiar to them—and they are more likely to listen to their messages. The media enhances the name recognition of candidates, whether through paid advertisements, personal appearances, coverage in news stories, or endorsements.[14]

Interacting with Opposing Candidates in Public Forums

Debates with opposing candidates are often important campaign events. They allow candidates to clarify their views and to distinguish them from opposing candidates; demonstrate they have a command of the issues; and place opponents on the defensive by questioning their positions or records.

Debate strategy needs to be carefully planned. Candidates need to anticipate likely positions and arguments of opponents, including how they might attack their own positions or records. They need, as well, to decide what issues to prioritize and what supporting arguments to use.[15]

Developing Positions on Issues and Demonstrating Positive Personal Qualities

Voters' decisions about who to support are shaped by many factors. In a two-person race, voters make their decisions by evaluating both candidates in terms of perceived positive and negative attributes, making an overall ranking of each candidate, and then selecting the candidate with the highest ranking. Each voter does the following:

- Decides what attributes are worth considering for each candidate, both positive ones and negative ones
- Decides what weight to give each attribute for each candidate
- Ranks each candidate on each attribute
- Decides, on balance, which candidate ranks the highest—and (if he or she votes) votes for that candidate

To illustrate this process, assume a voter decides that the following attributes are important when comparing two candidates: honesty, correct positions on three pivotal issues (abortion rights, promoting good schools, and supporting patient rights), and a successful track record in public service. The voter goes through a mental process that we can simplify with a hypothetical example. Suppose a voter ranks each candidate, say from −10 to +10, on each of these attributes and then selects the candidate with the highest score after weighting the relative importance of each attribute. In our hypothetical example our voter selects candidate B, with her positions on schools and, especially, her "positive track record" swinging the balance. (See Table 13.2.)

This example illustrates the tactical challenge faced by each candidate—assuming that large numbers of voters shared, roughly, the perspectives of this voter. Candidate A could try to enhance her positive scores on some attributes, paying particular attention to ones weighted heavily by the voter—such as a positive track record. Or she might try to increase negative scores of her opponent by challenging his record on issues where he scores heavily with voters, such as abortion rights, schools, and a positive track record. She might say that he has shifted his stand on abortion rights, has not consistently supported schools, and has many blemishes in his previous track record of public service. Or she might try to add new issues to the list of issues on which she thinks she will score more positively than her opponent. Perhaps she decides to add environmental pollution or recreational space to our community. Or she might try to change voters' weighting of specific issues by contending that honesty (now weighted

TABLE 13.2
A voter's
perception
of two
candidates

Issues	Candidate A	Candidate B
	Rank × Weight	Rank × Weight
Honesty (weight of 1)	$1 \times 1 = 1$	$-1 \times 1 = -1$
Pro Abortion Rights (weight 5)	$10 \times 5 = 50$	$8 \times 5 = 40$
Pro Schools (weight 2)	$5 \times 2 = 10$	$10 \times 2 = 20$
Pro Patient Rights (weight 1)	$-5 \times 1 = -5$	$8 \times 1 = 8$
Positive Track Record (weight 3)	$-5 \times 3 = -15$	$10 \times 3 = 30$
TOTAL	+41	+97

only 1) is the most important attribute voters should consider, perhaps adding some serious questions about her opponent's honesty.

A fluid situation often exists in campaigns.[16] At point 1, a candidate selects specific issues for top priority but then adds issues or puts different emphasis on some existing ones as the campaign unfolds. Sometimes she makes these changes in response to her opponent, wanting to counter his charges, locate vulnerabilities in his positions, or change the topic when she believes he is scoring points against her on specific issues. Sometimes she makes these changes in response to polling data or focus groups that suggest that different issues or different emphases on existing issues will allow her to gain ground. Sometimes candidates discover that certain lines or arguments draw a sympathetic response from particular audiences, leading them to emphasize them. Or, conversely, they may drop or de-emphasize issues or arguments that draw a weak audience response.

Candidates need to develop a set of campaign promises early in the campaign[17] that distinguish them from opponents. They give voters a sense that they will deliver results during their term of office rather than being inactive or ineffective. These campaign promises need to be carefully considered because candidates can assume that opponents will attack them and may contend that they are not feasible (such as overly costly) or that they are ill-advised, too numerous, too vague, or too few. Sometimes opponents might say that a candidate's campaign promises are contradictory, such as when a candidate proposes a costly new program but also promises to cut the budget or cut taxes.

Campaign promises are often linked, of course, to candidates' analysis of their electoral district. They want campaign promises that will mobilize likely supporters and appeal to some swing voters, and they want issues that will increase voter turn out.

Conducting Negative Attacks on Opponents

All candidates face a dilemma: whether to emphasize positive arguments or to make negative attacks on their opponents.[18] Take our example of candidates A and B in Table 13.2. Believing that she trails her opponent, candidate A could emphasize her accomplishments and positions regarding the various issues, as well as her own positive track record and honesty. Or she could attack her opponent's positions and, even more negatively, attack his character. Were she effective in doing this, some of Candidate B's positive numbers in Table 13.2 might diminish or even be converted to negative numbers. If she converted her opponent's position on having a positive track record from +30 to −50, for example, she would nearly catch up to him in the overall ratings.

However, negative attacks sometimes backfire. Candidate B might accuse Candidate A of running a negative campaign rather than discussing the real issues. Ethical issues exist, as well. (See Policy Advocacy Challenge 13.5.)

POLICY ADVOCACY CHALLENGE 13.5

When to Be Negative and When to Be Positive

BRUCE JANSSON, PH.D.

Most candidates face an ethical dilemma during their races. Knowing that voters are often less likely to vote for candidates with strong negatives on such personal traits as honesty, consistency, integrity, and diligence, they can often rapidly rise in polls by attacking opponents' personal traits. Sometimes they can find evidence of malfeasance, corruption, dishonesty, and lack of attention to citizens' needs (in the case of incumbents). When solid evidence is lacking, however, they can gain substantial advantage by making vague references, making allegations without credible evidence, or insinuating negative traits.

Why the temptation to go negative? Substantial polling data suggests that negative attacks can be efficient in lowering voters' opinions of opponents. Negative information is often effective in putting doubts into voters' minds about specific candidates. When used in television ads, negative messages are often particularly effective because they can be conveyed through vivid images—such as pictures of opponents in the company of unsavory people. Some candidates rationalize negative attacks by contending they merely want to beat their opponents to the punch. Yet considerable evidence shows that negative ads can backfire—or not be as effective as positive "advocacy" ads.[1]

What's lost in mud-slinging campaigns is intelligent discussion of important issues that ought to be the basis for deciding who wins and who loses. Negative ads often feature untrue or simplistic allegations that are not buttressed by facts.

So what should a candidate do in the following cases?

- She lags in the polls and believes her only hope is to attack her opponent's character.
- She wants to have a positive campaign, but finds her opponent has initiated a negative campaign against her.
- She believes her opponent lacks integrity and is dishonest, but lacks hard evidence to prove it.

[1] For a discussion of the pros and cons of negative ads, see Kahn and Kenney, "How Negative Campaigning Enhances Knowledge of State Elections."

Getting Out the Vote

Nonvoters shape election results as powerfully as voters, as a simple example suggests. Assume that 100,000 voters support Candidate A—and 80,000 of them turn up at the polls. Assume that 125,000 voters support Candidate B—but only 75,000 of them actually vote. In this example, the least popular candidate wins the election only because Candidate B could not get more of his voters to actually vote.

This result is not unusual. As Frances Piven and the late Richard Cloward discuss, voters in lower economic strata are considerably less likely to vote than relatively affluent

Americans, regardless of their ethnicity.[19] (See Policy Advocacy Challenge 13.6.) Since persons of color are disproportionately poorer than affluent Americans, they are considerably less likely to vote than Caucasians. So candidates with particular popularity among the less affluent members of our society and persons of color start electoral races with a significant disadvantage—unless they can entice their supporters to vote or can find offsetting support among more affluent persons. This is often not an easy task. While voter registration procedures have been greatly simplified across the nation to encourage registration, many poorer Americans still are not registered—and those who are registered vote in far fewer numbers than other voters. (Voters can now register when they obtain drivers' licenses and in many public agencies.)

POLICY ADVOCACY CHALLENGE 13.6

Empowering Homeless Persons by Helping Them Vote

BOB ERLENBUSCH, PH.D.

Go to **academic.cengage.com/ social_work/jansson** to watch this video clip

When a social workers recently lobbied a state legislator in Sacramento, California, he asked her whether "the kinds of persons" she helped actually voted. Before she could answer, he said, "Of course they mostly do not—and I therefore give them little attention as compared to my constituents who *do* vote."

Listen to Policy Advocacy Challenge Video 13.6 as Bob Erlenbusch, Chairman of the Board of the National Coalition on Homelessness and Executive Director of the Los Angeles Coalition Against Homelessness and Hunger, discusses how he and other advocates were able to get large numbers of homeless persons to vote in Los Angeles County. After you hear this video, consider these questions

- What effects did voting have on the politics of homelessness in Los Angeles County?
- Could similar projects be developed by social agencies that help other vulnerable populations?

Candidates can increase voter turnout by targeting populations and precincts having low turnouts with personal (or volunteer) contacts, leaflets, and advertisements. They can seek endorsements from leaders of low-turnout communities and populations. They can highlight the significance of the election to persons who would not normally vote and mount voter registration drives in areas where eligible voters are not registered. They can orchestrate Election Day activities, such as contacting voters by telephone and, in some cases, transporting them to the polls.

Securing Endorsements

Endorsements often carry considerable weight in elections—assuming they come from persons and organizations that are respected by the candidates' natural supporters and swing voters.[20] Candidates often vie for endorsements from newspapers, party leaders, public officials, and community leaders—endorsements that candidates often feature on their campaign literature and in their personal appearances. They also compete for the support of Political Action Committees (PACs), which channel funds to candidates from trade unions, interest groups, and professional associations like the National Association of Social Workers.[21] (We discuss NASW's PAC later in the chapter.)

Endorsements can take the form of public statements by organizations and people. In addition, an endorsement can be an agreement to be listed on invitations and advertisements as sponsors of campaign functions, such as fund-raising events or important speeches.

Candidates obtain endorsements in several ways. They often emanate from prior friendships or working relationships, such as when a candidate has worked with specific public officials on previous occasions. Candidates often meet personally with potential endorsers and work hard to convince them that they will be effective public servants on issues that are important to the endorsers. Candidates often must convince endorsers that they have a good chance of being elected. They might provide them with electoral data that demonstrates that they have considerable support in their district and that likely opponents are vulnerable.

Convincing Other Potential Candidates Not to Run

Considerable jockeying for position occurs before each election as persons decide whether to run for specific offices.[22] It is to the advantage of a candidate not to encounter a crowded field in primary contests—and not to encounter opponents in primary or final contests who possess widespread support and resources. Potential candidates cannot stop others from running, but they can try to discourage them by showing them that they will mount formidable campaigns. They can announce their intentions to run far in advance of the election to make clear that they will be serious contenders. They can talk to potential candidates in their own party to make clear their intention to run and to suggest that "if we beat up on each other in the primary, our likely opponent will have an easier time winning." They can approach campaign donors and seek early commitments as a way of showing potential candidates that they will have considerable resources. They can seek early endorsements from community leaders and public officials.

By starting early to build support and a campaign organization, candidates may also discourage some potential—and formidable—candidates from entering a race.

Gaining Support from Party, Trade Unions, and Other Groups

Candidates should assertively seek resources from organizations whose issues and perspectives are consonant with their own. Parties have resources to contribute to candidates, though they give priority to elections where they believe they can pick up seats. Unions distribute funds through their PACs to candidates who support union and union-backed issues. The National Association of Retired Persons not only contributes funds through its PAC, but sometimes organizes elderly volunteers to work in specific campaigns. As we discuss later, issue-oriented groups sometimes run advertisements during campaigns that take positions on specific issues like gun control and offer support for candidates who agree with these positions. (Supports from external groups become more important as candidates seek higher-level seats in county, state, and federal jurisdictions.)

Finding Resources

Resources have become increasingly important to campaigns as the cost of advertising has risen dramatically, whether in newspapers, television, radio, or mailings.[23] The funds spent on campaigns for high-level offices in the United States have become truly remarkable and troublesome. Several points should be considered at the outset. The amount of resources required for a campaign escalates as candidates seek higher or more visible seats. A race for a school board slot or a host of local positions is relatively inexpensive, but the cost rises for some county seats, most state-level seats, and all federal seats. Indeed, social workers who want to enter the electoral process almost always begin with local races that require relatively few resources as compared with high-level races. As they build a track record in initial offices, they develop contacts and reputations that allow them to raise larger sums in subsequent races for higher-level posts.

While extremely important in many races, resources are not, by themselves, a guarantor of victory as billionaire Ross Perot discovered in 1992 when his massive resources yielded him a distant third-place finish in the presidential race. Some candidates succeed even when greatly outspent by opponents, such as Senator Ross Feingold (D-Wisconsin) who won the U.S. senatorial race in 2000 after rejecting many sizeable contributions from wealthy donors and PACs.[24] Yet considerable evidence demonstrates that large imbalances in resources usually favor its more affluent candidate.

Resources pose troubling ethical issues in the United States because some candidates, regardless of their merit, obtain much greater resources than competing candidates. For example, incumbents can raise resources much more easily than most challengers—and wealthy individuals can underwrite their own campaigns. Some special interests, such as corporate entities, can contribute much more than others, such as groups representing disadvantaged and oppressed populations. Federal, state, and local legislation limiting the so-called hard money that candidates can raise is often circumvented by soft money spent by political parties and special interests on media advertising for specific issues. Precluded from giving more than a certain amount of money to individual candidates, for example, the National Rifle Association has given huge resources to parties and individual candidates that oppose control of guns. These ads help the candidate who opposes control of guns even when that candidate is not named in advertisements. Similarly, the major political parties can place issue-oriented ads in local races that favor their candidates—as can many other groups with deep pockets.[25] (Such tactics were partially limited by the enactment of federal campaign finance legislation in March 2002.)

The quest for resources has other troubling aspects. To the extent candidates devote more and more time to finding resources, they have less time to research and discuss issues. Even incumbents must devote considerable time to fund-raising while in office.

Yet resources are a fact of life in campaigns—and candidates for any office must devote considerable effort to raising funds so their opponents cannot buy their way into office.[26] Candidates need to estimate roughly what their opponents are likely to spend in a particular race so they can possess similar, if not greater, resources. Resources are needed to hire campaign staff, to hire political consultants, to advertise in the mass media, to produce campaign literature, and to make mailings. The cost of a 30-second ad in prime time on local television can range from $1,500 to $8,000 depending on the size of the market, though less expensive ads can be purchased on cable TV and radio, and in newspapers. Imagine the prospect of seeing your opponent appear frequently in these media outlets in the weeks preceding an election when you could not afford any of them.

Other campaign costs also exist. Consultants who can provide important information about the local electorate and campaign strategy are costly. Campaigns sometimes use advertising firms to craft their ads—firms that use focus groups and sophisticated electronics to fashion ads that will be effective. Bumper stickers, yard signs, and billboard ads are costly to print, install, and dismantle. Direct mail is very expensive. Campaigns sometimes use professional polling firms to get baseline data at a campaign's outset and tracking data as the campaign proceeds. Even a sample of 400 people can cost more than $10,000 each time data is collected.

Still another reason exists for trying to find resources. Absent them, candidates must perform some tasks that they might otherwise be able to turn over to staff. When candidates try to accomplish these tasks themselves, they have less time to devote to personal interactions with the electorate and to public appearances.

Every candidate gives priority to the recruitment of a resource that costs little but is worth its weight in gold: volunteers.[27] As they walk precincts, leaflet at highly frequented places in the community, or operate phone banks, volunteers operate as surrogates for candidates. Many of them, after brief training, are highly effective in these roles—often making the difference between winning and losing a campaign. Volunteers are also ambassadors of good will in the broader campaign with their extended families and with acquaintances. Candidates sometimes have the good fortune to find volunteers with technical skills like the ability to use computer technology to identify specific precincts or groups of voters. Many successful candidates are even more likely to give post-election access to volunteers than to contributors because they realize they donated their personal time and energy to the campaign rather than merely signing a check.

Creating a Campaign Organization

Campaign organizations are unlike most organizations because they are time-limited and have a single purpose: to gather as many votes as possible for candidates in a matter of several months. Everything about them is dedicated to this urgent task.

Candidates exist at the top of the organizational chart, but they differ widely in the actual roles they assume during the campaign. Some candidates delegate very little—making the key decisions and overseeing their implementation. Other candidates place extraordinary reliance on their staff and consultants, basically following their advice with respect to strategy and implementation decisions. No single style is best because the capabilities of candidates, staff, and consultants vary widely. Experienced candidates who possess political instincts often can and should play a more central role than candidates who lack these attributes. Problems occur when candidates who lack political instincts and savvy make too many decisions—as Ed Rollins recalls when discussing George Bush, Sr.'s lackluster campaign in 1992 when he was bested by Bill Clinton.[28] Falsely assuming that his popularity from winning Desert Storm would carry over into this election, Bush ignored domestic issues even when warned by Rollins and other advisers that this decision could cost him the election. When Clinton's staff adopted the motto, "it's the economy, stupid," they set the stage for a landslide victory over Bush.

The size and sophistication of a candidate's staff depends on the resources she can raise. In a campaign with extensive resources, staff could include a campaign manager, consultants, a director of research (polling and focus groups), a director of public policy, a media director, a recruiter and supervisor of volunteers, and a fund-raiser. In smaller campaigns for local seats, candidates may have virtually no staff—or may hire part-time consultants to help them with specific tasks. In some cases, candidates for local seats rely heavily on key volunteers with expertise in specific topics.

Because their work is so time-limited, effective campaign organizations are highly focused, work as a close team, and are highly motivated to succeed. While internal differences may emerge in the heat of the contest about strategy, effective campaign organizations quickly resolve them so they can develop a united strategy. Above all, effective campaign organizations believe in their candidates—and put everything on the line to try to get them elected.

Developing Campaign Strategy

Strategy Options at the Outset of a Campaign

We have already discussed many elements of campaign strategy. Even before a primary contest begins, and before a final contest or a run-off contest occurs, candidates need to do the following:[29]

- Conduct an analysis of the electoral population in their districts to ascertain what groups and geographic areas are in play.
- Link this analysis to the development of an initial set of positions and campaign promises. They may decide what issues to select and what kinds of positions to take initially with respect to them. They may decide what issues to avoid because they believe them to be unimportant or because they work to the advantage of opponents. With respect to some issues, they may decide not to commit themselves to a position or to leave the position relatively vague.
- As they are doing this analysis, they need to examine strengths and weaknesses of likely opponents, both in terms of their electoral support and in terms of their likely or stated positions on issues. Campaigns are competitions—and candidates cannot compete if they fail to analyze opponents' positions.
- Raise funds, recruit volunteers, seek endorsements, and develop a campaign organization.
- Set priorities by deciding what expenditures of time and effort will yield the highest return in terms of issues, geographic portions and populations of the electoral district, campaign advertisements in the media, campaign appearances, and priorities in phone banking and distribution of leaflets. The selection of priorities lies at the heart of campaign strategy; resources must be targeted at activities that will yield results, rather than scattered to many low-yield undertakings.
- Develop a master calendar of events, activities, and expenditures that build toward the final vote—whether the primary or the final or run-off election. Candidates cannot expend most of their resources in the early phase of a campaign, because they need to intensify their personal appearances, advertising, and outreach as the campaign nears its culmination—the final vote. Resources have to be rationed in the early and middle phases to allow an upsurge in the final phase. The early and middle phases must not be neglected, however, because candidates want to build momentum as they go.
- Develop an aggressive absentee ballot campaign so that votes of absentee supporters are counted.

Strategy During the Mid-Phase of a Campaign

Little is set in concrete as the campaign unfolds. Polls and focus groups will show that some issues and positions are not resonating with citizens in the geographic areas or populations that the campaign targets. New issues may arise, as well, from unexpected developments in the community, region, or nation—such as a sharp economic downturn or a crisis in local schools.

Strategy must often be changed to counter tactics of opponents.[30] Campaigns are like chess matches because each side develops strategies to offset or counter its opposition. As campaigns progress, candidates need to do the following:

- Analyze their opponents' strategy. Try to understand how the opponent answered the same questions they addressed in the early phase of their campaigns. (See the previous list.)
- Ask whether they need to strengthen their outreach and advertising to specific geographic areas or populations in light of their opponents' activities. Perhaps, for example, they discover through focus groups that opponents are making inroads on groups they had given high priority.
- Ask whether they should concentrate on new groups of voters who they had prematurely written off. Perhaps a focus group will suggest that certain kinds of swing voters are now up for grabs, whether because opponents have failed to try to reach them or have made serious errors in trying to reach them.
- Decide how to change the selection of issues and the positions on issues in response to opponents' selection and positions. Perhaps candidates need to offset or counter opponents' positions on specific issues if they seem to be gathering support from important parts of the electorate.
- Decide whether, when, and where to engage in public debates or forums with opponents. Candidates must decide how many public debates or forums to attend. If they are strong frontrunners and are not skilled debaters, they may want fewer of them—although excessive avoidance of debates or forums can work to the opponents' advantage. Persons who are long shots and good debaters will want more debates and forums to enhance their name recognition.
- Decide on an advertising strategy in the context of opponents' advertising strategy and how the campaign is progressing. There often is no need to advertise in areas that are already supportive of candidates, but advertising is very important if candidates lack name recognition (as compared with opponents), if opponents are aggressively advertising to specific populations that candidates had targeted, or if candidates are running behind in polls. If opponents are hoarding their advertising funds for a last-minute blitz, candidates may want to retain much of their advertising resources to counter that blitz.
- Decide to what extent positive versus negative messages should be included in advertisements and personal statements in the context of opponents' ads and statements. Many candidates have found that they suffer electoral damage if they do not quickly counter opponents' negative statements, but negative ads and statements sometimes can backfire.

End-Game Strategy   Campaigns gather intensity as candidates approach the final vote. They ask two questions: what last minute strategies have the most potential for persuading key voters to change their minds and what will make them turn out to vote? In some cases, of course, elections have already been decided by the last two weeks, but others still hang in the balance. Candidates need to do the following:

- Select final issues and positions that will change swing voters' minds
- Make the case to supporters that they need to turn out

- Place as many ads as the campaign budget allows in strategic places
- Mount an assertive get-out-the-vote drive on Election Day

Conducting Issue-Oriented Campaigns

During the Progressive Era at the start of the 20th century, reformers in the various states placed legislative proposals directly on the ballot, allowing citizens to bypass the state legislature. If supported by a majority of citizens, such propositions become law by referendum.

As policy advocates soon discovered, however, this option was a mixed blessing. If social reformers could get some of their ideas on the ballot, so could conservatives and special interests. When Proposition 13 was enacted in California in 1979, for example, it set off a wave of similar propositions in other states that slashed property taxes so markedly that many social programs had to be cut. Yet policy advocates have successfully supported the enactment of an array of measures of their own, such as ones dedicating revenues from marriage licenses to programs to stop child abuse and proposals to safeguard rights of gay men and lesbians.

Policy advocates must work on two fronts: They initiate propositions, and they battle those that others have initiated that they do not like. To initiate a proposition, they must draft it, campaign to secure enough signatures from registered voters to qualify it for the ballot, and raise funds for advertising and direct-mail efforts. If their proposition seeks to raise taxes, to establish major new programs, or to regulate powerful interests like gun dealers, they can expect considerable opposition from offended interests and conservatives.

Whether they support or oppose a specific proposition, policy advocates must use strategies similar to those used by candidates for office. They have to build a campaign organization that raises sufficient funds for a potent advertising campaign to be mounted. They need to recruit volunteers to distribute leaflets at shopping centers and other community sites, and they must enlist speakers who can make public appearances. They need strong liaison with editorial staff and reporters of newspapers so they get supportive coverage and endorsements of their positions. Since many propositions are on statewide ballots, they must decide which geographic areas in the state should be top priority.

Making Issue Campaigns and Electoral Politics Intersect

We noted earlier that electoral politics are sometimes influenced by issue campaigns. When propositions are on the ballot, candidates' positions on these propositions can shape elections' outcomes as well as the popularity of incumbents. When Republican Governor Pete Wilson endorsed Proposition 187 in 1994, which severely restricted the rights of undocumented immigrants, including their right to health care and use of public schools, his popularity plummeted among Latino voters with significant adverse electoral consequences for the Republican Party for more than a decade. Many Republican candidates subsequently lost key elections, allowing Democrats to gain the governorship and both chambers in California. Policy advocates can influence the outcomes of elections, then, by working on propositions—or on issue-oriented campaigns to secure specific legislation—in certain jurisdictions. They can assertively attempt to get politicians to state their positions on these issues in hopes that grass-roots support for them will influence the outcome of key issues. (See Policy Advocacy Challenge 13.7.)

POLICY ADVOCACY CHALLENGE 13.7

Smoking Out the Positions of a Conservative

ANNEKA SCRANTON, MSW, PH.D., COMMUNITY ACTIVIST AND FORMER CLINICAL PROFESSOR, SCHOOL OF SOCIAL WORK, UNIVERSITY OF SOUTHERN CALIFORNIA

Along with several other child advocates, I attended a League of Women Voters candidate forum in the fall of 1996. We were trying to flush out a radical right-wing candidate for the California State Senate. We had discovered that Phil Hawkins, as an assemblyman, had voted for corporal punishment in school. We therefore submitted several questions about this issue.

After several questions, Hawkins became overtly angry. He vehemently endorsed spanking and even held up caning in Singapore as admirable discipline.

Having got his enthusiasm for caning on video, we sent clips to the media and wrote numerous letters to the editor. Mr. Hawkins was handily defeated by a progressive family and child advocate who has become a leader on this issue in the State Senate: Betty Karnette.

➢ EXERCISE ➢

This case presents an interesting alternative to mud slinging: getting candidates to reveal their true beliefs by asking well-designed questions, and then sending these responses to the media.

When policy advocates do attack the motivations or character of an opposing candidate, do they act ethically?

What limits or boundaries should be placed on such negative attacks?

Is it true that candidates who do not resort to such tactics are usually defeated?

In some cases, issue-oriented organizations, such as the AFL-CIO, gun control organizations, the American Association of Retired Persons (AARP), and the National Association for the Advancement of Colored Persons (NAACP) target key electoral districts several years before specific congressional and presidential contests.[31] Their goal is to build a cadre of members who care deeply about specific issues that are relevant to their groups, including, in the case of unions, raising the minimum wage, improving work-safety policies, and expanding medical insurance to uninsured workers. They develop leaders in their membership, who then hold meetings and forums for other members. In the case of the NAACP, the organization mounts aggressive voter registration projects among African Americans. When the elections near, they identify the candidates who support their issues and work to help them by giving them resources, running issue-oriented ads, publicizing their endorsements, walking precincts, running phone banks, and distributing leaflets. Indeed, these examples tell us that campaigning begins long before many elections occur.

These tactics are not unique to relatively liberal groups. The Moral Majority, an umbrella term for conservative groups that include many fundamental protestant churches, as well as other conservative groups, were instrumental in electing scores of conservative candidates from 1980 to the present, by using precisely these kinds of tactics. It relied heavily on clergy in fundamentalist churches to obtain names and addresses of their congregations—and used these lists to target political advertisements and door-to-door campaigning to fundamentalist voters. These tactics were highly effective in helping Republicans gain majorities in one or both houses of Congress and the presidency during much of the 1980s and early 1990s—and then from 2000 to 2006.

The nexus between electoral politics and issue-oriented organizations is unlikely to disappear. Indeed, the Internet is increasingly used to link voters to larger movements and to political campaigns as illustrated by two examples that converged in the presidential election of 2004. Howard Dean, a contender for the Democratic nomination for president, used the Internet site, Meetup.com, to develop supportive groups in hundreds of communities across the nation. These local groups could be part of Dean's larger presidential campaign, yet could shape strategies and issues locally as well. This was a marked departure from usual top-down political advertising that most campaigns had used before this point. Within one year, 190,000 persons joined these local groups.[32] In yet another Internet project, Wes Boyd and Joan Blades formed MoveOn.org in 1998 to use the Internet to prevent Congress from impeaching President Bill Clinton. It created a membership of more than three million persons over several years through "viral marketing," where individuals pass on e-mails to friends and family to create a larger and larger membership.[33] It became a major force in the 2004 presidential election in marshalling votes for the Democratic presidential contender, John Kerry.

By getting involved in grassroots organizing that intersects with electoral politics, issue-oriented groups send a message to legislators and heads of government: support some of our issues or we will build grassroots pressure against you in the next round of elections.

Participating in Electoral and Issue-Oriented Campaigns

Policy advocates can assume major roles in political campaigns as well as ballot propositions—and some run for office, as we discuss subsequently. As volunteers, policy advocates can do the following:

- Work inside the campaigns of specific candidates performing myriad tasks, such as organizing and working on phone banks, precinct walking, distributing leaflets, helping with focus groups and data gathering, and helping to prepare policy positions on important issues
- Work on campaigns for or against specific propositions
- Work with specific issue-oriented organizations as they build grassroots and membership support for specific issues and as they try to link such support to electoral campaigns
- Work on voter registration, absentee ballot, developing forums, and get-out-the vote drives (See Policy Advocacy Challenge 13.8.)

POLICY ADVOCACY CHALLENGE 13.8

How Students Can Get Involved in Political Campaigns

Ramon M. Salcido, DSW, Associate Professor, School of Social Work, University of Southern California Jolene Swain, MSW, Field Coordinator, University of Southern California

Background

The electoral project was conceived by the authors as a school of social work project to heighten awareness of the importance of voting and participating in the 1996 presidential election—but they have repeated the project in succeeding elections and plan to repeat it in the elections of 2006 and 2008. The goal was to organize several activities that would result in students' participating in the election. The time frame for the project was 4 months. The activities included (1) voter registration, (2) an absentee ballots effort, (3) a forum rally, and (4) a get-out-the-vote drive.

The authors (a policy instructor and a field educator) initially took the lead in forming a planning committee, since students did not yet have the experience in organizing for an electoral campaign. Moreover, both authors had worked closely during the summer with both the national and the state NASW political action committee. The policy instructor also organized seven policy instructors and the field educator in the school to provide support to the students and to act as a link with the field agencies. A steering committee was organized, consisting of three student organization officers, four student volunteers, and the authors. The committee met once a week to do the planning and coordination.

Once the plan had been developed, the students took charge of implementation. Officers of the student organization, elected by students to represent them in the school's governance, met with the dean, presented the plan, and received approval.

Role of Student Organization

The school's student organization became the key in implementing the electoral drive, contacting students and informing them of coming events. On September 10, 1996, the student organization sent a memo to every student, announcing the electoral campaign and giving key dates for voter registration training, the forum rally, and the availability of information kits. Similarly, a memo was sent to interested agencies to inform them of the voter registration drive, to encourage them to support students in the field to initiate voter registration activities, and to invite them to participate in the forum rally.

Activities

Voter Registration   Several tasks are involved in voter registration activities. The first step was to obtain large numbers of mail-in voter registration forms from the county office of the registrar (election office). The second was to train the members of the steering committee and other students about how to register voters—and then to use this knowledge to register other students to vote. Eleven students were trained and promptly registered 32 other students to vote. Moreover, students registered 123 voters at 7 field agencies.

Absentee Ballots   The next activity was to have students participate in an absentee ballot effort. The faculty person contacted the county election office and obtained information on absentee ballot procedures, and two student members went to the county elections office to be trained on how to do absentee balloting. On September 30, 1996, the student organization sent another letter to each student, giving information on the steps in absentee voting, a request form for an absentee ballot, and a county number to call for information. A total of 420 information letters were sent to all students of the school.

Student feedback informed us that the absentee ballot drive allowed many students to vote by mail during midterm. From an informal count by the policy instructors, it is estimated that about 30 percent (129) of the student body voted by absentee ballot.

Organizing a Forum   A forum was organized to provide information on all of the state ballot measures, including the so-called Civil Rights Initiative (a proposition that proposed to eliminate affirmative action in California), to inform participants of NASW's position and endorsed candidates, and to stress the importance of social workers' being part of the political process.

The forum was publicized in many ways. For example, the dean sent a memo to all students and faculty two weeks before the event. Policy instructors also emphasized the importance of the forum and encouraged students to participate as part of a class assignment. The student body president served as master of ceremonies. Forum speakers included a state Cal-PACE person, who spoke about the state initiatives; a representative of a political action committee concerned with persons with disabilities, who spoke about the impact of the so-called Civil Rights Initiative on clients; and a Los Angeles city council person (Laura Chick, MSW), who spoke about the importance of voting and getting others to vote. The state NASW Cal-PACE and National PACE provided the forum with a list of NASW-endorsed candidates and information on the ballot initiatives. An attempt was made to be educational and nonpartisan. After the presentations, political district maps were displayed, and students were asked to locate their geographic location and identify their political representatives. Sign-in sheets showed a total of 82 students, 3 clients, 6 faculty, and 9 field instructors.

Get-Out-the-Vote Drive   One week before Election Day, the student organization sent letters to students reminding them to vote and asking them if they wanted to participate in any NASW-targeted races. A total of 120 students were personally contacted. About 62 students volunteered to work at NASW-targeted races, as well as in the effort to defeat the proposition that proposed to end affirmative action.

Suggestions

This kind of campaign project is only one of many possibilities for student participation in political campaigns. Other experiences could include participation in one NASW-targeted race as a school project, voter registration initiatives that include registering clients at field education sites, and students' organizing phone banks in a get-out-the-vote effort on Election Day. Our experience suggests the importance of (1) knowing the dates for voter registration completion and absentee ballots; (2) being familiar with the laws concerning electoral activities in the academy; (3) getting an endorsement from the dean; (4) realizing that students have time constraints; and (5) including in the planning field instructors representing social work training sites.

This case example of student involvement raises a number of interesting questions:

- Should schools of social work involve students in the electoral process?
- Should schools and fieldwork agencies engage in voter registration drives?
- Do policy courses motivate students to become involved in the electoral process?

Policy advocates can also work with a political action committee (PAC), such as NASW's PAC, which is called PACE. Because nonprofit organizations may lose their tax-exempt status if they engage in partisan politics, many of them have created these spin-off PACs. For example, the NASW formed PACE, its political action arm, in 1976. PACE solicits its funds from members of NASW, who make small annual contributions to PACE with their annual membership fee unless they choose not to—or who make contributions any time of the year to national or chapter NASW PACE. One-half of membership fee contributions are used at the national level and one-half are given to state chapters. PACE keeps these funds in a separate account from the funds of NASW and has its own board of directors.

The national unit of NASW PACE endorses candidates for federal offices, and chapter units in each state endorse state and local candidates and collaborate with the national unit on federal elections. PACE currently has 46 chapter PACE committees. NASW PACE also trains and mobilizes NASW members to vote and volunteer for endorsed candidates, funds field organizers in certain prioritized races, and lets members know how elected officials voted on issues tracked by NASW.

NASW PACE endorses candidates on the following criteria:

- Issues that candidates support or oppose
- Viability of the campaign in terms of money raised and name recognition
- Relationship to the social work community
- Leadership positions of candidates if they are incumbents
- Whether they come from an underrepresented group such as a racial minority group

NASW PACE staff interview candidates either in person or on the phone to obtain this information. PACE then determines the kind or kinds of support it will give, which can include a letter of endorsement, a financial contribution, publicity in NASW publications, volunteers, fundraisers, and photo opportunities.

PACE has grown steadily. It endorsed many candidates in the 2000 elections and contributed considerable resources to them. NASW PACE has identified 150 social workers who hold elected offices at all levels of government, including 6 in federal positions that include Senators Barbara Mikulski (D-Maryland) and Debbie Stabenow (D-Michigan) and Representatives Susan Davis (D-California), Barbara Lee (D-California), Ciro Rodgriguez (D-Texas), and Ed Towns (D-New York).

Deciding to Run for Office

Reasoning that they want to make policy decisions themselves, some policy activists run for office. (See Policy Advocacy Challenge 13.9.)

POLICY ADVOCACY CHALLENGE 13.9

My City Council Campaigns, Past and Future

VICTOR MANOLA, MSW, PH.D., ASSISTANT PROFESSORT, DEPARTMENT OF SOCIAL WORK, CALIFORNIA STATE UNIVERSITY AT LOS ANGELES

It was the case that led me into politics. I had just started working for child protective services when I received Brenda's case. Brenda had just given birth to her sixth child, who had a positive toxicology screen for cocaine and her five other children were in foster care. After a lot of hard work, Brenda had completed a drug treatment program and moved into a two-bedroom apartment with all six of her children.

Soon thereafter, I read that an initiative was going to be on the ballot that would sharply decrease AFDC payments in the state. I knew that Brenda used a large part of her AFDC check to pay her rent. I feared that any cuts in her AFDC payment would force Brenda and her newly reunited and very fragile family back down the road of substance abuse and child neglect.

I became very angry and I knew that I had to act. I decided to work on the campaign to defeat that initiative. Thankfully, we defeated that initiative, but the political onslaught on our clients—the poor, the undocumented, the oppressed—continued.

After working on political issues since then, I became frustrated with elected officials who had no idea how to address the needs of our clients. In the policy classes that I taught, I tried to convince students that social workers should be proactive, instead of reactive; making the policies, instead of reacting to policies. Well, I finally convinced myself! I knew that, when the time was right, I would run for office.

I discussed my intentions with my wife, friends, and colleagues, all of whom were very supportive of my decision. I did not have much experience in electoral politics. So, I decided to get involved in my city.

I started attending community events and city council meetings. I began writing letters to the editor to local newspapers. One editor liked my letters so much that she asked me to write a weekly column. As a result of my networking with city officials, I accepted an appointment to the city's planning commission, dealing with zoning and land use issues within the city.

In my two years on the commission, I've voted on issues ranging from affordable housing for seniors and granting permits to adult day health care centers, to upgrading our city parks and improving our commercial district. When I found out that there were three city council seats up in the next election, I knew that I could make a difference.

I called the city clerk to find out how to file to run for city council. After collecting nominating signatures from 25 registered voters in the city and filing papers with the city and with the state's fair political practices commission, I became an official candidate for city council.

It was less than three months until Election Day and I had a lot of work to do. I began by asking for campaign contributions and volunteer time from family, friends, and colleagues by telephone, in person, and by e-mail. I had social work students walking precincts and phone banking. Besides attending community events, talking

(continued)

to voters, and getting endorsements, I was putting up campaign signs late at night, designing and making copies of my campaign flyers, and preparing voter registration lists for volunteers.

I received endorsements from state and local elected officials, as well as from the California Chapter of NASW, the California Democratic Party, and the Long Beach Press Telegram. The local Lions Club hosted a candidate forum where I used my public speaking skills to my advantage. We had sent out two strong mailers and, going into Election Day, I felt really positive about my campaign.

On Election Day, I was a nervous wreck. We went to the polling places to make sure my supporters voted; if not, we called to remind them to vote. That evening, my friends went to city hall to get the vote count, because I was too stressed out. Unfortunately, when the precinct counts came in, my heart dropped—I knew that I would not have enough votes to win a city council seat.

Looking back upon the campaign, I realized, I was not running for one of three open seats against five other candidates, but I was really running for one open seat against four candidates. Two of the seats were being sought by two incumbents (who nearly always get reelected), while the remaining four candidates fought for one seat. The eventual winner of that seat was a Portuguese man who was supported by a very organized and influential Portuguese community and whose family name was very well known. I came in fourth. I learned the importance of knowing your opponents.

Although I was very disappointed, I believe that my campaign was very successful. Losing a campaign the first time out is not unusual and many influential people from the community have already encouraged me to run again. As a result of my campaign, more people in the community know me now and I have a strong base of supporters from which to build upon for the next election.

While the next election is 1½ years away, I am already beginning to make preparations. I have already been attending city council meetings, community events, and local club meetings, telling people that I am planning to run in the next election. I am learning more about the community and residents' concerns.

Next election, I will put together a campaign committee that will be responsible for running the campaign, so that I can focus on meeting voters. I will raise campaign money early, so that I will have my signs, flyers, and mailers ready to go three months before Election Day. Also, I will ask everyone that I know for campaign contributions. People are generous and they want to see you do well, but they will not give you money unless you ask!

Now that I know what it takes to run a good campaign, I am confident that I will improve my chances at winning a seat on the city council and using my social work knowledge and skills to bring people together to improve the city for everyone.

Reassessing My Priorities

While I was much more prepared for my next election, I lost by a mere 21 votes! Of course, this was a very disappointing loss, especially since I had spent more than one year preparing for the election.

Not only did losing the election force me to reassess my priorities, but the birth of my third child two weeks before the election also gave me great pause. Do I really want to take more time away from my family and my work to prepare for another election, especially when there is no guarantee of success? As an assistant professor, do I want to jeopardize my quest towards getting tenure? The next election was two years later, and, in considering my priorities, I decided to sit it out. I wanted to spend more time with my family and focus on my work.

Today, nearly five years after my first campaign, and three years since my last campaign, I am considering another run for city council, which is nine months away. One major difference for the next election is that there may be an open seat. One of the current city council members, who supported me in my last campaign, just won the Democratic primary election for the state legislature. If he wins in November, there will be an open seat, and I will have a powerful supporter.

I will be spending the next few months consulting with my family and my supporters to assess the viability of another campaign. No matter what I decide to do for this upcoming election, I know that, eventually, I will run for public office and win.

Selecting Other Public-Service Positions

Many social workers cannot or do not wish to run for office. Many other kinds of public-service trajectories are possible, however, including high-level administrative positions, civil service positions, and consultative positions. (See Policy Advocacy Challenge 13.10.)

POLICY ADVOCACY CHALLENGE 13.10

Considering a Public-Service Trajectory

CAROL TURNER, M.A. (SOCIAL WORK), SHARILYN TWIDWELL, MSW, AND MICHELLE WILSON, MSW

While many social workers develop outstanding careers "in the trenches" in child welfare, mental health, health, and other organizations, some venture into public-service realms where they interact with legislators, high-level civil servants, and other policy makers. Here are three examples of social workers who branched into public service.

Bio-Sketch: Carol Turner, A.M., Education Advocate, Office of the Mayor, Portland, OR

You can be a good clinician and still decide to go into public service—as my career illustrates. I received training at the University of Chicago in psychiatric social work, graduating in 1965. My husband and I moved to Portland, Oregon, where I held clinical positions with nonprofit agencies over several decades, in addition to having a small private practice. I was not particularly "political," identifying myself professionally as a clinician.

I was very concerned about public education, however. The Portland School District, which my two children attended, was sorely in need of new leadership and ideas. Somebody asked me one day if I wanted to run for an opening on the school board—something I had not considered before. After making inquiries and deciding I might actually win, I entered a heated race in 1985—and, to my amazement, won the seat.

Since that point, my career has completely changed. I served on the Portland School Board for 12 years where I took part in scores of decisions that shaped policies of the District. For example, I dealt with significant school reform; curriculum development; policies related to prevention—such as alcohol and drug use by students and increasing student, family and community assets; and the impact of gang violence and AIDS on a school district. As chair of the board for three terms, I was intimately involved with

(continued)

POLICY
ADVOCACY
CHALLENGE 13.10

(continued)

making major budget decisions and—the most important work of such boards—hiring a new superintendent. I also served as the president of the statewide association of school board members, in which I worked primarily on funding issues.

In 1997, I was offered a position with the Oregon Department of Human Services and worked in a consultative role with local agencies working on service integration and community development.

I was invited by the Portland Mayor in 1998 to join her staff to give her advice on educational matters. My focus in my five years in this post has been on developing ways that the city can help local school districts be successful in such arenas as stabilizing school funding, increasing volunteerism in schools, expanding after-school programs, and leading a community reading initiative and further developing early childhood programs.

I have found my public-service career to be highly fulfilling. I have brought my social work experience and perspectives to the table on many occasions, helping to develop policies and programs that will help youth obtain an array of services that might otherwise not be available to them. Also, such clinical skills as listening carefully and understanding the complexities of human motivation have definitely come in handy in dealing with the pressures from various political constituencies.

So you don't have to be a macro student to get into public service or to run for office. You just have to have a willingness to take some chances and expand your horizons!

Bio-Sketch: Sharilyn Twidwell, MSW, Director of Governmental Relations and Political Affairs for NASW California Chapter

I was a high school teacher in the Boston, Massachusetts, area, and I was tired of running into roadblocks when I and other teachers tried to help students with problems outside their academic life. The mental health worker on our campus was a social worker, and one day when I was complaining to him, he said, "You should look into becoming a social worker so you can actually do something about all this." So I did.

When I entered the MSW program at USC, I was absolutely convinced that I should choose the Mental Health concentration, work as a direct practitioner for about five years (until I was an "expert," hah), and then I would be ready to work in mental health policy. Once I got through the first semester, however, and it was time to make a decision about my concentration, I was torn between the clinical and the macro tracks. I spoke to everyone I possibly could have spoken to, but there was one person in particular who finally changed my mind, and my life, forever.

Dr. Rino Patti sat me down in his office, and we talked about what my ultimate goals were, and what the best path for me might be, and I'll never forget what he said, "Social work needs leaders so badly, Shari. If you feel like you have any inkling towards leadership at all, and I think you do, you would have an incredible path before you in this profession." Something about those words just made sense. I chose the macro concentration called Community Organization, Planning, and Administration (COPA).

My second-year internship was with NASW California's southern California office, where I did various needs assessment and community organization projects, as well as some legislative advocacy work. I also applied for a fellowship with the California Legislature, which I received and accepted shortly after graduating with my MSW.

(Applying for this fellowship took some courage because competition is intense to receive it.)

I worked through the fellowship in the capitol building in Sacramento, for a state assemblywoman named Carole Migden (D-San Francisco), where I became completely addicted to legislative process. I staffed bills for the assemblywoman that changed the face of California's emancipation process for foster youth, and that increased benefits for registered domestic partners.

At the end of that legislative session, I became its Director of Governmental Relations and Political Affairs for NASW California. I still cannot believe my luck in having the role models I did throughout my graduate education, and then in the state legislature. They changed my life forever.

Bio-Sketch: Michelle M. Wilson, MSW, Program Analyst, National Institute for Occupational Safety and Health, Centers for Disease Control and Prevention

Since the beginning of my career in social work, I have always had a passion and respect for those in macro practice. Early on, I realized that social workers in macro practice play a vital role in the success and survival of any social policy or program. As macro practitioners, we are the advocates, evaluators, organizers, planners, researchers, and change agents for programs that affect people's everyday lives. We bring unique perspectives to the table. We look at things form a systems perspective, advocating and creating change at the macro, mezzo, and micro levels of society.

As I was finishing the second year of my MSW curriculum, I decided to apply for the Presidential Management Intern Program. It was an easy decision, but I had to compete with hundreds of other applicants for a few slots. But I knew that I brought to the interviews unique perspectives stemming from my social work education and internships. My second-year field placement was at the Los Angeles County Department of Mental Health, where I primarily focused on program planning and evaluation and policy research surrounding the issue of Institutes for Mental Disease. During my second year of graduate school, I also had the opportunity to work for the United Way of Greater Los Angeles. During this time, I conducted community-based research, looking at the overall development of children in Los Angeles under the age of 6, which has now become a major social issue for Los Angeles County. My drive and passion for becoming a macro practitioner has also been inspired by past professors Rino Patti, Jacquelyn McCroskey, Vince Ornelas, and colleagues Marge Nichols and Jenny Gross, who in their own ways have opened my eyes to the need for macro practitioners and have encouraged me to become a "squeaky wheel" within the public sector.

When I learned that I was successful in receiving a Presidential internship, I chose a 2-year internship at the Centers for Disease Control and Prevention (CDC), where I could couple my passion for macro practice and public health. (I had received a B.S. in Applied Behavioral Science and Epidemiology at University of California, Davis.) A job with the U.S. CDC would give me, I decided, the means to become a change agent at the federal level, affecting social policies and programs from the top down. Within my job in the Director's Office at the National Institute for Occupational Safety and Health (NIOSH), I was involved in research analysis, project planning, strategic planning, performance measurement, policy formulation and analysis, and program evaluation. I then became a public health analyst in the office of the Director of the CDC where I now work.

Why Social Policy Often Hinges on Elections

All elections have import for social policy because they determine what kinds of people with what values will enact social policies relevant to vulnerable people. Held every two years, Congressional elections are particularly important because the federal government has resources and powers far greater than state and local governments. The United States holds its Congressional elections every two years. These Congressional elections shape social policy in the United States profoundly, even when they are "off-elections" not coupled with the once-per-four-years presidential elections. (See Policy Advocacy Challenge 13.11.)

POLICY ADVOCACY CHALLENGE 13.11

Why Ballot-Based Advocacy Can Powerfully Shape Social Policies

BRUCE JANSSON, PH.D.

The party that possesses a majority in specific chambers of Congress has extraordinary power. It selects the chairpersons of each of the Congressional committees and its subcommittees. It prevails on many votes within committees. It prevails on many votes on the House and Senate floors. It can control the scheduling of votes by controlling the chairpersonship and the votes in the House Rules Committee.

If this *same* party controls *both* the Senate and the House *and* the presidency, it truly has extraordinary power. The president can often secure most of his policy agenda through a Congress that is generally acquiescent when his party controls both chambers.

The Republican Party had this extraordinary power from 2001 through 2006 because it controlled both Houses of Congress and the presidency during the presidency of George W. Bush—with the minor exception of a brief interlude from May 2001 through 2002 when the Democrats had a majority in the Senate when Senator Jim Jeffords from Vermont left the Republican Party to become an independent—but this interlude ended in the Congressional election of 2002 when Republicans regained their Senate majority and widened their majority in the House.

This extraordinary Republican power often meant that:

- Only Republicans could place items on the policy agenda in the Congress. If Democrats tried to initiate policy proposals in specific committees, they usually found that they were not scheduled for hearings or even discussed.
- Only Republicans could get legislation assigned to committees in the House, since the Rules Committee acts as a scheduler.
- Republican committees in the House could send bills to the House floor under "closed rules" that allowed virtually no debate or discussion.
- Republicans could stop investigations of many Congressional activities because they controlled the chairs and the membership of oversight committees. (Review Policy Advocacy Challenge 10.4 and the documentary by Bill Moyers, "Capitol Crimes" on the PBS Web site, page 358)
- The Republican president could mostly get his way with a Congress controlled by his own party.

Had the Democrats controlled even a single chamber *or* the presidency, as they did during the presidency of Bill Clinton, they could at least have placed issues on the policy agendas of the committees of that chamber—or been able to use the presidential "bully pulpit" to get public support for some of their policies.

Go to **academic.cengage.com/ social_work/jansson** to watch this video clip

While Republicans had remarkable power from 2001 to 2006, it is important to remember that *moderate* Republicans often voted differently than *conservative* Republicans on many issues—and often joined ranks with many Democrats. These moderate Republicans included, for example, Senator Olympia Snowe of Maine, Senator Lincoln Chafee of Rhode Island, and Senator John McCain of Arizona who, along with Independent Jim Jeffords of Vermont, often averted spending cuts and other policies favored by conservative Republicans. Operating at the fringes of the Republican Party, however, Republican moderates in the Senate and the House often had scant influence on policies favored by the conservative mainstream of the Republican Party.

Only a small number of Republican moderates were elected to Congress in 2000, 2002, and 2004, so Republican conservatives' control of national politics had enormous repercussions for social policy. Imbued with a philosophy that emphasized individualism and decreasing the power and size of government, they downsized many programs. They opposed Democrats' efforts to increase the eligibility levels for federal funding of foster care, for example, so that most of its costs had to be borne by local and state governments—often leading to short funding that led to excessive caseloads for child welfare workers. They cut the Medicaid program and tried to disentitle it. They opposed increases in the minimum wage so that it remained at its lowest level in real dollars since 1969. They proposed replacing Medicare and Medicaid with medical savings accounts, but set at such low levels for these accounts that they would not cover the medical costs of many seniors and low-income persons. They made such huge cuts in taxes and increases in military spending that the nation developed huge deficits as opposed to the budget surpluses that existed at the end of Bill Clinton's presidency.

It is true: the Democratic Party and its office holders had their own faults. They, too, could be guilty of corruption. They, too, could get the United States into ill-advised military actions abroad, as well as a bloated military budget. Yet clear differences existed between the two parties on social legislation—with the Democrats favoring governmental regulations and programs to a greater extent than Republicans.

As the Congressional elections of 2006 loomed, it became clear that they could be a so-called transformational election where one party's dominance might be challenged.[1] Transformational elections don't occur very often: the last one had been in 1994 when Republicans took control of both chambers of Congress, as well as many governorships and state legislatures. To make the elections of 2006 transformational, Democrats would have to capture at least one chamber of Congress and reduce the size of the Republican majority in the other chamber. Even better for them, they would take control of both chambers. And even better for them, they would regain the presidency in 2008. Were Democrats to regain control of the House, they would need to have a net gain of at least 15 seats in the 435 elections for House seats—and they would need a net gain of six seats to take control of the Senate in the 33 elections for Senate seats. (Only one-third of Senators come up for election during each Congressional election since they serve staggered terms of 6 years as compared to 2 years for members of the House.)

Nobody knows precisely why transformational elections take place, but they are probably triggered by shifts in public opinion. When Republicans took control

---

[1] Bob Benenson, "Blue State Special," *Congressional Quarterly Weekly*, August 14, 2006, pp. 2224–2241.

(continued)

of Congress in 1994, they were helped by scandals in the Clinton Administration, Clinton's failure to get his national health insurance legislation enacted, dislike of Hilary Clinton, disenchantment with large federal deficits, and disenchantment with long-term Democratic control of one or both chambers of Congress.

Transformational elections are also triggered by high voter turnout by one party, particularly among their base of loyal supporters. Republicans were able to turn out their conservative base in extraordinary numbers in 1994—centering upon evangelical and conservative persons in the South, Midwest, and mountain states. It was, to say the least, a political massacre; not a *single* incumbent Republican governor or legislator was defeated in 1994—and many incumbent Democrats were defeated—as Republicans gained solid majorities in both chambers of the Congress and in many state legislatures.

Many Republicans feared that the Democrats would return the favor in the Congressional elections of 2006. Even in spring, President Bush's job approval rating had fallen to 31 percent. By August, public approval of Congress had fallen below 30 percent. Polls in October showed that Bush's ratings had only barely improved. Moreover, only 40 percent of voters believed the United States had "done the right thing" in taking military action against Iraq—and only 38 percent of the public believed the Republican Party "comes closer to sharing your moral values" as compared to 47 percent for Democrats. Remarkably, only 46 percent of persons approved of the way President Bush had handled the campaign against terrorism despite his efforts to publicize his counterterrorist initiatives—down from almost 90 percent soon after the destruction of Twin Towers in New York City in fall 2001. A solid majority of the public believed, moreover, that the Bush administration had lied to get the public to support the invasion of Iraq, such as alleging links between Saddam Hussein and Al Qaeda found later not to exist. A majority of the public believed that the Iraq war made the United States even more vulnerable to terrorist attacks stimulating the growth of terrorists in the Middle East.

The Republicans were bedeviled, as well, by corruption. Jack Abramoff, a high-powered lobbyist, was indicted on multiple counts for laundering money and offering illegal kickbacks to politicians in return for helping such clients as offshore corporations and Indian casinos. Abramoff, in turn, was linked to Tom Delay, the House Majority leader—who resigned as he was indicted by Texas authorities for illegal donations of corporate money to Texas political campaigns. Bob Ney, a Republican Congressman from Ohio, resigned when he became a focus for influence-peddling. Even though some Democrats were likely, too, to be indicted, Abramoff had links with far more Republicans—even frequently meeting with Karl Rove, President Bush's chief political advisor.

Added to these discontents was a scandal involving Representative Mark Foley (R., Fla.) that broke in September. Foley resigned from office when e-mails were discovered and made public that contained sexual advances on male House pages. As the public perceived a cover-up of this scandal by Republican House leaders—or at least a failure to take action when informed of the Congressman's behavior—public opinion turned against both the Republican Congress and the Republican leadership. This scandal was harmful to Republicans in yet another way: it soured many conservative voters on the GOP who strongly believed in family values and who disliked homosexuality. Republicans feared low voter turn-out among the very group of evangelical and conservative voters that had powered them into control of Congress and the presidency during the prior decade.

The Republicans' problems with public opinion and their conservative base energized, moreover, many Democrats who saw the prospect of substantial gains in the 2006 elections after years of bad news at the polls. Not only could they be expected to turn out in record numbers, but they gave substantial sums of money to Democratic candidates.

All elections—save for the presidential election—are local, involving opposing candidates in congressional districts or in states. Using poll data and other information, political experts characterized these local elections in August as falling into seven categories: safe Republican, Republican favored, Republican leaning, No clear favorite, Democrat favored, Democrat leaning, and safe Democrat.[2] (In so-called safe seats, an upset was almost impossible, but in all the other races, upsets were deemed possible, especially in "leaning" districts but even in some "favored" districts.) These experts contended that a sufficient number of election districts or states existed where Democrats had a significant chance of winning that they could regain the House majority that they had lost in 1994—and that they might even regain control of the Senate that they had lost in 2002.

As the nation moved from August to early October, experts raised the number of districts that were toss-ups or that leaned toward Democrats. Even between August and October, the trend favored Democrats with as many as eight additional GOP House seats estimated by experts to be "at risk" of a Democratic victory. If 40 Republican seats had been "in play" in the House in August, as many as 48 districts were now estimated to be in play.[3]

The ultimate results would depend upon the campaign strategies of candidates in multiple districts and states. Candidates from both political parties would try to get their liberal or conservative bases to turn out in large numbers—and then to supplement them with moderate voters whether from the ranks of the opposing party or from independent voters.

Democrats who had typically focused on urban voters in so-called blue states where they had prevailed in Congressional elections of 2004, like California and New York, realized that they would have to convince rural and suburban voters in red states that had voted strongly for President Bush in 2000 and 2004 to switch their votes to their party. In the Senate, for example, Democrats had a chance to unseat six Republican incumbent Senators in Arizona, Missouri, Montana, Ohio, Tennessee, and Virginia—but they would need considerable votes from relatively conservative rural voters to achieve this result. Claire McCaskill, the Democratic contender for the Senate seat in Missouri against incumbent Republican Senator Jim Talent, criss-crossed the state talking with rural voters.[4]

To get votes from relatively conservative rural persons, McCaskill chose to assert her own religious faith as well as her family values. While Democrats as a group are less likely to attend church once a week or more as compared to Republicans, many of them are religious—or share the religious values of Christians, Jews, Muslims, and others.

---

[2] Ibid., p. 2226.
[3] Adam Nagourney, "In House Races, More G.O.P. Seats Are Seen At Risk," *New York Times*, October 7, 2006, p. 1.
[4] Ronald Brownstein, "Democrats Aim at the Red," *Los Angeles Times* (October 11, 2006), pp. 1, 22.

(continued)

Why not, McCaskill decided, publicize her own religious background? McCaskill also criticized the administration's prosecution of the Iraq war not just because of her personal convictions, but because she knew that war had become unpopular with many rural voters, whose communities had borne a disproportionate share of fatalities and injuries in American military forces.

Democrats discovered, as well, that rural voters often resonated to environmental and social issues that they experienced in their own communities.[5] Roughly 9 percent of the nation's 600,000 homeless persons live in small towns—and often are homeless because of plant closures, economically distressed farms, and rising housing costs. Citizens in rural areas experience relatively high rates of suicide, mental illness, family violence and substance abuse—issues where Democrats and moderate Republicans are more likely than conservatives to favor public spending and programs. Many citizens in rural areas realize that their communities need affordable housing that can only be constructed with federal subsidies. Many women in rural areas favor choice when women have unwanted pregnancies. By talking about these issues in rural areas, such candidates as McCaskill hoped to convert sections of red states into Democratic areas, as had already happened in a number of Rocky Mountain states stretching from Montana down to New Mexico in the 2004 Congressional elections.

The challenge of securing victories in close races would be magnified by the formidable resources and campaign expertise of the Republican Party. Unlike the Democratic Party, Republicans had developed a huge nationwide database on voters that contained extraordinary details about them—details they used to target campaign literature to specific subgroups. Their database included, for example, information about which voters owned snow mobiles, so to such persons in Michigan they targeted campaign literature that asserted that the Democratic incumbent senator from Michigan, social worker Debbie Stabenow, had supported environmental regulations that limited access of snow mobile users to certain areas—an attack meant to help her Republican opponent, Detroit sheriff Mike Bouchard, gain their votes. With extraordinary corporate contributions, as well as contributions from relatively affluent persons, the GOP usually had a significant lead over Democrats in the resources it could spend on pivotal elections. Jim Webb, the opponent against the incumbent Republican senator from Virginia, Senator George Allen, had only $424,000 in cash on hand in July, for example, as compared to 15 times that amount for Allen.

Another pivotal battle pitted incumbent Senator Rick Santorum (R., Pennsylvania) against his opponent, Democrat Bill Casey, Jr., and state treasurer. This election had extraordinary symbolic importance because Santorum had become a pivotal leader among Republican conservatives in the Senate and the nation, often championing anti-gay legislation, banning of day-after birth control pills, and strongly supporting President Bush's foreign policy.

Policy advocates' involvement in electoral contests was particularly essential in political races that experts viewed as up for grabs. Many of these races might be settled by a mere percentage point or less of the popular vote. Those candidates with the most volunteers, the most house-to-house contacts, the most effective campaign literature, the most resources, and the most sophisticated use of the Internet would prevail in

---

[5] Randal Archibold, *New York Times*, October 11, 2006, pp. 1, 25.

close elections. Social workers' involvement in tight elections might even make the difference in some of them.

While Democratic candidates often led in the polls leading up to the 2006 elections, they faced a formidable GOP machine at turning out votes on election day. Republicans had a national strategy for getting nearly every Republican to vote through phone calls and home visits. In the so-called 72-Hour project in Ohio, for example, volunteers worked phone banks on October 7 where they contacted 100,000 potential Republican voters and knocked on the doors of 50,000 voters. Not to be outdone, Democratic volunteers also completed 100,000 calls. Voters' opinions about candidates would be important, but so, too, would these practical organizing efforts.[6]

The Democratic Party won a resounding victory in 2006 Congressional elections. Not only did Democrats McCaskill, Stebanow, Casey, and Webb win, but many others—resulting in a Democratic take-over of both the House and the Senate.

Policy advocates in New Orleans encountered a particularly difficult problem: large numbers of low-income persons had left the city, leaving a more conservative and white population that had existed in the city prior to Hurricane Katrina. Listen to Ron McClain, JD, MSW, LCSW, President and CEO of Family Service of Greater New Orleans, as he discusses this problem on Policy Advocacy Challenge Video 13.11, as well as why low-income persons are less likely to vote than more affluent persons.

Some questions to ponder:

- Is it true that moderate Republicans and Democrats are more likely to support policies helpful to vulnerable populations than conservatives?
- Why have Democrats not asserted religious and family values as assertively as many conservative Republicans?
- What close elections in your geographic area or state are looming—and how might policy advocates assist those candidates most concerned with helping vulnerable populations?
- Do Ron McClain's comments in Policy Advocacy Challenge Video 13.11 about low-income persons not voting in the same proportion as more affluent persons suggest that policy advocates should devote considerable time to registering them to vote and getting them to the polls?

---

[6] Robin Toner, "Democrats Have an Intensity, but GOP Has Its Machine," *New York Times*, October 15, 2006, pp. 1, 25.

What You Can Now Do	# CHAPTER SUMMARY

You are now equipped to do the following:

- Assess candidates' odds of winning seats by analyzing their districts, their name recognition, and other factors, while realizing that many electoral contests are highly unpredictable
- Identify an array of power resources used by candidates to influence voters' views and actions
- Understand the importance of resources for campaigns, while realizing that resources, alone, do not guarantee victory
- Understand what campaign organizations are

- Be able to discuss an array of campaign strategies that arise at the outset, mid-phase, and end-games of campaigns
- Work in issue-oriented campaigns
- Understand how issue-oriented campaigns and electoral politics often intersect
- Be able to participate in various roles as policy advocates during electoral campaigns and issue campaigns
- Work with NASW's PACE
- Consider whether to run for office at some future time
- Understand different public-policy career trajectories
- Identify close pending elections where the involvement of policy advocates is particularly needed, whether in local, state, or federal jurisdictions

We are now ready to examine in the next two chapters what happens after policies are enacted, when policy advocates participate in policy implementation and assessment.

NOTES

1. Robert E. DiClerico, *Political Parties, Campaigns, and Elections* (Englewood Cliffs, N.J.: Prentice-Hall, 2000), pp. 191–250.
2. Robert Biersack, Paul Herrnson, and Clyde Wilcox, *After the Revolution: PACs, Lobbies, and the Republican Congress* (Boston: Allyn & Bacon, 1999), pp. 77–93, 134–143.
3. Bruce Jansson, *The Sixteen Trillion Dollar Mistake: How the U.S. Bungled Its National Priorities from the New Deal to the Present* (New York: Columbia University Press, 2001), pp. 330–333.
4. Ibid., pp. 295–299.
5. Darrell West and Burdett Loomis, *The Sound of Money: How Political Interests Get What They Want* (New York: W.W. Norton, 1998) and Jeffrey Birnbaum, *The Money Men* (New York: Crown, 2000), pp. 3–48. For discussion of campaign finance at the state level, see Joel Thompson and Gary Moncrief, *Campaign Finance in State Legislative Elections* (Washington, DC: Congressional Quarterly, Inc., 1998.)
6. Anne Bedlington, "The Realtors' Political Action Committee: Covering All Contingencies," In Biersack, Herrnson, and Wilcox, *After the Revolution*, pp. 170–183.
7. Gary Jacobson, *The Politics of Congressional Elections* (New York: Longman, 1997), pp. 1–51.
8. Ibid. and Ann Beaudry and Bob Schaeffer, *Local and State Elections* (New York: Free Press, 1986).
9. Jacobson, *The Politics of Congressional Elections.*
10. Thompson and Moncrief, *Campaign Finance,* pp. 99–114.
11. Beaudry and Schaeffer, *Local and State Elections,* pp. 18–37.
12. Jacobson, *The Politics of Congressional Elections;* Beaudry and Schaeffer, *Local and State Elections,* pp. 20–21.
13. Ibid., pp. 20–22.
14. Bruce Newman, The Mass Marketing of Politics: Democracy in an Age of Manufactured Images (Thousand Oaks, CA: Sage Publications, 1999), pp. 71–86; and Karen Johnson-Cartee and Gary Copeland, *Inside Political Campaigns* (Westport, Conn.: Praeger, 1997), pp. 149–184.
15. Public debates assume greater importance as candidates run for "higher" offices in mayoral, congressional, and presidential contests.
16. See Jacobson, *The Politics of Congressional Elections.*
17. Richard Scher, *The Modern Political Campaign* (Armonk, NY: M. E. Sharpe, 1997), pp. 88–111.
18. Kim Kahn and Patrick Kenney, "How Negative Campaigning Enhances Knowledge of Senate Elections," in James Thurber, Candice Nelson, and David Dulio, *Crowded Airwaves* (Washington, DC: Brookings Institution, 2000), pp. 65–95; and Kathleen Hall Jamieson, Paul Waldman, and Susan Sherr, "Eliminate the Negative? Categories of Analysis for Political

Advertisement," in Thurber, et. al., *Crowded Airwaves*, pp. 44–64.

19. Frances Fox Piven and Richard Cloward, *Why Americans Don't Vote and Why Politicians Want It That Way* (Boston: Beacon Press, 2000).

20. Beaudry and Schaeffer, *Local and State Elections*, pp. 13, 102–103, 136–138, 169.

21. Biersack, Herrnson, and Wilcox, *After the Revolution*, pp. 1–17.

22. Kim Kahn and Patrick Kenney, *The Spectacle of U.S. Senate Elections* (Princeton, N.J.: Princeton University Press, 1999), pp. 3–29.

23. Gary Moncrief, "Candidate Spending in State Legislative Races," in Thompson and Moncrief, *Campaign Finance*, pp. 37–58.

24. William Cassie and David Breaux, "Expenditures and Election Results," in Thompson and Moncrief, *Campaign Finance*, pp. 99–114.

25. Birnbaum, *The Money Men*, pp. 225–230.

26. David Breaux and Anthony Gierznski, "Candidate Revenues and Expenditures in State Legislative Primaries," in Thompson and Moncrief, *Campaign Finance*, pp. 80–114.

27. Beaudry and Schaeffer, *Local and State Elections*, pp. 187–205.

28. Ed Rollins, *Bare Knuckles and Back Rooms* (New York: Broadway Books, 1996), pp. 216, 264.

29. Beaudry and Schaeffer, *Local and State Elections*, pp. 2–205.

30. Kahn and Kenney, *The Spectacle of U.S. Senate Elections*.

31. Robin Gerber, "Building to Win, Building to Last: AFL-CIO COPE Takes on the Republican Congress," in Biersack, Herrnson, and Wilcox, *After the Revolution*, pp. 77–93.

32. Allison H. Fine, *Momentum: Igniting Social Change in the Connected Age* (San Francisco: Jossey-Bass, 2006), pp. 150–160.

33. Ibid, p. 46.

SUGGESTED READINGS

Campaigns

Karen S. Johnson-Cartee and Gary A. Copeland, *Inside Political Campaigns* (London: Praeger, 1997).

Richard A. Scher, *The Modern Political Campaign* (Armonk, N.Y.: M. E. Sharpe, 1997).

Political Parties

William J. O'Keefe, *Parties, Politics, and Public Policy in America*, 7th ed. (Washington, DC: Congressional Quarterly Press, 1994).

Robert E. DiClerico, *Political Parties, Campaigns, and Elections* (Upper Saddle River, N.J.: Prentice-Hall, 2000).

Political Consultants

James Thurber and Candice Nelson, eds., *Campaign Warriors: the Role of Consultants in Elections* (Washington, DC: Brookings Institution Press, 2000).

Campaign Finance

Joel A. Thompson and Gary F. Moncrief, *Campaign Finance in State Legislative Elections* (Washington, DC: Congressional Quarterly Inc., 1998).

Campaign Advertising

James Thurber, Candice Nelson, and David Dulio, eds., *Crowded Airways: Campaign Advertising in Elections* (Washington, DC: Brookings Institution, 2000).

Connections Between Issue and Electoral Politics

Megan Twohey, "Gunfights at the State Corrals," *National Journal* (2000), pp. 2376–2377.

Hedrick Smith, *The Power Game: How Washington Works* (New York: Ballantine Books, 1996).

Political Action Committees

Robert Biersack, Paul Herrnson, and Clyde Wilcox, *After the Revolution: PACs, Lobbies, and the Republican Congress* (Boston: Allyn and Bacon, 1999).

Political Strategy

Kim Kahn and Patrick Kenney, *The Spectacle of U.S. Senate Campaigns* (Princeton, N.J.: Princeton University Press, 1999).

Gary Jacobson, *The Politics of Congressional Elections* (New York: Longman, 1997).

Voting Behavior

Frances Fox Piven and Richard Cloward, *Why Americans Don't Vote and Why Politicians Want It That Way* (Boston: Beacon Press, 2000).

Marketing in Politics

Bruce Newman, *The Mass Marketing of Politics* (London: Sage Publications, 1999).

TROUBLESHOOTING AND ASSESSING POLICIES

Having enacted policies, policy advocates must now turn to the implementation of enacted policies. This is a critically important part of policy advocacy because many meritorious policies are inadequately implemented. We discuss policy advocacy strategies during implementation, which we call troubleshooting, in **Chapter Fourteen.** We briefly discuss policy assessment since policy advocates must work to see if specific implemented policies are achieving successful outcomes. Only as we assess policies can we find evidence-based ones that can be used to promote policy reforms.

CHAPTER

14

Troubleshooting and Assessing Implemented Policies

POLICY PREDICAMENT

Policies become effective *only* as they are implemented. We provide three case examples of policy implementation in this chapter. One of them (Policy Advocacy Challenge 14.7) focuses on implementation *within* specific organizations—how social workers can work to promote hospitals and other health providers to provide patients with advance directives (or living wills) in their work with patients. The other two of them (both are discussed in Policy Advocacy Challenge 14.8) focus on two episodes of implementation associated with Hurricane Katrina: the failure to provide effective disaster relief to citizens of New Orleans during and immediately after Hurricane Katrina and the mixed results in implementing programs to rebuild New Orleans in the year following Hurricane Katrina.

Someone who says that a policy exists only on paper suggests that the enacted policy has little effect on the implementers, such as the direct-service staff of a social agency. When people say that direct-service staff members only halfheartedly implement a policy, they suggest that staff members honor it only marginally. As these examples suggest, implementation is vital to policymaking; without it, official policies are meaningless.

This chapter provides a framework for understanding policy implementation, including alternative strategies that policy advocates can use to improve the implementation of policies. We discuss the following in this chapter:

- The importance of implementation to policy practice and policy advocacy
- A systems approach to implementation
- The importance of interorganizational processes to implementation

- How implementation is often powerfully shaped by contextual factors
- How some innovations are more difficult to implement or have a bleaker prognosis than others
- How policy advocates can troubleshoot implementation to identify shortcomings
- How policy advocates have many options for improving the implementation of innovations
- How policy advocates must sometimes sabotage specific policies
- How policy advocates must draw on a range of skills to improve implementation

A Framework for Implementing Policy

We can conceptualize policy implementation in relatively simple systems by means of a systems diagram that includes (1) the context of implementation (2) policy innovations, (3) oversight organizations and staff, (4) primary implementing organizations, (5) implementing processes within specific agencies, (6) interorganizational processes, (7) external pressures on implementers, and (8) the evaluation of policy outcomes. (See Figure 14.1.) This systems framework is useful because it allows us to track a policy's implementation from its enactment to its final outcome and to place it in its political, economic, and legal context throughout its implementation. It allows us to identify and analyze the action system that springs into place once a policy innovation is enacted. It allows us to troubleshoot how the implementation process is flawed—and what kinds of reforms we might seek to secure more effective implementation.

The implementing system in Figure 14.1 helps us analyze the implementation of specific innovations or policies in relatively simple situations where a single agency takes the lead. In the case of child welfare policies or hospital-based health policies, specific child welfare agencies or hospitals become the lead or primary agency that implements specific innovations or policies. While they might collaborate with other agencies, as depicted in Figure 14.1, they are the lead agencies.

In more complex implementing situations, such as disaster relief or the rebuilding of New Orleans in the wake of Hurricane Katrina, it may not even be clear who the lead agency is. A welter of different agencies and public officials from different levels of government—not to mention the public and private sectors—shape relatively ill-defined innovations and policies. Indeed, we can replace "policy innovation" at the top of Figure 14.1 with two massive problems in the case of New Orleans: meeting the survival needs of citizens of New Orleans during and immediately after Hurricane Katrina and rebuilding the city in the years following it. Contextual political, economic, and many other factors intrude—such as the president's ideology, partisan conflict, budget resources, and conflict between officials in different levels of government over who should take the prime responsibility for specific tasks at a given point in time.

We will use Figure 14.1 to orient our discussion through most of this chapter—but will return to more complex implementing situations in Policy Advocacy Challenge 14.5 when we discuss the implementation issues in the wake of Hurricane Katrina in New Orleans.

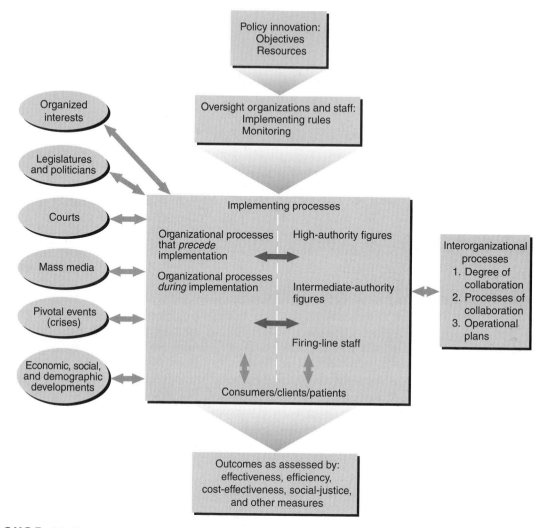

FIGURE 14.1
Implementation
action system

Considerable information can be obtained about the implementation of some social programs from the Web and from think tanks such as the Center on Budget and Policy Priorities (see Policy Advocacy Challenge 14.1. The mass media is highly useful as well; for example, you can read the *Times-Picayune* (http://www.nola.com) to find problems in programs implemented to help the citizens of New Orleans post Katrina.

POLICY ADVOCACY CHALLENGE 14.1

Using the Web to Learn About Troubleshooting: The Watchdogs— Investigative Agencies and Think Tanks

STEPHANIE DAVIS, RESEARCH LIBRARIAN, UNIVERSITY OF SOUTHERN CALIFORNIA, IRVINE

Once a policy is implemented, the effect of the policy needs to be assessed. There are several places on the Web that you can find evaluations, reports, studies, editorials and other information on the impact of policies. Government agencies, community groups, think tanks and nonprofit organizations all fulfill this purpose.

Resources:

- Government Accountability Office **http://www.gao.gov**
- RAND **http://www.rand.org**
- Center on Budget and Policy Priorities **http://www.cbpp.org**
- National Institute for Research Advancement (NIRA): World Directory of Think Tanks **http://www.nira.go.jp/ice/nwdtt/index.html**

⌒ EXERCISE ⌒

Visit the GAO and RAND Web sites to become familiar with the mission and the political perspective of each organization. Next, visit the NIRA's World Directory of Think Tanks, and compare and contrast at least three other think tanks listed in the directory, including international think tanks.

The Context of Implementation

The context of implementation can powerfully shape how specific policies are implemented. (See the various factors on the left side of Figure 14.1.) Implementation never occurs in a vacuum.

The implementation of many policies is closely linked to ideology and partisan politics. Remember that chiefs of government agencies are political appointees who usually reflect the viewpoints of the heads of government who appointed them. On such issues as substance abuse, family planning, health care, welfare, homelessness, juvenile delinquency, and social security, real differences exist between leaders of the two major parties—differences that are reflected in their appointments to agencies that administer policies in these areas. We have noted how many high officials in the administration of George W. Bush brought their free-market ideology into play as they implemented programs in New Orleans before, during, and after Hurricane Katrina.

We should not forget the role of courts, which frequently make rulings that influence the implementation of specific policies. Indeed, an entire field of administrative law exists that contains rulings on administrative procedures, rights of recipients, policies concerning commitments, and interpretation of statutes.

When a policy innovation is enacted, powerful contextual factors assist—or impede—its implementation. Take, for example, the Adoption Assistance and Child Welfare Act of 1980, which proposed a major overhaul of the child welfare system. Before its enactment, many people were alarmed by the dramatic increase in the number of children placed in foster care because of their parents' alleged abusive behavior or neglect of basic needs. (The number of children in foster care had risen from 177,000 in 1961 to more than 500,000 in 1979.) The framers of the act wanted to dramatically reduce the number of children in foster care by inducing local child welfare departments either to reunite children with their natural parents or to place them with adoptive families.[1] To secure this change, they did the following:

- Required child welfare departments to provide additional funds to the child welfare system to hire social service staff to give services to natural families
- Required each state to have a tracking system to monitor each child's progress so that no children became lost in the foster care or institutional system
- Required each state to have external reviewing bodies (either the courts or administrative bodies) assess each child's progress
- Mandated a case review after a child had been in foster care for 6 months and again at 12 months to make sure that caseworkers had planned permanent arrangements, either by reuniting children with natural families or placing children with adoptive parents
- Mandated a formal review at 18 months to ensure that the permanency plan had been implemented, meaning that the child had either been returned to the natural parents or adopted
- Increased subsidies for adoptive parents, hoping that many African-American and Latino parents would decide to adopt minority children, who, along with teenagers, had proved most difficult to place with adoptive parents

The Act seemed an ingenious solution to a vexing problem. As child welfare authorities were soon to learn, however, this policy innovation (actually a set of innovations) would prove not to be a panacea. Indeed, by the late 1990s, foster care caseloads approached levels that had existed in 1980 before the legislation had been passed.

The problem resided partly in contextual factors that, singly and in tandem, frustrated the work of child welfare departments. *Negative factors* in the nearly two decades after the enactment of the 1980 legislation included the following:

- Top administrators of child welfare in state and county positions were so preoccupied with responding to child-abuse and child-neglect cases that they lacked time to give intensive services to children or natural families.
- Rigid hierarchies in social services precluded top officials' communication with low-level staff.
- In light of allegations that many children had been harmed when prematurely returned to their natural parents, many high-level administrators emphasized child removal, rather than efforts to improve the parenting skills of natural parents.
- The unions representing direct-service and clerical staff emphasized pay, fringe benefits, and workloads, rather than service-related issues.
- Many legislators did not believe that powerful constituents supported major improvements in child welfare programs.
- State legislatures and county boards of supervisors did not fund child welfare services sufficiently to allow caseloads to be reduced, because of local tax revolts and the absence of political or community constituencies concerned about child welfare.
- Institutions that received funds for children who stayed with them had economic incentives not to return children to their natural families or to place them with adoptive families.

- Because of declassification, in which many local and state governments removed professional training requirements from specific jobs, many supervisors and direct-service staff in child welfare departments lacked training in social work. Lacking treatment skills and concepts, they could not easily perform the complex tasks required by the new legislation.
- Many natural parents viewed the child welfare staff and juvenile court as adversaries that primarily wanted to take their children from them. Because direct-service staff were so burdened with child removal and investigation, they had scant interaction with natural parents. (Increasing numbers of natural parents obtained attorneys.)
- Many parents neglected their children because they lacked sufficient financial resources—a problem that worsened with the growing economic inequality in the United States in the 1980s and 1990s. Thus, many children were insufficiently fed and clothed. Moreover, poverty contributed to some abusive behavior by exacerbating intrafamilial tension. Yet no system existed in child welfare agencies for providing job training or employment referral for parents.
- Innovative services, such as residential centers where troubled families can reside while receiving counseling, did not exist in most localities.
- Child welfare agencies often had few collaborative relations with schools, job-training agencies, or health services, so they could not develop innovative partnerships that might allow some natural families to surmount their economic difficulties.
- An epidemic of infants who were born drug-addicted occurred in the 1990s, leading to an infusion of hundreds of thousands of infants into the child welfare system. (Addicted newborns were often automatically placed in foster care soon after birth.)
- As child welfare agencies did reunite many children with their natural families, some of them were again abused or neglected, leading to widespread popular and political opposition to reunification. (Indeed, by the late 1990s, the pendulum had swung back to the extensive use of foster care!)
- While the welfare reforms enacted in 1996 were in their infancy in the late 1990s, some critics feared that they would exacerbate poverty among single-headed households as mothers were forced to take low-wage jobs, thus creating even more neglect and child abuse.
- Large numbers of adoptive parents for minority children, teenage children, and children with physical and mental problems did not emerge, even with adoption subsidies.

Of course, these negative contextual factors were somewhat offset by *positive ones*. Indeed, we can guess that, had the Adoption Assistance and Child Welfare Act of 1980 not been passed, far greater numbers of children would have entered and remained in foster care. Positive factors included the following:

- Because rapid increases in foster care became extraordinarily costly to local and state governments, they wanted to make the system more efficient.
- Subjected to litigation and adverse publicity stemming from scandals, such as ill-advised placement decisions and poor foster care, many officials and staff in child welfare departments wanted to reform their services.

- Finding it difficult to recruit foster care parents or adoptive parents, particularly for handicapped, ethnic, and adolescent children, many state and local officials were eager to cooperate with legislation to decrease the numbers of children in foster care and to promote adoptions.
- Many juvenile-court justices wanted to assume a more active role in reviewing cases and promoting permanent arrangements.
- Attorneys had increasingly publicized and defended natural families' rights to due process in court proceedings. This development made juvenile courts and child welfare staff less inclined to remove children quickly from their natural families.
- African-American and Latino communities had developed considerable interest in same-race adoptions, rather than transracial adoptions, thus enlarging the pool of adoptive parents in ethnic communities.
- By the late 1990s, many local child welfare agencies had developed partnerships with an array of local agencies—and had even begun to subcontract with them to help natural families remain intact.

The Adoption Assistance and Child Welfare Act illustrates that major policy innovations are rarely panaceas for complicated problems like child abuse and child neglect. They must battle an array of contextual factors that exacerbate the problems they seek to solve. If positive contextual factors outweigh negative ones—and if negative ones do not gather momentum as time passes—the prognosis for implementation improves.

As shown in Figure 14.1, many kinds of contextual factors may affect implementation. In the case of public policies, legislatures and politicians watch implementers carefully, sometimes holding oversight hearings when they want to examine problems that have come to their attention. Litigation is sometimes initiated to question specific decisions by implementers or to question provisions in legislation. The mass media sometimes cover facets of implementation, whether through positive stories that discuss successes, or through negative stories that highlight failures. Crises and pivotal events sometimes shape the course of implementation, such as wrongdoing by implementers or incorrect decisions that adversely affect the lives of clients. (Numerous stories in the mass media about children being reunited with natural families only to be abused or neglected again powerfully undermined the basic premise of the Adoption Assistance and Child Welfare Act that large numbers of abused and neglected children should be returned to their natural families.) Economic, social, and demographic developments also influence implementation, as the problem of addicted babies mentioned earlier suggests with respect to the 1980 legislation.

As these factors pressure implementers, so also do organized interests, such as unions, professional associations, and interest groups. As the welfare reforms of 1996 were implemented, for example, governors and their directors of welfare as organized into the American Public Welfare Association assumed powerful roles. Organized interests will support or oppose specific changes in the federal legislation based on their own experiences with its implementation. Leaders of professional groups like the National Association of Social Workers will seek to soften implementation so safeguards and exemptions are provided for women on welfare who cannot find work or who can only find work that does not meet their family's survival needs. (See Policy Advocacy Challenge 14.2.)

POLICY ADVOCACY CHALLENGE 14.2

How Does the Context Shape the Rebuilding of New Orleans After Hurricane Katrina?

BRUCE JANSSON, PH.D.

When Hurricane Katrina slammed into New Orleans in August 2005, New Orleans and the State of Louisiana had many traditions in place that would both facilitate and hinder the rebuilding of the city. On the positive side of the ledger, many persons who lived in New Orleans loved their city with its culinary and jazz traditions, its longstanding family networks, its rich community life, and its national reputation that attracted millions of visitors over many decades. On the negative side of the ledger, the city was among the most segregated in the United States with extraordinary rates of poverty, disease, illiteracy, and crime. Its public systems of education and health were not only under-funded, but poorly regarded by experts in these fields and in national rankings. Both the city and the state had traditions of political corruption even if considerable progress had been made against them. New Orleans' city council was mostly a nonproductive group that followed the mayor's lead. Nor had Governor Blanco and the state legislature been proactive in addressing New Orleans' major social and economic problems. New Orleans also had a deteriorating economy—actually losing a significant part of its population during the several decades preceding Hurricane Katrina.

Nor were the citizens of New Orleans united. Some relatively affluent and Caucasian persons were even happy that the hurricane had required huge numbers of low income African Americans to leave the city—and some of them even hoped they would not return. These persons often were not supportive of the development of low-income housing in their communities for low-income persons whose residences had been destroyed. The power base of the low-income African American community was greatly depleted by the forced evacuation of many of them to other cities and towns, making it more difficult for them to influence the plans that the residents of different parishes were developing in fall 2006.

The rebuilding of New Orleans would take place, as well, in a national context. On the positive side of the ledger, the enormity of the disaster—much like the terrorist attack on Twin Towers on September 11, 2001—triggered national sympathy for the citizens of New Orleans. This sympathy, in turn, generated great pressure on members of Congress and the president to enact scores of pieces of legislation to give assistance to New Orleans and other jurisdictions in the Gulf Coast region. The initial tepid response of the Bush administration to the disaster, moreover, created such outrage that the president knew that he would encounter political trouble if he did not become proactive and did not commit major resources to the relief and rebuilding efforts. On the negative side of the ledger, the president and his advisors were inclined to rely on private markets to solve the city's problems. He opposed creation of a commission or authority that would oversee the city's rebuilding. He faced a huge budget deficit even before the hurricane devastated New Orleans—not to mention distractions such as the wars in Iraq and Afghanistan.

Listen to Ron McClain, JD, MSW, LCSW, President and CEO of Family Service of Greater New Orleans in Policy Advocacy Challenge Video 14.2 as he discusses ideological factors that impeded the rebuilding of New Orleans.

Some questions to ponder:

Go to **academic.cengage.com/ social_work/jansson** to watch this video clip

- What additional contextual factors—positive or negative—do you think will influence the effort to rebuild New Orleans?

(continued)

- To what extent does the context *change* through time—becoming *either* more *or* less supportive of a specific innovation or project? For example, do you think that national public opinion supportive of the rebuilding of New Orleans will become more muted as time goes by and as people forget about New Orleans' plight?

Policy Innovations or Major New Initiatives

A specific policy innovation (i.e., newly enacted legislation or a proposal for new programs in agencies) at the top of the diagram in Figure 14.1, is the starting point for implementation. Or a major social problem or issue can provide the impetus to implementation, such as the destruction caused by Hurricane Katrina in New Orleans—or the homelessness problem in Los Angeles County. Many kinds of policy innovations and social problems or issues exist. Some are simple, such as a new policy that modifies an agency's intake services in a minor way. Others are highly complex, such as the rebuilding of New Orleans or the Personal Responsibility and Work Opportunities Act of 1996, which contained myriad items pertaining not only to single heads of household, but also to disabled persons, legal immigrants, and food stamps. The legislation wanted not only to get recipients off welfare rolls, but also to get them into employment. It wanted to free the states to establish their own programs, but to exert specific federal controls over them, such as setting minimum time schedules for reducing the welfare rolls. Some policy innovations or social problems require the collaboration of many people and agencies; others can be implemented by relatively few persons and one agency. Some policy innovations or social problems involve only a single task, such as changing intake procedures; others involve a sequence of tasks—or, in the case of New Orleans—a sequence of housing, economic, levee repairs, clean-ups of toxic waste, debris removal, repairing of infrastructure, and many other developments. Some policy innovations or social problems require vast amounts of resources, but others need few resources. Some are mandated by higher authorities and are highly detailed; others are vaguely defined. Some policies are relatively noncontroversial, and others are opposed by powerful interests. Some innovations require implementers to make only modest changes in their traditional practices; others demand sweeping changes.[2]

Some social policy innovations or social problems, we should remember, are not programs like Head Start or TANF, but *regulations*. Regulations include rules governing work safety, requirements that cigarette companies not market their products to teenagers, laws protecting confidentiality of patients and clients, laws prohibiting child labor, the federal minimum wage law, laws requiring states to provide abortions in the first trimester, regulations regarding public loitering (that apply to homeless persons), regulations regarding the licensing and training of social workers and other professionals, regulations governing affirmative action, and regulations giving patients certain rights when using health maintenance organizations. These regulations are often controversial, such as those regarding abortion and affirmative action. Some regulations are rigidly enforced; others are not. So regulations become a critical part of policy advocacy as advocates take positions on them, try to influence whether they are enforced, and (in some cases) try to amend or end them.

Even this cursory discussion suggests that some policy innovations and some efforts to address social problems are simpler to implement than others. A straightforward change in an agency's intake procedure that requires few resources and that the executive director has defined precisely can usually be implemented without much difficulty. Contrast this simple change with an ambitious, nationwide effort to make sweeping reforms in the child welfare system or to rebuild New Orleans. We can hypothesize that innovations and efforts to address social problems become more difficult to implement when they require major changes from the status quo, when they require many institutions to collaborate, when they are costly, when a sequence of tasks must be accomplished, when they are controversial, and when they ask implementers to discard their traditional practices.

Policy innovations and efforts to address social problems also become more problematic when they contain *internal contradictions* and *flawed strategies.*[3] Assume, for example, that a policy innovation seeks ambitious changes in existing programs but allocates only minimal resources. This internal contradiction is illustrated by the Family Support Act of 1988 and the Personal Responsibility and Work Opportunities Act of 1996. In each case, the policy innovations sought sweeping changes, such as the elimination of welfare as we know it and the employment of large numbers of welfare recipients, but the resources allotted to these sweeping goals were modest. Similarly, New Orleans can be rebuilt only if massive resources are available over an extended period of time

It is easy to overlook the actual substance of policy innovations when predicting their fate. A policy is likely to be unsuccessful if it proposes ill-conceived strategies, as illustrated once again by the Family Support Act of 1988 and the welfare reforms of 1996.[4] The legislation proposed giving jobs to many women on welfare when well-paying, blue-collar jobs were in sharp decline and when women had minimal access to unionized jobs in the trades, such as plumbing and carpentry. Moreover, many studies revealed that most female welfare recipients had educational deficits; indeed, many of them had not even completed high school. Both the Family Support Act and the 1996 welfare reforms proposed lifting numerous welfare recipients into jobs without addressing these fundamental economic and educational realities, proposing only modest training, educational, and day-care remedies. (An economic upturn in the late 1990s, remarkable in its scope and duration, proved to be a lucky break for the 1996 reforms, since many TANF recipients found jobs, although they often were relatively low-paying ones—and many TANF recipients were able to find jobs in the period from 2000 to 2006 when national unemployment remained relatively low.) The legislation did not acknowledge that the net economic condition of many women might deteriorate if they lost access to Medicaid, public housing, and food stamps, even after obtaining low-paying jobs. By requiring the states to contribute a considerable share of the training and education costs, the legislation overlooked many states' budget deficits, which restricted the resources available for these training and educational programs. While the Family Support Act had some effect on reducing the welfare rolls, many critics assessed the rapid reductions in the rolls in the year following enactment of the welfare reforms in 1996 as resulting from the booming economy that ensued following its passage. Moreover, as discussed in Chapter Six, many people feared that hundreds of thousands of recipients would take low-paying jobs that would leave them considerably poorer than they had been on the AFDC rolls.[5] Their predictions were partly borne out, though many former recipients graduated from minimum wage jobs to ones that paid between $7 and $10 per hour. (For a discussion of contradiction between theory and reality in New Orleans in the wake of Hurricane Katrina, see Policy Advocacy Challenge 14.3.)

POLICY ADVOCACY CHALLENGE 14.3

A Fatal Contradiction Between Theory and Reality in New Orleans?

BRUCE JANSSON, PH.D.

The rebuilding of New Orleans, too, would be hindered by a contradiction between the economic theories of the Bush administration and the extent of destruction of houses and businesses that occurred when Hurricane Katrina hit the city. Private markets, which the Bush administration emphasized, cannot work when a vicious circle of destruction and lack of incentives for businesses and residents exist—particularly in low-income areas. A chicken-and-egg problem existed in New Orleans. Many people had to return to New Orleans to provide customers for local businesses, just as many businesses had to return to New Orleans to provide the amenities needed to attract evacuees and others to the city. Private markets left to their own devices could not solve this problem since businesses would not return without many customers. Neither persons nor businesses would return to New Orleans, moreover, if other public amenities did not exist, such as good schools, acceptable levels of community safety, removal of debris, and restoration of an environment not compromised by pollution left in the city by contaminated water. Under these circumstances, only a carefully orchestrated redevelopment plan by governmental or civic leaders could synchronize the return of residents and businesses as well as many public amenities.

It is true: left to themselves, private markets might *eventually* promote the rebuilding of New Orleans, but this effort might take many years, even decades. Moreover, private markets might yield housing and development choices not helpful to low- and moderate-income populations, since private housing developers often seek higher profits associated with housing for relatively affluent persons. Here, too, a broad-based plan to meet the needs of all segments of the population would require a publicly orchestrated plan.

The use of governmental authority is not a panacea, as many failed projects suggest. Yet it is essential when private markets don't suffice. Even 15 months after Hurricane Katrina, the rate of the rebuilding of New Orleans was dishearteningly slow as only about half of the city's population had even returned to it. It was not just the physical structures that remained unrepaired, but the social fabric of some parts of the city. If New Orleans had had a very high number of homicides even before Hurricane Katrina, for example, the number of homicides per month in fall 2006 came to equal the number prior to Hurricane Katrina—even when the city only had roughly half the population that existed before the storm. High rates of violence existed, as well, in many public schools, which lacked resources to hire sufficient staff to contain it. Here, too, private markets could not provide the safety and good schools that New Orleans needed, but only community policing projects, safe neighborhood groups, programs for youth, and an array of publicly-financed schools.

Even before a policy innovation has been implemented or a major problem addressed, we can estimate the likelihood that it will be actualized during the implementation process. (See Table 14.1.)[6] Of course, we may be pleasantly surprised when our estimations prove to be excessively pessimistic, just as we may be disappointed when our estimations are too optimistic. Of course, many worthy projects have an uncertain prognosis, so we should not abandon them but redouble our efforts to make them work effectively.

Once the implementation of policy innovations or efforts to address social problems begin, a battle over priorities often ensues. Different people give priority to some of the provisions and place less emphasis on others. Success for different persons or

TABLE 14.1
The prognosis for the implementation of specific policies

Characteristics of the policy innovation	Positive prognosis	Less positive prognosis
1. Extent to which collaboration is needed	Relatively little	Extensive
2. Extent to which a lengthy sequence of tasks is needed	Short	Long
3. Amount of resources needed	Few	Considerable
4. Extent to which policies are clear	Clear	Vague
5. Extent to which large change from the status quo is needed	Little	Major
6. Extent to which innovation is controversial	Noncontroversial	Controversial
7. Extent to which internal contradictions exist in the innovation	Few	Many
8. Extent to which the theory and assumptions behind a policy innovation are flawed	Not flawed	Flawed

groups means the achievement of different objectives. Indeed, as the 1996 reform legislation moved toward full implementation in the summer of 1997, the protagonists had already staked out positions. People like Newt Gingrich emphasized reducing the welfare rolls and curtailing federal expenditures on welfare. More liberal politicians did not want to reduce the rolls at the expense of placing women in jobs (public or private) that consigned them to unacceptable poverty or unsafe working conditions.[7] (Since the legislation kept some federal rules but gave the states wide latitude, the battles over the implementation of welfare reform occurred at both the federal and the state levels.) At the federal level, President Clinton's administration made key rulings instructing the states to require the minimum wage in public service jobs—a ruling strongly protested by some conservatives who believed it coddled former recipients.[8]

Policy innovations carry not only objectives or goals with them, but usually resources. As discussed in Chapter Four, public policies are funded by the authorization and appropriation processes of federal, state, and local governments. Authorizations put a maximum on the resources that can be allocated to specific policy innovations, and appropriations determine the actual amounts, which are often far lower than the authorization level. Policy advocates need to prioritize the appropriations process if they want the resources to match the intentions or goals of many policy innovations or efforts to address social problems.

Oversight Organizations and Staff

In the case of publicly funded programs, oversight agencies are public funding agencies, such as the federal Department of Health and Human Services, specific state agencies, county-level agencies, and municipal agencies. In the case of privately funded programs, oversight agencies include foundations, the United Way, the Jewish Federation, and other private entities that provide funds to nongovernment agencies.

In the case of the rebuilding of New Orleans, it is unclear who the oversight organization is. Since no commission or authority was developed to oversee its rebuilding, authority is dispersed between a vast number of city, state, and federal agencies—each with its own programs and resources. While President Bush had appointed a "coordinator" of New Orleans' rebuilding, he reported directly to the president rather than to a commission or authority located in the city or in the Gulf Coast region. Private entrepreneurs operate on their own to purchase land and build structures on it—but their actions are not linked to broader plans for the city. In this welter of agencies, levels of government, and the private sector, the rebuilding of New Orleans is taking place haphazardly and unevenly. In relatively affluent areas, such as the Garden District, market forces *do* work because it suffered much less damage than many low-income areas such as the Ninth Ward and because many businesses and relatively affluent persons chose to remain, or to move, to it, sustaining markets for its businesses. Low-income areas are far less fortunate with even much of their debris mostly remaining untouched and relatively few persons able to return to their communities—or local businesses.

Oversight agencies are critically important to the implementation of policy. They have clout over agencies because they provide them with resources, which they can withdraw if they believe the agencies are not performing adequately. They often monitor programs that they fund, though the degree of monitoring varies widely. Monitoring may include periodic visits, analysis of program statistics, and audits of budgets. They may provide constructive technical assistance to help agencies better accomplish specific tasks.

With respect to programs established by legislation, public oversight agencies often establish *administrative regulations*, that is, rules governing the implementing process that were not defined in the original legislation. (Recall from Chapter Ten that legislation is often vague regarding many facets of programs, partly because legislators do not anticipate implementing details or because they wish to avoid conflict by simply leaving them out of the legislation.) These administrative regulations, which define many intake, service, budget, and other details of publicly-funded programs, have the force of law. Not only are executives and staff required to know about them, but they can suffer legal penalties if they violate them. (See Policy Advocacy Challenge 14.4.)

POLICY ADVOCACY CHALLENGE 14.4

Finding and Reading Administrative Regulations

<small>STEPHANIE DAVIS, RESEARCH LIBRARIAN, UNIVERSITY OF CALIFORNIA AT IRVINE</small>

To find federal administrative regulations online that are contained in the *Federal Register* from 1994 to the present, go to **http://www.access.gpo.gov**, then click on "access to government information products and go to the federal register." You can search by keywords, enabling law, and issuing agency.

Policy advocates not only need to know about administrative regulations: they need to try to influence their content. They are aided in this undertaking by the fact that oversight agencies are required to publicize proposed regulations before they are enacted, to hold public hearings about them, to invite written comments, and to take public sentiment into account before they issue the final versions. In other words, policy advocates can make certain that the oversight agencies receive input from citizens and agencies before they finalize or change administrative regulations.

In the case of policies that are initiated within agencies and funded from an agency's own resources, the executives and the agency board assume responsibility for oversight. They decide the content of intake, service, and other policies—and decide what funds to allocate to specific programs.

Oversight organizations often use purchase-of-service contracts when giving funds to specific agencies. These contracts are often awarded in the course of a bidding contest where agencies are asked to say what they would charge for a specified amount of services. Oversight organizations sometimes select a specific agency to provide services, rather than using a bidding contest, when they establish that only that agency has the competency to provide a specific service.

These contracts are a critical part of the implementing process because they define the amount of services to be provided, such as 2,000 hours of counseling services or after-school services to 250 children. The contracts often establish minimum standards, like the qualifications of staff and the parameters of service. (The after-school services might specify tutoring and recreational components.) An evaluation component is often attached to contracts, where providers must develop an evaluative mechanism to gauge client satisfaction and outcomes. Contracts impose specific auditing and budget provisions.

These contracts have burgeoned in the 1980s, 1990s, and the first years of the 21st century as government agencies have turned increasingly to nongovernment agencies (NGOs) to implement an array of services. For-profit agencies have become dominant players in many jurisdictions, even running the bulk of welfare reform services. Indeed, most nongovernmental agencies now receive the bulk of their funding from these kinds of contracts.

Contracts therefore have become a central part of the implementing process. Because often they define standards and content of services, as well as fund them, they should be viewed as policy documents. Sometimes, they contain provisions that detract from quality services, such as contracts that specify unrealistic goals in light of the funding they provide for specific projects. And sometimes bidders are awarded contracts primarily because they gave low bids and not because they possessed the competence to provide quality services.

Many contracts were issued by governmental agencies to private businesses in New Orleans in the wake of Hurricane Katrina. In the rush to clear some of the debris and to undertake other projects, however, some of them were no-bid contracts that were given to businesses that had links to specific public officials. Since no bids were sought, some of these contracts paid excessive amounts to the businesses that received them. Other contracts were poorly monitored, leading to nonperformance of contract objectives.

Primary Implementing Organizations

Once a policy is launched, its fate hinges on the beliefs and actions of various people and groups. We emphasize *evolving* beliefs and actions of decision makers, executives, staff, and clients when we discuss implementing processes, because these beliefs may shift as implementation takes shape.

The beliefs, interpretation, and mind-sets of those directly involved in the implementation shape its evolution. Direct participants include high- and intermediate authority figures, firing-line staff, and consumers.[9]

High-authority figures can choose to fully support a policy with verbal, financial, and time resources, or they can ignore a policy, neglect to address it, or actively oppose it. When analyzing the success or failure of a policy's implementation, we often examine the sort of leadership that is exerted in its behalf. Leaders' values, commitments, and priorities often influence whether they will lend their prestige, authority, time, and resources to a policy's implementation. When executives believe that a policy is unwise or intrusive, they are more likely not to enforce some of its goals or provisions. By contrast, when executives like an innovation, they may monitor its implementation, invest their own political capital to ensure its success, allocate resources to it, and ask staff members to go the extra mile.

Intermediate-authority figures, such as supervisors and administrative staff, are critical participants in implementation because theirs is a mid-level position between executives and line staff. When they favor a policy, they will report to higher-level executives any problems or issues they see in its implementation, and they will carefully monitor line staff to be certain that they implement the policy. In their proximity to line staff, they can be troubleshooters who help overcome barriers to implementation, whether in logistics or in the skills or orientations of line staff. If they dislike an innovation, they can sabotage it by opposing it or by failing to address implementation barriers.

We discussed in Chapter Ten (pp. 366–368) the considerable autonomy of *firing line staff*.[10] When staff members have considerable discretion, we must examine their perspectives. How do staff members understand a policy? How committed are they to its implementation? Do they have enough technical training to understand and implement it? Is the agency's informal culture supportive of the policy? If the staff is unionized, do the union leaders support the policy, or do they attempt to hinder its implementation?

The political scientist Michael Lipsky invented the term "street-level bureaucrats" to describe firing-line staff who are critical of the implementation of any policy. Direct-service workers can both implement and sabotage policies. If they fully understand and support a policy and are given technical supports in implementing it, if the agency's informal cultural is consonant with it, and if supervisors skillfully assist them in implementing it, the prognosis for its implementation rises considerably. The converse is true, as well. As Lipsky suggests, the power of firing-line staff is often augmented by their relative autonomy. What they do with specific clients, patients, or consumers, for example, is largely beyond the earshot of agency supervisors and directors, not to mention external monitors. So they have considerable latitude, which they can use to implement or to ignore a specific policy directive. Their personal views are often reinforced, or even shaped, by the informal policies and norms of other staff.

We should not overstate the autonomy of firing line staff, however. Some of their activities can be closely monitored, such as what eligibility standards are used during intake, how many persons they serve, and what kinds of referrals they make.

Although usually ignored in the burgeoning literature on implementation, *consumers* profoundly shape the course of implementation. For example, high-level officials, wanting to get homeless people off the streets, may fund a project in which outreach workers attempt to persuade homeless people to enter shelters. Even if the workers implement this policy diligently, they will fail if large numbers of homeless people refuse to enter shelters, either because they see the outreach workers as unwelcome authority figures or because they believe the shelters are inferior to life on the streets. Indeed, social marketing theory, discussed in Chapter Seven, suggests that consumers will reject programs whose benefits do not seem to offset the costs and risks associated with them. If consumers perceive the time and effort involved in using services as greater than the actual benefits received, they are likely to refrain from using a program. If they do use a program, they decide how much effort to invest in it and what kinds of advice or directive to heed or not to heed. Even in the case of involuntary use of programs, such as when a person is required to attend a counseling program by a court, consumers can decide whether merely to make perfunctory appearances or whether to invest themselves in it.

We have discussed each layer of staff as though it was independent of the others. In fact, interactions between different layers of staff powerfully influence the course of implementation. In organizations where lower-level staff like their leaders, for example, an innovation is likely to be taken seriously if the organization's leaders support it. But the converse is likely in organizations where the leaders are not highly regarded. Consumers also pick up cues from firing-line staff. If they sense that the staff does not favor an innovation, they may be less likely to participate in it. Organizational processes that precede an innovation often provide valuable clues to whether and how prime organizations, and their collaborators, will implement a policy innovation.

Before implementing a specific policy innovation, organizations have *standard operating procedures* that their staff members have evolved, such as techniques for reaching their clientele, organizing waiting lists, addressing their clients' needs, and making referrals. These standard operating procedures may prove to be well suited to a particular innovation, but they also may frustrate its implementation by being contrary to the procedures needed to implement a new policy.[11]

As discussed in Chapter Four, organizations also have missions, that is, goals that define their approach to specific problems as well as their priorities. When a mission is congruent with a policy innovation, staff and leaders are more likely to implement it. But a mission can also deter implementation. Take the case of a school district that is asked by higher authorities to cut the dropout rates of its students by engaging in aggressive outreach programs and intensive counseling. If the staff in some schools view students' attrition as outside their central mission of providing educational services to students who do attend classes, they may not invest energy in this new policy.

Organizations' patterns of resource allocation may profoundly shape a new policy's fate. If an agency has had to make numerous budget cuts before initiating a costly policy, its officials and staff members may not support its implementation. If they have given higher priority to other kinds of activities in their budget, they may be unwilling to shift resources to a new policy.

Interorganizational Processes

As implementation unfolds, prime implementing organizations are often joined by *collaborating organizations* that perform tasks, provide services, and otherwise interact with the prime implementers. (See Policy Advocacy Challenge 14.5.) Sometimes, these collaborations are planned, or are even mandated in the policy innovation itself, such as when policies require case management services, referral systems, or even the merging of several different agencies to provide a specific service. In other cases, collaborations emerge accidentally or serendipitously as the prime implementers undertake their work. Perhaps a child welfare agency develops links with local schools even though the legislation does not require these links.

POLICY ADVOCACY CHALLENGE 14.5

Crossing Organizational Boundaries

Patsy Lane, MSW, Director, Department of Human Services, City of Pasadena

As City Child Care Coordinator, my primary job was to implement the city child-care policy adopted by the mayor and the city council. The goal of this policy is to expand the supply, quality, affordability, and accessibility of child care throughout Los Angeles, by working with city staff in various departments, elected officials, consumers, employers, providers, developers, and others who affect child care in Los Angeles.

Since the policy did not approve any mandates for child care, one focus of this work involved trying to find incentives to get planners, land developers, and builders to include child care as they designed and built workplaces and residential communities. In order to find opportunities for such incentives, I had first to become familiar with the permit and approval process for property development in Los Angeles. After meeting with city staff in several departments that issue such permits and approvals and learning how the process works, we sought input from people from the development community about problem areas in the process and possible opportunities for improvements or changes that might offer incentives. There were lots of suggestions that were not "do-able" because of financial, regulatory, or political constraints, for example, to eliminate or greatly reduce city fees or eliminate steps in the review process. However, one area (among several) that seemed possible involved long delays in securing sewer permits. We found that the city sewer system was very close to capacity, so new building projects had to wait until sewer capacity became available (generally because of the demolition or elimination of an old property) before getting the sewer permit—often a delay of several months. On further investigation with the department responsible for issuing sewer permits, we learned that the city's elected officials had approved a set-aside of a small percentage of the available sewer for "priority" projects to add developments that include space dedicated to licensed child care for at least a minimum number of children. Thus, developments like new office buildings, condominium or apartment buildings, and business parks could save up to several months of waiting (which to date had cost both time and money) by including dedicated space for licensed child care.

Outcome

Within the first three months of implementation, there were some four project applications under the new child-care set aside for sewer permits—as opposed to only four major commercial or residential developments proposing to include child care in the prior year.

Lessons Learned

Among the many lessons learned on this project, the primary ones include the following:

- Sometimes, to accomplish a social policy goal, one must step out of one's "comfort zone" (i.e., the social service world) and understand that field's process, players, practices, and so on to find opportunities for implementing the original goal.
- Looking for such opportunities requires learning more than one perspective. In this case, we reviewed both the official city permit process (walking it through from start to finish) and the customer's experience with that process. Without those perspectives, we might have created an incentive that would be opposed by staff and/or elected officials, or one that had no value to the customer and therefore would not increase licensed child-care space in L.A.

> • Sometimes, you have to look and learn in many unexpected areas. As a social
>   worker, I never envisioned having to learn all about how sewer permits are issued—
>   but I'm very glad I did!

Whether interorganizational linkages develop among organizations charged with helping specific clients or consumers is a fascinating issue in implementation. Everyone realizes that clients, patients, and consumers often need assistance from many kinds of agencies and programs—such as children nearing age 18 who are about to be released from foster care. They often need job training, educational counseling, specialized counseling or substance-abuse services, housing, a supportive network of friends, and resources. Yet getting interorganizational collaboration is often no easy matter. As Catherine Alter discusses, it can be associated with such costs or difficulties (for a specific agency) as delays in solutions due to problems with communication, loss of autonomy, conflict over goals and methods, and loss of resources and time.[12] On the other hand, interorganizational collaboration can result in better services for clients, sharing costs, learning new technologies, finding innovative solutions, and gaining resources.

Interorganizational collaborations include a spectrum from relatively incidental, for example occasional interactions of two agencies in providing services to specific clients, to integration, where two or more agencies actually merge. Clearly, the incidental collaborations are simpler to put in place, such as joint referral systems and collaboration on modest projects. Even with these simple collaborations, staff from the two (or more) agencies must establish communication, develop common approaches, and trust one another. As collaboration becomes more ambitious, such as when agencies develop major programs jointly, it is more difficult to orchestrate. Such collaborations require extensive negotiations to decide who does what and how resources are shared. They can excite considerable fears by staff in all agencies involved, such as whether one agency will take undue resources or credit or will contribute equal effort. In more ambitious projects, some kind of joint governance is needed to allow decisions to be made as joint projects evolve.

The most ambitious interorganizational collaborations are called service integration, where an actual merger occurs, whether programmatically or budgetarily. In such cases, clients or consumers are not aware that separate agencies even existed. Such ambitious collaborations are relatively rare in the human services—not because they are not needed, but because of turf and funding realities. Executives of specific agencies are often reluctant to give up their autonomy and resources to interorganizational projects or mergers—even when they might provide consumers with a broader package of services. In fairness, however, collaborations and mergers can consume considerable time on the part of executives due to their logistical challenges. In some cases, moreover, specific agencies can lose visibility and resources in merged agencies as compared to other parts of the merged organization.

Interorganizational collaborations are often frustrated by fragmentation in funding from high-level sources. Look at our example of foster children nearing emancipation at age 18.[13] Since child welfare, education, health, and counseling agencies receive their resources from different oversight agencies or from different legislation, no mechanism often exists for pooling their funds to serve specific populations like children in foster care.

Case management is not a panacea for spanning organizational boundaries even if it is often highly useful—precisely because it is usually not a joint program but a one-way referral system from one agency to other agencies. Case managers often lack resources to purchase services from other agencies, which makes them vulnerable to rejections of their referrals by them. When cases are referred to other agencies by a case manager absent resources, they often are given less priority than are cases in which funders provide resources.

Interorganizational collaborations still remain, then, at the frontier of human services. They often arise from the determined efforts of staff at the grassroots level rather than from high-level edicts. While little data exists, we can surmise that some interorganizational collaborations improve the well-being of clients when compared with single agency services, precisely because they provide a fuller set of services that address various needs in tandem.

At a minimum, executives in agencies with services germane to a specific population, like foster children about to "graduate" from foster care at age 18, should not only meet together, but gather data and plan services that will meet their clients' needs. We know, for example, that a high percentage of emancipated foster children become homeless, unemployed, and substance abusers. Minus pooled services that address all of these needs in tandem, their plight will remain unmitigated by human services. This same observation holds for other populations, such as persons with AIDS, homeless persons, substance abusers, school drop outs, and persons released from correctional institutions. (See Policy Advocacy Challenge 14.6.)

Another collaborative approach utilizes persons from different professions *within* a single organization. Persons with diabetes should receive assistance not only from physicians, but from dieticians, physical therapists, and social workers in hospitals—as should persons with other chronic diseases such as cancer and heart disease.

POLICY ADVOCACY CHALLENGE 14.6

Needed Collaboration in FEMA's Trailer Camps

BRUCE JANSSON, PH.D.

The rebuilding of New Orleans required remarkable levels of coordination between disparate agencies to address residents' needs. When the Federal Emergency Management Agency (FEMA) set up temporary trailer camps within and outside of New Orleans to house thousands of evacuees, it needed to coordinate its efforts with police, social service, welfare, medical, school, and other agencies. Were it not to make these links, these trailer communities would provide a destructive environment for their residents. Already traumatized by their displacement from their homes as well as the injuries or deaths of friends, neighbors, or relatives, many of the residents needed counseling and substance-abuse services. With high rates of unemployment, the residents needed help in finding jobs. They needed help from the police to avert excessive rates of crime. They needed relocation counseling so that they could leave the trailer camps as soon as possible. Policy advocates should work to enhance collaborations when they have good reason to believe that they can enhance the well-being of specific populations. Understaffed and not accustomed to maintaining such large trailer parks—and under extreme time pressure—FEMA often failed to link residents with these kinds of services. In fairness to FEMA, its staff also had to contend with depleted services and schools, since many of their staff also left the city or found their facilities damaged or destroyed by Hurricane Katrina.

Diagnosing Implementing Processes

Once a policy innovation is in place or a major social problem addressed, we want to analyze critically the organizational processes that follow its initial implementation to find errors or problems. The following questions can determine whether internal implementing processes have been initiated that will support the innovation or the effort to address a major issue or problem:[14]

- Is the policy innovation clearly communicated and explained to implementing staff so they are familiar with its goals and provisions?
- Did the implementers have timely and good information and data to help guide implementation, such as demographic and other data about communities they serve, clients or persons they serve? They also need information about factors that could make the problems that they address even more formidable. For example, a program serving homeless persons would want to know if economic or other factors might markedly increase the number of homeless persons in a specific jurisdiction in the near future.
- Do high level officials understand the innovation they wish to implement as well as existing policies that are germane to the implementing process? For example, do they understand federal and state legislation as well as other guidelines?
- Have clear goals been established at the outset of an innovation or a project? Are implementing processes monitored to see if the guidelines have been met—and, if not, are corrective actions planned?
- Are clear time lines established that are realistic and are they met?
- Have appropriate logistical tasks been accomplished? If a project serves homeless persons, for example, have outreach staff and shelters been positioned so that they are truly accessible to them? Have sufficient numbers of staff been hired to implement key tasks?
- Does role clarity exist so that implementing staff know who has responsibility for what?
- Is someone charged with overseeing the implementation of the policy innovation at its outset and in ensuing time periods? And does she or he have the authority and expertise to engage in troubleshooting when snafus develop?
- Is in-service training provided to staff that lack skills needed to implement the innovation?
- Is implementation of the policy innovation built into staff promotion and performance review?
- Does staff receive bonuses or other rewards for additional work on the innovation?
- Is new staff hired to perform key tasks in the innovation?
- Do executives in the primary organizations demonstrate real leadership, carefully monitoring the innovation and troubleshooting its implementation?
- Does the prime organization allocate new resources to the policy innovation when they are needed or seek them from external sources?
- To the extent that belief systems of implementers impede or interfere with the implementation of an innovation, have efforts been made to change them? If, for example, persons working with homeless persons *do* view them primarily in criminal terms (i.e., illegally occupying public spaces), these views would need to be addressed and changed if the project meant to provide homeless persons with caring and nonjudgmental services.

When few of these internal actions and processes accompany the implementation of a policy innovation, the prognosis for effective implementation declines.

We also want to analyze implementation processes that are (or are not) initiated across organizational boundaries, particularly when a policy innovation's objectives require collaborations with other agencies and the community:[15]

- Are collaborative relationships with external organizations fashioned in a timely manner?
- Are contracts with outside agencies established with clear performance and cost standards—and are they monitored regularly? Is corrective action taken if they are not appropriately implemented?
- In the case of public or governmental agencies, do they interface sufficiently with the private sector and the nongovernmental organizations (NGOs), as well as community institutions such as churches, synagogues, and temples, and advocacy groups and community groups?
- Are outreach and community education initiated to the extent that a policy innovation's objectives require these activities?

Policy innovations sometimes specify collaboration among primary organizations and other organizations. An educational establishment, for example, may be required to involve health agencies providing family-counseling information to teenagers. Increasingly, federal and foundation grants favor projects that propose collaborations. Whether and how these collaborations actually develop will have important ramifications for a policy innovation.

Accidental or serendipitous collaborations may also emerge. As an agency implements a policy innovation, it may have to depend on other organizations for certain tasks or services that are essential to the policy innovation. Interactions between primary organizations and oversight agencies also figure prominently in implementation processes. To what extent do these oversight agencies actually monitor the work of the primary organization?[16] Do they provide technical assistance?

While many collaborations between social agencies *did* arise in Hurricane Katrina's wake, the rebuilding process was hindered by the relative absence of planned and mandated coordination of agencies and programs on the grand scale needed in a city that was so devastated. Minus such coordination that meshed the economic, social, housing, transportation, education, and medical systems, many of the city's residents would not find their needs adequately addressed in the months and years following Hurricane Katrina.

Implementation of policies is a dynamic process. Policies in action are different from written policies because they are shaped by this dynamic process. All social workers are part of this process, whether they are firing-line staff, supervisors, or administrators—or whether they work in governmental or nongovernmental agencies.

Actual Outputs: The Evaluation of Implemented Policies (Policy Assessment)

The framers of policy innovations want them to achieve specific goals, such as social justice, fairness, effectiveness, and cost-effectiveness, but it is not always easy to evaluate outcomes objectively. We often rely on reports and statistics from those who actually implement a policy to ascertain whether it has been implemented. However, agencies and providers may slant these data in order not to jeopardize continued funding from higher officials. Program evaluations that assess policies' implementation require considerable time and resources to complete, as well as the cooperation of the agencies that implement specific policies.

Perceptions of program outcomes, whether based on empirical studies, secondhand reports, or informal observations, often become an important part of a policy's context. When some legislators believe that implementing staff have not complied with existing policy, they may cut the funding of a program or try to modify the original legislation to make the official policy more precise. For example, at many points in the last three decades, conservative politicians have sought to tighten welfare programs because they believed that agency staff was not enforcing the work requirement provisions

It is particularly a challenge to evaluate complex and multi-faceted projects such as the rebuilding of New Orleans. It is difficult to define what constitutes success or failure—or to obtain data that tells evaluators to what extent indicators of success have been achieved. For example, should evaluations focus on the rate of rebuilding of structures in the city and the extent jobs have returned to the city? Or should evaluations focus upon rates of school drop-outs, crime, mental illness, or other social indicators? Or should evaluations focus on some combination of these factors?

Even when evaluators agree on the outcomes that they wish to measure, they often discover mixed results when the look at their data. The welfare reforms enacted in 1996, for example, did markedly reduce the size of welfare rolls in the succeeding decade and did lead to some recipients receiving relatively high-paying jobs. Yet many women who left the rolls remained under or near official poverty levels. Researchers sometimes face the conundrum of determining whether their evaluation suggests that the glass is half full or half empty.

Reforming the Implementation Process

Our discussion thus far may falsely suggest that various forces determine a policy's fate once it has been initiated. In fact, implementation processes evolve in the months and years after an innovation has been enacted. While some policy innovations are poorly implemented in their initial phase, implementation may improve markedly as leaders and staff take corrective action, whether because they favor the innovation or because they are pressured by external authorities. Innovations ultimately succeed or fail not because of abstract forces but because of the actions or inactions of implementing staff.

Policy advocates have several options when they want to improve implementation. They can target one or more of the facets of implementing action systems that we portrayed in Figure 14.1. (See Box 14.1.)

Amending the Policy Innovation Policy advocates can amend the original policy innovation. In the case of legislation, they can offer amendments or even seek to annul it. Legislation is not written in stone. In subsequent legislative sessions, policy advocates can convince legislators that they made some mistakes in the original version. Advocates often find it difficult to reopen the original legislation for amendments in the years immediately following its enactment, because legislators, having developed the legislation through elaborate compromises, are reluctant to reopen Pandora's Box. Moreover, some legislators may argue that a specific problem must be addressed by changes in the administrative regulations, not in the legislation itself or by changes in

BOX 14.1 | Reform Options for Policy Advocates During Implementation

1. Changing the policy innovation itself: its content, its objectives, or its funding
2. Changing the activities or nature of oversight organizations: their administrative regulations or their monitoring
3. Naming different agencies or adding new agencies to be primary implementing agencies, or requiring new collaborations by these agencies
4. Changing the internal and external implementing processes of primary implementing organizations
5. Modifying the context
6. Influencing the assessments (evaluations) of policy outcomes
7. Obtaining Additional Resources
8. Place pressure on implementing agencies through whistle-blowing or other forms of pressure

the implementation processes. However, if they can make a good case that the legislation was fundamentally flawed, advocates can get changes in the original legislation by following the strategy guidelines discussed in Chapter Twelve. As one example, the Adoption Assistance and Child Welfare Act of 1980 was modified several years after its initial passage to allow adopted children to retain their eligibility for Medicaid. Advocates hoped that this amendment would encourage people to adopt children with disabilities or children with other health problems.

Modifying Policies of Oversight Agencies   Policy advocates can try to change the administrative regulations that guide implementation, as when the Clinton administration required that minimum wages be paid to welfare recipients placed in public workfare programs. Advocates can also seek greater or improved monitoring of implemented programs. They can try to alter the content and nature of specific purchase-of-service contracts so they have better goals, policies, and funding.

Modifying the Choice of Primary Implementing Organizations   Policy advocates can modify the choice of agencies charged with implementing a policy innovation, for example, by adding new agencies, withdrawing contracts or funds from some agencies, or promoting new partnerships.

Intervening in Implementing Processes   Policy advocates can intervene in implementing processes in various ways, such as by insisting that the policy innovation be communicated more forcefully to staff, that in-service training be provided, and that staff be rewarded (or punished) as they do (or do not) implement the program.

Intervening in Interorganizational Processes   Policy advocates can try to enhance interorganizational collaboration to foster more effective services. They might seek specific negotiated agreements between organizations that promote specific kinds of collaboration, or they might agree to share resources to create a joint project. They might decide also to institute exchanges of technical knowledge.

Modifying the Context   Policy advocates can try to modify the context by offsetting negative factors and strengthening positive ones. If they publicize problems or faults in the implementation of a policy, for example, they can build pressure on implementers from the outside, such as activating an advocacy group that demands corrective action. They also might draw the attention of the media to flawed implementation or develop task forces that try to solve specific implementation problems in a collaborative fashion, such as an interorganizational task force.

Influencing the Evaluation of a Policy's Outcomes   Advocates should seek evaluations of a policy's implementation. When the genuine accomplishments of a policy's implementation are not understood, policy advocates can publicize its achievements to the mass media, to legislators, and to citizens. When evaluation suggests negative outcomes, advocates should ascertain whether they stem from defects in implementation or in the policy itself.

Working for Enhanced Funding   Some meritorious policies fail to be implemented because insufficient resources are allocated to them. In this case, advocates can put pressure not on the implementers, but on the funders, such as county or state legislators or public officials, or federal legislators.

Whistle-Blowing   When fraudulent or illegal activities occur during implementation —or when the well-being of clients, patients, or consumers is violated—social workers should engage in whistle-blowing if other remedies do not work.

Do Policy Advocates Ever Sabotage Policies?

We have assumed, so far, that policy advocates usually want to enhance the implementation of policy innovations. But what if policy advocates dislike a policy innovation, such as some of the reforms set in place by the Personal Responsibility and Work Opportunities Act of 1996?

This situation is both similar to and different from whistle-blowing, which we discussed in Chapter Ten. Distressed by wrongdoing in organizations, such as fraud or other illegal activities, whistle-blowers divulge information to outsiders. In the sabotaging of policies, however, policy advocates themselves take actions to subvert an existing policy. They can openly defy it, try to subvert it surreptitiously (perhaps by not implementing it in certain cases), or logjam it by creating logistical snafus that render it difficult to administer. Consider the case of the Medicare policy requiring older patients to be discharged rapidly after surgery. Assume that a social worker believes that this policy sometimes harms older patients who have experienced considerable physical or mental trauma in the wake of surgery. An inventive social worker could contend that a shortage of beds exists in convalescent homes (when no such shortage exists), obtain a physician's statement that medical complications preclude discharge (when, in fact, patients with similar medical assessments frequently are discharged), "lose" the required paperwork to delay discharge, or coach the patient to demand non-discharge, hoping this insistence will intimidate medical officials.

Is such sabotage ethical? Outright and continuing sabotage of official policy represents substantial risks and ethical dilemmas for social workers in specific settings. If a social worker is hired to implement the welfare reform of a specific state and cannot in good conscience enforce its provisions, she or he could be dismissed or even prosecuted for knowingly violating the law. In such cases, social workers may have to resign and work against the policy as policy advocates on the outside. Yet bending the rules for specific individuals often is ethically permissible. In such cases, social workers pit beneficence against compliance, deciding in egregious cases to help clients escape specific provisions that threaten their well-being. Who is to doubt that some older patients do need a delay in discharge after surgery, when immediate discharge threatens their well-being? To those who say that social workers play God in such cases, policy advocates can reply, "But doesn't professional training and experience equip us to determine when clients' well-being is endangered?" Moreover, in some cases, policy advocates do not violate existing policy but take advantage of loopholes or ambiguities in it that do allow for exceptions.

Case Study of Implementation

A case study of implementation that takes place largely within organizations is presented in Policy Advocacy Challenge 14.7. The case discusses troubleshooting skills used to analyze why a specific piece of federal legislation was unevenly implemented—and what might be done about this.

POLICY ADVOCACY CHALLENGE 14.7

A Case Example of Implementation *Within* Specific Organizations: The Patient Self-Determination Act of 1990

ASSOCIATE PROFESSOR SARAH-JANE DODD, SCHOOL OF SOCIAL WORK, HUNTER COLLEGE

On November 5, 1990, President George Bush signed the Patient Self-Determination Act (PSDA) into law as part of the Omnibus Budget Reconciliation Act of 1990. The act was sponsored by Senators John Danforth (R-Missouri) and Patrick Moynihan (D-New York) and by Representative Sandor Levin (D-Michigan). This act's implementation illustrates concepts in Figure 14.1 and Box 14.1.

The Policy Innovation

The PSDA was the first federal legislation to address patient decision making concerned with medical treatment at the end of life.[1] It was an effort to readjust the balance in the relationship between health care consumers and providers, intending "to empower people to take part in decisions that affect the duration and condition of their life."[2] Within PSDA, an advance directive is defined as a "written instruction such as a living will or durable power of attorney for health care recognized under state law and relating to the provision of such care when an individual is incapacitated."[3] The PSDA directly affects any hospitals, skilled-nursing facilities, home-health agencies, hospice organizations, and health maintenance organizations serving Medicare and Medicaid patients. Under the provisions of the act, these facilities are required to inform patients (adults aged 18 and older) of their rights to refuse treatment and to prepare advance directives. Specifically, the facilities are required to develop and maintain written policies and procedures describing (1) an individual's rights under state law to make decisions about his or her medical care, including the right to accept or refuse medical and surgical treatment; (2) an individual's rights under state law to formulate

[1] C. Soskis and T. Kerson, "The Patient Self-Determination Act: Opportunity Knocks Again," *Social Work in Health Care* 6 (1992): 1–18.
[2] F. Rouse, "Patients, Providers, and the PSDA," *Hastings Center Report* (September–October, 1991): p. S2.
[3] N. Paridy, "Complying with the Patient Self-Determination Act: Legal, Ethical and Practical Challenges for Hospitals," *Hospital and Health Services Administration* (1993): 291.

advance directives, such as a living will or a durable power of attorney for health care, when the individual is incapacitated; (3) the policies and procedures that the institution has developed to honor these rights; (4) a policy and procedure for documenting in the patient's medical record whether she or he has an advance directive; (5) a policy against discrimination in admission, treatment, or setting up conditions based on the existence or lack of an advance directive; and (6) a program of education about the act for the institution's staff, patients and their families, and the wider community.[4]

The act requires providers to present two documents to patients: a summary of the Patient Self-Determination Act and a description of the facility's policies concerned with patients' rights.[5] These two documents are to be made available at the following times: when a patient is admitted to a hospital or to a skilled-nursing facility as an inpatient; when an individual is admitted to a nursing home as a resident; when an individual comes under the care of a home-health agency; and when an individual begins to receive care from a hospice program. The PSDA does not override state laws that permit providers to decline to comply with an advance directive when they find it conflicts with their religious or moral beliefs, as long as the patient has been informed of their position.[6]

Context of the Patient Self-Determination Act

The PSDA can be seen as affirming rights and principles that have their "roots both in common law and constitutional law dating back to the late 19th century."[7] These rights involve choice concerning the kind of health care individuals wish to receive. However, few individuals exercised these rights. In addition, medical advances blurred the line between life and death to such an extent that an increasing number of individuals were being held hostage to technology and entered a suspended state between life and death.[8] Circumstances changed with the consumer rights movement of the 1960s and 1970s.

Patients became more aware of their rights as consumers of medical care—and began to assert these rights increasingly.[9] These events provide the backdrop for the emergence of PSDA. Four additional factors played a major role in the inception of PSDA: advances in medical technology, increased legal action concerning patient self-determination, changes in the political climate, and support by professional organizations.

Advances in Medical Technology The U.S. health care system is characterized by an unyielding dedication to and focus on acute care and curative interventions driven by the latest technological advances in health care. The use of life-sustaining technology has resulted in high medical costs and growing confusion about the line

---

[4] Soskis and Kerson, "The Patient Self-Determination Act," pp. 4, 6.
[5] Ibid.
[6] J. Luce, "Physicians Do Not Have a Responsibility to Provide Futile or Unreasonable Care If a Patient or Family Insists," *Critical Care Medicine* 23 (1995): 760–766.
[7] M. White and J. Fletcher, "The Patient Self-Determination Act: On Balance, More Help Than Hindrance," *Journal of the American Medical Association* 266 (1991): 410.
[8] R. Cranford, "A Hostage to Technology," *Hastings Center Report* (September–October 1990): 9–10.
[9] W. Pinch, P. Miya, K. Boardman, A. Andrews, and P. Barr, "Implementation of the Patient Self-Determination Act: A Survey of Nebraska Hospitals," *Research in Nursing and Health* (1995): pp. 59–66.

(continued)

between life and death, with an increasing number of individuals suspended in a "'living death,' technically alive but incapable of thinking, knowing, feeling, and responding."[10] In 1993, the American Medical Association estimated that daily, "approximately 10,000 individuals are in a persistently vegetative state or an otherwise permanently unconscious state and are maintained by tube feeding,"[11] placing an immense emotional and financial burden on families and society. The use of medical technology has been complicated by the fact that individuals increasingly spend their last days in institutions rather than at home.[12] The American Medical Association estimated that 70 percent of Americans will be involved in decisions concerning life-sustaining treatment for themselves or a family member.[13]

Legal Action Concerning Patient Self-Determination

The courts assumed a significant role in highlighting the need for legislation addressing patients' rights. Before the 1970s, court interventions were minimal, decisions were not consistent, and decisions were ambiguous regarding the right of an individual to refuse medical treatment.[14] Subsequent decisions consistently affirmed the competent patient's right to refuse medical treatment, even if it remained unclear how to determine the wishes of patients who were deemed incompetent.

Three cases were particularly instrumental: those of Karen Ann Quinlan (1976), Mary O'Connor (1988), and Nancy Cruzan (1990). In the Quinlan case the "New Jersey Court held that an individual's constitutional right to privacy outweighed the state's interest in preserving life, and therefore, the life sustaining measures could be withdrawn."[15] This decision confirming the desire of Karen Ann Quinlan's family to withdraw life-sustaining supports for their comatose daughter substituted their judgment on her behalf.

In the O'Connor case in October 1988, the New York State Supreme Court ruled that "life-sustaining treatment must be given unless there is 'unequivocal evidence' that the patient would have chosen to refuse it."[16] This ruling came even though O'Connor worked in an emergency room and had stated on several occasions that she did not want life support, though she had never made specific reference to her wishes regarding a feeding tube. Mary O'Connor died in August 1989 with a feeding tube still in place.[17] This decision fostered widespread support of policies that would encourage people to make their wishes explicit through such vehicles as advance directives.

Highlighting the confusion regarding what constitutes adequate evidence is the Cruzan case. Nancy Cruzan was involved in a car accident that left her in a coma in 1987. After aggressive treatment options had been tried, it emerged that she would remain in a persistent vegetative state (PVS), where she could not chew, swallow, or respond, even though she probably did not experience pain or suffering. Able to breathe, patients can

---

[10] Soskis and Kerson, "The Patient Self-Determination Act," p. 3.
[11] Paridy, "Complying with the Patient Self-Determination Act," p. 288.
[12] Ibid., pp. 287–296.
[13] Ibid.
[14] Ibid.
[15] Ibid., p. 289.
[16] B. Lo, F. Rouse, and L. Dornbrand, "Family Decision Making on Trial: Who Decides for Incompetent Patients?" _New England Journal of Medicine_ 322 (1990): 1228.
[17] Ibid., pp. 1228–1232.

remain in this condition indefinitely as long as nutrition and hydration are provided. As her condition worsened, Cruzan's parents wanted to remove the feeding tube to end her life, but Missouri law required "clear and convincing" evidence of a patient's wishes before such actions. The case proceeded through the Missouri court system as lower courts ruled that such evidence was unavailable. The U.S. Supreme Court ruled against the Cruzans in June 1990, indicating that "due process did not require the state to accept the substituted judgment of close family members without substantial proof that their views reflected those of the patient."[18] However, the Court did not determine exactly what constituted "clear and convincing" evidence of a person's wishes, with the justices urging the development of procedures that would facilitate the documentation of patients' wishes and the delegation of decision-making authority.[19] With new testimony from Cruzan's former coworkers about statements she had made regarding not wanting to be kept alive, the Cruzan case returned to the Missouri courts. Nancy Cruzan died on December 26, 1990, after the Missouri courts allowed nutrition to be removed. This dramatic case aroused broad support for federal policies to promote advance directives.[20]

Changes in the Political Climate   The political setting for PSDA is interesting as it had bipartisan authorship. Not surprisingly, the two authors of the PSDA (Senators Danforth of Missouri and Moynihan of New York) came from the states where the Cruzan and O'Connor cases had taken place. The issue cut across party lines, since members of both parties had had personal experiences with life-sustaining treatment. Moreover, self-determination is a right that is widely supported by politicians in both parties.

Bipartisan support was also based on the fact that advance directives can save considerable money. A significant portion of health care expenditures occurs during the last few months of life. In fact, 40 percent of Medicare expenditures on patients during their last year of life occur during their last month of life, a percentage suggesting huge savings from the termination of heroic measures for terminally ill persons.[21] It is therefore not surprising that PSDA was passed as part of the Omnibus Budget Reconciliation Act, a deficit reduction measure.[22] Of course, the potential cost-saving aspect of the act presented possible ethical problems: Was the primary motive behind PSDA to increase patient self-determination or to decrease health care costs? And would some patients be pressured to terminate treatment even when they desired it?

Professional Support for the PSDA   The PSDA was supported by many professional and advocacy organizations, including the National Association of Social Workers, the American Hospital Association's Society for Hospital Social Work

---

[18] Soskis and Kerson, "The Patient Self-Determination Act," p. 5.
[19] Ibid., pp. 1–18.
[20] Ibid.
[21] E. Emanuel and L. Emanuel, "The Economics of Dying," *New England Journal of Medicine* 330 (1994): 540–544.
[22] H. Osman and T. Perlin, "Patient Self-Determination and the Artificial Prolongation of Life," *Health and Social Work* 19 (1994): 245–252.

(continued)

Directors, the American Medical Association, the American Academy of Neurology, Concern for Dying, the Society for the Right to Die, and the Hemlock Society.[23]

Unfortunately, however, this strong support by professional health care workers has not often translated into implementation, because many health care workers do not adhere to the provisions of PSDA in their daily work.

While PSDA has the potential of advancing patient self-determination, its promise has been compromised by several barriers to its successful implementation. Let's return to concepts in Figure 14.1 and Box 14.1 to examine why PSDA has had mixed implementation.

Oversight Organizations

The secretary of the Department of Health and Human Services (DHHS) is responsible for a national education campaign to inform the public about PSDA, to distribute information to organizations that are Medicare and Medicaid providers, and to help the states develop information to present to patients.[24] Given their relatively passive role, which emphasizes the dissemination of information, the succession of secretaries of the DHHS have not been active advocates for PSDA—and have failed to put monitoring and enforcement policies in place. Nor have the states—also vested with disseminating information to PSDA providers—assumed leadership with respect to PSDA, mostly letting the health care providers develop their own policies with scant technical assistance or enforcement.[25]

Implementing Processes

Many physicians have been reluctant to inform citizens about advance directives—or to comply with them. Many believe that the Hippocratic Oath requires them to offer treatment to patients even when their health has a minimal chance of improving. To these doctors, even initiating a discussion of patients' rights and certainly complying with patient wishes to stop curative treatment are perceived as conflicting with beneficence.[26] Some doctors fear that a discussion of withholding life-sustaining treatments will delay their patients' recovery.[27] Doctors are also concerned that a discussion of advance directives might contribute to an adversarial posture by patients toward physicians, reducing the patients' faith in the doctors' curative powers.[28] Many doctors are uneasy, moreover, about discussing death with their patients, since they are schooled in preserving life.[29]

Many physicians are reluctant even to honor the patient's desires stated in advance directives. Palliative care, which aims to make terminal patients comfortable rather

---

[23] Soskis and Kerson, "The Patient Self-Determination Act," pp. 1–18. Also L. Emanuel, M. Barry, J. Stoekle, L. Ettleson, and E. Emanuel, "Advance Directives for Medical Care—A Case for Greater Use," *New England Journal of Medicine* 324 (1991): 889–895.

[24] Rouse, "Patients, Providers, and the PSDA," pp. S2–S3.

[25] Paridy, "Complying with the Patient Self-Determination Act," pp. 287–296.

[26] Osman and Perlin, "Patient Self-Determination," pp. 245–252.

[27] J. La Puma, D. Orentlicher, and R. Moss, "Advance Directives on Admission: Clinical Implications and Analysis of the Patient Self-Determination Act of 1990," *Journal of the American Medical Association* 266 (1991): 402–405.

[28] Davidson, C. Hackler, D. Caradine, and R. McCord, "Physicians' Attitudes on Advance Directives," *Journal of the American Medical Association* 262 (1989): 2415–2419.

[29] A. Kott, "Findings of RWJF Study on Dying Prompt Education Campaign to Stimulate New Approaches," *Advances* 1 (1996): 3.

than to cure them, has long been devalued in a profession that concentrates on curative measures. Indeed, caregiving has traditionally been devalued in Western medical culture and associated with the less prestigious professions of nursing and social work.[30] Thus, many doctors do not implement patients' wishes even when they are clearly stated in advance directives.

PSDA implementation is also impeded by the culture of many medical institutions. Many physicians and medical staff view providing information about advance directives as a legal issue that is outside the scope of medical services.[31] This orientation makes them see PSDA as an irritating distraction from their primary work rather than an integral part of it.

Since the act requires only that information be disseminated to patients at intake, it would seem that intake procedures could be easily modified to enhance implementation. While most health organizations have added information about advance directives to the intake process, the burden of intake paperwork often results in the mere addition of information about advance directives to the pile of other forms already given to patients. Moreover, many nurses and clerks are disinclined to discuss advance directives because the intake procedure is emotionally charged for many patients and their families, and is characterized by pain and fear.[32] Intake workers often fear that patients, already stressed by illness, cannot be cognitively receptive to information about advance directives. So, many intake workers take a minimalist approach to the implementation of PSDA, merely passing forms to patients and checking boxes rather than engaging patients in a discussion of advance directives. By taking this minimalist approach, they undermine the objective of PSDA to educate patients about their rights and to promote patients' self-determination.

Staff who do favor extended discussions with patients about advance directives, and scrupulously honoring patients' wishes are often placed on the defensive in this atmosphere. Some social workers and nurses are torn between organizational norms and their desire to advance patients' self-determination.[33]

Implementation of PSDA also is impeded by medical administrators' belief that it negatively affects their budgets, because organizations must bear the costs of developing, producing, and disseminating PSDA information to patients. When staff devote time to discussing advance directives with patients, they are drawn away from other tasks. Some medical administrators may even fear that a reduction of medical services to terminally ill persons will diminish their revenues from Medicare, Medicaid, or private insurance.

Of course, some positive economic incentives promote the implementation of PSDA. Medical institutions that receive fixed payments for the medical care of patients, such as members of health maintenance organizations, gain financially as heroic treatments for terminally ill persons are curtailed. The families of terminally ill persons, often financially devastated by these treatments, also have an economic incentive to curtail them.

---

[30] Paridy, "Complying with the Patient Self-Determination Act," pp. 287–296.

[31] Rouse, "Patients, Providers, and the PSDA," pp. S2–S3.

[32] H. Silverman, P. Tuma, M. Schaeffer, and B. Singh, "Implementation of the Patient Self-Determination Act in a Hospital Setting," *Archives of Internal Medicine* 155 (1995): 502–510. Also Soskis and Kerson, "The Patient Self-Determination Act," pp. 1–18.

[33] Osman and Perlin, "Patient Self-Determination and the Artificial Prolongation of Life," pp. 245–252.

(continued)

Moreover, compliance with PSDA is mandatory for any institution receiving Medicare or Medicaid funding. If institutions do not comply, they may risk their Medicare or Medicaid funding, even though the act does not specify enforcement provisions other than loss of funding in the case of noncompliance.[34] (No organization has had Medicare or Medicaid funding withdrawn as a result of noncompliance.)

The lenient approach of federal administrators has given the organization administrators a covert message concerning the importance of the policy. In turn, this attitude is passed down to the line staff—doctors, nurses, social workers, and clerical staff—who have their own internal hierarchy. The result of this lack of accountability has been that each discipline, and sometimes each individual, interprets the requirements of the policy and its importance differently, fostering misunderstandings among patients, physicians, and other medical staff. Many patients believe physicians are responsible for initiating a discussion of advance directives, whereas many physicians believe patients should initiate such discussion.[35] Aggressive compliance with both the letter and the nature of the law has often been restricted to institutions where an administrator has vigorously asserted the policy because of her or his own individual values and motivations. The result has been extremely different responses to the policy in different organizations.[36] This inconsistency has further frustrated implementation of the law when patients are transferred between facilities. Organizations do not necessarily transfer records regarding advance directives with the patient. Thus, a patient may wrongly think that he or she does not have to worry about discussing advance directives in the new institution because he or she has already declared his or her wishes elsewhere.

Sometimes the relatives, loved ones, and persons named by patients to be decision makers when they are incompetent hinder the implementation of PSDA. Even when patients have clearly stated their desire to have heroic treatment withheld, relatives who do not feel comfortable with the advance directive may intervene and seriously impede the process of fulfilling the patient's wishes.[37] Simply by questioning the medical staff, relatives raise doctors' fears of malpractice suits, causing them to provide heroic treatment.

The likelihood of noncompliance with patients' wishes is increased by the fact that there has never been successful litigation against individuals or organizations who implemented family wishes to prolong life against a patient's wishes.[38] By contrast, extensive litigation has been brought against physicians who stopped heroic treatment, sometimes even when the patient had requested this action in an advance directive. Without pressure from the courts, physicians are likely to continue overriding patient wishes. Advocacy organizations, such as the American Civil Liberties Union, must champion the rights of incompetent patients whose explicit wishes are overridden by relatives and physicians.

Perceptions of Policy Outcomes

Unfortunately, evidence suggests that the PSDA has not been implemented as intended. A 1996 national survey of 650 home health care directors found that only 67 percent of the agencies complied with the PSDA requirement that they make available to clients

---

[34] Paridy, "Complying with the Patient Self-Determination Act," pp. 287–296.
[35] La Puma, Orentlicher, and Moss, "Advance Directives on Admission," pp. 402–405.
[36] Soskis and Kerson, "The Patient Self-Determination Act," pp. 1–18.
[37] Ibid.
[38] Osman and Perlin, "Patient Self-Determination and the Artificial Prolongation of Life," pp. 245–252.

their policies on advance directives and life-sustaining treatment decisions.[39] This finding was consistent with that of an earlier study by the Medicare Advocacy Project in Los Angeles County that only 65 percent of hospitals and 33 percent of skilled-nursing facilities provided written materials concerning advance directives.[40] In facilities where policies do exist, patients may still not receive adequate information to facilitate self-determination. A study of one hospital indicated that only 57 percent of patients had received written materials on advance directives and, of those patients, only 55 percent reported having read the brochure.[41] Even if there is formal compliance by giving patients brochures, the intent of the legislation is often violated by not engaging patients in discussions to ensure that the brochure is read and understood. Furthermore, two-thirds of doctors who receive reports of patients' wishes about life-sustaining care do not even look at the reports.[42]

Of course, the defects in the implementation of PSDA ought not to obscure the real gains. Some providers do comply with the PSDA's requirements. And even limited compliance is better than the situation that existed before PSDA, when advance directives were seldom discussed with patients except by a few avant-garde institutions and providers.

Advocates' Options for Reforming the Implementation of PSDA

Following are summaries of a variety of strategies for improving the implementation of policy innovations that apply not only to PSDA but to other policies.

Changing the Content of the Policy   A basic problem with PSDA is that it provides only a minimum standard, requiring only superficial notification about advance directives by giving patients printed materials at intake.[43] What is needed is bolder legislation that covers patient education and patient rights more explicitly.

- Policy advocates can insist that physicians initiate discussions of advance directives in their offices rather than when emergency care is required.[44] This timing would greatly reduce the anxiety and urgent nature of the discussion. It would also answer the criticism that providing information regarding advance directives has become an administrative rather than a medical task, which undermines the serious nature of the topic. This fact was highlighted in a survey of patient reactions to the PSDA: The patients revealed a desire to discuss advance directives earlier in the treatment process.[45]

---

[39] J. Davitt and L. Kaye, "Supporting Patient Autonomy: Decision Making in Home Health Care," *Social Work* 41 (1996): 41–50.

[40] S. Risdon, V. Flack, and G. Dallek, *Implementing the Patient Self-Determination Act (PSDA): A Survey of Selected Hospitals and Skilled Nursing Facilities in Los Angeles County* (Los Angeles: Medicare Advocacy Project, 1993).

[41] Silverman et al., "Implementation of the Patient Self-Determination Act," pp. 502–510.

[42] S. Brink, "The American Way of Dying," *U.S. News and World Report* (December 4, 1995): pp. 70–75.

[43] White and Fletcher, "The Patient Self-Determination Act," pp. 410–412.

[44] Paridy, "Complying with the Patient Self-Determination Act," pp. 287–296. Also L. Emanuel, "PSDA in the Clinic," *Hastings Center Report* (September–October 1991): S6–S7.

[45] M. Pfeifer, J. Sidorov, A. Smith, J. Boero, A. Evans, and M. Settle, "The Discussion of End-of-Life Medical Care by Primary Care Patients and Physicians," *Journal of General Internal Medicine* 9 (1994): 82–88.

(continued)

- Policy advocates can ask the states to provide a legal waiver, that is, to respect the legal documentation of an individual's state of residence when its advance directives, living wills, or durable powers of attorney differ from those used in states where an individual currently lives. When people travel or move to a new state, they often find that the forms used in their first state of residence are not honored in the new state.
- Educational programs that involve patients in meaningful discussions of advance directives should be required in all health care institutions. It simply does not work merely to give patients brochures without also involving them in a discussion of the purpose of advance directives. There is some evidence that educational intervention programs are successful. In one such study, an intense intervention carried out by a social worker with patients, their families, and their health care proxies resulted in 71 percent of the subjects (all of whom were 65 years or older) completing advance directives, a considerably higher rate than the average completion rate of 15 percent.[46]

Changing the Context   The PSDA's implementation has been impeded by widespread public ignorance about advance directives.

- Policy advocates can insist that the federal government, as well as health providers, launch an aggressive advertising campaign similar to the one developed in 1997 to promote the donation of organs and tissue. Advertising spots during prime time on major channels, as well as on radio stations, should invite citizens to complete advance directives—and should give toll-free numbers so people can call for more information and counseling.

Changing Actions of Oversight Agencies   To improve implementation of the PSDA, policy advocates can seek changes in the administrative regulations to clarify several ambiguous points. They also can improve high-level monitoring of the PSDA's implementation, and they can seek the following:

- Clearer guidelines regarding who should initiate such discussions in the hospital setting. A coordinated effort among physicians, nurses, ethics committees, social workers, and clergy would provide optimal coverage. While physicians must be involved to some degree because advance directives involve medical issues, other staff should be empowered to initiate discussion, which should be approached as an ongoing dialogue rather than a one-time discussion.[47]
- Increased monitoring by the administrators of Medicare and Medicaid funding. A potential solution to pulling Medicare and Medicaid funding was offered by A. Capron, who called for the federal government to "reward physicians and other care providers who encourage advance planning."[48] Providing financial incentives has the potential to encourage implementation more effectively than the current mechanism, which is nothing more than an empty threat.

---

[46] M. Luptak and C. Boult, "A Method of Increasing Elders' Use of Advance Directives," *The Gerontologist* 34 (1994): 409–412.

[47] Paridy, "Complying with the Patient Self-Determination Act," pp. 287–296.

[48] A. Capron, "The Patient Self-Determination Act: Not Now," *Hastings Center Report* (September–October 1990): 35–36.

Changing Implementation Processes Even in the early part of the 21st century, health staff in many institutions remain unclear about the implementation of the PSDA. Policy advocates can do the following:

- Request vigorous efforts to educate health care providers about their potential role in the process. To the extent that they are unwilling to initiate discussions with patients because of their personal discomfort with discussing death or medical complications, they need assistance in surmounting these personal fears. Social workers can play an important role by acting as catalysts in the implementation of the act in their health care setting.
- Make the documents given to patients more readable. The current forms tend to be in legalistic language that is difficult to understand.[49] The average reading standard of the documents is at the 11th-grade level, but most Americans read well below this level.[50] Current documents discriminate against persons who are unable to read documents, especially those who speak English as a second language. (The poor reading skills of many patients also highlight the responsibility of health care workers to discuss this issue with patients rather than simply supplying them with written information.)
- Require health care providers to tailor written materials and verbal discussions to cultural diversity. Individuals from certain cultures—for example, the Navajo or Chinese American cultures—view discussions of death as unlucky.[51] In the Chinese American culture, "suggesting that the patient might become mentally confused or incompetent activates feelings of shame on the part of the patient."[52] Staff education and training efforts should highlight the possibility of such culturally based reactions. In addition, outreach and education programs in culturally diverse communities can ease the confusion and provide an opportunity for advance directives to be beneficial. When advance directives are being discussed, ethnic and racial minorities often misinterpret the motives of medical staff, believing they want to save money. In addition, a study of African Americans revealed the belief that they will receive less care if they complete an advance directive.[53] Education efforts aimed at ethnic and racial minorities—as well as the general public—are necessary to allay such fears, such as reframing advance directives as an opportunity to exercise personal rights rather than an effort to curtail medical services.
- Encourage the appointment of health care proxies to surmount the often vague or ambiguous instructions that patients place in their advance directives. (Health care proxies are persons empowered by patients to make decisions for them when they become incompetent.)

---

[49] Soskis and Kerson, "The Patient Self-Determination Act," pp. 1–18.
[50] Silverman et al., "Implementation of the Patient Self-Determination Act," pp. 502–510.
[51] J. Carrese and L. Rhodes, "Bioethics on the Navajo Reservation: Benefit or Harm?" *Journal of the American Medical Association* 274 (1995): 826–829. Also L. Fung, "Implementing the Patient Self-Determination Act (PSDA): How to Effectively Engage Chinese-American Elderly Persons in the Decision of Advance Directives," *Journal of Gerontological Social Work* 22 (1994): 161–174.
[52] Fung, "Implementing the Patient Self-Determination Act (PSDA)," p. 167.
[53] Silverman et al., "Implementation of the Patient Self-Determination Act," pp. 502–510.

(continued)

- Develop well-conceived implementation projects within specific hospitals. A leadership team can be identified within the hospital that cuts across medical, nursing, and social work disciplines. Engage all staff in small group discussions about the importance of advance directives. Engage all staff in small group training sessions. Give leadership awards for staff who assume major roles in implementing advance directors. Monitor the process with random reviews of patient records to see if advance directives were discussed with patients. Develop processes for educating patients, so that their concerns or fears or questions can be addressed. Troubleshoot with specific staff when they do not implement the securing of advance directives—or do not honor them when they give medical services to patients. Establish ways that patients can appeal medical decisions when they run counter to their advance directives.

Improving Interorganizational Collaboration   It would seem at first glance that few opportunities exist for interorganizational collaboration with respect to this policy. Hospitals could, however, develop some innovative collaborations, such as with clergy and the legal community. Perhaps patients would be more open to signing advance directives if they viewed this policy not primarily as a medical one, but as a moral and legal one. Consultation with the clergy and/or lawyers might expose them to different perspectives. Concerning persons of specific ethnic groups, it might make sense to connect with grassroots groups to see if they could facilitate problem solving around this issue.

Securing Evaluations of Policy Outcomes   To the extent that the PSDA is making a difference by curtailing the use of heroic treatment for terminally ill people, policy advocates should obtain data that demonstrate its effectiveness. To the extent that it is not meeting its objectives, policy advocates should obtain data demonstrating its ineffectiveness, using this information to secure support for the kinds of reforms in implementation that have just been discussed.

Participating in Community-Based Advocacy Projects   Once the administrative regulations have been issued and the program is operating, policy advocates can often exert external pressure on policy makers. For example, the Medicare Advocacy Project in Los Angeles conducted research on whether the PSDA was being effectively implemented. By disseminating data to the mass media, this project pressured local, state, and federal officials to improve PSDA's implementation.

Two Examples of Implementation Projects in New Orleans Post-Hurricane Katrina

The destruction wrought by Hurricane Katrina demanded two different kinds of implementation: disaster relief during and immediately after the hurricane and rebuilding of New Orleans in the months and years following it. (See Policy Advocacy Challenge 14.8.)

If the implementation of the Patient Self-Determination Act in the prior Policy Advocacy Challenge occurs primarily *within* specific organizations, the implementation system for responding to disasters like Hurricane Katrina *and* the rebuilding of New Orleans takes place *across* organizations.

Hurricane Katrina provides, then, two episodes of implementation: the immediate response to the hurricane (Episode #1) and the rebuilding of New Orleans in its aftermath (Episode #2). Virtually everyone agrees that the first episode was grievously bungled by city, state, and federal authorities—and it seemed in late fall 2006 that the second episode had achieved only mixed results.

Implementation Episode #1: Addressing Citizens' Immediate Survival Needs

The Federal Emergency Management Agency (FEMA) was established in 1979 to deal with major natural disasters. After more than 20 years of dealing with disasters—including a particularly successful period during the presidency of Bill Clinton—FEMA was then consolidated into the Homeland Security Agency (HSA) when the HSA was developed to house programs to deal not only with natural disasters but with terrorist attacks on the United States in the wake of the destruction of the Twin Towers in New York City on September 11, 2001.

The HSA and FEMA operate within the provisions of the federal Stafford Act, which gives the federal government the power to respond both to "emergencies" and to "major disasters" like Hurricane Katrina. Two scenarios are possible with respect to major disasters: a president can wait to respond until after specific local and state governments request federal assistance because they have discovered themselves to be overwhelmed by the sheer magnitude of citizens' needs, or the federal government can provide federal assistance *prior* to a disaster when a major disaster appears imminent without even waiting for specific requests from state or local governments. Because key federal officials were informed by experts that Hurricane Katrina might both be a Category-5 hurricane and might hit New Orleans, the president and federal officials did not have to wait until Mayor Ray Nagin or Governor Kathleen Blanco requested assistance.[1]

Two key innovations were developed in 2003 by DHS at the instruction of the president to help it cope with natural and man-made disasters. It developed a *National Response Plan* (NRP) that described how the HSA (and FEMA) would integrate the efforts and resources of all levels of government as well as the private sector and nongovernment organizations to deal with domestic disasters. It established federal coordinators during specific disasters who would respectively deal with such needs as transportation, firefighting, and public health/medical services—as well as mass care/housing/and human services. It also established a *National Incident Management System* that recognized that disasters differ in their scope, but that specifically defined "catastrophic disasters" as ones so large in their damage and inflicted casualties that

Go to **academic.cengage.com/ social_work/jansson** to watch this video clip

[1] See U.S. House of Representatives, *A Failure of Initiative*, Final Report of the Select Bipartisan Committee to Investigate the Preparation for and Response to Hurricane Katrina, February 15, 2006, pp. 29–58

(continued)

"the federal government may have to mobilize and deploy assets before local and state governments request them via normal protocols because timely federal support may be necessary to save lives, prevent suffering, and mitigate severe damage."[2]

The federal agencies, directives, and machinery were therefore in place prior to Hurricane Katrina—*and* federal, state, and local staff had done a "dry run" over one year prior to Hurricane Katrina on what to do if a Category-5 hurricane were to strike New Orleans. (Operation PAM is discussed in the PBS video discussed in Policy Advocacy Challenge 1.10 on page 35.) Yet the implementation of disaster relief was sorely lacking in Katrina's wake. Many persons were not evacuated. Medical needs were often not met for those who remained in New Orleans, not to mention their food and other survival needs. Many elderly persons in nursing homes and hospitals died or were harmed by the failure to attend to their needs in New Orleans or to evacuate them. Rotting corpses floated for days in the storm water that had submerged the city—and other persons begged for assistance from relief workers from the roofs of their homes, at the Superdome, or from freeways and bridges. Persons who congregated in the Superdome lived in horrible conditions for days before they were evacuated. Civil disorder, such as looting and shooting, existed in some areas as many members of the New Orleans Police Department left their jobs often because their families, too, had lost their homes.

Specific factors frustrated the competent implementation of federal disaster directives including:

- Lack of key information or intelligence as manifested by the widespread unwillingness of local, state, and federal officials to heed warnings by hurricane experts that Hurricane Katrina could be a category-5 storm rather than a less powerful one. Only *after* the hurricane made landfall did people realize how potent it was despite numerous pre-storm warnings from hurricane experts.[3]
- Under-funding of hurricane preparations at local, state, and federal levels. FEMA's budget had been slashed in the Bush administration. Budget allocations were not forthcoming to put into effect recommendations established during Operation PAM, which specified precisely what public officials and NGOs would need to do if a Category-5 hurricane struck New Orleans.
- Apparent misunderstanding of federal guidelines by FEMA Director Michael Brown, as well as HSA Secretary Michael Chertoff, leading them falsely to believe they had to wait until Mayor Ray Nagin or Governor Kathleen Blanco asked for assistance before they actually gave it. Once they heard that Hurricane Katrina might be a category-5 storm, they should have immediately moved federal troops and assets into position even before it made landfall. Nor were Mayor Nagin and Governor Blanco sufficiently assertive in demanding federal involvement even before the hurricane made landfall.
- Lack of sufficient communication between key people including:

  1. Brown's failure to tell Chertoff about the magnitude of the catastrophe
  2. Failure of key agencies to communicate with one another, partly because they lacked communication systems that were compatible with one another and

---

[2] Ibid, p. 36

[3] For discussion of these various defects, see Ibid., pp. 1–6 as well as U.S., Senate, *Hurricane Katrina: A Nation Still Unprepared, Executive Summary*, Report of the Senate Committee on Homeland Security and Governmental Affairs, May 2006, pp. 1–21.

that survived Hurricane Katrina. FEMA could not communicate with local or state officials. The New Orleans Fire Department could not communicate with the Police Department. Holed up in a hotel for days, Mayor Nagin was mostly out of touch with other officials.

3. Insufficient communication between Mayor Nagin and Governor Blanco about transportation needs to evacuate low-income persons before and after the hurricane hit New Orleans

- Poor leadership from key public officials at all levels of government including by:

1. The president, who did not even leave his ranch in Texas, where he was on vacation, until two days after the hurricane made landfall
2. Governor Blanco, who failed to send busses to New Orleans to evacuate citizens
3. Mayor Ray Nagin, who gave a belated evacuation order and failed to make school buses available for evacuating low-income persons
4. Incompetence by Brown and Chertoff—the two lead federal officials—who failed to take fast action in Hurricane Katrina's wake. Chertoff had focused primarily on counterterrorism rather than natural disasters, so he was insufficiently involved in preparing for hurricanes. A political appointee by President Bush with no experience in disaster relief, Brown lacked the knowledge, initiative, and communication skills to deal with the hurricane. Rather than communicating with Chertoff, he mostly communicated with the White House—thus further isolating Chertoff from unfolding events.

- Failure to accomplish key logistical tasks including:

1. The failure to pre-position sufficient water, food, and other essentials before the hurricane hit—and to place them in accessible locations that citizens could access once the hurricane had hit
2. The failure to place essentials at such key sites as the Superdome before the hurricane hit
3. The failure to make plans so that the needs of first responders, whose homes and families often were in jeopardy would be met immediately after the hurricane hit so that they could, in fact, continue their work. In fact, many police and fire personnel, as well as medical personnel, exited the city after the hurricane hit, so they were unavailable to help residents.
4. The failure of the New Orleans Police and Fire Departments to possess sufficient boats, greatly undermining their ability to rescue people in the hurricane's aftermath
5. The failure to develop an evacuation plan for persons who did not have automobiles, who did not have ready access to the mass media, and who were relatively isolated from social networks, including churches, even though it was known years earlier that tens of thousands of residents fit within these categories.

- Lack of clear agreements between FEMA, HSA, and such federal agencies as the Department of Defense, as well as such state entities as the National Guard and the Louisiana and U.S. Department of Transportation. In catastrophic disasters,

(continued)

only the military possessed equipment and personnel sufficient in size to deal with them, such as ships, planes, helicopters, and troops. The National Guard belatedly became involved in New Orleans because advance approval from the state had not been obtained. Busses and trains needed to evacuate persons were not made available because of lack of agreements between state and federal transportation departments and the city of New Orleans.

- Belief systems that undermined a rapid response to the needs of victims of Hurricane Katrina including:

1. Ideology that biased the president and some of his top aides from taking assertive government action before or after the hurricane hit New Orleans. Their anti-government ideology made it difficult for them to use the powers and resources of the federal government to plan for natural disasters of this magnitude or to implement post-storm relief. Only when faced with widespread public criticisms of their lethargy did FEMA and the HSA, as well as the Defense Department, become fully involved in helping citizens in Hurricane Katrina's aftermath.

2. Even if overt racial discrimination had been alleviated by civil rights and other legislation in prior decades, New Orleans was a deeply segregated city before Hurricane Katrina struck, so some local public officials were not used to making plans for vulnerable populations. The delayed and inadequate response to the hurricane by the Bush administration can partly be explained by the fact that most of its stranded victims in the city were African Americans who attracted less sympathy from some public officials and from the general public than would have more affluent Caucasians.

Apologists for the administration and for other public officials and agencies involved in relief efforts after Hurricane Katrina correctly note that Hurricane Katrina caused unprecedented destruction—so that no one could have been fully prepared for it. Yet public officials had rehearsed for just such a hurricane more than a year earlier in the PAM exercise—and federal directives were in place that gave the federal government the ability to intervene *before* a catastrophic disaster occurred. Many precedents existed, such as the numerous hurricanes that had struck Florida, Texas, and the Gulf Coast during the preceding century, sometimes with devastating consequences. It had been widely predicted that the levees surrounding the city might fail if a Category-5 hurricane hit the city.

Implementation Episode #2: The Rebuilding of New Orleans in the First 15 Months After Hurricane Katrina

Difficult as the implementation of disaster relief to address the immediate survival needs of residents of New Orleans was during and immediately after Hurricane Katrina, the rebuilding of New Orleans proved to be even more difficult. Everyone realized that persons would not settle in New Orleans—and that many evacuees would not return—because of absent housing, businesses, social services, an education system, repaired infrastructure, and many other community amenities. These different community assets would need to be repaired in tandem to attract citizens and businesses back to New Orleans. Even if housing was made available to them, many persons would not return to New Orleans *before* businesses, grocery stores, and banks, for example, were reestablished. If the rebuilding of New Orleans was delayed for many years, many evacuees would decide to stay in their new places of residence where they had established roots. If New Orleans were rebuilt but in a manner that was less satisfactory to evacuees than those cities and towns where they had settled, many of them would choose not to return.

Not only would the rebuilding of New Orleans require huge resources to clear its debris, to construct new houses and businesses, to rebuild schools and other public facilities, and to rebuild its infrastructure, but the rebuilding would require extraordinary cooperation between different agencies, different levels of government, and the public and private sectors.

Even more difficult would be the reconstruction of the lower Ninth Ward, a community that had mostly been occupied by low-income African Americans for generations. Its citizens had often lived in dilapidated housing, experienced high crime rates, were impoverished, used inferior schools, and suffered police brutality. Since much of the Ninth Ward lay about nine feet below sea level, it was flooded for weeks—and would be vulnerable to further flooding if other Category-4 or -5 hurricanes hit New Orleans in coming years. Living in mostly dilapidated housing, why would the Ninth Ward's residents return if conditions were *even* worse than before Katrina—particularly if they had established roots in other major cities such as Houston and Baton Rouge? (For a map of New Orleans, go to **http://gnocdc.org**—and find the Ninth Ward, the Garden District, and other parishes surrounding New Orleans.)

The implementation of the Ninth Ward's reconstruction would have to occur in the context of a gauntlet of governments, NGOs, and faith-based groups—as well as private markets. (See Figure 14.2.) It would take place, moreover, in a political context that depended upon decisions made by President George W. Bush, members of Congress, scores of Congressional committees, the governor and legislators of the State of Louisiana, and the mayor and city council members of New Orleans. It would require huge resources.

Natural disasters had taken place in other cities in the United States such as the San Francisco earthquake (and subsequent fire) that had killed 3,000 people and destroyed 28,000 buildings in 1906, or the hurricane that hit Galveston in 1900 where 10,000 people were killed (or 25 percent of its residents) and 8,000 buildings destroyed. In each case, the government had played a central role in instilling confidence in ordinary citizens and investors by:

1. Ensuring public safety by constructing sea wall and raising the grade of the entire city by 1 to 15 feet (Galveston) or by having the federal government guarantee a bond issue equal to 10 percent of total damages to help San Francisco repair its infrastructure and housing
2. Allocating and spending large sums of money from all levels of government to give employment to the homeless and jobless, to rebuild public buildings, and by making interest-free loans to local governments and businesses
3. Putting nonpartisan experts in charge of reconstruction to avert charges of corruption
4. Pressuring insurers to pay claims rather than seeking not to pay them on grounds they were not liable for damage from natural disasters
5. Establishing the confidence of private investors to bring businesses and development into the area expeditiously

(continued)

FIGURE 14.2
A resource map
for rebuilding
the Ninth Ward

**POLICY
ADVOCACY
CHALLENGE 14.8**

(continued)

These same steps seemed essential to reconstruct New Orleans' Ninth Ward. Why would businesses and residents return if they were not assured that the Army Corps of Engineers and other government agencies would quickly develop and implement an effective plan to bolster the city's levees to protect it against future Category-5 hurricanes? How could the economy rekindle absent huge public investments to create jobs, and to stimulate businesses to reopen even when most residents had not yet returned to the city? With its sales taxes and property taxes greatly reduced, how could the city of New Orleans or the State of Louisiana invest resources in the Ninth Ward absent grants or zero-interest loans from the federal government? If the reconstruction effort was not vested under the direction of nonpartisan experts with no conflicts of interest with corporations that bid for government contracts, how could citizens and businesses trust the reconstruction effort?

Implementation of the Ninth Ward's reconstruction would require, as well, high-level leadership or resources might pour into it in a chaotic fashion. Housing, schools, businesses, public services, and social services had to be provided in a timed sequence that could only occur if someone exercised leadership. The "someone" might be a federal official, an authority or commission with a director and board, the governor, the mayor, or some combination of these persons or entities. Examples of leadership existed at many points in American history. New Dealers created the Tennessee Valley Authority (TVA) to oversee the development of river systems of Tennessee. Many cities, such as New York, had an array of "authorities" or commissions to develop specific areas or projects. Public systems of health in many cities are placed under commissions.

High-level leadership *had* to involve the president and Congress if only to set in motion the authority or commission that would redevelop New Orleans. As can be seen in Figure 14.2, the federal government alone had the resources and agencies that could address the various problems of New Orleans, whether the Army Corps of Engineers or Departments of Education; Health and Human Services; Labor, and Transportation—or the Small Business Administration, FEMA, and Home Security Agency. *Only* the federal government could make New Orleans immune from devastation from future Category-5 hurricanes. *Only* the federal government could consider paying resources as high as $250 billion for New Orleans' reconstruction. (The entire budget of Louisiana in FY 2005 was only $17.5 billion—and the budget of the city of New Orleans was only $620 *million*.)

Whatever high-level leadership was developed, it had to develop goals and time tables to guide its efforts. Its goals had to include statements about the kind of city—and Ninth Ward—that it wanted to develop. New Orleans had been possibly the most segregated large American city by class and race before Hurricane Katrina hit. Not only did it have huge concentrations of low-income African Americans, but it had affluent mostly Caucasian areas in the Garden District and in suburban areas. It made sense to decrease this segregation in the reconstructed city and Ninth Ward by developing neighborhoods that mixed classes and races. If so, the high-level leadership would have to scatter low-income persons throughout the greater New Orleans area with use of Section-8 federal housing, as well as by requiring private developers to include affordable housing units within their projects *and* requiring surrounding parishes to accept some low- and moderate-income housing in the areas where more affluent housing had been destroyed by Hurricane Katrina.

To truly revitalize itself, New Orleans not only needed to help many low-income persons settle in surrounding and more affluent parishes, but to attract middle-income citizens into New Orleans in areas previously occupied exclusively by low-income African Americans. This goal would not be realizable, however, without substantial reforms of New Orleans public schools—one of the worst systems in the United States prior to Hurricane Katrina. The city would have to attract amenities that would be attractive not only to a range of citizens, including grocery stores and other businesses in the Ninth Ward and elsewhere. It would have to place parks and recreation areas in neighborhoods. It would have to improve public systems of transportation. It would have to improve municipal services and police protection.

(continued)

Unless the high-level leadership wanted to return to the segregated city and Ninth Ward of the past, then, it would *have* to engage in sophisticated planning that would lead to reformed and better neighborhoods than the segregated neighborhoods of the past. It would have to direct and sequence resources and programs into the Ninth Ward from an array of federal, state, and city agencies.

It would have to establish time lines. If it waited too long to accomplish a substantial part of the rebuilding of the Ninth Ward and the city—say 10 years—it would risk sabotaging the entire effort. Not establishing relatively short time lines would discourage many evacuees of all social classes from returning. It would discourage small businesses from returning and investing in new equipment and facilities. Yet high-level leadership might also undermine confidence in its work if it set unrealistic goals that it could not meet—or if it failed to meet those goals that it did establish.

To be effective, moreover, the reconstruction effort had to avoid *any* appearance of misconduct. With huge sums of money involved, fraud and misuse of resources would inevitably occur minus vigorous monitoring—such as was established during the New Deal when President Franklin Roosevelt established a "Division of Progress Investigation" that scrupulously audited expenditures, contracts, and bids of work-relief projects when not a single instance of malfeasance was discovered. The monumental Tennessee Valley Authority was unscathed by scandal despite its huge size.

Even at the outset of reconstruction, then, we can identify some factors that would be associated with the successful implementation of efforts to rebuild New Orleans. (See Table 14.2.)

The implementation of New Orleans' and the Ninth Ward's reconstruction could be compromised by many obstacles. The president and his top aides were skeptical about providing federal leadership, insisting that local government should take the lead even when city and state governments lacked resources for the reconstruction effort. They wanted private enterprise and market forces to be the primary engine of reconstruction, mostly unfettered by plans even though market mechanisms would hardly facilitate the rapid emergence of businesses and homes in areas mostly devastated by Hurricane Katrina—and even though many private developers would focus on relatively affluent clientele. Some critics wondered if the "new New Orleans" and the "new Ninth Ward" might be dominated by hotels, condominiums, and high-rent apartments that served tourists and patrons of rebuilt casinos rather than helping low-income African-American residents displaced by the storm.

The president and his top aides had not made clear by December 2005 whether (and by what date) they would immunize New Orleans and the Ninth Ward from Category-5 hurricanes—and then reconstructed levees by late summer 2006 sufficient only to protect the city against Category-3 hurricanes. Minus this decision, reconstruction could not proceed with use of public funds or with use of resources provided by private investors because persons and institutions would fear huge losses if the city was hit by another hurricane. Miraculously, New Orleans was spared being hit by a hurricane in summer and fall 2006, possibly because the climate condition known as *El Nino* in the Pacific Ocean had interrupted the normal development of hurricanes in the Atlantic Ocean. Ominously, climate experts predicted it would dissipate by the next hurricane season in summer and fall 2007.

The procedures used by the Bush administration to clear New Orleans and the Ninth Ward from rubble in the wake of Katrina did not inspire confidence in its intention to avoid malfeasance. Often without a bidding process, contracts were let

TABLE 14.2   Implementation guidelines to rebuild New Orleans and the Ninth Ward

---

1. Making the area secure from future flooding—a logistical requirement

2. Establishing high-level leadership that is formalized in some kind of implementing authority, such as a redevelopment authority or commission

3. Developing strong federal involvement in this high-level leadership in light of the resources needed to be successful; as well as successful partnering of the State of Louisiana and the city of New Orleans with the federal government

4. Establishing social and economic goals at the outset, such a reconstructing the Ninth Ward so that it is a multi-ethnic and multi-class area with its low-income residents offered the option to choose affordable housing within the Ninth Ward *or* in other neighborhoods in New Orleans and its environment

5. Committing huge resources at the outset, with most of them coming from the federal government in light of the fact that the State of Louisiana and the city of New Orleans revenues were greatly diminished by Hurricane Katrina

6. Sequencing investments into the area so that housing, creation of business, and other local improvements proceed simultaneously

7. Establishing realistic timelines—and meeting them

8. Encouraging private investors to participate fully in the rebuilding of New Orleans and the Ninth Ward, but within guidelines established by high-level leadership (for example, developers would be required to include specified percentages of affordable housing units in their projects)

9. Improving local schools so that they are attractive to multi-ethnic and multi-class families

10. Improving infrastructure and local transportation

11. Adding parks and other local amenities

12. Scrupulously monitoring contracts and bids so that no malfeasance occurs—and making all decisions transparent

---

to corporations to perform this work. Some critics feared that large corporations with links to top officials in the administration would get the lion's share of contracts, much as the Halliburton Company which had received huge contracts for work in Iraq that had been widely viewed as priced at excessive levels.

Nor was it clear what resources the Bush administration would dedicate to the reconstruction of New Orleans and the Ninth Ward. While it received commitments from Congress for more than $50 billion in fall 2005, it had spent or committed less than half of these resources by the start of 2006 and had large upspent balances even in fall 2007. While the president pledged about $110 billion by fall 2006, it remained unclear if these were sufficient sums.

Ominously, moreover, no federal commitments had been made to the former residents of the Ninth Ward, who were allowed to tour their neighborhood for the first time on December 1, 2005. On that day, members of New Orleans' city council castigated the Bush administration for back-tracking on earlier promises for a "massive reconstruction," fearing that their city would be abandoned.

(continued)

It was discouraging to residents of, and evacuees from, New Orleans in late fall 2006 that vast sections of New Orleans remained in precisely the same condition as in the weeks following Hurricane Katrina. Much of the city remained a huge field of rubble. With no higher-level plan developed, each parish began its own planning process in fall 2006 using funds from the Rockefeller Foundation to develop plans that would then be approved by the city and the state. In a city devastated to this extent, however, it was unclear whether this decentralized and belated planning process could deal with problems that occurred on a *regional* level. How could strictly local plans deal with:

- Developing of mixed-income housing throughout the region rather than allowing more affluent areas to develop plans with scant regard for the needs of low-income persons from devastated areas like the Ninth Ward?
- Addressing regional economic needs such as developing roads, bridges, and business facilities so that businesses would want to return to the area?
- Developing regional transportation networks?
- Establishing realistic time lines that would be met, so that evacuees and businesses would feel sufficiently confident that they would return to New Orleans in a reasonable period?

Listen to Policy Advocacy Challenge Video 14.8 with Ron McClain, JD, MSW, LCSW, President and CEO of Family Service of Greater New Orleans, who discusses some implementation challenges in putting plans into action in the Ninth Ward of New Orleans.

Policy Assessment

Policy advocates do not know if their policy initiatives have been successful if they do not obtain evidence about outcomes that followed their implementation. The fundamental logic of policy assessment is strikingly similar to policy analysis—except that it is conducted *after* a policy has been enacted and implemented. Evaluators have to identify and weigh those criteria to be used to determine whether an implemented policy has been successful. They have to develop a credible research design to rule out whether extraneous factors led to a policy's success. They have to use statistical measures to determine if the magnitude of change or outcomes caused by a specific policy might be due to chance rather than to the effects of the policy. They need to use an array of quantitative and qualitative tools and measurements.

Policy advocates should seek to develop evidence-based policies just like many clinical practitioners want evidence-based practice guidelines. These policies can be located only by subjecting existing policies to empirical scrutiny.

Policy advocates not only need to encourage and facilitate policy assessment, but they need to draw upon research findings when they develop specific policy initiatives—such as specific findings that suggest certain interventions for specific kinds of homeless persons are likely to be effective.

What You Can Now Do

CHAPTER SUMMARY

You are now equipped to do the following:

- Analyze whether specific policy innovations are being implemented
- Diagnose why specific policies are not implemented by using a systems framework
- Analyze implementation both within and across organizational boundaries
- Initiate strategy to improve implementation

Policy advocates also can use data, such as from program evaluations, to check on the merits of specific implemented policies.

NOTES

1. For an overview of the strategy, see Congress, House, Ways and Means Committee, Subcommittee on Public Assistance, *Hearings on Amendments to Social Services, Foster Care, and Child Welfare*, 96th Cong., 1st Sess., March 1979, pp. 22–157.
2. Robert Montjoy and Laurence O'Toole, "Toward a Theory of Policy Implementation," *Public Administration Review* 39 (September–October 1979): 465–476.
3. Jeffrey Pressman and Aaron Wildavsky, *Implementation* (Berkeley and Los Angeles: University of California Press, 1974).
4. Ibid.
5. Mary Jo Bane, "Welfare as We Might Know It," *American Prospect* (January–February 1997): 47–55.
6. Laurence O'Toole and Robert Montjoy, "Toward a Theory of Policy Implementation," *Public Administration Review* 44 (November/December 1984): 491–503.
7. Richard Berk, "Gingrich Promises to Fight Clinton on Welfare Law," *New York Times* (August 23, 1997): 1, 9.
8. Jason DeParle, "White House Calls for Minimum Wage in Workfare Plans," *New York Times* (May 16, 1997): 1.

9. Mary Ann Scheirer, *Program Implementation: The Organizational Context* (Beverly Hills, CA: Sage, 1981).
10. Michael Lipsky, *Street Level Bureaucracy* (New York: Russell Sage Foundation, 1980).
11. Yeheskel Hasenfeld, "Implementation of Social Policy Revisited," *Administration and Society* (February 1991).
12. Catherine Alter, "Interorganizational Collaboration in the Task Environment." In Rino Patti, ed., *The Handbook of Social Welfare Management* (Thousand Oaks, CA: Sage Publications, 2000), pp. 283–302.
13. Jane Waldfugel, "The New Wave of Service Integration," *Social Service Review* (September 1997): 463–484.
14. Scheirer, *Program Implementation*.
15. John O'Looney, "Beyond Privatization and Service Integration," *Social Service Review* (December 1993): 40–54.
16. Bruce Jansson, "The Political Economy of Monitoring: A Contingency Perspective," in Harold Demone and Margaret Gibelman, *Services for Sale* (New Brunswick, NJ: Rutgers University Press, 1989), pp. 343–359.

SUGGESTED READINGS

Theoretical Perspectives on Implementation

Erwin Hargrove, *The Missing Link: The Study of the Implementation of Social Policy* (Washington, DC: Urban Institute Press, 1975).

Yeheskel Hasenfeld, "Implementation of Social Policy Revisited," *Administration and Society* 22 (February 1991): 451–479.

Robert Montjoy and Laurence O'Toole, "Toward a Theory of Policy Implementation," *Public Administration Review* 39 (September–October 1979): 465–476.

Carl Van Horn and Donald Van Meter, "The Implementation of Intergovernmental Policy," in Charles Jones and Robert Thomas, eds., *Public Policy Making in the Federal System* (Beverly Hills, CA: Sage, 1976).

Models of Interorganization Collaboration

John Fleischman et al., "Organizing AIDS Service Consortia: Lead Agency Identity and Consortium Cohesion," *Social Service Review* (December 1992): 501–534.

John O'Looney, "Beyond Privatization and Service Integration," *Social Service Review* (December 1993): 40–54.

Privatization and Links to Informal Systems

Charles Hoch and George Hemmens, "Linking Informal and Formal Help: Conflict along the Continuum of Care," *Social Service Review* (September 1987): 434–447.

Julie Kosterlitz, "Unmanaged Care?" *National Journal* (December 10, 1994): 2903–2907.

Lester Salamon, "The Marketization of Welfare: Changing Nonprofit and For-Profit Roles in the American Welfare State," *Social Service Review* (March 1993): 16–39.

Structural-Political Perspectives on Implementation

Jeffrey Pressman and Aaron Wildavsky, *Implementation* (Berkeley and Los Angeles: University of California Press, 1974).

Political-Economy Perspectives on Implementation

Eugene Bardach, *The Implementation Game* (Cambridge, MA: MIT Press, 1977).

Micro or Agency Perspectives on Implementation

Yeheskel Hasenfeld, "The Implementation of Change in Human Service Organizations," *Social Service Review* 54 (December 1980): 508–520.

Mary Ann Scheirer, *Program Implementation: The Organizational Context* (Beverly Hills, CA: Sage, 1981).

Staff Perspectives on Implementation

Michael Lipsky, *Street-Level Bureaucracy* (New York: Russell Sage Foundation, 1980).

Ethical Issues in Policy Implementation

Sissela Bok, "Blowing the Whistle," in Joel Fleishman, Lance Liebman, and Mark Moore, eds., *Public Duties: The Moral Obligations of Government Officials* (Cambridge: Harvard University Press, 1981), pp. 204–220.

Robert Goodin, *Reasons for Welfare: The Political Theory of the Welfare State* (Princeton, NJ: Princeton University Press, 1988), pp. 184–223.

Donald Warwick, "The Ethics of Administrative Discretion," in Fleishman, Liebman, and Moore, *Public Duties*, pp. 93–127.

NAME INDEX

SUBJECT INDEX